Abstracts of Marriages and Deaths

and Other Articles of Interest

In the

Newspapers of

Frederick

and

Montgomery

Counties, Maryland,

From 1831-1840

Compiled by
L. Tilden Moore

Heritage Books
2008

HERITAGE BOOKS
AN IMPRINT OF HERITAGE BOOKS, INC.

Books, CDs, and more—Worldwide

For our listing of thousands of titles see our website
at
www.HeritageBooks.com

Published 2008 by
HERITAGE BOOKS, INC.
Publishing Division
100 Railroad Ave. #104
Westminster, Maryland 21157

Copyright © 1991 L. Tilden Moore

All rights reserved. No part of this book may be reproduced or transmitted in any form or by any means, electronic or mechanical, including photocopying, recording or by any information storage and retrieval system without written permission from the author, except for the inclusion of brief quotations in a review.

International Standard Book Numbers
Paperbound: 978-1-55613-478-4
Clothbound: 978-0-7884-7031-8

TABLE OF CONTENTS

Date ....Page

FREDERICKTOWN HERALD
1831 1
1832 28

FREDERICK HERALD
1833 60
1834 91
1835 132
1840 140

THE WEEKLY TIMES
1832 141
1833 147
1834 156

THE CITIZEN
1831 159

THE FREDERICK CITIZEN
1836 159

THE REPUBLICAN CITIZEN
1837 161
1838 168
1839 178

THE TIMES AND DEMOCRATIC ADVOCATE
1837 179
1838 193

FREDERICK TIMES AND DEMOCRATIC ADVOCATE
1838 201
1839 210

Date ....Page

FREDERICK VISITER AND TEMPERANCE ADVOCATE
1839 211

THE VISITER
1840 235

POLITICAL EXAMINER AND PUBLIC ADVERTISER
1835 257

POLITICAL EXAMINER
1836 267
1837 298
1838 311
1839 318
1840 328

MARYLAND JOURNAL AND TRUE AMERICAN
1831 330
1832 335
1833 338
1834 342
1835 343
1829 343
1831 343

EMMITSBURG GAZETTE
1839 344

FREDERICKTOWN HERALD
1831 345

INDEX.................347

INTRODUCTION

This is a compilation of events taken from the newspapers of Frederick and Montgomery Counties, giving many details about other activities besides marriages and deaths that were transpiring in the two counties during this period.

The newspapers of Frederick County account for most of the available articles of the two counties. Some of the newspapers in Frederick did carry some events that took place in Montgomery County. They also carried information about familes that had moved to other states, but still had ties in Frederick County.

The *Frederick-town Herald* was established around 1802; in 1832, it changed to the *Frederick Herald*. The *Weekly Times* was established around 1832, with various titles and continued until 1835. The *New Citizen* was organized in 1821, and like the *Weekly Times* had a variety of titles. The *Times and Democratic Advocate* was established around 1835, in 1838 it changed its name to *The Frederick Times and Democratic Advocate*, and continued until 1839. The *Frederick Visiter and Temperance Advocate*, established in 1838, changed to *The Visiter* in 1840, until 1841. The *Emmitsburg Gazette* was established in 1839. The *Political Examiner* was organized in 1813, with several title changes. The *Maryland Journal* started publishing in 1825, and changed to the *Maryland Journal and True American* in 1834.

There has been no change in spelling of names from the newspapers. You will see the names in the papers sometimes are spelled correctly, other times letters may be added or deleted which may or may not affect the pronunciation of the person's name. Printers of yester-year made mistakes, just as they do today.

Each article is arranged in numerical order, and the index is keyed the to the article number. The code at the end of each date indicates the location of origin (original newspapers or microfilm).

CBAL - On microfilm at the C. Burr Artz Library, Frederick, Maryland.

MHS - Original newspapers at the Maryland Historical Society, Baltimore, Maryland.

LC - Original newspapers located at the Library of Congress, Washington D.C.

EP - On microfilm at the Enoch Pratt Library, Baltimore, Maryland.

Abbreviations code used:

Co./co.	= County	F	= Fire
Col.	= Colonel	Inst	= Instant (This Month)
D	= Death	M	= Marriage
Dr.	= Doctor	Ult	= Ultimo (Last Month)

1831

FREDERICKTOWN HERALD

January 1, 1831 (CBAL)

1. (M) On Tuesday evening last, by the Rev. David F. Schaeffer, Mr SPEALMAN, to Miss MARY BIRTSCH.
2. (M) On Friday evening, the 24th ult., by the Rev. David Martin, Mr DANIEL KOLB, to Miss CAROLINE BRENGLE, all of this co.
3. (D) On Sunday, the 25th ult., aged 74 years, and 5 days, Mrs JOSHAN MONTGOMERY, wife of John Montgomery, Sen. She leaves a large family of children, and grandchildren.

January 8, 1831 (CBAL)

4. (D) On Wednesday last, the 29th of December, Mr NEWEY, who lived in Harbaugh's Valley, was murdered along with his wife, two children, father-in-law, and apprentice boy. The house was set a fire, and consumed. Mr. Flaut, who lived 400 yards away, saw the fire, he found Mr Newey lying on the floor nearly consumed with his wife lying by his side. Mrs Newey was nearly partly consumed with stab wounds. The two children partly consumed, still lying with bloody bed clothes under them, the old man, and boy both consumed. Newey, sleeping in the front, was first stabbed, he reached for his wife and was prostrated with blows on the head with a ax, and killed. The two children were killed in bed, the father-in-law who lived in the upper chamber came down and was killed as he entered the room. The boy started out the door when he was killed. Mr JOHN MACKLEY, nephew of the Newey's, is suspected for this murder. He was sent to imprisonment in the penitentiary for stealing from the Newey's. He stole a wedding suit of clothes, a watch, and $250.00, on October 26th, 1825.

January 15, 1831 (CBAL)
5. Arrested in Baltimore, on Sunday night last, Mr JOHN MACKLEY, by W. Walker, who was assisted by two citizens. He was taken before Justice Blair who committed him to prison.

January 22, 1831 (CBAL)
6. Examination of JOHN MACKLEY, took place on Saturday last. Mr King, who identified some of the clothing of Mr Newey. Mackley, was turned back over to jail and will be returned to the Frederick Co., Sheriff for his trial.
7. (F) Mr FREDERICK STALEY's Mill, situated about 4 miles from Frederick, was entirely destroyed by fire on Wednesday night last.
8. (D) On the 21st ult., in the 45th year of her age, at the residence of her brother-in-law in New Market, Mrs DAVIS, relict of the late Asabel Davis, of Harpers Ferry.
9. (D) On Friday morning last, Mr JOHN SCHISSLER, an old inhabitant of this place.
10. (D) On the 8th inst., Mr WILLIAM T. JOHNSON, aged 43 years, after a lingering illness.

January 29, 1831 (CBAL)
11. (M) On the 9th inst., by the Rev. Mr Schaeffer, Mr JOHN HOLTZ, to Miss ELIZABETH SMITH, all of this co.
12. (M) On Sunday last, by the same, Mr RICHARD H. EDWARDS, to Mrs SUSAN HOFFMAN, all of this co.
13. (M) On the 27th inst., by the Rev. John H. Smaltz, Mr ELIAS SCHOLL, to Miss SUSANNA SHARER, both of this co.
14. (D) At Richmond, VA., on Sunday the 16th inst., PETER FRANCISCO, Sergeant-at-Arms of the House of Delegates. A soldier of the Revolution, famous for his extraordinary personal powers. His dying request was that he might be buried with the Honors of War. The legislature adjourned over from Monday evening to Wednesday, to attend his funeral.
15. (D) In Baltimore, on Sunday the 15th inst., in the 34th year of his age, the Rev. YELVERTON T. PEYTON, of the Methodist Church.
16. (D) On Thursday last, in this city, Mr GEORGE DAVIDSON, a druggist of the firm of Haff and Davidson.
17. (F) On Sunday night, at 8 o'clock, a small dwelling near the outskirts of town, which was occupied by a colored woman, was consumed by fire.

February 5, 1831 (CBAL)
18. JOHN MACKLEY, arrived in the city on Wednesday night last, following a morning examination. He was brought before Judge Shriver, who committed him for trial at the next term of Criminal Court, which will commence in May.
19. (D) In this town, on Thursday last, Mr. JACOB DERR, (carpenter,) an old and respectable citizen.
20. (D) At Alexandria, D.C., EDWARD STABLER, a minister of the gospel, in the Society of Friends, aged 61 years.
21. (D) In Emmittsburg, on the 26th of January, Mrs ELIZA WATERS, consort of Henry G. Waters, aged 36 years.
22. (D) On Saturday last, MARGARET M., child of Mr John D. Smith, of this town, aged 3 years.

February 12, 1831 (CBAL)
23. (D) Melancholy accident - Mr JOHN KUHN, a wagoner, employee of William Tilgham, of Washington Co., was accidently killed on Wednesday last while driving his team on the road from this city to Hagerstown, at about 100 yards from Getzendanner's Tavern. While attempting to mount one of the horses his foot slipped, in consequence of the ice in the road. Falling to the ground he was caught by one of the wheels which crushed his body without passing over it. He was released with the help from other wagoners and was able to stand, but soon expired, in consequence of blood vessels.
24. Appointments by the Governor and Council for Frederick County: Judges of the Orphans' Court: HENRY KEMP, PETER MANTZ, and JACOB STEINER. Levy Court: JACOB SHRIVER, GRAFTON DUVALL, MOSES WORMAN, JAMES SIMMONS, ABRAHAM JONES, WM. MILLER, SINGLETON WOOTTON, DAVID FOUTZ, MARTIN EICHELBERGER, FREDERICK TROXALL, SOLOMON FORREST. Coroners: WM. R. KING, HENRY BAER, HENRY BOTELER, GEORGE TITLOW, GEORGE PRICE, ALEXANDER McIlHENNY, DENNIS D. HOWARD, GEORGE HUGHES. Magistrates: JAMES C. ATLEE, JACOB BAER, HENRY BAER, BELT BRASHEAR, HENRY BAKER, JNO. BAUMGARTNER, S. BAUMGARTNER, C. H. BURKHART, DAVID BUCKEY, DAVID BOYD, EDWARD BUCKEY, HENRY BANTZ, MALACHI BARNARD, ROBERT BOONE, TILGHMAN BISER, G. BECKENBAUGH, CHRISTIAN BROWN, PETER BANKER, WASH. BURGESS, GEO. P. BUCKEY, JOHN COST, ABNER CAMPBELL, JACOB COBLENTZ, PETER COBLENTZ, WM.

COOKERLY, JOHN COLE, JOHN R. CURTIS, JACOB CRAMER, G. CASSELL, of J., WM. CUGHLAN, JACOB CASSELL, JESSE CLARY, EZRA CRAMER, THOMAS DUVALL, ROBERT DAVIS, ISAAC DERN, DANIEL DUVALL, JOHN W. DERR, CHARLES DEVILBISS, WM. DUDDERAR, JAS. DURBIN, of T., ISAAC DUNHAM, JOHN EBERT, GEO. W. ENT, JONATHAN EADOR, JOHN ERB, of P., DANIEL ENGLE, NATHAN ENGLAND, WM. FLANAGAN, JACOB FLOOK, JACOB FIROR, H. FUNDENBURGH, WM. P. FARQUHAR, NIMROD FRIZZLE, JAMES FISHER, JACOB FOX, GEORGE FLAUT, GEORGE P. FOX, J. GETZENDANNER, of Nathan., WM. GRIMES, GEORGE GROVE, STEPHEN GORSUCH, JOHN HOFFMAN, NICHOLAS HOLTZ, JOHN L. HARDING, WILSON HAYS, BENJ. HEFFNER, BARTON HACKNEY, H. A. HAMILTON, JACOB HOFFMAN, TOBIAS HORINE, H. HERSHBERGER, PERRY HILLEARY, DANIEL HOOVER, JACOB HAHN, JOHN HINES, JNO. H. HOPPE, N. E. HAMMOND, PLUMMER IJAMS, W. JARBOE, of J., T. JOHNSON, of W., ISAAC JAMES, Jr., JOSHUA JONES, WILLIAM JONES, JOSEPH JAMES, D. J. KRAMMER, LEWIS KEMP, J. KEEFAUVER, of G., JOHN KINZER, WM. KNOX, M.D., ZEBULON KUHN, GEORGE KUHN, EDWARD KNOTT, FREDERICK KELLER, JACOB LAMBERT, Sen., NELSON LUCKETT, LLOYD LUCKETT, WALTER A. LIGHTEN, JOHN LOWE, MICHAEL LEASE, PAT. McGILL, Senr., JER. G. MORRISON, LEWIS MOTTER, ALEX. McIIHENNY, JOHN McDONALD, PHIL. S. McELFRESH, WM. MURPHY, Sen., THOS. MAYBERRY, JOHN McNEIL, PAT. McGILL, Jr., W. L. McELFRESH, WILLIAM MOONEY, SAML. McKEEHAN, GEORGE MATTHIAS, Jr., JOHN MONTGOMERY, CHRIST. MUSSETER, JONATHAN NORRIS, NICHOLAS NORRIS, HENRY NELSON, WILLIAM NORRIS, NAT. H. OWINGS, LEVI O'BRIAN, NOAH PHILLIPS, WM. H. POOLE, THOMAS POWELL, JOHN W. PRAFT, W. B. PITTINGER, GEORGE PRICE, JACOB POUDER, Jr., GEORGE PHELPS, GEORGE ROHR, ELIHA H. ROCKWELL, GEORGE RINER, ANDW. SHRIVER, DAVID STEINER, HENRY STEINER, Jr., DAVID SCHLEY, JACOB SOUDER, JOHN J. SMITH, PETER SCHLOSSER, JOHN SHAFFER, JAMES SMITH, SEBASTIAN SULTZER, WILLIAM SULLIVAN, MICHAEL SULLIVAN, JOSHUA SMITH, Jr., R. B. STEVENSON, THOS. C. SHIPLEY, GEORGE SMITH, GEORGE TITLOW, JACOB THOMAS, JOSEPH TANEY, Jr., BENJAMIN TODD, ABDIEL UNKEFER, W. VAN BIBBER,

ABRAM. WAMPLER, S. D. WARFIELD, ZACH. T. WINDSOR, S. R. WATERS, ISAAC WYSONG, LEVIN WEST, JOSEPH WEST, CHARLES WILLIAR, HENRY YOUNG, DANIEL YOUNG, GEORGE YANTIS, J. M. A. ZOLLICKOFFER, JACOB ZIMMERMAN, JOSEPH TANEY.

25. Corporation election - Candidates for the Common Council: Ward #1. GEORGE WISSENGER, HENRY STEINER, Jr. Ward #2. GEORGE M. CONRADT, JOHN RIGNEY. Ward #3. DAVID B. DEVITT, JACOB LITTLE. Ward #4. JACOB ENGLEBRECHT, WILLIAM FISCHER. Ward #5. JOHN ENGELBRECHT, DAVID SPRENGLE. Ward #6. DANIEL KOLB, THOMAS CARLEN. Ward #7. WILLIAM ELY, JACOB ROWE.

February 19, 1831 (CBAL)

26. (D) Melancholy accident - Mr JOHN WILLYARD, who lived near Buckeystown, was killed on Thursday last. In consequence of the limb of a tree falling upon him, while engaged in cutting wood.

27. (D) In this town on Saturday morning the 12th inst., the Rev. JOHN FRANCIS PETERS, S.J., in the 32nd year of his age. For the last 16 months he exercised his duties as minister in this town and its vicinity. The decease was a native of Belgium and came to this country in 1829.

28. (M) On Tuesday evening the 8th inst., by the Rev. Thomas H. W. Monroe, Mr JOHN PHILLIP, to Miss MARY ANN, third daughter of Amos Norris, Esq., near Liberty-Town.

29. (M) On Tuesday last the 5th of February inst., by the Rev. John N. Hoffman, Mr LENARY LEADER, printer, of Bradford Pa., to Miss MARIA JENNINGS, of Taney-Town, MD.

30. Election of officers for the Independent Hose Company: President - LEWIS RAMSBURG, Vice President - SAMUEL CARMACK, Secretary - W. V. MORGAN, Treasurer - JACOB ENGELBRECHT. Directors - WILLIAM FISCHER, and GORDON BANTZ, Principal Engineer - DAVID B. DEVITT, Assistant Engineers - WILLIAM SMALL, PETER HALLER. Standing Committees from the following appointments: Property Guard - WM. SCHLEY, DAV. STEINER, EVAN CARMACK, and JOHN FESSLER, Lane-men - S. GAITHER, P. TORMEY, I. WYSONG, W. C. RUSSELL, M. E. BARTGIS, Ladder-men - ALEX. TRUSCOTT, JOHN JONES, Superintendents of fire plugs - JOHN STRAEFFER, JOHN HANSHEW, Ax-men - D. SPRENGLE, T. EADER, Hosemen - WM. STEINER, V. J. BRUNNER, JOHN HALLER, G. W. SHARP,

J. DOLL, G. M. CONRADT, J. SCHELL, P. REICH, H. M. JAMISON, H. YOUNG, EDWARD TRAIL, Pipe Director - L. RAMSBURG, Hose Director - SAML. CARMACK, Engine Director - WM. FISCHER, Lane Director - G. BANTZ. The balance of the members are enginemen. W. V. MORGAN, Sect.

February 26, 1831 (CBAL)

31. (M) On the 15th inst., by the Rev. John H. Smaltz, WM. BAUGHER, of Frederick Co., to Miss ELIZABETH ZIMMERMAN, of Washington Co.
32. (M) Near Middletown MD., on the 10th inst., by the Rev. J. C. Bucher, Mr STEPHEN CARPENTER, of Boonsboro, to Miss MARIA SHANK, daughter of Mr Jacob Shank, of this co.
33. (M) On the 13th inst., at Mount Saint Mary's Seminary, by the Rev. John B. Persell, Mr PATRICK NOWLAND, to Miss CECELIA LIVERS, all of this co.
34. (M) On the 13th inst., by the Rev. Mr Greer, Mr BENJAMIN SHUNK, to Miss REBECCA GRASON, both of this co.
35. (M) In Baltimore, Mr JOHN L. STONER, (merchant) to Miss MARIA M. WYGERT.
36. (M) On the 22nd inst., by the Rev. John H. Smaltz, Mr HENRY BOTELER, to Miss ANN REBECCA LEVY, all of this city.
37. (M) On Thursday evening last, by the Rev. D. F. Schaeffer, Mr ALEXANDER GETZENDANNER, to Miss MARIA HILL, both of this co.
38. (D) At his residence near Middleburg, on Thursday morning the 18th inst., Mr MATTHIAS HANN, aged 91 years, 9 months and 21 days. He leaves a large family of children.
39. (D) Departed this life on the 16th inst., Mrs SOPHIA WINEBRENNER, consort of Jacob Winebrenner, and daughter of John Gephart, of the "Frederick Examiner."

March 12, 1831 (CBAL)

40. (D) At Bloomsburg near Frederick-Towne, Frederick Co., Md., on the 3rd inst., Major ROGER JOHNSON, in the 83rd year of his age. A highly respected citizen, and friend to the poor, and a sincere Christian, and a honest man.
41. Rev. Mr JONES, will preach in the Baptist Meeting House, on Sunday next at 3 o'clock.
42. Rev. JOHN V. RIGDON, will preach at the Methodist Episcopal Church, tomorrow morning at 10 o'clock.

43. Appointed by the Executive for Frederick County, Justices of the Peace: ARTHUR TANZEG, JACOB EVERHART, THOMAS HOOK, JOHN HINDS, CHRISTIAN BOWERS, BENJAMIN F. BARTGIS, JAMES SUMMERS, MICHAEL BALTZELL, JACOB T. C. MILLER.
44. Council elected yesterday: Ward #1. GEORGE WISSINGER. Ward #2. WM. SMALL. Ward #3. D. B. DEVITT. Ward #4. GIDEON BANTZ. Ward #5. JOHN ENGELBRECHT. Ward #6. DANIEL KOLB. Ward #7. No election, equal number of votes.

March 19, 1831 (CBAL)

45. (D) On Sunday evening the 6th inst., near Liberty-Town, after a lingering illness of complicated disease, Miss CATHARINE, daughter of Amos Norris, in the 22nd year of her age. Services were held on Tuesday the 8th inst., by the Rev. James Riley.

March 26, 1831 (CBAL)

46. (M) On the 8th inst., by the Rev. J. C. Bucher, Mr JACOB RICHMOND, to Miss REBECCA, second daughter of Mr Peter Coblentz, Sen., all of Middletown.
47. (D) Near Middletown, Frederick Co., on the 28th of February, Mr JOHN HENRY BEIGHLY, age 72 years, 8 months and 22 days.
48. (D) On Friday last the 8th inst., in this city, Mr JOHN KELLER, in the 78th year of his age.
49. (D) On the 19th inst., JOHN HOFFMAN, Esq., in the 76th year of his age. A native of Lancaster PA., but resided upwards of 56 years of the latter part of his life in this co. For many year he engaged in mercantile business and latterly in farming and milling business.

April 2, 1831 (CBAL)

50. (M) On Thursday evening, by the Rev. Mr Schaeffer, Mr JOHN YARDEY, to Miss MARY POOLE, both of this co.
51. (D) In New York, on Saturday the 26th ult., the Rev. FREDERICK C. SCHAEFFER, D.D., Pastor of the Evangelical Lutheran Church of St. James, in that city, and President of the Synod and a Professor of the German Language and Literature in Columbia College. Active member of the Scientific and Literary Association. Pulmonary complication terminated his life, for some time he layed unable to speak, about 5 o'clock, P.M., he suffered no more, in the

39th year of his age. He spoke "Victory, Victory," and repeated a German Scripture, then folded his arms over his breast, and his spirit left him.
52. (D) Departed this life, at his residence on Linganore, on the 14th inst., Mr ARMOND HAMMOND, in the 77th year of his age.
53. (D) Departed this life, on Sunday morning the 20th inst., of a pulmonary consumption, MATILDA SHIVERS, second daughter of Mrs Susan Ader, of this village, age 23 years. Liberty-Town, March 23, 1831

April 9, 1831 (CBAL)
54. (M) On the 31st of March, by the Rev. Mr Stier, Mr WILLIAM NICHOLS, of Anne Arundel Co., to Miss HARRIET EVANS, of this co.
55. (M) On Thursday last, by the Rev. John A. Gear, Mr JOHN SLIFER, to Miss DOROTHEA WATERS, both of Merryland Tract, in this co.
56. (M) On the 26th of March, by the Rev. John H. Smaltz, Mr THOMAS O. BLACKWOOD, to Miss SUSAN MARTIN, both from VA.
57. (M) On the 3rd of April, by the same, Mr EPHRAIM SHEETS, to Miss SARAH ANN APPLEBEE, both of this co.
58. (M) On Sunday evening last, by the Rev. Robert Scott, RICHARD ORPUT, Esq., to Miss ELIZABETH LAMBERT, both of this co.

April 16, 1831 (CBAL)
59. JOHN MACKLEY, confessed to the murder of the Newey family.
60. JOHN MORELAND, was confinded in jail for debt. He escaped on Friday night the 8th inst., during a storm. He scaled the wall with the aid of a rope. A pursuit commenced and was stimulated by a $1,000.00 reward offered by the Sheriff for his recovery. He was arrested in Lancaster, PA., and was on the verge of leaving for Philadelphia in the stage. Sheriff Brengle has left to return said person in custody.
61. (F) Sunday last, about 11 o'clock, A.M., two barnes and a few stacks of wheat and rye, on the farm of Major JOHN GRAHAME, a short distance from the city, was destroyed by fire. It is believed it started from a spark from the chimnies of the dwelling or quarters.

62. (M) In this place, on Tuesday evening last, by the Rev. J. E. Jackson, the Rev. CHARLES MANN, Rector of Christ Church, in Alexandria, D.C., to Miss MARY C. JACKSON, daughter of Rev. Thomas Jackson.
63. (M) On Thursday evening the 7th inst., by the Rev. Mr Reek, Mr ROBERT FINLEN, merchant of Delaware, Ohio., to Miss ELIZABETH, daughter of Thomas Lamar, Esq., of Frederick Co., MD.
64. (M) On the same day, by the Rev. Mr Bucher, GEO. B. RICE, Esq., to Miss CATHERINE ANN, daughter of Stephen House, Esq., all of this co.
65. (M) On Sunday evening last, by the Rev. D. F. Schaeffer, Mr JACOB LEIS, to Miss SABINA HENRY, all of this city.
66. (M) Near Middletown, on the 17th of March ult., by the Rev. J. C. Bucher, Mr JOSHUA WINKS, to Miss MAHELA DUDDERER, youngest daughter of John Dudderer.
67. (M) On the 20th inst., by the same, Mr JAMES NAYLOR, to Miss HARRIET KUHN, all of Middletown Valley.
68. (M) On the 24th ult., by the same, Mr JACOB FLOOK, Jr., to Miss MARY ANN, eldest daughter of Mr Thomas Castle.
69. (M) On Tuesday evening last, by the Rev. D. F. Schaeffer, Mr GEORGE KETRO, to Mrs CATHARINE GETZENDAN-NER, daughter of Frederick Kemp, Esq., all of this co.
70. Election of officers for the Frederick County Savings Institute - Meeting was held on Monday night last, at Capt. N. TRUBUTT's Hotel. The members of the Board of Managers were: SAMUEL CARMACK, DAVID BOYD, WILLIAM C. SMALLWOOD, DAVID F. SCHAEFFER, WILLIAM FISCHER, VALENTINE J. BRUNNER, JACOB FAUBEL. Following officers were appointed: STEUART GAITHER - President, DAVID STEINER - Secretary, JOHN McPHERSON - Treasurer.

April 23, 1831 (CBAL)

71. (D) Dr. ELISHA DEBUTTS, Professor of Chemisty of the University of Maryland died in Baltimore, on the 3rd inst., after a teclious illness.
72. (D) In New York, JAMES LLOYD, Esq., formerly a distinguished member of the United States from Massachusetts.
73. (D) Recently at Worcester Mass., venerable and beloved ISAIAH THOMAS, father of American Printers, in his 86th year of his life.

April 30, 1831 (CBAL)

74. Justices of the Levy Court appointed on the 18th of April 1831. Ditrict #2. MOSES WORTHINGTON - President. District #1. JAMES SIMMONS. District #3. THOMAS SPRINGER. District #4. MARTIN EICHELBERGER. District #5. FREDERICK TROXEL. District #6. DAVID FOUTZ. District #7. ABRAHAM WAMPLER. District 8. ABRAHAM JONES. District #9. SINGLETON WOOTTEN. District #10. SOLOMON FORREST. District #11. WILLIAM MILLER. District #12. JOHN COST.
75. (M) On Thursday last week, by the Rev. Mr Drane, Mr JOSEPH I. MERRICK, Esq., to Mrs SOPHIA B. HAYS, both of Hagerstown, MD.
76. (M) At Washington City, on the 19th inst., Col. R. W. WILLIAMS, of Tallahassee, to Miss REBECCA B. BRANCH, daughter of the Hon. John Branch, of North Carolina.
77. (M) On the 15th inst., by the Rev. J. H. Smaltz, Mr EPHRAIM DOYLE, to Miss CATHERINE HAMILTON, both of this co.
78. (M) On Tuesday evening last, by the Rev. C. B. Young, Mr WILLIAM CRUM, to Miss ANN PHILLIPS.
79. (D) On Wednesday evening the 13th inst., after a lingering pulmonic disease Mrs ELIZABETH W. DUVALL, consort of Dr. Grafton Duvall, and youngest daughter of of the late Tho. Hawkins, Esq., of this co. In the 46th year of her age, a lady of exemplary piety and christian benevolence.
80. (D) On Monday the 25th inst., of a pulmonic consumption, at the 25th year of his age, Mr JOHN ORNDORFF. For several years a clerk in the store of Basil Norris, of this city.

May 14, 1831 (CBAL)

81. (M) On the 5th of May, at Mr Wm. Hape's Inn, by the Rev. Mr Wachter, Mr RICHARD BURGESS, to Miss HARRIET STIMBLE, both of Frederick Co.
82. (M) At Newton, Middletown Valley, Frederick Co., MD., on the 9th of May, by the Rev. J. C. Bucher, Mr ENOCH G. DAY, to Miss JULIA ANN ENGLAND, all of Frederick Co., MD.
83. (M) On the 10th near Middletown, Frederick Co., MD., by the same, Mr DANIEL SEINBACH, to Miss CATHERINE BEAGLEY, youngest daughter of Mr John H. Beagley, deceased, all of Frederick Co.
84. (D) On Tuesday morning the 3rd ult., departed this mortal life in the 37th year of her age, after a sudden attack of

epilepsy, Mrs MARY YANTIS, wife of Mr Daniel Yantis, of this village. Services were conducted by the Rev. Mr Steger, of Union Church, with verses from Revelation, Chapter 7, Verse 9. (Liberty-Town)
85. (D) On the 8th inst., at Middletown, after a distressing illness of several weeks, JONA. BOWLUS, eldest son of Mr Andrew Bowlus, in the 8th year of his age.

May 21, 1831 (CBAL)

86. JOHN MACKLEY's trial - He was found guilty of murder in the first degree of Mr JOHN NEWEY, and his wife Mrs LYDIA NEWEY.
87. (M) At Graceham, Frederick Co., by the Rev. Mr Heike, CHARLES WORTHINGTON, Esq., to Miss ELVIRA HART, both of Creagerstown.
88. (M) On Thursday morning last, by the Rev. David F. Schaeffer, HENRY S. SKINNER, Esq., to Miss ANN W. D. RILY, all of this co.
89. (M) In Allegany Co., on Thursday evening the 5th inst., by the Rev. L. H. Johns, WILLIAM J. ROSS, Esq., of Frederick, to ANN MARIA DAVIS, daughter of John Davis, Esq., of Flinestone.
90. (M) On the 19th inst., by the Rev. John H. Smaltz, Mr CHRISTIAN STONER, to Miss ANN MARIA SMITH, both of Frederick Co.
91. (D) Departed this life on the morning of the 4th inst., at the house of his father in Frederick, MD. The Rev. BASIL D. HIGGINS, late worthy member of the Baltimore annual conference, in the 24th year of his age.
92. (D) On Sunday evening last in Gettysburgh, PA., Mrs REBECCA, consort of Mr John Norris Starr, in the 22nd year of her age. A member of the Lutheran Church, her remains were deposited in Taney-Town, MD., the place of her nativity on Tuesday following.

May 28, 1831 (CBAL)

93. JOHN MACKLEY - Was sentenced by Chief Justice Buchanan, to be executed. (long article)
94. Appointment of Judges to Frederick Co., by the Levy Court: District #1. JOHN HOSSELBOCK, OTHO THOMAS, PETER BROWN. District #2. JOHN EBERT, HENRY BAER, NICHOLAS HOLTZ. District #3. HENRY COST, GEORGE BEER, JOHN STALEY. District #4. FREDERICK OTT, JAS. CROCKET, JOHN COLE. District #5. PATRICK

OWINGS, JOHN NICKUM, M. SLUSS. District #6. WM. SHEPHERD, JACOB BOMGARDNER, Jr., THOMAS JONES. District #7. JOHN WAMPLER, MOSES SHAW, P. WEAVER. District #8. JOHN GILSAN, GEORGE COA, EDEN HAMMOND. District #9. HENRY McELFRESH, THOMAS DUVALL, HENRY SMITH. District #10. WILSON HAYES, JOS. SMITH, GEORGE HARMAN. District #11. ELIAS CRUTCHLEY, JOSEPH WOOD, JACOB HYDER. District #12. H. OHR, BEN. BOONE, JOSEPH WEST. Constables appointed by the Levy Court: District #1. PETER STITCHER, JAS. STEPHENS, JOHN CAREY, ADDISION WHITE, F. J. KRAMMER, GEORGE W. WINDSOR, DANIEL DUDDERER, ARTHUR DELASHMUTT, and GEORGE STONER. District #2. FRED'K STONER, JAMES CARLIN, CHARLES PETERS, JOSHUA DILL, EZRA GADULITIG, JOHN BENDER, JOHN M. LOWE, JACOB MYERS, FREDERICK HARMAN, and JOHN W. METZ. District #3. JAMES CASTLE, JACOB LUDWICK, JOS. WILLIAMSON, P. J. KEPHART, ABRAHAM MILLER, PETER YOUNG, JACOB STOTTLEMYER, JESSE M. LITTLE, THOMAS H. PHILIPS, ELISHA HOUSE, CHRISTIAN TABLER. District #4. CYRUS WALKER, HENRY NEED, SAMUEL FAVOURITE, ABRAHAM KUNTZ, JACOB LIDY, and JOHN KING. District #5. JESSE MARTIN, ISAAC WILSON, and FREDERICK BLACK. District #6. JOHN CLABAUGH, JACOB FRINGER, PETER GELMITH, and JAMES RODGERS. District #7. JACOB FRINGER, Jr., JOHN KROUSE, JOHN D. WOODS, WM. C. WRIGHT, FREDERICK YINGLING, JEREMIAH CURRY, JAMES LONG, JOHN LITTLE. District #8. DAVID SWEADNER, JOHN H. CONDON, WM. DELL, JOHN F. STANSBURY, JOHN G. BAYNER, JOSEPH L. WAGNER, DANIEL ROOT. District #9. CHARLES STEVENS, HENRY HOUCK, GRAFTON BURGEE, R. W. PHELPS, GREENBURY SHEETS, NATHANIEL CLARY. District #10. WM. H. BROWN. District #11. SAMUEL WILHIDE. District #12. ADAM CUSTARD, ABSALOM CRAMER, JOHN BARNES. Trustees of the Poor for the current year: PHILIP RHOR. JOHN HOUCK, JACOB FAUBLE, GEORGE HAUER, DANIEL KOLB. Collector of Tax: GEORGE BALTZELL.

95. (D) Departed this life on Thursday evening last, Mr JOHN MORRISON, in the 66th year of his age, he leaves a small family. (Liberty-Town, May 20th 1831)

June 4, 1831 (CBAL)

96. Letter concerning details of the life of JOHN MACKLEY - He denys this sketch of his life, saying that the only person he has met with and knows the details of his life, is the Rev. Schaeffer.
97. The Rev. Mr JONES, will preach in the Baptist Meeting House, of this place, next Lord's Day evening at 3 o'clock.
98. (M) At Elmwood, the residence of Jacob Poe, Esq., on Wednesday the 25th inst., by the Rev. Mr Smaltz, DAVID SCHLEY, Esq., to Miss GEORGIANA M., daughter of the late Wm. Clemm, Esq., of Baltimore.
99. (M) At Cincinnati, Ohio., on Thursday the 19th ult., by the Rev. Lewis Myers, Mr MICHAEL STRAEFFER, formerly of Frederick, MD., to Miss ELIZABETH DRESSEL, of Cincinnati, Ohio.
100. (M) On Sunday evening last, by the Rev. D. F. Schaeffer, Mr PHILIP LOTS, to Miss EVE REDDICH, all of Frederick.

June 11, 1831 (CBAL)

101. (D) On Sunday morning the 1st inst., at the residence of William Dudderar, Esq., near Liberty-Town, CONRAD DUDDERAR, aged 93 years. His remains were interred in the family burial grounds.
102. (D) At his residence near Liberty, on Thursday morning the 3rd, Capt. JOHN FUNSTON, in the 54th year of his age, he leaves a widow, and numerous friends.
103. (D) Of a protracted disease of the lungs, on the 23rd last April, near Tallahasse in Florida, WM. N. RITCHIE, son of the late Col. Jno. Ritchie, of this place.
104. (D) On Wednesday morning the 1st inst., after a lingering illness, at Matteawan Fishkill Landing, New York, the Hon. ABRAHAM H. SCHENCK, age 56.

June 18, 1831 (CBAL)

105. Governor appointed next Friday the 24th, as the day for JOHN MACKLEY's, execution. To take place at the building called "The Barricks," adjoining the city. Sheriff Brengle read the death warrant on Monday last to the wretched criminal. He is a suspect for the murder of Mrs Cunningham, of near Harpers Ferry, in 1825. The Charlestown Free Press, states that Mackley formerly lived in Jefferson Co., when he committed a felony which sent him to prison for a year. (long Article)

106. (D) CHARLES MITCHELL, Esq., one of the distinguished members of the Baltimore Bar, died in that city on the 11th inst.
107. (M) At Mobile, Mr THOMAS W. McCOY, to Miss ANNA M., daughter of George Poe, Jr., Esq.
108. (M) On Thursday the 9th inst., by the Rev. Mr Morgan, Mr SAMUEL URNER, to Miss SUSANNA, eldest daughter of Amos Norris, Esq., all of this city.
109. (D) UPTON SWEADNER, departed this life on Saturday, the 28th ult., after a long and racking illness supposedly brought on by a injury of two years standing. (Libert. June 1831)

June 25, 1831 (CBAL)

110. (D) Melancholy accident - On Thursday evening last, JOSEPH BELL, and PHILIP CLOUSE, laborers of the B & O Railroad were killed by a large body of earth falling upon them. Digging a foundation of stone in the vicinity of the bridge over the Monocacy on the Georgetown turnpike. CLOUSE, was a resident of this city, and the latter of Alleg-any Co.
111. JOHN MACKLEY, was executed yesterday at 11 o'clock, according to the sentencing. In a field adjoining "The Barricks," in the suburbs of the city. Carried from the jail to the place of execution in a carryall, which contained the Sheriff, and Rev. Mr Schaeffer.
112. (M) On Sunday morning the 19th inst., by the Rev. Mr Smith, Mr JOHN C. HOWARD, merchant of Zanesville Ohio, to Miss MINERVA, daughter of Noah Philips, Esq., all of this co.

July 2, 1831 (CBAL)

113. Possible arrest of another subject, Mr CHRISTIAN FRY-DINGER, who may have been involved with Mackley, in the Newey family murder. He was brought before M. Baltzell, Esq., on Thursday last, who committed the subject to jail.
114. Public letter - By the Rev. David F. Schaeffer, who gives a narratived sketch of JOHN MACKLEY. (long article)
115. (M) At Mount Saint Mary's, on the 21st ult., by the Rev. Mr Wiseman, Mr RAYMOND BARNET, of Jefferson Co., VA., to Miss REBECCA OBERMEYER, of this co.
116. (M) At Winchester VA., on Thursday morning the 23rd ult., by the Rev. J. E. Jackson, Mr JAMES R. COBOURN, to Miss MARY ANN MORGAN, all of that town.

117. (D) Near Middletown, Frederick Co., MD., after a short but painful illness on the 12th of June, Mr JOHN DUTROW. He leaves a widow and three sons and four daughters.
118. (D) On the 21st, at his residence in Allegany Co., Mr SAMUEL JAMISON, formerly a inhabitant of this co.
119. Medical Chircugical Faculty - Has selected Drs. JOHN BALTZELL, and W. B. TYLER, as censors for this city. Drs. W. WILLIS, and JACOB BEAR, to represent the co.

July 16, 1831 (CBAL)

120. On Saturday last after a examination before Justice M. Baltzell, Mr CHRISTIAN FRYDINGER, was released from jail, and found to have no connection to John Mackley.
121. (D) Governor DANIEL MARTIN, died at his home in Talbott Co., after a three day illness caused from attack of gout in the stomach. He died on Monday last at 3 o'clock. Mr GEORGE HOWARD, of Anne Arundel Co., was appointed Governor of the State.
122. (M) On Sunday evening last, by the Rev. D. F. Schaeffer, Mr JONATHAN EBRECHT, to Miss REBECCA WILLS, both of this city.
123. (M) On the same evening, by the same, Mr JOHN TURNER, to Miss BARBARA HUGHES, both of this co.
124. (M) On Tuesday morning last, by the same, Mr DANIEL SLEIGH, Esq., of Hagerstown, to Mrs MARY ANN BECK, of this city.
125. (D) On Thursday evening the 22nd ult., Mrs ADELINE STONER, in the 87th year of her age, short and severe was the sickness.
126. (D) Of a pulmonary complaint, on Saturday the 9th inst., in the 12th year of her age, SARAH, eldest daughter of Mr Geo. Broadrupt, of Pleasant Dale Paper Mill, near this city.

July 23, 1831 (CBAL)

127. (D) On Wednesday morning last, after a short illness of 17 hours, VIRGINIA MARY, infant daughter of Henry J. Schriner, aged 19 months and 9 days.

July 30, 1831 (CBAL)

128. (D) Near Ridgeville, below New Market, on the morning of the 18th inst., Mr SAMUEL MENTZER, aged 61, and at 12 o'clock, the following night, his wife Mrs CATHERINE MENTZER, aged 54 years.

129. Rev. Mr JONES, will preach in the Baptist Meeting House of this city, tomorrow afternoon at 3 P.M.

August 6, 1831 (CBAL)

130. (M) In Baltimore, on the 20th ult., by the Rev. Mr Henshew, DANIEL KEMP, of Henry, of this co., to Miss MATILDA, daughter of Derrick Fahnestock, Esq., of Baltimore City.
131. (M) In Mount Pleasant, Frederick Co., MD., on the 31st inst., Mr MICHAEL MORRISON, to Mrs MARY HILLS.
132. (D) Near New Town (Trap,) Frederick Co., MD., on the 25th of July, Mr CHARLES GROSS, age about 85 years, this venerable citizen left eight children and many grandchildren.
133. (D) Suddenly at Winchester VA., on Wednesday last, ALFRED H. POWELL, Esq., highly distinguished for his talents and personal worth. He was seized with apoplexy while pleading in court, and died a few hours afterwards.
134. (D) At Charlottesville VA., on the 27th ult., EDWARD BRIEN, forth son of John Brien, Esq., of this co., in the 21st year of his age.
135. St. John's Female Institute, at last examination of the scholars of the institute, following have been found to merit distinction: 1st, English Grammar - 1st. TERESA LITTLEJOHN, (premium). 2d. TERESA MULLEN, (premium). 3d. MARY O'NEIL. 4th. SOPHIA HOLTZ. Geography - 1st. ELIZABETH WIEST, (premium). 2d. VICTORIA HUGHES (premium). 3d. MARY A. ROACH. 4th. TERESA LITTLEJOHN. History - 1st. MARY O'NEIL, (premium). 2d. TERESA LITTLEJOHN, (premium). 3d. ROSANNA McCHRYSTAL. 4th. SOPHIA SHULTZ. 5th. TERESA McMULLEN. Reading - 1st. ELEANOR MORGAN, (premium). 2d. VICTORIA HUGHES, (premium). 3d. ROSANNA McCRYSTAL. 4th. MARGARET LAWRENCE. Arithmetic - 1st. TERESA McMULLEN, (premium). 2d. TERESA LITTLEJOHN, (premium). 3d. SOPHIA SHULTZ. 4th. MARY O'NEIL. Writing - 1st. VICTORIA HUGHES, (premium). 2d. SOPHIA SHULTZ, (premium). 3d. ELIZABETH WIEST. 4th. TERESA LITTLEJOHN. 2d English Class: Grammar - 1st. ELIZABETH McVICKER, (premium). 2d. CATHARINE KEPHART, (premium). 3d. TERESA FLYNN. History - 1st. ELIZABETH McVICKER, (premium). 2d. CHARLOTTE BAUGHMAN, (premium). Reading and Spelling - 1st. TERESA FLYNN, (premium). 2d. MARGARET FINCH, (premium). Arithmetic - MARGARET SHULTZ, (premium).

2d. MARY McMULLEN, (premium). Writing - 1st. MARY BIRELY, (premium). 2d. CONSTANTIA KNOTT, (premium). 3d. English Class - 1st. ELIZABETH BRUNNER, (premium). 2d. MARGARET SHULTZ, (premium). 3d. MARY McMULLEN. 4th. Class - 1st. HARRIET LITTLEJOHN, (premium). 2d. SAVINIA ABBOTT, (premium). 3d. RACHAEL LAMBRECHT, (premium). 4th. MARY BRUNNER. 5th. Class - 1st. CONSTANTIA KNOTT, (premium). 2d. MARGARET DOLL, (premium). 6th. Class - 1st. BARBARA BRUNNER, (premium). 2d. CATHARINE ELBERT, (premium). 3d. RACHAEL LAMBRECHT, (premium). 4th. MARY FRAZIER. 7th. Class - 1st. HENRIETTA WIEST, (premium). 2d. ZENOBIA HUGHES, (premium). 8th. Class - 1st. ROSE DONNELLY, (premium). 2d. FLORIDIA HUGHES, (premium). 9th. Class - 1st. JULIA ARMOUR, (premium). 2d. MARY STICKLE, (premium). 3d. CATHERINE MAGLAUGHLIN. Music - 1st. VICTORIA HUGHES, (premium). 2d. ELIZABETH WIEST, (premium). 3d. MARGARET LAWRENCE. For regular attendance to all school duties, respect to teachers, strict observance of rules: 1st. SOPHIA SHULTZ. 2d. TERESA McMULLEN. JNO. McELROY.

August 13, 1831 (CBAL)

136. (M) On Sunday last, at Middletown, by the Rev. Mr Reck, Mr JOSHUA JAMES, to Miss CATHERINE HALLER, both of Frederick.
137. (D) On Tuesday the 2nd inst., of pulmonary affliction, Miss JULIANA WALLING, daughter of Mr John Walling, this city.

August 20, 1831 (CBAL)

138. (D) Melancholy accident - Regret to state that Mr JACOB WISSINGER, the only son of Mr George Wissinger, was thrown from his horse on Wednesday last, his skull so badly fractured as to cause his death yesterday morning.
139. (D) At his residence, in this city on Thursday evening last, after an illness of four weeks, Mr DANIEL HAUER, in the 85th year of his age Deceased was an inhabitant of this city upwards of 60 years.
140. (M) On the 11th inst., by the Rev. David F. Schaeffer, Mr HIRAM TULEY, to Miss RUTH HERD, of this place.
141. (M) On Tuesday evening last, by the same, Mr ADAM FRE SHOUR, to Miss LYDIA A. FAUBLE, all of this city.

August 27, 1831 (CBAL)
142. (D) On Tuesday last, Mrs ANNA MARGARET HEICHLER, at the advanced age of 91 years and 23 days.
143. (D) On Sunday night the 14th inst., Mrs ANNA MARIA BAYER, consort of Mr Jacob Bayer, in the 64th year of her age.
144. (D) Another Revolutionary Patriot gone - DAVID WILLIAMS, the last of the captor of Major Andre, died at Renssalaerville, N. Y., on Tuesday week, in the 79th year of his age. His remains were on Thursday interred with full military honors, at Livingstonville, Schoharie Co.
145. (D) On Saturday morning last, Mr STEPHEN CURTISS CRUBB CROMWELL, son of Mr Richard Cromwell, in the 23rd year of his age.
146. (D) On Sunday evening last, Mrs HANNAH HOFFMAN, consort of Mr William Hoffman, in the 28th year of her age.
147. (D) Departed this life, on the 17th inst., at the residence of his father near Liberty-Town, ALEXANDER A. WARFIELD, son of Suratt D., and Matilda Warfield, late a student of Kenyon College in the state of Ohio, in the 17th year of his age.

September 10, 1831 (CBAL)
148. (M) At the house of Mr Rives, Minister of the United States at the French Court, NATHANIEL NILES, Esq., Secretary of the American Legation, to Mrs ROSELLA DE MILHAU, of Baltimore, widow of the late Dr. John Sue of Paris.
149. (M) On Tuesday evening last, by the Rev. D. F. Schaeffer, Mr CHARLES SCHISLER, to Miss AMELIA SHIELDS, of this co.
150. (M) Yesterday morning, by the same, Mr PHILIP BAER, to Miss CYRENE JOHNSON, all of this co.
151. (M) On the same day, by the same, Mr SAMUEL SLIFER, Esq., to Miss MARY SLIFER, both of Middletown Valley.
152. (D) At about 2 o'clock, on the morning of the 2nd inst., in Baltimore, aged nearly 22 years, ROBERT DUER NILES, printer, and son of Hezekiah Niles, editor of the "Weekly Register," the decease was fifth but third surviving son. He had never been altogether healthy; yet on Tuesday morning, previous to his death with only a moments warning as it were, received his death blow-repeated and violent convulsions from which he was unexpectedly recover through the energy of his physician and friends, to linger a little longer, and became sensible of his condition generally

being in possession of his mind, and greatfully acknowledging the efforts made to relieve him of his pain. His remains were interred in the Friends burying grounds.

153. (D) On Friday evening the 2nd inst., at a quarter before 9 o'clock, in the 27th year of his age, ALEXANDER THOMAS HAWKINS, only son of James L. Hawkins, Esq., of Baltimore. He was educated at Yale College, and graduated in 1826. His parents had designed him for the profession of the law, but enthusiastic attachment to agriculture pursuits, he prevailed on his father to purchase a farm in Frederick Co., where he was about to settle when he was attacked with a pulmonary affection which terminated his mortal existence.

154. (D) In New York, on the 7th inst., Dr. SAMUEL L. MITCHELL, the justly celebrated philosopher and antiquarian.

September 17, 1831 (CBAL)

155. (M) On the 27th ult., by the Rev. Mr Smaltz, Mr JOHN HEFFERMAN, to Miss ELIZABETH CRANE, both of this co.

156. (M) On Tuesday evening last, by the same, Mr THOMAS L. ARVARD, to Miss MARTHA ANN ROSE, both of District of Columbia.

157. (D) On Thursday last, Mr. PETER HALLER, (carpenter,) after a illness of a few days.

158. (D) Another hero of the Revolution gone - Died on Saturday last, at his farm in this co., Major JOHN LEATHER, a soldier of the Revolution, in the 77th year of his age. Major Leather, distinguished himself in the War of Independence, by many acts of valor and was wounded in several engagements with the enemies of his Country. Was in the Battles of Trenton, Monmouth and Germantown, and various other engagements, in all of which he distinguished himself by his bravery and soldier-like conduct, as a citizen, he was universally respected:-mild and amiable in his manners, as a Christian, he was a example of meekness and piety, worthy of imitation. (Citizen.)

159. Rev. Mr JONES, of Rockville, Montgomery Co., will preach in the Baptist Meeting House of this place, on next Sunday evening at 3 o'clock, P.M.

September 24, 1831 (CBAL)

160. (M) On Thursday last, by the Rev. D. F. Schaeffer, Mr THOMAS BERGER, to Miss ANN REBECCA HOUSE, all of this co.

161. (M) On the 20th inst., by the Rev. Mr Hayden, Mr LAWRENCE JAMISON, of Allegany Co., MD., to Miss MARGARET JOSEPHINE, only daughter of Thomas Hayden, Esq., of Bedford PA.
162. (D) On Friday the 16th inst., of pulmonary complaint, at Mr Jacob Cramers, on Israel Creek, JESSE W. STARR, in the 20th year of his age, his remains were deposited in the graveyard of Mr Amos Norris, near Liberty-Town.
163. (D) In this city on Saturday morning the 16th inst., of a paralytick affection which she survived for 431/2 hours, in the 61st year of her age, Mrs CATHERINE CONTEE TYLER, wife of Dr. John Tyler. Though she had suffered much for several years past, from ill health, death was most sudden and unexpected. She had resided in Fredericktown for 50 years, she had been married to Dr. Tyler for 44 years.
164. (D) On the same day, Mrs ------ MARTIN, consort of Rev. David Martin, of this city, at an advanced age.
165. (D) In this city on Thursday evening last, after a short illness, Mrs CATHARINE THOMAS, wife of Dr. John Thomas, she leaves infant children.
166. (D) On Monday mornig last, after a short illness, Mr WILLIAM KELLEY, a native of Ireland.
167. (D) On the 14th inst., MARGARET, wife, and on Monday last, THOMAS, son of John H. Abbott, all of this city.

October 1, 1831 (CBAL)

168. On Sunday morning last the family of NOAH PHILIPS, Esq., a highly respectable inhabitant of Woodsboro District in this co., was poisoned by drinking coffee, in which seeds of Jamestown weed, or stramonium had been mixed. Medical aid was promptly afforded, and we are happy to state that the persons poisoned, consisted of Mr Philips, his wife, son, and daughter and neice, are rapidly recovering. A negro woman, and two men, the property of Mr P., have been committed to prison on charges of being concerned in the diabolical act.
169. (M) On Sunday morning last, by the Rev. Mr Schaeffer, Mr ISRAEL SWEENY, to Miss ANN MARIE WILHIDE, all of this co.
170. (M) On the same day, by the same, Mr CASPER MILLER, to Miss CATHARINE KEIL both of this co.
171. (M) On Thursday the 22nd ult., by the Rev. Mr Smaltz, Mr SOLOMON STALEY, to Miss SUSANNA BARBARA STALEY, of this co.

172. (M) At Union Mills, Frederick Co., on Tuesday the 20th ult., by the Rev. Mr Fiddler, Mr WM. T. STEIGERS, of Baltimore, to Miss ANN M. S. SHRIVER, daughter of Andrew Shriver, Esq.
173. (M) On the 21st ult., Mr ABNER M. PLUMMER, to Miss RUTH HAINES, all of Pipe Creek.
174. (D) In this city, on Thursday the 22nd of September of one week sickness, in the 30th year of her age, Mrs CATHARINE CONTEE THOMAS, wife of Dr. John M. Thomas, and daughter of the late Thomas Turner, Accountant of the Navy Department, and resident of Georgetown, D.C.

October 8, 1831 (CBAL)

175. (M) On Sunday morning last, by the Rev. David F. Schaeffer, Mr PETER BRUNNER, to Miss ANN SOPHIA SHAFER, all of this co.
176. (M) On Sunday evening last, by the same, Mr GEORGE RICE, to Miss MARGARET MICHAEL, all of this city.
177. (M) On Tuesday last, by the same, at Liberty, Mr JOSIAH GETZENDANNER, of this city, to Miss HARRIET HULL, of the former place.
178. (D) In Carlisle PA., WILLIAM RAMSEY, Esq., a member of the Congress of the United States from PA., he was about 50 years old.

October 15, 1831 (CBAL)

179. (M) On Wednesday evening last, by the Rev. D. F. Schaeffer, Mr PETER L. STORM, to Miss HARRIET RHEIL, both of this co.
180. (M) On Thursday last, by the Rev. John H. Smaltz, Mr JOHN D. LATE, to Miss MARY ANN BAUMBAUGH, both of this co.
181. Mr LEWIS MEDTART, candidate for Mayor.

October 22, 1831 (CBAL)

182. A Miss CLIFTON, who was educated at Emmitsburg, MD., only 17, played in New York as Lady MacBeth.
183. (M) On the 20th inst., at the house of M. E. Bartgis, Esq., by the Rev. John H. Smaltz, Mr JNO. HOCKENSMITH, to Mrs ELIZABETH SMITH, all of this co.
184. (M) On the same day, by the same, Mr JOSEPH DEVILBISS, to Miss CAROLINE STOUFFER, all of this city.
185. (M) In Hagerstown, Washington Co., on the 13th inst., by the Rev. Mr Draine, DANIEL MARTIN, Esq., to Miss MARY

BARTIN HAMILTON, both of Petersville, Frederick Co.
186. (D) On Tuesday last, of an apoplectic attack, Mr JOHN GOMBAR, at advanced age, an a soldier of the Revolution.
187. (D) Recently, at the city of Washington, Mrs SARAH ELLIOTT, wife of Jonathan Elliott, printer.
188. (D) Mrs MARY THOMPSON, sister of the famous Charles Thompson, Secretary of the Revolutionary Congress, died at the house of her nephew John Thompson, Esq., at Newark Del., on the 20th ult., aged 93 years. There were five brothers, and one sister, of this family the youngest died at 79, the oldest Charles, at 95 the sum of their ages being 531 years, or an average of 88 1/2 years.
189. Rev. Mr JONES, will preach in the English Presbyterian Church, this evening at early candle light.

October 29, 1831 (CBAL)

190. (D) Melancholy accident - By letter received from Baltimore yesterday, we leaned that the body of Mr JOHN HUGHES, who formerly resided at Locust Level in vicinity of this city, was discovered on Wednesday morning last, floating in the dock at the foot of Bond Street, Fell's Point near Capt. Kerr's Wharf. A inquest was held upon it and a verdict of death by drowning was returned. In the pockets of the decease was found a small sum of money in notes on the Frederick County Bank, and a pair of pocket pistols. He was last seen four or five days previous to the discovery of his body, at about 1 o'clock in the morning, without his boots, hat or coat. It is suppose that while laboring under mental derangement, he met his melancholy end by falling into the basin. The body was disfigured from the fish and crabs, made it difficult to recognized by some our of our citizens.
191. Mr WILLIAM J. THOMSON, Esq., has presented to us an apple of a kind called "English Red Streak," which measured 13" in circumference, and weighted one pound.

November 5, 1831 (CBAL)

192. Candidates announced for Mayoralty: JOHN RIGNEY, LEWIS MEDTART, THOMAS CARLTON, JOSHUA DILL.

November 12, 1831 (CBAL)

193. (M) On the 6th inst., by the Rev. Mr McElroy, Mr PHILIP DAWSON, to Miss ANN PHEOBUS, all of this co.

194. (M) On the 8th inst., by the Rev. Mr Barber, Mr JOHN HIMMILL, to Mrs CATHERINE LEASE, all of this co.
195. (D) In the village of New Market, on Tuesday the 8th inst., Mr AMBROSE INGMAN, in the 49th year of his age-long a resident of this place. He leaves a widow, and a number of children. His funeral with Masonic Honors will take place on Sunday the 20th inst.
196. (D) On Tuesday last, after a few hours illness, HENRY KOONTZ, Esq., an old and most worthy citizen of Frederick.
197. (D) On Monday last, Mr MICHAEL MARQUART, and old and respectable inhabitant of Frederick.
198. (D) Departed this life on the 8th inst., in the 51st year of his age, at his residence near this city, STEPHEN RAMSBURG, leaving a disconsolate widow. He had been afflicted for the last two to three years with and inveterate cutaneous disease which defied the skills of the most able physicians more immediate cause of death was a bilious attack.
199. At the 11th annual meeting of the Young Mens Bible Society, of Frederick County, held at the Luthern Church in Frederick, on Monday, the 31st of October. The following gentlemen were elected Directors, for the ensuing year: AUGUSTUS F. EBERT, JAMES M. SHELMAN, VALERIUS EBERT, Dr. ALBERT RITCHIE, A. P. BEATTY, WILLIAM OGDEN NILES, JOHN HANSHEW, JONA. E. WOODBRIDGE, SETH NICHOLS, WILLIAM J. ROSS, JOHN L. SAUNDERS, HORATIO McPHERSON, GIDEON BANTZ, Jr., NEILSON POE, JACOB RAMSBURG, VALENTINE BIRELY, GEORGE L. L. DAVIS, THOMAS RITCHIE, WILLIAM WEBER, GEORGE ENGLISH, MEREDITH DAVIS, GEORGE SALMON. At the meeting of the Directors, held on Monday the 7th inst., the Board elected the following officers for the ensuring year: JAMES M. SHELMAN - President, JONATHAN E. WOODBRIDGE - Vice President, WM. OGDEN NILES - 2nd Vice President, AUGUSTUS F. EBERT - Corresponding Secretary, Doct. ALBERT RITCHIE - Treasurer, GIDEON BANTZ, Jr., - Recording Secretary, Rev. DAVID F. SCHAEFFER - Agent of the Depository.

November 19, 1831 (CBAL)

200. (M) On Thursday evening the 10th inst., by the Rev. James Day, Mr RICHARD D. SALMON, to Miss DORCAS KINLEY, all of this co.

201. (M) On Sunday last, by the Rev. D. F. Schaefffer, Mr DIEDER BERGSTRASSER, to Miss CATHERINE E. PIETER, of Chambersburg, PA.
202. (M) At Hagerstown, on the 1st inst., by the Rev. Mr Hoshour, Mr WILLIAM STICKLE, of Williamsport, to Miss SARAH RIDENOUR, of the former place.
203. (M) On the 10th, by the Rev. D. F. Schaeffer, Mr JOHN HOVES, to Miss MARGARET LAYMAN.
204. (M) On Thursday evening last by the same, Mr GEORGE STULL, to Miss SUSAN HEDGES, all of this co.
205. Rev. Mr JONES, of Rockville Montgomery Co., will preach at the Baptist Meeting House of this city on to-morrow afternoon at 3 o'clock.
206. At a public meeting in the city of Frederick held at the Court House on Saturday evening last. THOMAS CARLTON, Esq., Mayor of this city, was called to the chair, and CYRUS MANTZ, was appointed Secretary. A resolution was approved to appoint a committee of thirty to make appropriate arrangement to testify the high gratification which will be felt by the city of Frederick, at the completion of that part of the railroad which is to unite more intimately the commerical and social relations of the city of Baltimore and Frederick. The following gentlemen were appointed to this committee: THOMAS CARLTON, RICHARD POTTS, ABRAHAM SHRIVER, FRANCIS THOMAS, WILLIAM ROSS, GIDEON BANTZ, Dr. WILLIAM TYLER, GEORGE W. ENT, JOSEPH M. PALMER, Dr. JOHN BALTZELL, WILLIAM FISCHER, WILLIAM SCHLEY, WM. M. BEALL, GEORGE BALTZELL, Dr. W. B. TYLER, F. A. SCHLEY, J. P. THOMPSON, W. OGDEN NILES, G. M. EICHELBERGER, JOHN RIGNER, NEILSON POE, T. C. WORTHINGTON, JOHN McPHERSON, HENRY SCHLEY, DANIEL KOLB, GEO. W. SHARP, W. S. McPHERSON, J. H. McELFRESH, M. E. BARTGIS, GEO. WISSINGER, MADISON NELSON.

November 26, 1831 (CBAL)

207. The Baltimore and Ohio Railroad is officially open between Baltimore and Frederick. (long article)
208. Mr CLAY, is expected to arrive in this city on Tuesday or Wednesday next.

December 3, 1831 (CBAL)

209. (M) At Elmwood, residence of Jacob Poe, Esq., on Wednesday evening last, by the Rev. Mr Jackson, Mr NEILSON

POE, to Miss JOSEPHINE E., second daughter of the late Wm. Clemm, Esq., of Baltimore.

210. (M) On Thursday evening last, at Hagerstown, by the Rev. M. L. Fullerton, Mr WILLIAM MARSHALL, to Miss ELIZABETH, youngest daughter of Capt. Lodowick Leeds, formerly of Baltimore.

211. (M) On Tuesday last, by the Rev. John H. Smaltz, Mr JAMES DURBIN, to Miss ANN ELIZABETH, daughter of John Stoner, Esq., all of this co.

212. (M) On Tuesday evening last, in Baltimore, by the Rev. Mr Pierce, JOHN THOMAS SCHLEY, of this city, to GEORGIANA VIRGINIA, daughter of the late John McClure, of Baltimore.

213. (M) On the same evening, in Baltimore, by the Rev. Mr Johns, GEO. W. COX, to ANN ELIZA, daughter of Richard M. Hall.

214. (M) On Thursday the 10th inst., by the Rev. Mr Porter, Mr NATHAN HAMMOND, of Linganore, to Miss MARY SIMS, of the vicinity of Woodsboro.

215. (M) On Tuesday last, by the same, Mr CHARLES MEYER, to Miss CATHERINE HESSON, both of this co.

216. (M) At Westminster, MD., by the Rev. Mr Burnap, Mr EVAN GAITHER, of Baltimore Co., to Miss SARAH ANN SELMAN, daughter of Mr Wm. Shipley of Westminster.

217. (M) On the 20th ult., by the Rev. David F. Schaeffer, ISAAC HANNA, Esq., to Miss SARAH YOUNG.

218. (M) On Sunday last, by the same, Mr BALDWIN WOODWARD, to Miss LYDIA A. WOODWARD, both of this city.

219. (M) On Thursday the 16th of Nov., by the Rev. Alfred Griffith, Mr GREENBURRY BUCKENHAM, to Miss CATHERINE ROWHAN, both of Liberty-Town.

220. (M) At Philadelphia on Thursday last week, by the Rev. Mr Barnes, ANDREW JACKSON, Jr., Esq., son of the President of the United States, to Miss SARAH, daughter of the late Peter Yorke, of that city.

221. Last Summer an individual named DANIEL SHAEFFER, was committed to the jail of this co., upon a volunteer confession of murder made by him to a magistrate of this city. The particulars was forward to Lancaster Co., Pa., where the murder occurred, and was found to be true. The prisoner was soon afterwards forward to Lancaster's jail, by the Sheriff of that co. Trial took place last week, our Mayor was summoned as a witness, but returned home before it terminated. A letter received by him yesterday stating that

on Saturday evening last, the jury, after retiring for 4 1/2 hours returned with a verdict of "Guilty of murder in the first degree." The murder was committed on the person of an aged female. The Lancaster paper, perhaps will give particulars of the trial.

December 10, 1831 (CBAL)

222. (M) On the 8th inst., by the Rev. John H. Smaltz, Mr GEORGE KLEIN, to Miss SARAH ANN SHUP.
223. (M) On the same day, by the same, Mr NATHANIEL CLAREY, to Miss CASSANDRA THOMAS, all of Frederick Co.
224. Mr CLAY, passed through this city on Sunday last, and during his brief stay he was waited on by a large number of citizens.
225. At the funeral of Mr JONA. WOODMAN of Newburryport, the pallbearers were all soldiers of the Revolution, the oldest being 82, and the youngest 70 years old; their united ages were 463.

December 17, 1831 (CBAL)

226. (M) On the 24th ult., by the Rev. Charles Weyle, Mr THOMAE SLICK, to Miss RACHEL MAUS, both of Frederick Co.
227. (M) On the 24th ult., by the Rev. John N. Hoffman, Mr JOHN RECK, to Miss ELIZABETH FAIR, both of Taney-Town.
228. (M) On the 6th inst., by the Rev. D. F. Schaeffer, DANIEL LAMBERT, Esq., to Miss CATHERINE HILDEBRAND, all of this co.
229. WM. NILES, WM. FISCHER, our worthy fellow citizens will be supported as a candidate for the office of Alderman at appointed election.
230. Rev. Mr JONES, will preach in the Baptist Meeting House on tomorrow, at 3 o'clock in the afternoon.

December 24, 1831 (CBAL)

231. (M) On Tuesday evening the 20th inst., by the Rev. David Englar, Mr EPHRAIM ENGLAR, to Miss AGNES, fourth daughter of Mr Christian Ely, all of Frederick Co.
232. (D) Departed this life on the 18th inst., at the house of the brother-in-law, Wm. Ross, Esq., in FrederickTown, Mrs CAROLINE W. G. GRAHAME, relict of the late Thomas J.

Grahame, youngest daughter of the late Col. Baker Johnson.
233. Relief of the poor - Meeting was held at the Court House on Friday evening last week. Mayor THOMAS CARLTON, Esq., was called to the Chair, and JOHN BRUNNER, of J., was appointed Secretary. The following gentlemen were appointed to make collections in their respected Wards. Ward #1. JOHN LUGENBED, GEORGE WISSINGER. Ward #2. NICHOLAS TURBUTT, JOHN RIGNEY. Ward #3. STUART GAITHER, PATRICK TORMEY. Ward #4. LEWIS MEDTART, JAMES M. SHELMAN. Ward #5. EDWARD TRAIL, GEORGE WEBSTER. Ward #6. TH. C. PRINCE, MICHAEL BALTZELL. Ward #7. L. P. W. BALCH, JOHN McDONALD. The following gentlemen were appointed by the chairman as a committee to receive and disburse the funds: R. POTTS, P. O'NEAL, DAVID BOYD, ABRAHAM KEMP, and HENRY NIXDORFF.

December 31, 1831 (CBAL)

234. (M) On the 29th inst., by the Rev. John H. Smaltz, Mr GEORGE ZIMMERMAN, paper maker, to Miss MARY ANN MARTZ, daughter of Maj. Martz.
235. (M) On the same day, by the same, Mr JACOB BARRICK, to Miss CATHERINE SMITH, all of Frederick Co.
236. (D) In Baltimore, on the night of Wednesday the 21st inst., Mr THOMAS PEACOCK, proprietor of the American Hotel, Pratt Street.
237. (D) In Philadelphia, on Monday last, STEPHEN GIRRARD, Esq., aged 85 years. Probably the richest merchant in the world, he rose from humble poverty, and his net capital is estimated at about ten million dollars. He has resided here for about 50 years.
238. Mr GEO. WOODBRIDGE, acknowledges receipts of the following contributions from citizens &c, of Frederick, to the Society for Education of Pious Young Men for the Ministry of the Protestant Episcopal Church. Rev. Mr JACKSON: $10.00, Dr. WM. TYLER: $10.00, HORATIO McPHERSON: $5.00, Mite Society: $50.00, Dr. W. B. TYLER: $10.00. Ladies of All Saint's Church for furnishing room at seminary, $50.00. Making together a total of $135.00.

1832

January 7, 1832 (CBAL)

239. (D) On Saturday last, at his residence in this co., MATTHEW BROWN, Esq., aged about 65 years. Former editor and one of the proprietors of the Baltimore Federal Gazette, which he conducted for 12 years.
240. (D) On Tuesday morning last, Mrs CATHARINE NUSZ, consort of Frederick Nusz, Esq., in the 58th year of her age.
241. (D) On Thursday the 29th ult., after a protracted illness of nearly seven years, Mrs DOROTHEA M. A. STUCHBURY, in the 57th year of her age, a resident of this city for the last 30 years.
242. The following gentlemen are respectfully announced to the city of Frederick as candidates for Alderman: GIDEON BANTZ, ABRAHAM KEMP, GEORGE SHUTZ, DANIEL KOLB, and WM. FISCHER.

January 14, 1832 (CBAL)

243. (M) On Wednesday evening last, by the Rev. Mr Wachter, GEORGE G. HENDERSON to Miss MARY ANN WEAVER, all of this co.
244. (M) On Tuesday last, by the Rev. David F. Schaeffer, Mr JOHNSEY EASTON, to Miss SARAH STIMMEL, all of this co.
245. (M) On the same day, by the same, Mr BASIL LUGENBEEL, merchant of this city, to Miss SYBILLA SMITH, daughter of H. Smith, Esq.
246. (D) At Liberty-Town on Wednesday morning, 4th inst., CHRISTIAN VAGNER, in the 64th year of his age, after a long and lingering illness. The deceased was one amongst the oldest resident of that place. His remains were followed to the grave by his widow and six children, was interred in the Catholic Church burying grounds on Thursday last.
247. (D) Last week, in Baltimore Co., Mrs MARY STINCHCOMB, wife of Beal C. Stinchcomb, Esq., and daughter of John Hamilton, Esq., in the 35th year of her age.
248. (D) On the 27th ult., WILLIAM P. FARQUHAR, Esq., formerly a representative from this co., in the Legislature of MD.
249. Rev. Mr JONES, will preach in the Baptist Meeting House of this city, on to-morrow, at 3 o'clock, P.M.

January 21, 1832 (CBAL)
250. (D) On Sunday last, Mrs BUCKEY, consort of Mr Michael Buckey, of this city.
251. (D) On Sunday night last, Mr JOHN L. ATWOOD, in the 56th year of his age, a respectable citizen of this co.
252. (D) In Baltimore, on the 18th inst., aged 84 years, the Hon. ALEXANDER McKIM, for several years past the presiding judge of the Orphan's Court, of Baltimore Co., and previously one of the representatives of that district in Congress. Was numbered among the most respectable citizens of Baltimore, for nearly 60 years.
253. (M) On Thursday evening the 19th inst., in Frederick, by the Rev. John Johns, of Baltimore, Mr JAMES HOWARD, of Baltimore, to Miss CATHERINE M. ROSS, eldest daughter of William Ross, Esq., of Frederick.
254. (M) On Sunday eveninng last, by the Rev. D. F. Schaeffer, Mr JAMES FINNEY, to Mrs CHARLOTTE BEAR, daughter of the late Christian Keefer, Esq., all of this co.
255. A committee of fifteen was appointed by Chairman JAMES DIXON, to draw up articles of association and to apply to the Legislature for an Act of Incorporation for the "Mechanics Institute and Frederick Lyseum" The following gentlemen was appointed to serve on the committee: RICHARD POTTS, F. A. SCHLEY, Dr. JOHN BALTZELL, WILLIAM M. BEALL, VALENTINE BIRELY, GEO. W. ENT, D. B. DEVITT, GEORGE M. EICHELBERGER, GEO. ENGELBRECHT, SAMUEL CARMACK, WM. FISCHER, WM. OGDEN NILES, G. W. SHARP, JOHN McPHERSON, GIDEON BANTZ, and BENJAMIN PRICE, appointed as Secretary.
256. Candidates for the position of Mayor: THOMAS CARLTON, LEWIS MEDTART, JOHN L. HARDING. For Alderman: MICHAEL BALTZELL, GIDEON BANTZ, WM. FISCHER, JACOB FAUBEL, TH. W. MORGAN, GEORGE SHULTZ, WM. KOLB, Sr., FREDERICK LOEHR, ANDREW HEIM, HENRY SCHOLL, DAVID B. DEVITT, WM. S. McPHERSON, HENRY NIXDORFF, LEWIS BIRELY, JOHN KUNKEL, JOHN S. MILLER, G. W. ENT, SAMUEL CARMACK, NICHOLAS TURBUTT, DANIEL KOLB, DAVID BOYD, ABRAHAM KEMP, JOHN McDONALD, JACOB BERGER, CASPER QUYNN, PHILIP HAUPTMAN, JOHN FESSLER. For Councilmen: 1st Ward: GEORGE WISSINGER. 2nd Ward: WILLIAM SMALL. 3rd Ward: VALENTINE BIRELY, JACOB LITTLE. 5th Ward: JAMES WALLING, SAMUEL B. LEWIS,

and GEORGE WHIPP. 6th Ward: GEORGE B. SHOPE, JOSEPH PAYNE, and HENRY KEHLER, Sen.

January 28, 1832 (CBAL)

257. (D) At his residence at "Rockdale Factory" near Emmitsburg, on the 24th inst., in the 65th year of his age, after a protracted illness, WILLIAM GREASON, Sen'r., a native of Ireland. He came to this Country soon after the close of the Revolution, to enjoy the blessings purchased by some of the noblest blood of his native and adopted Country. Was an ardent admirer of the political institution of this Country and sympathized in the suffering of his friends and the Country of the "Emerald Isle." He leaves a widow and four children.
258. (D) Departed this life near Newtown Trap, on Saturday the 4th inst., Mrs ELIZA LYNCH, in the 35th year of her age. After a long and lingering illness, she leaves a husband and eight children.
259. (D) Departed this life on the 31st of December last, at the residence of Elisha S. Johnson, Esq., in Baltimore Co., Mrs MARTHA WORTHINGTON, widow of Samuel Worthington late of that co., in the 78th year of her age.

February 4, 1832 (CBAL)

260. (F) Fire broke out yesterday morning at about 2 o'clock in the Tailor's Shop of Messer CROMWELL and STONE, on Patrick near Market Street, and ajoining the Dry Goods store of Mr WM. ROCHESTER. Before it was discovered it had consumed a portion of the partition which separated Mr R's., store from the Tailors' Shop, and we reget to state that material injury was done to the Dry Goods &c. A young man who was, fortunately, sleeping in the store discovered the fire before it had made such progress. Mr R's., goods were insured, the fire was caused by a most culpable and dangerous practice, by placing warm ashes from the stove or fire place in wooden vessels. In this instance they were put in a barrel, after starting it rapidly moved in to the wooden partition. Question? What amount of property is insured in this city? Probably not one twentieth.
261. J. L. HARDING, is not a candidate for Mayor, and Dr. WM. S. McPHERSON, declines being a candidate for Alderman.

February 11, 1832 (CBAL)
262. (M) On Sunday morning last, by the Rev. David F. Schaeffer, Mr CHARLES BRENGLE, to Mrs SARAH ANN BAER, all of this city.
263. (M) On Tuesday evening by the same, Mr HENRY KESSLER, to Miss PRISCILLA BOSWELL, all of this city.
264. (D) On the 4th inst., Mr CHARLES BENTZ, aged 25 years.
265. (D) In Baltimore, on Sunday the 5th inst., Mr JOHN LEE POTTS, of Frederick Co., in the 44th year of his age. His remains were interred on Tuesday the 7th in the graveyard of St. Paul's Church, in Baltimore.
266. (D) On the 3rd inst., Mrs CAROLINE DOLL, wife of Mr Thomas Doll, of this town, in the 28th year of her age.

February 18, 1832 (CBAL)
267. (M) On Thursday the 9th inst., by the Rev. William Armstrong, Mr GEORGE W. BEALL, to Miss CAROLINE C. COCKEY, all of this co.
268. (M) On Sunday last, by the Rev. D. F. Schaeffer, Mr JOHN M. SCHNEIDER, to Miss ANNA HEIST, both of this co.
269. (M) On Tuesday last, by the same, Mr DANIEL EYSTER, to Miss MAGDALENA MILLER, both of this co.
270. (D) On Saturday last, in the 25th year of his age, Mr WILLIAM RICE, of this city.
271. (D) In this city, on Monday morning 13th inst, Mr JOHN McALEER, a native of Tyrone Co., Ireland, after a illness of several weeks.

February 25, 1832 (CBAL)
272. (M) On the 14th inst., by the Rev'd. John Smaltz, Mr JOHN NICHOLAS ZIMMERMAN, to Miss ELIZABETH ALBAUGH, both of this co.
273. JOSEPH B. WEBB, has been appointed flour inspector for this city.
274. Mayor DANIEL HUGHES, declines being considered as a candidate for the Common Council.
275. Appointments for Frederick County, for the year 1832. Judges of the Orphans' Court: HENRY KEMP, PETER MANTZ, and JACOB STEINER. Levy Court: JACOB SCHRIVER, GRAFTON DUVALL, MOSES WORMAN, JAMES SIMMONS ARAHAM JONES, WM. MILLER, SINGLETON WOOTTON, DAVID FOUTZ, MARTIN EICHELBERGER, FREDERICK TROXALL, SOLOMON FORREST. Coroners: WM. R. KING, HENRY BOTELER, GEORGE TITLOW,

GEORGE PRICE, ALEXANDER McIIHENNY, DENNIS D. HOWARD, GEORGE HUGHES. Justices of the Peace: JACOB BAER, BELT BRASHEAR, HENRY BAKER, SAMUEL BOMGARDNER, CHARLES H. BURKHART, HENRY BANTZ, MALACHI BERNARD, TILGHMAN BISER, PETER BANKERT, WASHINGTON BURGESS, CHRISTIAN BOWER, MICHAEL BALTZELL, GEORGE BLESSING, HENRY BURHMAN, PHILIP BIRELY, DANIEL S. BISER, ABNER CAMPBELL, JACOB COBLENTZ, JACOB CRAMER, GEORGE CASSELL, of Jno., JACOB CASSELL, GIDEON D. CRUMBAUGH, WM. DURBIN, ROBERT DODDS, ISAAC DERN, DANIEL DUVALL, JOHN W. DERR, CHARLES DEVILBISS, WM. DUDDERAR, JAMES DURBIN, of Jno., JOSHUA DOUB, LLOYD DORSEY, JOHN EBERT, DANIEL ENGLE, WM. FLANAGAN, HENRY FUNDENBURG, JAMES FISHER, GEORGE FLAUTT, WM. GRIMES, STEPHEN GORSUCH, WM. R. GILLELAN, JOHN L. HARDING, WILSON HAYES, BENJAMIN HEFFNER, BARTON HACKNEY, H. A. HEINBLETON, JACOB HOFFMAN, THOMAS HOOK, JOHN HINDS, WM. R. HEAD, JOHN W. HOPPE, LEWIS I. HOBBS, DANIEL HUGHES, WM. C. HOFFMAN, MAHLON HARLEY, NELSON HOFFMAN, THOS. JOHNSON, of Wm., JOSHUA JONES, WM. JARBOE, Dr. THOS. W. JOHNSON, WM. KNOX, ZEBULON KUHN, GEORGE KUHN, EDWARD KNOTT, JOSEPH KEEFER, JACOB LAMBERT, Sr., LLOYD LUCKETT, MICHAEL LEASE, JACOB LEASE, PATRICK MAGILL, JEREMIAH G. MORRISON, LEWIS MOTTER, ALEX'R McIIHENNY, JOHN McDONALD, PHIL. S. McELFRESH, WM. MURPHEY, Sr., JOHN McNEEL, WM. MOONEY, GEORGE MATHIAS, Jr., JOHN MONTGOMERY, MICHAEL MEALY, WM. V. MORGAN, NICHOLAS NORRIS, BURGESS NELSON, N. H. OWINGS, LEVI O'BRIEN, NOAH PHILLIPS, WM. H. POOLE, THOMAS POWELL, JNO. W. PRATT, GEORGE PRICE, JACOB POWDER, Jr., GEORGE PHELPS, GEORGE ROHR, ELIHU H. ROCKWELL, GEORGE RINER, GEORGE RICE, ANDREW SHRIVER, DAVID SCHLEY, JOHN L. SMITH, JAMES SMITH, SEBASTIAN SULTZER, MICHAEL SULLIVAN, JOSHUA SMITH, Jr., JAMES SUMMERS, NOAH A. SHAFER, DANIEL SWEADNER, JACOB THOMAS, JOSEPH TANEY, Sr., WASHINGTON VANBIBBER, SARAT D. WARFIELD, SOMERSET R. WATERS, ZACH. T. WINDSOR, CHARLES WILLARD, HENRY YOUNG, GEORGE YANTIS, JNO. M. ZOLLICKOFFER.

276. Candidates for Mayor: THOMAS CARLTON, LEWIS MEDTART. Following gentlemen are proposed candidates for Alderman: MICHAEL BALTZELL, GIDEON BANTZ, WM. FISCHER, JACOB FAUBEL, TH. W. MORGAN, GEORGE SHULTZ, WM. KOLB, Sr., FREDERICK LOEHR, ANDREW HEIM, HENRY SCHOLL, DAVID B. DEVITT, HENRY NIXDORFF, LEWIS BIRELY, JOHN KUNKEL, JOHN S. MILLER, G. W. ENT, SAMUEL CARMACK, NICHOLAS TURBUTT, DANIEL KOLB, DAVID BOYD, ABRAHAM KEMP, JOHN McDONALD, JACOB BERGER, CASPER QUYNN, PHILIP HAUPTMAN, JOHN FESSLER. For Councilmen: 1st Ward: GEORGE WISSINGER. 2nd Ward: WILLIAM SMALL. 3rd Ward: VALENTINE BIRELY, JACOB LITTLE. 5th Ward: JAMES WALLING, SAMUEL B. LEWIS and GEORGE WHIPP. 6th Ward: GEORGE B. SHOPE, JOSEPH PAYNE and HENRY KEHLER, Sen.

March 3, 1832 (CBAL)

277. Levy Court - Following is a correct list of the Levy Court recently appointed for this county. The list published in our last comprised the members who were first appointed for last year. District #1. MOSES WORMAN. District #2. JAMES SIMMONS. District #3. THOMAS SPRINGER. District #4. MARTIN EICHELBERGER. District #5. FREDERICK TROXALL. District #6. DAVID FOUTZ. District #7. ABRAHAM WAMPLER. District #8. ABRAHAM JONES. District #9. SINGLETON WOOTTEN. District #10. SOLOMON FORREST. District #11. WM. MILLER. District #12. JOHN COST.

278. City election, which was held on Monday last for the officers of the corporation, which resulted as follows. For Mayor: THOMAS CARLTON - 298, LEWIS MEDTART - 236. For Alderman: DANIEL KOLB - 300, GIDEON BANTZ - 292, THOS. W. MORGAN - 257, DAVID BOYD - 217, ABRAHAM KEMP - 200, CASPAR QUYNN - 176, JACOB FAUBLE - 117, GEO. W. ENT - 108, SAML. CARMACK - 106, ANDREW HEIM - 93, WM. KOLB - 77, JOHN KUNKLE - 70, GEO. SHULTZ - 69, WM. FISCHER - 62, HENRY NIXDORFF - 59. For the Common Council; following gentlemen were elected: 1st Ward: GEORGE WISSINGER. 2nd Ward: WM. SMALL. 3rd Ward: JACOB LITTLE. 4th Ward: PHILIP ROHR. 5th Ward: SAMUEL B. LEWIS. 6th Ward: GEO. B. SHOPE. 7th Ward: WILLIAM ELY.

March 10, 1832 (CBAL)

279. (D) At Rockville, MD., on Wednesday morning last, Mr JOHN PORTER, editor of the "Free Press." Deceased was a native of Westmoreland Co., Pa., where he was brought up to the profession of a practical printer. At the close of his apprenticeship, he came to Frederick where he chiefly resided until he established himself at Rockville. He was foreman in the "Citizens" office, for 18 months. About 2 years since he commenced the Free Press, in Montgomery Co.
280. (D) Departed this life on the morning of the 6th inst., Mr GEORGE DOYLE, a native of this place.
281. (D) Near Middletown, Frederick Co., MD., on the 6th of Feb., after a protracted and distressing illness, Mrs SUSANNA HAY, consort of Mr Jacob Hay, age about 70 years. She leaves nine children and a husband to mourn her loss.
282. (D) On the 12th of Feb., in Middletown Valley, after an afflicting illness, Mr JOHN SUMAN, who was aged about 72 years, he leaves a disconsolate widow and four children.
283. (D) On Tuesday the 21st of February, Mr WASHINGTON HOFFMAN, in the 22nd year of his age.
284. (M) On the 1st inst., by the Rev. John H. Smaltz, Mr WILLIAM HEATH, to Mrs D. PAXTON, both of Loudon Co., VA.
285. (M) On Wednesday last, by the Rev. David F. Schaeffer, Mr JOSEPH SHAWEN, to Miss ELIZABETH MOTTER, all of this co.
286. (M) Near Middletown, Frederick Co., MD., on the 26th of Feb., 1832, by the Rev. J. C. Bucher, Mr THOMAS CARNELL, to Miss CATHARINE ARNOLD, of Middletown Valley.
287. (M) On Thursday the 1st inst., by the Rev. Mr W. R. Rhinehart, Mr HENRY CUTRO, to Miss ELIZABETH GITTINGER, both of this co.
288. (M) On the 8th inst., by the Rev. John H. Smaltz, Mr JOHN F. CLINGAN, to Miss MARIA SHARER, both of Frederick Co.

March 17, 1832 (CBAL)

289. (M) Near Middletown, Frederick Co., MD., on the 8th, March 1832, by the Rev. J. C. Bucher, Mr JOHN ROUTZAHN, to Miss SARAH COBLENTZ, daughter of Mr John Philip Coblentz, all of the Middletown Valley.
290. (M) On the 15th ult., in Port Gibson, MS., at the residence

of A. K. Shaifer, Esq., Mr HENRY S. GOSLIN, to Miss SUSAN CATHERINE ROBERTSON, all of Clairborne Co.

291. (M) On Monday morning last, by the Rev. Mr Jackson, Mr WILLIAM OTIS, Esq., of New York, to Miss MARY A. C. LATE, daughter of the late Michael Late.

292. (D) It is with feelings of deep regret that we announce the death of the Hon. OCTAVIUS TANEY, of the State of MD. Mr Taney, was a residence of Calvert Co., where he had been engaged in the practice of medicine for many years. He visited Baltimore about ten days ago, and was taken suddenly ill, on the night of his arrival, and died on the 6th inst., in the 39th year of his age. Leaving a wife, brother and sisters. His remains were taken to his late residence, attended by a joint committee of both branches of the Legislature on Friday morning.

March 24, 1832 (CBAL)

293. (D) Departed this life on Saturday the 17th inst., after a protracted illness of nearly 3 years, Dr. MILTON JOHNSON, youngest son of the late John Johnson, Esq., in the 30th year of his age. He leaves a young wife and brother.

294. (M) Near Middletown, Frederick Co., MD., on the 8th of March 1832, by the Rev'd. J. C. Bucher, Mr JAMES MICHAEL, to Miss ELIZABETH, daughter of Mr Solomon Renner, all of said co.

295. (M) On the same day, by the same, Mr PETER WERNFELS, to Miss SUSANNA GROVER, all of Frederick Co., MD.

296. (M) On Wednesday last, by the Rev. D. F. Schaeffer, Mr CHARLES P. McMULLIN to Miss ELIZABETH HAUER, daughter of George Hauer, Esq., all of this city.

March 31, 1832 (CBAL)

297. (M) In New York, on Sunday the 11th inst., by the Rev. Mr McClay, Mr ELISHA HALLER, (formerly of this place,) to Miss FANNEY BETES, both of New York.

298. (M) On the 8th inst., by the Rev. Mr Young, Mr DENNIS MANAHAN, to Miss ELIZABETH BROWN, both of this co.

299. (M) On the 15th, by the same, Mr WILLIAM B. LAMAR, to Miss ELIZABETH HARLEY, both of this co.

300. (M) On the 15th., by the Rev. Mr Hoffman, Mr JOHN MEHRING, Jr., to Miss AMY SHOEMAKER, both of this co.

301. (M) On the 6th inst., by the Rev. Mr Weyl, Mr GEORGE MEYERLY, to Miss SUSAN CLABAUGH, of this co.

302. (M) On Linganore, on Tuesday the 20th inst., by the Rev. James M. Hanson, Mr THOMAS E. SOLLERS, the only son of Major Sabritt Sollers, to Miss BARBARA ANN, third daughter of Nathaniel Hammond, deceased.
303. (M) On Tuesday evening last, by the Rev. D. F. Schaeffer, Mr JOHN MATTERN, to Miss ELIZA MASBURY, all of this co.
304. (D) Departed this life on Saturday evening last, after a short illness, Mrs MARY THOMSON, wife of John P. Thomson, Esq., the former editor and proprietor of the "Frederick Herald," in the 59th year of her age.
305. (D) On Thursday morning the 22nd inst., between the hours of 6 and 7, FRANCES COLUMBIA NELSON, youngest daughter of John Nelson, Esq., age 23 months.
306. (D) On the 14th inst., Mrs MARTHA BRACKENRIDGE, of Taney-Town, aged 74 years.
307. (D) Departed this life on Monday evening last, after a short illness, at her residence near Middleburg, Mrs MARY ROOT, consort of Mr Jacob Root, in the 19th year of her age. She leaves a husband and infant to mourn her departure.
308. (D) Departed this life on the 8th inst., Mr PETER LUGENBEEL, Post-Master at Unionville, in this co., in the 30th year of his age.

April 7, 1832 (CBAL)

309. (D) In Magnolia Florida, whither he had gone for the recovery of his health, HENRY WILLIS, Esq., formerly of this co.
310. (M) On Thursday morning 29th inst., by the Rev. Mr Jackson, MAHLON TALBOTT Esq., to Miss LOUISA B. CHARLTON, all of this city.
311. (M) On Thursday evening last, by the Rev. D. F. Schaeffer, Mr EZRA SMITH, to Miss MARY MYERS, eldest daughter of Mr E. Myers.
312. (M) On the same evening, by the same, Mr EZRA HALLER, to Miss ELIZABETH BUCKEY, all of this city.
313. Rev. Mr JONES, will preach at the Baptist Meeting House of this city, on next Sabbath, at 3 o'clock P.M.

April 14, 1832 (CBAL)

314. (M) On Thursday last, by the Rev. D. F. Schaeffer, Mr ANDREW HAINES, to Miss SARAH SWIGART, all of this co.
315. (M) On the 10th inst., by the Rev. J. H. Smaltz, Mr

JOSEPH STUB, to Miss ELIZABETH HOUCK, both of Frederick Co.
316. (M) On Tuesday morning, by the Rev. D. F. Schaeffer, Mr WILLIAM SMITH, to Miss ANN MARIA ZIMMERMAN, all of this co.
317. (D) Departed this life yesterday morning, Mrs CATHARINE TEHAN. The decease has left an affectionate husband, and four children, one of whom is only six days old.

April 21, 1832 (CBAL)

318. (D) In Baltimore on Sunday evening the 15th inst., Mr JOSEPH RUDDACH, leaving a wife and four children.
319. (M) On the 12th inst., by the Rev. John H. Smaltz, Mr PETER CRAMER, to Miss LUCY BENNETT, both of Fred'k Co.
320. (M) At Washington, at the mansion of the President, on the evening of the 10th inst., by the Rev. Mr Hawley, LUCIUS J. POLK, of Tenn., to Miss MARY A. EASTIN, a member of the President's family.

April 28, 1832 (CBAL)

321. (M) At Mount Prospect, near Baltimore, on Tuesday evening the 17th inst., Mr NICHOLAS CROMWELL, of Frederick Co., to Miss CATHARINE, eldest daughter of the late Wm. Clemm, Esq., of Baltimore.
322. (M) On Thursday evening last, by the Rev. D. F. Schaeffer, Mr JOHN A. STUBBINS, to Miss ANN SOPHIA KLEIN, all of this city.
323. (M) On Tuesday last, by the Rev. D. F. Schaeffer, Mr OWEN HENESTOFEL, Esq., to Miss ELIZABETH ANN DAVIS, all of this co.
324. Following gentlemen were appointed delegates to the Young Men's National Republican Convention, to be held in Washington, on the 7th of May next: BENJAMIN PRICE, JAMES M. COALE, JOHN W. PRATT, NEILSON POE, WM. OGDEN NILES, WM. COST JOHNSON, FRANCIS BRENGLE.
325. Appointments of the Governor and Council to the Levy Court, on April 20th 1832. PHILIP HINES, Jr., as additional Justice of the Peace of Frederick Co. Test. TH. CULBRETH, clk.

May 5, 1832 (CBAL)

326. (D) Melancholy accident - We regret to state that a promis-

ing lad the son of Mr PETER MANTZ, was drowned by falling into Town Creek, on Wednesday last, near Mr Nimrod Bantz's water-wheel, in which his body was discovered much buised and with a number of broken bones.

327. (D) On Saturday the 28th April, near Middletown, Mr JOEL JACOBS, in the 83rd year of his age.

328. (D) On Sunday evening 29th inst., WILLIAM GIBSON, late clerk of Baltimore County Court, in the 79th year of his age.

329. (D) On Sunday morning last, after a short illness, ANN S. GAMBRILL, wife of Chas. A. Gambrill, and eldest daughter of Judge Shriver, of this city.

330. (D) On Monday night last, at 12 o'clock, JOHN THOMAS, merchant of this city, after an illness of six days. The death of Mr J. Thomas, deprives us of one of our most active an enterprising and experienced merchants. Although misfortune in business and heretofore attended him.

331. (M) On Saturday evening by the Rev. D. F. Schaeffer, Capt. EDWARD HALE, to Miss ELIZABETH BENTZ, all of this co.

332. (M) On Tuesday by the Rev. D. F. Schaeffer, Mr GEORGE FISHER, to Miss MARIAN HARGATE, all of this co.

333. (M) On the 1st inst, by the Rev. John H. Smaltz, Mr DAVID FAUBEL, to Miss MARGARET DEGRANGE, both of this city.

334. (M) On Tuesday morning last, by the Rev. Mr Hank, Mr GEORGE R. WEBER, of New York, to Miss SUSAN SHEPHERD, of Shepherdstown VA.

335. The First Light Infantry, and Morgan Rifle Corp, paid a visit on Monday last, and remained until Wednesday morning, when they departed for Baltimore.

336. (F) Destructive fire - The Saw and Chopping Mills of our esteemed fellow citizen, JOHN McPHERSON, Esq., situated near the George Town Bridge over the Monocacy, with 1600 bushels of rye, were destroyed yesterday morning, and with great difficulty the grist mill was saved. The fire, was suppose to have been caused by friction of the machinery, owing to neglect of oiling it. Loss is estimated at $3,000.00. The Miller, who was a sleep in the mill, escaped with some difficulty.

May 12, 1832 (CBAL)

337. (M) On Thursday last, by the Rev. D. F. Schaeffer, Mr

ISAAC STOLEY, of this co., to Miss SUSAN SHAFER, of Loudoun Co., VA.

338. (M) On the 2nd inst., by the Rev. C. B. Young, Mr DENTON J. SNYDER, to Miss HARRIET ANN EASTERDAY, both of this co.

339. (M) On Tuesday morning the 8th inst., by the Rev. John H. Smaltz, Mr JOHN RAMESBURG, to Miss MARGARET JANE McCOUBERY, both of this city.

340. (D) At his residence, near this borough, on Tuesday morning last, in the 42nd year of his age, THOMAS WETHERALD, a preacher of the Society of Friends. (York Gazette)

341. (D) On Sunday last, after a short illness, in the 23rd year of her age, Miss CATHARINE NICHOLS, daughter of Mr Peter Nichols, of this city.

May 19, 1832 (CBAL)

342. (D) On Tuesday the 15th inst., after a protracted illness, Miss MARGARET BRUNNER, in the 21st year of her age, eldest daughter of Mr Jacob Brunner, of this city.

343. (D) On Sunday evening the 13th inst., Mr EZRA F. NUSZ, in the 33d year of his age.

344. (M) On Tuesday last, by the Rev. John Johns, of Baltimore, Mr WILIAM G. HARRISON, of Baltimore, to Miss ANN E., second daughter of William Ross, Esq., of this city.

345. (M) On the 16th inst., by the Rev. John H. Smaltz, Mr ALFRED F. BRENGLE, to Miss LOUISA BRENGLE, both of this co.

346. (M) On the 15th inst., by the Rev. Dr. Hawley, the Hon. GEORGE POINDEXTER, United States Senator, from Mississippi, to Miss ANN HEWES, daughter of Samuel Hewes, Esq., of Boston.

347. (M) On the 10th inst., by the Rev. John H. Smaltz, near Hagerstown, Mr JONATHAN BRUNNER, of Frederick Co., to Miss SARAH MIDDLEKAUF, of Washington Co.

May 26, 1832 (CBAL)

348. (M) On Sunday last, by the Rev. D. F. Schaeffer, Mr FREDERICK SHIPMAN, to Miss ELIZABETH CUSHMAN, both of this co.

349. (M) On the same day, by the same, Mr PETER POWELL, to Mrs JULIAN HETHINGTON, both of this co.

350. (M) On Tuesday morning, by the same, Mr BARTON GARROTT, to Miss MARY J. ANDERSON, both of this co.

351. (M) On the 17th inst., by the Rev. John N. Hoffman, Mr MICHAEL HELMAN, of this co., to Miss SUSAN FISHER, of Adams Co.
352. (M) At Middletown, Fred'k Co., Md., on the 20th of May, 1832, by the Rev. J. C. Bucher, Mr MICHAEL KELLER, to Miss MARGARET CREAGER, all of Middletown. (Amor non est medicabilis herbis, "Sed vinvit omnia et conjunget.")
353. (D) At her residence in Uniontown, on Wednesday the 9th of May, after a protracted illness, Mrs GRIZELDA JAMISON SHAW, consort of Mr Moses Shaw, aged 63 years, and 7 months.
354. (D) In this town on Wednesday night last, after a short illness, THOMAS PERRIN SMITH, Esq., was editor of the "Republican Star," a paper he established in this place, and conducted to the day of his death, a period of nearly 33 years. (Easton Gazette)

June 2, 1832 (CBAL)

355. (M) On Thursday evening the 17th inst., in Winchester, Chester Co., PA., W. P. JONES, Esq., of Frederick Co., MD., to Miss MARGARET, eldest daughter of Peter Askew, Esq., of Cecil Co., MD.
356. (M) On Tuesday evening last, by the Rev. D. F. Schaeffer, Mr JACOB NICKLES, to Miss ELIZABETH RAGAN, both of this city.
357. Flour inspector of Frederick, JOSEPH B. WEBB, Esq., with the return of flour inspected by him in the quarter ending on the 30th ult., amounting to 7,526 barrels, in which amounted the 1/2 barrels are included.
358. On Saturday last, JOSEPH SCHELL, Esq., was appointed Collector of this co., Vice: GEORGE BALTZELL, Esq., was not a candidated for reappointment
359. The following gentlemen composed the committee to meet delegates from several districts in County Convention: MOSES WORMAN, RICHARD POTTS, BENJAMIN PRICE, ABRAHAM KEMP, JAMES M. COALE, ISRAEL MYERS, JACOB GETZENDANNER, GEORGE BALTZELL, GIDEON BANTZ, and CHARLES BURKHARL.
360. The following appointments have been made by the Levy Court of Frederick County, for 1832. Constables: District #1. JAMES STEVENS, JOHN CAREY, ALLEN SAIN. District #2. JAMES CARLIN, FREDERICK STEINER, JOHN KLISE, AARON H. BALTZELL, FREDERICK HAWMAN, JOHN M. LOWE, CHARLES PETERS, JOSIAH DAYHOFF.

District #3. ISAAC WILLIAMSON, CHRISTIAN TABLER, ABRAHAM MILLER, JACOB LUDWICK, JACOB YOUNG, of Dewalt, THOMAS PHILLIPS, of Levi, PETER YOUNG, WILLIAM KLEIN. District #4. CYRUS WALKER, JOSEPH WILLHIDE, JACOB BARNHART, JACOB LIDAY, HENRY REED. District #5. JESSE MARTIN, ISAAC WILSON. District #6. DAN'L. McKINSIE, JOHN CLABAUGH, JACOB FRINGER. District #7. JOHN D. WOODS, JEREMIAH CURREY, JACOB FRINGER, Jr., JAMES LONG, JOHN LITTLE, FREDERICK YINGLING, JOHN CROUSE. District #8. JOHN H. GORDON, JOSEPH L. WAGNER, DANIEL ROOTE, DANIEL SWEADNER. District #9. LEVI VAN FOSSEN, NATHANIEL CLERY, JOHN DARBY. District #10. HORATIO N. HARNE, JACOB POORMAN. District #11. JOSEPH LYNN, SAMUEL WILLHIDE, JACOB STITLEY. District #12. ABSALOM CRAMER, FRANCIS B. HAMILTON, THEOPHILUS BEALL. Judges of Election: District #1. OTHO THOMAS, P. H. BROWN, LEWIS KEMP. District #2. JOHN EBERT, HENRY BAER, NICHOLAS HOLTZ. District #3. GEO. BAER, TH. JOHNSON, of Wm., J. M'NEILL. District #4. FRED'K. OTT, JAS. CROCKETT, JOHN COLE. District #5. PATRICK OWINGS, JNO. NICKUM, MICHAEL SLUSS. District #6. W. SHEPHERD, J. BAUMGARDNER, Sr., J. SMITH. District #7. MOSES SHAW, ISRAEL NORRIS, DAVID UHLER. District #8. JOHN GLISAN, Sr., G. COX, WM. A. ALBAUGH. District #9. JOSHUA RUSSELL, THO. DUVALL, HENRY SMITH. District #10. WILSON HAYES, JOS. SMITH, GEO. HARMAN. District #11. ELIAS CRUTCHLEY, MID. SMITH, JACOB HYDER. District #12. HENRY OHR, BENEDICT BOON, J. N. HOSKINS. Trustees of the Poor: DANIEL KOLB, JACOB FAUBEL, GEORGE HAUER, PHILIP ROHR, VALENTINE DOUB.

June 16, 1832 (CBAL)

361. (M) At New Market, on Tuesday the 5th inst., by the Rev. J. H. Brown, Mr JOHN FALCONER, to Miss ANN, eldest daughter of G. W. Falconer, of this place.

362. (M) In Philadelphia, on Tuesday evening the 5th inst., by the Rev. Mr Hughes, JOHN LEE, Esq., formerly representative of this District in Congress, to HARRIET CARROLL, daughter of the late Charles Carroll, Esq., of Baltimore.

363. (M) On Tuesday evening last, the 12th inst., by the Rev. Michael Wachter, Mr PETER H. ROUSE, to Miss BELINDA E. BALTZELL, both of this co.
364. (D) At Statesburg, on the 1st inst., Gen. SAMUEL SUMPTER, a brave and distinguished soldier of the Revolution.
365. (D) In Tennessee, on the 27th ult., in the 79th year of his age, JOHN RHEA Esq., for many years a member of Congress from that state.
366. (D) The Rev. Mr COLTON, author of Lacon, has committed suicide by cutting his throat.
367. Medical and Chirurgical Faculty of Md., at annual convention of the faculty held in Baltimore on the 5th inst. The following gentlemen were elected censors for this section of the State.
Frederick City: Dr. W. B. TYLER, Dr. JOHN BALTZELL.
Frederick County: Dr. O. H. OWINGS, Dr. W. WILLIS.
Washington County: Dr. W. D. MAEGILL, Dr. P. BODMAN.
Montgomery County: Dr. O. WILLSON, Dr. W. MAGRUDER.
Allegany County: Dr. J. M. LAURENCE, Dr. S. P. SMITH.

June 23, 1832 (CBAL)

368. (D) On Sunday morning last, after a long illness, Mr WILLIAM GORDON, a native of Ireland, aged --- years.
369. (D) At Mount Vernon, on the 14th inst., Mr JOHN A. WASHINGTON, Esq., proprietor of that estate.
370. (D) Melancholy accident - Sunday night last, C. C. JOHNSON, Esq., one of the representatives of Congress from Va., was drowned in the dock at Alexandria, D.C. Circumstances of his death are thus given; he had gone to Alexandria to visit a friend, he passed the evening with his friend and left his house in the midst of the storm then raging, to go to the wharf, with a view to take passage on the mailboat Sydney, which leaves for the city at about 9 o'clock, P.M. He was attended by a servant, who left him in sight of the wharf. It is beyond a doubt that he walked into the slip, and struck his head in falling, or he would have saved himself, being a expert swimmer. His body was found on Monday afternoon.
371. (M) On Sunday evening last, by the Rev. D. F. Schaeffer, Mr JOHN ABBOTT, to Miss JULIANNA DORF, all of this city.
372. (M) On Sunday the 10th inst., by the Rev. John H. Baker, Mr GEORGE HUFFER, to Miss SARAH ANN McNEILL, daughter of John McNeill, Esq., all of this co.

373. (M) On the 3rd inst., by the Rev. Mr Barber, Mr PETER BLUME, to Miss DORCUS HEDGES, both of this city.
374. (M) On Thursday last, by the Rev. D. F. Schaeffer, Mr JOHN SCHOLL, to Miss ELIZABETH STROUP, all of this co.
375. The following appointments were made by the Executive of Maryland, on the 13th inst. JOHN G. BAYNE, MAHLON TALBOT, and JAMES M. HARDING, additional Justices of the Peace for Frederick Co. WILLIAM SMALL, Capt. DANIEL KOLB, and EDWARD A. CARLTON, Lieuts, for the 16th Regiment, Frederick Co. A Uniform Infantry Company: SAMUEL CARMACK, Capt., JACOB FAUBLE, Lieut. VALENTINE J.BRUNNER, Ensign, of a Uniform Rifle Company. MAHLON TALBOT, Adjutant; Vice: GLENN, moved away.
376. BENJAMIN S. FORREST, Esq., of Montgomery Co., agent to settle and adjust the claims of the State upon the general government.
377. Following gentlemen have been named as the National Republican Central Committee for Frederick Co: WM. S. McPHERSON, THO'S. C. WORTHINGTON, GIDEON BANTZ, GEO. BALTZELL, CHAS. H. BURCKHART, WM. FISCHER, BENJ. PRICE, JOHN P. THOMSON, ISRAEL MYERS, DANIEL BUCKEY, DANIEL GETZENDANNER, JACOB BRUNNER, VALENTINE ADAMS, SAMUEL OGLE, JOHN GRAHAME, JOHN DOYLE, WILLIAM R. THOMAS, WM. J. ROSS, GEO. TRISLER, DANIEL KOLB, SAM'L. CRONICE, JACOB LITTLE, THOS. W. MORGAN JAMES M. COALE, ENOS SCHELL, LEWIS MEDTART, WM. R. SANDERSON, Jr., L. P. W. BALCH, G. M. EICHELBERGER, PHILIP ROHR, WM. SCHLEY, DANIEL HUGHES, JOHN McPHERSON, EZRA DOLL, ABRAHAM KEMP, JACOB DOLL, JONATHAN T. WILSON, PATRICK TORMEY, EDWARD MANTZ, JOHN BALTZELL, EDWARD TRAIL, G. ADAM EBERT, LAWRENCE BRENGLE, N. TURBUTT, PATRICK O'NEILL, HENRY KEMP, HENRY BAER, FREDERICK NUSZ, JONATHAN GETZENDANNER, LEWIS BIRELY, GEORGE RICE, JACOB REASER, LEWIS RAMSBURG, JOHN MARKELL, NOAH A. SHAFER, FREDERICK HAWMAN, JAMES CARLIN, JOHN EBERT, WM. WHITE, FRANCIS BRENGLE, STUART GAITHER, DAVID STEINER, CYRUS MANTZ, PETER NICHOLS, WM. OGDEN NILES, JAS. RAYMOND, JACOB WEIST, PETER McKERNAN, DANIEL SCHOLL, BALTZER FOUT, EDWARD B. McPHERSON, R. POTTS, HENRY SMITH, GEO. DARTZEBAUGH, WALTER POOL,

DAVID KEMP, EZRA BOUB, BENJ. HEFFNER, PHINEAS WATSON, PETER SHOOK, ISAAC HEDGES, GEO. FOX, WM. WILLS, J. P. FLEMMING, WM. V. MORGAN, JOHN LANE, P. S. STALEY, JACOB BRENGLE, JOHN BAILEY, WORTHINGTON JOHNSON, NICHOLAS CROMWELL, MOSES WORMAN, CHRISTIAN BRENGLE, THOS. A. FLEMMING, V. J. BRUNNER, JOHN DILL, JOHN ENGELBRECHT, WM. C. HOFFMAN, WM. C. SMALLWOOD, JOHN McDONALD, JACOB DADISMAN, FRED'K. LOEHR, PHILIP REICH, JACOB FAUBEL, BENJ. RUTHERFORD, NEILSON POE.

June 30, 1832 (CBAL)

378. (M) In Washington, on Tuesday evening, by the Rev. O. B. Brown, ISAAC SHELBY REED, Esq., of Mississippi, to ANN LAURA, daughter of Gen. Duff Green.
379. (D) In Baltimore, on the evening of the 21st inst., EDWARD G. WOODYEAR, Esq., in the 48th year of his age.

July 7, 1832 (CBAL)

380. (D) As the mail stage was proceeding Westward, on Tuesday morning last, and within a short distant beyond Clearsprings, in this co., the front axle-tree gave way, and a passenger, seated with the driver, was precipitated under the stage and instantly killed. His name was ENOCH EDMONSTON, a printer, lately in employment in the telegraph office in the city of Washington, (where he leaves a wife and two or three children) he was on his way to Cincinnati, to establish a press there. It is supposed that in attempting to leap from the seat, as the body of the stage was descending, he became entangled in some of the straps or harness, and thus thrown immediately under the stage, which fell with its whole weight upon his breast. (Williamsport Banner)
381. (D) In Washington, on Monday 25th inst, Mr FREDERICK STEINER, formerly of this place

July 14, 1832 (CBAL)

382. (M) On Thursday evening the 5th inst., by the Rev. Mr Hamner, Mr EZRA M. GOMBER, to Miss MARGARET FISCHER, both of this city.
383. (D) On Saturday morning last, ROBERT EICHELBERGER NILES, infant son of Wm. Ogden Niles.

384. (D) On Monday morning the 25th inst., after a long and protracted illness, Mr THOMAS O'BRIEN, a native of Ireland.
385. (D) A man named MICHAEL CONNER, was drowned in the Monocacy yesterday.

July 21, 1832 (CBAL)

386. (D) On Tuesday night last, the Rev. DAVID MARTIN, long a resident of this city, and a zealous and active minister of the Methodist Episcopal Church.
387. Messrs; MILLER, THOMPSON and CARLTON, have established a line of stages, running from this city to Emmitsburg, to Gettysburg and Carlise, &c.

July 28, 1832 (CBAL)

388. The Hon. ROGER B. TANEY, Attorney General of U. States, accompanied by his lady, arrived in this city on Thursday last, on his way to the Springs. It will occasion general and deep regret in this community, when we state that his journey is occasioned by the protracted and severe illness of Mrs Taney.
389. (D) Melancholy accident - Mr FRANKLIN FAIRBANKS, driver of one of the stages attached to "The Blue Lines," was killed on Thursday, last by being thrown from the box while the stage was descending the mountain, about five miles from Middletown. Supposed to be aged about 26 years, and is believed to be a native of Maine.
390. (M) On Sunday last, by the Rev. D. F. Schaeffer, Mr JAMES PROBY, to Miss RACHAEL WATTS, all of this co.
391. (M) On Tuesday evening last, by the same, Mr SAMUEL M. HUNTER, to Miss REBECCA MICHAEL, both of this co.
392. (D) On Monday last, MARIA, infant daughter of Mr Charles A. Gambrill, of this city, age 8 months, 12 days.
393. (D) On Monday last, near New Market, Mr JOHN SMITH, Sr.
394. The Rev. Mr JONES, will preach in the Baptist Meeting House, to-morrow afternoon at 3 o'clock, P.M.
395. CHARLES W. JACOBS, a minister of the Methodist Protestant Church, will preach in the Court House on Wednesday evening next.

August 4, 1832 (CBAL)

396. (M) In Baltimore, on Wednesday evening last, by the Rev. J.

P. K. Henshew, Mr DAVID MARKEY, to Miss SUSAN BENTZ, both of Frederick Town.
397. (M) On Sunday morning last, by the Rev. David F. Schaeffer, Mr LEWIS HEIM, to Miss REBECCA R. SHAWEN, all of this co.
398. (M) On Monday the 23rd ult., by the Rev. J. C. Bucher, Mr JAMES COOK, to Mrs CATHARINE BOWLUS, both of Middletown, in this co.
399. (D) On Saturday last, after a illness of 2 months, Mr DANIEL KELLER, (housejoiner,) of this co., aged 30 years.

August 18, 1832 (CBAL)

400. (M) Near Middletown, Frederick Co., MD., on the 29th of July, 1832, by the Rev. J. C. Bucher, Mr VALENTINE WISE, to Miss LYDIA WEISTLER, all of said co.
401. (M) On the 4th day of August, by the same, at Berlin, Frederick Co., MD., Mr ANTHONY LOFFUS, to Miss MARY DEVINE, both of said co.
402. (D) At Middletown, on the 13th inst., Mrs ELIZABETH LORENTZ, wife of Mr Jacob Lorentz, Sr., in the 76th year of her age.
403. (D) Suddenly near Middletown, on the 2nd of Aug., Mrs ELIZABETH WELCH, consort of Mr Vachael Welch. The deceased leaves 3 very young children, an afflicted husband to lament her early departure, aged 26 years, 6 months and 13 days.
404. (D) On the 31st ult., at the residence of his father-in-law, William Plummer, in New Market, ISAAC P. TAYLOR, of Philadelphia, in the 48th year of his age.
405. (D) On Friday the 10th inst., at Williams' Ferry, near this place, after a illness of a few days, Mr JAMES H. BALDWIN, architect, of Oxford, Chenango Co., N. York, aged about 35 years.
406. (D) In Baltimore, on Saturday last, after a short illness, Mr WILLIAM W. TAYLOR, Esq., in the 63rd year of his age.
407. (D) In Baltimore, Mr THOMAS BARRETT, printer, aged 45 years, after a lingering illness of 3 months.
408. The Rev. H. V. JONES, will perform devine services in the Episcopal Church, to-morrow morning at 10 o'clock, A.M.

August 25, 1832 (CBAL)

409. (M) Near Middletown, Frederick Co., MD., on the 19th of Aug., by the Rev. J. C. Bucher, Mr WM. GREENWOOD, to

Miss ELIZABETH, daughter of Mr Jacob Houck, all of Middletown.
410. (D) On Wednesday, 15th inst., at the residence of his father in this co., Mr JOHN C. GROFF, of Ohio, in the 35th year of his age. He was a delegate to the Clay Convention, which assembled in Washington in May last.
411. The Rev. JOSEPH JONES, will preach in the Baptist Meeting House, to-morrow evening, 3 o'clock, P.M.
412. The Rev. EDWARD SMITH, will preach in the Methodist Episcopal Church, on to-morrow morning, and evening.
413. CHAS. W. JACOBS, a minister of the Methodist Protestant Church, will preach in the Court House on Wednesday evening next at early candle light.

September 1, 1832 (CBAL)

414. (D) Yesterday morning after a lingering illness in the 76th year of his age. The Rev. SAMUEL KNOX, for many years the President of the Baltimore College. His funeral will take place this evening at 4 o'clock, from his late residence.
415. (M) On Tuesday the 21st ult., by the Rev. Mr Wachter, Mr DAVID LEE, of Hartford Co., to Miss BARBARA, daughter of Major Charles Baltzell, of this co.
416. (M) On Thursday the 16th, by the same, Mr ALEXANDER STEWART, to Miss ELIZABETH SHOUP, both of this co.
417. (M) On Thursday last, by the Rev. D. F. Schaeffer, Mr JOHN B. STEWART, to Miss ANNA MARY LINK, all of this co.
418. (M) On Tuesday last, by the Rev. Henry Robinson, Mr SAM'L. H. FRAZIER, to Miss MARY ANN WATERS, daughter of Hazel Waters, Esq., all of this co.
419. By devine permission, Rev. EDWARD SMITH, will preach in the Methodist Episcopal Church, on to-morrow morning.

September 8, 1832 (CBAL)

420. (M) Near Middletown, Frederick Co., Md., on the 30th of August 1832, by the Rev. J. C. Bucher, Mr DANIEL BRANDENBURG, to Miss SUSANNA SMITH, daughter of Mr Jacob Smith, all of Middletown Valley, of said co.
421. (M) On Thursday the 6th inst., by the Rev. D. F. Schaeffer, Mr ISAAC LEWIS, to Miss MARGARET OGLE, all of this city.
422. (M) On the same day, and by the same, at the house of Mr Murray, Mr ALBERT B. WARD, to Miss MARIAN FISH, all of this co.

423. (M) On Thursday last, in the Lutheran Church of this city, by the Rev. Mr Schaeffer, Mr SAMUEL THOMAS, to Miss JULIET C. JOHNSON, all of this co.
424. (D) In Baltimore, on Thursday, the 30th of Aug., at 7 o'-clock, P.M., at hospital No. 3, Sister MARY FRANCES, was found in the morning attending patients in the hospital, and was stricken about 8 o'clock and by 7 in the evening was a corpse. Was carried to the grave early yesterday morning, attended by the Mayor of the city, and Board of Health. (Baltimore Patriot)
425. (D) Departed this life in Baltimore, on Tuesday morning, BENJAMIN EDES, Esq., Brigadier General of the 14th Brigade of M.M., and a respectable and well known printer. Born in Massachusetts, but for the greater part of his life has resided in Baltimore. In whose defense he so nobly displayed himself as an officer in the late battle against an invading foe, he was an officer of the 27th Regiment of M.M.
426. (D) On Sunday morning last near Frederick, in the 19th year of his age, Mr JOHN HENRY STULL, eldest son of Otho H. W. Stull, Esq., of this town. His remains were interred in the Episcopal burying grounds near town, on Monday. (Torch Light)
427. Rev. JONATHAN FORREST, will preach the funeral sermon of the late Rev. David Martin, in the Methodist Episcopal Church, of this city, on Thursday next, 13th inst., at 11 o'clock, A.M.
428. ISAAC WEBSTER, a priest of the Methodist Protestant Church, will preach in the Court House, on Wednesday evening next, at candle light.

September 15, 1832 (CBAL)

429. (M) On Tuesday last, by the Rev. James G. Hamner, Mr HENRY M. PETTIT, to Miss MARY JANE BEALL, daughter of William M. Beall, Esq., of this city.
430. (M) On Sunday last, by the Rev. D. F. Schaeffer, Mr JOHN BRADLEY WEBSTER, to Miss MAHALA FRAZIER, all of this co.
431. (M) On the same day, by the same, Mr GEORGE MEAZLE, to Miss MARGARET MARTZ, second daughter of Major Martz, of this co.
432. (M) On Tuesday evening last, by the Rev. Mr Wachter, Mr ANDREW LUGENBEEL, of Tiffrin Sepeca Co., Ohio, to Miss ELIZABETH, daughter of Major Charles Baltzell, of this co.

433. (M) On Thursday last, by the same, Mr SAMUEL BARRICK, of New Philadelphia, Ohio, to Miss HETTY CRUM, of Fred'k Co.
434. (D) In Baltimore, on Saturday last, after a short illness, THOMAS SHAW, Esq., formerly cashier of the Frederick Branch of the Farmer's Bank of MD.
435. (D) In this city, at the residence of H. Schley, Esq., on Friday evening 7th inst., ELIZABETH RACHAEL, daughter of Dr. Edward H., and Elizabeth Worrall, of Easton MD., in the 6th year of her age, from affection of the liver.
436. (D) On Monday evening last, after a short illness in the 46th year of her age, Mrs HOFFMAN, consort of Mr George Hoffman, of this city.
437. (D) On Monday last, Mrs MARY GETZENDANNER, aged about 67 years, long a resident of this city.
438. (D) On Friday night last, the 7th inst., in Baltimore, after a illness of 2 days, Miss BELLE JANE PEACOCK, in the 21st year of her age.
439. Rev. HENRY V. D. JOHNS, accepted the call of the Vestry of the All Saints' Church, Friday, Divine services may be expected next Sunday, as usual.
440. By Divine permission, Rev. EDWARD SMITH, will preach in the Methodist Episcopal Church, on to-morrow, morning and evening.

September 22, 1832 (CBAL)

441. (M) On Thursday last, by the Rev. D. F. Schaeffer, Mr DAVID STUB, to Miss SUSAN BAST, all of this co.
442. (M) On Wednesday last, at Bloomsburg, Frederick Co., by the Rev. Mr McElroy, McCLINTOCK YOUNG, of Baltimore, to SUSAN BIRD NEWMAN, youngest daughter of the late Francis Newman, of Charles Co.
443. (D) On Sunday last, of the prevailing epidemic, Mr JACOB HOFFMAN, of this city, aged about 67 years.
444. (D) On Tuesday last, of the prevailing epidemic, Mr JOSEPH WORLEY, Inn Keeper, of this city.
445. (D) Departed this life, on Thursday night, the 6th inst., in the 25th year of her age, Miss BETSY GALLAHER, of Liberty-Town, after a illness of but a few days.
446. (D) In Lexington, KY., on the 26th of August, in the 86th year of her age, Mrs SUSANNA HART, widow and relict of the late Col. Thomas Hart, and mother of Mrs Henry Clay.

447. (D) On Thursday last, of the pulmonary consumption, Miss JANE JOHNSON, daughter of Dr. Thomas W. Johnson, of this co.
448. (D) On 15th inst., in Washington, D.C., of the prevailing epidemic, after and illness of 48 hours, Dr. THOMAS SIM, for many years a distinguished practitioner of that city.

September 29, 1832 (CBAL)

449. (M) On the 25th inst., by the Rev. J. H. Smaltz, Mr SOLOMON CHARLESWORTH, to Miss MARY McVICKER, of this city.
450. (M) On the 27th inst., by the same, Mr DANIEL STEINER, to Mrs JULIA ANN LARKIN, all of this city.
451. (M) On Sunday last, by the Rev. D. F. Schaeffer, Mr ELI POOLE, to Miss SUSAN BIGGS, all of this city.
452. (M) On the 23rd inst., by the Rev. Mr Henry Robinson, PERRY G. THOMAS, of Jefferson, MD., to Miss MARY ANN D. RICE, youngest daughter of Perry Rice, Sen., of this city.
453. (D) Departed this mortal existence, of a pulmonary affection, JANE, eldest daughter of Dr. Thomas W. Johnson, at his residence in Frederick Co., MD., on Wednesday evening last, in the 18th year of her age. (Baltimore Patriot)
454. (D) On Saturday the 22nd ult., Mr JOHN HALLER, in the 36th year of his age.
455. (D) On Sunday evening last, of the prevailing epidemic, Mr DAVID SPRENGLE, in the 37th year of his age.
456. (D) On Sunday night last, Mrs MARKEL (widow,) at an advanced age.
457. (D) On Friday morning the 21st inst., after a illness of a few days, in the 43rd year of her age, CAREY ANNA, wife of Gen. John Spear Smith of Baltimore Co.
458. (M) On Thursday evening last, by the Rev. D. F. Schaeffer, Mr MICHAEL H. HALLER, to Miss CHARLOTTE C. BIRELY, all of this city.
459. Young Men's Bible Society held their annual meeting in the German Reformed Church, on the 17th inst., the following gentlemen were chosen Directors for the ensuing year: Lutheran Church: AUGUSTUS F. EBERT, VALERIUS EBERT, JOHN HANSHEW, WILLIAM D. HEIM. Presbyterian Church: JAMES M. SHELMAN, Doct. ALBERT RITCHIE, W. OGDEN NILES, Doct. S. L. McKEEHAN. Methodist Church: JAMES L. NORRIS, WILLIAM WINULL, MEREDITH DAVIS, WILLIAM WEBER. German Reformed Church: JOHN L. SAUNDERS, GIDEON BANTZ, Jr., SETH

NICHOLS, JACOB RAMSBURG. Episcopal Church: HORATIO McPHERSON, STUART GAITHER, WILLIAM J. ROSS, NEILSON POE. Baptist Church: THOMAS RITCHIE, ENOS B. REED, GEORGE ENGLISH, HENRY RIGGS, Jr. At the meeting of the Board of Directors held on Monday evening Sept. 21. The Board was organized by the election of the following gentlemen as officers of the Society for the ensuing year: President - JAMES M. SHELMAN, 1st Vice President - WILLIAM J. ROSS, 2nd Vice President - NEILSON POE, Corresponding Sec. - AUGUSTUS F. EBERT, Treasurer - Doct. ALBERT RITCHIE, Recording Sec. - GIDEON BANTZ, Jr. Agt. of Depository - Rev. D. F. SCHAEFFER.

October 6, 1832 (CBAL)

460. (M) On Thursday last, by the Rev. Mr Samsden, Mr CHARLES T. McELFRESH, to Miss FANNY S. WAGGONER, all of this co.
461. (M) On Thursday evening last, by the Rev. D. F. Schaeffer, Mr JAMES BARTLEY, to Miss AGNES SPONSELLER, all of this city.
462. (M) On Tuesday evening the 2nd inst., by the Rev. Mr Young, Mr ISAAC H. HOWARD, to Miss SARAH ANN DORSEY SPRIG, both of this co.
463. (M) At Shepherdstown, VA., on the 23rd inst., by the Rev. Mr Medtart, Mr JOHN B. WEBER, Jr., (formerly of Frederick,) to Miss SARAH WOLTZ, eldest daughter of Mr John B. Woltz, of Shepherdstown.
464. (D) On Saturday evening last, after a very short illness, Miss MARY LEATHER, aged 19 years, 6 months and some days.
465. (D) On Monday morning the 1st inst., of the prevailing disease, Mrs EXILE JAMISON, wife of Henry Jamison, aged about 28 years. Leaving affectionate husband and 3 infant children, a member of the Catholic Church, and in the cemetery of which her remains were interred.
466. (D) On Sunday last, of the prevailing epidemic, ELIZABETH LAWRENCE, of this city, at an advanced age.
467. (D) On Sunday last of cholera, Mrs MARY ANN WALLING, late of Philadelphia, wife of Henry Walling, aged 23 years.
468. (D) On Monday last, of the prevailing epidemic, Mr JOHN H. ABBOTT, of this city.
469. (D) At New York, on the 26th ult., after a painful illness of several weeks, Mrs SUSAN WEBER, wife of George R.

Weber, and daughter of Mr Thos. Shepherd, of Shepherdstown, VA.

470. ISAAC WEBSTER, a minister of the Methodist Protestant Church, will preach (God willing,) in the Court House on Wednesday evening next, at 2 o'clock.

October 13, 1832 (CBAL)

471. (D) On Wednesday last, after a very short illness, Mrs SARAH MATILDA HALLER, wife of Henry Haller, aged 41 years, 5 months and 10 days.
472. (D) On the 31st inst., of the prevailing epidemic, Miss CATHARINE BROWN, of this city, in the 32nd year of her age.
473. (D) On the 4th inst., Mrs MAGDALEN BROWN, of this city, aged 71 years.
474. (D) On Sunday evening last, SARAH ELLEN WYSONG, daughter of Isaac and Elizabeth Wysong, aged 8 years and 5 days.
475. (D) MICHAEL SPONSELER, merchant, was so unfortunate, on the evening of the late election, at Westminster, as to have one of his legs broken, to be mangled by a fall from his horse. He was brought home on Wednesday last, but the fracture being a most severe one, mortification soon commenced and progressed so rapidly that he died on Friday last, a little after 12 o'clock, and from the state of his body; were obliged to bury him on the same evening. He leaves a young widow, and 2 infant children. (Union Town, Md.) October 8, 1832

October 20, 1832 (CBAL)

476. (D) On Saturday last, after a lingering illness, Mrs CATHARINE NICHOLS, wife of Mr Seth Nichols, of this city.
477. (D) On Monday night last, at the residence of his grandfather, in Frederick Co., Md., THOMAS TURNER, aged 3 years, 7 months, son of Dr. John M. Thomas, of Washington City. On Sunday he was in good health, early Monday morning, symptons of scarlet fever made there appearance which lasted for 24 hours.
478. (D) On the 4th inst., in the 14th year of his age, FRANCIS McDANIEL, a native of Ireland. But for the past 62 years, a resident of Baltimore, and Frederick Co's., he served in the Revolutionary War as Quartermaster of a battalion.
479. (D) At Stockholm, on the 7th of Aug., last, LAURA SOPHIA,

wife of Christopher Hughes, Esq., Charge De Affairs of the U. States of America, and daughter of Gen. Saml. Smith.

480. (D) On Monday night the 8th ult., at the residence of Dr. West, of Frederick Co., MD., after 6 days of severe suffering, THOMAS TURNER, only son of Thomas Turner, Esq., of George-Town, D.C., aged 5 years, 9 months and 17 days.

481. (D) On Thursday night, the 9th inst., Mrs CATHERINE BRENGLE, consort of Mr Lawrence Brengle, residing near this city, and daughter of Andrew Shriver, Esq., of near Westminster.

482. (M) On the 3rd ult., by the Rev. Mr Albert, Mr SAMUEL WEAVER, of Gettysburg, PA., to Miss ELIZABETH REINHART, of Westminster.

483. (M) On Thursday evening last, by the Rev. John Smaltz, Mr ELIAS RAMSBURG, to Miss CATHERINE HOUCK, daughter of Mr John Houck, all of this co.

484. (M) On Tuesday evening last, by the Rev. D. F. Schaeffer, Mr DANIEL MILLER, to Mrs CATHARINE RIEHL, both of this city.

485. (M) On the same evening, by the same, Mr GEORGE FREYTAG, to Miss MARIA GOES, both lately from Europe.

486. Rev. Mr JONES, will preach in the Baptist Meeting House, to-morrow at 3 o'clock.

487. (D) The cholera has reappeared in Hagerstown and destroyed many most worthy citizens, there has been 18 deaths by cholera, since Thursday the 11th inst., among the victims are: JOHN McIIHENNY, THOMAS KENNEDY, "editor of the Mail," WILLIAM MOFFETT, JOHN MILLER, JOHN McGLANGHLIN, MASTER FRITCH, Miss SNIDER, and a child of JOHN SCHLEIGH.

October 27, 1832 (CBAL)

488. (M) On Sunday last, by the Rev. D. F. Schaeffer, Mr CHRISTAIN L. STEDING, to Miss CATHERINE FISCHER, all of this city.

489. (M) In Baltimore, on Tuesday evening, at Mr R. Gilmor's, by the Rev. Mr Johns, JOHN McPHERSON BRIEN, Esq., of Frederick Co., to Miss ISABEL ANN BARON, daughter of the late Dr. Baron, of Charleston.

490. (M) On Thursday evening the 11th inst., at the residence of Mrs Dandridge, in Berkley Co., VA., by the Rev. Mr Matthews, THOS. ELIE BUCHANAN, Esq., (son of the Hon. John Buchanan of this co.,) to Miss ANN S., and at the same time and place, and by the same, ANTHONY KENNE-

DY, Esq., of Ellicott Mills, MD., to Miss SARAH, daughter of the late A. S. Dandridge, of Berkley Co., VA.
491. (M) On Sunday evening the 21st inst., by the Rev. David Engler, Mr DAVID E. STONER, to Miss ESTHER, youngest daughter of Mr John Foutz.
492. (M) At Louisville, KY., HENRY CLAY, Jr., to MARIA JULIA, daughter of the late Thomay Prother.
493. (D) In Annapolis, on Friday evening, the 19th inst., after a severe illness of 10 days, JAMES WILLIAMSON, Esq., a delegate elected to the Legislature of Maryland from that city.
494. (D) In Baltimore, on Friday evening, the 19th inst., in the 66th year of his age, Mr WM. WARREN, for many years manager of the Baltimore and Philadelphia Theatres. Was a native of England, and for more than 30 years he has been a residence of this Country. He is a Shakespearean actor, a widow and a large family survives him. (Baltimore Patriot)
495. (D) Death of the editor of this paper, THOMAS KENNEDY, Esq., he expired at 3 o'clock, on Thursday morning, in the 56th year of his age, after a few hours illness of cholera. For many years he had been either in the House of Delegates or in the Senate of Maryland. He was presently serving in the House of Delegates. (Hagers-Town Mail)

November 3, 1832 (CBAL)

496. (M) On Thursday last, by the Rev. John H. Smaltz, Mr ARNOLD S. STONEBRAKER, of VA., to Miss SOPHIA RAMSBURG, near Jefferson, Frederick Co.
497. (M) Near Mount Pleasant, MD., on Thursday the 1st inst., by the Rev. Mr Smith, Mr EDMUND STARR, to Miss ANN BEAUMONT, both of this co.
498. (D) Near Hagerstown, on Friday the 26th ult., Mr PARKER BLOOD, bookseller of that town, in the 34th year of his age.
499. (D) At Hagerstown, on Sunday the 21st ult., of the prevailing epidemic, VACHEL W. RANDALL, Esq., was a native, and for many years a resident of this co. Having studied the profession of law-he located himself at Hagerstown, and was actively engaged in the practice, at the period of his decease.
500. Appointments by the Governor and Council: JOHN L. HARDING, Justice of the Orphans' Court, Frederick Co.

ADDISSON WHITE, Justice of the Peace and Col. WILLIAM DURBIN, Armourer for Frederick Co.
501. Rev. ISAAC WEBSTER, will on Wednesday evening next at 1/2 past 6 o'clock, at the Court House explain the causes which originated the Methodist Protestant Church, and contrast its government with that of the Methodist Episcopal Church.

November 10, 1832 (CBAL)
502. (M) On the 8th inst., by the Rev. John H. Smaltz, Mr MICHAEL HOUCK, to Miss CATHARINE BLOOM, all of this co.
503. (D) In Gettysburg, PA., on the 5th inst., in the 84th year of his age, WILLIAM RUNKEL, D.D., formerly a resident of this city.
504. (D) Departed this life on the 27th of Oct., Mr JOHN GEPHART, in the 82nd year of his age, 65 of which he was a resident of Frederick.
505. (D) Of a paralytic affection, on the 26th of October, Mr GEO. SMITH, in the 57th year of his age.
506. (D) Judge McMECHON, of the Baltimore City Court, departed this life on Sunday morning last, after a long illness. At the meeting of the Court on Monday morning a respected tribute was paid to his memory.
507. Appointments by the Executive of Maryland: JOHN THOMAS, Junr, Captain, EMANUEL THOMAS, 1st Lieutenant, and MICHAEL THOMAS, 2nd Lieutenant of the 28th Regiment of a Uniform Rifle Company near Jefferson, MD.

November 17, 1832 (CBAL)
508. (M) On the 13th inst., by the Rev. John H. Smaltz, Mr JACOB HOLTZ, to Miss AGNES SNOOK, both of this co.
509. (D) Departed this life on Thursday the 11th inst., after a tedious and protracted illness, in the 40th year of his age, Mr HENRY HEICHLER HALLER. He leaves 7 children and 1 infant, whose mother died a month ago.
510. (D) On Sunday the 11th inst., GEORGE MURDOCH, youngest son of Mr George M. Potts, of Fountain Rock, Frederick Co.
511. (D) Departed this life on Monday morning last, after a few days illness, Miss CHARLOTTE HOFFMAN, in the 17th year of her age, daughter of George Hoffman, of this city.

512. (D) On Monday night last, after a very short illness, JOHN SPRINGER, youngest son of Daniel Springer, in the 3rd year of his age.
513. Serious accident - As Mr MYERLY and his wife, from near Westminster, Frederick Co., Md., were on their way to Huntington Co., in this State, in a dearborne wagon. They were upset off the turnpike near Capt. John P. Mertz's in this co., on Saturday the 20th of October last, both were seriously hurt-of which Mrs Myerly died on the 3rd inst. Mr M., is doing well, and recovering fast as can be expected
514. Rev. Mr JONES, will preach in the Baptist Meeting House, on to-morrow afternoon, at 3 o'clock.

November 24, 1832 (CBAL)

515. (M) At Point of Rocks, on Tuesday the 13th inst., by the Rev. Daniel J. Hauer, Mr ROSWELL P. JACOBS, to Miss SUSAN R. PLASTER.
516. (M) At Middletown, MD., on the 8th of November, 1832, by the Rev. J. C. Bucher, Mr ASA LEWIS, of Williamsport, Washington Co., to Miss HANNAH JANE BARNES, of Frederick City, MD.
517. (D) On Friday the 6th inst., at Washington, after a severe illness, EDWARD J. COLE, Esq., formerly of Baltimore.
518. (D) On the 19th inst., at Brown's Hotel, in the city of Washington, the Hon. PHILIP DODDRIDGE, a Representative of Congress, from the State of VA., aged about 60 years.
519. An Irish potatoe raised on the farm of PETER GROSSNICHOL, Esq., of Middletown, it weighted 30 1/2 ounces.

December 1, 1832 (CBAL)

520. (F) The mill of JACOB CRONICE, situated on Linganore Creek, was burnt, with all its contents, on Wednesday the 14th inst. It contained a considerable amount of flour and grain, together with the millhouse, was entirely destroyed. The property was insured to the amount of $4,000.00 which is not sufficient to protect the property against loss. The fire was supposed to have been the work of an incendiary.
521. (M) On the 27th inst., by the Rev. John H. Smaltz, Mr WM. MICHAEL, to Miss ANN ZEALER, all of this city.
522. (D) On the 7th inst., after a short and painful illness, Miss ELIZA HALLER youngest daughter of Christopher Haller, deceased was in the 29th year of her age.

523. (D) In Salem, Massachusetts, Mr JOSEPH VINCENT, aged 96 years, and 7 months. When the news of the Battle of Bunker Hill reached Salem, he immediately repaired to the field of action, accompanied by a number of his townsmen, too late to take part in the battle. At this time he carried on a large cordage manufactory and supplied the army besieging Boston with matches, ropes, and the boats with cordage, when the sloops of war was built at Newburyport, Mr Vincent was called upon to furnish the cordage for them. This article at the time was not easily to be obtained, and he refused to sell to the merchants there using these words, "my Country first until she is supplied, I have nothing for you." He took the promise to pay of the State of Massachusetts gold-this "promise to pay," was never fulfilled-he later received an adequate compensation, being compelled to take Continental money. In 1777, a number of apprentices, and a colored servant in his family, wishing to enter the Army, he equipped them at his own expense. He afterwards joined the Army under Washington as a volunteer.

524. The Rev. ISAAC WEBSTER, of the Methodist Protestant Church will preach in the Court House on Wednesday evening next, at 1/2 pass 6 o'clock.

December 8, 1832 (CBAL)

525. (M) At yesterday, in Montgomery Co., MD., on the 27th ult., by the Rev. Mr Mines, Dr. JOHN M. THOMAS, formerly of this city, to Miss HARRIET MARGARET, daughter of the late James Dunlop, Esq., of George-Town.

526. (M) On Thursday evening the 29th ult., by the Reve. L. Deborah, Mr GEORGE T. ROSENSTEEL, of Baltimore, to Miss LOUISA CLAPSADDLE, of Uniontown, Frederick Co., MD.

527. (D) Departed this life on Saturday the 17th of November, Mr FRANCIS S. MILLER, son of Mr John S. Miller, this city. In early period of boyhood he was visited with a debility in one of his legs, (supposed to have been originated by bathing when in a state of perspiration) which shocked his growth and rendered him a cripple and a invalid for life. His skills as a engraver were excellent and being self taught. In 1827, he made his attempt at engraving; rud was the product. His work upon copper will bear comparison with the generality of that kind of engraving and we think his work on wood has seldom been surpassed by the delicacy

of the lines and the near imitation of copperplate that he effected. His greatest achievement in this art may be accounted in the cutting of an entire set of steel dies, for steel work. More recent, Mr Miller devoted a portion of his attention to drawing card painting. The accuracy of his copies, in portraits though few in number has been admitted, and admired by all who have seen them. (He required the constant use of crutches) The illness that terminated his earthly career was the dropsy which discovered itself, but a few weeks before is dissolution. He was in the 27th year of his age.

December 15, 1832 (CBAL)

528. Conviction of rape - In the Criminal Court of this co., now in session, LEVI HENRY, a bright mulatto, was found guilty, on Thursday last, of committing a rape upon a white girl, not 20 years of age. The crime was committed near Reisterstown, Baltimore Co., the trial was removed to Frederick. The sentence of the court has not been pronounced.
529. (M) On Sunday evening last, by the Rev. D. F. Schaeffer, LEVI T. UPTON, to Miss ADELIA EMELINE MICHAEL, all of this city.
530. (M) At Tankerville, Loudon Co., VA., on Tuesday 2nd inst., by the Rev. D. J. Hauer, Mr JOHN WENNER, to Mrs SARAH EVERHART.
531. (M) On Thursday the 6th inst., by the same, Mr ADAM COOPER, to Miss HARRIET EDWARDS.
532. (M) On The same day, by the same, Mr JOHN YEAKEY, to Miss MARY BEEMER. all of Tenhevila.
533. (D) On the 10th ult., JACOB SHOLL, aged 27th years, on the 19th ult., Mrs SHOLL, aged 25 years, and on the 5th inst., SARAH ANN HARDEN, aged 19 years, the two last named were children of Mrs ---- Harden.
534. (D) On yesterday afternoon, HOWARD H., son of Dr. Wm. S. McPherson, in the 5th year of his age. The funeral will take place this afternoon at 1/2 pass 3 o'clock.
535. (D) On the 2nd inst., aged 2 years and 8 months, HENRY CLAY, youngest son of Thomas Hammond.

December 22, 1832 (CBAL)

536. (M) On Tuesday last, by the Rev. Mr Bosler, Mr GEORGE WEAVER, to Miss MARY ANN TROXELL.

537. (D) On the 19th inst., Miss ESTHER CHARLOTTE, youngest daughter of Mr Michael Straeffer, of this co., in the 12th year of her age.
538. (D) On Friday the 14th ult., in the 26th year of his age, Mr LAWRENCE NOLAND, leaving a helpless mother and sister to deplore the loss of their only support. His death was occasioned by a railroad car passing over his body, fracturing both of his legs and mangling his whole body.
539. (D) Departed this life, on the 31st of Oct., ELIZA AMELIA, aged 13 months and 16 days. And on the 14th inst., MARY ANN REBECCA, aged 2 years 7 months and 14 days, daughter of John T. Simmons, of this co.
540. (D) On the evening of the 14th inst., SARAH ANN, eldest daughter of Dr. Wm. S. McPherson, in the 13th year of her age.
541. (D) Departed this life, at Liberty-Town, on the 12th inst., after a illness of 5 weeks, RICHARD G. DORSEY, in the 32nd year of his age. Service was conducted by the Rev. Mr McGee, in the Methodist Episcopal Church, service was from the 2nd Corinthians, 5th Chapter 1st Verse.

December 29, 1832 (CBAL)

542. (M) On the 25th inst., by the Rev. John H. Smaltz, Mr DANIEL SHOOK, to Miss SUSANNA STALEY.
543. (M) On the same day, by the same, Mr SAMUEL TRIG, to Miss ELIZABETH PARE.
544. (M) On Thursday, the 16th inst., by the Rev. John H. Baker, JONATHAN MANRO, Jr., M.D., to Miss RACHEL M. S. WATERS, youngest daughter of the late Dr. Richard Waters, of Montgomery Co.
545. (M) On the 20th inst., by the Rev. D. F. Schaeffer, Mr JOSEPH STIMMEL, to Miss SUSAN MORNINGSTAR, all of this co.
546. (D) Suddenly on Sunday evening the 23rd inst., at his residence near Westminster, Mr JOHN HAMBLETON, in the 77th year of his age.
547. (D) Last week was announced the death by scarlet fever, HOWARD, son of Dr. William S. McPherson, of this place. Since then the unpitying destroyer has twice sped his fatal shafts into the bosom of the same afflicted family. On Monday night last, the 24th inst., HENRY, their youngest son, aged about 3 years.

1833

FREDERICK HERALD

January 5, 1833 (CBAL)

548. (M) On the 16th inst., by the Rev. D. Engler, Mr JAMES WOOD, to Miss ELEANOR ZEGAFOOSE, all of this co.
549. (M) On the same day, by the Rev. D. Sailer, Mr GEORGE ZUMBRUN, to Miss SUSANNA P. FOUTZ, all of this co.
550. (M) On the 21st ult., at Fairfax Court House, VA., by the Rev. D. Baxter, Mr JAMES G. SHIED, of Frederick City, to Miss EMILY WALPOLE, of this former place.
551. (M) On Thursday evening last, by the Rev. C. B. Young, Mr REASIN HOBBS, to Miss MARGARET GALEZIO, all of this city.
552. (M) On the 1st inst., by the Rev. John H. Smaltz, Mr DANIEL JULIUS, to Miss SARAH WOLFENSBERGER, both of Hagerstown, Washington Co., MD.
553. Dinner for Mr JOHN NELSON, took place on Saturday last at Thoma's Hotel. The following persons were chosen to serve on the two committees. Committee for the Toast: W. O. NILES, F. A. SCHLEY, J. A. McELFRESH, JAMES DIXON, NEILSON POE, WM. SCHLEY. Committee for the Dinner: JAMES M. SHELMAN, Dr. JOHN BALTZELL, Dr. WM. B. TYLER HENRY SCHLEY, JOHN RIGNEY, BENJAMIN PRICE, THOMAS CARLTON.
554. GEO. WISSINGER, an applicant for the benefit of the insolvent laws, is not Geo. Wissinger, victualler, of Frederick.
555. A young man named OSGOOD, having shaken a large glass bottle containing alcohol, which was sitting upon a stove, threw the liquor over his person, which became ignited. He was dreadfully burnt in all the fore parts of his body, from his face to his feet. He lingered 2 days in great agony.

January 12, 1833 (CBAL)

556. (M) On Tuesday evening last, by the Rev'd. Mr Shriner, Mr JOHN MURPHY, to Miss NELLY SHEHAUN, of this co. (Verse: The sex admit, with humbled pride, that Nelly is a splendid bride, and John, so manly firm and true, is handsome and good natured too.)
557. (M) On Thursday evening last, by the Rev. J. G. Hamner, Mr JAMES L. DAVIS, to Miss ELIZABETH G. HAMMER, all of this city.

January 19, 1833 (CBAL)

558. (M) On Thursday the 10th inst., by the Rev. D. F. Schaeffer, Mr HEZEKIAH MASON, to Miss MARY POOLE, all of this co.
559. (M) On the 10th inst., by the Rev. Mr Bucher, Mr NATHAN KINNA, to Miss MARY ANN DELAWTER, all of Middletown Valley.
560. The notice of marriage published in the newspaper of the 2nd inst., of Mr JAMES G. SHEID, of Frederick, to Miss WALPOLE, of Va., was unauthorised, no such event having taken place. (Baltimore American)
561. (D) On Monday evening last, at his residence near Emmitsburg, PATRICK OWINGS, Esqr., for the last 20 years a resident of this co. He leaves a widow and a interesting family of children.
562. (D) On the 14th inst., after and illness of more than 3 weeks, of scarlet fever, MARY ELEN, in the 4th year of her age, daughter of Charles Nagle.
563. (D) On Wednesday last, in this city, Maj. PETER MANTZ, one of the Judges of the Orphan's Court of Frederick Co.

January 26, 1833 (CBAL)

564. (M) On Tuesday the 22nd inst., by the Rev. Mr Birkly, Mr DANIEL G. SMITH, of Leesburg, Va., to Miss ELIZA, daughter of Mr Peter Buckey of this vicinity.
565. (M) On Tuesday last, by the Rev. D. F. Schaeffer, Mr HIRAM WHITE, to Miss ELIZABETH POOLE, all of this co.
566. (M) On Thursday last, by the same, Mr FREDERICK W. KROMMER, to Miss MARGARET SCHOLL, all of this co.
567. (M) On the same evening, by the same, Mr JACOB LAMBRIGHT, to Miss NANCY G. DAYHOFF, of this city.
568. (M) On Thursday evening last, by the Rev. Mr Johns, ROBERT Y. STOKES, to HARRIET D., daughter of Dr. William Bradley Tyler, all this city.
569. Corporation election: JOHN TITLOW, is a candidate for the Common Council for the 6th Ward, and to represent the 7th Ward: EZRA DOLL.

February 2, 1833 (CBAL)

570. (M) On the 31st ult., by the Rev. John M'Enally, Mr JESSE W. RINE, to Miss LUCY ANN BROOKOVER, all of this co.
571. (D) Departed from this scene of transitory existence, on Monday the 14th ult., in New Market, Frederick Co., MD.,

after a few days illness, Mrs SARAH ELLIOTT, in the 82nd year of her age.
572. BOURNE'S, collection of engravings now exhibiting at City Hall, and to be sold this evening at auction, is really very beautiful, and well worthy of public patronage.

February 9, 1833   (CBAL)

573. (D) At Graceham, on Sunday the 27th ult., LOUIS DUNKIN, youngest son of Wm. Pittinger, Esq., of that place, aged 4 years, 5 months and 22 days.
574. (D) On Thursday the 10th ult., Mrs FINNETTA COOMES, consort of Mr Jesse Coomes, of this co. She leaves a infant 9 days old, her death was occasioned by falling down stairs.
575. New Post Office called Urbana, has been established 7 miles from Frederick on the Washington Road, LORENZO B. WINDSOR, has been named Post-Master.

February 16, 1833   (CBAL)

576. (M) On the 5th inst., by the Rev. Mr Brown, Mr THORNTON POOLE, to Miss RACHAEL RUTH, eldest daughter of Dr. Thomas B. Owings, all of this co.
577. (D) In Washington City, on Thursday the 7th inst., in the 14th year of his age, DECIMUS EUGENE M., son of Dr. Tobias Watkins, of that city.

February 23, 1833   (CBAL)

578. (M) In Cincinnati, on the 1st of Jan., Mr JAMES L. LYON, (late of Frederick,) to Miss ELIZABETH KENT, of Cincinnati.
579. (M) On the 10th inst., by the Rev. D. F. Schaeffer, Mr HENRY SCHMAL, to Miss MARIA KLEIN, both from Germany.
580. (M) On the 14th inst., by the same, Mr MICHAEL WALDMAN, to Miss SUSAN SHIELDS, all of this co.
581. (M) On Thursday the 14th inst., by the Rev. Mr Rice, Mr JOHN C. WILSON, of the Point of Rocks, to Miss SUSAN HILLIARY, of Maryland Tract.
582. (M) In Clinton Township, Franklin Co., near Columbus Ohio, on the 7th inst., Mr WASHINGTON LAKIN, late of Frederick Co., to Miss ANNA REBECCA EASTERDAY.
583. (M) On Thursday evening last, by the Rev. John H. Smaltz, the Rev. GEORGE A. LEOPOLD, late of the Theological Seminary, at York, PA., to Miss JANE M. ARMOUR, of this city.

584. (D) On Sunday morning last, in the 8th year of his age, WILLIAM, only son of William Schley, Esq., of this city.
585. Mr RANDOLPH, has left his home on a visit to Washington.
586. Corporation election: Mr JACOB FAUBLE, a candidate for Ward #1, GEORGE M. CONRAD, to represent Ward #2, Mr JACOB KELLER, candidate for Ward #3, WILLIAM FISCHER, candidate for Ward #4, SAMUEL B. LEWIS, will represent Ward #5, JOHN TITLOW, candidate for Ward #6, JOHN W. MILLER, Mr RICHARD ENGLISH, EZRA DOLL, are all candidates for Ward #7, PHILIP ROHR, JOHN RIGNEY, GEORGE W. ENT, GEORGE B. SHOPER, WILLIAM ELY, ANDREW HEIM, PATRICK TORMEY, are recommended to the voters, in their respective Wards. These persons are all candidates for the Common Council. PATRICK TORMEY, declines, being considered as a candidate.
587. Dr. JAMES W. PRYOR, has commenced the practice of medicine in Frederick. Any messages left at the bar of Mr Thomas' Hotel, will receive immediate attention. (Feb. 23.)

March 2, 1833 (CBAL)

588. (D) In Tottenham England, on the 24th December, Rev. GEORGE WHITFIELD, the celebrated Methodist Preacher, aged 79 years.
589. (D) On the 9th inst., at New Goshenhoppen, Montgomery Co., Pa., the Rev. JOHN FABOR, Pastor of the German Reformed Church at that place, in the 60th year of his age. The decease was preaching a funeral sermon a few days before his death, and near the close of his discourse was stricken with the palsey. It is something worthy of remark, that a number of years before, the father of Mr F., also a minister of the gospel, in the same pulpit, and while preaching a funeral sermon, was attacked with the same disease, and died in a few days.
590. (D) Departed this transitory pilgrimage, on the morning of the 17th inst., after a long and distressing infirmity, Mrs ELIZABETH GILSON, in the 68th year of her age. Has been 48 years since her marriage, she has left an aged husband, 8 children, 65 grandchildren and 3 great grandchildren. On Monday her remains were removed from her late dwelling to the family burying grounds. (Liberty-Town, February 1833)
591. Corporate election results for members of the Common Council, were held on Monday last, with the following

gentlemen elected: Ward #1. JACOB FAUBEL. Ward #2. GEORGE M. CONRADT. Ward #3. JACOB KELLER. Ward #4. PHILIP ROHR. Ward #5. SAMUEL B. LEWIS. Ward #6. JOHN TITLOW. Ward #7. WILLIAM ELY.

March 9, 1833 (CBAL)

592. (D) On Wednesday evening last, PETER BRENGLE, Esq., Sheriff of Frederick Co.
593. (M) On Tuesday last, by the Rev. D. F. Schaeffer, Mr JACOB BYERS, to Miss HENRIETTA SAYLOR.
594. (M) On Thursday last, by the same, Mr JOHN CULLERYS to Miss MARIA SMITH.
595. (M) On the same evening, by the same, Mr JOSEPH HENDERSON, to Miss ANN BALLINGER.
596. (M) On the 3rd inst., by the Rev. John H. Smaltz, Mr DANIEL KEAFAUVER, to Miss SARAH BECHTOL, both of Middletown Valley.
597. (M) On the 7th inst., by the same, Mr JACOB STULL, to Miss EVE ELIZABETH STALEY, both of this co.
598. In consequence of the death of PETER BRENGLE, Esq., MATTHIAS E. BARTGIS, Esq., the next highest on the return at the last election, became Sheriff of this co., until the end of this term, which expires next Oct.
599. Escape of prisoners - 3 old offenders, RINEHART, KELLY and HURST, made their escape from the Maryland Penitentiary on Saturday evening last. Being attached to the bakery, they worked longer than time allotted for the return of prisoners to their cells-they obtained clothing left by those that had just entered for service, with which they made their escape over the walls-outside they left their prison uniforms and escaped in citizens dress. The keeper of the penitentiary has forward the following description. JOHN RINEHART, from the city of Frederick, convicted for robbing a gentlemen of this co., is about 50 years of age, 5'10" high, dark complexion, dark eyes, and hair, shows the loss of his jaw-teeth, a hatter by trade. PATRICK KELLY, about the same age, 5'11" high, sallow complexion, grey eyes, dark hair, was born in Ireland, a baker by trade. JOSEPH HURST, 5'11" high, fair complexion, blue eyes, brown hair. They took with them one green, and one brown frock coat, four shirts marked "Bond," and four marked "T. Murray," one fur hat marked under the leather lining "Bond Maryland." A reward of $20.00 will be paid for each prisoner. (Baltimore Patriot)

March 30, 1833 (CBAL)

600. (M) On Sunday last, by the Rev. Michael Wachter, Mr JOSIAH BLACK, to Miss CATHERINE GREENALL, all of this co.
601. (M) On Thursday last, by the same, Mr LEWIS ALBAUGH, to Miss SUSAN FOX, both of this co.
602. (M) On Thursday the 21st inst., by the Rev. George Roberts, Mr SAMUEL BARNES, (printer, late of Frederick,) to Miss ELLEN RIDGELY LOCKE, daughter of Nathaniel Locke, Esq., of this city. (Baltimore Republican)

April 6, 1833 (CBAL)

603. (M) In Baltimore, on the 2nd inst., by the Rev. J. Gibson, Mr JOSEPH MILTON BAKER, of Winchester, Va., to Miss ELIZABETH BERASTON BREVITT, second daughter of Dr. Joseph Brevitt, of Baltimore.
604. (D) On Tuesday, the 5th ult., Mr JOHN COLE, after a illness of 15 days. A member of the Church of God, he leaves affectionate wife.
605. (D) At Shippensburg, on the 22nd ult., the Rev. DIETRICH GRAVES, in the 58th year of his age. A minister of the German Reformed Church, he commenced his ministerial course in the neighborhood of Uniontown and Taney Town, in this co., for some time. When he was called to Woodstock, in VA., after 5 years he was called back to his former station in Md. From there he removed to Shippensburg last fall.
606. (D) In Baltimore on the 3rd of April, the Rev. ROGER SMITH, Rector of the Cathedral in the 43rd year of his age. After a short but very severe illness.
607. WILLIAM C. JOHNSON, Esq., and JOHN LEE, Esq., are candidates for Congress to represent the Congressional Districts, composed of Montgomery and part of Frederick Co., in the 23rd Congress of the United States.

April 13, 1833 (CBAL)

608. (M) On Thursday the 11th inst., by the Rev. D. F. Schaeffer, Mr FREDERICK EBERTS, to Miss CATHERINE WINPIGLER, all of this co.
609. (M) On the 9th inst., by the Rev. Daniel Zollicoffer, Mr SAMUEL McKINSTRY, son of Evan McKinstry, Esq., to Miss MARY ANN, daughter of the late Mordeca Clemson, all of this co.

610. (M) On Monday evening, in Baltimore, at Saint Mary's Chapel, by the Rev. Mr Elder, Mr JOSEPH GIGAN, Esq., to CATHARINE ANN, second daughter of Thomas Whelan, Esq., all of this city.
611. (D) At Etna Glasshouse, on Monday morning the 9th inst., Mr BENJAMIN JOHNSON, nephew of the late Gov. Thomas Johnson, in the 73rd year of his age. He resided not more then 5 miles away from Frederick for the last 35 years. His visit to this town was about the same during that time. While conducting the glassfactory, he became occupied with agricultural labours. Having around him an indigent population who occupied the huts which have been erected during the operation of the glassfactory. He devoted much time to reclaiming of the drunkards, and promoting the comforts of their wives, and children. By agreements he would remunerate their services with bread and clothing for their families, and pay the balance of their earnings in money to their wives, for the benefit of their families and to prevent the husband from laying it out in liquor. He was a indulgent husband and a kind master.

April 20, 1833 (CBAL)

612. (M) On Tuesday evening last, by the Rev. James G. Hamner, SAMUEL TYLER, Esq., Attorney-at-law, to Miss CATHARINE BAYLEY, daughter of John Bayley, Esq., all of this city.
613. (M) On the 1st inst., by the Rev John H. Smaltz, Mr THOMAS CAPES, to Miss ELIZABETH McVICKER, both of this city.
614. (M) On the 10th inst., by the same, Mr CHRISTIAN NEIHOFF, to Miss SUSANNA KEEFER, all of this city.
615. (D) Departed this life, on the 5th inst., at his residence in this co., Mr PETER ENGEL, in the 54th year of his age. Retiring to bed the evening previous in as good health as usual (which was weakly for several years, occasioned by a wen on his throat,) was known to be as well as usual at 12 o'clock at night, and was found a corpse, at 4 in the morning; having died without a struggle or a groan as the posture of his body and features plainly indicated and by not awakening his wife, who was in bed with him. He was a kind father, and left an aged mother, a disconsolate wife and 8 children.
616. GEO. C. WASHINGTON, Esq., is a candidate for Congress to represent the Congressional District, composed of

Montgomery and part of Frederick Co. Mr FRANCIS THOMAS, Esq., is a candidate for re-election in the Congressional District of Washington and Allegany and part of Frederick Counties. Mr JOHN LEE, has withdrawn his candidacy.

April 27, 1833 (CBAL)

617. (M) In Middleburg, on Sunday last, the 21st inst., by the Rev. Mr Houblestine, Mr JOHN STRINE, to Miss MARY ANN ECKER, all of this co.
618. (D) Departed this life, on the morning of the 17th inst., after a short illness at her residence in Frederick, Mrs ELIZABETH STEINER, relict of the late Henry Steiner, deceased.
619. (D) In Port Gibson, MS., after an illness of only 1 week, SARAH ANN, eldest daughter of A. K. Shaifer, Esq., formerly of this co.

May 4, 1833 (CBAL)

620. (M) Near Middletown, MD., on the 23rd of April, by the Rev. J. C. Bucher, Mr HENRY, second son of Mr Jno. Cobentz, to Miss ANN MAGDALENE, daughter of Mr Benjamin Routzaun deceased, all of Middletown Valley, Frederick Co., MD.

May 11, 1833 (CBAL)

621. (M) On Tuesday evening last, by the Rev. John H. Smaltz, Mr ABRAHAM W. GETZENDANNER, to Miss MARY E. BUCKEY, all of this co.
622. (M) On Thursday morning last, by the same, Mr JOHN C. TURNER, to Miss ELIZABETH T. LITTLEJOHN, all of this city.
623. (M) On Sunday evening the 28th inst., at the house of Jacob Appler, Sr., in Union Town, by the Rev. Henry Hablistone, JOSEPH MUNDSHOWER, to CHARITY HOLLENBERGER, both of this co.
624. (M) On Wednesday evening last, by the Rev. Mr Wachter, Mr PAUL ANDERS, to Miss MARY ELLEN OTTO, all of this co.
625. (M) On Thursday last, by the same, Mr JONATHAN WELLER, to Miss ELIZABETH BOMGARDNER, both of this co.
626. (M) On Sunday evening last, by the Rev. D. F. Schaeffer,

Mr ACQUILLA BATES to Miss MARGARET HERRING, of this city.
627. (M) On the same evvening, by the same, Mr WILLIAM HARPER, to Miss ANN SHAWEN, all of this co.
628. (D) On Saturday morning last, in the 7th year of his age, JOHN, eldest son of Horatio McPherson, Esq., of this city. He fell victim to that disease which has caused so much mourning in this city.
629. (D) On Sunday last, near Taney Town, at the residence of Sterling Galt, (her son-in-law,) whither she had gone on a visit, Mrs AGNES GRAYSON, relict of William Grayson, deceased, in the 68th year of her age, she leaves 4 children.
630. (D) Near Middletown, Fred'k. Co., MD., on the 2nd inst., Mrs CATHARINE HOYBERGER, sister of Mr Christopher Michael. The deceased, has left an aged and much affected husband in the care of kind friends, she was aged 75 years, 3 weeks and 4 days.
631. (M) At Middletown, MD., on the 2nd inst., by the Rev. J. C. Bucher, Mr JOHN POFFENBEAGER, to Miss REBECCA, fourth daughter of Mr Christopher Michael, all of Middletown Valley, Frederick Co., MD.

May 18, 1833 (CBAL)

632. (M) On Thursday evening May 9th, by the Rev. Thomas McGee, Rev. THOMAS W. H. MUNROE, of the Baltimore Conference, to Miss SARAH ANN WARFIELD, of Frederick Co., MD.
633. (M) On the 23rd ult., in Harford Co., by the Rev. Mr Stephenson, Mr WILLIAM H. GILPIN, to Miss MARGARET A. PRICE.
634. (M) On the 9th inst., by the Rev. Daniel J. Hauer, Mr THOMAS TRITTEPO, to Miss SARAH HOFFMAN.

May 25, 1833 (CBAL)

635. (M) At Mr Shepherds, near Union Bridge, on Thursday the 8th of May, Mr WILLIAM GAMBLE, to Miss ELIZABETH FISHER, both of this co.
636. (M) Near Frederick City, on the 17th of May, by the Rev. John L. Saunders, Mr DANIEL KLINE, to Miss MARGARET ELLIS, all of this co.
637. (M) On Tuesday last, by the Rev. D. F. Schaeffer, Mr JONATHAN SEARS, to Miss CASSANDRA ANN SEARS.
638. (D) After a short illness near Middletown, MD., on the 19th

day of May 1833, Mr HAYBERGER, aged 75 years and about 5 months.
639. (D) On Thursday morning last, ANN REBECCA, second daughter of John Stoner, Esq., of this co.
640. A man named MICHAEL KUSER, of Middletown Valley, was convicted in the Frederick County Court, on Wednesday last, of having committed rape. The victim of this outrage, is a woman LETITIA CAIN, a native of Ireland, and for some years past a resident of the city of Baltimore. She left Baltimore about a year ago, and proceeded to Brownsville, in Pa., where she remained until a few weeks since, she left that place for the purpose of returning to Baltimore. The crime was perpetrated in Middletown Valley. (Citizen)

June 1, 1833 (CBAL)

641. (M) On the 30th ult., by the Rev. John H. Smaltz, Mr NATHAN PLOUGHMAN, to Miss ADRIAN LYONS, of this city.
642. (M) Near Middletown, Fred'k, Co., MD., on the 26th ult., by the Rev. J. C. Bucher, Mr WILLIAM SLIFER, to Miss LYDIA ANN WALDECK, all of Middletown Valley, MD.
643. (M) On Sunday morning last, by the Rev. D. F. Schaeffer, Mr JAMES MOSER, to Miss REBECCA MILLER, both of this co.
644. (M) On Tuesday last, by the same, Mr GEORGE BREEDY, to Miss ANN ELIZABETH BUTLER, both of this co.
645. (M) On the same evening, by the same, Mr EMANUEL SMITH, to Miss MARGARET HOUCK, daughter of Mr John Houck, Esq., both of this co.
646. (M) In Baltimore, on Monday the 20th ult., by the Rev. Mr Gibbson, Mr FRANICS J. CROPSEY, merchant of Brooklyn, L.I., to Miss MIRANDA E. STOUFFER, formerly of Frederick City.
647. (D) Near Middletown, Fred'k, Co., MD., on the 22nd ult., after a short an distressing illness, Mrs ELIZA SHAWAN, consort of Mr Richard Shawan She leaves a husband to lament her early dissoultion.
648. (D) On the morning of the 24th ult., near Middletown, after a short distressing illness, Mr JACOB WEIST, aged 39 years, 6 months and 6 days.
649. (D) On the 14th inst., at the residence of her son-in-law, Rev. Robert Henry, in Greensburgh, Penn., Mrs ELIZABETH BUCHANAN, in her 67th year. She was the mother

of James Buchanan, Esq., now minister at the Court of all the Russians.

650. Reform Convention - The following gentlemen, comprising those of both political parties, have already been selected to attend the Reform convention to be held in Annapolis on the 10th inst. J. D. MAULSBY, THOMAS ARCHER, ABEL ANDERSON, JAMES NELSON, ABRAHAM JARRET ALBERT CONSTABLE, JAMES W. WILLIAMS, JAMES STEEL, RICHARD F. HOLLIS WILLIAM G. DRONE, BENJAMIN PRICE, JAMES DIXON, JOHN W. THOMAS, G. TOWNSEND, WILLIAM JENKINS, WM. S. WINDER, JAMES TURNER, NICHOLAS R. MERRYMAN, ROBERT HOWARD, JONAS GREEN, JOHN C. DESHON, ABRAHAM DeGROFT, JAS. P. HEATH, SAM'L. McCLELLAN, GEORGE WINCHESTER, NAT. F. WILLIAMS, WM. H. MARRIOTT, JOHN BERRY, SAM'L. MOORE, JOHN K. ROWE, WM. H. FREEMAN, PHILIP LAURENSON, JOB SMITH, Jr., CORNELIUS McLEAN, JOHN J. GROSS, THOMAS FINLEY, HUGH ELY, THOMAS HARKLEY.

651. MICHAEL KUSER, convicted at the recent session of Frederick County Court, of committing a rape upon Letitia Cain, has been sentenced to 5 years imprisonment in the penitentiary. During the trial several facts were elicited which divested the crime of that enormity which rumor attached to it.

June 8, 1833 (CBAL)

652. JOHN WARNER, of the neighborhood of Westminster, in this co., was apprehended on Friday last, and confined in the jail of Bedford, Co., PA. The Frederick County Grand Jury, at the May term issued a bill of indictment for passing counterfeit $10. notes on the Bank of Westminster. He was arrested near Bedford, by Messrs; John Crouse, and Jacob Fringer, of Westminster.

653. Destructive tornado - Passed over the mountains about 6 miles above Mechanicstown on Sunday last. The principal sufferer is Mr ZOLINGER, every building on his farm was unroofed grable ends and chimneys of his brick dwelling, torn down every apple-tree in his orchard, nearly all his fencing prostrated, and the bacon in his meat house scattered over the fields. It carried the roof nearly a mile from the site. The family is safe, his wife, and daughter was in no peril from the falling bricks. The tornado did not extend more then 5 or 6 rods in width.

654. On Monday last fall, the following gentlemen were elected to the Frederick County Bank, for the ensuing 12 months: JOHN P. THOMSON, JAMES TORRANCE, Dr. JOHN BALTZELL, HENRY SCHLEY, F. A. SCHLEY, GEO. M. EICHELBERGER, Dr. W. B. TYLER, *WILLIAM GAITHER, MOSES WORMAN, JOHN C. FRITCHIE, *ABRAHAM JONES, GRAFTON HAMMOND. On Tuesday, at the meeting of the above Directors: JOHN P. THOMSON, Esq., was reelected President, and HENRY DOYLE, Esq., reelected cashier. (* new members)
655. (M) On Thursday evening, by the Rev. D. F. Schaeffer, Mr JOHN YOUNG, to Miss MARGARET GRUMBINE, all of this city.
656. (M) On the 6th inst., by the Rev. John H. Smaltz, Mr MICHAEL ZIMMERMAN, to Miss CHRISTIANA E. STALEY, both of this co.
657. (M) At Richmond, VA., on Thursday evening the 30th ult., by the Rev. Bishop Moore, THOMAS GREENE, Esq., to Miss MARY ROANE RITCHIE, second daughter of Thomas Ritchie, Esq., editor of the "Richmond Enquirer."
658. (D) At his residence in the city of Baltimore, on Saturday the 18th ult., in the 28th year of his age, of a protracted pulmonary disease, ROBERT COLEMAN BRIEN, formerly of Catoctin, Frederick Co., MD.
659. (D) At Maysville, Ky., GEORGE BREATHITT, Esq., (brother of the Governor of KY.,) who had occasionally acted as private secretary to the President of the United States.

June 15, 1833 (CBAL)

660. Mrs S. CHAPMAN, and Messrs: WILLIS and CUDDY, will give a concert on Monday evening next, at the City Hall. Mrs Chapman, a delightful vocalist and a great favorite in Baltimore. Messrs: W. & C., are unrivalled on their respective instruments.
661. (M) On Thursday morning the 13th inst., by the Rev. John H. Smaltz, Mr JOHN STOCKWELL, to Mrs FRANCES ANN MILLER, both of Washington City.
662. (M) On the same morning, by the same, Mr JOHN BUTCHER, to Miss MARGARET ANN GEHR, both of this co.
663. (M) On Thursday the 6th inst., by the Rev. D. F. Schaeffer, Mr GEORGE FOX, to Miss ELIZABETH WATSON, all of this co.
664. (M) On Sunday evening last, by the same, Mr DANIEL

CATZEBERGER, to Miss ELIZABETH EIDENMILLER, both from Germany.
665. (M) On Tuesday evening last, by the same, Mr SAMUEL HALLER, to Miss CHARLOTTE LEAB, all of this co.
666. (M) On Thursday the 6th inst., by the Rev. M. Wachter, Mr NIMROD NORRIS, to Miss ELIZABETH BIRELY, all of this co.
667. (M) On the same day, by the same, Mr GEORGE M. OLCOTT, of Hartford, Conn to Miss MARY ANN BAKER, eldest daughter of Brook Baker, Esq., of Woodsborough.
668. (D) On Monday last, after a painful and protracted illness of several months, Miss BARBARA SMITH, of this city, in the 57th year of her age.
669. (D) Yesterday morning at the residence of her father, Wm. Ross, Esq., Mrs ANN E. HARRISON, wife of Wm. G. Harrison, Esq. of Baltimore.

June 22, 1833 (CBAL)

670. (M) On Tuesday evening, by the Rev. D. F. Schaeffer, Mr PETER HERMAN, of Baltimore, to Miss CATHARINE SHELLI, of this city.
671. (M) On Sunday morning last, by the same, Mr HENRY KOESTER, to Miss CHRISTIANA ROELKE, all of this co.
672. (M) On the same evening, by the same, Mr JACOB BUCKEY, to Miss JULIANA TITLOW, all of this city.
673. (M) On Thursday last, by the Rev. Mr Wachter, Mr SYLVESTER BIDWELL, of Conn., to Miss SARAH ANN ELIZABETH BARRICK, of this co.
674. (M) At Rambler retreat, on Tuesday last, by the Rev. Mr Johns, Mr JAMES GIDDINGS, to Miss LOUISA C. JOHNSON, all of this co.
675. (D) Departed this life, on the morning of the 14th inst., at the residence of her father, ANN ELIZABETH, daughter of William Ross, of Frederick, and consort of William G. Harrison, of this city, in her 21st year of age. (Balt. Am.)
676. (D) On the 6th inst., at New Philadelphia, Ohio, Mr MICHAEL DOLL, in the 39th year of his age, a native of this place, he leaves a wife and 7 children.
677. (D) In Upper Marlborough, Prince George's Co., on the 11th ult., PHILIP KEY, Esq., in the 55th year of his age.
678. (D) At Maysville, KY., on the 12th inst., Mr WILLIAM J. DORSEY, son of the late Wm. H. Dorsey, of Montgomery Co., in the 33rd year of his age. He fell victim to the diso-

lating disease which is now producing so much distress throughout the Western part of our Country.

July 13, 1833 (CBAL)

679. Mr PALMER'S troop of equestrians, is now performing at the Pavilian Circus which is erected on Dr. Wm. Tyler's Lot on the West end of 3rd Street.
680. (M) On Monday evening last, at Harlem Heights, by the Rev. Dr. Bogart, Col. AARON BURR, to Mrs ELIZA JUMEL.
681. (M) On Wednesday evening 3rd inst., by the Rev. Mr Hughes, at St. John's Church, JOSEPH R. CHANDLER, Esq., editor of the United States Gazette, to Mrs MARIA H. JONES, daughter of Benjamin Jones, all of Philadelphia.
682. (D) On Saturday night, the 30th ult., Mrs MARY ANN PHILLIPS, consort of Mr John Phillips, near Liberty Town, aged 22 years, 5 months and 3 days. For the last 2 weeks of her life, she laboured under an inveterate disease that baffled the skills of most judicious physicians. She was a member of the M. E. Church for the last 4 to 9 years.
683. (D) The Hon. A. M. SCOTT, Governor of Mississippi, died at Jackson, (Miss.,) of cholera.
684. (D) EDMUND KEAN, the celebrated actor, died in London on the 15th of May, aged 45.
685. (D) On Sunday evening last, Mrs ANN MARIA CHRISTINAH HILTON, in the 62nd year of her age, after an illness of many years. The last 18 months of her life, her suffering were extreme and painful.

July 20, 1833 (CBAL)

686. (D) Distressing accident - On Sunday afternoon the 14th inst., while Mrs NEEL, wife of Joseph Neel, formerly an Inn Keeper on the Frederick and Washington Road, about 7 miles from this village. She was sitting with her child in the upper story of their dwelling when the house was struck by lighting, which passed into the room where Mrs Neel was sitting, and killed her instantly, while we understand the child was not injured.
687. On the same afternoon, a carriage belonging to JOHN COOK, Esq., of this village, was struck while in a house near his dwelling, and materially injured, but unfortunately no other damage was done. We have also been informed that a house belonging to JAMES HAWKINGS, Esq., near Darnestown, was also materially injured. (Rockville Free Press)

688. (M) In Franklin Co., Ohio, on the 27th of June, Mr DANIEL LAKIN, formerly of Frederick Co., to Miss DORCAS FLANAGAN, of Ohio.
689. (M) On Tuesday last, by the Rev. Mr Wachter, Mr CHARLES W. MORGAN, to Mrs ANN SMITH.
690. (M) On Tuesday the 16th inst., in New Market, by the Rev. James Higgins, Mr JAMES M. ARNOLD, to Miss ELIZABETH PHEBUS., both of this city.
691. (M) On Tuesday the 16th inst., by the Rev. Mr Joseph Smith, Mr JOHN KNIGHT, of Natchez, Miss., to Miss FRANCES Z. S. BEALL, daughter of Wm. M. Beall, Esq., of this city.
692. (D) On Friday the 28th of June last, Miss MARGARET BENTZ, daughter of the late Mr George Bentz, of this city.
693. The Rev. Mr JOHM H. SMALTZ, will preach in the Baptist Meeting House, on Sunday next, at 10 o'clock. July 20th.

July 27, 1833 (CBAL)

694. (M) On Saturday last, by the Rev. Mr Schaeffer, Mr JOHANNES FERTICH, to Miss CATHARINE ROTHAUVER, both from Germany.
695. (M) On Sunday last, by the same, Mr CHARLES G. ROW, to Miss ELIZABETH CLOSE, both of this city.
696. (M) On the same day, by the same, Mr A. P. GORSUCH, of Baltimore, to Miss ANN SOPHIA ARNOLD, of this city.
697. (M) On the 23rd inst., by the Rev. J. McEnelly, Mr WILLIAM MOORE, to Miss ELIZABETH HOFF.
698. (D) At the Parsonage of St. Marks, on the 21st inst., Rev. JARED RICE, aged 32, he leaves a wife and infant children.

August 3, 1833 (CBAL)

699. (M) On Thursday last, by the Rev. D. F. Schaeffer, Mr GEORGE MYERS, to Miss MARY FORTNEY, all of this co.
700. (M) On same evening, by the same, Mr GEORGE W. CROMWELL, to Miss MARY A. STORM, all of this city.
701. (M) On Sunday the 28th inst., at the Coppermines, in Frederick Co., by the Rev. Henry Hablistone, Mr DENNIS SHOEMAKER, to Miss MARY ANN STEELE, both of this co.
702. (M) On Sunday the 13th inst., by the same, Mr GEORGE M. LIGHTNER, of York PA., to Miss ELIZABETH YOST, of New Market, Baltimore Co., Md.
703. (M) At Middletown, MD., on the 28th inst., by the Rev. J. C. Bucher, Mr JOSEPH RHODNICK, to Miss MARY ANN

EVERHART, daughter of Mr William Everhart, all of Frederick Co., MD.

704. (D) In this city, on the 26th inst., Mr JOHN M. BRISH, in the 36th year of his age, he leaves a wife and 4 children.

705. (D) In this city on Friday the 19th inst., after a short but painful illness, Mr PAUL PROVOST, a native of GermanTown, near Philadelphia, in the 33rd year of his age. He leaves a wife and 2 children. A few days before his death, he embraced the Roman Catholic Religion, and had received all the rites and sacraments of the Church.

706. The Revd. Mr SMALTZ, will preach God willing, to-morrow (Sunday) morning, in the Baptist Church, divine service is to commence, at 10 o'clock. August 3.

707. National Republican Meeting of the 2nd Election District was held in the Court House in this city, on Saturday evening the 27th inst. PHILIP ROHR, Esq., was called to the chair, and CYRUS MANTZ, appointed Secretary. A committee of 3 were appointed to draught resolutions: JAMES M. COALE, WM. FISCHER and FRANCIS BRENGLE, Esqr. They drafted a resolution, calling upon the chairman to appoint a committee of correspondence, consisting of 7 persons. They also recommended that the chairman appoint 9 persons to represent this election district at the convention. In pursurance of this resolution, the chairman appointed: MOSES WORMAN, WM. S. McPHERSON, CHARLES H. BURKHART, WILLIAM FISCHER, DANIEL KOLB, JAMES M. COALE, BENJ. PRICE, L. P. W. BALCH, and NEILSON POE, to represent the 2nd election district in the county convention. For the committee of correspondence, the chairman appointed: Dr. WM. B. TYLER, Col. JOHN McPHERSON, WILLIAM J. ROSS, ISRAEL MYERS, PATRICK TORMEY, FRANCIS BRENGLE, GEORGE ADAM EBERT, and ABRAHAM KEMP, for the 2nd Election District.

708. St. John's Literary Institution announces the results of the annual examination, which ended on the 22nd inst., is as follows: Department of Languages. Greek: The premium of excellence was awarded to THOMAS SAPPINGTON, FRANCIS SAPPINGTON, CHARLES JENKINS. Latin: 1st class: Premium of excellence: AUGUSTINE L. McMULLEN, 2nd premium: WILLIAM CUNNINGHAM. 2nd Class: Premium of excellence: BERNARD MAGUIRE, 2nd Exequo: CHARLES JENKINS, ROGER BROOKE, Accessit: T. SAPPINGTON. 3rd Class: Premium of excellence:

GEORGE PRICE, Accesserunt: R. BOONE, JOHN LOFTUS. French: 1st Class: Premium of excellence: A. L. McMULLEN. 2nd Class: Premium of excellence: ENOCH L. LOWE, Accesserunt: B. MAGUIRE, C. JENKINS, R. BROOKE. English: Elocution - Premium of excellence: A. L. McMULLEN, Accesserunt: B. MAGUIRE, E. L. LOWE. Compostion and 1st Class of Grammar premium of excellence: G. PRICE, 2nd premium: R. BOONE, Accessit: F. SPONSSELLER. 2nd Class: Premium of excellence: OLIVER C. GEPHART, 2nd premium: JOHN W. BAUGHMAN, Accesserunt: T. GRIFFIN, J. GITTINGER. Premium for reading: JOHN A. SCHISSLER, Accessit: JOSEPH CARLIN. Geography: 1st Class: Premium of excellence: A. L. McMULLEN, 2nd premium : B. MAGUIRE, accessit: THOMAS SAPPINGTON. Premium for the projection of maps: FRANCIS SAPPINGTON. 2nd Class: Premium of excellence: WM. H. WARD, accesserunt: ROBERT BOONE, J. LOFTUS, J. O'NEILL. Mathematics. Algebra: Premium of excellence: A. L. McMULLEN, accesserunt: B. MAGUIRE, E. L. LOWE. 1st Class of Arithmetic: Premium of excellence: J. O'NEILL, accesserunt: GEO. PRICE, O. C. GEPHART. 2nd Class premium of excellence: JOHN W. BAUGHMAN, 2nd Premium: J. LOFTUS, accesserunt: CHARLES STONE, R. BOONE, W. H. WARD. 3rd Class: Premium of excellence: THOMAS GRIFFIN, 2nd Premium: JOSEPH CARLIN, accesserunt: J. SCHISSLER, J. GITTINGER. Elementary School: Reading, Writing and Arithetic: 1st Class: Premium of excellence: THADDEUS PROVOST, 2nd premium: WM. GRANTHAM, premium of improvement: JACOB KUNKEL, accesserunt: CHARLES ARMOUR, J. Q. A. CARLIN. 2nd Class: Premium of excellence SIMON GEPHART, 2nd premium: ANDREW WEAVER, accesserunt: GEORGE DILL, JOSEPH STONE. 3rd Class: Premium of excellence: JOHN H. GITTINGER, 2nd premium: GEORGE GEPHART, accesserunt: JAMES MAGENNIS, WM. COOPER SMALLWOOD. Christian Doctrine: 1st Class: Premium of excellence: BERNARD MAGUIRE, accesserunt: A. L. McMULLEN, R. BROOKE, 2nd Class: Premium of excellence: J. LOFTUS, accesserunt: T. GRIFFIN, R. BOONE, GEO. PRICE. 3rd Class: Premium of excellence: WM. TEHAN, 2nd premium: J. MAGENNIS, 4th Class: Premium of excellence: CHA'S. ARMOUR, 2nd premium: JAMES TEHAN. The school will be opened, after vacation, on the 1st Monday in September. JOHN McELROY. (Frederick, July 27, 1833)

August 10, 1833 (CBAL)

709. The Rev. EDWARD CHOAT and THOMAS POTEET, will preach in the Baptist Meeting House, next Sabbath the 11th inst., at 10 o'clock.

August 17, 1833 (CBAL)

710. (D) On Friday the 9th inst., at his residence on Carroll's Manor, in the 65th year of his age, Mr JOHN SHAFER, one of the oldest members of the Lutheran Church in this place.

711. (D) Death of Mr SCHOLL, a citizen of this place, age of 55 years. After a short but painful sickness. After giving his wife several instructions as to particular persons whose benefactor he was, he folded his hands and fell to sleep. He discharged his duties of a Elder of the Lutheran Church, in this place for 6 years past with faithfulness. By his will which he made 5 years ago, he leaves to the President and Directors of the Evangelical Lutheran Theological Seminary $500. (Examiner)

712. (D) Died in this city on the 29th inst., of a lingering illness, JOHN L. DORSEY, M.D. Mr D., was 25 years of age, and son of Mr Evan Dorsey of Frederick Co., Md. He studied his profession with Dr. W. Bradley Tyler, of Frederick Town, and graduated from the University of Pennsylvania in 1829. He emigrated to this city and commenced his practice, in the house of his uncle Mr Ely Dorsey, where he received his last illness. (Cincinnati Chronical)

713. (D) At his residence in New Windsor, on the 27th ult., after a long illness, Mr ROBERT DODDS, in the 48th year of his age.

714. (D) On Thursday last, Mrs CATHARINE, wife of Jacob Boston, in the 39th year of her age.

715. St. John's Female School, at the late general examination, the following pupils have merited distinction, and as inducement to future exertion, their names are thus made public: 1st Class Grammar: TERESA McMULLEN, 1st premium, ROSANNA McCHRYSTAL, 2nd premium, accesserunt: TERESA FLYNN, 3rd premium, CAROLINE MURPHY, 4th. premium. 1st Class Reading and Spelling: ELLEN MORAN, 1st. premium, TERESA McMULLEN, 2nd. ROSANNA McCHRYSTAL, 3rd. TERESA FLYNN, 4th. 1st

Class History: TERESA McMULLEN, 1st premium, ROSANNA McCHRYSTAL, 2nd. TERESA FLYNN, 3rd. ELLEN MORGAN, 4th. Natural History: T. McMULLEN, 1st premium, R. McCHRYSTAL, 2nd. T. FLYNN, 3rd. C. MURPHY, 4TH. 1st Class; Geography: T. McMULLEN, 1st. E. MORGAN, 2nd. C. MURPHY, 3rd. R. McCHRYSTAL, 4th. 1st Class Writing: A. SCHROEDER, 1st. E. MORGAN, 2nd. C. MURPHY, 3rd. T. FLYNN, 4th. 1st Class Arithimetic: T. McMULLEN, 1st. A. SCHROEDER, 2nd. T. FLYNN, 3rd. E. MORGAN, 4th. 2nd Class Grammar: CHARLOTTE BAUGHMAN and CATHERINE ELDER, equal premiums, MARY McMULLEN and ELIZABETH DULANY, equal premiums, HELEN STONE, premium for improvement. 2nd Class Reading and Spelling: CATHERINE KESSLER and CHARLOTTE BAUGHMAN, equal premiums. 2nd Class History: C. BAUGHMAN, 1st. C. ELDER, 2nd. E. DULANY 3rd. E. KLINE, 4th. 2nd Class Writing: 1st Division: SARAH GRANTHAM, 1st. C. BAUGHMAN, 2nd. 2nd Division: EMMA WALLING, 1st. SARAH JANE MORGAN, 2nd. 2nd Class Arithmetic: 1st Division: M. M'MULLEN and C. ELDER, equal premiums. 2nd Division: S. GRANTHAM, 1st. E. KLINE, 2nd. Junior division of 2nd class: VIRGINIA RUTHERFORD, a premium for improvement in reading and writing, M. PROVOST, a premium for grammar and spelling. SARAH J. MORGAN, a premium for grammar and spelling. SOPHIA R. MORGAN, a premium for reading. ELLEN STONE, MARY JANE TORMEY and LOUISA HARDING, premiums. 3rd Class Grammar: ELLEN NUSBAUM, 1st premium, ELIZABETH OGLE, 2nd. 3rd Class Reading and Spelling: E. NUSBAUM, 1st premium, MARY ENGLAND, 2nd. ELIZABETH McGINNIS, 3rd. SUSAN YONITZ, 4th. 3rd Class History: E. NUSBAUM, 1st premium, RACHAEL NUSBAUM, 2nd. MARY QUYNN, 3rd. MARGARET QUYNN, 4th. 3rd Class Writing: CONSTANTIA KNOTT, 1st premium, ELIZABETH OGLE, 2nd. 3rd Class Arithmetic: MARGARET QUYNN, 1st premium, ELIZABETH OGLE, 2nd. 4th Class Reading and Spelling: MARTHA WALLING, 1st premium, MICHAEL McGINNIS, 2nd. CAROLINE FRAZIER, 3rd. REBECCA WITTER, 4th. 5th Class Reading and Spelling: MARGARET MORGAN, 1st premium, JANE WALLING, 2nd. MARGARET MOORE, 3rd. ELIZABETH WITTER, 4th. 6th Class Reading and Spelling: ANN E. ROBINSON, 1st premium, MATILDA CARLIN, 2nd. MINERVA KOONTZ, 3rd. ELIZABETH PORTER, 4th. 7th

Class Reading and Spelling: L. HALLER, 1st premium, ELLEN REARDON, 2nd. BRIDGET DOUGHERTY, 3rd. MARY MARTIN, 4th. 1st premium in Music awarded to MARY A. SALMON, 2nd premium to CAROLINE MURPHY. 1st premium in Drawing awarded to ELIZABETH DULANY, 2nd premium to ARABELLA SCHROEDER, 3rd premium to ELIZA O'NEILL. Bead-work: CHARLOTTE BAUGHMAN, 1st premium, ELIZABETH KLINE, 2nd premium. Ornamental neddle work: M. A. SALMON. The school will be opened on the first Monday in September, for the reception of boarders and day scholars.

716. By Divine permission the Rev. M. SMALTZ, will preach in the Baptist Church to-morrow morning. Divine service to commence at 10 o'clock. August 17th.

August 24, 1833 (CBAL)

717. (M) On Thursday last, by the Rev. Mr Wachter, Mr BALTZER FOX, to Miss LYDIA STITELY, all of this co.
718. (M) On Thursday last, by the Rev. D. F. Schaeffer, JOSIAH S. COVER, to Miss SUSANNA ENGLE, all of this co.
719. (D) JANE OLIVIA RIDGELY, consort of Nicholas H. Ridgely, Esq., and daughter of the late Samuel Vincent of Baltimore. She died on Tuesday evening the 6th inst., after a short illness of cholera. (St. Louis, (MO) Republican)
720. (D) Departed this life, in this place, on Thursday morning the 22nd inst., of cholera infantine, MARGARET WILSON, aged 15 months and 18 days. Only daughter of Mr Alexander B. Hanson, formerly of Kent Co., Eastern Shore of this state.
721. (D) At the residence of William Ross, Esq., in this city, on the 17th inst., WILLIAM ROSS, infant son of Wm. J. Ross, Esq., aged 12 months and 17 days.
722. National Republican voters of Creagerstown District convened at the house of GEORGE BECKENBAUGH, on Saturday the 17th of August. On motion ZEBULON KUHN, Esq., was called to the chair, and Dr. ROB'T. C. CUMMING, appointed secretary. The following gentlemen were selected to draft resolutions to be submitted to the consideration of the meeting. VALENTINE SHRYOCK, FREDERICK OTT, HENRY A. BRIEN, JOSEPH EICHELBERGER, and GEO. BECKENBAUGH. They nominated the following candidates to represent Frederick Co., in the next legislature of Maryland: JOHN W. DERR, VALENTINE SHRYOCK, Col. JACOB CRAMER, JACOB D. SHRYOCK, Dr. ROBERT C. CUM-

MING, LEWIS L. HOBBS, GEORGE BECKENBAUGH, ADAM SNOOK of A., WM. B. PITTINGER, JOSEPH EICHELBERGER, GEORGE KUHN, WM. BIGGS of J., FREDERICK OTT, WM. B. HEAD, SAMUEL GRIMES, HENRY A. BRIEN, JOHN BUCHANAN, LEONARD PICKING, HENRY FUNDENBURG, Dr. L. W. GOLDSBOROUGH, WM. COOKERLY, JOHN W. MILLER, J. P. ZIMMERMAN, CYRUS WALKER, and ZEBULON KUHN, be the committee to represent this district in said convention. And that Dr. ROB'T. C. CUMMING, LEONARD PICKING, Dr. L. W. GOLDSBOROUGH, WM. H. GRIMES, GEORGE BECKENBAUGH, MAHLON HARLEY, and MARTIN EICHELBERGER, be a committee of Correspondence for this election district. And that Dr. ROB'T. C. CUMMING and HENRY A. BRIEN, be delegates from this district to the Reform Convention to be held in Baltimore on the 27th of this month.

723. National Republican voters of Middletown District, met at Mr PERRY'S Tavern, on the 19th inst., Mr DANIEL ROUTZAHN, was called to the chair and JOHN KEAFAUVER, appointed secretary. The following gentlemen were appointed delegates to the convention: Dr. THOMAS SPRINGER, JOHN McNEILL. GEO. BLESSING, HENRY HERSHBERGER, JACOB THOMAS of Jno., THOMAS CASTLE, JOSEPH ROUTZAHN, JOHN J. SMITH, JOSEPH SMITH, HENRY SNELSER, Sr., GEORGE BEAR, JONATHAN HERRING, CHRISTIAN RAMSBURG, SAM'L. THOMAS, GEORGE DAUB, JACOB HOOK of Jno., and WM. PERRY. Committee of Correspondence: Dr. THOMAS SPRINGER, GEO. BEAR, BENJAMIN ROUTZAHN, WASHINGTON SMITH, ADAM KELLER, and JOSHUA WINKS.

724. The National Republicans of Emmitsburg of the 5th District convened at the Union Academy in Emmitsburg, on Tuesday the 20th inst. ROBERT FLEMING, Esq., was appointed chairman, ISAAC E. PEARSON, Secretary. A committee of 5 were appointed to draft resolutions: JEFFERSON SHIELDS, JOSEPH WELTY, ISAAC MOTTER, SAMUEL BAUMGARDNER, and ROBERT ANNAN. The committee to meet the convention: JNO. CRAPSTER, Dr. JEFFERSON SHIELDS, JACOB WINEBRENNER, ROBERT FLEMING, ISAAC MOTTER, ISAAC E. PEARSON, JNO. H. DAVIS, JNO. SLUSS, JOSHUA WELTY, and DAVID KEPHART. A committee of Correspondence: JOSHUA BAUGHER, JOSHUA MOTTER, ROBERT ANNAN, and SAMUEL BAUMGARDNER, were selected for this election district.

August 31, 1833 (CBAL)

725. Messrs, RAYMOND & OGDEN'S, menagerie has arrived and is now exhibiting on Dr. Wm. Tyler's lot, West end of 3rd Street. It is the best collection of animals in the United States, among them is the celebrated rhinoceros or unicorn.
726. M. BOUDET'S, picture of the "Raising of Lazarus" is now being exhibited at City Hall.
727. (D) On Sunday the 18th inst., at his residence in Shepherds Town, VA., of asiatic cholera, Mr JOHN MOTTER, in the 65th year of his age.
728. The Rev. Mr SMALTZ, will preach in the Baptist Meeting House to-morrow (Sunday) morning, divine service to convene at 10 o'clock. August 31.
729. JNO. M. PALMER, Esq., has written a letter to the editor of the "Citizen" in which he declines the nomination as a candidate for the Legislature.

September 7, 1833 (CBAL)

730. (M) At Point of Rocks, on Tuesday the 13th inst., by the Rev. D. J. Hauer, Mr JOHN BANTZ, to Miss SUSAN OWINGS.
731. (M) On Thursday the 22nd inst., by the same, Mr JOHN POTTS, to Miss RUTH TULLY.
732. (M) On Thursday last, by the Rev. David F. Schaeffer, Mr THOMAS JEFFERSON MYERS, to Miss CATHARINE SHOLL, all of this co.
733. (M) On the same day, by the same, ALEXANDER O'BEALL, to Miss CAROLINE WALL.
734. (M) On the same day, by the same, Mr WAYNE McKIMMEL, to Miss ELIZA ANN WRIGHT, of Loudoun Co., VA.
735. (M) On the same day, by the Rev. Joseph Smith, Mr SAMUEL BAKER, of Rodney Mississippi, to Miss MARTHA A McLANAHAN, of this city.
736. (M) On the 5th inst., by the Rev. John H. Smaltz, Mr DAVID MAHONEY, to Miss SARAH DRONESBURG.
737. (D) In Baltimore Co., on Thursday evening the 29th ult., in the 60th year of his age, Col. ADAM SHOWERS, served this county as a legislator and a soldier.
738. We are informed that a discourse will be delivered on to-morrow morning, in the German Reformed Church, by the Rev. CHARLES REIGHLY on the analogy between natural and revealed religion.

739. Elder ELI SCOTT, will preach in the Baptist Meeting House, on next Sabbath, at 3 o'clock in the afternoon.
740. Montgomery County Convention - At a meeting of the delegates, appointed by the several election Districts of Montgomery Co. Held its meeting at the Court House on Saturday the 31st of August. WILLIAM DARNE, Esq., was called to the chair and ZADOCK M. WATERS and JOHN H. BEALL, appointed secretaries. JOHN A. CARTER, Esq., made the following resolution; that the delegates from each election district retire, and return, and present to the consideration of the convention, a suitable person to represent their county in the General Assembly, and 5 persons to represent their respective districts in convention to be held on the 11th of September next, at New Market. Whereupon the several districts retired, and returned and made the following nominations; Medley's District: For the Assembly: Dr. STEPHEN N. C. WHITE. For delegates to the convention: BENJAMIN WHITE, of Nathan, Gen. THOMAS T. WHEELER, DAVID TRUNDELL, Sen., GEO. W. DAWSON, Dr. HENRY A. OFFUTT. Cracklin District, for the Assembly; HENRY C. GAITHER. For the convention: EPHRAIM GAITHER, NATHAN COOK, HENRY GRIFFITH, of Lyde, JOHN W. DARBY, and CASSAWAY WATKINS. Clarksburg District; for the Assembly: HENRY C. GAITHER. For the convention: Dr. HORACE WILLSON, ZADOCK M. WATERS, LYDE GRIFFITH, Jun., JOSHUA PURDOM, and LOTT LINTHICUM. Rockville District; for the Assembly: JOHN A. CARTER. For the convention: SAMUEL T. STONESTREET, WILLIAM DARNE, LEMUEL CLEMENTS, JOHN G. ENGLAND, and RICHARD I. BOWIE. Berry's District; for the Assembly: ROGER B. THOMAS. Delegates to the convention: AMOS FARQUHAR, THOMAS WORTHINGTON, of Wm., ROBERT G. BOWIE, HENRY HOWARD, and BERNARD GILPIN. Nomanation made by Dr. HENRY HOWARD, that a vote on the nominations be taken, any person opposed to a nominee that his name be left off the ticket. If a person does not receive a majority of the whole number of members attending, that the gentlemen retire and make a new nomination. The convention proceeded to ballots, upon counting the ballots, it appeared that STEPHEN N. C. WHITE, ROGER B. THOMAS, HENRY C. GAITHER, and J. A. CARTER, had received a majority of the whole number of votes. The above were confirmed by the convention.

741. ROBERT LYLES, Esq., was nominated as Sheriff.
742. MADISON NELSON, Esq., has declined the nomination as a candidate for Congress.
743. JOSEPH M. PALMER, Esq., has accepted the nomination as a candidate for the Assembly.
744. Trial of Miss CRUNDALL, is postponed or continued till the next County Court, in December next because the jury did not agree on a verdict.
745. National Republican Ticket - For the Assembly: DAVID DUVALL, L. P. W. BALCH, THOMAS HAMMOND, JOHN LEE. Candidates for Congress, for the District composed of Frederick, and Washington and Allegany Counties: JAMES DIXON, FRANCIS THOMAS. For the district composed of part of Frederick and Montgomery Counties: WILLIAM C. JOHNSON, GEORGE C. WASHINGTON, RODERICK DORSEY.

September 14, 1833 (CBAL)

746. (D) EDWIN RANDOLPH, son of the late P. Randolph of Richmond Va., blew his brains out in Charlestown, Jefferson Co., VA., a few days ago.
747. (D) On Sunday last, Miss NANCY WITTINGER, in the 65th year of her age, long a worthy and respected resident of this city.
748. The Rev. Mr SMALTZ, will preach in the Baptist Meeting House, to-morrow (Sunday) morning. Divine service to commence at 10 o'clock.

September 21, 1833 (CBAL)

749. Military visit - The "Jefferson Greys" beautiful and well-drilled rifle corp, arrived in this city on Thursday evening last, escorted by the Everhart Greys.
750. (D) On Tuesday morning last, at his residence in Hager-Town, Rev. MATTHEW L. FULLERTON, for several years pastor of the English Presbyterian Church of that town.
751. For Congress from Frederick and Montgomery Counties only WILLIAM C. JOHNSON name remaines. For the Jackson ticket for Congress: RODERICK DORSEY.

October 5, 1833 (CBAL)

752. (M) On Tuesday the 24th ult., by the Rev. D. F. Schaeffer, JOHN WAR, Esq., to SUSANNAH FOX.
753. (M) On Saturday last, by the same, Mr GEORGE KEEFER, to Miss ANN MARIA KREBY.

754. (M) On Monday evening last, by the same, Mr SAMUEL HOLTZMAN, of VA., to Miss MARGARET ADKINS, of this co.
755. (M) On Sunday last, by the Rev. Mr Wachter, Mr WILLIAM BOSTION, to Miss CATHARINE LOCK, all of this co.
756. (M) On the 25th ult., in Baltimore, by the Rev. Mr Duncan, Mr RICHARD T. DAVIS, to Miss ANNE R., eldest daughter of the late John Bear, all of Baltimore.
757. (D) On Thursday last, after a short illness, MARY, third daughter of Eli Baiderston, of this city, in the 20th year of her age, deceased who recently a resident of this city.
758. (D) Melancholy event - In Cumberland, on the morning of Tuesday last, Dr. CHARLES V. SWEARINGEN, resding near Cresaptown, in this co., shot a young man, Mr BAYARD THISTLE, son of Mr Geo. Thistle, of this co., in the back; and then in about 10 minutes afterward, he shot himself. The tragical circumstances, were as follows: Mr Thistle was on a visit to Dr. Swearingen's, where he was kindly received by the Dr., not the least animosity being shown by him towards Mr T., but the Dr., was evidently somewhat deranged in his mind, and had been so for several days- saying that some person was after him, and intended to kill him, or take him off to jail, &c.-and on the above morning, as Mr Thistle stepped to the door to look out, Dr. S., was in the room, and all of a sudden, looking very wild out of his eyes he said some man was then about in the house, who intended to kill him, and snatching down the gun, he fired at Mr T., whilst standing in the door, the contents of the gun entering his back, and he fell upon the porch. Dr. S., then went into the kitchen, and putting his head out of the window enquired what was the matter. Being told that he had shot or killed Thistle, he said he would kill himself; and he then came out, went around a corner of the house, and re-loaded the gun. His father went into the yard, and requested him to give him the gun, he refused, unless he would shoot him with it-his father refused. His father could not get the gun away from his son, walked into the house, to the aid of young Thistle. In a few minutes after, the report of a gun was heard, going off, outside, was found lying on the ground lifeless. The load of the gun having entered his left breast. The manner in which he effected his purpose related by his little daughter, who was the only person who witnessed deed, was by placing the butt end of the gun on the fence, and holding the muzzle against his

breast with one hand, with the other, with a long stick, he pushed back the trigger. Dr. Swearingen has left an amiable wife and 3 young children. Mr Thistle is now lying the house of his grandfather, Maj. J. H. Bayard, of this town; there are hopes of his recovery, but we learned that his physician still considers it doubtful whether he can survive the injury he has received. Mr Thistle is a younger brother of the lawyer of that name, and not the lawyer as stated in some of the papers. He had just returned from New York, where he had resided for the last 2 or 3 years.

759. The Fredericksburg area says: Col. JOHN THOMAS, once a distinguished leader of the Freeland Party, in Frederick Co., MD., has been appointed Navy Agent for the Baltimore Station, our friend Blackford is in error; Col. Thomas, of Baltimore, is a distinguished member of the Democratic Jackson Party, has been thus distinguished.

October 12, 1833 (CBAL)

760. Military visit - Yesterday the Hagers-Town Infantry, Capt. ARTS, and the Rifle Greens, under Capt. ROBINSON, were escorted by the Frederick Volunteers and Everhart Greys, arrived from Hagers-Town. On Thursday they were paraded through the streets.

761. (M) In Frederick Co., at the residence of Capt. Thomas Hammond, on Thursday morning 26th of September, by the Rev. Mr McGee, Mr ALPHEUS WATERS MARRIOTT, late of Anne Arundel Co., to Miss ADELIA HAMMOND, only daughter of the late Charles Hammond, Esq., of Frederick Co.

762. (M) On the 1st inst., by the Rev. D. F. Schaeffer, Mr JACOB RUCK, to Miss BARBARA LOTZ.

763. (M) On Thursday the 3rd inst., by the Rev. Jas. M. Brown, CHARLES JAMES FAULKNER, Esq., to Mrs MARY, daughter of Gen. Elisha Boyd, all of Berkeley Co., VA.

764. (D) At Harper's Ferry, VA., on Monday evening last, Mr WM. M. ROLLINGTON, formerly of this place, in the 27th year of his age.

765. Election returns for Frederick Co. Assembly: National Republican Candidates: DUVALL - 3014, LEE - 2771, BALCH - 2962, HAMMOND - 2877. Jackson Candidates: SCHLEY - 3470, UNKEFER - 3364, PALMER - 3359, SIFFORD - 3325. For Sheriff: TALBOTT - 3222, BARTGIS - 2838, CAMPBELL - 1322, LOWE - 816, GURLEY - 1548. For Congress 6th District: JOHNSON - 2300, DORSEY -

1784. Montgomery County: JOHNSON - 763, DORSEY - 658. 7th District: THOMAS - 1483, DIXON - 647. For Washington County: THOMAS - 1951, DIXON - 1961. For Allegany County: THOMAS - 651, DIXON - 854. Mr THOMAS won by a majority of 581.

October 19, 1833 (CBAL)

766. (M) On Tuesday last, by the Rev. D. F. Schaeffer, Mr CHARLES DUNCAN, to Miss HANNAH CANON.
767. (M) On Thursday last, by the same, Mr JACOB STULL, to Miss NANCY STONE.
768. (M) On Tuesday the 24th ult., by the Rev. Thomas McGee, Mr PERRY GAITHER, of Anne Arundel Co., to Miss HENRIETTA HANSON, youngest daughter of the late Dennis Poole, Esq., of Frederick Co., MD.
769. (M) On Sunday evening last, by the Rev. Chas. Reighly, Mr WILLIAM D. HEIM, to LOUISA BENTZ, all of Frederick.
770. (D) On the 7th inst., at his residence near this city, Mr JOHN WHITE, aged 69 years, a man of sterling worth. He commenced the career of life under circumstances of proverty and discouragement, few have surpassed him for a life of industy. Has long been a member of the Presbyterian Church, and a ruling Elder.
771. (D) Departed this life, in Cumberland, on the 3rd inst., at the residence of his grandfather (Maj. John H. Bayard,) Mr. BAYARD THISTLE, in the 24th year of his age, son of Mr George Thistle, of Allegany Co. The unfortunated youth was shot in the back by the late Dr. Charles V. Swearingen, on the 17th ult.
772. (D) On Sunday the 29th ult., in Hagers-Town, after a protracted illness, ARTHUR, second son of Arthur Johnson, Esq., of Hagers-Town, in the 26th year of his age.
773. The Rev. Dr. PURCELL, late President of Mount Saint Mary's Seminary at Emmitsburg, Md., was on Sunday last, consecrated Bishop of the Diocess of Cincinnati Ohio. The ceremonies took place at the Catheradral in this city, in the presence of 4000 persons, discourse was delivered by the Rev. Mr Eccleston, with performances by the choir, vocal and instrumental under the direction of Mr Gilles. (Baltimore Chronicle)

November 2, 1833 (CBAL)

774. The store of Mr GEORGE TRISLER, of this city, was forcibly entered on Monday night last, and robbed of a considerable

sum of money and a variety of valuable dry goods were taken. They forced the lock with an iron lever, which they took from the railing in the court house yard.

775. (M) On Thursday the 24th ult., by the Rev. P. Kinzer, Mr DAVID F. ANGELBERGER, to Miss CATHARINE RAMSBURG, both of this co.

776. (M) On the same day, by the Rev. Mr Wachter, Mr JACOB CASHOUR, to Miss CATHERINE KUNKLE, all of this co.

777. (D) On Monday last, Mr THOMAS GORDON, a resident of this city.

778. (D) At Henderson KY., RICHARD, son of Mr John Cromwell, formerly a resident of this city.

779. (D) Died in MIddletown Valley, on Tuesday morning the 29th October, MARY CATHERINE, daughter of John Cole, aged 3 years, 1 month and 20 days

780. Meeting of the African Colonization Society was held on Wednesday evening last, at the German Reformed Church, to afford Rev. Mr McKENNEY, agent of the Maryland State Society, to explain, and recommend the objective of a new settlement at Cape Palmas. Dr. WM. BRADLEY TYLER, President of the Frederick County Auxiliary Society was requested to act as chairman. After Rev. Mr M., speech, Mr RICHARD POTTS, Esq., made a resolution to appoint a committee from Frederick County Auxiliary Society to solicit donations from citizens. The following gentlemen were appointed: LEWIS MEDTART, ROBERT McCLEARY, GEORGE WEBSTER, JAMES M. SHELMAN, WM. OGDEN NILES, Dr. SAMUEL L. McKECHAN, NEILSON POE, CHESTER COLEMAN, Col. LEWIS KEMP, GRAFTON HAMMOND, Dr. JACOB BAER, and EZRA DOLL.

781. Rev. EDWARD CHOAT, will preach in the Baptist Meeting House, next Sabbath Morning, at 10 o'clock.

782. Rev. CHARLES REIGHLY, will deliver a sermon to the young men of Frederick, in the German Reformed Church, tomorrow evening.

November 9, 1833 (CBAL)

783. (M) On Thursday evening last, by the Rev. David F. Schaeffer, Mr GEORGE McGACHIN, to Miss MARIAN LAMBRECHT, all of this city.

784. (M) On Sunday last, by the Rev. M. Wachter, Mr WILLIAM BARNHART, to Miss ELIZABETH DUNDDAR, all of this co.

785. (D) On the 29th of October, at Mount PLeasant, the residence of Mr John P. Zimmerman, near Creagerstown, of the

scarlet fever, Miss ANN CATHARINE PATTERSON, daughter of John and Ruth Patterson, after a short and painful illness of 3 days.

786. (D) Departed this life at 12 o'clock on Monday the 14th inst., DANIEL OURAND, Esq., Postmaster at Walkers-ville, in the 41st year of his age. As a mechanic, Mr Ourand had not only attained the highest degree of eminence in the manual part of his business, from his extensive reading, he was enable to combine and render science tributary to his profession. He leaves a wife and infant son.

787. Cheaspeake and Ohio Canal has been filled with water for several days. On Wednesday last a canal-boat, with passengers, was drawn by a single horse from Harpers Ferry to Seneca, 40 miles, in 4 hours. The canal holds water well, and not a single break has occurred in it.

788. (D) At Somerset Ohio, on the 23rd ult., of a violent attack of apoplexy which terminated his existence in less then 30 minutes, Rev. JOHN F. MOELLER, of the Evangelical Lutheran Church. The decease was pastor of the Church in this place for several years.

789. Elder ELI SCOTT, will preach in the Baptist Meeting House, next Sabbath, at 10 o'clock.

November 23, 1833 (CBAL)

790. (M) At Jefferson, Frederick Co., MD., on the 20th of November 1833, by the Rev. J. C. Bucher, of Middletown, Mr GEORGE THOMAS, to Mrs MARY KRAMER, eldest daughter of Mrs Rachel Kessler, all of Jefferson, MD.

791. (M) On Saturday last, by the Rev. D. F. Schaeffer, Mr NICHOLAS KEEFER, to Miss SOPHIA FRESHOUR, all of this city.

792. (M) On the same day, by the same, Mr NICHOLAS ROTH, to Miss PHAEBE HESS, all of this co.

793. (M) On Thursday last, 14th inst., by the Rev. M. Wachter, Mr THOMAS CURLEY Jr., to Miss AMANDA STULL, both of this co.

794. (M) On Sunday evening last, by the Rev. Wm. McSherry of George-Town, D.C., Mr JAMES CARLIN, to Miss ELIZA A. HEMSWORTH, all of this co.

795. (M) On Thursday evening last, by the Rev. Charles Reighly, Mr DANIEL BENTZ to Miss ELIZABETH SCHOLL, all of this city.

796. (M) On Wednesday the 13th ult., at Montivieu, Frederick Co., MD., by the Rev. Mr Allen, Dr. RICHARD S. BLACK-

BURN, of Berryville, Frederick Co., VA., to Miss SARAH A. E. THOMAS, daughter of Col. John Thomas, of the former place.

797. (M) On Thursday last, in the Glade near Frederick City, by the Rev. J. W. Hoffmeier, Mr JOHN F. BEST, to Miss CATHARINE, daughter of Mr Henry Cramer, of the Glades.

798. (D) On Monday the 11th inst., in Creagerstown, after a short illness, JANE ELIZABETH, second daughter of George Beckenbaugh, Esq., in the 4th year of her age.

799. (D) On the 7th inst., at Mt. Pleasant, Mr JACOB ALEXANDER ZIMMERMAN, in the 22nd year of his age. Son of George Zimmerman, deceased.

800. (D) On Sunday last, after a lingering illness, ADRIANN ELIZABETH, daughter of Ethelbert Taney, of this co., aged 8 months and 10 days.

November 30, 1833 (CBAL)

801. (M) On Thursday the 21st inst., by the Rev. D. F. Schaeffer, Mr HENRY EATON, to Miss MARY HIMBURY, all of this city.

802. (M) On Thursday the 21st inst., by the Rev. M. Wachter, Mr ISAAC DERN, to Miss SARAH ANN ANDERS, all of this co.

803. (D) On Saturday last, after a severe illness, Mrs ELIZABETH NICKEL, wife of Adam Nickel, in the 40th year of her age, she leaves a husband and 8 children.

December 7, 1833 (CBAL)

804. Rev. E. H. SCOTT, will preach in the Baptist Meeting House, to-morrow morning, at 10 o'clock.

December 14, 1833 (CBAL)

805. (M) On Thursday the 5th inst., in George-Town D.C., Mr FREDERICK W. DeKRAFT, of Washington City, to Mrs ROSANNA RITCHIE, of the former place.

806. (M) On Wednesday the 11th ult., by the Rev. John McElroy, JOHN SHAFFNER, Sergent of the U. S. Army, to Miss JULIANN HOOVER, both of Boonesborough.

807. (M) On Tuesday morning last, by the Rev. Joseph Smith, Mr GEORGE W. SHARP, formerly the editor of "The Citizen," to Miss CAROLINE R. SNYDER, daughter of Capt. Nicholas Snyder, both of this city.

808. The following gentlemen composed the Petite Frederick Co. Petite: BROOKE BAKER, S. BAUMGARDNER, JOHN

COLEGATE, JACOB CARMACK, TOBIAS COVER, GEO. DERTZBAUGH, STERLING GALT, S. GRIMES, Sen., ELIAS A. GROSHON, JACOB GROVE, JACOB HARBAUGH, WILSON HAYS, DAVID HULL, ABRAHAM JONES, JOHN KEAFAUVER, CHRISTIAN KEEFER, A. LIGHTENWALTER, LLOYD LUCKET, WILLIAM MUROCK, JOHN W. PRATT, JOHN RIGNEY, JOHN SIMMONS, JONAS. SMITH, JOHN THSEN, JACOB TROXELL.

December 21, 1833 (CBAL)

809. Mr STEPHEN STEHLEY, Pastor of the German Reformed Church, in Shepherdstown, VA., will preach by Divine permission on the morning of the 29th of December inst., at 10 o'clock, in the Manor Church, near Buckeys-Town.

December 28, 1833 (CBAL)

810. (D) A negro child aged about 2 years was burnt to death in this city, during the last week. Its mother, left her in charge of her daughter, who having placed it in a chair, left the house-from the chair the child rolled into the fire, and, in the language of our informant was "burnt to a crisp!"

811. (M) On Wednesday last, by the Rev. D. F. Schaeffer, Mr JEREMIAH BUTLER, to Miss CHARLOTTEE JACKSON, daughter of Mr Charles Jackson, all of this co.

812. (M) On Thursday last, by the Rev. David F. Schaeffer, Mr ISAAC HEDGES, Jr., to Miss REBECCA KLEISZ, all of this co.

813. (M) Near Middletown, MD., on the 19th inst., by the Rev. J. C. Bucher, Mr DANIEL DERR, eldest son of Mr Jacob Derr, to Miss ELIZABETH, daughter of Mr John P. Coblentz, all of Middletown Valley.

814. (M) On the 14th inst., by the Rev. Robert Cadden, Mr JACOB HOFFMAN, to Miss SARAH ANN LIFE, all of this city.

815. (M) On Sunday last, by the Rev. Charles Reighley, Mr JOSEPH C. PERKINS, to Miss ELIZA ANN COOK, all of this co.

816. (M) At New Market on Thursday the 19th Dec., by the Rev. R. Cadden, of Frederick City, Mr HENRY M. SNYDER, merchant of that place, to Miss ALMEDA PHILIPS, of the same place.

817. (M) On Thursday evening the 24th inst., by the Rev. D. F. Schaeffer, Mr EZRA STALEY, to Miss SOPHIA BRUNNER, all of this vicinity.

818. (D) On Tuesday morning, the 24th inst., Mrs RACHAEL CRONISE, wife of John Cronise, Esq., aged about 45.
819. A wagon and 3 valuable horses, the property of Mr PHILEMON CROMWELL, Jr., were lost on Tuesday last, in an attempt to cross the Monocacy at Biggs Ford, the 4th horse was saved only thro the intrepidity of Mr C., who cut him lose from the harness at great personal risk.
820. A new Post Office has been established in Foxville, Frederick Co., MD., on the road from Hagers Town to Mechanicstown, GEORGE KING, Post Master.

1834

January 4, 1834 (CBAL)

821. Mr NICHOLAS TURBUTT, Esq., was appointed to fill the vacancy in the Orphans Court, with the death of Col. H. Kemp.
822. (M) On Thursday evening, the 26th ult., by the Rev. D. F. Schaeffer, Mr WILLIAM GLESSNER, to Mrs REBECCA INGLES, all of this city.
823. (D) Departed this life, on Thursday the 23rd ult., at the residence of Mrs Herbert, of Baltimore Co., Mrs HELENA JENKINS, of this town, in the 37th year of her age, after a long and protracted illness, her remains arrived here on the evening of the 15th, and were interred in the Catholic Cemetery.
824. (D) On the 13th ult., near Middleburg, Frederick Co., Mrs MARGARET DELPHY, wife of Philander Delphy, aged 36 years, leaves a husband and 8 children.
825. (D) On Saturday morning last, in the 71st year of his age, Col. HENRY KEMP President of the Orphan's Court of this co.
826. We may confer a favor upon numerous persons in the County who have required the services of Mr W. D. JENKS, by stating that he has returned from his professional tour thro VA., and may be found at his room in Capt. Turbutt's, Hotel.
827. The Grand Jury for Frederick County visited the jail on Friday Dec. the 20th., and reported the jail in very healthy and comfortable conditions: THOS. CARLTON, JOHN HEAD, NICHOLAS NORRIS, MICHAEL SULLIVAN, THOMAS C. BRASHEAR, JOSHUA SMITH, Jr., JOHN YOUNG, JOHN

JONES, JOHN SMITH, of Geo., DANIEL YEISER, JACOB POWDER, JOSEPH TALBOTT, JOSEPH WELTY, EDWARD McBRIDE, WM. DURBIN, JAMES CASTLE, GEO. H. WAESCHE, JOHN LEASE, PETER NICHOLS, GEORGE POTTS, GEORGE HARMAN, JOHN SMITH, of Jn., WM. GAITHER.

January 11, 1834 (CBAL)

828. (D) A man named LINGENFELTER, who resided in Middletown Valley, whilst engaged the other day, in killing hogs, was slightly bitten by one of the animals. The puncture was very small, but causing considerable pain, he applied to a physician in the vicinity, from whom he received some medicine, but had swallowed it only a short time when he swooned and died. The presumption is that a subtle poison was communicated to his system from the hog's tooth.

829. (M) At Columbia, (Tenn.) on Thursday the 12th ult., by the Rev. Labaree, Dr. WILLIAM McNEILL, to Miss MARY CROCKETT, daughter of the Hon. David Crockett, a member of Congress from Tenn.

830. (M) On Thurday the 2nd inst., by the Rev. D. F. Schaeffer, Mr HENRY STEWART, to Miss SARAH MATTERN, all of this co.

831. (M) Near Middletown, MD., on the 2nd of January 1834, by the Rev. J. C. Bucher, Mr ELIAS DUTROW, to Miss SALLY, eldest daughter of Mr Daniel Shuemaker, all of this valley, Fred'k. Co., Md.

832. (M) On Thursday evening last, by the Rev. Mr Johns, Capt. JOHN SAUNDERS, of this city, to Mrs MARY SCHLEIGH, of Hagerstown.

January 18, 1834 (CBAL)

833. (D) At Cincinnati, Ohio, on Sunday night the 29th of December last, Rev'd. Dr. THOMAS SARGENT, formerly of Philadelphia, aged 58 years. He had commenced preaching, when he was seized while speaking with an apoplexey and survived about an hour. For about 40 years a minister of the Methodist Episcopal Church.

834. (D) On Wednesday last, in Hagers-Town, DANIEL MALOTT, Esq., Sheriff of Washington Co., Mr Fitzhugh, who is upon the return will again succeed to this vacated office.

835. (D) At Sam's Creek, on Friday morning the 10th inst., JOSIAS V. MANTZ, youngest son of Daniel Mantz, Esq., aged 13 months and 15 days.
836. (D) Near Middletown, Md., on the 11th inst., after a protracted an distresssing illness, Miss SUSANNA BECKENBAUGH, aged 72 years.
837. (D) At his residence, near Creagers-Town, on the 28th ult., after a brief illness, in the 86th year of his age, Maj. W. B. HEAD.
838. (M) On Wednesday last, by the Rev. D. F. Schaeffer, Mr ELIAS WHEELER, of Baltimore Co., to Miss ELIZABETH ROWE, of Emmittsburgh, Frederick Co., MD.
839. (M) On the 9th inst., by the Rev. Thomas McGee, Mr MAURICE T. STARR, to Miss AUGUSTA ANN, youngest daughter of Noah Phillips, Esq., all of this co.
840. Corporate election - Candidates for the Common Council to represent their distinguish Wards. NOAH A. SHAFFER, EZRA DOLL, and JOHN W. MILLER, for Ward #7. JOSHUA DILL, JOHN FAUBLE, for Ward #6. PETER MANTZ, JACOB ENGLEBRECHT, for Ward #4.

January 25, 1834 (CBAL)

841. (D) Departed this life, on Monday the 13th inst., in the 31st year of her age, Mrs SARAH JONES, wife of Mr John Jones, near this place. The disease which terminated her earthly career, was a lingering consumption.
842. Flour inspection laws - The Millers, Farmers and others, on the East side of Monocacy, who feel themselves aggrieved by the existing "Flour Inspection Laws," are requested to meet at James Wood's Tavern, Unionville, on Monday the 27th inst., at 1 o'clock, for the purpose of co-operating with the meeting of Farmers and Millers held in Frederick on the 11th inst. In memorializing the legislature of Maryland for a revision of the laws respecting the inspection of flour: ANTHONY KIMMEL, WM. A. ALBAUGH, THORNTON POOLE, PRADBY JAMES, JOSEPH JAMES, WILLIAM LOWE, ALEXANDER LOWE, JOHN S. LAWRENCE, GEORGE DEVILBISS.
843. The Hon. DAVID CROCKETT, has recently stated in a letter to this paper, that a daughter of his was not married at Columbia (Tenn,) is a mistake, he says there is a heap of Crocketts in that part of Tenn., and from that no doubt the mistake arose, but none of my family lives there.

844. Corporate elections - Candidates for the Common Council to represent their distinguish Wards. JACOB KELLER, for Ward #7. SAMUEL B. LEWIS, for Ward #5. GEORGE LOWE, representative of Ward #7. GEORGE M. CONRADT, for Ward #2.

February 1, 1834 (CBAL)

845. (M) On Thursday last, by the Rev. Mr Wachter, Mr HEZEKIAH DUDDERER, to Miss MARY ANN, youngest daughter of Wm. Miller, Esq., all of this co.
846. (M) On the same evening, by the same, Mr NIMROD BECK, to Miss MARY ANN ELIZABETH, eldest daughter of Wm. Grimes, Esq., all of this co.
847. (M) On the 21st inst., by the Rev. D. F. Schaeffer, Mr CHRISTIAN BICKLE, to Miss BARBARA FICHTER, all of Frederick Co.
848. (D) At his residence, on Maryland Tract, Doct. WILLIAM HILLEARY, in the 59th year of his age, he labored under a painful disease for upwards of 15 years, which baffled the skills of the medical profession. His symptom, though maturally vigorous, gradually gave way to the ravages of his disease. Doct. Hilleary was a very skillful physician.
849. (D) In this city, on Thursday the 29th inst., in the 27th year of her age, Mrs SUSAN POOLE, wife of Mr Eli Poole, of this place.
850. Candidate for the Common Council, for Ward #5: JOHNATHAN EADER.

February 8, 1834 (CBAL)

851. (D) Suddenly at Monocacy, January the 28th, after a 11-hour illness, Mr WILLIAM BIGGS, Sr., in his 80th year.
852. (D) Death of LORENZO DOW, died in George-Town, D.C., on the 2nd inst., a well known Itinerant preacher. A native of Coventry, Conn., travelled extensively in England and Ireland, and respectedly visited almost every portion of the United States. A public preacher for more then 30 years, wrote several books particularly a history of his own life. He was a Methodist in principal, a wander through life. It is believe he was a sincere Christian Pilgrim in search of a havenly country.
853. (M) On Tuesday the 28th ult., by the Rev. D. F. Schaeffer, Mr FRANCIS SHOEMAKER, to Miss CATHARINE SHARER, all of this co.

854. (M) In Baltimore, on Tuesday evening the 28th ult., by the Rev. Dr. Henshaw, Dr. J. H. McCULLOH, to Miss DOROTHEA JOHNSON, both of Baltimore.
855. (M) On the 16th ult., by the Rev. J. C. Bucher, Mr WM. TOFF, to Miss THERESA WALDECK, daughter of Mr John Waldeck, of Frederick Co., MD.
856. (M) On Tuesday evening last, by the Rev. D. F. Schaeffer, Mr WILLIAM ROBERTS, of Baltimore, to Miss SOPHIA ELIZABETH, daughter of Mr John Rigney, of this town.
857. The Rev. JOSEPH H. JONES, will preach in the Presbyterian Meeting House, this evening at early candle light.
858. Candidate for the Common Council to represent Ward #4. URIAH BANTZ.

February 15, 1834 (CBAL)

859. (M) In Baltimore on Tuesday morning the 14th inst., by the Rev. Dr. Damphoux, Mr JOHN BEAHEY, of Fred. City, to Miss MARGARET A., youngest daughter of Thomas Kelly, Esq., of Baltimore.
860. (D) On the 6th inst., Mrs ELIZABETH SIEVER, in the 65th year of her age.
861. Suicide - A man named DAY, a stone mason, put a period to his existence on Monday last by hanging himself, at a public house in this city. We have heard no cause assigned for the commission of the rash act, except that the deceased was in extremely indigent circumstances, and dreaded the prospect of still more abject want. He is said to have been of intemperate habits.
862. The Rev. Mr CHOAT will preach in the Baptist Meeting House, on next Sabbath at 10 o'clock.

February 22, 1834 (CBAL)

863. (M) On the 11th inst., by the Rev. D. F. Schaeffer, Mr FREDERICK BRENEMAN, of Baltimore, to Miss MATILDA TROUT, of this co.
864. (M) On Thursday last, by the Rev. M. Wachter Mr BURGESS N. CLARY, to Miss SARAH ZIMMERMAN, all of this co.
865. (D) In this city on Monday last, Mrs ROHR, wife of Jacob Rohr, Postmaster.
866. (D) On the same day, Mr GEORGE BUCKEY, an old and respectable inhabitant of this city.
867. (D) Departed this transitory life, on Tuesday morning last, Mr JOSEPH HARTZ, a resident of this city.

868. (D) Near Middletown, MD., on the 10th of Feb., after a very short illness, Mr JACOB TIPPIS, an aged and respectable citizen in his 80th year.
869. (D) On the 11th inst., after an illness of about 8 hours, Mrs MARY ALEXANDER, consort of Mr Henry Alexander, in her 66th year. She leaves a husband and 9 children to deplore her loss.
870. (D) On Wednesday the 12th inst., Mr THOMAS MAYBERRY, a respectable inhabitant of this co.
871. The Rev. Mr EVERT will preach in the Baptist Meeting House, on next Sabbath morning at 10 o'clock.
872. DAVID HANE, is a candidate for the Common Council to represent Ward #2.

March 1, 1834 (CBAL)

873. (D) On Monday last after a short illness of 9 days, Miss ELIZABETH LOVEDER, in the 14th year of her age.
874. (D) Near Taney-Town, MD., Mrs ANN HERBERT, wife of Dr. Herbert.
875. (D) At his farm near Graceham, on the 21st inst., HENRY KUHN, Esq., in the 73rd year of his age. He was a native of this co., until a few years past, a resident of this city. He has held several public offices, for the past 20 years, served as one of the Judges of the Orphans' Court, he was a good husband and father.
876. (D) Near Union Bridge, on the 20th of February, Mr JOHN STITELY, in the 79th year of his age.
877. (D) At his residence, near Johnsville on the 21st of February, Mr DAVID FUNDENBURG, in the 73rd year of his age.
878. The following gentlemen were on Monday last, elected members of the Common Council for the ensuing year: Ward #1: JACOB FAUBLE, Ward #2: GEORGE M. CONRADT, Ward #3. EZRA BENTZ, Ward #4. URIAH BANTZ, Ward #5. SAMUEL B. LEWIS, Ward #6. JOSHUA DILL, Ward #7. JOHN W, MILLER.
879. The Frederick County Court commenced it February session on Monday last. The following gentlemen composed the jury: HENRY BAER, MICHAEL BALTZELL, ROBERT BOONE, GEORGE BOWLUS, WILLIAM COALE, ROBERT FLEMING, SOLOMON FOREST, DAVID FOUTZ, JACOB HOLTZ, THOS. JOHNSON, of Wm., GEORGE KEPHART, JOHN KINZER, Jr., JACOB MATHIAS, JOHN McNEALE, AMOS NORRIS, LEONARD PICKING, JACOB ROOT, JACOB SHAFER, BENJAMIN SHANK, SOLOMON STICKLE,

GEORGE THOMAS, FREDERICK TROXELL, JOSEPH WIL HIDE, SAMUEL WRIGHT.

March 8, 1834 (CBAL)

880. (M) On Sunday last, by the Rev. D. F. Schaeffer, Mr DAVID SWIGERT, to Miss MARY ANN LEAMAN, all of this city.
881. (M) On the same day, by the Rev. M. Wachter, Mr JOSEPH STULL, to Miss MARGARET HUFFNER, all of this co.
882. (M) On the same day, by the same, Mr PETER EYLER, to Miss MARY ANN ENGLE, both of this co.
883. (M) On the same day, by the same, Mr JOHN McCROSKY, to Miss ANNA MARY C. WOLF, both of this co.
884. (M) On Tuesday the 4th of March inst., by the Rev. Daniel Zollickoffer, Mr STEPHEN HAINES, of Frederick Co., to Miss ESTHER COOKSON, of Adams Co., PA.
885. (D) Near this city, on Sunday the 23rd ult., Mrs ELIZABETH STALEY, consort of Mr J. Staley, deceased, in the 55th year of her age. The decease leaves 5 children to deplore her loss.

March 15, 1834 (CBAL)

886. (M) On Thursday last, by the Rev. David F. Schaeffer, Mr FREDERICK D. MILLER, to Miss CHARLOTTE BURKHARD, of this co.
887. (M) On Sunday evening last, by the same, Mr CHARLES GETZENDANNER, to Miss ANN MARIA JONES, all of this city.
888. (M) Near Middletown, Frederick Co., MD., on Thursday last, by the Rev. J. C. Bucher, Mr DANIEL GROVE, to Miss JULIANN, youngest daughter of Mr John Williard, Sr., all of Middletown Valley.
889. (M) Near the Glade, by the Rev. Mr Hoffmier, Mr JACOB BOWERSOX, of Utica, to Miss SUSAN, daughter of Mr John Gittinger, deceased.
890. (D) On the 23rd ult., Mr HENRY THOMAS, in the 51st year of his age, a highly and valuable citizen of this co.

March 22, 1834 (CBAL)

891. (F) On yesterday morning about 7 o'clock, the Hotel of M. E. BARTGIS, Esq. was discovered to be on fire. The wind blew a gale, at the time and the most serious apprehensions were entertained for the safety of the building, buth through the activity and zeal of our fire company the fire was got under control before it had done to much injury.

892. At a meeting of the Alderman and Common Council of Frederick, held in the City Hall on Monday the 17th inst., the following persons were elected officers of the corporation: JAMES M. SHELMAN - Printer, DAVID STEINER - Register, HENRY BAER - Collector of the tax, FREDERICK NUSZ, ROBERT M'CLEERY, ANDREW HEIM - Commissioners of the Tax, JOHN FESSLER - City Commissioner, FREDERICK STONER - Suprt. Str. Wells & Pumps, C. HILTON - Market Master, JACOB STOUFFER, C. HILTON - Lamp Lighters, JOHN FESSLER - Clock-winder, CHRISTOPHER MYERS - Messenger, C. HILTON, JOHN MARTIN, JAMES CARLIN, JOHN BENDER - City Constables.
893. (M) Near Middletown, MD., on the 16th inst., by the Rev. J. C. Bucher, Mr PETER BISER, to Miss MAHALA, youngest daughter of Mr Henry Brown, all of the valley.
894. (M) On the 5th inst., by the Rev. J. Caren, Mr LEVI NOLL, of Frederick Co., MD., to Miss JANE CLEVELAND, of Petersburg. (York Springs)
895. (D) Near Burkittsville, Frederick Co., on the 9th inst., after a protracted illness, in the 84th year of her age, Mrs ELIZABETH BISER, widow of Daniel Biser, deceased nearly 17 years since. She lived to enjoy a posterity of 99 souls.
896. (D) In Middletown, on the 13th inst., after a very painful illness, JOHN WILLIAM, son of Mr Henry Cochran, in the 10th year of his age.
897. (D) On Friday evening the 14th inst., at Gettysburg PA., Mrs SARAH McPHERSON, relict of the late Wm. McPherson, Esq., deceased of that borough, in the 58th year of her age.

March 29, 1834 (CBAL)

898. (M) On the 20th inst., in Pleasant Valley, Washington Co., MD., by the Rev. J. C. Bucher, Mr SAMUEL NORRED, of Jefferson, MD., to Miss ISAVENA N. SHOUMAN, of Pleasant Valley.
899. (M) On the same day, by the same, near Burkittsville, MD., Mr HARRY KEAFAUVER, to Miss MARIAH, daughter of Mr Daniel Biser, Sr., of Daniel, all of Middletown, MD.
900. (M) On Thursday the 20th inst., by the Rev. Daniel Zollickoffer, Mr HENRY SHEETS, to Miss HANNAH COPPERSMITH, both of this co.
901. (M) Near Liberty-Town, on Thursday the 13th inst., by the Rev. Webster, Mr SOLOMON CANE, to Mrs ELIZABETH BARKER, both of Fred., Co.

902. (M) On the same day, at New London, by the same, Mr CHARLES ARTHUR, to Miss HARRIET MEALY, both of Fred., Co.
903. (M) On Tuesday last, by the Rev. David F. Schaeffer, Mr WILLIAM DIXON, to Miss REBECCA STALLINGS, both of this co.
904. (M) At Leesburg, VA., on the 25th inst., by the Rev. Mr Dorsey, Mr AUGUSTUS G. SMITH, to Miss ANN M. JOHNSTON, of the former place.
905. (M) On Thursday evening last, in New Market, by the Rev. J. L. Pitts, Mr DAVID REINHART, to Miss JANE REBECCA, second daughter of Jacob Cronise, Esq., all of this co.
906. At the annual meeting of the Washington Hose Company, held at the house of Capt. NICHOLAS TURBUTT, on the 4th of January. The following persons were elected officers for the ensuing year: JOHN ENGELBRECHT - President, MICHAEL BUCKEY - Vice President, GEORGE W. ENT - Treasurer, GODFREY KOONTZ - Secretary, LEWIS MEDTARDT, JAMES CARLIN - Directors, JACOB HART - Principal Engineer, THOS. C. PRINCE, JAMES CARLIN - Assistant Engineers, SAMUEL B. LEWIS, JACOB LITTLE - Axe-men, FRANCIS LUEBER, HIRAM KEIFER - Supts. of Water Plugs, JOHN ENGLEBRECHT, EZRA SCHELL, HORATIO WATERS, GODFREY KOONTZ, WM. OGDEN NILES, WM. BRENNER - Hose-men, W. R. SANDERSON, JOHN KUNKLE - Property Guards. The balance of the company are Engine men. By order of the company. GODFREY KOONTZ, Sec'y. March 29.

April 5, 1834 (CBAL)

907. (M) On Thursday the 20th ult., by the Rev. James L. Higgins, Mr JOHN., eldest son of Noah Philips, Esq., to Miss RUTH., daughter of Mr Nicholas Hoy, near Liberty, MD.
908. (M) On the same day, by the Rev. M. Wachter, Mr FREDERICK E. KLISE, to Miss CATHERINE ALBAUGH, both of this co.
909. (M) On the same day, by the same, Mr WASHINGTON A. BENET, to Miss ELIZABETH GEESEY, both of this co.
910. (M) On the same day, by the same, Mr JOHN SMITH, to Miss ELEANOR WICKUM, both of this co.
911. (M) In the evening, by the same, Mr ARTHUR ETZLER, to Miss MIRANDA STEELE, both of this city.

912. (M) On Sunday evening last, by the Rev. D. F. Schaeffer, Mr JOHN HAGAN, to Miss MARIA SIFFORD, both of this city.
913. (M) On Monday evening last, by the Rev. C. Reighley, Mr SAMUEL D. WAYS, to Miss SUSAN WALLING, both of this co.
914. (M) In New Market, by the Rev. J. T. Reese, Mr HAMILTON STIER, of Baltimore, to Miss HARRIET D., youngest daughter of the late Nathan Hammond, of Frederick Co.
915. (D) On the 3rd inst., near Hyatts-Town, Montgomery Co., MD., after a very protracted illness, GEORGE BAER, Esq., recently President of the Frederick County Bank, and formerly a member of Congress of the United States.
916. (D) Departed this life, at Mount Saint Mary's College, on March 24th, after and illness of 3 weeks, in the 18th year of his age, THOMAS SIM LEE HORSEY, eldest son of the Hon. Outerbridge Horsey, for many years a Senator of the State of Delaware, and grandson of the Hon. Thomas Sim Lee, late Governor of Maryland. He was a member of the senior class at Mount Saint Mary's College, and would have graduated at the ensuing commencement, had his life and health been spared.

April 12, 1834 (CBAL)

917. (D) Death of WILLIAM GAITHER, Esq., at his residence near Liberty, in this co. He died after a few hours of illness in the vigor of manhood, in the midst of a career illustrated by every virtue which could adorn the higher relations of life and the character of a patriotic citizen.
918. (D) In Baltimore on Monday last, Mr EBENEZER PERKINS, recently of this city, in the 93rd year of his age.
919. (M) On Tuesday 1st inst., by the Rev. Mr Higgins, Capt. WILLIAM LEEKINGS, to Mrs SARAH ANN GALLION, both of this co.
920. (M) On the 8th inst., by the Rev. Henry Brown, of Baltimore City, Mr WILLIAM TAYLOR, of Hampshire Co., VA., to Miss SARAH ANN BENNETT, of Baltimore Co., MD.
921. (M) On Sunday evening last, by the Rev. M. Wachter, Mr JACOB WOLFE, to Miss MARY SHORB, all of this co.
922. (M) On Wednesday last, by the same, Mr DANIEL FERREE, of Adams Co., PA., to Miss ELIZA DIXON, of this co.
923. (M) In Fort Ball, Seneca Co., Ohio, on Sunday the 30th of March, by Levi Davis, Esq., Mr JOHN FLEMING, to Miss CATHARINE KESSLER, both formerly of this co.

924. (M) On Thursday the 20th ult., by the Rev. Mr Reck, EMANUEL SLIFER, Esq., to Miss SARAH, daughter of John Biser, Esq., all of this co.
925. (M) On Monday the 31st ult., by the Rev. Mr Tabler, Mr WM. B. TABLER, to Miss LOUISA, daughter of Henry Crum, Esq., all of this co.
926. (M) On the same day, by the Rev. Mr Reck, Mr LLOYD GITTINGS, to Miss CATHARINE, daughter of Henry Crum, Esq., all of this co.
927. (M) On Thursday the 10th inst., by the Rev. Mr Finkle, Mr ELIJAH CURRAN, to Mrs AMELIA J. RINEDOLLAR, all of Taney-Town.
928. (M) On Thursday the 27th ult., near Ellicotts Mills, Mr JOHN HALLER, of Boonesboro Washington Co., MD., to Miss JANE MARTIN, of Baltimore Co.
929. (M) On Thursday the 31st inst., by the Rev. D. F. Schaeffer, Mr SAMUEL YOUNG, to Miss MARIAN MATHIAS, both of this co.

April 19, 1834 (CBAL)

930. (M) On Wednesday evening the 9th inst., by the Rev. Mr Cadden, Mr ABRAHAM FURRAY, to Miss ELIZA RINGLAND, both of Liberty-Town.
931. Concert - Mr ARTHUR KEENE' a distinguished vocalist has been induced to visit this city, and to give a concert here at City Hall on Monday evening next, he ranks among the top vocalist in the Country and plays the piano. Tickets were on sale for 50 cents for adults, children were 1/2 price. A list of selections to be sung is published as well.
932. The Rev. WM. A. GOOD, of Hagers-Town will preach, with Divine permission, on next Lord's Day, (to-morrow) in the German Reformed Church in this city-in the morning in the German Language-in the evening in the English language. The exercise will commence at the usual time
933. JAMES HENSHALL, of Baltimore, a reforming Baptist, will deliver a discourse on the Christian Religion, on Sunday (to-morrow) at 3 o'clock P.M., and at candle light of the same day, in the Baptist Church.

April 26, 1834 (CBAL)

934. (M) On Thursday last, by the Rev. Charles Reighley, Mr CHARLES WILSON, to Miss MARY, daughter of the Hon. Judge Schriver, all of this city.

935. (M) On Sunday evening last, by the Rev. Mr Finkle, Mr JACOB LEILICH, to Miss CATHARINE BLUMINOUR.
936. (M) On Thursday evening last, by the same, Mr JAMES B. BEALL, Esq., of Montgomery Co., to Miss LOUISA WILCOXON, of this co.
937. (M) Near Jefferson, on the 10th inst., by the Rev. J. C. Bucher, Mr FRANCIS A. KNOTT, to Miss RUTH SLAGLE, both of Middletown Valley.
938. (D) On Thursday last, Mrs ELIZABETH HOWARD, in the 58th year of her age.

May 3, 1834 (CBAL)

939. C. J. HADERMAN, formerly of this city, has been appointed professor of Modern Languages, and Adjunct professor of Mathematics, in Jefferson College, Cannonsburg, PA.
940. (D) Mr V. FERRON, who taught fencing and dancing in this city during last Summer, has committed suicide a few days since, whilst confinded in Lexington, KY., hospital. He effected his death by strangling himself with a silk handkerchief.
941. (D) On Tuesday the 15th inst., after a lingering illness, CHRISTIAN YONITZ aged 22 years.
942. (D) On Monday the 16th., at his residence near Utica Mills, Mr HENRY KEMP, in the 73rd year of his age, one of the old an esteemed citizens of this co.
943. (D) At Rockville, Montgomery Co., MD., on Sunday morning last, Mr CALVIN ZIMMERMAN, age about 18 years, son of the late George Zimmerman, of this co. Its but a few months since the widowed mother of this young man was called to mourn the loss of a promising son.
944. (D) On the 22nd April, at the residence of her father, Luke Teirnan, Mrs ANNA E. BRIEN, wife of the late Coleman Brien, Esq., of Catoctin MD.
945. (D) In Baltimore on Monday last, in the 64th year of his age, PHILIP MOORE Esq., President of the Franklin Bank of that city, and of the Second Branch of City Council.
946. (M) On Tuesday morning last, by the Rev. Mr Heiner, Mr JACOB SNYDER, to Miss SABILLA TROXELL, all of Emmittsburg.
947. (M) On Thurday the 10th inst., by the Rev. J. Rebaugh, Mr CHARLES MANTZ, of Frederick City, to Miss MARY, youngest daughter of John D. Grove Esq., of Sharpsburg.
948. (M) On Sunday evening last, by the Rev. David F. Schaeffer, Mr CHARLES W. McKINSTRY, to Miss ANN LOVEDER.

949. (M) On the same evning, by the same, Mr JOHN P. GARDNER, to Miss ELIZABETH BERGER, all of this city.
950. (M) On Tuesday morning, by the same, Mr RICHARD HARPER, to Miss SOPHIA KELLER, all of this city.
951. (M) On Thursday the 24th of April, at York, PA., by the Rev. Mr Cares, Mr GIDEON BANTZ, Jr., of this city, to Miss JULIA, daughter of Mr John Hartman, of the former place.
952. (M) On Thursday last, by the Rev. M. Wachter, Mr CASPER HOLBRUNNER, to Miss LOUISA REYNOLDS, of Washington Co.
953. Mr JOSEPH H. JONES, will preach in the Baptist Meeting House, next Sabbath evening, at candle light.

May 10, 1834 (CBAL)

954. (M) On Thursday evening, by the Rev. D. F. Schaeffer, Mr JAMES HOPWOOD, to Miss MARY ANN WALKER, both of this city.
955. (M) On the same evening, by the same, Mr DANIEL GILBERT, to Miss JANE TOMPKINS, both of Jefferson Co., VA.
956. (M) On the 3rd inst., by the same, Mr WILLIAM REID, to Miss HENRIETTA FISH both of this co.
957. (M) On the 4th inst., by the same, Mr ELI SMALL, to Miss MARIAN HOLMES, both of this city.
958. (M) On the 5th inst., by the same, Mr NICHOLAS YOUNG, to Miss MARGARET BOLABAUGHER, from Germany.
959. (M) In the Glade, on Thursday last, by the Rev. J. W. Hoffmeier, Mr SOLOMON CREAGER, to Miss SUSAN, eldest daughter of Mrs Frederick Barrick.
960. (D) In Boston, on the 25th of April, Mr WILLIAM PRENTISS, age about 30 years. He was a eminent teacher, in Baltimore, and much esteemed for his private worth.
961. Mr WILLIAM GILMORE, will preach in the Baptist Meeting House, on Wednesday evening next, at candle light.

May 17, 1834 (CBAL)

962. (M) On Thursday the 1st of May inst., near Antietam Iron Works, Mr JOHN A. MANTZ, of this city, to Miss ELIZA ANN SHOWMAN, only daughter of Mr David Showman.
963. (M) On Thursday evening last, in Martinsburg, (VA,) by the Rev. J. Howell, Mr JACOB JEFFREYS, formerly of Frederick (MD,) to Miss ANN ELIZA, daughter of the late Mr Alexander Kennedy, of Martinsburg.

964. (M) On the 15th ult., by the Rev. Dr. Neill, Mr DAVID EWING, of Frederick-Town, MD., to MARTHA ANN, daughter of Zenas Wells, of Germantown, PA.
965. (M) On Thurday the 8th inst., by the Rev. Mr Reighley, Mr REASON M. PEDICORD, to Miss LYDIA EURY, all of this co.
966. (M) Near Middletown, MD., on the 1st of May 1834, by the Rev. J. C. Bucher Mr JOHN DARNER, to Miss JULY ANN ARNOLD, both of the valley.
967. (M) On the 12th inst., by the same, Mr JAMES WRIGHT, to Miss MATILDA, daughter of Mr Leonard Miller, all of Frederick City, MD.
968. (D) On the 8th inst., at Ridgeville, General HENRY BARRICK, aged 77 years a soldier of the Revolution.
969. The Rev. CHARLES REIGHLEY, will preach by Divine permission, before "The Christian Missionary Society," in the German Reformed Church, at Middletown, on Whit-Monday, at 2 o'clock, P.M., when and where the congregation will elect new officers and managers for the purpose of conducting the business of the society during the ensuing year.
970. The Criminal Court of Frederick County, commenced its May session on last Monday. The following is a list of the names of gentlemen who compose the Grand and Petit Juries, for the present term. Grand Jury: ANTHONY KIMMEL - Foreman, JOHN ANNAN, JACOB BRUNNER, JOHN COST, JOHN W. DERR, JACOB FAUBLE, GEORGE GROVER, BASIL HAYDEN, JOSHUA MURRY, JEREMIAH G. MORRISON, WM. B. PITTINGER, JOHN SMITH, JOHN BAUMGARDNER, JACOB CRAMER, SAMUEL CARMACK, JOSEPH FLEMING, GEORGE FLAUTT, THOMAS HOOK, THOMAS MEDCALF, ALEXANDER McIIHENNY, P. S. McELFRESH, MICHAEL SHUNK, AB'M. P. SHRIVER. Petit Jury: WILLIAM ALBAUGH, PHILIP BIRELY, JOHN BRUNNER of J., ADAM CUSTARD, ISAAC DERN, WILLIAM GALT, THOMAS HAMMOND, JOHN HARRITT, JOHN H. HILLEARY, EZRA HOUCK, ZACHARIAH T. WINDSOR, JACOB HYDER, ADAM KELLER, JOHN McELFRESH, WILLIAM NORRIS, THOMAS C. PRINCE, LEWIS SHARER, JOHN H. SIMMONS, MICHAEL SLUSS, JOHN B. STIMMEL, ABRAHAM WAMPLER, CHARLES WILLIAR, PETER YOUNG, JOHN HOUCK, HENRY ZIMMERMAN.

May 24, 1834 (CBAL)

971. (M) In Hagers-Town, on Tuesday evening last, by the Rev. Mr Winecoop, BENJAMIN PRICE, of this city, to SARAH ANN, eldest daughter of John Kennedy, Esq., of the former place.
972. (M) On the 22nd inst., by the Rev. D. F. Schaeffer, Mr LEWIS A. BRENGLE, to Miss ANN REBECCA, second daughter of Thomas Carlton, Esq., Mayor of this city.
973. (D) On the 18th inst., near Middletown, Mrs FANNY POFF, aged 89 years and 8 months.
974. (D) Departed this life at New Market, on Sunday the 18th inst., in the 4th year of her age, ELIZA, daughter of Dr. E. W. Mobberley.
975. (D) On Tuesday last, at his residence near the Monocacy, Mr EDWARD CAMPBELL.
976. Meeting of the Second Election District of Frederick Co., opposed to the recent measures of the National Administration. Col. JOHN McPHERSON, was called to the chair, and WM. OGDEN NILES, appointed secretary. NEILSON POE, Esq., made the following resolution, which was seconded by FRANCIS BRENGLE, Esq. It called for the chair to appoint 15 persons to represent this district in the general convention for the pursuance of nominating a ticket to be supported in the next House of Delegates, and to appoint 7 persons to act as a Committee of Correspondence for the election district, with the power to increase their number as they deemed necessary. Dr. JAMES W. PRYOR, then rose and addressed the meeting. The resolution was accepted by those presenced. For the Committee of Correspondence: GIDEON BANTZ, JAS. M. COALE, Dr. WM. WATERS, W. J. ROSS, NEILSON POE, FRANCIS BRENGLE, WM. OGDEN NILES. For the 15 persons to represent this district: WM. S. McPHERSON, URIAH S. BANTZ, JONATHAN EADER, DANIEL GETZENDANNER, LAWRENCE J. BRENGLE, AUGUSTUS EBERT, EDWARD TRAIL, JACOB FAUBLE, GEORGE SHULTZ, PATRICK TORMEY, L. P. W. BALCH, BENJAMIN PRICE, CHARLES BURCKHART, SAMUEL CRONISE, ISRAEL MYERS.

May 31, 1834 (CBAL)

977. Most severest thunderstorm ever seen hit the town, several of the conductor attached to the houses in town were said to be struck. A very large portion of fluid was discharged upon the steeple of the German Reformed Church, tearing

off the shingles of the roof for 10 to 12 feet, and scattering the railing and posts around the belfry, then descended down the steeple until it reached the stone work, when it turned and passed horizentally through the wall, and tracing its way along the outside of the wall of the main building, then was safely conducted to the ground by the water spout.

978. (F) A small log barn situated on the land of CASPER MANTZ, near this town was set on fire and confirmed.

979. JOHN BUSH, from Ohio, was robbed on Tuesday night last, on his way home from Baltimore, of a pocketbook, containing $1100.00 in money, besides notes of hand, and other papers. The act was perpetrated 1 mile West of Frederick, by 2 stout athletic men, who stopped his horse, and forcibly wrested the pocketbook from him. A reward of $300.00 is offered for the apprehension of the robbers, and recovery of the pocketbook.

980. (M) At Washington, on Tuesday evening the 27th ult., by the Rev. Mr McCallum, JAMES MASON CAMPBELL, Esq., of Baltimore, to Miss ANNA ARNOLD, daughter of Hon. R. B. Taney.

981. (M) On Wednesday morning, at the house of Richard Osborn, Esq., George-Town, by the Rev. Mr Hanson, Mr E. BENTZ, of Frederick, MD., to Miss PRUDENCE ASHBURY, of the former place.

982. (D) At his residence in Frederick Co., on the 29th inst., Major BENJAMIN MURDOCK, aged 76 years, who entered the Revolutionary War at a very early age.

June 7, 1834 (CBAL)

983. (M) On Sunday evening last, near Taney-Town, by the Rev. J. W. Hoffmier, Mr ELI THOMAS, to Miss CHRISTAINA SHUK, all of this co.

984. (M) At Taney-Town, on the 20th of May, by the Rev. Mr Finkle, GEORGE A. FARQUHAR, Esq., of Union Bridge, to Miss MARY R. CLABAUGH, of Taney-Town.

985. Appointments by the Levy Court of Frederick County, for the year 1834. Constables: District #1. JOHN CAREY, WM. CRAWFORD, ARTHUR DELASHMUTT, THOMAS KOHLENBURG, WM. CLARKE. District #2. JAMES CARLIN, LEWIS CROSS, FREDERICK STONER, JACOB MYERS, JOSHUA DILL, JOHN M. LOWE, HUGH MULLEN, JOSIAH DAYHOFF, DANIEL HALLER, SAMUEL McDADE, JOHN BENDER, FREDERICK HAWMAN. District #3.

JOHN ALEXANDER, JAMES WILLIAMSON, ABRAHAM MILLER, WM. KLEIN, JACOB YOUNG of Dewalt. District #4. CYRUS WALKER, HENRY NEED, GEORGE KUHN, BENJAMIN OGLE, NATHANIEL RICE. District #5. JESSE MARTIN, ISAAC WILSON, SAM'L. DUPHORN, JAMES BOYLE. District #6. JOHN CLABAUGH, DANIEL McKENZIE, WM. R. GILLIN, WILLIAM KUHN, TOBIAS COVER. District #7. JACOB FRINGER, JOHN CROUSE, JOHN D. WOOD, ISAIAH PIEREE, FREDERICK YINGLING, DANIEL BANKER, WILLIAM COOPER, JOHN FEASER. District #8. DANIEL SWEADNER, DANIEL ROOT, JOEL WOOD, JOHN H. CONDON. District #9. WM. P. HAUSER, LEVI VAN FOSSEN, JONATHAN BROWNING. District #10. DANIEL KLINE, WM. H. BROWN. District #11. JOSEPH BIRELY, FRED'K. GRIMES. District #12. JACOB J. OHR, F. G. HAMILTON, GEO. W. WINDSOR. District #14. JACOB B. HALLER, W. B. TABLER. CHRISTOPHER MYERS-Keeper of the Court House. SOLOMON GETZENDANNER-Keeper of the Court House Yard. Judges of Election: District #1. OTHO THOMAS, F. H. BROWN, SAMUEL THOMAS, of Thomas. District #2. JOHN EBERT, HENRY BAER, NICHOLAS HOLTZ. District #3. GEORGE BEAR, JOHN J. SMITH, JOHN YOUNG, of Peter. District #4. FREDERICK OTT, JAMES CROCKETT, VALENTINE SHRYOCK. District #5. JEFF. SHIELDS, MICHAEL SLUSS, DANIEL HOOVER. District #6. EVAN McKINSTRY, SAMUEL GALT, JACOB ZUMBRAN. District #7. MOSES SHAW, ISRAEL NORRIS, DAVID UHLER. District #8. JOHN GLESSAN, Sen., GEORGE COX, W. A. ALBAUGH. District #9. JOSHUA RUSSELL, HENRY SMITH, JOHN WOOD. District #10. WILSON HAYS, JOSEPH SMITH, GEORGE HARMAN. District #11. ELIA CRUTCHLEY, JACOB HYDER, JOHN D. CRUMBAUGH. District #12. HENRY OHR, JOHN N. HOSKINSON, and BENEDICT BOONE. District #14. THOMAS JOHNSON, of Wm., JOHN SIMMONS, THOMAS LAMAR. Trustees of the Alms House: DANIEL KOLB, VALENTINE DAUB, DANIEL HAUER, PHILIP ROHR, JACOB FAUBEL.

June 14, 1834 (CBAL)

986. (M) On Tuesday the 3rd of June, by the Rev. Mr McGee, Mr JESSE COOMES, to Miss THOMAS SHIVERS, both of Frederick Co.

987. (M) On the 5th inst., by the Rev. Mr Cadden, Mr JOHN J. MULLEN, to Miss MARY ANN PATRICK, both of Liberty-Town.

988. (M) Near Middletown, on the 23rd of May, by the Rev. J. C. Bucher, Mr SOLOMON, son of Mr Daniel Coblentz, to Miss MALINDA MICHAEL, both of Middletown Valley, MD.

989. (M) On the same day, by the same, Mr MAHLON RODRICK, to Miss MARY ANN, daughter of Mr Henry Flook, deceased, both of Middletown Valley.

990. (M) At Philadelphia, on the 7th inst., by the Rev. Bishop White, Mr PIERCE BUTLER, of Philadelphia, to Miss FANNY KEMBLE, of England, daughter of Mr Charles Kemble.

991. (D) At sea on board the packet ship Lorenz, on her voyage from Harve to New York, when 2 days out, ROBERT GOODLOW HARPER, youngest son of the late General Harper, and brother of Charles Carroll Harper, Esq., of Baltimore, in the 20th year of his age.

992. (D) At 11 o'clock, on Sunday the 8th inst., at his residence near Liberty Town, Mr EDEN HAMMOND, of a malignant fever. He was followed to the family interment of his father-in-law, by a number of relations

993. Appointment by the Governor and Council of Maryland for Frederick County. Lieut. Col. JAMES M. SHELMAN, Colonel 16th Regiment. Vice Col. KEMP, removed out of the county. Major BENJAMIN PRICE, Lieut. Col. ditto. Vice Lieut. Col. SHELMAN, promoted. EDWARD A. LYNCH, Esq., Adjutant; ditto. Vice Adjutant TALBOTT, resigned. Dr. WILSON W. KOLB, Surgeon, ditto.

994. Military visit - Grey's of Middletown, under the command of Capt. JOHN KEFAUVER. They were escorted into the city by the Everhart Grey's, under the command of Capt. SAMUEL CARMACK, along with the Frederick Volunteer's, under the command of Capt. WILLIAM SMALL. The parade took place on Saturday last, in the afternoon.

995. Three murders, of the most foul and inhuman character, were perpetrated on Friday and Saturday nights, on the line of the canal, near the Point of Rocks. A man named CREED, who was confinded, on some criminal charges, in our jail, last winter, is one of the victims. His body, as we learned from respectable authority, was dreadfully mangled. The names of the others were unknown to our informant. All the sufferers and no doubt their murderers were the laboring Irish on the canal.

996. City appointed the following men to a committee for the July 4th celebration. THOMAS CARLIN, MAHLON TALBOTT, HENRY NIXDORFF, WM. OGDEN NILES, NEILSON POE, SAM'L. L. McKEEHAN, FRANCIS BRENGLE, Col. G. M. EICHELBERGER, Col. JOHN McPHERSON, Col. JAMES M. SHELMAN, Maj. JAMES M. COALE, Maj. HENRY SCHLEY, Capt. GEO. W. ENT, Capt. M. E. BARTGIS, Capt. SAM'L. CARMACK, Capt. WM. J. SMALL.

997. At a meeting of the Delegates from Taney-Town and Westminster Districts, appointed as Committee of Conference, to take into consideration the various plans suggested for the formation of a new county, held at Union-Town, on the 31st day of May. Dr. WILLIAM B. HEBBARD, was called to the chair, and J. K. LONGWELL, appointed Secretary. A sub-committee consisting of Col. THOMAS HOOK, Dr. WILLIAM WILLIS, J. A. M'KALEB, JOSHUA SMITH, Jr., and ISAAC SHRIVER, Esquires, to draft resolutions expressing the views of the conference. The committee requested that a committee of 5 persons be appointed to petition the General Assembly for their signatures to form a new County. The persons appointed to this committee are: Dr. WILLIAM WILLIS, Col. T. HOOK, JACOB MATTHIAS, Esq., J. A. M'KALEB, Esq., and J. K. LONGWELL.

June 21, 1834 (CBAL)

998. (M) On Thursday last, by the Rev. David F. Schaeffer, Mr PHILIP WACHTER, Jr., to Miss SUSAN REES, all of this co.

999. (M) On the same day, by the same, Mr WILLIAM MESSLER, to Miss SUSANNA SMITH, all of this co.

1000. (M) On Tuesday morning the 10th inst., by the Rev. R. S. Grier, Mr ANDREW GALBRAITH EGE, of Carlisle, PA., to Miss MARGARET ANN, daughter of Major John M'Kaleb, of Taney-Town.

1001. (D) On Thursday the 12th inst., in the 22nd year of her age, of puerperal fever, Mrs SUSAN SCHOLL, wife of Elias Scholl, all of this co.

1002. The Rev. CHARLES REIGHLEY, will (God willing) preach on the subject of Temperance in the German Reformed Church at Middletown, on tomorrow morning, the 22nd inst., at 1/2 past 9 o'clock.

1003. The parade Marshalls, for the 4th of July celebration have been chosen. The Grand Marshall is JOHN McPHERSON, the Deputy Marshalls are: WM. OGDEN NILES, Lt. Col.

BENJ. PRICE, WM. H. DAINGERFIELD, and JOHN BRUNNER, of J.

June 28, 1834 (CBAL)

1004. (M) On Sunday the 22nd inst., Mr JOSEPH KEANS, to Miss DRUSILAH HARRIS, both of this co.
1005. (M) On Thursday evening last, by the Rev. D. F. Schaeffer, Mr JOHN C. DIETERICH, of George-Town, D.C., to Miss ANNA MARY TREFZER, all of Germany.
1006. Drs. WILLIAM WILLIS, and JEFFERSON SHIELDS, JAMES A. SCHROB, and T. H. T. COCKEY, were appointed censors for this county, at the last annual meeting of the Medical and Chirurgical Faculty of the state.
1007. Candidates for the next Mayoralty election are: Mr THOMAS C. PRINCE, Capt SAMUEL CARMACK, and JACOB TALBOTT.

July 5, 1834 (CBAL)

1008. (D) Mr CHRISTIAN THOMAS, respectable citizen of this co., residing about 1 1/2 miles from this city, was killed by lightning, during the storm which raged so furiously on Thursday last. He was sitting at the dinner table and died instantly after receiving the stroke-whilst a lad sitting near him escaped uninjured, 3 servants, who were also at the dinner, received shocks with such violence they were thrown on the floor-but not seriously hurt. Lightning first struck the top of the chimney, shattered the adjoining end of the building, passed down into the front room along the chimney, until it was attracted by a gun which was standing in the corner-it then passed out on the opposite side of the room, through a partition wall into the passage, where it met a current of air. The plastering in front and back room was detached in several places. The house was not ignited, but a barrel of whiskey, standing on an end in the second story, took fire and was nearly 1 1/2 consumed, before discovered.
1009. (M) On Sunday last, by the Rev. Mr Wachter, Mr JOSHUA MURPHY, to Miss LOUISA SLICK, all of this co.
1010. (M) On the same day, by the same, Mr JOHN GEESEY, to Miss ELIZABETH HANKEY, both of this co.
1011. (M) On Thursday the 19th ult., by the Rev. Finckle, Mr WM. THOMPSON, of New York, to Miss ELIZA RECH, of Taney-Town.

1012. (D) On Sunday the 22nd ult., in the 74th year of his age, Mr JACOB FRINGER, Sen., an old and respectable citizen of Westminster.
1013. (D) On Tuesday the 17th ult., EMANUEL, son of Mr David Root, aged 18 months.
1014. (D) On Sunday the 22nd ult., in the 72nd year of her age, Mrs ELIZABETH LLOYD, consort of Mr William Lloyd, of the vicinity of Westminster
1015. Candidates for the next election: JACOB FAUBEL, MICHAEL BALTZELL, JOSHUA DILL, DANIEL KOLB.

July 12, 1834 (CBAL)

1016. (M) On the 22nd ult., Mr HENRY McLEAN, to Miss BARBARA, daughter of Mr Michael Wagoner, all of the Westminster District.
1017. (M) On Thursday last, by the Rev. Mr Gutelius, Mr DAVID WEAVER, to Miss MARGARET FOWLER, both of Westminster.
1018. (M) On the 26th ult., by the Rev. Mr Ruthrauff, Mr JOHN SMITH, of Adams Co., to Miss ELIZA ANDERS, of Taney-Town.
1019. (M) On Sunday evening last, by the Rev. David F. Schaeffer, Mr MICHAEL BROMETT, to Mrs ELLEN ROLLINGTON, all of this city.
1020. (D) Departed this life, on Saturday night the 5th inst., Mrs ELIZABETH KELLER, consort of the late Conrad Keller, in the 63rd year of her age.
1021. Candidate for the Mayorality election: Capt. NICHOLAS H. TURBUTT.
1022. Foul and atrocious murder on Friday night last, on Saturday morning last, Mr BENDER one of our constables, was aroused by one of the female tenants of a house of infamous character, and apprised that one of her guilty companions living in same house, had been murdered. Mr B., found lying in the entry of a house on 5th Street, long known as the abode of the most abandoned of the female sex, the body of a woman, who had died of stab wounds, which she had received in the back, a little below the armpit. The adjoining room showed signs of a struggle covered with blood.

July 19, 1834 (CBAL)

1023. (M) In Christ Church, Baltimore, on the 17th ult., by the Rev. Dr. Henshaw, JOSPEH R. SNYDER, of that city, to

MARGARET ANN, daughter of Dennis Lackland, of Montgomery MD.
1024. (M) In Hagers Town, by the Rev. Mr Bucher, Capt. JOHN KAUFAUVER, to Miss CATHARINE YOUNG, all of Middletown MD.
1025. Meeting on Thursday evening the 10th inst., Capt. GEO. W. ENT, was called as chairman, EDWARD SHRIVER, Esq., as secretary. They appointed a committee to make plans to honor the memory of LaFayette. HENRY NIXDORFF, Capt. WM. SMALL, Capt. SAMUEL CARMACK, FREDERICK A. SCHLEY, WILLIAM ROSS, M. E. BARTGIS, MICHAEL BALTZELL, made up the committee. The committee selected to hold a funeral procession on July 24th, at 9 A.M., to the memory of the late General. The following persons were selected to act as pallbearers: LAWRENCE EVERHART, HENRY BAER, PHILIP ROHR, MOSES WORMAN, CASPAR MANTZ, Capt. JOHN BRENGLE, Dr. JOHN TYLER, JOHN P. THOMPSON. For the funeral procession the following persons were appointed as Assistant Marshals: Capt. NICHOLAS SNIDER, Capt. ALEXANDER B. HANSON, Capt. GEORGE W. ENT, Maj. HENRY SCHLEY, Capt. LEWIS BIRELY Capt. THOMAS W. MORGAN, Mr. EDWARD TRAIL, and Mr JOHN TITLOW.
1026. The Rev. Mr SMITH, being unavoidably absent, there will be no service in the Presbyterian Church to-morrow.

July 26, 1834 (CBAL)
1027. (M) On Tuesday last, by the Rev. D. F. Schaeffer, Mr JACOB MORELOCK, to Mrs SUSANNA BROWN, all of Westminster District.
1028. (M) On the 31st ult., by the Rev. Thomas Kill, Mr JOHN LITTLE DILL, to Miss FANNY B. HILL, both of Kent Co. (Their cup of life may pleasure fill. May death be far from Mr Kill. Though Mr Kill has killed Miss Hill, and Hill is turned to little Dill.)
1029. (D) Near Liberty, on Thursday night the 17th inst., in the 62nd year of his age, Maj. SABRETT SOLLER.

August 2, 1834 (CBAL)
1030. (D) At his residence in Liberty Town, on Tuesday morning the 22nd inst., in the 74th year of his age, Mr RICHARD COALE, Sen. As a volunteer he entered at an early period of the Revolutionary War, and before he had attained the age of maturity. In a expedition for the protection of the

city of Annapolis which was being menaced with attack by water, whilst acting in temporary capacity, of assistant surgeon on board of an American vessel of inferior grade. He was captured by a British Man-of-War, and carried to Edinburgh in Scotland, and detained for many months, a prisoner on parole. Upon being liberated he returned to this country. Abandoning the profession of medicine for agriculture, then he settled in the vicinity of his late residence. Several years ago he erected on his land a neat and durable church for the benefit of the Catholic Congregation at Liberty-Town, whose communion he accepted; and place upon the record prior to late restrictive legislation on subject of deeds of manumission for all of his slaves to the number of 50, and upwards. To his children he was the best of fathers to the poor, and needy a generous benefactor.

1031. (D) In the vicinity of Union Bridge, in this co., on the 23rd inst., after a lingering illness, Mrs SUSANNA SHEPHERD, wife of Mr Solomon Shepherd, in the 82nd year of her age.

1032. (D) On the 15th ult., at her residence near Burkettsville, Mrs ASNETH SLIFER, aged 86 years, 11 months and 25 days.

1033. (D) On Sunday last, at Bedford Springs, whither he had gone for the benefit of his health, Mr JOHN BRIEN, Senr. A respectable citizen of Frederick Co., and proprietor of Catoctin Iron Works, near Creagerstown.

1034. (D) On the evening of the 28th ult., Miss CATHERINE DAVIS, only daughter of Dr. A. Ritchie, aged nearly 15 months.

1035. (D) Near Middletown, on the 25th of July, after a short illness Mr DANIEL BISER, of Daniel, in the 52nd year of his age, he leaves a large family and friends.

1036. (D) On the 27th of July, ANN CECELIA SOPHIA CATHERINE MOTTER, only daughter of Mr William Motter, at an very early period of her life

1037. (D) On the 22nd of July, DAVID SYLVESTER SMITH, in the 3rd year of his age, and son of Mr J. J. Smith.

1038. (D) On the 26th of July, in the 14th year of her age, Miss MARY ANN KLINE daughter of Mr William Kline, near Middletown, MD.

1039. The Creagerstown District meeting of the Whig party has appointed the following delegates to the convention: JOSEPH WILHIDE, HENRY FUNDENBURG, WILLIAM B. PITTINGER, JOHN W. DERR, Col. J. CRAMER, JOS.

EICHELBERGER, WILLIAM GRIMES, WILLIAM COOKERLY, Doct. L. W. GOLDSBOROUGH, HENRY A. BRIEN, JOHN BUCHANAN, JOHN KNOUFF, PARMENIO R. HARRY, WM. JONES, and ZEBULON KUHN.

1040. The Liberty District meeting of the Whig party was held at JOSEPH L. WAGNER'S, Tavern in Liberty-Town, on the 26th inst., to appoint delegates to the convention to be held in Frederick on Saturday the 2nd of August. WILLIAM WORMAN, Esq., was called to the chair and NICHOLAS NORRIS, appointed secretary. Capt. JOHN DUDDERAR, WILLIAM JONES, WILLIAM H. POOLE, WILLIAM LOWE, NATHAN H. OWINGS, DAVID DUDDERAR, DAVID W. NAILL, HENRY REPP, HENRY BOUGHER, DANIEL ALBAUGH, DANIEL SWEADNER, JOSHUA STEVENSON, WM. A. ALBAUGH, ANTHONY KIMMELL, SURATT D. WARFIELD, RICHARD SIMPSON, JAMES DOUTY and JACOB CASSELL, be delegates to the convention. ABRAHAM JONES, Dr. RICHARD DORSEY, Dr. HENRY BAKER, THOMAS HAMMOND and DANIEL SWEADNER, were appointed as a committee of correspondence.

1041. Jefferson District meeting of the Whig party was held at S. S. CHURCH'S Inn on the 26th inst. The meeting was organized by appointing HENRY COST, chairman and AMOS CURR, secretary. Col. THOMAS JOHNSON, JACOB THOMAS, SEBASTIAN REMSBURG, Jr., LEVI PHILIPS and WILLIAM TABLER, were appointed to draft resolutions. JACOB B. HALLER, CHRISTIAN TABLER, WILLIAM JARBOE, CHRISTIAN WEAVER, GEORGE WILLIARD, RICHARD JOHNSON, Col. THOMAS JOHNSON, WM. TABLER, JOHN CULLER, Jr., FIELDER THOMSON, LEWIS RODRICK, WM. NORRED, HENRY GROSS, HENRY CRUM, PATRICK McGILL, Jr., LLOYD LUCKETT, Col. N. LUCKETT, SAMUEL NORRED, WM. NEIGHBOURS, JOHN BURKETT, AMOS CURR, RICHARD CHILCOTE, JAMES FORRANCE, ANDREW JONES, DAVID CARLISLE, WILLIAM ERVING, WM. REMSBURGH, Dr. G. W. CRUM, HENRY SUTER, PATRICK McGILL, Sr., JAMES T. CASTLE, WILLIAM BUCKINGHAM, MICHAEL GEARY, JACOB DUBLE, JOHN SHAFER, GEORGE C. BISER, A. J. DOUGLASS, THOMAS BOTELER, JOSEPH CATZENDAFFER, GEO. POTTER, MARTIN MILLER, WILSON SPARROW, NELSON HOFFMAN, WM. S. JOHNSON, Dr. VAN BURSKIRK, JOHN NEIGHBORS, ROBERT WILLIAMS, PETER W. GARDNER, JOSEPH STOCKMAN, WILLIAM LAMAR, JONATHAN FEASTER,

DAVID CULLER, PERRY RICE, Sr., PHILIP CULLER, and WILSON L. PHILIPS, constitute a committee of vigilance whose duty in part will be to see that every Whig voter is at the poles on the first Monday in October next.

1042. Meeting of the Taney-Town, District National Republicans were held at Sultzer's Hotel, on Saturday the 26th inst., JACOB BAUMGARTNER, Esq., was called to the chair, and JAMES SMITH, Esq., appointed assistant chairman, SAMUEL McKINSTRY, was appointed secretary and ELIAS HEITER, assistant secretary. A committee was appointed to draft resolutions expressing the views of the party: FRANCIS SPALDING, THOMAS HOOK, J. A. McKALEB, JOHN N. STARR, and JOHN COVER, of Jacob. The following citizens were appointed to attend the convention: WILLIAM B. HEBBARD, STERLING GALT, JACOB BAUMGARTNER, JOHN McKALEB, Dr. SAMUEL SWOPE, J. A. M'KALEB, GEO. A. FARQUHAR, JAMES SMITH, JOHN MATTHIAS, ABRAHAM NULL, JACOB HAHN, Jr., JAMES A. M'KALEB, DANIEL M'KINSTRY, DAVID KEPHART, PETER ERB, WILLIAM L. CRAPSTER, CHARLES A. WRIGHT, THOMAS HOOK, ELIAS GRIMES, JOHN COVER, of Jacob, and WILLIAM RUDISCEL.

1043. Woodsboro, District meeting of the Whig party was held at ISAAC LYNN'S Tavern on the 26th inst., PAUL CARMACK, Esq., was appointed chairman and MASON PARSONS, secretary. The following persons were appointed to represent this district at the annual convention, to be held in Frederick: SAMUEL BIRELY, JACOB ROOT, NOAH PHILIPS, MASON PARSONS, HENRY W. DERR, Capt. ROBERT FURRON, Dr. THOMAS W. JOHNSON, DAN'L. CREAGER, GEORGE BARRICK.

1044. To represent the Petersville District at the convention, the following gentlemen were appointed: JOHN COLE, JOHN ALLSTON, JOHN LEE, EMANUEL SLIFER, JOHN N. HOSKINSON and JOSEPH WAITMAN.

1045. The Whig party of New Market District assembled at the house of Mr ENOS SCHELL, on Saturday the 26th day of July. The meeting was organized by calling Dr. BRASHEAR to the chair and appointed WASHINGTON BURGESS secretary. J. CRONICE, made a motion to appoint a committee to represent their district at the convention in Frederick. The following gentlemen were appointed: ABRAM JOHNS, SINGLETON WOOTEN, MICHAEL LEASE, NATHAN NELSON, JOHN KLAY, GRAFTON HAMMOND, SAMUEL

STEVENSON, REZIN STEVENS, JACOB CRONICE, THOMAS C. BRASHEAR, PLUMMER IJAMS, Sr., JOHN HOUCK, ABEL RUSSELL, WM. MORSELL, ENOS SCHELL, Dr. HUGHES, JOHN LOWE, G. P. BUCKEY, NATHAN HAMMOND, of O., THOMAS DUVALL, NICHOLAS BRENGLE, GEO. RINER, ELIAS BRASHEAR, ELISHA NELSON, WILLIAM COCKEY, JOHN MILLER, JESSE RUSSELL, JOHN WOOD, SAMUEL RUNKLES. The following gentlemen were appointed to serve on the Committee of Correspondence: Dr. BELT BRASHEAR, WASHINGTON BURGESS, FREDERICK SMITH, Sr., THOMAS M. PLUMMER, JOHN LEASE, DENTON HAMMOND, JOHN McELFRESH, WM. NORRIS, BENJAMIN TODD, Dr. HUGHES, CORNELIUS KLAY, THOMAS MOUNT and BENJAMIN GREENTREE.

1046. Meeting of the Buckeystown Whigs met at the house of ALLEN LAIN, on Saturday the 26th inst., Capt. CONRAD RUDDERAR, was called to the chair and MARTIN M. MAHONEY appointed secretary. The following gentlemen were appointed to represent this district at the convention in Frederick: Dr. JONATHAN MANRO, HENRY KEMP, CHRISTIAN KEMP, DANIEL DUVALL, OTHO THOMAS, JAMES L. DAVIS, J. G. COBBS, J. C. OSBORN, RICHARD CROMWELL, Major JAMES SIMMONS, WILLIAM MURPHY, CHARLES JOHNSON, ELISHA HOWARD, RICHARD MURDOCK and PHILEMON S. McELFRESH.

1047. At a meeting of the Whigs of the 5th Election District, which was held at the Union Academy in Emmittsburg, on Saturday the 26th inst., the meeting was organized by calling ROBERT FLEMING, Esq., to the chair, and appointing I. E. PEARSON Secretary. On motion, THOMAS HAYS, Esq., Dr. ANDREW ANNAN and JOSEPH WELTY, were appointed to draft resolutions expressing the sense of the meeting. The following gentlemen were appointed as Committee of Correspondence for the district: Capt. JACOB WINEBRENNER, SAMUEL BAUMGARTNER, Esq., ROBERT ANNAN, Esq., JOSHUA MOTTER and ISAAC BAUGHER. That Dr. J. SHIELDS, Captain M. SLUSS, JOHN ANNAN, ISAAC MOTTER, FELIX B. TANEY, JOSEPH TROXELL, ISAAC E. PEARSON, JOHN CRAPSTER, DANIEL HOOVER and JOSEPH BAUGHER, to represent this district in the convention of delegates to meet at Frederick on the 2nd of August next.

1048. At a respectable meeting of the voters of District No. 3, in Middletown, at the house of WM. PERRY. They called

JOHN J. SMITH to the chair and appointed WM. H. CREAGER Secretary. The chair appointed the following committee to report resolutions expressing the sentiment of the meeting: GEORGE BOWLUS, THOS. CASTLE, Dr. SPRINGER, JOHN SHINDLER and CHRISTIAN RAMSBURG. A committee of 15 be appointed to attend the convention of next Saturday: DANIEL YOUNG, JACOB FLOOK, THOMAS CASTLE, JACOB THOMAS, PETER COBLENTS, HENRY R. SMELTZER, CHRISTIAN REMSBURGH, JOHN J. SMITH, Dr. JACOB BAER, GEO. BOWLUS, Dr. THOMAS SPRINGER, DANIEL COBLENTZ, JONATHAN HERRING, JACOB LEATHERMAN and GEORGE BLESSING compose said committee.

1049. A highly respectable meeting of the Whig voters of Westminster District, convened at Uniontown, on Saturday the 26th of July inst. WASHINGTON VANBIBBER, Esq., was called to the chair and Dr. J. JONES appointed Secretary. The chair appointed a committee of 5 to draft resolutions, the following gentlemen were appointed: A. F. SHRIVER, WILLIAM ROBERTS, MOSES SHAW, JOHN HYDER and A. M'IIHENNY, Esqrs. The following gentlemen were appointed to attend the general county convention to be held in Frederick, on the first Saturday of August next, for the purpose of nominating candidates to be supported by the Whig party at the coming election: MOSES SHAW, JOHN ROBERTS, JAMES C. ATLEE, Dr. J. L. WARFIELD, DANIEL ENGLE, A. F. SCHRIVER, JACOB REESE, ISAAC NICODEMUS, GEO. CASSELL, of John., JACOB MATHIAS, EMANUEL GERNAND, CHARLES DEVILBISS, JOSHUA SMITH, Jr., ABRAHAM WAMPLER.

August 16, 1834 (CBAL)

1050. (M) Near Middletown, on the 7th inst., by the Rev. J. C. Bucher, Mr HANSON RUDY, to Miss CATHARINE ANN, eldest daughter of Mrs George Schaeffer, all of Middletown Valley, MD.

1051. (M) On Tuesday week, by the Rev. F. Rathrauff, Mr MICHAEL BROWNER, of Adams Co., PA., to Miss ANN E. FIEZER, of Frederick Co., MD.

1052. (M) On Tuesday week, by the Rev. Joshua Wells, Mr ALEXANDER B. DAVIDSON, to Miss ANNA LOUISA, daughter of the late Dr. Walls, all of Baltimore.

1053. (M) On Sunday evening, by the Rev. D. F. Schaeffer, Mr HENRY RILING, to Miss BARBARA SMITH, all of this city.

1054. (D) Near Jefferson, MD., on the 5th of August, in her 2nd year, MARGARET ANN ELIZABETH, daughter of Mr Lewis Rodrick.

1055. The following persons were elected Directors of Farmer Bank of Maryland: WILLIAM ROSS, JOHN TYLER, GEORGE BALTZELL, RICHARD POTTS, DANIEL HUGHES, LEWIS MEDTARD, JOHN BRIEN, JONA. T. WILSON and NOAH PHILIPS, WILLIAM S. McPHEARSON.

1056. Civil appointments by the Executive of Maryland for August 1834: For the 16th Regiment of Milita, Fred'k., Co. CHARLES H. BURKHART, Major V. PRICE, promoted. For the 28th Regiment of Frederick Co. MICHAEL THOMAS, 1st Lieutenant, of Capt. JOHN THOMAS, Uniform Rifle Co. Vice; E. THOMAS, resigned. SAMUEL NORRIS, 2nd Lieutenant, Vice; MICHAEL THOMAS, promoted.

1057. Candidate for Alderman: G. W. ENT.

August 23, 1834 (CBAL)

1058. (D) At Martinsburg, VA., on the 15th inst., in the 68th year of age, Mrs MARY JAMESON, relict of the late Leonard Jameson, formerly a respectable citizen of this co.

1059. (D) Departed this life on the 12th day of August, in Petersburg, VA., in the 16th year of her age, Miss ELIZA H. LYNCH, daughter of Mrs Sarah Lynch. (Petersburg Constellation)

1060. On Saturday last the Jackson convention was held in this city. The following gentlemen were selected as candidates for the legislature: JOHN SIFFORD, JOHN HARRITT, CHRISTIAN GETZENDANNER and ABDIEL UNKEFER.

1061. The Rev. JOSEPH H. JONES, will preach in the Baptist Meeting House this evening, at early candle light.

1062. The Rev. JOHN HEALY, on the following evening, at early candle light.

1063. The Rev. Mr BRECKENBRIDGE, from Washington City, will preach in the German Reformed Church in this city on Sunday morning next.

1064. The Rev. Mr SHELMAN, will preach in the English Presbyterian Church tomorrow morning, at 10 o'clock.

August 30, 1834 (CBAL)

1065. (M) On Thursday the 21st inst., by the Rev. David F. Schaeffer, JOHN CONTER, Esq., of Shepherdstown, VA., to Miss CATHERINE NUSZ, daughter of the late Henry Nusz, of this city.

1066. (M) On Monday the 25th inst., by the same, Mr JOHN DAVIS, to Miss MARY BISHOP, all of this co.

1067. (D) On Thursday the 14th inst., Mrs CATHARINE KOONTS, wife of Isaac Koonts, and daughter of William Miller, Esqr., in the 30th year of her age.

1068. (D) On Saturday the 16th inst., ELIZA JANE, infant daughter of Dr. Thomas Sims, of Woodsborough.

1069. (D) On Wednesday the 20th inst., after a long painful illness, Mr JUSTINIAN MAYBERRY, in the 70th year of his age. A highly respected citizen of Frederick, and until a short time since overseer of the Alms House of this co.

1070. (D) On the 25th of August, after a short but painful illness, FREDERICK PETER, son of Geo. Hardt, in the 8th year of his age.

September 6, 1834 (CBAL)

1071. Military visit - The Marion Rifle Corps, one of the most beautiful and efficient military company of Baltimore, accompanied by splended music, will visit on the 12th.

1072. (D) On Tuesday the 26th ult., near this city, Mrs SOPHIA RUTHERFORD, wife of Benjamin Rutherford, Esq. She leaves a husband and a number of children.

1073. Candidates for the office of Mayor of Frederick: THOMAS C. PRINCE, JOSHUA DILL, SAMUEL CARMACK, JOSEPH TULBOTT, JACOB FAUBEL, MICHAEL BALTZELL, DANIEL KOLB, G. W. ENT.

September 13, 1834 (CBAL)

1074. Appointed by the Governor and Council of Maryland, an additional Justice of the Peace for Frederick Co. Mr PETER STEM, Esq.

1075. Military visit - The Marion Rifle Corp, was met at the Monocacy bridge by a committee from the Everhart Grey, under the command of Capt. W. G. COOK, they were quartered at Bartgis's Hotel. The next day a parade was held, along with a public dinner in their honor. At 4 o'clock, they visited the college yard to witness the ballon ascension, followed by a concert in the evening.

1076. (M) On Thursday evening the 4th inst., by the Rev. D. F. Schaeffer, Mr JACAMIAH SEAMAN, to Miss MARY ANN B. POTTS, all of Loudoun Co., VA.

1077. (M) On Tuesday last, by the same, Mr EPHRAIM RIDDLEMOSER, to Miss JULIA ANN TABLER, both of this co.

1078. (M) On Sunday 1st., by the Rev. Mr Wachter, Mr MANASSUS CREAGER, to Miss MARGARET RIDENOUR, both of this co.
1079. (M) On the same day, by the same, Mr ELIAS WALTZ, to Miss BARBARA KINZEY, both of this co.
1080. (D) On Tuesday the 2nd inst., in the 74th year of his age, Capt. MICHAEL HOUSER, a most respectable inhabitant of this city.
1081. (D) Near Middletown, MD., on the 29th of August, Mr JOHN HENRY FEETE, in the 79th year of his age.
1082. (D) On Thursday last, after a short but painful illness, Miss ELIZABETH OTT, in the 17th year of her age.
1083. (D) Departed this life, on Saturday the 6th of September, at Waterford, VA., DANIEL W. THOMAS, formerly of Winchester, aged 74 years.
1084. Mr SIMPSON, succeeded in making an ascension yesterday evening at 1/2 past 6 o'clock, and proceeded about a mile in a North-Westerly direction, at the height of 250 feet.

September 20, 1834 (CBAL)

1085. Dr. GROVER, shot a 150 pound bear last week in the vicinity of Emmittsburg.
1086. (M) Near Middletown, on the 11th inst., by the Rev. J. C. Bucher, Mr GEORGE L. ROUTGANER, to Miss EVE, daughter of Mr John P. Coblents, all of Middletown Valley.
1087. (M) On Thursday last, by the Rev. D. F. Schaeffer, Mr REZIN STEPHENS, to Miss SUSANNAH KESSLER, all of this co.
1088 (M) At New Windsor, by the Rev. R. Cadden, on Thursday morning Sept. 6th Mr ISAAC BLIZZARD, to Miss LOUISA ANN BRAWNER.
1089. (M) On the same day, by the same, in Woodsborough, Mr DENNIS ESTLER, of Liberty, to Miss ANN ELIZABETH DOLL, of that place.
1090. (M) At Locust Grove, on Thursday morning last, by the Rev. H. L. Baugher, Mr JOSEPH SCHELL, to Miss CATHARINE ANN, daughter of Mr John Grabile, all of this co.
1091. (M) In Philadelphia, on Tuesday evening, the 2nd inst., by the Rev. Mr Brinckley, Mr ARTHUR F. KEENE, of the city of Dublin, Ireland, to Miss ELIZABETH LEVIS, eldest daughter of Mr Aaron Clement of the former place.
1092. (D) In this city on the 25th of August, after a protracted and painful illness, Mrs SARAH JOHNSON DORSEY, consort of Mr Eli Dorsey, was the daughter of Maj. Roger

Johnson, of Bloomsburg, Frederick Co., MD. (Cincinnati Chronicle)

1093. Candidates for the Legislature from Frederick County, selected for the Whig party; DAVID DUVALL, FRANCIS BRENGLE, ROBERT ANNAN, WILLIAM ROBERTS. For the Jackson party: ABDIEL UNKEEFER, JOHN SIFFORD, C. GETZENDANNER, JOHN HARRITT.

1094. The Rev. JOSEPH H. JONES, will preach in the Baptist Meeting House, tomorrow at 3 o'clock, in the afternoon.

1095. The Rev. THOMAS P. C. SHELMAN, will preach in the Presbyterian Church, tomorrow at 10 o'clock, A.M.

1096. Members of the Frederick Debating Society, are requested to meet at the office of NICHOLAS H. PITTS, Esq., this evening at 7 o'clock.

September 27, 1834 (CBAL)

1097. The attention of the charitable ladies of Frederick, is invited to the destitute condition of a female living in the back part of Mr JOHN MAGRATH's store, on Patrick Street. She has recently lost her husband and one of her children, three of whom are the surviving pariah takers of the extremest proverty.

1098. At an adjourned meeting of the Whig voters of Frederick City, which convened at JOHN DILL's Tavern, in Frederick, on Wednesday the 24th inst., Dr. WM. BRADLEY TYLER, in the chair, and WM. OGDEN NILES secretary. JAMES M. COALE, Esq., presented several resolutions; one of them called for a Committee of Vigilance be appointed for this district, to consist of every Whig voter in it, whose circumstances will permit him thus to act, in sustaining the character and prosperity of his country. In pursuance of that resolution, the following Committee of Vigilance for this city was appointed: C. B. ARTZ, JOHN ABBOTT, JOSEPH ADLUM, JOHN BAYLEY, VALENTINE BIRELY, L. A. BRENGLE, VALENTINE J. BRUNNER, GIDEON BANTZ, Jr., GIDEON BANTZ, Sen's., URIAH S. BANTZ, LEWIS BIRELY, HENRY BAER, L. P. W. BALCH, JACOB BRUCHA, JACOB BRUNNER, JAMES BRUNNER, MARK BISHOP, Jr., CHARLES BRENGLE, JAMES BARTLY, CHRISTIAN BRENGLE, Jr. JACOB BUCKEY, G. M. CONRADT, GEORGE CROMWELL, JAMES CARLIN, JAMES M. COALE, JAMES S. CROCKEN, JACOB CRUMBINE, GEORGE COLEMAN, ABNER CAMPBELL, ANDREW DAYHOFF, R. E. DORSEY, ISAAC DUNHAM, WM. DURBIN, Jr., JACOB

DADISMAN, LEWIS DUNHAM, DAVID B. DEVITT, WM. DURBIN, Sr., WM. DIXON, JOS. DAUGHERTY, THOS. DOLL, CHARLES DeBUTTS, JOHN DILL, MEREDITH DAVIS, GEORGE DOLL, EZRA DOLL, JOSIAH DAYHOFF, AUGUSTUS EBBERT, GEORGE M. EICHELBERGER, JACOB ENGLEBRECHT, VALERIUS EBERT, GEORGE A. EBBERT, GEORGE ENGLEBRECHT, EZRA ELY, JACOB FAUBEL, ADAM FISHER, ADOLPHUS FEARHAKE, THOMAS A. FLEMING, JOHN FAUBEL, ADAM GETZEN- DANNER, GEORGE C. GELWICKS, LEWIS GEPHART, DAVID HANE, NICHOLAS HALLER, GEORGE HOFFMAN, JOHN HOOPER, FREDERICK HAUMAN, RICHARD HARPER, PHILIP HAUMAN, PHILIP HALLER, ABRAHAM HOOPER, Capt. DANIEL HAUER, GEORGE HAUER, WM. HAUER, HENRY K. HILTON, SAMUEL R. HOGG, WILLIAM HILTON, JOHN HANE, Major DANIEL HUGHES, JOHN HENSHEW, JOHN L. HARDING, JAMES M. HARDING, WILLIAM HARDING, NORMAN HARDING, ASBURY H. HUNT, JOSHUA INGMAN, WM. COST JOHNSON, HENRY KESSLER, PETER KEPHART, DANIEL KOLB, JOHN KOONTZ, HIRAM KEEFER, ABRAHAM KEMP, WM. KAUFFMAN, RICHARD M. LOVIER, HENRY LARE, SAMUEL B. LEWIS, GEORGE LARE, MOUNTJOY B. LUCKETT, FREDERICK LOEHR, JOHN M. LOWE, JACOB LITTLE, CYRUS MANTZ, THOMAS MARMAN, WM. MICHAEL, JOHN S. MARTIN, LEWIS MEDTART, JOHN McPHERSON, JOSEPH MERCHANT, THOMAS W. MORGAN, WM. V. MORGAN, JOHN McDONALD, LEVI MOBBERLY, PETER McKERNAN, CHARLES NAGLE, WM. OGDEN NILES, FREDERICK NUSZ, JOHN NIGH, Sr., PETER NICHOLS, PETER OTT, J. O'BOYLE, JONATHAN PLAIN, ELI POOL, BENJAMIN PERSEY, NICHOLAS H. PITTS, BENJAMIN PRICE, RICHARD POTTS, Dr. JAMES W. PRYOR, NEILSON POE, JOHN RICHARDS, PETER ROHR, JAMES RAYMOND, PHILIP ROHR, WM. J. ROSS, JOHN RAMSBURGH, PHILIP REICH, JOHN REICH, Dr. A. RITCHIE, ROBERT G. RUSSELL, CONRAD RITENMYER, LEWIS RAMSBURGH, JACOB SHELLMAN, DANIEL SPRINGER, WM. STEINER, JOHN STRAFFER, FREDERICK SHELLY, DAVID STEINER, WM. R. SANDERSON, JAMES STEINER, JOHN SCHREIN- ER, CHRISTIAN SEAMAN, WM. SMALLWOOD, WILLIAM SYKES, WILLIAM SCHLEY, JOHN SHOLL, CHARLES STINGER, GEORGE STINGER, FREDERICK STONER, Sen'r., CHRISTIAN STEINER, NOAH A. SHAFER, EZRA

SCHELL, HENRY SHOTTS, ABIJAH SHEPHERD, DENNIS SCHOLL, JOHN SPONSELLER, WM. R. THOMAS, BERNARD TEASE, GEORGE TRISLER, AQUILLA TULLY, PATRICK TORMEY, EDWARD TRAIL, MAHLON TALBOTT, Dr. JOHN TYLER, HENRY THOMAS, JOHN P. THOMPSON, EDWARD TURBUTT, WILLIAM WILCOXEN, CHARLES WILSON, VALENTINE WEAVER, GEORGE WILLS, THOMAS C. WORTHINGTON, J. B. WEBB, JAMES WHITEHILL, Dr. WM. WATERS, WM. H. WILLIAMS, JOHN WRIGHT, JACOB WEIST.

October 4, 1834 (CBAL)

1099. (M) On the 20th ult., by the Rev. D. F. Schaeffer, Mr JOHN REDDICK, to Miss DEBORAH LIGGINS, all of this co.
1100. (M) On Thursday the 18th ult., by the same, Mr FREDERICK FRENCHBAUGH, to Miss SUSAN BLASKEY, of this co.y
1101. (M) On Thursday the 25th ult., by the same, Mr JONATHAN FOX, to Miss MARGARET E. DOUR, all of this co.
1102. (M) On the same day, by the same, Mr JAMES E. CASSELL, to Miss MARY ANN HOFFMAN, all of this co.
1103. (M) On Sunday the 28th ult., by the same, Mr PHILIP MARKER, to Miss ELIZABETH BOCK, both from Germany.
1104. (M) On Sunday evening the 21st ult., by the Rev. Mr Wachter, Mr DANIEL DERR, to Miss CATHARINE DERTZBAUGH, all of this co.
1105. (M) On Tuesday evening last, by the Rev. Mr McGee, Mr THOMAS MAYNARD, to Miss ADRIANNA, daughter of the late Major Sabrett Sollers, both of the vicinity of Liberty-Town.
1106. (M) On Thursday evening the 25th ult., in Hagerstown, by the Rev. R. Drane, JOHN R. KEY, Esq., to Miss VIRGINIA, daughter of the late General Samuel Ringgold, all of Hagerstown.
1107. (D) On Saturday the 20th ult., Mr DANIEL FICKLE, of the neighborhood of Union Bridge, aged about 62 years.
1108. (D) On Saturday the 20th ult., Mr MICHAEL ZIMMERMAN, (merchant) of New Windsor.
1109. The Rev. WM. M. RICHARDS, will preach in the Baptist Meeting House next Lord's Day, at 3 o'clock, P.M.
1110. The Rev. JOSIAH VARDEN, will preach in the Baptist Church on Sunday next, at 10 o'clock, A.M.

October 11, 1834 (CBAL)

1111. (M) On Tuesday evening last, by the Rev. M. Wachter, Mr JACOB KEEFER, to Miss ELIZABETH STEIN, all of this co.
1112. (M) In George-Town, (D.C.) on Sunday evening the 21st ult., by the Rev. Mr Hanson, Mr JAMES DAVIS, to Miss SOPHIA SMITH, formerly of this city.
1113. (M) On the 1st inst., in York, PA., by the Rev. Charles Reighley, the Rev. E. HEINER, of Emmitsburg, to MARY E., only daughter of the late _____ Wolfe, Esq., of the former place.
1114. (D) On Thursday last, after a very painful illness, Mr CHARLES PETERS, in the the 41st year of his age. He leaves a wife and 4 children to larment his loss.
1115. (D) On Thursday the 25th of September last, ELIZA JANE, infant daughter of Thomas and Elizabeth Gapes, aged 9 months and 6 days.
1116. There are 377 person confinded in the Maryland Penitentiary, of whom 312 are males and 67 females.

October 18, 1834 (CBAL)

1117. (D) At the residence of Capt. Brashear of Frederick Co., on Wednesday the 1st of October, Mr DENNIS F. MAGRUDER, a resident of Baltimore, in the 49th year of his age. He had been for several months gradually wasting away by consumption, and sometimes during the summer he left for his residence in Baltimore, to enjoy the more salacious breezes of the country. But his disease so rapidly exhausted his strength, and impaircd his physical energies, that a return to Baltimore was very soon rendered impracticable. He was compelled to spend the remnant of his days where he had intended to remain but a few weeks. He was a man of honesty and integrity. He was unhappy because he was destitute of religion. Soon after his removal to this county, he was visited by a clergyman to whom he freely communicated his feeling, his views and his disease. Soon he was made to feel the efficacy of Divine Grace in his soul, and the love of God and Holy Ghost.
1118. (D) We are sorry to learn that Mr JOSEPH L. HARP, one of our most active and efficient police officers, died on Saturday in Philadelphia, from cholera. (New York Star)
1119. The pastor of the Lutheran Church will be absent tomorrow, the Rev. Dr. SCHAEFFER, from Philadelphia, will, by Divine permission conduct the service in the morning, in the German Language.

1120. The Rev. JOSEPH H. JONES, will preach in the Baptist Meeting House next Lord's Day (to-morrow) at 3 o'clock, P.M.

October 25, 1834 (CBAL)

1121. (D) In Baltimore, on Sunday morning last, the Right Rev. JAMES WHITEFIELD Archbishop of the Roman Catholics in Baltimore.

November 1, 1834 (CBAL)

1122. (M) On Thursday evening the 16th inst., by the Rev. D. F. Schaeffer, Mr DAVID M. HOFFMAN, to Miss MARGARET ANN REBBECCA, only daughter of James Castle.
1123. (M) On Thursday the 23rd inst., by the Rev. D. F. Schaeffer, Mr JAMES H. MURPHY, to Miss SARAH DAVIS, both of this city.
1124. (D) On Sunday the 26th ult., near Petersville, in the 28th year of his age, Mr ALEXIUS BOONE, highly respectable citizen of this co.
1125. (D) On Tuesday the 28th inst., after a illness of a few days, Mr STUART GAITHER, late merchant of this city. In the 44th year of his age
1126. (D) On the morning of Sunday the 19th, SALLY, only daughter of Thomas Duckett, Esq., of Annapolis City.
1127. WILLIAM ROBERTS, ROBERT ANNAN, FRANCIS BRENGLE, DANIEL DUVALL, are the official members of the Maryland Legislature for the House of Delegates.
1128. Messrs: JACOB and BENJAMIN HAYS, arrested a young man named BAILEY PATTERSON on Friday last. Mr P., was deputy Post Master in the town of Staunton, VA., of forging a bank draft for another person in the amount of $500.00.
1129. On Friday last, as Mr PHILIP POULTNEY, was coming from his farm on the York Road in his rig, while descending the hill, near Jenkins Tannery, his reins broke, and horse took flight. It threw Mr P., out against the fence with such force it broke his back. It is doubtful if he will ever recover. He was taken in to Mr Jenkins where he still remains. (Patriot)
1130. Meeting in behalf of the Bible cause was held in the German Reformed Church, on the evening of Sunday the 19th ult. Col. JAMES M. SHELMAN was called to the chair and Mr J. C. WHEAT chosen secretary. The meeting was addressed by the Rev. Mr EASTER, Rev. H. V. D. JOHNS,

Rev. C. REIGHLY and R. POTTS, Esq. On motion of Rev. Mr EASTER and seconded by Rev. H. V. D. JOHNS: That American Bible Society be sustained in its efforts to supply the world with the Bible. On motion by Rev. H. V. D. JOHNS and seconded by Rev. C. REIGHLY: Whilst we view the Bible as the common property of the human family, we deem it our duty, as far as we can, to render it universally accessible. Motion by R. POTTS, Esq., seconded by Dr. WM. BRADLEY TYLER: As the sense of this meeting, that the pledge of the Young Men's Bible Society meet our approbation, and we most cheerfully engage to sustain them in their efforts to raise 1 1/2 thereof for the District of Frederick. The meeting was adjourned with prayer by the Rev. H. V. D. JOHNS.

November 8, 1834 (CBAL)

1131. Meeting of the Young Men's Bible Society was held in the German Reformed Church on Monday evening October 27th 1834. The following gentlemen were elected Directors for the ensuing year: Episcopal Church: WILLIAM J. ROSS, NEILSON POE, J. C. WHEAT, T. BARROW. Presbyterian Church: JAMES M. SHELMAN, Dr. ALBERT RITCHIE, SAMUEL R. HOGG, DAVID B. DEVITT. Methodist Church: JAMES L. NORRIS, ASBURY H. HUNT, MEREDITH DAVIS, SAMUEL SMITH. Lutheran Church: VALERIUS EBERT, AUGUSTUS F. EBERT, J. L. HANSHEW, WM. D. HEIM. German Reformed Church: GEORGE MARKELL, J. REMSBURG, HENRY RHODES EDWARD TURBUTT. Baptist Church: ENOS B. REED, GEORGE ENGLISH. At a meeting of the aforesaid Directors; held on Thursday Nov. 6th 1834. The Board was organized by the election of the following gentlemen as officers for the ensuing year: President: JAMES M. SHELMAN, 1st Vice President: WM. J. ROSS, 2nd Vice President: ASBURY HUNT, Treasurer: Dr. ALBERT RITCHIE, Corresponding Sec'ry: AUGUSTUS F. EBERT, Recording Sec'ry: EDWARD TURBUTT, General Agent of the Society: Rev. DAVID F. SCHAEFFER.

1132. The Rev. J. P. KRAUTH, was inaugurated at Gettysburg, as President of the PA., College, on Thursday the 30th ult.

1133. (M) On Thursday evening the 30th inst., by the same, Mr HENRY BICKLE, to Miss ELIZABETH SCHUGAR, both of this city.

1134. (M) On the 29th inst., by the Rev. Henry Robinson, Maj. LEVI N. RICE, to Miss ANN R. THOMAS, eldest daughter of Maj. Jacob Thomas, both of this co.

1135. (M) On Tuesday evening the 28th inst., by the Rev. David F. Schaeffer, Mr STEPHEN KLINE, Jr., to Miss MARY ANN POOLE, both of this city.

1136. (D) On Tuesday evening last, GEORGE MORLIMER RIGNEY, youngest son of Mr John Rigney, of this place, at the age of 4 years, 1 month and 17 days.

November 15, 1834 (CBAL)

1137. (M) On Tuesday morning last, by the Rev. David F. Schaeffer, Mr JACOB RAMSBURG, of George-Town, D.C., to Miss ANN REBECCA, only daughter of John Ebert, Esq., of this city.

1138. (M) At Philadelphia, on Thursday evening the 6th inst., by the Rev. Dr. Delaney, ROBERT WALSH, Esq., editor of the National Gazette, to Miss ELIZABETH STOCKER.

1139. (M) Near the Glade, on Tuesday morning, by the Rev. John Wm. Hoffmeier, Mr JACOB DUDDERO, to Miss SUSAN ERAST.

1140. (M) On Thursday evening last, by the same, near Liberty, Mr WASHINGTON OWINGS, to Miss HANNAH, eldest daughter of Capt. George Reiner.

1141. (D) On Saturday morning last, after a long an painful illness, Mr GEORGE EVITT, in the 48th year of his age.

1142. (D) In Baltimore, on Sunday last, in the 65th year of his age, JOHN OGSTON, Esq., a highly respected and worthy citizen.

1143. (D) On Saturday evening last, of a paralytic affection, MARGARET E., only daughter of Dr. Wilson W. Kolb, aged 10 months and 1 day.

1144. (D) Of congestive fever on Sunday the 19th of October, in the 27th year of his age, HENRY A., only son of Mr Frederick Slager, of Middle-Town Valley.

1145. The Rev. JOSEPH H. JONES, will preach in the Baptist Meeting House, this evening, at candle light.

1146. The Rev. Mr OTIS A. SKINNER, an universalist preacher from Baltimore, will preach in the Court House on Tuesday evening next, the 18th inst., at 1/2 past 6 o'clock.

November 22, 1834 (CBAL)

1147. THOMAS C. PRINCE, declines being a candidate for the Mayoralty.

1148. The Hon. HENRY CLAY, passed through the city yesterday, on his way to Princeton, N. J., where his son is at college.

November 29, 1834 (CBAL)

1149. (M) On Tuesday evening, near the Glade, by the Rev. John W. Hoffmeier, Mr WILLIAM, eldest son of Mr George Barrick, to Miss LEAH MARY, youngest daughter of Mr Daniel Creager.
1150. (D) Departed this life on the morning of the 20th inst., at his residence in New Market, Dr. BELT BRASHIER, aged 70 years.
1151. (F) The barn of Mr JOHN GLISON, adjoining the town of Liberty in this co., was destroyed by fire on Tuesday night last, the loss of property is considerable.
1152. On the 18th inst., the Rev. J. JOHNS, of this city, was unanimously elected Rector of St. Andrew's Church, Philadelphia. We know that soon after the vacancy occurred in that church, he was earnestly urged to permit a call to be forward to him, but that he felt it his duty to repress the application; and we are authorised to say that he has now declined the formal call. (Balt. Amer.)
1153. The Railroad between Point of Rocks, and Harpers' Ferry will open on Monday next.
1154. The citizens of Frederick are requested to meet at JOHN DILL's Tavern, this evening, to take measures for immediate establishment of a Lyceum in Frederick.
1155. Meeting of the citizens of Frederick Co., was held at the Court House in Frederick, on Saturday evening last. When THOS. CARLTON, Esq., was appointed chairman and Col. JOHN McPHERSON, secretary. FRANCIS THOMAS, Esq., presented several resolutions which was adopted. One called for a committee of 25 persons, including the chairman of this meeting, be appointed by the chair to represent the people of this co., in said convention. The other one, called for a committee of 12 persons be appointed by the chairman to correspond with similar committees elsewhere on the subject, to deliberate on which the convention at Baltimore is to assemble on the 8th of December next, to deliberate on the expediency and best means of providing for the future prosecution of the Chesapeake and Ohio Canal. The following gentlemen were appointed: Hon. OUTERBRIDGE HORSEY, Col. JOHN THOMAS, RICHARD JOHNSON, of Wm., JOHN COST, Major JAS. SIMMONS, SOMERSET R. WATERS, RODERICK DORSEY, PLUMMER

IJAMS, ANTHONY KIMMEL, JOHN KINZER, ISSAC SCHRIVER, WASHINGTON VAN BIBBBER, JOHN McKALH, Dr. W. GWYNN, ISAAC BAUGHER, JOHN STEWART, MARTIN EICHELBERGER, WILLIAM TODD, JACOB POE, BROOKE BAKER, Dr. WILLIAM TYLER, JOHN H. McELFRESH, THOMAS CARLTON, GEO. BOWLUS, JOHN SIFFORD. For the Committee of Correspondence: Dr. WM. B. TYLER, Col. GEORGE M. EICHELBERGER, GEORGE W. ENT, FREDERICK A. SCHLEY, Dr. J. BALTZELL, WM. M. BEALL, WM. SCHLEY, CASPAR MANTZ, GEORGE BALTZELL, Dr. WM. M. B. WILSON, MOSES WORMAN, MICHAEL BYRNE.

1156. Candidates for the Mayoralty: JACOB FAUBEL, JOSHUA DILL, SAMUEL CARMACK, JOSEPH TALBOTT, MICHAEL BALTZELL, DANIEL KOLB, G. W. ENT.

December 6, 1834 (CBAL)

1157. (M) In Taney-Town, on Tuesday last, by the Rev. N. Zocchi, Mr SAMUEL ORENDORFF, (merchant,) to Miss MARY, daughter of Jacob Mathias, Esq., both of Westminster.

1158. (M) On Thursday last, Mr BEAL SELLMAN, to Miss ANN CASSELL, daughter of Mr George Cassell, of Pipe Creek.

1159. (M) In Emmitsburg, on Thursday last, by the Rev. Mr Butler, Mr ANDREW MARTIN, of Baltimore, to Miss ELIZA J., third daughter of Mr Joseph Beahey, of Emmitsburg.

1160. (D) On Friday last, Mrs CATHERINE MYERHEIFFER, in the 77th year of her age.

1161. A meeting was held at the National Hotel, on Saturday evening last, for the purpose of taking measures to establish a Lyceum. Meeting was organized by calling the Rev. D. F. Schaeffer, to the chair and appointing GEO. F. STONE, secretary. A motion by RICHARD POTTS, Esq., that 14 gentlemen be appointed by the chair, to "Act to Incorporate the Mechanics' Institute and Frederick Lyceum," as commissioners to open subscription books for stock, and to solicit subscriptions in several Wards. The following gentlemen were then appointed: Ward #1: AUGUSTUS F. EBERT, JACOB FAUBEL. Ward #2: Dr. R. E. DORSEY, CYRUS MANTZ. Ward #3: GEO. W. ENT, VALENTINE BIRELY. Ward #4: GEO. I. FISHER, JAMES M. SHELMAN. Ward #5: DAVID BOYD, GEORGE WEBSTER. Ward #6: JOHN HANSHEW, L. P. W. BALCH. Ward #7: M. E. BARTGIS, WM. R. THOMAS.

December 13, 1834 (CBAL)

1162. (M) In Baltimore on Monday evening last, by the Rev. Mr Musgrave, ENOCH M. MAYO, of this city, to ELIZABETH MARTIN, of the former place.

1163. (M) On Tuesday evening the 2nd inst., by the Rev. Mr Ellis, Mr JOHN A. SIMMONS, to Miss ROSANNA C., second daughter of Mr John Fessler, of this city.

1164. (M) On Thursday evening the 4th inst., by the Rev. Mr McGee, Mr JOHN SNYDER, to Miss REBECCA SPRINGER, both of this city.

1165. (M) On Tuesday the 2nd of December, by the Rev. Mr Monroe, Mr JOHN KINZER Jun'r., of this co., to Miss ANN GORE, of Baltimore Co.

1166. (D) On the 11th inst., WILLIAM BRIEN, youngest son of the late John Brien Esq.

1167. (D) On Saturday evening last near this city, Mrs BARBARA KEEFER, in the 81st year of her age.

1168. (D) On the 24th of November, Mr SEBASTIAN GRAFF, in the 65th year of his age. He was a native of PA., and settled in the neighbourhood of this town, about 40 years since on a farm which he had purchased.

1169. The convention on Internal Improvements assembled at the Masonic Hall, in Baltimore on Monday last, and elected GEO. C. WASHINGTON, Esq., President, ELISHA WHITTLESEY, of Ohio, ELIJAH BOYD, of VA., WM. BRADLEY, of D.C., Vice Presidents and J. P. KENNEDY and JOSEPH SHRIVER, Secretaries. A committee was appointed to determine what measurers should be considered, which reported resolutions to appoint a committee to memorialize Congress and the Legislatures of MD., VA., and PA., on the behalf of the Chesapeake and Ohio Canal--also committee to address the Councils and citizens of Baltimore on the same subject, to ascertain the probable cost and time necessary to complete the canal to its Eastern and Western sections, respectively, to prepare a report of the probable amount of revenue from the same, to urge the U. S. to make a survey of the Potomac and its tributary streams, &c. The committee appointed to solicit the states of MD., VA., and PA., to pledge their credit for the payment of the interest on the additional stock, which may be subscribed in aid of the canal, is composed of Messrs: HEZEKIAH NILES, J. McCULLOCH, J. P. KENNEDY, D. SHRIVER, J. P. INGLE, J. McKNIGHT and A. HUNTER. Messrs: R. S. COXE, E. BOYD, H. M. WATTS, WM. M. STEWART, A.

BRUCE, S. ETTING and R. JOHNSON, of W., composed the committee to memorialize, Congress for futher aid.

December 20, 1834 (CBAL)

1170. (D) In Baltimore on the morning of the 11th inst., at the residence of her daughter, Mrs Shaw, Mrs ANNA MARIA MORRIS, late of Frederick.
1171. (D) At the Antietam Iron Works, on Thursday morning the 11th inst., after a short illness, Mr WM. COLEMAN BRIEN, youngest son of the late John Brien, Esq., in the 22nd year of his age.
1172. (D) On Monday morning last, after a severe illness, Mr JACOB BOYER, one of the oldest inhabitants of this city, and who for the last 30 years, was crier in the Court of Frederick Co., in the 80th year of his age.
1173. (D) On Thursday the 11th of December, at Washington City, Mrs ELIZABETH RAYCLIFF, in the 56th year of her age. On Saturday the 13th, she was followed to her place of interment, at her former residence near New Market, Frederick Co., MD.
1174. (D) On Wednesday morning the 10th inst., after a long an painful illness, Mr LEWIS WELTZHEIMER, an old and highly respectable citizen of Frederick, in the 69th year of his age.
1175. (M) In Baltimore on Thursday morning last, by the Rev. Jas. G. Hamner, JOHN P. THOMSON, Esq., of this city, to Miss MARY HAMNER, of the former place.
1176. (M) On Sunday evening last, by the Rev. D. F. Schaeffer, Mr ELI POOLE, to Miss ELIZABETH BIGGS, all of this city.
1177. (M) On Tuesday morning the 18th of November, 2 hours before daybreak, by the Rev. Thos. C. Brexton, JUDGE-MATICAL WRIGHT, of Westmoreland Co., VA., near Middleton Cross Roads, to Miss LUCY PURSLE, of Richmond Co., near Whearleburn. The happy bridegroom was 73 years old, and the lady 53.
1178. The trial of JOSEPH O'CONNER, for the murder of MARY ANN GOWER. Counsel for the State was Mr RAYMOND, Attorney General, and Mr F. A. SCHLEY. For the prisioner, Messre: WM. SCHLEY, DIXON and LYNCH. The Juniors: JAS. C. ATLEE, foreman, EDWARD T. HEBB, SAMUEL NAILL, ANDREW HORNER, JACOB HOFFMAN, JOHN AGNEW, ELISHA HOWARD, WM. WILCOXEN, RICHARD SIMPSON. Talis-men: R. CROMWELL, TOBIAS COVER, W. B. PITTINGER. He was found guilty of murder in the

second degree, sentenced to 18 years imprisonment, and 18 months of it to be spent in solitary confinement.

December 27, 1834 (CBAL)

1179. (M) On Sunday last, by the Rev. D. F. Schaeffer, Mr FREDERICK LAMBRECHT, to Miss ANNA MARIA MILLER, both of this city.
1180. (M) On Monday last, by the same, Mr EZRA DADISMAN, to Miss CATHARINE KELLY, both of this city.
1181. (M) On Thursday the 18th inst., by the same, Mr JOHN LYNTAN, to Miss REBECCA ADKINS, both of this city.
1182. (M) Near Freedom, Baltimore Co., on Thursday evening the 18th inst., by the Rev. Mr Bean, GEORGE HOSSELBOCK, Esq., of Frederick Co., to Miss SARAH ANN HARDING, of the former place.
1183. (D) On Saturday morning last, Mr EDWARD A. CARLTON, eldest son of Thomas Carlton, Esq., his remains were accompanied to the grave on Monday by two military companies of this city, (one of which he was the 2nd officer.) At a meeting of the Frederick Volunteers held in the Court House, on Saturday evening the 20th inst., a resolution and preamble were offered by Mr Lewis Stone, and unanimously adopted. Sect. George Hardt.
1184. (D) Departed this life on the 8th inst., in the 70th year of her age, Mrs ELIZABETH STEINER, relict of Mr Jacob Steiner, and a native of Frederick.
1185. Honorary degree of Dr., of Medicine, was conferred by the Washington Medical College of Baltimore, on JOHN W. DORSEY, of Liberty-Town, Frederick Co. Surgeon in the Navy of the United States during the Tripolitan War, under Commodore Edward Preble.

1835

January 3, 1835 (CBAL)

1186. (M) On Thursday last, by the Rev. David F. Schaeffer, Mr JONATHAN KLINE, to Miss ANN CATHARINE TROUTMAN, all of Middletown Valley.
1187. (M) In Baltimore on Monday last, by the Rev. J. G. Hamner, the Rev. T. P. C. SHELLMAN, of Louisville, GA., to Miss HENRIETT A STEINER, of this city.

1188. (M) On Wednesday morning last, by the Rev. John L. Pitts, Mr JOHN EDWARD BROMWELL, of Baltimore, to Miss ELIZABETH HALL, daughter of Thomas C. Shipley, Esq., of this co.

1189. (D) After a few hours illness, at Weston, Lewis Co., VA., Mrs CATHARINE CARMACK, consort of Mr Evan Carmack, formerly of this city, until the 18th inst., when she ended her pilgrimage in triumph.

1190. The Rev. Mr F. P. PHELPS will preach in the Presbyterian Church, to-morrow morning at 10 o'clock.

1191. At a meeting of citizens on the 1st inst., in pursuant of the notice of the Mayor, to consider and devise measurers for the relief of the poor. A committee of two from each Ward be appointed to solicit subscriptions and donations to relieve the poor during the inclement season, and that the committee be requested to investigate the condition of poor families in their respective Wards, and to report to the distributing committee. A distributing committee of seven be appointed, for the prudence appropriation of the collections of charity, such appropriation be particularly used for the relief of the sick, and the supply of wood to the destitute. The following gentlemen were appointed to represent their respective wards. Ward #1. ANDREW HEIM, HENRY NIXDORF. Ward #2. GEO. M. CONRADT, EDW'D TURBUTT. Ward #3. D. B. DEVITT, DANIEL KOLB. Ward #4. VALENTINE J. BRUNNER, JAMES M. SHELMAN. Ward #5. GEORGE WEBSTER, DAVID BOYD. Ward #6. MICHAEL BALTZELL, ABRAHAM KEMP. Ward #7. J. W. MILLER, EZRA DOLL. Distributing Committee: The Mayor, Rev. H. V. D. JOHNS, Rev. THOMAS McGEE, PATRICK TORMEY, LEWIS MEDTART, Rev. D. F. SCHAEFFER, JOHN KUNKLE. THOMAS CARLTON, Mayor. LEWIS MEDTART, Secretary.

1192. JOSHUA DILL, has declined to be a candidate for Mayor.

January 10, 1835 (CBAL)

1193. (M) In New Philadelphia, Ohio, on Wednesday the 17th inst., by the Rev. James B. Morrow, the Rev. EMANUEL GREENWALD, Pastor of the Evangelical Lutheran Church in that town, to Miss LIVINIA, daughter of Peter Williams, Esq.

1194. (M) On Wednesday evening, the 30th ult., by the Rev. D. F. Schaeffer, Mr DANIEL ELDRED, to Miss MARY ELIZABETH LAMB, both of this co.

1195. The Rev. Mr JONES, will preach in the Baptist Meeting House to-morrow at 3 o'clock, P.M.
1196. MATHIAS E. BARTGIS & JOHN McDONALD, JOSHUA DILL, as candidates for Alderman at the next election for corporation officers. Other candidates for the above positions are: Dr. ALBERT RITCHIE, ABRAHAM KEMP, DAVID BOYD, GIDEON BANTZ, T. W. MORGAN, WM. SMALL, (Brewer,) and GEORGE HART.
1197. Mr JOHN TITLOW, slaughtered this day 4 hogs, 18 months old, the weight of which was as follows: 469 1/2, 423, 426,425 /4, the average length from nose to the root of the tail was 6 ft., and their girth 3 ft., 6 inches.
1198. The distributing committee for the poor, met at 10 o'clock, A.M. Present: THOMAS CARLTON, Esq., Rev. H. V. D. JOHNS, Rev. D. F. SCHAEFFER, PATRICK TORMEY and LEWIS MEDTART. The committee was organized by appointing THOMAS CARLTON, Esq., chairman and LEWIS MEDTART, secretary, the Rev. Mr McGEE was absent. Mr JOHN KUNKLE, declined serving, whereupon; GIDEON BANTZ, was elected to fill the vacancy. Mr LEWIS MEDTART was appointed treasurer to receive the collection and distribute the charity to the poor upon the orders of anyone of the committee. The treasurer acknowledges the receipt of the following articles: Mr DAVIS RICHARDSON, Mr JACOB KELLER, JOSEPH McCLEARY, each gave 1 load of oak wood. From Mrs CUNNINGHAM, 3 barrels of corn and some pork.

January 17, 1835 (CBAL)

1199. (D) In Baltimore, on Tuesday morning, Dr. WILLIAM DONALDSON, a distinguished physician of that city.
1200. (D) On Friday night the 9th inst., in this city, at the house of Mr Ramsey, in Carroll Street, Mr WILLIAM RODES, late of Butler Co., PA., in the 23rd year of his age, after a protracted illnesss of about 3 months.
1201. (D) Departed this life on Sunday last, in this city, Dr. JOHN M. THOMAS, of the United States Army, late of Washington. He leaves a wife and several fatherless children.
1202. Candidates for the position of Alderman: Dr. ALBERT RITCHIE, ABRAHAM KEMP DAVID BOYD, GIDEON BANTZ, T. W. MORGAN, WM. SMALL, (Brewer,) and GEORGE HARDT. For the Common Council from Ward #7. PERRY RICE. Ward #6. FREDERICK NUSZ. Ward #5. JOHN

FESSLER. Also for Alderman: JOSHUA DILL, JACOB BRUNNER, M. E. BARTGIS, JOHN McDONALD.
1203. A 1/2 load of hickory wood was received for the poor from the following persons: Mr H. ZIMMERMAN, Dr. W. S. McPHERSON and ABRAHAM KEMP.
1204. Candidates for the position of Mayor: JACOB FAUBEL, JOSEPH TULBOTT, JAMES SHELMAN, MICHAEL BALTZELL and DANIEL KOLB.

January 24, 1835 (CBAL)

1205. (D) At Raleigh, N.C., on the 12th of December inst., J. U. ARMOR, aged 50 years. Mr A., for many years a residence of Frederick.
1206. (D) In the city of Washington, on Monday the 12th inst., of pulmonary disease, Mrs SARAH M. CONVERSE, wife of Freeman Converse, Esq., formerly of this city, and daughter of Mr Alexander McDonald, of the former place.
1207. The Post office at the Point of Rocks, has been abolished by the the Post-Master General.
1208. The Rev. Mr VARDEN will preach in the English Presbyterian Church on Tuesday evening next.
1209. ABRAHAM KEMP, THOMAS W. MORGAN, PERRY RICE, has declined to be a candidate in the up-coming election.

January 31, 1835 (CBAL)

1210. (D) Departed this life at his residence on Sam's Creek, in this co., on Tuesday morning the 6th inst., ALEXANDER WARFIELD, Esq., in the 71st year of his age, after a protracted and distressing illness. As a professor of the religion of Christ, he honored his profession by a holy and consistent life. For nearly half a century he had been a member of the Methodist Episcopal Church; and the history of that church in this co., is closely connected with his own. He was one of the early hearers of Mr Strawbridge, (perhaps the first Methodist preacher who came to America, about the year 1765, settled in the neighborhood of Pipe Creek, about 2 miles from the residence of Mr Warfield:) From whose ministry, and the pious exhortation of his revered mother, he was introduced to give his heart to God, and become a subject of regenerating grace. He had represented this county in the Legislature of Maryland, and filled several other important offices. In his relations as husband, father, master, and neighbor, he sustained the same pure, upright and honorable character. His children (who loved him with the tenderest affection) are so many strong proofs of his excellent paternal character. Some of them have already left the shores of mortality-but they died strong in faith. All who remain are members of the church of which he was an ornament. His humanity as a master maybe inferred from the unaffected sorrow which his old servant manifested at his decease whose universal exclamation was "Our best friend is gone!" On Thursday the 8th inst., his corpse was attended to the grave by a large consourse of his friends. A deeply interesting funeral sermon was preached on the occasion by the Rev. James Reiley, from 2nd Timothy, 4th chap., 6th, 7th, 8th, verses, and some very pertinent remarks made by the Rev. B. Nelson, "He is gone-but he has gone to live forever may we follow him as he followed Christ."

1211. (D) On Friday night of the 23rd inst., Mrs MARY F., wife of Worthington Johnson, Esq., of this city. In apparent good health, visiting her connections on the previous Saturday, attending with deep interest in the House of God. On Sunday, to the comforting assurance of the last text, permitted to the sound of her ears, that "the gift of God is eternal life through Jesus Christ our Lord." She was thence summond through 5 days of severe suffering to the place prepared for her, in her Father's House. The mother of 5 tender children, too young to be conscious of bereavement.

1212. (D) At his residence in Union-Town, in this co., on Wednesday morning last, of an affection of the liver, Major ALEXANDER McIIHENNY, in the 56th year of his age. He served in the Army of the United States with credit and usefulness, in the late war. Since it termination he has resided in this co., and served in the Legislature, for many years past, he acted as a Justice of the Peace.

1213. (D) On Sunday evening the 25th inst., after a painful illness of about 4 weeks, Mr WILLIAM KOLB, Sen'r., in the 60th year of his age. A native of Frederick, he met death with firness and resignation.

1214. (D) On Monday last, Mr ELISHA NELSON, in the 51st year of his age--an old and highly respectable citizen of this co.

1215. JAMES M. COALE, Esq., is a candidate to represent the 6th District in the next Congress of the United States. (Taney-Town)

1216. The Treasurer of the Poor Fund acknowledges the receipt of a load of oak wood from Mr John T. Schley.

1217. Appointment by the Executive for Frederick County Justices of the Peace: REZIN E. TILLARD, EBENEZER POMEROY.
1218. Candidates for the Mayoralty: JACOB FAUBEL, JOSEPH TALBOTT, JAMES M. SHELLMAN, MICHAEL BALTZELL, DANIEL KOLB. Candidates for Alderman: DAVID BOYD, M. E. BARTGIS, GIDEON BANTZ, JACOB BRUNNER, LEWIS BIRELY, EZRA BENTZ, JOSHUA DILL, GEO. W. ENT, WILLIAM ELY, GEORGE HARDT, ANDREW HEIM, JOHN HANE, HENRY KEHLER, Sr., JACOB KELLER, JOHN McDONALD, THOMAS C. PRINCE, Dr. ALBERT RITCHIE, SOLOMON STICKLE, WILLIAM SMALL, (brewer) GEO. WISSINGER. Candidates for the Common Council: Ward #1. DAVID FAUBEL, JOHN JONES, PETER MANTZ. Ward #2. GEO. M. CONRADT, JACOB LITTLE. Ward #3. DAVID B. DEVITT. Ward #4. URIAH S. BANTZ. Ward #5. JOHN FESSLER, HIRAM KEEFER, PATRICK TORMEY, JAMES WHITEHILL. Ward #6. FREDERICK NUSZ, GEORGE HOSKINS. Ward #7. JOHN W. MILLER, WINCHESTER CLINGAN.
1219. FREDERICK LAMBER, declines being a candidate for Alderman.
1220. G. B. SHOPE, declines being a candidate for the Common Council for the 6th Ward. RICHARD J. WEBB, declines being a candidate for the Common Council from Ward #7.

February 7, 1835 (CBAL)
1221. (M) In Tiffin, Ohio, on the 20th ult., by the Rev. Adam Minear, the Rev. JOHN L. SANDERS, to Miss LYDIA E. SPAYTH.
1222. (M) In Lynn, Massachussetts, on the 9th of December, Mr AMOS RHODES, to Miss LYDIA, daughter of Winthrop Newhall, Esq.
1223. (M) On Thursday evening, 5th Feb., by the Rev. L. H. Johns, Mr BARTHOLOMEW BOTELER, to Miss MARY ANN CARROLL, all of Pleasant Valley.
1224. (M) At Ellicott's Mills on Tuesday last, by the Rev. James Munroe, Mr JAMES SUNDERLAND, to Miss ANN F. HUGHES, all of Harford Co.
1225. (D) On Monday night, January 12th, about 11 o'clock, at Jefferson, HENRY W., son of William S., and Anne Rebecca W. Johnson, aged 7 months and 11 days.
1226. An agent for the sale of the Rev. C. F. CRUSE's translation of the Ecclesiastical History of Bishop Eusebme, is now in

the city for the purpose of soliciting subscribers to the work.

1227. (D) Melancholy accident - Very sudden death and under the most awful circumstances. On Tuesday morning last, Mr THOMAS HAINES of Little Pipe Creek, went out into the woods in the company with another individual to cut down some timber, for the purpose of building a barn; and whilst engaged in felling a large tree, one of the braches was broken off, and falling, struck Mr Haines across the forehead and fractured the skull so badly that he died in a few minutes after receiving the blow. On Wednesday last, his remains were interred.

February 14, 1835 (CBAL)

1228. On Saturday evening the 7th of February inst., the citizens of Frederick and its vicinity, friendly to the banking system upon a sound and stable foundation, assembled at the City Hotel, at 7 o'clock. Capt. GEORGE W. ENT, and Dr. WM. S. McPHERSON, were called to the chair, and EDWARD A. LYNCH, Esq., appointed Secretary. Mr McPherson explained the purpose of the meeting; which was a plan of a bank founded upon Real Estate as a sound practical and beautiful scheme. Several resolutions were presented and passed, one resolution called for the appointment of a 6 man committee, to present these resolutions to the Senators and Delegates from this county in Annapolis. The committee appointed by the chair, including the two chairmen were, Messrs: OUTERBRIDGE HORSEY, WM S. McPHERSON, GEORGE W. ENT, EDWARD A. LYNCH, THOMAS HAMMOND, JAMES WHITEHILL, RODERICK DORSEY and WILLIAM SHAW.

February 21, 1835 (CBAL)

1229. (M) On Thursday evening last, by the Rev. David F. Schaeffer, Mr WILLIAM ODEN, to Miss ELIZABETH PICKINS, all of this co.

1230. (M) In Hagerstown, on Tuesday the 10th inst., by the Rev. Mr Wynkoop, Mr GEORGE J. FISCHER, to Miss ISABELLA JOHNSTON, daughter of Arthur Johnston, Esq., of the former place.

1231. (D) Near this city, on Sunday night the 8th inst., after a short illness, Mrs ANNA MARIA THOMAS, consort of Mr George Thomas of H., in the 32nd year of her age. She leaves a husband and 5 children, one of which is quite

young. On Tuesday afternoon, her remains were interred in the family cemetery on the farm.
1232. (D) On the 13th inst., near Frederick, of a lingering disease, Mr OTHO FOUT, in the 31st year of his age.
1233. (D) On Thursday the 12th inst., after a lingering illness, Mrs MARY ANN CRAILEY, in the 39th year of her age.
1234. (D) On Friday evening, the 13th inst., in this city, of a lingering pulmonary disease, WILLIAM STEINER, Esq., in the 41st year of his age. He was for the last 15 years the Chief Clerk in the office of the Register of Wills of this co. No one could be more punctual, obliging or assiduous in the discharge of the duties which this station devolved upon him.
1235. A large an respectable meeting of the citizens of Woodsborough District, was held at the Tavern of Mrs YANTIS, in Woodsborough, for the purpose of considering the proposed project of a Real Estate Bank. Capt. JOSEPH WOOD, was called to the chair and Mr JOSHUA DOUB, appointed secretary.

February 28, 1835 (CBAL)

1236. The Senate on Monday last, confirmed the nomination of Capt. NICHOLAS SNIDER, of this city, as Marshal of the District of MD.-notwithstanding we utterly despise the barbarous policy which caused the President to dismiss the late incumbent, we take pleasure in saying that the successor of Mr THOS. FINLEY is a worthy citizen who will prove a valuable officer.
1237. Dr. JOHN O. WHARTON, of Washington Co., and FRANCIS THOMAS and DAVID SCHLEY, Esqrs., of Frederick are nominated in the Citizen of yesterday, as candidates to represent this district in the next Congress.
1238. Corporation election - The election of Mayor, Alderman and Common Council of this city took place on Monday last. It resulted in the choice of Mr DANIEL KOLB as Mayor. Messrs: SMALL, KELLER, BENTZ, BANTZ and KELLY as Alderman. Messrs: JONES, LITTLE, DEVITT, ENGLEBRECHT, KEEFER, HOSKINS and MILLER, as members of the Common Council. The following is a result of the vote for Mayor and Alderman: Mayor: KOLB - 222, FAUBEL - 177, BALTZELL - 217, Scattering - 33. For Alderman: SMALL - 236, BENTZ - 186, KELLER - 200, BANTZ - 178, KELLY - 174, WISSINGER - 170, ELY - 165, HANE - 149, PRINCE - 149, RITCHIE - 130, ENT - 128, DILL - 127,

BARTGIS - 126, BOYD - 108, STICKLE - 95, HEIM - 89, BIRELY - 86, CONRADT - 82, BRUNNER - 75, McDONALD - 62.

1239. WM. OGDEN NILES, Esq., of Frederick City, has been appointed Aid to the Governor, with the rank of Colonel.
1240. (M) In Washington Co., on the 10th inst., by the Rev. John Dorcas, Mr JOHN WESLEY REED, to Miss EVILINE CONNER, of Frederick Co., MD.
1241. (M) On the 22nd inst., by the same, Rev. JOHN HANEY, of Washington Co., to Miss JANE REBECCA RAMSBERG, of Frederick Co., MD.
1242. (M) On Tuesday evening last, by the Rev. D. F. Schaeffer, Mr WILLIAM HEISELY RIGNEY, to Miss MARY ANN HENDERSON, both of this city.
1243. (D) Yesterday morning at 2 o'clock, Miss RACHEL REBECCA, third daughter of the late Capt. Henry Steiner, in the 6th year of her age.
1244. (D) Departed this life, yesterday, at 12 o'clock, at the house of the Rev. D. F. Schaeffer, Mrs ROSANA SCHAEFFER, consort of Dr. F. D. Schaeffer, in the 71st year of her age. The friends of the family are particularly invited to attend her funeral, to-morrow, at 3 o'clock, P.M.

1840

November 14, 1840 (LC)

1245. (M) Near Lewistown, on the 31st inst., by the Rev. William F. Colliflower Dr. TIDEMAN HULL, formerly of the Dutchess Co., New York., to Miss ELIZA, only daughter of John W. Derr, Esq., of Frederick Co.
1246. (D) At Washington, Gurnsey Co., Ohio, on Monday the 2nd inst., JOSEPH EVITT, aged 1 year, 11 months and 4 days, and on Friday the 6th inst., ANN CECELIA NICHOLS, aged 10 years, 5 months and 15 days, both of scarlet fever.

1832

THE WEEKLY TIMES

May 10, 1832 (MHS)

1247. (M) On the 1st inst., by the Rev. John H. Smaltz, Mr DAVID FAUBEL, to Miss MARGARET DEGRANGE, both of this city.

May 17, 1832 (MHS)

1248. (M) On Thursday last, by the Rev. D. F. Schaeffer, Mr DANIEL RAMSBURG, to Miss MARIA HYATT, all of this co.

July 12, 1832 (MHS)

1249. At a meeting of a number of gentlemen called to witness the efforts of Mr MULKEY's, new method of teaching children to read. Messrs: STUART GAITHER, DAVID BOYD, WM. SMALL, F. CONVERSE, N. VERNON and SAMUEL MARKELL were appointed a committee to have a conference with Mr M., and obtain a more perfect knowledge of his method of imparting instruction, and to report on the subject. The report they gave which highly approved it and recommended it to the consideration of the citizens of Frederick.

July 26, 1832 (MHS)

1250. On Monday last upon a bill of complaint of VALENTINE BIRELY, of this city, an injunction was issued by the Hon. THOMAS BUCHANAN, against the corporate authorities of Frederick, their servants, labourers &c, enjoining and prohibiting them from cutting down, and grading All Saints Street, for the purpose of introducing the Railroad into the streets of this city.

August 9, 1832 (MHS)

1251. (M) On Wednesday the 25th ult., at Middletown, by the Rev. J. C. Bucher, Mr JACOB BYERS, to Miss CATHARINE ERNST, both of Shepherdstown, VA.

1252. (M) At Baltimore by the Rev. Mr Johns, Colonel THOMAS HAMMOND GIST, of Baltimore Co., to Miss JULIA ANN MACUBBIN, daughter of Mr Jno. L. Hammond of that city.

1253. (M) At the Associate Reformed Church, by the Rev. John M. Duncan, the Hon. RICHARD THOMAS, Speaker of the House of Delegates of Maryland to Miss JANE ARMSTRONG, youngest daughter of the late James Armstrong, Esq.
1254. (M) On Sunday evening last, by the Rev. Michael Wachter, Mr JOHN EYLER, of Peter, to Miss CATHARINE STRINE, both of this co.
1255. (D) On Tuesday night 25th ult., at the Point of Rocks, OTHO BEATTY, of Cumberland Allegany Co.
1256. (D) In this city, on Monday the 6th inst., MARIA A. JOHNSON, wife of William Johnson, and daughter of the late William H. Dorsey, of Montgomery Co., in the 39th year of her age. She died from a protracted illness of several months, and on the same day, ELIZA, her infant daughter, aged 4 1/2 months.

August 16, 1832 (MHS)

1257. (D) Departed this life, in Emmitsburgh, on Thursday evening the 26th ult., after a painful illness of 9 days, in the 50th year of her age, Mrs CATHARINE HARRITT, wife of Major John Harritt, besides her husband she leaves a family of 6 children.
1258. (D) On the 7th inst., in the 77th year of her age, Mrs ROSANNAH BARRICK, wife of Mr Jacob Barrick, one of the oldest an respectable inhabitant of this co.
1259. (D) In Jefferson, at the residence of her father, Patrick McGill, Esqr., Senr., on Tuesday the 31st ult., after a severe and lingering illness of more then 7 weeks, Mrs ELEANOR, consort of Nelson Luckett, Esqr.

August 23, 1832 (MHS)

1260. On Thursday evening last, in the City Hall by Delegates appointed from each Ward, which met for the purpose of taking into consideration the appointing of a Board of Health. Thus 3 persons from each Ward were appointed to constitute a Board of Health. Ward #1. HENRY NIXDORFF, PETER HALLER and JACOB FAUBLE. Ward #2. NICHOLAS TURBUTT, JOHN RIGNEY and G. M. CONRADT. Ward #3. MICHAEL BUCKEY, CASPER QUYNN and GEORGE SALMON. Ward #4. NEILSON POE, LEWIS MEDTART and HENRY M. JAMISON. Ward #5. GEORGE WEBSTER, DAVIS RICHARDSON and EDWARD TRAIL. Ward #6. L. P. BALCH, GEORGE W. SHARP and JOHN

TITLOW. Ward #7. EZRA DOLL, JOHN L. HARDING and JACOB KNOUFF.

September 6, 1832 (MHS)

1261. (M) At Hagerstown, Mr JOHN BLAIR, to Miss MARY ANN HALLEY, of Frederick.
1262. (D) At Sulphur Springs, near Westminster, VA., on the 20th ult., DAVID HOLMES, late Governor of MS., and U. S. Senator from that state.
1263. (D) At the residence of his father in this co., Mr JOHN C. GROFF, of Ohio, in the 35th year of his age.

September 13, 1832 (MHS)

1264. (D) Sudden death of JACOB STEINER, Esq., one of the Justices of the Orphan's Court. On Monday morning he attended as usual his duties of his station-was attacked with cholera early in the evening and by 3 o'clock, on Tuesday morning was a corpse. On opening of the Court yesterday, his deceased was announced by Colonel Eichelberger, the Register of Wells.

September 20, 1832 (MHS)

1265. Report of he Board of Health of Frederick. Tuesday 12 o'clock, September 18, 1832. Remaining from the last report, 4 cases; since which there have occurred 19 cases, making an aggregated of 23 cases, of which 11 have died, 9 recovered, and 3 remaining. Of the 11 decease, 8 were citizens, 6 whites and 2 colored and 3 foreigners.
1266. (M) On Tuesday morning the 11th inst., by the Rev. Mr Duncan, Mr JOHN H. KAUFFMAN, of Frederick, MD., to Miss ELIZABETH JOHNSON, only daughter of the late Mathias Johnson, of Baltimore.
1267. (D) On Monday week last, after a short but severe illness, ELIE WILLIAMS STULL, in the 11th year of his age, second son of O. H. W. Stull, Esq., of Hagers-Town.

September 27, 1832 (MHS)

1268. Meeting of the Board of Health of Frederick, Tuesday 25th. 21 deaths have occurred in the city, the last week, from Tuesday 18th to this date. Of the 21 deaths, there were 15 citizens, 6 whites and 9 colored-and 6 foreigners.
1269. (D) Near Harpers-Ferry, VA., on the 2nd inst., in the 68th year of his age, Mr JOHN HINKLE, for many years a respectable residence of the vicinity of Frederick.

October 4, 1832 (MHS)
1270. Report of the Board of Health of Frederick,Tuesday October 2, 1832. 17 deaths by cholera have occurred since last week, from Tuesday September 25th, to this date - of which 13 were citizens - 10 whites, 3 colored, and 4 foreigners, total 17. LEWIS MEDTART, Secretary.
1271. Election returns for Frederick County. National Republicans: JOHNSON - 3472, OWINGS - 3368, SHEPHERD - 3361, HAMMOND - 3371. Jackson Party: SCHLEY - 3375, RAMSBURG - 3337, UNKEFER - 3331, PALMER - 3289.

October 11, 1832 (MHS)
1272. Report of the Board of Health of Frederick, Tuesday October 9th, 1832, - 12 o'clock. 5 deaths by cholera have occurred the last week, from Tuesday Oct. 2nd., to this date - 3 citizens - 2 foreigners. Since last Friday not a death has occurred by cholera; the Board of Health, therefore, deem a futher report unnecessary, as the state of the health, of the town is as good as it generally is at this season of the year.

October 25, 1832 (MHS)
1273. (M) On Tuesday last, by the Rev. D. F. Schaeffer, Mr WALTER C. HAMMOND, to Miss MARY SHIPLEY, all of this co.

November 1, 1832 (MHS)
1274. (M) On Sunday last, by the Rev. D. F. Schaeffer, Mr CASPAR ZECHER, to Miss MARGARETTA A. FINK, both lately from Europe.

November 8, 1832 (MHS)
1275. (M) At Canondaigua, Oct. 24th, by the Rev. Mr Eddy, ASHER B. BOTES, Esq., Counselor at Law, Detroit M. T., to Miss LUCILIA, daughter of Thomas Beall, Esq., of the former place.
1276. There has been a new office established at Johnsville, Frederick Co., MD., formerly called Frog Town, under the direction of BASIL ROOT, Esq., as Post-Master.

November 15, 1832 (MHS)
1277. The Rev. JOSEPH JONES, will preach in the Baptist Meeting House, on Sunday afternoon at 3 o'clock.

November 22, 1832 (MHS)

1278. Meeting of the Hickory Club #1., for Frederick County convened at the house of WM. KOLB, on Saturday evening the 17th inst. Officers were chosen by ballot in the following order. Presidents - Dr. WILLIAM TYLER, WILLIAM M. BEALL, Esq., and Capt. GEORGE W. ENT. Vice Presidents - JOHN RIGNEY, Esq., Capt. WILLIAM SMALL, THOMAS CARLTON, Esq., Maj. N. HOLTZ, and CHRISTIAN GETZENDANNER. Record-ing Secretaries - GEORGE W. SHARP, JOHN LUGENBEEL, J. MARKELL, Esqrs. Corresponding Secretaries - NICHOLAS SNYDER, and J. G. SHEID, Esqrs. Treasurer - HENRY NIXDORFF. Messenger - DANIEL HALLER.

1279. (D) Death of CHARLES CARROLL of Carrolton, the last of the signers of the Declaration of Independence, departed this life Wednesday morning about 4 o'clock, at the residence of his son-in-law, R. Caton, Esq., in Water Street. Pallbears, mourners, and the Rev'd. Clergy, physicians, will assemble at the dwelling of Richard Caton Esq., at 8 o'clock in the morning. Mayor and City Council, President and Directors of Baltimore & Ohio Railroad, and all city officials assemble at City Hall. Governor, Executive Council, Heads of Departments, Senators, members of Congress and State Legislators, and Foreign Ministers and Counsels, Cincinnatti, and Soldiers of the Revolution, Officers of the Army and Navy assemble at the Exchange. Citizens to assemble in Baltimore Street, extended from Gay Street, to Exeter Street and fall into the procession, as Assistant Marshals direct. Bells to commenced tolling and minute guns firing at 1/2 past 8 o'clock, A.M. After services at the Catherdral on Charles Street. The corpse was conveyed on the Frederick Turnpike to the Manor for interment, aged 96 years.

1280. (D) At Cincinnati, Ohio, on the 5th inst., Mr CHARLES BALTZELL, Jr., late of this co., and eldest son of Charles Baltzell, of this co.

November 29, 1832 (MHS)

1281. To present Frederick County at the next Legislature of Maryland, the following gentlemen: WM. C. JOHNSON, DAVID SCHLEY, and *ABDIEL UNKEFER, *THOMAS HAMMOND. (*new members)

Decmeber 13, 1832 (MHS)

1282. List and dates of death of all the signers of the Declaration

of Independence: THOMAS LYNCH, of South Carolina,
June 1779, BUTTON GWINNET of GA., May 27, 1777,
JOHN MORTON, of PA., December 1777, PHILIP LIVING-
STON of N.Y., June 12, 1778, GEORGE ROSS of PA., July
1779, JOSEPH HEWES of N.C., JOHN HART of N.J., 1780,
GEORGE TAYLOR of PA., February 23, 1781, RICHARD
STOCKTON of N.J., February 28, 1781, CEASAR RODNEY
of DE., 1783, STEPHEN HOPKINS of R.I., July 13, 1785,
WM. WHIPPLE of N.H., November 28, 1785, ARTHUR
MIDDLETON of S.C., January 1, 1787, THOMAS STONE of
MD., October 5, 1787, JOHN PENN of N.C., September
1788, THOMAS NELSON, Jr. of VA., January 4, 1789,
BENJAMIN FRANKLIN of PA., April 17, 1790, WILLIAM
HOOPER of N.C., October 1790, BENJAMIN HARRISON of
VA., April 1791 FRANCIS HOPKINSON of N.J., May 8,
1791, LYMAN HALL of GA., 1791, ROGER SHERMAN of
CT., July 23, 1793, JOHN HANCOCK of MA., October 8,
1793, RICHARD HENRY LEE of VA., June 19, 1794, JOHN
WITHERSPOON of N.J., November 1794, ABRAHAM CLARK
of N.J., 1794, JOSIAH BARTLETT of N.H., May 19, 1795,
SAMUEL HUNTINGTON of CT., January 5, 1796, CARTER
BRAXTON of VA., October 10, 1797, FRANCIS LIGHTFOOT
LEE of VA., 1797, OLIVER WOLCOTT of CT., December 1,
1797, LEWIS MORRIS of N.Y., January 1798, JAMES
WILSON of PA., August 28, 1798, GEORGE READ of DE.,
1798, WILLIAM PACA of MD., 1799, EDWARD RUTLEDGE
of S.C., January 23, 1800, MATT. THORNTON of N.H.,
June 24, 1803, SAMUEL ADAMS of MA., October 1, 1803,
FRANCIS LEWIS of N.Y., December 30, 1803, GEORGE
WALTON of GA., February 2, 1804, ROBERT MORRIS of
PA., May 8, 1804, GEORGE WYTHE of VA., June 6, 1806,
JAMES SMITH of PA., 1806, THOMAS HAYWARD of S.C.,
March 1809, SAMUEL CHASE of MD., June 19, 1811,
WILLIAM WILLIAMS of CT., August 2, 1811, GEORGE
CLYMER of PA., January 23, 1813, BENJAMIN RUSH of
PA., April 19, 1813, ROBERT T. PAINE of MA., May 11,
1814, ELBRIDGE GERRY of MA., November 23, 1814,
THOMAS M'KEAN of DE., June 24, 1817, WILLIAM
ELLERY of R.I., February 15, 1820, WILLIAM FLOYD of
N.Y., August 4, 1821, JOHN ADAMS of MA., July 4, 1826,
THOMAS JEFFERSON of VA., July 4, 1826, CHARLES
CARROLL of MD., November 14, 1832.

December 27, 1832 (MHS)
1283. (M) On the 13th inst., by the Rev. David F. Schaeffer, Mr MICHAEL DORSEY, to Miss MARGARETH BUSH, all of this co.

1833

January 3, 1833 (MHS)
1284. (M) On the 25th inst., by the Rev. John H. Smaltz, Mr DANIEL SNOOK, to Miss SUSANNA STALEY.

January 10, 1833 (MHS)
1285. (M) On Sunday last, by the Rev. David F. Schaeffer, Mr JOHN McDEVITT, to Miss MARY KLINE, all of this co.

January 17, 1833 (MHS)
1286. (D) On Saturday evening the 12th inst., ROBERT, youngest child of W.C. Smallwood, aged 11 months and 6 days.
1287. (D) On Thursday the 10th inst., GEORGE GAITHER, a man of steady industrious habits came to his death in a most melanchol mannor. The decease was a laborer in the employment of Mr Frederick Smith, near New Market, was in the act of watering two horses. He was riding one and leading the other. The horse he was leading had a bridle thrown over his neck, and became frighten in an effort to escape, he pulled the decease from back of the horse he was riding. In the fall, the reins of his bridle seem to become entrangled around his ankles. He was dragged from the mill of Mr. Smith, through Bush Creek, and over very rough roads, a distance of 150 yards. Along the railroad, a distance of 1 1/2 miles passing over the ends of the steepers of the roads. The horse was stopped by persons engaged in quarrying stone on the side of the road. The body was released, it was torn and mangled and not recognized by persons who released it, Mr Smith, had the body taken to his house.
1288. During the prevalence of the cholera, we, the undersigned inhabitants of the Point of Rocks, having been much alarmed on account of the prevailing epidemic, and whereas our physican having left this place, we are obliged to seek remedies elsewhere, and found Dr. "Isaac Lyon's antibillious pills as well as his anti-spamsmodic tincture."

Most efficacious medicine, the former as a safe cathartic, and the latter a speedy relief for cramps in the stomach and limbs. We recommend this to the public generally, and particulary to those persons who are unable to have a family physician. October 11th. WILSON HOLMAN, JOHN LINDSEY, JACOB CREEP, LINVEL PURVEST, JOHN O'FARRELL, WM. RHODES, MARTIN LAWLER, THOS. ABEARM, JOSEPH MARTIN, JOHN CONNELLY, DAVID MULLEN, JAMES CARROLL, PATRICK DANAHEW, PATRICK O'BRIEN, CHARLES DEVINE, WM. SCHLEY, MICHAEL MARONEY, JAMES GRAHAM, PATRICK BUTLER, MICHAEL M'GOWAN, JOHN MURPHY, THOMAS REEL, THOS. McMANUS, MORRIS KERLY, JOHN McMANUS, THOS. A. HEARN, Sr., OWEN McMANUS, EDWARD KELLY, JOHN DUNNE, THOS. WARE, JOHN PLUMMER, MICHALE BOURK, ALEXANDER McDONALD, DENNIS MORRARTY, WM. BARRITT. January 17,-3m.

January 24, 1833 (MHS)
1289. (D) On Sunday evening last, BENJAMIN, son of W. C. Smallwood, in the 6th year of his age.

January 31, 1833 (MHS)
1290. (M) On Sunday evening by the Rev. D. F. Schaeffer, Mr FREDERICK LAMBERT, (merchant) to Miss CATHERINE E. LAMBRECHT, all of this city.
1291. (M) On the same evening by the same, Mr FREDERICK SCHAEFFER, to Miss ELIZABETH ORTNER, all of this city.
1292. (M) At Columbia, S.C., on the 3rd inst., by the Rev. Mr Henry, Mr A.P. CALHOUN, eldest son of the Hon. J. C. Calhoun, to Miss EUGENIA CHAPPELL, eldest daughter of Col. J. J. Chappell.
1293. (D) Departed this life on Saturday morning the 26th inst., Mrs SARAH MACKLIN, the wife of Mr Rives Macklin, and daughter of the Reverend Richard Sneath, of the Methodist Church.

February 7, 1833 (MHS)
1294. (M) On Tuesday the 5th inst., by the Rev. Michael Wachter, Mr EZRA SMITH, to Miss MARY BEARD.

February 14, 1833 (MHS)
1295. (D) On Saturday morning last, SUSAN AMELIA, daughter

of Mr George Salmon, of this city, aged 1 year, and 7 months.

1296. (D) On yesterday morning, CHARLOTTE LUCRETIA, aged 4 years, and 6 days, youngest daughter of Henry H. Haller, (deceased) of this city, funeral today at 2 o'clock, P.M.

February 28, 1833 (MHS)

1297. Appointments for 1833, for Frederick County, by the Governor and Council. Justices of the Orphan's Court: DAVIS RICHARDSON, Esq. Coroners: WM. R. KING, GEORGE HUGHES, DAVID KEPHART, DENNIS D. HOWARD, JACOB BAER, HENRY BAER, ALEX'R. McIIHENNY, HENRY BOTELER. Justices of the Levy Court: MOSES WORMAN, MARTIN EICHELBERGER, JAMES SIMMONS, FREDERICK TROXELL, WM. WORMAN, SOLOMON FOREST, ELISHA NELSON, JACOB MATHIAS, WM. MILLER, JOHN COST, DAVID FOUTZ, THOMAS SPRINGER. Justices of the Peace: JACOB BAER, BELT BRASHEAR, HENRY BAKER, SAMUEL BAUMGARDNER, CHARLES H. BURKHART, MALACHI BERNARD, HENRY BANTZ, TILGHMAN BISER, PETER BANKHERT, WASHINGTON BURGESS, CHRISTIAN BOWERS, MICHAEL BALTZELL, GEORGE BLESSING, PHILIP BIRELY, DANIEL S. BISER, A. L. BARNEY,* JOHN A. BAYNE,* ROBERT BOONE,* JACOB COBLENTZ, JACOB CRAMER, GEORGE CASSELL, of Jno., GIDEON D. CRUMBAUGH, THOMAS COE,* JOHN W. CHARLTON,* JOSEPH M. CROMWELL,* ROBERT DODDS, ISAAC DERN, DANIEL DUVALL, JOHN W. DERR, CHARLES DEVILBISS, WM. DUDDERAR, JAS. DURBIN,* (of Thos.,) JOSHUA DOUB, LLOYD DORSEY, HENRY W. DERR,* A. T. H. DUVALL,* JOHN EBERT, DANIEL ENGLE, WM. FLANAGAN, HENRY FUNDENBURG, JAMES FISHER, GEORGE FLAUTT, GEO. A. FARQUHAR,* WM. GRIMES, STEPHEN GORSUCH, JOHN GITTING,* WILSON HAYES, BENJAMIN HEFFNER, H. A. HAMBLETON, JACOB HOFFMAN, THOMAS HOOK, JOHN HANDS, WM. B. HEAD, JOHN H. HOPPE, THOMAS J. HAMMOND,* HENRY HERSHBERGER,* LEWIS L. HOBBS, GEORGE HANER,* JAS. M. HARDING,* THOS. JOHNSON, of Wm., JOSHUA JONES, THOS. W. JOHNSON, JACOB JOHNSON,* WM. KNOX, ZEBULON KUHN, EDWARD KNOTT, JOSEPH KEEFER, JACOB LAMBERT, Sen'r., LLOYD LUCKETT, MICHAEL LEASE, JOHN S. LAWRENCE,* ABH'M. LIGHTENWALTER,* PATRICK

MAGILL, Sen'r., PATRICK MAGILL, Jr.,* J. G. MORRISON, LEWIS MOTTER, ALE'X. McIIHENRY, JOHN McDONALD, P. S. McELFRESH, WM. MURPHY, Sr., JOHN McNEILL, WM. MOONEY, GEORGE MATHIAS, Jr., JOHN MONTGOMERY, MICHAEL MEALEY, Jr., WM. V. MORGAN, DANIEL MORGAN,* JOHN McDOWELL,* MARTIN MAHONEY,* NICHOLAS NORRIS, NATHAN H. OWINGS, LEWIS O'BRIEN, NOAH PHILIPS, JACOB POWDER, Jr., GEORGE PHELPS, WM. B. PITTINGER,* GEORGE ROHR, ELIHU H. ROCKWELL, GEORGE RINER, GEORGE RICE, JAMES ROGERS,* WILLIAM ROBERTS, ANDREW SHRIVER, JOHN J. SMITH, JAMES SMITH, SEBASTIAN SULTZER, MICHAEL SULLIVAN, JOSHUA SMITH, Jr., JAMES SUMMERS, NOAH A. SHAFER, ABRAHAM F. SHRIVER,* THOS. SMITH, of Jos.,* BENJAMIN SHUNK,* HENRY STEPHENSON,* JACOB SMITH,* JACOB THOMAS, JOSEPH TANEY, Jr.,* MAHLON TALBOTT, W. VANBIBBER, SURAT D. WARFIELD, SOMERSET R. WATERS, ZACHARIAH T. WINDSOR, CHARLES WILLIARD, ABRAHAM WAMPLER,* WILLIAM WILLIS,* HENRY YOUNG, GEORGE YANTIS, JOHN M. A. ZOLLICKOFFER. (* not commissioned last year.)

1298. (M) On the 19th, by the Rev. David F. Schaeffer, Mr NICHOLAS MATTOX, to Miss EMILY HICKMAN, both of this co.

1299. (M) On the same day by the same, Mr WILLIAM KARNE, to Miss ANN R. CROBY, both of this co.

1300. (M) On Wednesday last, by the same, Mr JOHN L. STOUT, to Miss MARGARET WILLIS, both of this co.

1301. (M) On yesterday, by the same, Mr JOHN CRUM, to Miss MARY ANN GETZ, all of this city.

1302. (M) At Friends Meeting House, on 21st of Feb., Mr JOHN TALBOTT, Jr., merchant of Baltimore, to Miss MARY, eldest daughter of Mr Wm. Coale, of New Market.

March 7, 1833 (MHS)

1303. Appointed by the Governor and Council: HORATIO G. O'NEAL, surveyor for Frederick Co.

1304. (F) Night of February 26th, about 11 o'clock, a tenant house on the farm belonging to Mount Saint Mary's College took fire and burnt down. No loss, except a house, some furniture, it was a considerable distant from the college, fire started in the kitchen.

1305. (M) On Thursday last, by the Rev. D. F. Schaeffer, Mr JOHN G. MANE, to Miss SUSAN BROWN, all of this co.

March 14, 1833 (MHS)

1306. Election of officers for the Independent Hose Company of Frederick. At a meeting held at the Hotel of M. E. BARTGIS, on the evening of Friday 2nd, 1833. President - DAVID B. DEVITT, Vice President - SAMUEL CARMACK, Secretary - WILLIAM FISCHER, Treasurer - JACOB ENGLEBRECHT, Directors - MATTHIAS E. BARTGIS, WILLIAM FISCHER, Principal Engineer - WILLIAM SMALL, Assistant - HENRY HANSHEW, GEORGE HOSKINS, Property Guards - JOHN FESSLER, DAVID STEINER, WILLIAM SCHLEY, EVAN CARMACK, Lane-men - STUART GAITHER, WILLIAM C. RUSSELL, PATRICK TORMEY, FREDERICK A. SCHLEY, ISAAC WISONG, Ladder-men - ALEXANDER TRUSCOTT, SOLOMON ALBAUGH, Ax-men - THOMAS EADER, WILLIAM BROWN, Superintendent of fire plugs - JOHN STRAEFFER, JOHN HANSHEW, Hosemen - WILLIAM STEINER, JOSEPH SCHELL, VALENTINE J. BRUNNER, PHILIP REICH, GEORGE W. SHARP, JOHN SCHREINER, JACOB DOLL, HENRY YOUNG, GEORGE M. CONRADT, EDWARD TRAIL, GIDEON BANTZ, Pipe Director - DAVID B. DEVITT, Hose Director - SAMUEL CARMACK, Engine Director - WILLIAM FISCHER, Lane Director - MATTHIAS E. BARTGIS.

March 21, 1833 (MHS)

1307. Laying the corner-stone, of the new Catholic Church in this city, will take place on Monday next, the 25th inst., at 3 o'clock, P.M.

April 11, 1833 (MHS)

1308. WM. C. JOHNSON, and JOHN LEE, Esq., Candidates for Congress in the District of Montgomery and part of Frederick Counties.

May 16, 1833 (MHS)

1309. ALEXANDER, engineer, and JULIUS F. DUCATEL, assistant engineer, are to make a map of the State. J. W. McCULLOH, Esq., ex-Governor CHAS. GOLDSBOROUGH, and the Hon. B. S. FORREST, Representative of the State in the Joint Stock Company, in which the State holds stock. Additional Justices of the Peace for Frederick County;

JAMES G. HARDING, GEORGE BRECKENRIDGE, and etc. HENRY CULLER, Esq., Justice of the Levy Court from the 14th (Jefferson) District.

1310. Meeting of a number of stockholders of the Frederick Water Company, Dr. WM. BRADLEY TYLER, was called to the the chair, and LEWIS MEDTART, appointed secretary.

June 6, 1833 (MHS)

1311. The names of the Post-Masters within the County are as follows: JOHN THOMAS, Jr., Jefferson, ALEXANDER H. BROWN, Point of Rocks, B. A. CUNNINGHAM, Buckeystown, FRANCIS RICHMOND, Middletown, BASIL ROOT, Johnsville, D. W. NAIL, Sams' Creek.

June 27, 1833 (MHS)

1312. Appointment by the Governor: THOMAS C. WORTHINGTON, WILLIAM M. BEALL, EDWARD A. LYNCH, Esqrs., Visitors of Saint John's Literary Institute, of Frederick, MD.

1313. Judges of Election for Frederick County. District #1. OTHO THOMAS, PETER H. BROWN, LEWIS KEMP. District #2. JOHN EBERT, HENRY BAER, NICHOLAS HOLTZ. District #3. GEORGE BISER, JOHN McNIEL, JOHN J. SMITH. District #4. FREDERICK OTT, JAMES CROCKETT, VALENTINE SHRYOCK. District #5. JEFFERSON SHIELDS, MICHAEL SLUSS, DANIEL HOOVER. District #6. EVAN McKINSTRY, JACOB BAUMGARDNER, JAMES SMITH. District #7. MOSES SHAW, ISRAEL NORRIS, DAVID UIILER. District #8. JNO. GLISON, GEO. COX, WM. A. ALBAUGH. District #9. JOSHUA RUPEL, THOMAS DUVALL, HENRY SMITH, District #10. WILSON HAYS, JOSEPH SMITH, GEO. HARMAN. District #11. ELIAS CRUTCHLEY, JACOB HYDER, JOHN D. CRUMBAUGH. District #12. HENRY OHR, BENEDICT BOONE, JOHN N. HOSKINS. District #14. THOMAS JOHNSON, JOHN SIMMONS, THOMAS LAMAR. Trustees of the Poor: DANIEL KOLB, PHILIP ROHR, GEORGE HAUER, JACOB FAUBLE and VALENTINE DAUB.

July 18, 1833 (MHS)

1314. Candidates for Congress: MADISON NELSON, Esq., from the 4th District. JACOB CRONISE, of Monrovia, Fred'k. Co.

August 8, 1833 (MHS)
1315. RODERICK DORSEY, in the Congressional Election to represent part of Frederick and Montgomery Counties.

August 22, 1833 (MHS)
1316. A contract has been entered into for making the McAdamised Road, from Frederick to the Monocacy, on the Liberty Road. The contractor for the building of the turnpike, is Mr DANIEL K. CAHOON.
1317. The Jackson Republican County convention which was held in this city on Saturday last, nominated; DAVID SCHLEY, JOSEPH M. PALMER, ABDIEL UNKEFER and JNO. SIFFORD, candidates for the next Legislature of MD.

August 29, 1833 (MHS)
1318. Appointment by the Governor and Council: Notaries Republic: EDWARD TURBUTT, Frederick. JACOB REESE, Westminster. Military appointment: JAS. COALE.

September 19, 1833 (MHS)
1319. Col. WM. COST JOHNSON, has been nominated by the National Republicans convention, held in New Market on Wednesday the 11th inst., as candidate for Congress in the 6th Congressional District, composed of Montgomery and part of Frederick.
1320. Sheriffalty candidates: MAHLON TALBOT, MATHIAS E. BARTGIS, ABNER CAMPBELL, WILLIAM LOWE, THOMAS GURLEY.

September 26, 1833 (MHS)
1321. Appointment by the President of the U. States: R. B. TANEY, Esq., was yesterday appointed Secretary of the Treasury of the U.S. He resigned the office of Attorney General.

October 24, 1833 (MHS)
1322. At a public meeting in the Court House on Saturday evening the 19th inst. Mr LEWIS BIRELY, called to the chair and JAMES M. SHELMAN, as secretary. A resolution to appoint a committee of 5, was presented by R. POTTS, to establish a carpet manufactory in Frederick. The chair appointed; Major D. HUGHES, FRED'K. A. SCHLEY, Esq., STUART GAITHER, EDWARD TRAIL, Col. J. M. SHELMAN.

November 7, 1833 (MHS)
1323. Appointment of Deputies for Frederick County, by MAHLON TALBOTT, Esq. Creagerstown & Hauver, Emmitsburg, Taney Town, & Westminster Districts: THOMAS GURLEY. Woodsborough, & Liberty DIstricts: MASON PARSONS. New Market, Buckeystown Districts: HENRY HOUCK. Jefferson, Middletown, & Petersville Districts: CHRISTIAN TABLER. Jailor: WILLIAM ELY.

November 14, 1833 (MHS)
1324. FRANCIS S. KEY, has been dispatched by the President of the U. States, to the State of Alabama, in consequence of the difficulties in that state's relative to the Indian land.
1325. (M) On Thursday last, by the Rev. M. Wachter, Mr ELI GILBERT, to Miss SOPHIA HEFFNER, both of this co.
1326. (M) On Thursday the 7th inst., by the Rev. D. F. Schaeffer, Mr EDWARD LARE, to Miss REBECCA KELLER, both of this place.

November 21, 1833 (MHS)
1327. At the annual meeting of the Young Men's Bible Society, held in the Lutheran Church, on Monday evening Nov. 18th, 1833. The following gentlemen were elected Directors for the ensuing year. Lutheran Church: AUGUSTUS F. EBERT, WILLIAM D. HEIM, JOHN HANSHEW, VALERIUS EBERT. Presbyterian Church: JAMES M. SHELMAN, Dr. S. L. McKEEHAN, Dr. A. RITCHIE, SMAUEL R. HOGG. Methodist Church: WILLIAM WEBER, ASBURY H. HUNT, MEREDITH DAVIS, JAMES L. NORRIS. Ger. Ref. Church: SETH NICHOLS, JOHN RAMSBURG, EDWARD LARE, GIDEON BANTZ, Jr. Episcopal Church: WILLIAM J. ROSS, NEILSON POE, J. C. WHEAT, Dr. J. W. PRYOR. Baptist Church: GEORGE ENGLISH, ENOS B. REED, JAMES D. ROMAN, HENRY RIGGS, Jr. At a meeting of the Board of Directors, held on Monday, Nov. 18th, 1833, the Board was organized by the election of the following gentlemen as officers for the ensuing year. President: J. M. SHELMAN, 1st Vice President: E. B. REED, 2nd Vice President: J. HANSHEW, Cor. Secretary: A. F. EBERT, Treasurer: Dr. A. RITCHIE, Agent Depository: Rev. D. F. SCHAEFFER. GIDEON BANTZ, Jr., Rec. Secretary.

December 5, 1833 (MHS)
1328. (M) On Thursday evening last, by the Rev. D. F. Schaeffer,

PETER GOODMANSON, to Miss WILHELMIMINA EBERTS, all of this city.
1329. (M) On Tuesday evening last, by the same, Mr DANIEL BRENGLE, son of Capt. John Brengle, to Miss CAROLINE E. THOMAS, all of this city.
1330. (M) On Thursday last, by the Rev. M. Wachter, Mr BENJAMIN STULL, to Miss EDITH SHARPE, all of this co.
1331. (M) In Baltimore, on Wednesday morning the 27th inst., by the Rev. Daniel Zollikoffer, Dr. JAMES L. BILLINGSLEA, to Miss SUSAN, daughter of the late Daniel Haines, all of Frederick Co., MD.

December 12, 1833 (MHS)

1332. The following gentlemen composed the Grand and Petit Juries at the present term of the criminal court of Frederick County Grand Jury: THOS. CARLTON, NICHOLAS NORRIS, JOSEPH WELTY, DANIEL YEISER, JAMES CASTLE, JOHN HEAD, JOHN SMITH, of John., JOSEPH TALBOT, THOS. C. BRASHEAR, JOSHUA SMITH, Jr., JOHN JONES, WM. GAITHER, GEORGE POTTS, GEO. H. WAESCHE, WM. DURBIN, JOHN YOUNG, JOHN SMITH, of Geo., JOHN LEASE, GEORGE HARMAN, PETER NICHOLS, EDWARD McBRIDE, MICHAEL SULLIVAN, JACOB POWDER. Petit Jury: BROOKE BAKER, S. BAUMGARDNER, JACOB CARMACK, JOHN COLEGATE, ELIAS A. GROSHON, JACOB GROVE, JACOB HARBAUGH, WILLIAM HAYS, DAVID HULL, ABRAHAM JONES, JOHN KEAFAUVER, CHRISTIAN KEEFER, A. LIGHTENWALTER, LLOYD LUCKET, WILLIAM MURDOCK, JOHN W. PRATT, JOHN RIGNEY, JOHN SIMMONS, JONAS SMITH, JOHN THSON, JACOB TROXELL, TOBIAS COVER, GEO. DERTZBAUGH, STERLING GALT, S. GRIMES, Sen.

December 19, 1833 (MHS)

1333. (M) On Tuesday last, by the Rev. M. Wachter, Mr JACOB BEARD, Jr., to Miss CATHARINE SMITH, all of this co.
1334. (M) On Monday evening last, by the Rev. D. F. Schaeffer, Mr JACOB BOSTON, to Miss CHRISTIANNA ENGLES, all of this city.

December 26, 1833 (MHS)

1335. (M) On Thursday 12th inst., by the Rev. Charles Reighley, Mr GEORGE SNOUFFER, to Miss MARY WIRTS, both of this city.

1336. (M) On the 17th inst., by the Rev. David F. Schaeffer, Mr TOBIAS KEIL, to Miss CATHERINE BREAHAN, both of this city.

1834

January 23, 1834 (MHS)
1337. (M) On Thursday evening the 9th inst., by the Rev. Robert J. Breckenbridge, Mr NEWTON H. GIST, formerly of Frederick, to Miss AMELIA A. BACON, of Baltimore.

March 6, 1834 (MHS)
1338. Election of officers for the Independent Hose Company, was held on the 27th of January 1834. President - EDWARD TRAIL, Vice President - SAMUEL CARMACK, Secretary - A. P. BEATTY, Treasurer - NIMROD BANTZ, Directors - GIDEON BANTZ, VAL. J. BRUNNER, Pipe Engineer - DAVID B. DEVITT, Assistant - HENRY HANSHEW, GEORGE HOSKINS, Property Guard - JOHN FESSLER, WM. SCHLEY, DAVID STEINER, VALENTINE BIRELY, Lane men - STUART GAITHER, PATRICK TORMEY, URIAH S. BANTZ, WM. C. RUSSELL, FRED'K A. SCHLEY, Laddermen - CHARLES PETERS, SOLOMON ALBAUGH, Superintendent of fire plugs - JOHN STRAEFFER, JOHN HANSHEW, Ax-men - THOMAS EADER, WM. BROWN, Hosemen - WILLIAM STEINER, GEO. SALMON, LEWIS RAMSBURG, JOSEPH SCHELL, GEO. W. SHARP, PHILIP REICH, JACOB DOLL, J. SCHREINER, GEO. M. CONRADT, CASPER QUYNN, HENRY YOUNG, Pipe Director - EDWARD TRAIL, Hose Director - SAMUEL CARMACK, Engine Director - VAL. J. BRUNNER, Lane Director - GIDEON BANTZ.

March 13, 1834 (MHS)
1339. Appointments by the Governor and Council of Maryland for Frederick County. Levy Court: MOSES WORMAN, JACOB MATHIAS, JAMES SIMMONS, THOMAS SPRINGER, WM. WORMAN, HENRY CULLER, WM. MILLER, J. L. HIGGINS, M. EICHELBERGER, JAMES SMITH, FREDERICK TROXELL, J. G. MORRISON, SOLOMON FORREST. Justices of the Orphans' Court: JOHN L. HARDING, DAVIS RICHARDSON, NICHOLAS TURBUTT. Justices of the Peace: JACOB BAER, BELT BRASHIER, HENRY BAKER, SAM'L BAUM-

GARTNER, CHAS. H. BURKHARDT, HENRY BANTZ, MALACHI BERNARD, TILGHMAN BISER, PETER BANKERT, WASHINGTON BURGESS, CHRISTIAN BOWER, MICHAEL BALTZELL, GEORGE BLESSING, P. BIRELY, D. S. BISER, AL BARNEY, JOHN A. BAYNE,* GEO. BECKENBAUGH, GEO. BOWLUS, JACOB COBLENTZ, JACOB CRAMER, G. CASSELL, of Jno., G. D. CRUMBAUGH, THOMAS COE, JOHN N. CHARLTON,+ THOMAS CRAMPTON, THOMAS CARLTON, ISAAC DERN, DANIEL DUVALL, JOHN W. DERR, CHARLES DEVILBISS, WM. DUDDERAR, JAMES DURBIN, of Tho., JOSHUA DOUB, LLOYD DORSEY, HENRY W. DERR, WM. DURBIN, DANIEL ENGLE, HENRY FUNDENBURG, JAMES FISCHER, GEORGE FLAUTT, SOLOMON FORREST, WM. GRIMES, STEPHEN GORSUCH, JOHN GITTING, WILSON HAYS, BENJ. HEFFNER, HENRY A. HAMILTON, JACOB HOFFMAN, THOMAS HOOK, JOHN HINES, THOS. J. HAMMOND, LEWIS L. HOBBS, GEORGE HAUER, JAMES M. HARDING, HENRY HOUCK, THOMAS HAYS, TH. JOHNSON, of Wm., JOSHUA JONES, TH. W. JOHNSON, JACOB JOHNSON, JOHN JONES, ZEBULON KUHN, EDWARD KNOTT, JOSEPH KEEFER, GEORGE KUHN, JACOB LAMBERT, Sen., LLOYD LUCKETT, MICHAEL LEASE, JOHN S. LAWRENCE, ABH'M. LIGHTENWALTER, PATRICK McGILL, Sen., PATRICK McGILL, Jr., J. G. MORRISON, LEWIS MOTTER, ALEX. McIlHENNY, JOHN McDONALD, P. S. McELFRESH, WM. MURPHY, Sen., JOHN McNEIL, WM. MOONY, GEO. MATHIAS, Jr., JOHN MONTGOMERY, MICHAEL MEALY, Sen., WM. V. MORGAN, JOHN McDOWELL, M. M. MAHONY, J. MANRO, NICHOLAS NORRIS, BURGESS NELSON, N. H. OWINGS, LEVI O'BRIEN, NOAH PHILIPS, JACOB POWDER, Jr., GEORGE PHELPS, W. B. PITTENGER, GEORGE PRICE,+ B. PUSEY, GEORGE ROHR, E. H. ROCKWELL, GEORGE RINER, JAMES ROGERS, JACOB REESE, ANDREW SHRIVER, JOHN J. SMITH, JAMES SMITH, SEBASTIAN SULTZER, MICHAEL SULLIVAN,* JOSHUA SMITH, Jr., JAMES SIMMONS, NOAH A. SHAFER, TH. SMITH, of Joshua, DANIEL STONESIFER, EMANUEL SLIFER,* JACOB HOOK, JOSEPH TANEY, Sen., JOSEPH TANEY, Jr., ARTHUR TANZEY, JOSEPH TALBOTT, WASH. VAN BIBBER, S. D. WARFIELD, SOMERSET R. WATERS, ZACH. T. WINDSOR, CHARLES WILLIARD, ABRAHAM WAMPLER, HENRY YOUNG, GEORGE YANTIS, J. M. A. ZOLLICKOFFER, WM.

ZOLLICKOFFER. Coroners: HENRY BAER, JACOB BAER, HENRY BOTELER, DENNIS D. HOWARD, GEORGE HUGHES, DAVID KEPHART, WM. R. KING, ALEX. McIIH- ENNY. *Probably - JOHN G. BAYNE, +Probably - JOHN W. CHARLTON, +Probably - GEORGE RICE.

1340. A pig killed by EPGRAIM WILLYS, Esq., of Manchester, on the 5th inst. After it was dressed, it weighted in at 672 1/2 pounds. It was sold to FREDERICK WOODBRIDGE, Esq., of Manchester.

March 20, 1834 (MHS)

1341. Appointment by the Governor and Council: HORATIO G. O'NEAL, to be surveyor for Frederick County.

March 27, 1834 (MHS)

1342. (M) On Tuesday morning the 18th inst., at Emmitsburg, by the Rev. Mr Heiner, Mr MICHAEL HELMAN, of Taney Town, MD., to Miss LYDIA A. SMITH, of the former place.
1343. (M) On Thursday the 20th inst., by the same, Mr ELIAS HARBAUGH, of Frederick, Co., to Miss ELIZABETH EYLER, of Adams Co., PA.
1344. (M) On Tuesday morning last, by the Rev. M. Wachter, Mr JOHN FULTON, to Miss SABINA WILHIDE.
1345. (M) On the same day by the same, Mr JOSHUA HERRING, to Miss SUSAN HARMAN.
1346. (M) On the evening last, by the same, Mr JAMES THOMAS, to Miss SARAH ANN HARDMAN, all of this co.

April 3, 1834 (MHS)

1347. (M) On Sunday evening last, at the residence of Governor Floyd N. Richmond, by the Rev. Mr O'Brian, ROBERT B. RANDOLPH, Esq., late of the U. S. Navy, to Miss EGLAN- TINE BEVERLY, of Alexandria, D.C.

June 26, 1834 (MHS)

1348. (M) On Sunday evening last, by the Rev. Mr Albert, Mr BENJAMIN MATHIAS, to Miss CASSA ANN, daughter of Mr Daniel Stonesifer, both of Westminster District.
1349. (M) On Tuesday the 24th inst., by the Rev. Mr Cadden, Mr PERRY BENNETT, of Baltimore Co., to Miss ELEANOR HIGGINS, of Frederick Co.
1350. (M) On Thursday the 19th ult., near Middletown, by the Rev. J. C. Bucher Mr HENRY DUDDEROW, to Miss E. LUDY, all of this co.

1351. The Rev. JOSEPH H. JONES, will preach at the Baptist Meeting House on next Lords Day, at 3 o'clock, in the afternoon.

November 6, 1834 (MHS)

1352. JAMES M. SHELMAN, attorney at law, and solicitor in Chancery, has removed his law office, to the office of the "Times" in Church, Street.

1831

THE CITIZEN

December 9, 1831 (CBAL)

1353. A handsome wood cutting of the splendided railroad car "Frederick," will be found in our advertisement columns, from the graver of our ingenious townsmen FRANCIS S. MILLER. Mr Miller is a skillful artist, entirely self taught, and deserves encouragement.

1354. A raddish of uncommon size grew this fall on the farm of M. L. J. BRENGLE, near Frederick. The following were its dimensions - length 23", circumference 18", and weighing 9 pounds.

1836

THE FREDERICK CITIZEN

January 29, 1836 (MHS)

1355. (F) The house of Mr GEORGE RAMSBURG, on the road leading from this city to the Point of Rocks, was burnt to the ground on Sunday night last. All that was in the house was consumed, including a consideral amount of money, and securities. Some members of the family were considerly injuried by the fire, they were all driven out at midnight by the merciless fire. The fire was occassioned by falling of the sparks from the stove on wood lying in the hearth.

1356. (M) On the 17th inst., by the Rev. John W. Hoffmier, Mr J. EBERLY, to Miss MARY ANN HAMMOND, both of Johnsville, Frederick Co., MD.

1357. (M) In Pleasant Valley, Washington Co., on Tuesday the 5th inst., by the Rev. R. H. Philips, MR JOHN NORRIS, of said co., to Miss SARAH ANN POSEY, late of Charles Co., MD.
1358. (M) On Thursday the 21st inst., by the Rev. David F. Schaeffer, Mr DAVID S. MERTZ, eldest son of Major George Mertz, to Miss HARRIET, daughter of S. Wachter, Esq., all of this co.
1359. (D) Departed this life on Wednesday last, at the residence of his son in this city, the Rev. Dr. F. D. SCHAEFFER, late Pastor of Zion and Michaels Churches, in the city of Philadelphia, aged 76 years. He labored for the Lord upwards of 50 years, for many years held the office of Senior Reverend Ministeral of the Lutheran Church. Funeral will be held on Saturday at 2 o'clock, P.M., at the residence of the Rev. D. F. Schaeffer.
1360. (D) On Friday the 15th inst., at St. John's Literary Institution, Mr JAMES MAGUIRE, in the 24th year of his age, after a severe and painful illness of 2 weeks, from bilious pleurisy.
1361. (D) On the 12th inst., Major CHARLES BALTZELL, near Woodsborough, of paralysis in the 63rd year of his age.
1362. (D) Departed this life, on the 19th inst., in the 25th year of her age, Mrs SEVILLA HARBAUGH, daughter of Mr George Doffler, of this city. She leaves 3 children, one of whom if but 3 months old.
1363. (D) On Tuesday the 19th inst., Mrs CATHARINE ROHR, wife of Mr Philip Rohr in the 74th year of her age.
1364. Candidates for the Common Council: Ward #1. PETER MANTZ, A. P. BEATTY, JACOB FAUBEL. Ward #2. JACOB LITTLE, GEORGE MORE, CHARLES GETZENDANNER. Ward #3. JOHN H. KAUFFMAN, DAVID B. DEVITT. Ward #4. SAMUEL MILLER, JACOB ENGELBRECHT. Ward #5. JAMES WHITEHILL, JAMES WALLING, HIRAM KEEFER. Ward #6. GEORGE HOSKINS. Ward #7. JOHN W. MILLER, SAMUEL ALBAUGH, JAMES BRUNNER.

April 22, 1836 (MHS)

1365. (M) On Sunday evening last, by the Rev. D. F. Schaeffer, Mr LEONARD AUGUSTUS DILL, to Miss ANN LAVINA CANNON, both of this city.
1366. (M) On Tuesday evening last, by the Rev. Daniel Zacharias, Mr JACOB SINN, to Miss EMILY COLE, all of this city.

1367. (M) On Tuesday evening the 19th inst., by the Rev. John McElroy, Mr PATRICK KELLY, of Emmittsburgh, to Miss CATHARINE ROSANNA PITTENGER, of this city.
1368. Magistrates Court appointees: Buckeystown: Dr. JONATHAN MONROE, PHILEMON S. McELFRESH, and Z. T. WINDSOR. Frederick District: GEO. BALTZELL (declines serving,) GIDEON BANTZ, and JOHN H. BEALL. Middletown: GEO. BOWLUS, Dr. JACOB BAER, and JACOB HOFFMAN. New Market: GEO. PHELPS, WASHINGTON BURGESS, and GEO. RITNER. Woodsboro: JACOB POE, NOAH PHILLIPS, and WILLIAM GRIMES. Creagerstown: ZEBULON KUHN, GEO. BRECKENBAUGH, and WM. B. PITTINGER. Westminister: WASHINGTON VAN BIBBER, JACOB MATHIAS, and JOSHUA SMITH, Jr. Union Town: WM. SHEPHERD, THOMAS HOOK, and JOHN ROBERTS. Taney Town: JOHN SWOPE, JAMES SMITH, and JOHN BAUMGARTNER. Emmittsburg: LEWIS MOTTER, SAMUEL BAUMGARDNER and WILSON HAYS. Liberty: THOMAS SAPPINGTON, ABRAHAM JONES, and THOMAS HAMMOND.

1837

THE REPUBLICAN CITIZEN

April 28, 1837 (MHS)

1369. (M) On Tuesday evening last, by the Rev. Mr Kepler, Mr ALFRED B. BEATTY, to Miss SARAH, only daughter of the Rev. Joseph Trapnell, all of this city.

May 19, 1837 (MHS)

1370. A steer purchased by Mr WM. KOLB, of this place from STEPHEN MARTIN, of Washington Co., MD., was weighted upon the hay scales here yesterday morning, and weighted 1955 pounds, measured 5'9" in height, and 7'10" in grith and 9'4" in length, from poll of head to the root of the tail. It will be slaughtered to-day, and offered for sale at stall of Mr. K., on Saturday morning.
1371. A motion made by Dr. WILSON W. KOLB, that a committee of 17 persons be chosen from the city, 6 from Ramsburgh School House, 6 from Mount Zion, and 6 from the Manor,

to solicit funds by subscription for a monument with inscription to the memory of our beloved minister, Dr. DAVID F. SCHAEFFER, and that the bodies of his father, mother, wife and self be then deposited together. From town: MICHAEL ENGLEBRECHT, VALERIUS EBBERT, O. C. ENT, WM. REICH, FREDERICK LAMBERT, WM. THOMAS, THOMAS HALLER, CHAS. KELLER, HENRY KAUFFMAN, Jr., N. HALLER, P. L. STORM, A. P. BEATTY, MATHIAS EBBERT, PETER GARDENER, JACOB LIDAC, CHRISTIAN STEDDING. Ramsburgh's School House: GEO. FEAGEA, GEO. MARTS, JN. ROSE, GEORGE UNGLEBERGER, GEO. KETRO, and MICHAEL WACHTER. Mount Zion: HENRY KULLER, JAS. CASTLE, DAVID HEIM, J. A. SHAFER, CHRISTIAN SMITH, and JAS. STOOP, Manor: DANIEL KEMP, JACOB KEEFER, JACOB SHAFER, JON. HARGET, of P., and GEO. BRADY. HENRY NIXDORFF - Chairman, MATHIAS EBBERT - Secretary, JNO. McDONALD - Treasurer.

May 26, 1837 (MHS)

1372. Constables appointed by the Levy Court: District #1. JAMES L. SIMMONS, SAM'L. H. HANSER. District #2. JAMES CARLIN, JAMES M. DAYHOFF, JOSHUA DILL. District #3. MAHLON RODUCK, WARREN R. WILLIAMSON, ADAM RENNER, JOHN H. YOUNG, of H., P. YOUNG, JACOB YOUNG, JACOB YOUNG, of D., JOHN ALEXANDER. District #4. CYRUS WALKER, GEORGE KUHN, ARNOLD R. FAHS, WARREN F. GRIMES. District #5. SAMUEL DUPHORN, ISAAC WILSON, JOHN MARTIN. District #6. JONATHAN BROWNING, THOMAS INGMAN, THOMAS MOUNT, UPTON CLARY. District #8. DANIEL SWEADNER, DANIEL ROOT, AARON GOSNELL, JACOB WOOD, of D., OWEN BURGESS. District #10. HENRY REED. District #11. JOHN A. MARTIN, JOHN BARRICK, AARON T. NORRIS, LEVI BARRICK, CHARLES HESSER. District #12. JOHN G. DABBLESTEAD, HENRY BOTELER, of Ed. District #14. WM. B. TABLER, JESSE M. LITTLE, LLOYD A. RESSLER.

June 2, 1837 (MHS)

1373. Grand Jury of this co., after a full examination of all testimony for the State, against Mr EDWARD B. McPHERSON, they refused to find a bill, as every paper in the State of

Maryland has published the suspicion that had fallen on this gentleman at the time of the robbery.

1374. (M) On Tuesday evening the 25th inst., by the Rev. H. V. D. Johns, in Baltimore, Mr HENRY STEVENSON, of Frederick Co., MD., to Miss DEBORAH OWINGS, of the former place.

June 16, 1837 (MHS)

1375. (M) On Thursday the 1st day of June, by the Rev. Mr Buckley, Mr WM. EAGLE, of Frederick Co., to Miss RUTH ANN COOLY, of Montgomery Co.

1376. (D) In the city of Lancaster, on the 29th of May, Mrs GERTRUDE, wife of the Rev. John Hoffmire, in the 73rd year of her age.

1377. WILLIAM COST JOHNSON, Esq., as candidate to represent the 5th Congressional District, in the next Congress of the United States. If Col. ROBERT ANNAN will permit himself to be a candidate for Congress, in the 5th Congressional District, he will receive the cordial and active support of a large portion of the Whig Party of said district.

June 23, 1837 (MHS)

1378. The Rev. Mr BLOOD, will preach in the English Presbyterian Church, on next Sabbath, at 10 o'clock, A.M.

June 30, 1837 (MHS)

1379. Appointment by the Governor and Council: PATRICK O'NEILL, to be Justice of the Levy Court of Frederick Co., Vice: MOSES WORMAN, resigned.

July 7, 1837 (MHS)

1380. (M) On Sunday evening last, by Somerset R. Waters, Mr DAVID CLARKE, to Miss ELIZABETH WISE, both of Middletown Valley.

August 25, 1837 (MHS)

1381. (D) Departed this life on Friday the 4th inst., after a severe and protracted illness, JOHN STOOPS, Esquire of Kent Co., in the 60th year of his age. A graduate of Nassau Hall, N.J., and received the highest collegiate honors. A representative in the State Legislature, and a member of the Executive Council.

September 1, 1837 (MHS)

1382. Military appointments by the Governor and Council for Frederick, Co: JAMES M. COALE, Esq., Colonel of the 16th Regiment, Maryland Militia. Vice Col: SHELMAN, removed from this Co. SAMUEL CARMACK, to Lieutenant Colonel of the same. Vice: CHARLES H. BURKHART, resigned. DANIEL KEMP of Hy., Major of the same. Vice Major: COALE, promoted. For the 26th Regiment; BENJAMIN SMITH, Captain of a Uniform Rifle Company. GEORGE H. WEASCHE, Captain of a militia company. ELI OTTO, 1st Lieutenant, JOHN WARNER, 2nd Lieutenant, JAMES KRIDLER, Adjutant, THOMAS SIMIN, Surgeon.

1383. (D) On Wednesday the 23rd inst., in the 13th year of his age, LLOYD W. L. LUCKETT, son of the late Lloyd Luckett.

September 15, 1837 (MHS)

1384. (M) At Norfolk, VA., OLLENBOCKENOFFEN GRAPHENSTEINER, Dutch Consul to the United States, to the widow MARY SLANSLEUTE.

1385. (M) On Thursday evening last, by the Rev. Mr Hoffmier, Mr JACOB FUNK, to Miss SUSAN SHAW.

September 29, 1837 (MHS)

1386. (M) On Monday morning last, by the Rev. John L. Pitts, Mr KARL J. RYPMA, late of Germany, to CATHARINE A., youngest daughter of the late Wm. Thomas, of this co.

1387. (M) On the 12th inst., by the Rev. Mr Brown, Mr. LEVI BORIN, to Miss EVELINE HOCKERSMITH, both of Frederick Co.

October 6, 1837 (MHS)

1388. (D) Near Middletown, MD., on the 13th of September, after a painful illness, ELIZABETH LOUISA, daughter of Mr Samuel Remsburg, in the 5th year of her age.

1389. (D) On the 13th, near Middletown, MD., at the house of her son, Peter Schaffer, suddenly, Mrs ANN MARIA, relict of the late Mr John Schaffer, aged 83 years.

1390. (D) On the 15th, near Middletown, MD., ELI, infant son of Mr Peter Biser, in the 1st year of his age.

1391. (D) On the 16th, at Burkettsville, MD., after a painful illness MARY CATHARINE, daughter of Dr. Tilghman Biser, in the 2nd year of her age.

October 20, 1837 (MHS)
1392. (M) On the 15th inst., by the Rev. Daniel Feete, Mr JOHN RUSSLE, to Miss CATHARINE R. SMITH, all of Loudon Co., VA.
1393. (D) On Friday evening last, after a protracted and severe illness, CATHARINE H. KEMP, youngest daughter of Walter Kemp, in the 13th year of her age.

October 27, 1837 (MHS)
1394. October session of the Civil Court commenced on Monday last, the following gentlemen are named as jurymen: JOHN BAILY, MICHAEL BALTZELL, ISAAC BROWN, BASIL BAKER, PRESSLY J. BARTHOLOW, JOHN BUZZARD, JOHN H. T. COCKEY, THOMAS CASTLE, JOHN W. DORSEY, ABRAHAM DEAVER, ROBERT FLEMING, THOMAS JOHNSON, DANIEL KEMP, WILLIAM LYNCH, JOHN McDONALD, THOMAS METCALF, GEORGE M. POTTS, EDWARD SCHLEY, CORNELIUS STALEY, THOMAS C. SHIPLEY, JESSE WRIGHT, ISAAC WILSON, DEWALT WILLIARD, SAMUEL WOLF, SAMUEL YEAST.
1395. Civil appointments by the Executive: BENIDICT I. HEAD, a member of the Council, Vice: HARRIS, deceased. WILLIAM SCHLEY, a trustee of of University of Maryland, Vice: SOMERVILLE, deceased. HENRY HERSBERGER, a justice of the 3rd District Court of Frederick Co., Vice: BAER, resigned. WILLIAM P. JONES, a Justice of the 4th District Court of Frederick Co., Vice: PITTINGER, moved away. JAMES M. HARDING, a Justice of the 2nd District Court of Frederick Co., Vice: BEALL, moved away. ROBERT BOONE, a Justice of the Orphans Court of Frederick Co., Vice: HARDING, dec. NICHOLAS BREWER, Jr., Associate Justice of the 3rd Judicial District, Vice: KILGOUR, dec.
1396. Officer of the County Colonization Society: President - MOSES WORMAN, Vice Presidents - RICHARD POTTS, Dr. W. B. TYLER, F. A. SCHLEY, Corresponding Secretary - W. J. ROSS, Recording Secretary - GEORGE L. L. DAVIS, Treasurer - LEWIS MEDTART. Managers for the Frederick District - Dr. ALBERT RITCHIE, Dr. WILLIAM WATERS, EZEKIEL HUGHES, Rev. J. L. PITTS, LEWIS RAMSBURG, JACOB FAUBLE. Buckey's Town District - Maj. JAS. SIMMONS, JAMES L. DAVIS, Dr. JONATHAN MANRO, Dr. JAMES J. JOHNSON, THOMAS J. DAVIS, ROBERT SPENCER. New Market District - Dr. E. W. MOBBERLY, Dr. J. H. M. SMITH, Dr. GEORGE HUGHES, JOHN

BARTHOLOW, JOHN WOOD, GRAFTON HAMMOND. Liberty District - Capt. WM. DUDDERAR, Dr. RICHARD DORSEY, Dr. HENRY BAKER, Hon. THOS. SAPPINGTON, THOMAS HAMMOND, SURAT D. WARFIELD. Woodsborough District - Dr. THOMAS JOHNSON, Dr. THOMAS SIMS, JOSHUA DOUB, GEORGE M. POTTS, CHESTER COLEMAN, THOMAS I. WORTHINGTON. Emmittsburgh District - Dr. JEFFERSON SHIELDS, JOSEPH DARNER, ISAAC BAUGHER, ROBERT CROOKS, RICHARD GILSON, WILLIAM GREASON. Creagers-Town District - MARTIN EICHELBERGER, GEORGE BECKENBAUGH, Dr. L. GOLDSBOROUGH, HENRY A. BRIAN, WILLIAM TODD, WILLIAM JOHNSON. Hauvers District - HENRY BUSHMAN, Col. HOOVER, WILSON HAYS, HENRY SMITH, SOLOMON FORREST, ROBERT EYLER. Middletown District - Dr. JACOB BAER, SOMERSET R. WATERS, GEORGE BOWLUS, DANIEL ROUTZONG, JOHN BOWLUS, W. PATINGAL. Petersville District - Col. JOHN THOMAS, Dr. B. W. WEST, JOSEPH WEST, LLOYD THOMAS, HANSON MARLOW,, Dr. TILGHMAN BISER. Jefferson District - Dr. LLOYD DORSEY, Col. THOMAS JOHNSON, JOHN COST, GEORGE W. HOFFMAN, HENRY COST, JOHN SIMMONS.

November 3, 1837 (MHS)
1397. Candidates for Mayor - MICHAEL BALTZELL, JOHN BAILY, GEORGE HAUER, GEORGE HOSKINS, DANIEL KOLB, JOHN McDONALD, GEORGE RICE, MAHLON TALBOTT. For Alderman - ANDREW HEIM, JACOB KELLER, JACOB FAUBLE, MATHIAS E. BARTGIS, LEWIS BIRELY, WILLIAM KOLB, HORATIO WATERS, JACOB LITTLE, HENRY KAHLER, ALBERT RITCHIE, GIDEON BANTZ, DAVID BOYD, JOHN A. SIMMONS, THOMAS C. PRINCE.

November 17, 1837 (MHS)
1398. (M) Near Sharpsburg, on the 8th inst., by the Rev. J. W. Hoffman, Mr EZRA J. SNYDER, to Miss SARAH ANN STAUBS, both of Washington Co. MD.

November 24, 1837 (MHS)
1399. (D) On Friday morning last, near the mouth of Monocacy, Mrs REBECCA RANEBERGER, wife of Mr Philip Raneberger, in the 28th year of her age, she leaves a husband and 6 small children.

December 1, 1837 (MHS)

1400. (F) On Sunday evening last, the Tavern at Point of Rocks, occupied by Mr HAZEL BUTT, together with a store ajoining was burnt to the ground.
1401. (D) Near Burkettsville, on Sunday the 26th of November last, GIDEON BISER in the 26th year of his age, after a illness of 8 weeks.

December 8, 1837 (MHS)

1402. (M) On Thursday night last, at Chambers Hotel, by the Rev. J. L. Pitts, Mr JOHN W. CRAMPTON, to Miss SUSAN DEAVER, both of this co.
1403. (M) On the 23rd inst., at the same, by the Rev. Mr Brison, Mr. WM. RICHARDS, to Miss SARAH SHOEMAKER, both of Harpers Ferry.
1404. (D) At her residence in Tiffin, on the 10th inst., Mrs ELIZA HEDGES, consort of Josiah Hedges, Esq., of this place, aged about 40 years.

December 15, 1837 (MHS)

1405. December term of the Frederick County Court has commenced with the following gentlemen composing the juries: Grand - J. H. WORTHINGTON, JOHN WITHEROW, GEORGE HARMAN, LEONARD REDDICK, WILLIAM GRIMES, WILLIAM BROWN, HENRY HARBAUGH, FRANCIS SPALDING, THOMAS C. PRINCE, JOHN STONER, JACOB GROVE, GEO. ZIMMERMAN, JOHN HERRING, HENRY YOUNG, EPHRAIM McCOLLUN, JAMES McNULTY, PETER SCHLOSSER, HENRY KOONTZ, JOHN T. MITCHELL, JOHN RIGNEY, ISAAC WALKER, HENRY BOTELER, JOHN W. DERR. Petit - JOSHUA ADELSPERGER, NICHOLAS BRENGLE, GEO. C. BISER, JOHN BARTHOLOW, JOHN BARRICK, L. J. BRENGLE, WILLIAM COCKEY, JOHN CRAPSTER, JOHN COALE, HENRY DUNLAP, DANIEL DUVALL, ADAM EYLER, DANIEL FIROR, J. GETZENDANNER, JACOB HART, ANTHONY KIMMEL, JACOB KEEFER, WILLIAM LEAKIN, JOHN H. M. SMITH, GEORGE SALMON, ELI THOMAS, JACOB THOMAS, ABDIEL UNKEFER, MOSES WORMAN, ROBERT B. WINDSOR.
1406. The Rev. Mr BLOOD, will preach a sermon to the young men on the subject of infidelity, on next Sunday, in the Presbyterian Church, at 3 o'clock, and on the following sunday, at the same time, on the Doctrine of the Eucharist.

1407. Candidates for Alderman: HENRY KAUFFMAN, JAMES BRUNNER, ABRAHAM KEMP, HENRY KELLY, A. P. BEATTY, JOHN ENGLEBRECHT, CHRIST. STEINER, WM. C. HOFFMAN. For the Common Council: Ward #1. CASPAR CLINE, DAVID FAUBLE, WILLIAM WILCOXON. Ward #7. W. F. JOHNSON, PETER DEGRANGE.

December 22, 1837 (MHS)
1408. (D) At his residence in this co., on Sunday evening last, Mr ELISHA BELL, in the 93rd year of his age. Was a native of this co., entered the Army of the Revolution as a Lieutenant, attached himself to "The Flying Camp," during the Revolution, he was distinguished as a gallant soldier and devoted Patriot. After the War, his attention turned to agriculture, and continued to the day of his death. Services were held on Tuesday last.
1409. Gone on this date, for the position of Alderman: ABRAHAM KEMP, replaced by JOHN HANE. For Ward #6. DAVID J. MARKEY.

1838

January 9, 1838 (MHS)
1410. (D) On Saturday last, the 6th inst., at Oxford, the residence of his grandmother, Mrs Edwards, Mr JAMES EDWARDS FRIDBY, eldest son of Richard Frisby, Esq., in the 24th year of his age. Symptons of plumonary consumption manifested themself about 2 years ago. He was advised to try the effect of a West India climate, he did so, his devoted wife accompanied him, in residence of some months in the island of Cuba. The disease had taken deep roots, he returned during his last illness, he was resigned-and died with Baxter's Saints' resting in his hand.

January 26, 1838 (MHS)
1411. Candidates for the Common Council: Ward #1. SAMUEL HALLER, CASPAR CLINE, DAVID FAUBLE, WILLIAM WILCOXON, GEORGE METZGAR. Ward #2. DANIEL SPRINGER, JACOB RIEHL. Ward #3. PETER L. STORM, GEORGE McGAHAN. Ward #4. JACOB ENGLEBRECHT, PHILIP HAUPT. Ward #5. MICHAEL H. HALLER, HIRAM

KEEFER. Ward #6. DAVID J. MARKEY, WILLIAM BRENNER. Ward #7. W. F. JOHNSON, GEORGE SALMON, PETER DEGRANGE.

February 2, 1838 (MHS)

1412. Appointments by the Governor and Council: SAMUEL TYLER, Esq., Aide-de-camp. To Brigadier General: THOMAS C. WORTHINGTON, of the milita of this State.
1413. Candidates for the Common Coucil: Ward #2. CHARLES GETZENDANNER, HENRY BOTLER, and for Ward #7. JOHN W. MILLER.
1414. Election of officers for the Independent Hose Company: President - CASPAR QUYNN, Vice President - EZRA BENTZ, Secretary - GEORGE MARKELL, Treasurer - GIDEON BANTZ, Sr., Directors - ABRAHAM KEMP, J. HANSHEW, Engine Director - JOHN HANSHEW, Hose Director - ABRAHAM KEMP, Pipe Director - EZRA BENTZ, Lane Director - CASPAR QUYNN, Chief Engineer - WILLIAM C. MARTIN, Assistant Engineers - T. C. PRINCE, G. HOSKINS, Ax-men for the engine - EZRA M. GOMBER, H. RHODES, for the hose - DAVID J. MARKEY, Ladder men - HENRY YOUNG, DAVID BRENGLE, Lane men - HENRY HANSHEW, SAMUEL CARMACK, GIDEON BENTZ, PATRICK TORMEY, JOHN ENGELBRECHT, Hosemen - WM. E. SALTER, HIRAM KEEFER, JOSEPH SCHELL, EDWARD TRAIL, GEO. M. J. FISHER, FREDERICK KEEFER, EDWARD LARE, EZRA HALLER, JOHN HIMBURG, JAMES WHITEHILL, SAMUEL B. LEWIS, CALVIN PAGE, WM. TYLER, Jr., GEORGE TRISCOTT, EDWARD SHRIVER, LEVI MOBBERLY, DANIEL NICKLE, CHARLES SHRIVER, JOHN A. SIMMONS, DAVID B. DEVITT, Bucketmen - JOSHUA DILL, SOLOMON GETZENDANNER, SAMUEL R. HOGG, Enginemen - GEORGE SALMON, WM. C. RUSSELL, JACOB REIHL, FREDERICK A. SCHLEY, DANIEL HALLER, ISAIAH MEALEY, EDWARD MANTZ, LEWIS RAMSBURG, NIMROD BANTZ, JOHN RAMSBURG, JOHN RHODES, CAPAR KLINE, GIDEON BANTZ, Jr., GEORGE MARKELL, JOHN H. WILLIAMS, CHARLES WILSON, GEORGE MALAMBRE, PHILIP P. FOUT, JAMES HOPWOOD, JOHN REIHL, PERRY YOUNG, DAVID HALLER, GEORGE F. STAYMAN, HENRY HOUCK, HENRY SCHLEY, PHILIP ATTIG JOHN YOUNG, MICHAEL H. HALLER, GEORGE HARDT, GEORGE KOONTZ, JAMES REYNOLDS, A. B. HANSON, JAS. STEVENS, WM. C. SMALLWOOD, Doct.

WM. TYLER, ASBURY H. HUNT, GEORGE RICE, DAVID SCHLEY, GEO. M. TYLER, JOHN McPHERSON, JOS. LOKEY, GEORGE LARE, JOHN A. STEINER, JOHN DUVALL, RAYMOND SANDERSON, WM. T. PALMER, JACOB BUCKEY, DAVID C. STEINER, WM. MARKELL, JOHN E. SCHLEY, HENRY FESSLER, A. A. STAMBAUGH, DANIEL HIMBURG, JOSEPH LEONARD, DENNIS SCHOLL, WILLIAM J. ROSS, GEORGE A. PEARRE, FREDERICK A. RIGNEY, SOLOMON FAUBLE, THOMAS GURLEY, A. K. MANTZ, HENRY ZEIGLER, RICH'D. H. MARSHALL, PHILIP KUNKLE, AMBROSE INGMAN, NILES EICHELBERGER. Honorary members: DAVID STEINER, PATRICK TORMEY, FREDERICK A. SCHLEY, JAMES WALLING, ISAIAH MEALEY, ED. MANTZ, EDWARD A. LYNCH, A. D. O'LEARY, JOHN REIHL, HENRY SCHLEY, JAMES REYNOLDS, A. B. HANSON, WM. C. SMALLWOOD, Dr. WM. TYLER, DAVID SCHLEY, JOHN McPHERSON, WILLIAM J. ROSS, JOSHUA DILL, RICHARD C. MARSHALL.

February 9, 1838 (MHS)
1415. (D) In this city, on Thursday the 1st inst., Mr CHRISTIAN S. CARMACK, in about the 35th year of his age.

February 16, 1838 (MHS)
1416. (M) On the 13th inst., by the Rev. J. McElroy, Mr AMOS L. WELLING, to Miss JANE JUDY, both of Frederick Co.
1417. (D) In the city of Baltimore, on Thursday evening the 8th inst., Miss SEVILLA DAVIS, (formerly of this place,) in the 29th year of her age.

February 23, 1838 (MHS)
1418. (D) On Sunday morning the 14th inst., in Liberty Town, RACHEL ELIZABETH ROOT, daughter of Daniel and Mary Root, of this place, after a violent attack of about 21 hours, aged about 3 years.
1419. (D) Death of CHESTER RINGGOLD, Esq., a member of the Jefferson Bar, and lately chosen attorney for this district. He expired in Fayette, on Friday evening last, at about 10 o'clock. (Torch Light)

March 2, 1838 (MHS)
1420. (F) The barn of Mr MOSES WORMAN, said to be one of the largest and most costly in the county, togather with a quanity of wheat and oats, was entirely destroyed by fire on

Sunday last. Which is about 2 miles from the city. The alarm which was turned in a little before 12 o'clock.

1421. Jury for the County: MICHAEL BLESSING, JACOB BRUNNER, DANIEL BRENGLE, CHARLES BURKHART, WILLIAM CREAGER, NICHOLAS CROMWELL, THOS. A. FLEMING, C. GETZENDANNER, BASIL HAYDEN, J. HARBAUGH, of J., ANDREW HEIM, GEORGE KUHN, JACOB T. C. MILLER, WILSON L. McELFRESH, AMOS NORRIS, SEBASTIAN RAMSBURG, FRANCIS SHAW, JOHN SIFFORD, THOS. C. SHIPLEY, MICHAEL THOMAS, FELIX B. TANEY, LLOYD THOMAS, GEORGE THOMAS, SAMUEL WILHIDE, JACOB WETNIGHT.

1422. Corporate election results: Mayor: BALTZELL - 326, KOLB - 283. Alderman GEORGE HOSKINS, WILLIAM KOLB, MAHLON TALBOTT, EDWARD SHRIVER, JOHN A. SIMMONS. Common Council: Ward #1. GEO. METZGER. Ward #2. CHARLES GETZENDANNER. Ward #3. P. L. STORM. Ward #4. LEWIS MEDTART. Ward #5. HIRAM KEEFER. Ward #6. D. J. MARKEY. Ward #7. P. DEGRANGE.

March 9, 1838 (MHS)

1423. (D) On Monday 26th ult., at his residence near Salisbury, Somerset Co., MD., the Right Rev'd. WM. MURRAY STONE, D.D., Bishop of the Protestant Episcopal Church, in MD., died from gastrich fever.

1424. (D) On the 26th ult., DAVID BENJAMIN, infant son of Peter and Elizabeth Brain.

1425. (D) On Friday the 27th ult., Mr JACOB SUMMERS, residing about 4 miles from this place. He was hauling in gain, near his back yard, his son about 4 years old, when unobserved by the father, to get on board the wagon, and was caught between the wheels and the body of the wagon and instantly killed. (Williamsport Banner)

March 23, 1838 (MHS)

1426. (M) On Tuesday evening last, by the Rev. Dr. Johns, JAMES W. W. GORDON, M.D., to CATHARINE ELENORA, youngest daughter of Rezin Rowles, of Frederick Co., MD.

1427. (D) In Boston on Wednesday morning the 7th inst., of consumpton, contracted while a novice in the Charlestown Nunnery, Miss REBECCA THERESA REED, aged 26.

1428. Officers of the new Board of Alderman, and Common Council, were elected on Monday the 19th inst. GODFREY

KOONTZ, Register and Clerk to the Board of Alderman. HENRY BAER, Collector of Tax. EZRA DADISMAN, Clerk to the Board of the Common Council. JOHN FESSLER, City Commissioner. ROBERT McCLEARY, GEORGE HAUER, ANDREW HEIM, Commissioners of Tax. JOHN FESSLER, Clock Winder. C. HILTON, Market Master. C. HILTON, G. FAGAN, Lamp Lighters. GEO. KOONTZ, JOHN BENDER, City Constables and Superintendent of Streets. S. STICKELL, Hay Weighter. P. ROHR, Collector of Water Rents. JOHN H. WILLIAMS, Printer. C. MYERS, Messenger.

April 6, 1838 (MHS)

1429. (M) On Thursday morning last, by the Rev. S. R. Waters, Mr JOHN MILLER, to Miss MARY HOOVER, both of Middletown Valley.

April 13, 1838 (MHS)

1430. (M) On Tuesday evening last, by the Rev. John L. Pitts, Mr GEORGE COOKERLY, to Miss CELENA CAROLINE BEALL, both of this co.
1431. (M) On Thursday evening last, by the same, Mr DAVID O. THOMAS, to Miss ELIZABETH STAUFFER, both of this co.
1432. (M) On Thursday, March the 29th., by the Rev. Daniel Zacharias, Mr SAMUEL NUSSBAUM, to Miss CATHARINE REESE, all of this co.
1433. (D) At his residence in Montgomery Co., on the 3rd inst., Mr WILLIAM TRUNDLE, aged 33 years, after a short illness of 2 days. He leaves a widow and 4 children, and a member of the Church of Christ.

April 21, 1838 (MHS)

1434. WM. R. KING, Esq., has been appointed Post-Master, at the Point of Rocks.
1435. The Rev. JOSEPH SMITH, will preach in the Presbyterian Church, next Sabbath morning at 10 o'clock.

May 4, 1838 (MHS)

1436. Appointed by the Executive of Maryland, for Frederick County, as Justices of the Levy Court: MARTIN EICHELBERGER, FREDERICK TROXELL, SOLOMON FORREST, THOMAS SPRINGER, JEREMIAH G. MORRISON, WILLIAM LYNCH, WM. DUDERAR, PATRICK O'NEILL, ABEL RUSSELL, DANIEL DUVALL, and ELIAS CRUTCHLEY.

1437. Rev'd. STEPHEN WILLIAMS, will preach in the Presbyterian Church, next Sabbath morning at 10 o'clock.
1438. (D) Near Philadelphia, on the 30th ult., Mrs HENERIETTA WEAVER, consort of Mr James S. Weaver, of Baltimore, and daughter of George Trisler, Esq., of this place. Her remains were carried to the silent tomb from the residence of her father, yesterday afternoon at 2 o'clock, on the German Reformed burial grounds.

June 1, 1838 (MHS)

1439. (M) On Tuesday morning the 29th ult., by the Rev. Mr Elder, of Baltimore Mr CASPER MANTZ, to Miss ELIZABETH H. ELDER.

June 8, 1838 (MHS)

1440. (D) Departed this life on Tuesday night, May the 18th ult., at her residence near Emmittsburg, after a short illness, Mrs SARAH HOOVER, in the 56th year of her age.

June 15, 1838 (MHS)

1441. (D) At his residence in the County of Powhattan VA., on Saturday evening the 26th of May last, EDWARD F. BAUGH, Esq., in the 68th year of his age. (Richmond Enquirer)
1442. (D) On the 11th of May, in Saline Co., MO., Mr JAMES CLEMSON, in the 58th year of his age.

June 22, 1838 (MHS)

1443. (D) On Friday night the 8th inst., at his residence near Buckey's-Town, Frederick Co., MD., after a severe and protracted illness, Mr PETER STITCHER, aged 54 years. His remains were removed to Baltimore City, on Sunday and deposited in the family burial grounds.
1444. (D) On Thursday the 7th inst., at Oxford, the residence of Mr Edwards, Mrs ELENOR M. FRISBY, consort of the late James Edwards Frisby, in the 23rd year of her age. She leaves a infant daughter, she accompanied her sick husband to the West Indies, to try the effects of that climate. A short time after their return he fell victim to the fatal disease of consumption in a few months, she feel victim to the same disease. She will be laid beside her husband.

June 29, 1838 (MHS)

1445. (D) At the residence of her brother-in-law, Barent Hoes,

Esq., in the village of Kinderhook, (N.Y.,) on the 19th inst., Miss JANE VANBUREN, sister of the President of United States, in the 59th year of her age.

July 6, 1838 (MHS)

1446. (M) Thursday evening last, by the Rev. Mr Perry, LOT NORRIS, Esq., to Miss ELIZABETH ANN, daughter of the late William Gaither, Esq., all of this co.
1447. (M) On the 7th of June, by the Rev. S. W. Harkey, Mr DAVID STOCKMAN, to Miss ELIZABETH WASKEY, all of this co.
1448. (M) On the 25th inst., by the same, Mr JOSHUA J. ZIMMERMAN, to Miss SUSAN M. BEARD, all of this co.
1449. (M) On the 28th inst., by the same, Mr JACOB Mac RANDER, to Miss CATHARINE KING, all of this city.
1450. (D) At his residence near Emmittsburgh, on Friday last, ANDREW HORNER, in the 63rd year of his age.
1451. (D) Departed this life, on the 29th inst., ANN MALOINE, daughter of Nicholas W. and Eliza Ann Hammond, aged 17 months.

July 20, 1838 (MHS)

1452. (D) A black boy owned by Mr JACOB KELLER, of this city, was drowned on Sunday last, while bathing in the Monocacy.
1453. The Rev. BENJAMIN KURTZ, of Baltimore, will preach in the Lutheran Church, on next Sabbath, 22nd July.

August 3, 1838 (MHS)

1454. The Rev. W. H. SMITH, will preach in the Lutheran Church, on next Sabbath, August 3.

August 10, 1838 (MHS)

1455. (F) The barn of Mr JOHN GITTINGER, (in the Buckeystown District,) burnt to the ground on Wednesday night the 1st inst., the entire crop of wheat, (about 800 bushels of rye,) hay, a quanity of old oats, and corn. Is suppose to have been the work of incendiary, and was discovered about 11 o'clock, at night.
1456. (D) At his residence in Creagerstown in this co., on Tuesday morning the 7th inst., Mr FREDERICK EICHELBERGER, in the 76th year of his age.
1457. (D) Near Tallahassee, on the 13th inst., Col. BAKER JOHNSON, formerly of Frederick Co., MD., in the 50th year

of his age. He leaves a wife and 5 children. Col. Johnson, was the son of Col. Baker Johnson, of Frederick Towne, MD. One of the noble band of Patriots, who in the most gloomy time of the American Revolution, who commanded a regiment of volunteers, and in company with his brothers, Gen. Thomas and Col. Johnson, marched to Jersey, and with their regiments, and the Maryland Milita, formed the greatest part of Gen. Washington's forces, on the memorable winter of 1776 and 1777 Col. Johnson inherited all the virtues of patriotism which enobled his father, was always beloved and esteemed by his neighbors and friends, a christian gentleman and a friend in whom their was no guile.

1458. (D) On the 19th July, at his residence, near Liberty Copper Mines, MARTIN B. GARBER, in the 27th year of his age. He leaves a wife and 2 small children. During excessively warm weather, he became overheated from exertion, and died within 1 day. He was the Fife Major of the regiment, and was buried by the Woodsboro Rifle Company, with Honors of War.

1459. (D) On Thursday the 2nd inst., at her residence in Carroll Co., HANNAH H., consort of Charles W. Hood, and daughter of Walter Worthington Esq.

1460. At the Democratic Republican Convention, a resolution to compose a committee of 35 to represent this district in the county convention on the 18th inst., to act as excutive officers, as members of this delegation and that 10 members of it be also elected from the of the Democratic Republican Associations of young men, purpose of nominating a Senatorial candidate, and a Delegate ticket: PETER H. BROWN, NICHOLAS HOLTZ, NIMROD OWINGS, WILLIAM C. MARTIN, JOHN RIGNEY, GEORGE MALAMBRE, EZRA BENTZ, JOHN H. FOUT, THOMAS GURLEY, STEPHEN RAMSBURG, EZRA HOUCK, JOHN SCHOLL, GEORGE MARTZ, MICHAEL BYRNE, GEORGE SMITH, HENRY NIXDORFF, HENRY KEEFER, THOMAS H. O'NEALL, CORNELIUS STALEY, WILLIAM G. COLE, NICHOLAS WHITMORE, PETER GOODMANSON, GEORGE W. ENT, CHARLES SHRIVER, MATTHIAS E. BARTGIS, JOHN A. SIMMONS, JACOB SHRIVER, JAMES HERGESHEIMER, JOHN HOUCK, AMBROSE INGMAN, SAMUEL CARMACK, WILLIAM KOLB, JACOB MARKELL, JOHN McCARTHY, FREDERICK A. RIGNEY.

August 17, 1838 (MHS)
1461. The members of the Democratic Association of young men, are requested to meet at Mr CHAMBER's Hotel on Monday evening next at 8 o'clock, P.M., an address is expected.

September 7, 1838 (MHS)
1462. (F) Last week at Sugar Loaf, was accidently set on fire, was extinquished without much material damage. On Sunday the Catoctin Mountains was discovered to be on fire, in the neighborohood of Mr HENRY BRIEN's Iron Works. The dewelling, barn, out-houses and entire crop of grain on one of the farms of JAS. L. HAWKINS, Esq., on the Merryland Tract was destroyed on Sunday last, it is said to have originated from the negro children's playing with fire, during the absence of the family residing on the place.

October 26, 1838 (MHS)
1463. (M) In Gettysburg on the 18th inst., by the Rev. Mr Grier, Mr WILLIAM WILSON, of Huntington Co., PA., to Miss MARTHA GURLEY, daughter of Thomas Gurley, Esq., Sheriff of Frederick Co., MD.

November 2, 1838 (MHS)
1464. (D) Death of JAMES DIXON, District member of the Bar, addressed to the court of this co., by Mr Warfield, Mr Frederick A. Schley.

November 9, 1838 (MHS)
1465. Democratic Representives celebration, to be held at the court house square, on the 9th of October, at 12 o'clock. President - Dr. WILLIAM TYLER, Vice Presidents - Col. JOHN McPHERSON, Col. JOHN H. McELFRESH, Col. HENRY DUNLOP, Col. THOMAS JOHNSON, Maj. JOHN HARRITT, JOHN SIFFORD, EZRA CRAMER, JOSEPH SMITH, of Liberty, Dr. E. W. MOBBERLY, GEO. THOMAS, JOHN R. CUTIS, GEO. HARMAN. Chief Marshall - Capt. WILLIAM SMALL, Assistant Marshalls - Col. SAMUEL CARMACK, Capt. GEO. HOSKINS.
1466. (D) At Germantown, Ohio, on the 8th of February last, Mrs MARGARET ANN MUMMEY, consort of Mr Samuel J. Mummey, in the 28th year of her age.

November 23, 1838 (MHS)
1467. (D) On the 14th inst., at the residence of his son-in-law, Mr

Daniel Weller, near Creagerstown, Frederick Co., MD., Maj. FREDERICK WILLHIDE, a soldier of the Revolution, in the 85th year of his age. Born on the 2nd of Nov. 1762, enlisted in the German Regiment of this State for 3 years, during which period he was promoted to Orderly Sergeant in the company to which he was attached and served out his term of enlistment, afterwards acted as volunteer until the close of the war. Was present at the battles of Brandywine, Germantown, Trenton and Monmouth, and witnessed the closing of the glorius struggle at Yorktown. He afterwards commanded a company of volunteers and subsequencely commissioned a Major in the Old Maryland Line, he was never to see any active service after the war. The "Mechanics-Town Guard" accompanied his remains to the grave.

November 30, 1838 (MHS)

1468. (M) In Westminster, on Tuesday the 29th inst., by the Rev. Isaac Webster, Mr JACOB ECKER, of this co., to Miss SARAH DUDDERAR, daughter of William Dudderar, Esq., of Frederick Co.

1469. (M) At the same time and place by the same, Mr JOSIAH WORMAN, to Miss ELIZABETH DUDDERAR, daughter of William Dudderar, Esq., of Fred., Co., MD.

1470. (M) On the 19th inst., at Esperanza, by the Rev. J. G. Morris, Mr WILLIAM W. PLUMMER, of New Market, to Miss HARRIET L. FINCH, adopted daughter of Dr. Hopkins.

1471. (M) On Thursday evening last, (at Dorsey's City Hotel,) by the Rev. John L. Pitts, Mr TIMOTHY A. HERRINGTON, to Miss MARTHA GARFORD, both of VA.

1472. (M) On the same evening by the same, Mr THOMAS NICHOLS, to Miss BARBARA SPURRIER, both of Frederick Co.

1473. (D) On Friday the 16th inst., in the city, Mrs SUSAN, wife of Henry Rhodes, in the 69th year of her age, she leaves a husband and 4 small children.

1474. (D) In this city on the 17th inst., MARY ANN, infant daughter of William Elkins, Esq., in the 4th year of her age.

1475. (D) On the 17th inst., Mr HOFFMAN, of this co., in the 82nd year of his age.

1476. (D) At Bel-Air, on the 19th inst., EVAN POULTNEY, in the 45th year of his age.

December 14, 1838 (MHS)

1477. JOHN RIGNEY, Esq., has been appointed by the Post-

Master General, Post-Master at this place, in place of JACOB ROHR, Esq. Mr R., will enter upon his duties of office on the 1st of January.

1478. (D) Lately departed this life, ALEXANDER FULTON, at his residence near Mt. Vernon, (OH). A native of Ireland, and came to this Country more than 40 years ago, and resided the greater part of that time near Little Pipe Creek, in this co., about 2 years since he emigrated to Ohio.

1839

January 5, 1839 (MHS)

1479. (D) On Wednesday the 20th inst., Mr JACOB KITZMILLER, of Gettysburg, aged about 36 years.
1480. (M) Thursday evening last, at the Eagle Hotel in this city, by the Rev. Brison, Mr BENJAMINE RODRIC, to Miss ROSEBERRY, both of Jefferson Co., VA.
1481. (M) Thursday morning last, by the Rev. John L. Pitts, Mr FREDERICK COVELL, to Miss CATHARINE POOLE, both of this co.
1482. (M) On the 25th inst., Mr JAMES L. DAVIS, of Littlestown, to Miss CATHARINE, daughter of Col. Thomas Sappington, of Fred. Co., MD.
1483. The amount of flour inspected in Frederick City, with in the last 3 months up to the 1st of January 1838, is 1821 pounds flour, and 13 pounds rye flour. H. ROBINSON, Insepector.
1484. The line of stages from this city to Washington will on this day commence running daily.
1485. Candidates for Mayor - MICHAEL BALTZELL, JOHN BAILY, DANIEL KOLB, JOHN McDONALD. For Alderman - ANDREW HEIM, JACOB LITTLE, JACOB KELLER, HENRY KELLY, JACOB FAUBLE, ALBERT RITCHIE, MATTHIAS E. BARTGIS, GIDEON BANTZ, LEWIS BIRELY, DAVID BOYD, WILLIAM KOLB, JOHN A. SIMMONS, HORATIO WATERS, THOMAS C. PRINCE, HENRY KAUFFMAN, A. P. BEATTY, JAMES BRUNNER, JOHN ENGLEBRECHT, JOHN HANE, CHRISTIAN STEINER, WM. C. HOFFMAN. For the Common Council - Ward #1. CASPAR KLINE, DAVID FAUBLE, WILLIAM WILCOXON. Ward #6. DAVID J. MARKEY, WILLIAM BRENNER. Ward #7. W. F. JOHNSON, PETER DEGRANGE, GEORGE SALMON.

1837

THE TIMES AND DEMOCRATIC ADVOCATE

April 27, 1837 (MHS)

1486. (M) In York, on Wednesday morning the 5th inst., by the Rev. Dr. Mayer, Rev. SAMUEL R. FISHER, of Emmittsburg, MD., to Miss ELLEN E., daughter of Daniel M. May, Esq., editor of the "Republican Herald."

1487. (M) On Thursday evening last, by the Rev. S. W. Harkey, Mr DANIEL SINN, to Miss SUSAN LAMBRECHT, all of this co.

1488. (M) On Tuesday evening last, by the same, Mr JOHN NEIGH, to Miss JULIETTA GILBERT, all of this place.

1489. (M) On Tuesday last, by the same, Mr EDWARD C. CUNNINGHAM, of Warrenton, MO., to Miss ELIZABETH SLAGLE, of this co.

1490. (M) On Thursday afternoon, by the same, Mr MARTIN M. MAHARNA, to Miss MARGARET SHOTTS, all of this co.

1491. (M) On Thursday evening last, by the Rev. John L. Pitts, Mr NICHOLAS WAGNER, to Miss CHRISTIANNA SPONSELLER, all of this co.

1492. (M) On Thursday morning, by the Rev. J. Johns, Mr ALEXANDER NEILL, Jr., Esq., of Washington Co., to Miss MARY S., daughter of John Nelson, Esq., of Baltimore.

1493. (D) At Linganore, on Saturday the 1st of April 1837, after a short illness, MARIAN LOUISE, aged 3 years, 7 months and 3 days, and on Sunday the 16th inst., EDMUND CLEMSON, aged 6 years, 1 month and 23 days, oldest son, and only daughter of Col. Anthony and Sidney Ann Kimmel.

1494. (D) On Tuesday last, Mr JACOB GETZENDANNER, at the Poor House, of which he was the keeper, at advanced age.

1495. Appointment of Post-Masters for Frederick Co. LEWIS J. GROVE, Esq., Warfield's Stone, Carroll Co. JOHN H. T. COCKEY, Urbana, Frederick Co. WM. M. WATKINS, Sykesville, Carroll Co. GEORGE PARKS, Esq., Mechanicsville, Frederick Co. JAMES FRITZPATRICK, Old Town, Allegany Co.

1496. Candidate for Congress: JOSEPH H. PALMER.

May 4, 1837 (MHS)

1497. (M) On Saturday morning last, by the Rev. Mr Slicer, Mr

TOBIAS WALTZ, to Miss ELIZA ANN GREY, all of George-Town, D.C.

1498. The Rev. S. W. HARKEY, will deliver a Missionary Sermon, on this day, (being Ascension Day,) at 10 o'clock. The public are respectfully invited to attend.

1499. (D) At the residence of Levi Chambers, in Anne Arundel Co., JOSEPH PEDDICOARD, aged 84 years and 23 days.

1500. (D) On Friday the 14th inst., at Upton, his residence in Anne Arundel Co., CALEB DORSEY, of Thomas, in the 90th year of his age.

1501. Candidates for Congress: DAVID SCHLEY, Esq., FRANCIS THOMAS, Esq.

May 11, 1837 (MHS)

1502. (M) On Tuesday morning last, by Somerset R. Waters, Mr CHARLES MILLER, of Frederick Co., to Miss ROSANNA ROBECKER, of Washington Co., MD.

1503. (M) At Gettysburg, on Thursday week, by the Rev. James C. Watson, Mr JHU. ROYER, of Carroll Co., to Miss MARGARET TROXELL, of Frederick Co.

1504. (D) In Frederick Town, on Thursday morning last, the 5th inst., Mrs ANN J. GRAHAM, the relict of Major Jno. Graham, and eldest daughter of the late Governor Thos. Johnson, in the 69th year of her age.

1505. (D) On Tuesday last, in the neighborohood of Frederick, VALENTINE, son of Valentine A. Albaugh, in the 5th year of his age.

1506. (D) On The 29th ult., of a lingering disease, Mrs ROSANNA MARTZ, daughter of George Martz, Sen., of this vicinity, in the 56th year of her age.

1507. (D) On the 4th inst., in Frederick, at the residence of her son H. M. Jamison, Mrs MARGARET BELT, in the 59th years of her age.

1508. (D) On Friday afternoon the 5th inst., under the most afflicting and heartrending circumstances. The Rev. Dr. DAVID F. SCHAEFFER, fell a victim to the hand of death. He had disposed of his property, placed his children under suitable protectors and guardians, and retired to a private boarding house near this city.

1509. The Criminal Court of this county commenced its session on Monday last, the following are members of the jurors: Frederick - CASPAR QUYNN, HENRY SCHULTZ, JACOB ENGELBRECHT, JOHN BRUNNER, PHILIP UNGLEBERGER, JOHN DERR, JOHN TITLOW, NIMROD OWINGS.

Woodsborough - JOHN B. STIMMELL, BROOKE BAKER, ROBERT Y. STOKES, JACOB ROOT. Liberty - JOSEPH SMITH, DAVID ETZLER, HENRY BAKER, JACOB HALL. New Market - THOMAS NORWOOD, ELIAS BUTLER, THOMAS BRASHEAR, SAMUEL GEYER. Buckeystown - JAMES DAVIS, EDWARD HOWARD, WILLIAM R. KING, ELIAS L. DELASHMUTT. Middletown - ISRAEL RAMSBURGH, GEORGE W. SANDS, JACOB FLOOK, JOHN YOUNG, DANIEL HERRING. Hauver - JACOB HARBAUGH, GEORGE FOX, OVERTON HARM. Emmittsburg - ROBERT ANNAN, JOHN AGNEW, JOHN ZIMMERMAN, FREDERICK CRABBS, Jr. Creagerstown - JOHN P. ZIMMERMAN, JOSEPH EICHELBERGER, WILLIAM TODD, HENRY G. WATERS. Petersville - JOHN WILLIARD, JOHN BARNES, JEREMIAH G. MORRISON, TILGHMAN BISER. Jefferson - THOMAS LAMAR, JOHN DARE, PERRY HILLEARY, EMANUEL THOMAS.

May 25, 1837 (MHS)

1510. (M) On the 11th inst., by the Rev. S. W. Harkey, Rev. CHARLES MARTIN, of Martinsburg, VA., to Miss ELIZA CARLTON, daughter of the late Thomas Carlton, Esq., of this city.
1511. (D) Its with pain we have to announce the death of JOHN R. KEY, Esq., of Washington, attorney-at-law, and son of F. S. Key, Esq.
1512. (D) In this co., on the 25th ult., Mr YATE PLUMMER, in the 93rd year of his age.
1513. The Republican voters of election District #3, held its meeting at the Academy, ISRAEL RAMSBURGH, Esq., was called to the chair, and MICHAEL McCARTNEY, appointed Secretary. For the Congressional convention, to be held at Hagerstown on the 10th of June next: DAVID MAUGENS, DANIEL S. BISER, SOMERSET R. WATERS, JOHN SIFFORD, and SAMUEL YEAST. For the County convention: ISRAEL RAMSBURG, MICHAEL McCARTNEY, WM. HYATT, MARTIN S. GROVE, JOHN HAGAN, J. B. WISE, DAVID MAUGENS, DAVID SHINDLER, DANIEL S. BISER, JACOB WETNIGHT, JOHN SIFFORD, SAMUEL AHALT, SOMERSET R. WATERS, SAMUEL YEAST, EPHRAIM LONG, PETER PALMER, JOHN BOGNER, GEORGE GAVER, SOLOMON ROUTZONG, SAMUEL SUMMERS, JOHN YOUNG, JACOB MILLER, PHILIP COBLENTZ, Jr., DANIEL C. HERRING, LEONARD S. GROVE, GEORGE TITLOW, GEORGE W.

MARIS, ROBERT ALEXANDER, GEORGE KOONTZ, JOHN ALEXANDER, JOHN A. MAGRUDER, WILLIAM VORE, DAVID KAILOR, DAVID BOILEAM, and FRANCIS RICHMOND.

1514. The Hauvers District meeting of the Democratic Republican voters was organized in Sabillasville, on Saturday the 13th inst., JACOB HARBAUGH, of J., was called as chairman and THOMAS CONN, appointed secretary. A committee to draft resolutions was composed of: JOHN HARBAUGH, JOHN MILLER, SOLOMON HARBAUGH, JOHN McCLAIN, THOS. CONN, and CHARLES W. BIGHAM. One of the resolutions called for a committee to represent this district at the convention in Hagerstown on 10th day of June next: GEORGE ZOLLINGER, HENRY HARBAUGH, of C., SOLOMON HARBAUGH, GEORGE P. FOX, JOHN BUZZARD, GEORGE KLINE and HENRY HARBAUGH, of John.

1515. Meeting of the County Democratic Republicans was held at the Court House in this city, on Wednesday evening at early candlelight. On a motion of P. H. BROWN, Esqr., the meeting was organized by calling JOSEPH TANEY, and WM. WORTHINGTON, Esqrs., to the chair, and on motion MADISON NELSON, Esqr., BARZILLAI MARRIOTT, was appointed Secretaries. The chair appointed a committee of 5 to select 50 persons to compose a Central Committee, whose duties is to appoint sub-committees. (PETER H. BROWN, CHRISTIAN GETZENDANNER, JOHN RIGNEY, HENRY NIXDORFF, and JOHN AGNEW, Esqr.) The chair appointed a committee of 20 to represent it in the convention on the 17th June. GEORGE W. ENT, JOSEPH M. PALMER, GEORGE MARTZ, EDWARD SCHLEY, CASPAR QUYNN, NIMROD OWINGS, JACOB SHRIVER, MADISON NELSON, JOHN RIGNEY, NICHOLAS HOLTZ, JACOB YEAGLE, JOSEPH PAYNE, GEORGE SMITH, A. B. HANSON, NICHOLAS WHITMER, CONRAD STALEY, J. H. McELFRESH, JNO. A. SCHAEFFER, JNO. McPHERSON, HENRY NIXDORFF. Central Committee: GEORGE W. ENT, HENRY R. WARFIELD, JACOB MARKELL, JACOB KELLER, CASPAR QUYNN, CONRAD STALEY, EZRA BENTZ, WM. TYLER, Jun., FRED'K. LAMBERT, EDWARD SHRIVER, GEORGE SMITH, EZRA HOUCK, EMANUEL SMITH, NICHOLAS WHITMER, EDWARD KOONTZ, NIMROD OWINGS, FRED'K. LAMBRECHT, CORNELIUS STALEY, J. SHAWBAKER, NICHOLAS HOLTZ, WM. KOLB, MOSES STALEY, W. CLINGAN, MICHAEL BURNS, HENRY

KAUFFMAN, JNO. McPHERSON, WM. BRENNER, JOSEPH STOOP, GEO. MALAMBRE, WM. METZ, MADISON NELSON, JOHN TITLOW, GEORGE HOSKINS, JACOB SHRIVER, WM. C. MARTIN, EZRA DADISMAN, A. P. BEATTY, JOHN LAMBERT, ISAAC WILLIAMSON, DAN'L. SHAWEN, Sen., JNO. A. SIMMONS, PHILIP KIZER, SAM'L. NORRIS, ADAM STOLL, HENRY BANTZ, JOHN MEASELL J. H. McELFRESH.

June 1, 1837 (MHS)

1516. (M) At Middletown, MD., on the 23rd of May, by the Rev. J. C. Bucher, Mr DANIEL LEASER, to Miss MARY GRAVER, all of Middletown, Frederick Co., MD.
1517. (M) Near Middletown, on the 25th of May, by the Rev. J. C. Bucher, Dr. GEORGE W. MARIS, to Miss ELIZABETH ANN, only daughter of the late Mr George Motter, and his widow Susan, all of Middletown Valley, MD.
1518. Following persons were appointed Postmasters for the county. DANIEL MARTZ McKinstry's Mills, Frederick Co. WILLIAM WERTENBAKER, Monrovia, Frederick Co.

June 8, 1837 (MHS)

1519. (M) On the 11th ult., by the Rev. Dr. Boteler, Mr ANDREW KESSLER, Junior, to Miss LAURETTZ LAMAR, daughter of Thomas Lamar, Esq.
1520. (M) On Thursday evening last, by the Rev. Daniel Zacharias, Mr JOHN A. CASSELL, to Miss CATHARINE RHODES, all of this co.
1521. (D) Near Middletown, on Monday last, of a lingering illness, Mr JOHN WELKER, aged 66 years, 9 months.
1522. (D) At Charleston, S.C., on Friday the 18th inst., of consumption, 1st. Lieut. JOHN F. KENNEDY, of the Army of the Unitd States. Lieut. Kennedy was from Hagerstown, MD., aged 28 years, and said to have been a young man of great worth.
1523. The Republican voters of Liberty District met at the house of Daniel Root on a motion CHARLES WORTHINGTON, of J., was called to the chair, and JOSEPH SMITH, appointed secretary. The following persons were appointed to represent this district in the county convention, to be held in Frederick-Town, on the 17th inst. JOHN KINZER, WM. HOBBS, JOHN WOLF, JOHN GLISON, Sr., Esq., WM. MORRISON, ISAAC BROWER, Dr. JOHN W. DORSEY, BASIL HAYDEN, JOHN GAITHER, CHS. WORTHINGTON, of

J., JOSEPH SMITH, A. UNKEFER, PETER BOND, N. C. HAMMOND, DANL. HERRING, EPHRAIM COVER, T. P. WILLIAMS, LEONARD REDDICK, ELY BERRIER, PHILIP BERRIER, Dr. J. E. MORRIS, SOLOMON EARNST, JACOB DUDRER, WARFIELD SIMPSON, JACOB HOFFMAN, S. A. LAUVER, JOSEPH RADCLIFF.

June 15, 1837 (MHS)

1524. (M) At Columbus, Ohio, on Wednesday last, by the Rev. Mr May, Mr EDWARD F. WILLSON, formerly of Frederick Co., MD., to Miss VIRGINIA, eldest daughter of Mr Henry Matthias, of Madison Co., OH.
1525. (M) At Columbus, Ohio, on Tuesday last, by the Rev. S. C. Church, Mr W. A. HEBBARD, formerly of Frederick Co., MD., to Miss ANNA, eldest daughter of Col. J. Elwood, of Franklin Co., Ohio.
1526. (M) On Sunday last, by the Rev. John McElroy, Mr WILLIAM J. STEVENS, of Harpers Ferry, VA., to Miss ELIZABETH MICHAEL, youngest daughter of Andrew Michael, Esq., of this co.
1527. (M) On the 1st of June, near Woodsboro, by the Rev. J. W. Hoffmier, Mr MICHAEL GRINDER, to Miss MARGARET ANN, second daughter of Mr Samuel Wilhide, both of Frederick Co.
1528. (M) On Tuesday morning last, by the Rev. D. Zacharias, Mr DAVID HARGATE, to Miss REBECCA DUDROE, all of this co.
1529. (D) At the residence of her son, Geo. W. Poole, on Saturday the 10th inst., ACHASAH, relict of the late Brice Poole, Esq., aged 66 years, 4 months and 4 days.

June 22, 1837 (MHS)

1530. Democratic Republican nomination for Congress - FRANCIS THOMAS. For the Assembly - GEORGE W. ENT, EZRA CRAMER, JOHN W. GEYER, DANIEL S. BISER.

June 29, 1837 (MHS)

1531. (D) In New Market, on Friday the 16th of June inst., Mrs MARY ANN BURGESS, consort of Washington Burgess, after a severe and painful illness of many weeks duration. The decease was a member of the Methodist Episcopal Church. Her end was peaceful and in keeping with the tenor of her life.
1532. Candidate for the office of Sheriffalty: THOMAS C. PRINCE.

July 6, 1837 (MHS)

1533. (D) On Monday evening last, ELEANOR, infant daughter of Jacob and Mary Holler, in the 3rd month of her age.
1534. (D) On Tuesday morning last, IGNATIUS WATERS, fourth son of Somerset R. Waters, in the 6th year of his age.
1535. (D) On Tuesday the 27th inst., JOHN HENRY, son of John and Mary Richardson, aged 7 months and 14 days.
1536. The Whigs met in this city on Saturday last and nominated the following gentlemen as candidates for the General Assembly: GEORGE SCHLEY, of Frederick District. JOHN KEFAUVER, of Middletown District. GEORGE BRECKENBAUGH, of the Creagerstown District. NATHAN H. OWINGS, of the Liberty District.

August 24, 1837 (MHS)

1537. (D) On Friday evening last, after a few days illness, ANN ELIZABETH COCKEY HOFFMIER, daughter of Rev. J. W. Hoffmier, aged 6 months.
1538. (D) On Tuesday the 8th inst., after a short illness, LAWSON D. STOCKMAN, in the 19th year of his age.

August 31, 1837 (MHS)

1539. (M) On the 22nd inst., at Saint Thomas' Manor, Charles Co., MD., by the Rev. Thomas Lilly, S.J., Mr HENRY M. JAMISON, to Miss MARY AMANDA HOLMES.
1540. (M) On the 23rd inst., by the Rev. R. S. Grier, Mr ANDREW J. REA, (merchant,) of Emmitsburg, to Miss SARAH JAFE MALONY, of the same place.
1541. (M) On the 29th inst., by the Rev. D. Zacharias, Mr GEORGE W. LOCK, to Miss REBECCA ANN GORDON, both of Jefferson, VA.
1542. (D) Departed this life, on Tuesday 22nd inst., at the residence of Mr Joshua Chilton, in this co. The Hon. CHARLES J. KILGOUR, one of the Associate Judges of the 3rd Judical District of MD. Judge Kilgour had been to his farm in VA., and after leaving Mr Chiltons where he had spent the previous night, his horse took fright and running with full speed with the carriage against a tree, precipitated him into the road with such force as to cause his death in about a hour. (Rockville Free Press)
1543. (D) On the 7th int., in the 32nd year of her age, Mrs MINERVA NEAL.
1544. (D) On the 26th inst., FRANCIS EPHRAIM, son of Peter Thomas, aged 5 years 2 months and 22 days.

1545. (D) On Saturday last the 26th inst., at his residence on Carroll's Manor, Mr BAKER JAMISON, in the 53rd year of his age.

September 7, 1837 (MHS)

1546. (M) On Wednesday the 30th ult., by the Rev. E. Heiner, Mr EDWARD SHRIVER, attorney-at-law, of this city, to Miss ELIZABETH LYDIA, daughter of P. Reigart of Baltimore.
1547. (M) On Wednesday last evening, the 30th ult., by the Rev. Dr. Roberts, JOSEPH WEBSTER, of this city, to ELIZA G., second daughter of John M'Cabe, of Baltimore.

September 14, 1837 (MHS)

1548. (M) On Thursday evening last, by the Rev. D. Zacharias, Mr FREDERICK KEEFER, to Miss ELIZABETH HIMBURY, both of this city.
1549. (D) On the 31st ult., CHARLES EDWARD, infant son of Ezra Doll, aged 3 years, 6 months annd 27 days.

September 21, 1837 (MHS)

1550. (M) On Sunday the 3rd of September, in Fairfield, Adams Co., PA., by the Rev. Mr Paxton, Mr SOLOMON HARBAUGH, to Miss LYDIA WHITMORE.
1551. (M) On Tuesday the 5th nst., in Waynesburg, by the Rev. Mr Glessing, Mr JOHN BIRELY, to Miss SUSANNA H. MILLER, eldest daughter of Col. John Miller.
1552. (M) On the same day, by the same, Mr JOSEPH McCLANE, to Miss MARY EYCLER, daughter of Cove-Hollow, John Eycler.
1553. (M) On Thursday the 7th inst., Mr SAMUEL STRICKLAN, to Miss MARGARET STEM, daughter of Peter Stem, Esq.
1554. (M) On Friday the 4th ult., in Middletown, by the Rev. Mr Wachter, Mr SAMUEL SHANEBERGER, from the West, to Miss ELIZA ANN CASSELL, of Middletown.
1555. (M) On Thursday evening last, by the Rev. Mr Harkey, Mr JOHN LAYMAN, to Miss REBECCA BLESSING, all of this co.
1556. (M) On the same evening, by the same, Mr JOSEPH LONG, to Miss SALLY HITESHEW, both of this co.
1557. (D) In Burkettsville, ANN DRUSIL, daughter of Archibald and Susan Lamar, she was born January 23rd 1832, and departed this life on the 6th of September 1837, aged 5 years, 7 months and 14 days.

1558. (D) At Bloomsburg, Frederick Co., MD., on Friday the 8th inst., Mrs ELIZABETH JOHNSON, relict of Major Roger Johnson, in the 82nd year of her age.
1559. (D) At his residence in Baltimore Co., on the 27th ult., Rev. ANDREW HEMPHILL, of the M. E. Church.
1560. (D) In Annapolis, on the 8th ult., ROBERT EMMET CULBRETH, son of Thomas Culbreth, Esq., in the 26th year of his age.

September 28, 1837 (MHS)

1561. (M) On Thursday morning last, in Frederick City, by the Rev. John L. Pitts, Mr JOHN C. WHITEHILL, to Miss BARBARA D. WORMAN, second daughter of the late William Worman, Esq., both of this co.
1562. (D) At her residence near woodsborough, on Friday morning the 25th of August, after a short but severe illness, Mrs SABINA FULTON, in the 23rd year of her age. Consort of Mr John Fulton, and oldest daughter of Mr Samuel Wilhide.
1563. At City Hall an exhibition of Dr. COLLGER'S "Achromatic micro scope," this evening at 7 o'cock.
1564. (D) The little daughter of Mr MICHAEL WEANER, aged 10 years, near Harpers Ferry, VA., was burned to dath on the 4th inst., by her clothes taking fire.

October 5, 1837 (MHS)

1565. (M) On Thursday the 24th ult., by the Rev. Mr Wiser, ARCHIBALD B. KNODE, Esq., merchant of Dayton, Ohio, to Miss ISABELLA KEITH, youngest daughter of James Lagget, Esq., of Creagerstown, Frederick Co., MD.
1566. (M) On Tuesday last, in Hagerstown, by the Rev. Richard Wynkoop, J. DIXON ROMAN, Esq., to Miss LOUISA, youngest daughter of Mr John Kennedy, Esq.
1567. (M) On the 7th of September, by the Rev. J. C. Bucher, Mr WILLIAM ITHIRE, to Miss CATHARINE ANN, eldest daughter of Mr Joseph Leighter, all of Washington Co., MD.
1568. (M) On the 14th inst., by the same, Mr DANIEL YOUNG, to Miss ANN REBECCA, daughter of Mr George Kefauver, all of Middletown Valley, MD.
1569. (D) Near Middletown, MD., on the 23rd of September, after an afflicting illness, SARAH ANN MARIA, daughter of Mr Samuel Remsburg, in the 3rd year of her age.
1570. (D) Near Middletown on the 29th of September, JOHN, the third son of Mr John Michael, in the 7th year of his age.

1571. Election results - ENT - 2274, BISER - 2303, GEYER - 2287, CRAMER - 2219. Whigs - BRECKENBAUGH - 2425, SCHLEY - 2092, OWINGS - 2015, KEAFAUVER - 2099.

October 12, 1837 (MHS)

1572. (M) On Tuesday morning last, by the Rev. J. L. Pitts, Mr LOUIS D. WORLEY, to Miss HANNAH MENDENHALL, both of Waterford, Loudon Co., VA.
1573. (M) On Tuesday evening last, at the Eagle Hotel, Frederick, MD., by the Rev. Mr Brison, Mr DANIEL S. BOYLE, to Miss LOUISA BERLIN, both of Harpers Ferry, VA.
1574. (D) On Sunday the 4th inst., after a shorth illness, MARY HARTSOCK, aged 20 years. (Liberty-Town, Oct. 5, 1837)
1575. (D) On the 3rd inst., closed the exemplary life of JULIA ANN HARDING, only daughter of John and Hannah Harding, aged 13 years, 23 days.
1576. (D) On Sunday the 1st inst., at the residence of her grandfather, near Creagerstown, ANN ELIZABETH, eldest daughter of John Zimmerman, aged 5 years, 10 months and 5 days.
1577. (D) At New Orleans, of the prevailing epidemic, on the 19th ult., Mr ISAAC REICH, in the 27th year of his age. A native of this city.

October 19, 1837 (MHS)

1578. (M) On the 12th of Octobert, by the Rev. Mr Keller, Col. JOHN REAVER, of Piney Creek, near Fringer's Mill, Carroll Co., to Miss ANN ELIZABETH BOWERS, eldest daughter of Major Gen. John Bowers, of Adams Co., PA.
1579. (M) Another editor gone-married, in Hoosie, New York, JOHN C. HASWELL, editor of the Bennington Gazette, to Miss SAMALVA SHERWOOD, of Hoosie.
1580. (D) In Westminster, Carroll Co., on Monday morning the 9th inst., after a severe illness of 6 weeks, Mrs MARY TRUMBO, in the 81st year of her age. In her death, Westminster has lost one of their oldest and respectable citizens.
1581. (D) On Saturday the 9th inst., Mrs ELIZABETH GROVE, wife of Jacob Grove, Esq., of Westminster, aged 47 years.
1582. (D) On the same day, ANN, daughter of Conrad Moul, formerly of Hanover, PA., aged 18 years, 3 months and 27 days.

October 23, 1837 (MHS)

1583. (M) On Thursday evening last, by the Rev. D. Zacharias, Mr J. L. JOURDON, to Miss M. BUCKLES.

1584. (M) On Sunday evening the 15th inst., by the same, Mr OTHO REAL, of this vicinity, to Miss CATHARINE M. HANE, of Mr Mr John Hane, of this city.

1585. (M) On Thursday evening last, at Mr Bartgis Central Hotel, by the Rev. John L. Pitts, Mr JACOB MYERS, to Miss LYDIA INZOR, both of Carroll Co.

1586. (M) On Tuesday last, by the Rev. D. Zacharias, Mr GEO. GARRETT, to Miss SARAH SHRIVER, all of Mechaniestown.

1587. (M) On Tuesday the 17th inst., by the Rev. Robert S. Grier, Mr JOSEPH M. COOKS, of Franklin Co., PA., to Miss JANE EMMETT, of the vicinity of Emmitsburg.

1588. (D) At Middletown, Frederick Co., MD., on the 16th of October, after a protracted and distressing illness, Mrs ELIZABETH, relict of the late Mr Jonathan Levy, in the 56th year of her age.

1589. (D) On the 18th inst., Mrs SUSANNAH MAYU, of this co., in the 59th year of her age.

1590. (D) At his residence, in this city, on the 15th inst., Hon. JOHN L. HARDING, Chief Justice of the Orphan's Court of Frederick Co., in the 58th year of his age. His remains were respectfully interred in the Episcopal burying grounds of this place.

November 2, 1837 (MHS)

1591. (M) In Chambersburg, PA., on Wednesday morning the 25th inst., by the Rev. Mr Denny, the Rev. BENJAMIN KURTZ, editor of the Lutheran Observer, Baltimore, to Miss MARY CALHOUN, daughter of Alexander Calhoun, deceased, late cashier of the Bank of Chambersburg.

1592. (M) On Thursday evening last, by the Rev. J. L. Pitts, Mr HAMMEDATHA CECIL, of Frederick Co., to Miss MARY ANN, eldest daughter of Mr Richard Thompson, of Montgomery Co.

1593. (M) On the same day, by the same, Mr CORNELIUS CLEARY, to Miss EMMA WINDSOR, daughter of Zadock Windsor, Esq., all of this co.

November 9, 1837 (MHS)

1594. (D) On Saturday evening last, Mr JONATHAN EADER, an enterprizing and most worthy citizen.

1595. (D) On Saturday night last, WILLIAM MORGAN, oldest son of Mr Thomas Morgan, of this city.
1596. (D) On Wednesday morning last, at her residence in Hagerstown, Mrs SARAH PRICE, consort of William Price, Esq.
1597. (D) On Friday last, the 3rd inst., at his residence in this city, after an illness of a few days, Mr VALENTINE J. BRUNNER, in the 41st year of his age. He was for many years a leading member of the German Reformed Church, and took active part in the Sabbath School course. His remains were taken on Sunday last into the Church, where an appropate sermon was preached to a large audience, after which he was followed to the grave.
1598. (D) At Mount Vernon, Carroll Co., on Monday morning, the 30th ult., after a protracted illness of 12 weeks, JOHN HOOPER, eldest son of Joseph T. F. Hooper, of that place, aged 14 years, and 24 days.

November 16, 1837 (MHS)

1599. (D) On Sunday morning a week, WM. MORGAN, in the 19th year of his age, son of Thomas Morgan, of this city.
1600. (D) On the 18th inst., at New Orleans, after an illness of about 2 weeks, FREDERICA S. CONRADT, late of Baltimore, MD., a member of the of the Methodist Episcopal Church.
1601. (D) In this city, on Tuesday the 7th inst., Miss SENOVA HUGHES, a daughter of the late John Hughes.
1602. (D) On the 16th of Oct., last, near Vicksburg, Mr GEORGE KRBS SCHAEFFER, aged 18 years, son of the late Rev. Dr. Schaeffer, of this city. Only a few months have elapsed since he left our midst, in high health and full of youthful expectations.
1603. (D) At his farm near Point of Rocks, MD., on the 8th inst., after a protracted illness of more then 3 weeks, WILLIAM S. JOHNSON, son of the late John Johnson, in the 40th year of his age, he leaves a wife and 2 small children.
1604. (D) At his residencenear Unionville, on Tuesday the 7th inst., Mr MICHAEL SHRINER, in his 63rd year.

November 23, 1837 (MHS)

1605. (D) On Friday morning last, near the mouth of Monocacy, Mrs REBECCA RANEBERGER, wife of Mr Philip Raneberger, in the 28th year of her age. She leaves 6 motherless children and a disconsolate husband.

1606. (D) In this city on Tuesday evening the 14th inst., GEORGE KAUNTNER, Jun., in the 14th year of his age.
1607. (D) At Ridgeville, Frederick Co., on the 8th ult., Mr BRICE RUNKLES, aged 27 years. He was a industrious and worthy man.
1608. The Rev. WILLIAM GILMORE, will preach next Saturday evening at early candle light in the Methodist Meeting House, and on Sunday morning in the Baptist Meeting House.
1609. Candidates for Alderman: JAMES BRUNNER, A. P. BEATTY.

November 30, 1837 (MHS)

1610. (M) On Tuesday morning the 14th inst., by the Rev. Dr. Wyatt, Mr THOMAS J. DAVIS, of Frederick Co., to Miss ISABELLA WINN, of Baltimore City.
1611. (M) Married extraordinary - We copy the following notice from Indiana American, as a specimen of how they do things in Hoositerland. (Cincin. Whig)
On the 5th of October, by Rev. Daniel Wilson, Esq., Mr TIMOTHY GREEN, to Mrs JULIA JACOBS, all of Whitewater Township, Franklin Co. From the Justice who officiated at the above wedding. We learned the following rather extra ordinary particulars. The above named Mr Green is about 30 years old, and Mrs Julia is his second wife. But what is more and almost incridible, Mrs Julia Jacobs is about 50 years old and Mr Green is her 8th husband, all of whom are living except one. We wish some friends in white-water Township would furnish us, and the world a history of the above named Julia J., - and how she has disposed of so many husbands? It might be of benefit to some other unlucky dame who is tired of her yoke-fellow.
1612. (D) At his residence near Jefferson, on Sunday evening last, JOHN COST, Esq., at an advanced age.
1613. (D) In Baltimore, on Thursday night the 2nd inst., Mr RICHARD C. STOCKTON, in the 50th year of his age.
1614. (D) In Hagerstown, on Saturday the 11th inst., at the house of Mr George Coke, Mr JOHN ALLISON, (formerly of this city,) in the 33rd year of his age.

December 7, 1837 (MHS)

1615. (M) At Middletown, Frederick Co., MD., on Thursday evening last, by the Rev. J. C. Bucher, Mr JACOB YOUNG, to Miss ANN L. PERRY, all of Middletown.

1616. (D) Near Middletown, MD., on the 30th of Nov., JOHN HENRY, son of Mr John Shroyer, in the 3rd year of his age.

December 14, 1837 (MHS)

1617. (M) On Thursday evenig last, by the Rev. Samuel Brison, Mr HENRY C. LARE, to Miss MARIA O'NEAL, both of this city.
1618. (D) On Wednesday evening the 5th inst., of a painful illness of several months, BENSON STEWART, Esq., of Patapsco, Anne Arundel Co., in the 28th year of his age. He attended the Methodist Episcopal Church.
1619. (D) At his residence in Catoctin Valley, on the 2nd inst., Mr ROBERT PATTENGALE, in the 72nd year of his age. A native of the Parish of Paunell Co., of Norfolk, England. He emirgrated to this Country in 1820, and was for the last 12 years a citizen of this Valley.
1620. (D) On the 4th inst., at his residence near Utica, in Frederick Co., MD., after a short illness, Mr HENRY HILL, in the 50th year of his age. He leaves a disconsolated wife and son.

December 21, 1837 (MHS)

1621. (M) At the Glade, on Tuesday the 19th inst., by the Rev. Andrew P. Freez, Mr MICHAEL ZIMMERMAN, to Miss HANNAH WOOD, both of Frederick Co., MD.
1622. (D) At Liberty-Town, on Saturday Dec. 16th, Dr. HENRY BAKER, in the 60th year of his age. One of the elders and class leader in the Methodist Episcopal Church. As a magistrate, he was enlightened, independent, and impartial. On Monday his remains were removed to the brick meeting house cemetery on Israel's Creek, he leaves a widow to mourn his loss.
1623. The anniversary of the Young Men's Bible Society of Frederick Co., will take place on the 1st day of January next, at the German Reformed Church, at 2 o'clock, in the afternoon. The Rev. Mesrrs, KEPPLER, of the Episcopal, and BLOOD, of the Presbyterian Church, will address the meeting. ALBERT RITCHIE, LEWIS BIRELY, ASBURY H. HUNT committee of arrangement.

December 28, 1837 (MHS)

1624. (M) On Thursday last, by the Rev. J. L. Pitts, Mr GEORGE

S. CRUSHON, to Miss MARY DAVIS, both of Montgomery Co.

1625. (M) On Tuesday, Mr GEORGE POFFENBERGER, of Dauphin Co., PA., to Miss RACHEL POFFENBERGER, of Frederick Co., MD.

1626. (M) By the Rev. Mr Zacharias, at Mr Stevens' Tavern, on Thursday afternoon, last, Mr GEORGE MILLER, to Miss ELIZABETH YEAST, all of the Middletown Valley.

1627. (D) Suddenly on Friday evening last, ELIZABETH SHYLER, in the 55th year of her age.

1628. (D) At advanced age of 88 years, on Wednesday morning last, at his residence, Big Small Mill, Butler Co., Ohio. Captain THOMAS FLEMMING, formerly of this city. Was a Revolutionary Officer of the Maryland Line, and fought for American Independence and glory at the head of his company in the Battles of Brandywine, Germantown &c. He survived nearly all his contemporaries, and is survived by his wife and several small children.

1838

January 4, 1838 (MHS)

1629. (M) On Thursday last, the 28th of December, at Mr Stevens' Hotel, by the Rev. D. Zacharias, Mr HENRY RAMSBURG, to Miss CHARLOTTE GESEY, all of this co.

1630. (M) On Thursday the 21st inst., by the Rev. Wm. Runnels, JOHN J. STEINER, Esq., to Miss FRANCES HANNAH BOYER, all of this town. (Tiffin Gaz.)

1631. THOMAS W. VEASEY, Esq., has been re-elected Governor of Maryland, for the ensuing year. WILLIAM F. JOHNSON, JOHN McKENNEY, BENEDICT J. HEARD, THOS. F. HICKS, and THOS. G. PRATT, Esq., has been reelected members of the Executive Council of Maryland.

1632. Candidates for Alderman - HORATIO WATERS, THOMAS C. PRINCE, DAVID BOYD, ANDREW HEIM, GIDEON BANTZ, JOHN A. SIMMONS, JACOB KELLER, LEWIS BIRELY, WILLIAM KOLB.

January 11, 1838 (MHS)

1633. (M) On Sunday evening the 23rd of December, by the Rev. John Robinson, Mr PARIS DOWNS, to Miss JULIET DIGGS, all of Frederick Co.

1634. (D) On the 5th inst., Miss CHARLOTTE LARE, eldest daughter of Mr George Lare, of this city, in the 21st year of her age.

1635. (D) At the residence of her daughter in Frederick, on Sunday last, the 7th inst., Mrs ANN SPURRIER, formerly of Elkridge, A. A. Co., in the 77th year of her age. She was a kind and devoted parent, and full of hopes through the merits of the Redemer, the last survivor of her numerous kindred of the first degree in the collateral and last but one in the descending line.

1636. (D) On Sunday morning last, at his residence on the mountains, of a long and painful illness, MORDECAL VORE, Esq., aged about 60 years. He leaves an aged widow and 4 children. His remains were deposited in the Friends burying ground at New Market.

January 18, 1838 (MHS)

1637. (M) On Tuesday evening last, by the Rev. John L. Pitts, Mr DENNIS STONER, of Ohio, to Miss CHARLOTTE SMITH, of this co.

January 25, 1838 (MHS)

1638. (M) On Tuesday the 9th inst., near Woodsboro, by the Rev. R. Weiser, Mr PETER HANKEY, to Miss MARY ANN KRISE, of this co.

1639. (M) On Thursday the 11th inst., by the Rev. R. Weiser, Mr NOAH HOY, to Miss SUSAN STULL, youngest daughter of Mr Stull, near Woodsboro.

1640. (M) On Thursday the 5th inst., by the Rev. Mr Keller, Mr THOMAS RUDISEL, of Taney-Town, to Miss ANNA MARY SNIDER, daughter of Captain Nicholas Snider, of Frederick Co.

1641. (D) At Fort Brooke, East Florida, on the 9th of September last, JOHN HENRY HALL, of the 6th Regiment, United States Infantry, in the 29th year of his age, an a native of this co.

1642. (D) Near Libertytown, on Tuesday the 16th inst., of scarlet fever, after an illness of 5 days, WILLIAM HENRY, son of Mr William A. Albaugh, in the 13th year of his age.

1643. (D) Another Revolutionary Patriot gone - Died in Allegany Co., of which he has long been a resident, at an advanced age, Colonel WILLIAM LAMAR, officer during the Revolutionary War.

1644. (D) Departed this life, on Sunday the 14th inst., after a short but severe illness, Miss SOPHIA JANE GRAFF, in the 18th year of her age.
1645. Temperance Society in Woodsboro, met on 1st of January. The address was delivered by the Rev. D. F. WEISER, and Rev. THOMAS MYERS. On the 13th inst., a meeting was held and a constitution was adopted and the following officers appointed for one year. President - THOMAS WORTHINGTON, Vice President - Rev. D. P. WEISER, Secretary - HENRY W. DERR, Esq. Directors - JAMES KRIDLER, and MALACHI BERNARD, Esq., JOHN A. BAKER.
1646. The Rev. Mr SUDDARELS, of Grace Church, Philadelphia, will preach in the Episcopal Church, in this place, this evening at 7 o'clock. January 25th.

February 1, 1838 (MHS)

1647. (M) In Summer Co., Tennessee, Mr JAMES LYON, to Miss SARAH LAMB. (The Scriptures are fulfilled-for the Lyon and the Lamb have laid down together.)
1648. (M) On Tuesday the 23rd inst., at Winchester, Cona., by the Rev. Mr Marsh Doct. J. H. T. COCKEY, of Frederick Co., MD., to ELIZABETH ANN, daughter of L. Hurlbut, Esq.

February 8, 1838 (MHS)

1649. (M) In Baltimore, on Thursday evening last, by the Rev. Mr Merriken, Mr GREENBURY PHILLIPS, to Miss ELIZABETH PEACOCK, all of that city.
1650. (M) In Baltimore, on Thursday evening last, the 1st inst., by the Rev. Mr Merriken, Mr WILLIAM O'ROUKE, to Miss ANNA MARIA LINTHICUM.

February 15, 1838 (MHS)

1651. (M) In Hagerstown, on Tuesday evening the 7th inst., by the Rev. Mr Wiley, Mr JAMES M. SCHLEY, of this city, to Miss ELLEN N., daughter of O. H. W. Stull, Esq., of Hagerstown.
1652. (M) On Thursday, by the Rev. John L. Pitts, Mr MOSES TAILER, to Miss SUSAN KEY, all of this city.
1653. (D) In this city, on Wednesday last, Mr GEO. LARE, in the 50th year of his age.

February 22, 1838 (MHS)

1654. (M) On Tuesday last, by the Rev. Dr. Reese, Mr PETER KEMP, of Dublin, to Miss ELIZA DUTROW, of this co.
1655. (M) On Thursday evening last, by the Rev. Jno. L. Pitts, Mr HARRISON CONLEY, to Miss ROSANNA E. SCHELL, both of this city.
1656. (M) On Tuesday morning last, by the Rev. S. Bryson, Mr WILLIAM W. MARKELL to Miss MARY A. E. SALMON, both of this city.
1657. (M) On Thursday evening, Feb. 8th, by the Rev. Wm. Prettyman, the Rev. BENJAMIN C. FLOWERS, a local minister of the M. E. Church, to Miss MARY ANN, daughter of the late Rev. Joshua Jones, of Sam's Creek.
1658. (M) On the 1st inst., by the Rev. James Pearre, Mr THOMAS I. MOLESWORTH, to Miss MARY A. CALN, both of this co.
1659. (M) On the 11th inst., by the same, Mr MOSES DOUTY, of Baltimore, Co., to Miss MARTHA E. COCHRANE, of Frederick Co.
1660. (D) At her residence near Emmittsburg, on Tuesday the 13th inst., Mrs ABIGAIL EMMITT, in the 64th year of her age.
1661. (D) On Thursday morning last, MARY JANE YOUNG, daughter of Perry Young, aged 11 months and 9 days.
1662. (D) In this city, on the 15th inst., Mr ISAAC LEWIS, in the prime of life.
1663. (D) In this city, on the 15th inst., Mrs SARAH RHINEHART, aged 94, residing in East Church Street.
1664. (D) In this city, on the 14th inst., Mrs MILLER, a widow, residing in East 3rd Street.
1665. (D) Suddenly on Sunday night last, Mrs KELLER, consort of Henry Keller, Esq., of Jefferson.
1666. Candidates for Alderman: EDWD. SHRIVER, JOHN HAVE. Common Council: PHILLIP HAUPTMAN.

March 1, 1838 (MHS)

1667. (M) On Wednesday the 14th inst., by the Rev. R. S. Grier, of Adams Co., PA., Mr WILLIAM C. LANDERS, of Franklin Mills, to Miss SARAH A., youngest daughter of Mr Daniel Runzer, both of this city.
1668. (M) On Thursday evening last, by the Rev. Daniel Zacharias, Mr JOHN B. HIMBUY, to Miss JULIAN HOOPER, all of this co.

1669. (M) On Tuesday evening last, by the Rev. John L. Pitts, Mr JOHN WATKINS, to Miss MARGARET A. HANER, both of Frederick.
1670. (D) In New Market, on Wednesday evening last, at the residence of his father Thomas Anderson, Esq., Dr. JOHN HAMILTON ANDERSON, in the 24th year of his age, and died of bronchitis consumption.
1671. Corporate election results: Alderman: HOSKINS - 358, SHRIVER - 352, KOLB - 304, SIMMONS - 199, TALBOTT - 178, HAVE - 168, KELLY - 154, FAUBLE - 161, BRUNNER - 132, KELLER - 147, BARTGIS - 114, ENGLEBRECHT - 109, BOYD - 86, HEIM - 86, STEINER - 83, PRINCE - 68, LITTLE - 54, KAUFFMAN - 53, HOFFMAN - 40, BIRELY - 36, BEATTY - 36 WATERS - 32.

March 8, 1838 (MHS)

1672. (M) Near Middletown, MD., at the public house of Mr John Lidy, on Tuesday evening Feb. 27th 1838, by the Rev. J. C. Bucher, Mr DAVID WM. OYSTER, of George-Town, D.C., to Miss ELIZA ANN THOMPSON, of Frederick Co., MD.
1673. (M) At the parsonage of the German Reformed Church, Middletown, MD., on the 1st of March, by the Rev. J. C. Bucher, Mr AARON YOURTE, to Miss CATHARINE McDADE, both of Pleasant Valley, Washington Co., MD.
1674. (M) On Sunday evening last, by the Rev'd. D. Zacharias, Mr JOHN DUVALL, to Miss CHRISTIANNA KNOXE, all of this city.
1675. (M) On the 22nd ult., by the Rev. Mr Wiley, WM. B. CLARKE, Esq., of the D.C., to Miss SOPHIA, daughter of Wm. Price, Esq., of Hagerstown.
1676. (M) In Greencastle, on Monday the 19th inst., by the Rev. Mr Lipsicomb, Mr ADAM EYLER, to Miss MARY BESORE, daughter of Captain Daniel Smith, all of Harbaugh's Valley.
1677. (D) At the residence of his father, Edward McBride, in Emmittsburg, JOHN A. McBRIDE, aged 24 years, 4 months, after a long and painful illness.
1678. (D) In Jefferson, MD., on the 4th inst., CHARLES BEDFORD, young son of Perry G. Thomas, aged 1 year, 3 months and 6 days.

March 15, 1838 (MHS)

1679. (M) On Tuesday evening last, by the Rev. Mr Zacharias, Mr DANIEL BRENGLE, to Miss CAROLINE HOFFER, both of this co.

1680. (D) On Friday evening last, LAWRENCE BRENGLE, infant son of Edward Turbutt, of this city, aged 1 month.

March 22, 1838 (MHS)

1681. (M) On Sunday evening last, by the Rev. D. Zacharias, Mr DAVID C. STEINER, to Miss ELIZABETH WIEST, all of this co.
1682. (M) On the 8th inst., by the Rev. I. P. Haines, Mr JONATHAN HIDE, of Frederick Co., to Miss REBECCA STONE, of Carroll Co.
1683. (M) On the 8th inst., by the same, Mr JACOB SMITH, formerly a native of Germany, to Miss CATHARINE DEAFOBOUGH, both of Carroll Co.
1684. (M) In Washington, on Wednesday March 7th., by the Rev. Mr Hawley, Lieut. JOHN NAVARRE McCOMB, to Miss CZARINA, daughter of Maj. Gen. Alexander McComb.
1685. (M) On Tuesday evening the 13th inst., by the Rev. John Johns, Mr JOHN NELSON, Esq., to MATILDA, daughter of the late Thomas Tenant, all of Baltimore.
1686. (D) At her residence, in New Market, on Wednesday evening the 14th inst., Mrs JANE McELFRESH, in the 76th year of her age. Her last illness was short, and for some hours prior to her death, she was unable to speak or notice anyone.
1687. (D) On Friday night last, after a long and painful illness, RAYMOND SANDERSON, in the 21st year of his age.

March 29, 1838 (MHS)

1688. (M) On Thursday last, by the Rev. Michael Wachter, Mr DAVID CARLIN, to Miss MARY KENEGA.
1689. (M) On the same day, by the same, Mr HARRISON FEET, to Miss ELIZABETH A. MILLER, both of Middletown MD.
1690. (M) Near Jefferson, MD., at the house of Mr Henry Cost, on the 21st of March, by the Rev. J. C. Bucher, Mr JOHN POOLE, of Barnesville, Montgomery Co., to Miss ANN REBECCA, daughter of the late Capt. Christian Cost, of Jefferson, Frederick Co., MD.
1691. (M) Near Middletown, Frederick Co., MD., on the 22nd of March, by the same, Mr ELIAS SCHLOSSER, to Miss MALINDA STEHLEY, all of Middletown Valley.
1692. (M) On the same day, by the same, Mr JOSIAH REMSBERG, son of Christian, to Miss MARY ANN, daughter of Mr Henry Lighter, all of Frederick Co., MD.

1693. (M) On Thursday last, by the Rev. Daniel Zacharias, Mr WILLIAM STALEY, to Miss MARY ANN RAMSBURG, all of this co.
1694. (M) On Tuesday last, by the Rev. Michael Wachter, Mr JOHN ROUTZONG, to Miss MARY ANN SHEFFER, both of this co.

April 5, 1838 (MHS)

1695. (M) On Thursday morning last, by the Rev. S. W. Harkey, Mr WILLIAM KOLB, to Mrs CATHARINE FOUT, all of this city.
1696. (M) On evening of the same day, by the same, Mr ISRAEL C. O'NEIL, to Miss CATHARINE DOLL, all of this city.
1697. (M) On Monday morning last, by the Rev. Jn. L. Pitts, Mr JOHN BLOCHER, Esq., of Cumberland, to ELIZABETH, eldest daughter of Col. Wm. Durbin, of this place.
1698. (M) On the 13th inst., by the Rev. D. Reese, Mr PETER BOYER, Esq., to Miss MARY HERRING, widow of the late Geo. Herring, both of this co.
1699. Appointment by the Governor and Council, as Leather Inspector of Frederick City: Mr HORATIO WATERS.
1700. The Rev. Mr GUITEAU, from Baltimore, will preach in the Presbyterian Church, next Sabbath, at 10 o'clock, A.M.

April 12, 1838 (MHS)

1701. (D) On Monday morning last, Mr JOHN DERR, an old and respectable citizen, aged about 65.
1702. (D) On the 3rd inst., at his residence, FRANCIS WHARTHON, aged about 60.

April 19, 1838 (MHS)

1703. (D) On Tuesday the 10th inst., Mrs SUSANNAH REPP, consort of Mr Jacob Repp, aged about 49 years.
1704. (D) On the morning of the 12th inst., at the residence of his father, in this city, after a lingering and somewhat protracted illness of consumpton, Mr GEO. W. LYONS, in the 24th year of his age.
1705. (D) On Thursday morning last, at his residence in New Market, Mr ENOS SCHELL, aged about 55 years.

April 26, 1838 (MHS)

1706. (M) On Thursday the 19th inst., by the Revd. R. Weiser, Mr JOSEPH SHANK, to Miss SARAH LINK, all of this co.

1707. (M) By the same, on Tuesday, 17th inst., Mr SAMUEL GEISBERT, to Miss SUSAN SHOUP, all of this co.

May 3, 1838 (MHS)

1708. (M) On Tuesday last, by the Rev. Wm. Hunt, Mr LEWIS J. GROVE, merchant, of Warfieldsburg, to Miss CORDELLA BARNES, daughter of Mr Moses Barnes, of Carroll Co.
1709. (D) Another Revolutionary soldier gone - On Sunday evening last, at his residence near New Market, in this co., Col. PHILIMON GRIFFITH, in his 82nd year of his age. Throughout a long life he maintained an unblemished character.
1710. (D) On Friday the 13th day of April, Mrs ROSANNA CRUTCHLEY, wife of Elias Crutchley, Esq., in the 74th year of her age.
1711. (F) A thunder storm of uncommon severity swept the little village of Woodsboro on Saturday evening last, at about 3 P.M. Two large stables on the back street, owned by Mr JOHN BARRICK, and Mr JOHN MILLER, Sen., were totally enveloped in flames. The Methodist Episcopal Church was rescued from the impending danger several times. The barn of Mr SNYDER, one or two hundred yards East of town, was also on fire, which was extinguished by the exertion of himself and family, his house was also partly unroofed. The barn of Mr DANIEL BOWERS, 1/2 a miles South West of the village was also blown down, killing and clipping several of his cattle.
1712. It appears the Rev. UPTON BEALL, late of St. Andrews Church in Baltimore, has accepted the call of the Vestry of All Saints Church, Frederick, the Rev. Mr KEPPLER, has resigned. The latter gentleman takes charge of St. Andrews Church, as the successor of Mr Beall.

May 24, 1838 (MHS)

1713. (M) On Tuesday morning last, by the Rev. John L. Pitts, Nr THOMAS ERVIN, to Miss HARRIET PHELPES, both of this co.

May 31, 1838 (MHS)

1714. (M) On Thursday evening last, by the Rev. John L. Pitts, Mr ELI SOWER, to Miss SUSAN BUCKEY, all of this co.
1715. (M) On Wednesday mornng, 23rd inst., by the Rev. Dr. Wyatt, HANSON B. PIGMAN, attorney-at-law, of Cumber-

land, MD., to MARY E., daughter of John S. Shriver, Esq., of Baltimore.
1716. (M) On Tuesday morning the 29th inst., by the Rev. John L. Pitts, Mr STEPHEN B. CROMB, to HARRIET, daughter of Casper Kline, Esq., of this city.
1717. (M) On the 27th inst., by the Rev. D. Zacharias, Mr FREDERICK WINTER, to Miss CATHARINE BERGER.

1838

FREDERICK TIMES AND DEMOCRATIC ADVOCATE

June 1, 1838 (MHS)
1718. Appointments by the Levy Court for Frederick County. Collector of Tax: JOSEPH SHELL. Trustees of the Alms House: DANIEL KOLB, PHILIP ROHR, GEORGE HAUER, JACOB FAUBLE, VALENTINE DOUB. Constables: District #1. JAMES S. SIMMONS, SAMUEL H. HOUSER. District #2. JOHN H. HUFF, GEORGE KOONTZ, JAMES M. DAYHOFF, JOSHUA DILL, JOHN M. LOWE, SOLOMON MEASLER, JAMES CARLIN, ISAAC RENN. District #3. JOHN H. YOUNG, WARREN R. WILLIAMSON, JACOB YOUNG, of D., MAHLON RODERICK. District #4. CYRUS WALKER, WARNER T. GRIMES, SAMUEL HERD. District #5. SAMUEL DUPHORN, JOHN MARTIN, ISAAC WILSON. District #8. DANIEL SWEADNER, DANIEL ROOT, JOEL WOOD, AARON GOSNELL, OWEN BURGESS. District #9. JOHN W. BUXTON, THOMAS MOUNT, WM. HAMMOND, JONATHAN BROWNING. District #10. HENRY NEED. District #11. JOHN BARRICK, CHARLES HESSER, ADAM CREAGER, JEFFERSON BOON. District #12. JOHN G. DABEESTEIN, HENRY BOTELER. District #13. WM. B. TABLER, JESSE M. LITTLE, and LLOYD KESSLER. Election Judges: District #1. OTHO THOMAS, PATRICK MURPHY, and DANIEL KEMP. District #2. JOHN EBERT, HENRY BAER, NICHOLAS HOLTZ. District #3. GEORGE BISER, JOHN J. SMITH, JOHN YOUNG, of J. District #4. JACOB CRAMER, JAMES CROCKETT, and VALENTINE SHRYOCK. District #5. JEFFERSON SHIELDS, MICHAEL SLUSS and DANIEL HOOVER. District #8. GEORGE COX, ABRAHAM JONES, WM. A ALBAUGH. District #9. JOSHUA RUSSELL, JOHN WOOD, HENRY SMITH. District

#10. WILSON HAYS, JOSEPH SMITH, GEORGE HARMAN. District #11. JOHN D. CRUMBAUGH, GEORGE BARRICK, JACOB BIRELY. District #12. JOHN COLE, EMANUEL SLIFER, HARMAN MARLOW. District #14. SEBASTIAN RAMSBURG, Jr., THOMAS LAMAR, DANIEL CULLER. School Inspector: District #1. OTHO THOMAS. District #2. VALENTINE ADAMS. District #3. PETER SCHLOSSER. District #4. WILLIAM BIGGS. District #5. JEFFERSON SHIELDS. District #8. ANTHONY KIMMELL. District #9. WASHINGTON BURGESS. District #10. HENRY BURHMAN. District #11. DANIEL KEMP. District #12. JOHN COLE. District #14. THOMAS JOHNSON, of Wm.

June 7, 1838. (MHS)

1719. (M) In Anne Arundel Co., on the 24th inst., by the Rev. Thomas Myers, Mr PHILIP CISSELL, to Mrs SARAH CARR, all of said co.

1720. (M) On Thursday last, by the Rev. Daniel Zacharias, Mr NORMAN HARDING, to Miss ANN MARIA OGLE.

1721. (M) On the evening of the same day, by the same, Mr THOMAS SINN, to Miss CATHARINE LOVEDER.

1722. (M) On Thursday evening last, by the Rev. J. L. Pitts, at the Eagle Hotel Mr WILLIAM KUHN, to Miss ELIZABETH WILSON, all of VA.

1723. (M) On the same evening by the same, Mr CHRISTOPHER WARNER, to Miss LOUISA NICKLE, both of this city.

1724. (D) In this city, on Thursday evening last, Mr JACOB BALTZELL, in the 87th year of his age. Mr B., has been a resident of this town for upwards of 75 years, and now at a ripe old age, he has closed a long life of probity innocence and integrity.

June 14, 1838 (MHS)

1725. (M) On Tuesday morning 29th of May, by the Rev. John W. Porter, Mr SOLOMON FREEBORN CONOWAY, to Miss ANN REBECCA, daughter of Mr Haines Dixon, all of Frederick Co.

1726. (M) On the 12th of April, in this city, by the Rev. Tobias Riley, Mr RICHARD A. MORRIS, to Miss ELIZABETH HARRIS, both of VA.

1727. (M) At Jefferson, on Tuesday morning, 29th of May, by the same, Mr WM. MAHONEY, to Miss ELIZABETH ANN ERVINE, all of this co.

1728. (D) On the 27th ult., in this city, ELIZA HORSEY LEE, daughter of William Lee, Esq., of Needwood, Frederick Co., MD., of a lingering illness.

1729. (D) At White Hall, Illinois, on the 27th of May last, Mrs SOPHIA NICHOLS, daughter of Mr George Lambrecht, of Frederick, in the 34th year of her age.

June 21, 1838 (MHS)

1730. (M) On Sunday the 10th inst., by the Rev. R. Weiser, Mr MATTHIAS BEARD, to Miss MARY ANN SMITH, all of this co.

1731. (M) On Tuesday the 15th inst., by the Rev. M. Wachter, Mr. W. N. VORE, to Miss S. A. CHAMBERS, all of Middletown Valley.

1732. (M) On Wednesday evening last, by the Rev. C. G. M'Lean, Mr W. A. HEBBARD to Miss M. E. PATTERSON, both of Frederick Co.

1733. (M) On Tuesday evening last, Mr LUTHER RICHARDS, senior editor of the "Lancaster Examiner and Herald" to Miss ELIZABETH, daughter of the late John Reitzel, all of this city.

1734. (D) In Liverpool, England, on the 28th of March 1838, FLETCHER HUNT, in the 19th year of his age, late of Frederick Town, MD.

1735. DANIEL KEMP, of Buckeystown District, THOMAS ANDERSON, of New Market District, JACOB T. C. MILLER, are Independent Candidates to represent Frederick Co., in the next General Assembly.

1736. Dr. ABDIEL UNKEFER, of the Democratic Republican to serve in the next Legislature.

June 28, 1838 (MHS)

1737. (M) On Tuesday the 12th inst., by the Rev. Mr Hanks, E. M. BARTHOLOW, of Utica, Frederick Co., MD., to Miss MARY JANE, daughter of Mr James Given, of Columbia, PA.

1738. (D) On Friday evening, the 15th of June, at his residence in Uniontown, after an illness of 5 weeks, Mr SAMUEL ROBERTS, in the 32nd year of his age.

1739. (D) At the residence of her nephew, Dr. S. P. Smith, in this place, on Sunday evening last, at 6 o'clock, Miss REBECCA PRICE, aged 88 years, and daughter of the late Colonel Price, of Frederick Co., a member of the Protestant Episcopal Church. (Cumberland Civilian)

1740. MAHLAN TALBOTT, was former Sheriff of Frederick Co., is a candidate for the General Assembly.

July 12, 1838 (MHS)

1741. (M) By the Rev. R. Weiser, on the 21st ult., Mr WILLIAM FLEWETT, to Mrs ANN SHRYOCK, all of this co.
1742. (M) On Tuesday the 25th ult, by the same, Mr SAMUEL STAUB, to Miss SUSAN HAHN, all of this co.
1743. (D) On Saturday evening last, Mrs ANNA M. ROSS, wife of William J. Ross, Esq., of this place.
1744. (D) Departed this life, on Wednesday last, Mrs CATHARINE HOUCK, consort of Mr Geo. Houck, of this city, in the 57th year of her age.
1745. (D) Departed this transitory life, about 5 o'clock, on Saturday evening, the 7th inst., in the 35th year of her age. Mrs SOPHIA WAGNER, consort of Mr Joseph L. Wagner, of Liberty-Town, Frederick Co., MD. On Monday morning at 10 o'clock, an able and sympathising discourse from the 11th Chapter of St. John, 25th, and 26th verses was delivered by the Rev. James Bunting, of the Methodist E. Church. After which her remains were deposited in an ancient cemetery. (Liberty Town July 16.)
1746. DAVID SCHLEY, candidate for the Senate of Maryland.

July 19, 1838 (MHS)

1747. (M) On Monday evening last, by the Rev. Tobias Riley, Mr SIMEON HANES, to Miss ELIZABETH ANN SINCLAIR, both of VA.
1748. (M) In Baltimore, on Tuesday evening last, by the Rev. Dr. Roberts, Mr ROBERT MILES, to Miss ELIZABETH PEACOCK, all of that city.
1749. (D) On Saturday evening, the 14th inst., Mrs BARBARA LOWE, wife of John M. Lowe, of this place, in the 62nd year of her age.
1750. (D) On Wednesday evening last, MARY ELIZABETH, only child of Asbury H. Hunt, in the 10 month of her age.
1751. (D) On Thursday morning last, ELIZABETH, an infant daughter of William Maulsby, Esq., of Carroll Co., MD.

July 26, 1838 (MHS)

1752. (D) Departed this life, on Thursday afternoon last, at 6 o'clock, in the 47th year of his age, CHRISTIAN GETZENDANNER, Esq., the late proprietor of this paper. On Wednesday evening, he was healthy, lively, and cheerful as usual and yet less then 24 hours, he was struck down by the hand of death.

1753. (D) On Sunday morning last, at her residence in Emmittsburg, Mrs HUGHES, aged 75 years and 8 months.

1754. (M) On Tuesday morning, by the Rev. Dr. Wyatt, Mr LAMBERT N. HOPKINS, to MARY R., daughter of James Johnson, Frederick Co., MD.

1755. (M) In George-Town (D.C.,) on the 17th inst., by the Rev. Mr Slaughter, the Rev. J. JOHNS, D.D., of Baltimore, to MARGARET JANE SHAAFF.

1756. (M) At Columbus, GA., on the 19th inst., by the Rev. Mr Samford, LAUNCELOT GAMBRILL, formerly of MD., to ANN AMERICA, daughter of the Rev. Dr. Pierce, of the former place.

1757. (M) On the 8th inst., by the Rev. C. H. A. Albert, Mr JNO. G. WACHTER, late of Frederick Co., MD., to Miss FRANCES SHOUB, of Delaware, OH.

August 2, 1838 (MHS)

1758. (M) On the 8th ult., by the Rev. R. Weiser, Mr WALTER J. SLOAN, to Mrs MARY WELLER, all of Mechanicstown.

1759. (M) On the 26th ult., by the Rev. R. Weiser, Mr DAVID MISINGER, to Miss ELIZABETH WILHIDE, all of this co.

1760. (M) On Thursday evening the 12th of July, in Wooster, Wayne Co., Ohio, by the Rev. Mr Smidmer, Mr WILLIAM H. SMITH, to Miss ELIZABETH E. WINEBRENNER, second daughter of Jacob Winebrenner, formerly of Frederick Co., MD.

1761. (D) Near Woodsboro, on the 16th ult., Mrs SARAH SMITH, in the 49th year of her age.

1762. (D) Departed this life, on the 16th inst., Mrs ELIZABETH McELFRESH, relict of the late Charles McElfresh, in the 69th year of her age.

1763. (D) In Harbaugh's Valley, on the 5th inst., Mr DANIEL GORDON, aged 81 years, a soldier of the Revolution.

August 9, 1838 (MHS)

1764. (M) On the 2nd inst., at Mr Cunningham's Tavern, by the Rev. H. Robinson, Mr JACOB HEWET, to Miss ELIZABETH DERR, all of this co.

1765. (D) On Wednesday evening, July 25th, RACHEL RAITT, infant daughter of Warfield and Rachel Simpson, aged 4 months and 18 days.

1766. Mr ISAAC VANBIBBER, of Carroll Co., sewed an acre of ground with Spring Wheat, and obtained from it 85 dozen sheaves of the ordinary size.

August 16, 1838 (MHS)

1767. (M) On Tuesday morning last, by the Rev. John W. Everist, of Baltimore, Mr JOHN J. WILSON, to Miss ANNA L. P., daughter of Dr. Wm. Bradley Tyler, all of this city.

1768. (D) On Tuesday morning, the 14th inst., at Mount Pleasant, (his residence) after a short illness, Major DANIEL JAMES, a native of this co., aged 75 years, 3 months and 11 days.

1769. Whig convention met in this city on Saturday and nominated the following ticket: Senate - RICHARD POTTS, Esq. Assembly - GEORGE SCHLEY, GRAFTON HAMMOND, GEORGE BECKENBAUGH, SURAT D. WARFIELD, JACOB THOMAS, of Jno.

1770. Directors of Farmers Bank of Maryland: WILLIAM S. McPHERSON, WILLIAM ROSS, JOHN TYLER, RICHARD POTTS, DANIEL HUGHES, LEWIS MEDTART, NOAH PHILIPS, CASPER MANTZ, JOHN I. WILSON, GEORGE BALTZELL.

September 6, 1838 (MHS)

1771. (M) On Tuesday evening last, by the Rev. Daniel Zacharias, Mr VALENTINE SHARRER, to Miss JULIAN BOLLENBAUCHER, both of this co.

1772. (M) On the 21st ult., by the Rev. A. P. Freese, Mr DAVID HAMMETT, of Washington Co., MD., to Miss SARAH EIGENBRODE, formerly of Frederick Co., MD.

1773. Administration candidates: Senate - JOHN H. McELFRESH. Assembly - JOHN HARRITT, DANIEL S. BISER, JOHN W. GEYER, ABDIEL UNKEFER, JOHN McPHERSON.

October 4, 1838 (MHS)

1774. (M) On the 14th ult., by the Rev. George Rimel, Mr HIRAM H. MULLEN, of Leesburg, VA., to Miss ELIZABETH HOOVER, of Frederick Co., MD.

October 11, 1838 (MHS)

1775. (M) On Thursday last, in Carlisle, PA., by the Rev. Mr Thornton, Mr JOHN E. NORRIS, of Frederick, MD., to Miss ELIZABETH S., daughter of John Phillips, Esq., of Carlisle.

1776. (M) On Thursday evening last, by the Rev. J. W. Porter, Mr EZRA DUDEROW, to Miss MARGARET E. MYERS, all of this co.
1777. (M) In New Market, on the 4th inst., by the Rev. John L. Pitts, Mr GEORGE HARDT, of Frederick, to Miss ELIZA BALEY, formerly of Rockville.
1778. (D) On Thursday last, at the house of D. H. Schleigh, EDWARD BECK, in the 13th year of his age, after a lingering and painful illness of upwards to 4 weeks.
1779. Results of the election: Whig for Senate: POTTS - 2570. Van Buren candidate for Senate: McELFRESH - 2411. Whig candidates for the General Assembly: SCHLEY - 2534, HAMMOND - 2532, BECKENBAUGH - 2520, WARFIELD - 2493, THOMAS - 2494. Van Buren candidates for the General Assembly: McPHERSON - 2573, BISER - 2528, UNKEFER - 2506, GEYER - 2520, HARRITT - 2481.

October 18, 1838 (MHS)

1780. (D) On Saturday last, at the residence of Mrs Pipher, in East Patrick Street, AMELIA ANN BRENGLE, in the 14th year of her age.
1781. (D) On Friday evening last, HARRIET ANN REBECCA, infant child of George and Mary Ann Cromwell, aged 10 months and a few days.
1782. GEORGE KELLY, and JACOB KLEIM, of Uniontown, Carroll Co., MD., trotted off to the West, leaving the late properitor of this paper minus $10.00. Recently JACOB GLAZIER, of the same place, decamped, leaving him minus $5.00, and ourself $1.00. Some of these fellows may have gone to Cincinnati, Ohio, we want our friends of the "News" to have them "rode up on a rail."

October 25, 1838 (MHS)

1783. (D) On Wednesday the 17th inst., CHRISTIAN FRANKLIN, son of Daniel Kemp, Esq., near Buckeys-Town, in the 15th year of his age.
1784. (D) In this city, on Thursday the 16th inst., after a long and protracted illness, BENJAMIN RUTHERFORD, Esq., in the 51st year of his age.
1785. (D) In Frederick Co., Mr ISAAC SAUM, aged about 48 or 49 years old.

1786. (D) Departed this life, in Cumberland, on Thursday the 11th inst., Miss CHARLOTTE, youngest daughter of John and Eleanor Gephart, in the 17th year of her age.

November 1, 1838 (MHS)

1787. (M) On Tuesday last, by the Rev. John L. Pitts, Mr HENRY BOYER, to Miss ROSSANNA HILTON, both of Frederick.
1788. (M) On Thursday last, by the same, Mr JOHN WILLIAM BOWLUS, to Miss MARY ANN REBECCA BAKER, all of this co.
1789. (M) On the same day, by the same, Mr FREDERICK BENTLINGER, to Miss AMANDA ANN SPONSELLER, both of this co.
1790. (M) In New Market District, on Tuesday night the 9th ult., by the Rev. John Wood, Mr THOMAS HILLEARY, to Miss SARAH THOMPSON, all of this co.
1791. (M) Near Jefferson, on Thursday evening last, by the Rev. D. Zacharias, Mr JOHN H. REN, to Miss SARAH ANN R. HOUSE, all of this co.
1792. (D) On Sunday the 21st ult., MARY ELIZA, daughter of Col. John McPherson, in the 6th year of her age.
1793. (D) On Monday the 22nd ult., Mr JOHN TITLOW, in the 51st year of his age, he leaves a wife and 9 children to mourn his loss.

November 8, 1838 (MHS)

1794. (M) On Thursday last, by the Rev. John L. Pitts, Mr REUBEN SHETENHELM, to Miss ELIZABETH LEASE, both of this co.
1795. (M) On the same day, by the same, Mr JOHN FOX, to Miss JULIAN BEAL, both of this co.
1796. (M) On Tuesday morning, at Mr Wallings Tavern, by the Rev. John L. Pitts, THOMAS J. BOONE, to Miss ELIZABETH A. BOOCHER, all of this co.
1797. (D) On Friday the 2nd inst., Miss LOUISA WALLING, in the ---- years of her age.
1798. (D) On Sunday the 28th ult., at his residence in this co., JAMES COOPER, Sen., in the 75th year of his age.
1799. (D) On Saturday 1st., at the residence of his father, Nathan Hammond, Esq., SINGLETON WOOTON HAMMOND, in the 12th year of his age.

November 15, 1838 (MHS)

1800. (M) On Thursday morning last, by the Rev. John L. Pitts,

Mr THOMAS T. CROMWELL, to Miss CATHERINE STOUFFER, both of this co.

1801. (M) On the same day, by the same, Mr STEPHENSON PLAINE, to Miss ANN SPONSELLER, both of this co.

1802. (M) At Blenhiem, in this co., on the 2nd ult., the Rev. WM. PINKNEY, to Miss ELIZABETH LLOYD, daughter of Richard T. Lowndles, Esquire.

1803. (M) On Tuesday evening the 16th inst., by the Rev. Jno. B. Gildea, Mr SAMUEL BROWN, Jr., of Anne Arundel Co., to Miss ELIZABETH J., second daughter of Henry Jenkins, Esq., of this city.

1804. (M) On the 30th ult., by the Rev. Tobias Riley, Mr ANDREW DRONENBURG, to Miss CORNELIA RICHARDS, both of Frederick Co.

1805. (M) On the 31st ult., by the same, Mr CHARLES HALLER, to Miss SARAH B. PRESTON, both of Frederick Co.

1806. (D) At the residence of Wm. C. Russell, in this city, on Sunday the 4th inst., after a long and protracted illness, Madame ANN SEGAN, an old and respectable inhabitant of this city.

1807. JAMES DAVIS, Esq., of Georgetown, D.C., is our duly authorized agent for the District of Columbia.

December 6, 1838 (MHS)

1808. (M) In Baltimore, on Wednesday evening the 1st ult., by the Rev. Mr Lispcond, Mr OLIVER P. GARDINER, of this borough, to Miss ELIZABETH M. BUCKEY, of Frederick, MD. (York Republican)

1809. (D) Departed this life, at Ceresville, on Thursday morning the 29th ult., Mrs REBECCA SHRINER, wife of Cornelius Shriner, Esq., in the 31st year of her age.

1810. (D) At 1 o'clock, on Monday morning the 31st ult., at St. John's Female Academy, Frederick City, MARY A. R. GARLIN, of Waynesborough, Franklin Co., PA., in the 10th year of her age.

1811. Information wanted of one PHILIP ATTICK, who left this place for Cincinnati, Ohio. He owes us $1.00 which we would thank him to pay.

December 13, 1838 (MHS)

1812. (M) In Middletown Valley, on Tuesday last, by the Rev. Mr M. Wachter, Mr SAMUEL MILLER, to Miss SARAH ANN C. EASTERDAY.

1813. (M) On Tuesday last, by the Rev. R. S. Grier, Mr JOHN S. STEWART, to Miss MARGARET B., third daughter of John Witherow, Esq., both of Frederick Co.

1814. (M) On Tuesday evening the 4th ult., at the house of Mrs Keefer, near Frederick, by the Rev. S. W. Harkey, Mr DANIEL H. CANDLER, of Montgomery Co., to Miss ANNE E. BAER, of this co.

1815. (D) On Friday morning last, in the 7th month of his age, PHILIP ABRAHAM, son of Edward Shriver, Esq., of this city.

December 20, 1838 (MHS)

1816. (M) On Thursday evening last, by the Rev. John L. Pitts, Mr JOEL HALL, to Miss LUCINDA CLEARY, both of this co.

1817. (M) On the 27th of Nov., by the Rev. Mr Converse, Major ABRAHAM VAN BUREN, (eldest son of the President of the U. States,) to Miss SARAH ANGELICA SINGLETON, eldest daughter of Richard Singleton, at her father's house, in Sumpter District, South Carolina.

1818. (D) In Anne Arundel Co., on Friday the 25th ult., MARY, infant daughter of Wm. C. and Eleanor M. Tyler.

1819. (D) On Thursday morning last, aged 55 years, Mrs ELIZABETH SANDERSON, consort of Wm. R. Sanderson, of this city.

1839

January 3, 1839 (MHS)

1820. (M) On the 24th ult., by the Rev. Mr Summers, Mr WILLIAM HENRY FRESHOWER, late of Frederick, MD., to Miss ELIZA JANE KING, of Baltimore.

1821. (M) On Thursday last, in Hyattstown, by the Rev. John L. Pitts, Mr JOSIAH WOLF, to Miss ANN LEE BEALL.

1822. (M) On the 24th ult., by the Rev. D. Zacharias, Mr J. F. WORTHINGTON, to Miss DELILA DAVIS, both of this co.

1823. (M) On Thursday evening last, by the Rev. Mr Wiley, JERVIS SPENCER, Esq., to Miss CATHERINE, youngest daughter of Richard Ragan, all of Hagerstown.

1824. Junior Fire Company to raise money to purchase a new engine, which may cost approxinatel $1,500.00.

1839

FREDERICK VISITER AND TEMPERANCE ADVOCATE

January 10, 1839 (MHS)

1825. (M) On Thursday evening last, by the Rev. Tobias Riley, Mr AUBURY G. JONES, of Liberty District, to Miss MARY ANN BOYD, of this city.

1826. (M) On New Year's Eve, by the Rev. S. W. Harkey, Mr FREDERICK KELLY, to Miss MARGARET ELKINS, both of this city.

1827. (M) On Tuesday evening the 1st inst., by the Rev. John L. Pitts, Mr WILLIAM BAKER, to Miss DELILA DUVALL, both of this co.

1828. (D) At Frederick on the 28th ult., in the 15th year of his age, ROGER, eldest son of Madison Nelson.

1829. (D) At his residence near Frostburg, on Thursday morning, Dec. 27th, ANDREW BRUCE, Esq., a member of the State Senate of Maryland.

1830. A meeting was held at the court house on Wednesday evening last, to aid the poor. MICHAEL BALTZELL, Esq., was appointed chairman, and JOHN L. PITTS, as Secretary. A committee was appointed to solicit funds and contributions from their respective Wards. The following persons were appointed to represent their Wards. 1st Ward. GEO. METZGER, HORATIO WILCOXEN, and JACOB HARDT. 2nd Ward. MAHLON TALBOTT, PETER STOFFEL, JOHN FRITCHIE. 3rd Ward. JACOB KELLER, P. L. STORM, OTHO G. ENT. 4th Ward. GEORGE M. CONRADT, GEORGE WEBSTER, LEWIS MEDTART. 5th Ward. EDWARD TRAIL, ISAAC WYSONG, DAVIS RICHARDSON. 6th Ward. PHILIP ROHR, GEORGE HOSKINS, JOHN A. STEINER. 7th Ward. PETER DEGRANGE, GEO. SALMON, EZRA HOUCK.

1831. Meeting of the Young Men Bible Society of Frederick Co., was held in the Methodist Episcopal Church, on Tuesday evening the 1st inst. Meeting was open with a prayer by the Rev. T. RILEY, a chapter was read from the Bible, by the Rev. S. W. HARKEY. Report of the Board of Managers was read by Mr GEORGE L. DAVIS, one of the secretaries. Rev. J. SMITH, President of Frederick College and Pastor of the Presbyterian Church, addressed the gathering.

1832. At convention of the Temperance Society, held in the Lutheran Church, was organized by calling Dr. LLOYD DORSEY, of Jefferson, to the chair and appointing Dr. WM. M. KEMP, of Frederick, Secretary. Roll-call list of delegates to the convention: Frederick - Rev. Messrs: BEALL, PITTS, SMITH, ZACHARIAS, REILY, HARKEY. Messrs: LEWIS BIRELY, S. R. HOGG, J. KELLER, J. KUNKLE, GODFREY KOONTZ, C. MANTZ, Dr. WM. M. KEMP, Dr. ALBERT RITCHIE, S. CRONISE, R. HARPER, V. DOUB, G. M. CONRADT, L. P. W. BALCH, GEORGE L. DAVIS. Linganore - Rev. Mr PRETTYMAN, Col. DUDDERAR, GEO. W. DUDDERAR, BURGESS NELSON, Jr., WM. TRUNBULL. Jefferson - Dr. LLOYD DORSEY, HENRY CULLER, F. THOMSON. Woodsboro - Rev. WEISER, Rev. B. FLOWERS, H. W. DERR, T. WORTHINGTON. Mechanics-Town - Messrs: SAMUEL STEM, JOHN ARTHUR, W. SIFTON, G. STOKES, D. ZEPP, TOBIAS FAHS, F. RIDER, J. FLAHERTY, J. FREZE, ANDREW SIFTON, WALTER SLOAN J. SMITH. Middletown - Dr. JACOB BAER, J. FLOOK, of J., S. APPLEMAN, P. COBLENTZ, D. SMELSER, M. AHALT.

January 17, 1839 (MHS)

1833. (M) On Wednesday the 26th ult., by the Rev. Mr Creigh, Mr BENJAMIN HAMILTON, of Mercersburg, Franklin Co., PA., to Miss MARGARET ANN DEAN, of this co.
1834. (M) On Saturday the 5th inst., Mr WILLIAM HOGG, of Wilmington, DE., to Miss MARY ANN HALL, of this city.
1835. (M) In Middletown, on the 6th inst., by the Rev. J. C. Bucher, Mr PETER ORTNER, to Miss ANN REBECCA HAUPT, all of Middletown Valley.
1836. (M) On the 3rd inst., by the Rev. S. W. Harkey, Mr PETER WALTMAN, to Miss NANCY A. LONG, both of this co.
1837. (M) On Thursday evening the 10th ult., by the same, Mr IGNATIUS PAINTER, to Miss ELIZABETH COOK, both of this co.
1838. (D) Mr DANIEL KEMP, a member of the Lutheran Church, at the Manor. He departed this life, on Monday morning the 4th inst., at 8 o'clock, after a severe and violent illness of bilious congestive fever of 8 days. He leaves a devoted companion, and several small children.
1839. (D) In Middletown on Wednesday the 9th inst., PHILIP FISCHER, in about the 82nd year of his age. Was a Revolutionary soldier, and was buried at Middletown, with Honors of War. He enlisted under Captain Fistar, in the

Dutch Battalion, and was wounded in fighting the battles for his Country. The surviving worthies of the Revolution in this section were summoned together to see the last Honors of War paid to their old comrade.

1840. (D) On the 2nd inst., in the District of Columbia, in the 42nd year of her age, Mrs MARGARET BROADRUP, wife of George Broadrup, formerly of Frederick Co., MD., and daughter of George Burchart, Esq., of Paperville, TN.

January 24, 1839 (MHS)

1841. (D) On the 6th inst., Mrs ELIZABETH, wife of Stephen Ramsburg, in the 63rd year of her age. On Monday following, her remains were interred in the cemetery of the German Reformed Church, of this city.

1842. (D) In Frederick, on the 2nd of January inst., Mr JACOB HANE, in the 86th year of his age. Was one of the oldest citizens of Frederick, and partook in the Revolutionary War. He served in the Dutch Battalion, was taken sick in Philadelphia, which prevented him from participating in the Battle of Germantown.

1843. Election for Councilmen will be held on last Monday, (25th of Feb. next,) the judges for the election were appointed for the following Wards. Ward #1. DAVID SHAWEN, Sen'r. Ward #2. GEORGE MARQUERT. Ward #3. GEO. W. ENT. Ward #4. GEORGE HAUER. Ward #5. JOHN FESSLER. Ward #6. SOLOMON STICKLE. Ward #7. HENRY KAUFMAN. GODFREY KOONTZ, City Register.

January 31, 1839 (MHS)

1844. (M) On Thusday last, by the Rev. D. Zacharias, Mr ISRAEL MICHAEL, to Miss SOPHIA THOMAS, both of this co.

1845. (D) At his residence in this co., on Saturday the 19th inst., Capt. WILLIAM H. POOLE, aged about 42 years.

1846. (D) Suddenly on the 21st of December 1838, JUDITH KOHLHASS, near the Sugar Loaf Mountain, in this co., aged about 79 years.

1847 (D) On the 10th of January, 1839, HENRY KOHLHASS, husband of the above, an old and respectable citizen of this co., who emigrated, when young to this Country from Germany.

1848. (D) On Thursday morning the 24th inst., after a short illness, ABRAHAM, infant son of Mr Charles Shriver, in the 6th month of his age.

1849. (D) On the morning of the 9th inst., in Carlisle, in the 41st year of her age, Mrs ELLEN B. HAYS, wife of John Hays, leaving a husband and 3 children. For many years a member of the Presbyterian Church. (Carlisle, PA.)

February 7, 1839 (MHS)

1850. (M) On Tuesday last, by the Rev. John L. Pitts, Mr GEO. W. FRESHOUR, to Miss JULIAN BAER, both of this co.
1851. (M) On Thursday last, by the same, (at Dorsey's City Hotel,) Mr HENRY EATON, of Catoctin Furnace, to Miss SARAH A. BURCH, of Lewistown, both of this co.
1852. (M) On Tuesday evening the 5th inst., at the Eagle Hotel, by the Rev. S. W. Harkey, Mr ADAM LINK, Sen., to Miss ANN OSBURN, both of VA.
1853. (D) On the 30th of January, Mrs RACHEL B. HOGG, wife of Mr Samuel R. Hogg of this city, and daughter of the late Major William Boulden, Cecil Co., in the 38th year of her age, her illness was short and severe.

February 14, 1839 (MHS)

1854. (M) On Tuesday evening the 5th inst., by the Rev. John L. Pitts, Mr PHILIP RANNEBAGER, of this co., to Miss SARAH ELEANOR P. BEALL, of Montgomery Co.
1855. (M) Near Middletown, on the 31st ult., by the Rev. J. C. Bucher, Mr JACOB KEAFAUVER, to Miss LEONORA, youngest daughter of Mr J. P. Coblentz, all of Middletown Valley.
1856. (M) On Thursday the 24th ult., at Chambersburg, by the Rev. Ezra Keller, Mr E. SLAYBAUGH, to Miss E. HAKERSMITH, both of Frederick Co.
1857. (M) On the 3rd inst., by the Rev. J. C. Bucher, Mr JOHN HUTZELL, of John, of Washington Co., to Miss SARAH ANN, eldest daughter of Capt. John L. Smith, of Middletown Valley.
1858. (M) On the 31st ult., by the Rev. Ezra Keller, Mr GEORGE MILLER, of Taney Town, to Miss E. DELAPLANE, of Frederick Co.

February 21, 1839 (MHS)

1859. (M) On the 17th inst., by the Rev. D. Feete, Mr ISRAEL DERR, to Miss ELIZABETH CRISE, both of Carroll Co.
1860. (M) On the 14th inst., by the same, Mr HENRY G. BRENDEL, of Hagerstown, to Miss MARY A. FEETE, of Middletown.

1861. (M) On Thursday last, by the Rev. D. Zacharias, Mr JOSEPH FAUBLE, to Miss MARGARET REYNOLDS, both of this city.

1862. (D) At his residence in New Market, on Friday morning the 8th inst., JOSEPH HOLLAND, in the 80th year of his age. He was a volunteer in the service of his Country. His illness was protracted and often severe. On the Sabbath morning following, his remains were followed to the burying grounds of the Methodist Protestant Church, which he was a active member. He was interred with the Honors of War, by a fine troop under the command of Captain Richard Coale, of Liberty Town. (February 13, 1839)

1863. (D) In Baltimore, on Tuesday morning last, Col. WM. STEWART, aged 58 years. He filled several important offices, a member of the House of Delegates, and Executive Council, and Mayor of the city. A few days before his death, he was appointed by the Mayor the Collector of the city Taxes. In the late War, he acted as Lieutenant Colonel.

1864. (D) At Jefferson, on the 10th inst., MARY ELIZABETH, daughter of Lloyd and Catharine Gittings, in the 3rd year of her age.

1865. Rev. T. H. SCHROEDER, resigned as clergy of the Trinity Church, from regulations established by the Vestry, he considered it as interfering with his rights and which gives Rev. Dr. WAINWRIGHT, a precedence in some matters to himself.

February 28, 1839 (MHS)

1866. The ill health of WILLIAM W. MARKELL, Esq., compells him to abandon the printing business, and dispose of the establishment. The "Visiter," has been passed to the hand of THOMAS HALLER, Esq., who will continue publishing the said paper.

1867. (M) Near Middletown, Frederick Co., MD., on the 14th inst., by the Rev. J. C. Bucher, Mr DEWALT WILLIARD, to Miss ELIZABETH, eldest daughter of Mr Jacob Flook, of John, all of Middletown Valley, MD.

1868. (M) In Middletown, at the Parsonage, on the 21st inst., by the same, Mr JACOB S. TOMS, of Washington Co., MD., to Miss ELIZABETH SHOEMAKER, of Frederick Co., MD.

1869. (M) On the same day, by the same, at the Tavern of Mr George Titlow, Mr HENRY K. HILTON, to Miss MARGARET KNOUFF, all of Frederick Co., MD.

1870. (M) On Thursday last, by the Rev. D. Zacaharias, Mr SAM'L KEYSER, to Miss ANN C. POOL, both of this co.

1871. (M) On Thursday morning last, by the Rev. Jno. L. Pitts, Mr JAMES H. WATERS, to Miss ANN SCHLOSSER, all of Middletown Valley.

1872. (M) On the same day, by the same, Mr ROBERT MIX, to Miss AIRY TROUT, both of this co.

1873. (M) Near Harper's Ferry, on Monday evening last, by the Rev. Upton Beall, Mr CHARS. T. LIND, to Miss SARAH J. BENNETT, both of VA.

1874. (M) At Prince Anne, Eastern Shore, MD., Mr JOSHUA D. JOHNSON, formerly of this co., to Miss CHARLOTTE, daughter of H. K. Long, Esq.

1875. (M) On the 20th inst., at the residence of Mr Jno. Carmack, by the Rev. A. P. Freese, Mr JNO. FULTON, to Miss SARAH CARMACK, both of Frederick Co., MD.

1876. (D) In Frederick, on Saturday the 15th inst., in the 16th year of his age, MENELIUS HUDSON, son of the late Dr. Hudson, of Baltimore Co.

1877. (D) On the 17th inst., ANN MARY, infant, and only daughter of George Dofler, aged 2 years and 3 months.

1878. (D) On the 6th of January last, at Cumberland, CHRISTENIA DEATZEBACH, in the 85th year of his age.

March 7, 1839 (MHS)

1879. (M) On the 26th ult., by the Rev. John W. Hoffmier, at the house of Charles Mantz, (Antietam furnace,) Mr GREENBERRY FOUT, of Frederick Co., to Miss ANN ELIZABETH POST, daughter of John Grove, of Sharpsburgh, Washington Co., MD.

1880. (M) At Chambers Hotel, in February last, by the Rev. S. W. Harkey, Mr ADAM LINK, to Miss ANNE E. OSBORN, both of Jefferson Co., VA.

1881. (D) On Saturday the 16th ult., near Frederick, Mr JOHN GONSO, aged about 50 years.

1882. (D) In Buckeystown, on Saturday, the 16th ult., SUSAN ANN CECELIA, daughter of Samuel and Susan Ways, aged 3 years, 2 months and 6 days.

1883. (D) On the 24th ult., JOHN WESLEY, infant son of Washington and Catharine James, about 3 months.

March 14, 1839 (MHS)

1884. (M) On Tuesday evening last, by the Rev'd. D. Zacharias,

Mr THOMAS ZEPP, of Baltimore, to Miss JANE E. KOONTZ, of this city.

1885. (D) On Friday the 8th inst., Mrs CATHARINE PHILIPS, in the 66th year of her age, she was severely afflicted for a long time.
1886. (D) On Saturday night, the 9th inst., Mr PETER HOFF, at advanced age.
1887. (D) On Monday, the 11th inst., GLOVENIA, infant daughter of Mr Wm. Ely, aged 11 months.
1888. (D) Departed this life, at her residence in New Market on Friday the 8th inst., Mrs ANN BRASHEAR, relict of Dr. Belt Brashear, in the 72nd year of her age.

March 21, 1839 (MHS)

1889. (M) On the 5th inst., by the Rev. Mr Monroe, Mr EDWARD JONES, to ANN MATILDA, daughter of Mr Thomas J. Worthington, all of this co.
1890. (M) On Tuesday last, by the Rev. D. Zacharias, Mr GEO. W. BYER, to Mrs CATHARINE HELDEBRAND, all of this co.
1891. (M) On Tuesday evening last, by the Rev. Jos. H. Jones, LEBBEUS GRIFFITH, Esq., to Miss SARAH ANN, daughter of the Revd. John Wood, all of Frederick Co.
1892. (M) On the 12th ult., at the residence of Joseph Roop, Esq., near Ashland Ohio, by the Revd. Mr Shue, Mr DAVID ROOP, to Miss ELIZABETH HOFFMAN, of Richmond Co., Ohio, formerly of Carroll Co., MD.
1893. (M) On Thursday the 28th ult., by the Rev. Mr R. S. Grier, Mr JAMES THOMSON, to Miss MARY ANN, daughter of Jacob Hiltebridle, Esq., both of Taneytown District.
1894. (M) On the 14th ult., by the Rev. Mr Shue, Mr DAVID HOFFMAN, to Miss REBECCA, eldest daughter of Rev. Israel P. Haines, all of Richmond, Co., Ohio, formerly of Carroll Co., MD.
1895. (M) On Tuesday the 12th ult., by the Rev. Englar, Mr MICHAEL BARTHOLOW, to Miss ELIZABETH, daughter of Wm. Plane, all of Uniontown District.
1896. (M) On the 14th inst., near the mouth of Monocacy, by the Rev. Joseph Trapnell, Mr GEO. SPRING, to Miss CATHARINE JORDON, both of Frederick Co.
1897. (M) Near Poolesville, Montgomery Co., on the same day, by the same, GEORGE RHOADS, Esq., of VA., to Mrs JANE GREEN, of Montgomery Co.

1898. (M) On the 14th inst., by the Rev. A. P. Freese, Mr JACOB KEYSER, to Miss CATHARINE ZIMMERMAN, both of Frederick Co., MD.
1899. (M) On Wednesday the 13th inst., at Pleasant Retreat, residence of Joseph Gabby, Esq., by the Rev. Mr Buchanan, Dr. T. BUCHANAN DUCKET, of Hagerstown, to Miss ELIZA GABBY, daughter of Mr Gabby.
1900. (M) At the house of Mr Christopher Michael, on the 14th of March, by the Rev. J. C. Bucher, Mr JOHN NEWKIRK, of Washington Co., to Miss SUSAN, daughter of Mr Christopher Michael, of Middletown Valley, Frederick Co., MD.
1901. (D) On the 21st of February, Mr MICHAEL WAGONER, of Uniontown District, at aged of 87 years, 3 months and 15 days. He was interred at Emanuel Church.
1902. (D) On the 14th inst., of the croup, CHARLES HENRY, infant son of Mr George Sinn, of this city.
1903. (D) On the 15th inst., Mr JOSEPH MARSHALL, at an advanced age, leaving a widow and 5 children.
1904. (D) On the 17th inst., MARGARET REYNOLDS, daughter of Samuel Reynolds, Esq., formerly of this city.
1905. (D) Suddenly on the 8th inst., HENRY R. WARFIELD, Esq., auditor of the court of this co.
1906. (D) On Monday last, in the 14th month of his age, EDWARD GOLDSBOROUGH, son of Dr. Edward Y. Goldsborough, of this city.
1907. (D) On the 9th inst., at his residence, about 4 miles, from Emmittsburgh, Mr JOHN HARPER, aged 72 years. A cancerious affection which has been for many years making rapid and most painful progress, which terminated his existence.
1908. (D) In Shepherdstown, VA., on the 5th inst., of scarlet fever, JOHN MELVILLE, only son of Rev. D. G. Bragonier, aged 1 year, 10 months and 11 days. Also on the 9th inst., ELIZABETH S., infant daughter and only daughter of Rev. D. G. Bragonier, aged 2 months and 2 days.

March 28, 1839 (MHS)

1909. (F) On Monday evening last, in the rear buildings, to the property of Mr HORATIO WATERS, the origin is uncertain, it is thought it was the work of an incendiary.
1910. (M) On Thursday evening last, by the Rev. S. W. Harkey, Mr JOHN CONRAD, to Miss MARGARET TITLOW, both of this co.

1911. (M) On Tuesday evening last, by the Rev. J. L. Pitts, Mr WILLIAM BABYLON, to Miss BARBARA MARTIN, both of this co.

1912. (M) On the 13th inst., near Middleburg, by the Rev. Daniel Feete, Mr HANSON CARMACK, to Miss HARRIET, third daughter of John Clabaugh, Esq., of Carroll Co.

1913. (D) On Saturday the 16th inst., Mr KETROW, who resided a few miles Northwest of Frederick, at advanced age.

1914. (D) On the 20th inst., at his residence in Buckeystown, Mr JOHN STITCHER, aged 55 years, 11 months and 20 days.

1915. (D) On Sunday morning the 24th inst., at his residence near this city, Mr BALTZER FOUT, in the 60th year of his age.

1916. (D) On Saturday the 23rd inst., Miss MATILDA MANTZ, of this city, in the 31st year of her age.

1917. (D) On Tuesday evening, after a protracted illness, Mrs WALLING, in the _____ year of her age.

April 4, 1839 (MHS)

1918. (M) On the 14th inst., LEVI DAVIS, Esq., of Seneca Co., Ohio., to Miss JULIANNE, daughter of Isaac Shriver, Esq., of Westminster, MD.

1919. (M) On Thursday last, by the Rev. S. W. Harkey, WILSON SPARROW, to Miss ELIZABETH STOCKMAN, both of this co.

1920. (M) On Tuesday evening the 2nd inst., by the same, Mr JOHN REGG, to Mrs ELIZABETH FREDERICK, both of this co.

1921. (M) Near Middletown, Frederick Co., MD., on Tuesday evening the 26th of March 1839, by the Rev. J. C. Bucher, Mr SAMUEL McLEAN, to Miss HARRIET VORE, all of Frederick Co.

1922. (D) On the 8th of March inst., BELFORD, son of Washington Owings, of Liberty District, aged 2 years, 1 month.

1923. (D) On Wednesday evening the 20th inst., in the 36th year of her age, Mrs SARAH C. DAVIS, wife of Doct. Richard W. Davis, of this place, and daughter of the late Doct. Belt Brashear, of Frederick Co., MD.

April 11, 1839 (MHS)

1924. (M) On the 23rd of March, by the Rev. John L. Pitts, Mr DANIEL NUSBAUM, to Miss SARAH BORING, both of this co.

1925. (M) On the 9th of April, by the same, Mr JOHN HOWARD, to Miss ELIZABETH SPEELMAN, both of this co.
1926. (D) On Sunday morning the 31st of March, at his residence, Mr JACOB HARMAN, his remains were interred in the Lutheran cemetery.
1927. (D) The death of Mr HEZEKIAH NILES, took place yesterday morning in Wilmington, DE. For several years he had been in declining health, and was the publisher of the "Register," and was a printer by profession.
1928. (D) On the 9th inst., after a protracted and severe affliction, WM. W. MARKELL, Esq., former editor an proprietor of this paper.

April 25, 1839 (MHS)

1929. (M) On the 11th inst., in the Evangelical Lutheran Church, of Frederick, by the Rev. S. W. Harkey, Mr GEO. RINEHART, to Miss MARY M. FOUT, both of this co.
1930. (D) At Annapolis, on Sunday last, NICHOLAS BREWER, Senr., Esq., an old and respectable citizen of that place.
1931. (D) In Middletown, on Wednesday last, Mr DAVID BOWLUS, aged between 45 and 50 years of age. A influential, respected, and active citizen of Frederick Co.
1932. (D) Near Frederick, last week, Mrs MARY JOHNSON, relict of Benjamin Johnson, for a long time she had been in precarious health.

May 2, 1839 (MHS)

1933. (M) On Thursday evening last, by the Rev. J. L. Pitts, Mr ZACHARIAH SHAW, to Miss ELIZABETH RITER, both of this co.
1934. (M) On the 6th inst., in Emmittsburgh, by the Rev. Dr. Hickey, JOHN BEFORGODLEFEVER, to Miss MARGARET HOLODAY.
1935. (D) On Tuesday monring last, Mrs CATHARINE TURNER, after a lingering and painful illness. She leaves a husband, with 3 small children, and one only 3 months old.
1936. (D) On Sunday last, LUTHER BRENGLE, infant son of Charles and Sarah Brengle, aged 11 months and 11 days.
1937. (D) On the 14th inst., departed this life, Mrs HANNAH RICE, of Liberty, Frederick Co., MD., aged 81 years, 3 months and 14 days. She visited friends the previous day, and went to bed in prefect health and passed through death into life eternal. An appropriate and interesting

discourse was delivered by the Rev. Mr Munroe, from the 5th Chapter, 1st Verse, 2nd Corinthians.

1938. (D) On Saturday morning last, the 11th inst., Mrs ELIZABETH BEATTY, wife of Eli Beatty, Esq., of Hagerstown, aged 59 years.

1939. The Rev. Professor SMITH, of Marshall College, is expected to preach in the Reformed Church on next Sabbath morning.

1940. (D) At Annapolis, on Saturday last, after a lingering illness, Mrs ANN, wife of John N. Steel, Esq., of Dorchester Co., and daughter of Judge T. Buchanan.

May 9, 1839 (MHS)

1941. (M) On Thursday last, at the Parsonage of the Ev. Reformed Church, by the Rev. Daniel Zacharias, Mr JESSE MAINE, to Miss LYDIA SMITH, both of this co.

1942. (M) On the evening of the same, by the same, at the house of Mr Israel Myers, Mr JOHN RANDOLPH NICHOLS, of this city, to Miss CATHARINE MYERS, of this vicinity.

1943. (M) On the 17th inst., at the residence of Louis Bringerie, Esq., (Surveyor General of the State of LA.,) by the Rev. Mr Clapp, Maj. General EDMUND P. GAINS, of the U. S. Army, to Miss MARY CLARK WHITNEY, only daughter of the late Daniel Clark Whitney, Esq., of New Orleans.

1944. (M) On the 23rd of April, at Barnesville, Montgomery Co., by the Rev. Joseph Trapnell, Sen., HEZEKIAH L. TRUNDLE, to Miss MARY NICHOLLS, daughter of Col. Nicholls.

1945. (M) On May the 2nd, by the same, Mr WILLIAM MOTTER, to Miss COLUMBIA SPRIGG, both of Frederick Co.

May 16, 1839 (MHS)

1946. (M) On Thursday the 2nd inst., in Baltimore, by the Rev. J. Poisal, Mr ROBERT CROSS, to Miss HARRIET TIDY, formerly of Frederick.

1947. (M) On the 12th inst., by the Rev. D. Zacharias, Mr GRAFTON SHAWEN, to Miss CHRISTIANA BENTZ, both of this co.

1948. (M) On the same day, by the same, at the Parsonage of the Ev. Reformed Church, Mr HENRY BRANE, to Miss MARGARET LAWMAN.

1949. (D) On Sunday morning last, after a lingering illness, Mr JOHN MANTZ, of this city, aged 71 years, 9 months and 5 days.

1950. (D) On Saturday the 27th ult., MARTHA REBECCA, youngest daughter of Mr Michael and Rebecca Byrne, aged 2 years, and 6 months.
1951. (D) Near Liberty-Town, on Tuesday the 7th inst., after a protracted illness, of about 9 months, ALBERT, son of William A., and Sarah Albaugh, in the 11th year of his age.
1952. Following persons have been appointed by the Executive Committee of the Middletown Temperance Society as delegates to represent said society at the convention to be held in Frederick on whitmonday: Rev. J. C. BUCHER, Rev. J. CLEARY, Rev. M. WACHTER, S. R. WATERS, HENRY COBLENTZ, DANIEL KELLER, PETER COBLENTZ, JOHN APPLEMAN, DANIEL SMELTZER, MATHIAS AHOLT, JOHN DERR, PETER SCHLOSSER, LEWIS RECHTOL, JOHN KEAFAUVER, of Geo., JACOB DENN, GEORGE SHAFFER, JOSEPH ROUTZONG, DANIEL KEAFAUVER, DAVID RAMSBERG, DANIEL DERR, DAVID SHINDTER, JACOB THOMAS, of Jno., CHRISTIAN RAMSBERG, GEORGE BISER, JACOB FLOOK, of John, JACOB RUDY, PHILIP SHEFFER, SAMUEL YASTE, SAMUEL TOMS, JOHN KEPLAR, Jr., SAMUEL FILLER, HENRY CRONE, JACOB BEAR. S. G. HARBAUGH, Sec'y.
1953. At a meeting of the Executive Committee of the Frederick Union Temperance Society, the following resolution was adopted viz: Resolute; that Messrs: L. P. W. BALCH, GEORGE L. L. DAVIS, RICHARD POTTS, EZEKIEL HUGHES, LEWIS MEDTART, GEORGE SALMON, RICHARD HARPER, ANDREW BOYD, ABRAHAM HOFF, EDWARD TRAIL, ANDREW HEIM, JOHN A. STEINER, Dr. WILLIAM B. TYLER, VALENTINE BIRELY, ABRAHAM KEMP, JOHN FESLER, JOHN YOUNG, JACOB ENGLEBRECHT, GEORGE ENGELBRECHT, JOHN P. THOMPSON, ROB'T. McCLEERY, WILLIAM R. SANDERSON, SAMUEL CRONICE, VALENTINE DOUB, and CHESTER COLEMAN, in connection with the Executive Committee of the Frederick Union Temperance Society, and Protestant Clergry, be, and constitute the delegates to meet the county convention, to be held in Frederick City, on whitmonday. Resolved; that the Rv'd. Messrs: WEISER, and BROWN, be requested to address the convention. Resoluted: that L. P. W. BALCH, GEORGE L. L. DAVIS, and LEWIS BIRELY, be a committee to draft a constitution for the county society.

May 23, 1839 (MHS)

1954. (M) On the 16th inst., by the Rev. S. W. Harkey, Mr DANIEL WACHTER, to Miss CATHARINE ANN KEYSER, both of this co.
1955. (M) On the 9th inst., by the same, at the Parsonage of the Ev. Lutheran Church, Mr HENRY S. WILLIAMS, to Miss ANN CARNES, both of VA.
1956. (M) On the 20th inst., by the same, at the Parsonage of the Ev. Lutheran Church, Mr GEORGE FRAAS, to Miss MARGARETTA BARNHART, both of this city.
1957. (M) On the 17th inst., in the Lutheran Church in Taney-Town, by the Rev. Mr Keller, Mr PHILIP MILLER, of Frederick Co., to Miss ELIZABETH CRAMER, of Cattle Branch.
1958. (M) On the 16th inst., by the Rev. J. Cleary, at the residence of Mr Jacob Grove, Mr GRAFTON FOUT, to Miss LAURETTA, daughter of Jacob Grove both of this co.
1959. (D) On the 15th inst., BRIDGET ELIZA, daughter of John and Catherine Nooman, aged 4 years, and 3 months.
1960. (D) On the 6th inst., after a lingering illness of several months, Mrs SUSAN DERN, consort of Isaac Dern, Esq., of Taney-Town, District, in the 25th year of her age. She leaves a husband and 5 small children.

May 30, 1839 (MHS)

1961. (M) On Tuesday the 21st ult., (at Dorsey's City Hotel,) by the Rev. John L. Pitts, Mr JOSEPH SMITH, to Miss ELLEN MANDAVILLE, both of VA.
1962. (M) On the 9th inst., in Greencastle, DANIEL TROXELL, to Miss ELIZABETH DILLEHUNT, both of Frederick Co.

June 6, 1839 (MHS)

1963. (M) By the Rev. R. Weiser, on Thursday evening the 30th ult., Mr DAVID F. YANTIS, to Miss BELINDA, third daughter of Brooke Baker, Esq., of Woodsboro.
1964. (M) On the 24th of April, by the same, Mr SOLOMON BEARD, to Miss MARGARET EULER, all of this co.
1965. (M) On the 30th of April, by the Rev. J. Cleary, Mr HENRY BAKER, to Miss REBECCA DUVALL, both of Buckeystown.
1966. (D) In Middletown, on Saturday morning last, after a short illness, Mr MICHAEL PETERS.
1967. (D) On Tuesday last, JOHN HENRY, son of William and Rebecca Duvall, aged years, and 11 months.
1968. Meeting held in the Lutheran Church of this city, on whitmonday, May 20, 1839. Dr. LLOYD DORSEY, was

called to the chair, and Dr. ALBERT RITCHIE, as Secretary. Meeting open with a Hymm from the choir, and prayer by the Rev. S. W. HARKEY. Following gentlemen were present as delegates from their respective societies. Frederick Union Temperance: L. P. W. BALCH, G. L. L. DAVIS, GEORGE SALMON, RICHARD HARPER, J. A. STEINER, JOHN FESSLER, JOHN YOUNG, JACOB ENGELBRECHT, SAMUEL CRONISE, V. DOUB, Rv. J. L. PITTS, Rv. S. W. HARKEY, Rv. J. H. BROWN, LEWIS BIRELY, S. R. HOGG, JACOB KELLER, JOHN KUNKLE. Middletown: S. R. WATERS, H. COBLENTZ, D. KELLER, GEO. SHAFFER, JOSEPH ROUTZONG, D. SHINDLER, C. RAMSBURG, Rv. J. CLEARY, Dr. JACOB BAER. St. Johns: GEO. BLESSING, JACOB JOHNSON, JOSHUA SNYDER, J. GROSNICKLE, C. ROUTZONG. Linganore: JAMES PEARRE, BURGER NELSON. Mechanics-Town: J. SLOAN, LEVI HESSON, JAMES STOKES, J. FRAZER. Woodsborough: Rv. R. WEISER, JESSE WINCOUGH, J. A. BAKER.

June 13, 1839 (MHS)

1969. (M) On Thursday evening the 6th inst., by the Rev. E. Heiner, Mr C. K. THOMAS, of Fred'k, Co., to Miss EVELINA VIRGINIA, second daughter of Daniel Bucky, Merchant of Baltimore.

1970. (D) The body of a man was found in the Monocacy a few days since, drifted into shallow water by the current. We understand the body is that of an idiot who has been in this place for several weeks, named GEORGE CRAFT, his family we believe resides in York, PA.

June 20, 1839 (MHS)

1971. (M) On the 5th of June, by the Rev. John L. Pitts, Mr GEO. BRANE, to Miss SARAH A. HOFFMAN, both of this co.

1972. (M) On the 13th of June, by the same, at the Eagle Hotel, Mr LEONARD REDDICK, to Miss JAMIMAH WALTZ, both of this co.

1973. (M) On the 6th inst., by the Rev. B. Keller, Mr GREENBERY PEDICORN, to Miss MARIA CATHARINE KIPE, both of MD.

1974. (M) On the 3rd of June, by the Rev. A. P. Freese, Mr GEORGE F. ZIMMERMAN, to Miss ANN McNAIR, both of this co.

1975. (M) On Tuesday the 18th inst., by the Rev. James H. Brown, Mr FREDERICK COLEHORSE, to Miss JANE MARTIN, both of this co.

1976. (D) Near Middletown, Fred'k. Co., MD., on the 4th of June 1839, after a painful and distressing illness (scarlatina,) CORNELIUS, son of David Mahn, aged 4 years, 9 months and 17 days.
1977. (D) On the 14th inst., LOUISA ISABELLA QUYNN, aged 5 years, 2 months and 11 days.
1978. (D) Near Jefferson, Frederick Co., MD., on Friday the 7th of June 1839, after a protracted illness, MICHAEL THOMAS, Eqs., aged 45 years, 11 months and 6 days.
1979. (D) In Frederick, on the 12th inst., JOHN CASPAR HART, son of Jacob and Mary Hart, aged 5 years, 1 month and 20 days, and on the 13th., MARY ELIZABETH, aged 1 year, 8 months and 25 days.

June 27, 1839 (MHS)

1980. (M) On Sunday evening last, by the Rev. J. L. Pitts, Mr JOHN M. LOWE, to Mrs SARAH MORMAN, both of this city.
1981. (M) On Tuesday morning last, by the same, Mr AMBROSE INGMAN, formerly of New Market, to Miss CATHARINE LOUISA BUCKEY, of Frederick.

July 4, 1839 (MHS)

1982. (M) On Thursday morning last, by the Rev. John L. Pitts, Dr. GASAWAY GRIMES, to Miss SUSAN H., daughter of the late Upton Dorsey, Esq., all of Carroll Co.
1983. (M) On the 9th inst., by the Rev. William Monroe, Mr THOMAS LYNCH, of Boonesboro, to Miss MARY ANN JOY, late of Frederick Co.
1984. (M) At Emmittsburg, on Wednesday the 26th inst., by the Rev. John Hicky, Mr JOHN P. McMEAL, of St. Louis, MS., to Miss MARY A. GROVER, of Emmittsburg, MD.
1985. (M) On the 25th inst., at Highlands, Baltimore Co., by the Rev. Mr Backus, THOS. SANDERSON, to HANNAH A., daughter of Jas. Pearson.
1986. (D) On the 26th of June, near Mt. Zion Church, LUCRETIA PERMELIA RENN, daughter of Isaac and Martha Renn, aged 3 years, 1 month and 2 days.

July 18, 1839 (MHS)

1987. (M) On Sunday evening last, by the Rev. Jno. L. Pitts, Mr WM. CONROD, to Miss MARGARET STEINER, all of Frederick.
1988. (M) On Thursday the 12th inst., by the Rev. S. W. Harkey, Mr ABRAHAM E. GRUSHON, to Miss ANN MARIA, daughter

of Peter Eichelberger, Esq., of Lewistown, Frederick Co., MD.

1989. (M) On the same, by the same, Mr HENRY H. SCHRODER, to Miss JOANAH A. RETTGERING, both of this city.

1990. (D) On the 3rd inst., ANN MARIA STANISLAUS, infant daughter of John and Elizabeth A. Tehan, aged 8 months and 9 day.

1991. (D) On Monday morning, Miss ELIZA DUVALL, ceased to breath between 2 and 3 o'clock, in her 30th year. She leaves several younger sisters and brothers.

1992. (D) At Indianapolis, (Ind.) on Wednesday the 3rd of July, Mr JOHN T. DEVELBISS, merchant of that place, in the 22nd year of his age, after confinement of 3 weeks by consumption. He was from Maryland, and had just commence business there. He was at the time in the family of Dr. Dobbs, who took care of him and his mother.

1993. (D) Departed this life suddenly at his residence in Creagerstown, on Monday the 8th inst., Mr MICHAEL RAMICH, age about 60 years.

July 25, 1839 (MHS)

1994. The Rev. BISHOP WAUGH, of the Methodist Episcopal Church, is expected to be at the Buckeystown meeting, which commence on Saturday next.

1995. Meeting of the Executive Committee of the Frederick Union Temperance Society was held at the office of Dr. A. RITCHIE, on Tuesday evening July 23rd. The following 3 person were elected to draw up a report and present it in behalf of the society at the quarterly meeting of the County Society to be held in Middletown on 17th of August. L. P. W. BALCH, Esq., Rev. S. W. HARKEY, Mr JACOB KELLER. Executive Committee: Doct. WM. WATERS, Doct. WM. M. KEMP, Mr CYRUS MANTZ, Mr S. R. HOGG, Doct. A. RITCHIE, Mr G. KOONTZ, Mr JOHN KUNKLE, Mr LEWIS BIRELY.

August 1, 1839 (MHS)

1996. (M) On Sunday morning last, by the Rev. John L. Pitts, Mr ISRAEL BAST, to Miss MARY PARKS BURTON, both of this co.

1997. (D) On the 30th, in the 5th year of her age, ANN, only daughter of George and Ann M. Englebrecht.

1998. (D) On Thursday morning the 25th inst., ANN REBECCA HARDT, in the 5th year of her age.

August 15, 1839 (MHS)

1999. (D) Near Jefferson, on the 8th of July, MARY JANE, youngest dauhter of Mr Jacob Flook, aged 1 year, 7 months and 17 days.
2000. (D) On the 13th inst., in this city, after a lingering illness, Mr HENRY HEICHLER, aged 74 years, 3 months and 11 days.
2001. (D) On the 25th ult., Mrs ZERUIAH KNOX, relict of the late Rev. Samuel Knox, in the 56th year of her age.
2002. (D) At his residence in Frederick Co., MD., on the 13th ult., Mr JACOB BARRICK, in the 84th year of his age, was the son of John Barrick, who was among the early permanent settlers in this part of Frederick Co. He leaves 6 children and 37 grandchildren and 23 great grandchildren.

August 22, 1839 (MHS)

2003. (M) On the morning of the 1st ult., at the Institution for the Deaf and Dumb, in this city, by the Rev. Dr. Milnor, Mr J. R. BURNETT, of Livingston, N.J., to Miss PHEBE OSBORNE, of Castile Co., N.Y. (A pupil of that institution.)
2004. (M) On Tuesday the 17th inst., by the Rev. S. W. Harkey, Mr JOHN C. V. NAUMANN, to Miss MARY GEITZ, both of this city.
2005. (D) On Wednesday morning last, after an illness of 16 days, Mrs ANN SABINA SIDES, aged 79 years, 5 months and 22 days. She died at the residence of Mr Greenbury Shipley, of Carroll Co.
2006. (D) On Saturday last, after a few days illness, JOHN HENRY, only child of Adam W., and Rosanna Devilbiss, aged 7 months and 15 days.
2007. Preparation is now making for a "Firemen's procession" in the city, on Saturday next. The occasion of the procession is the first appearance of the "Junior Fire Company," who under the escort of the several fire companies of the city, the whole under the command of our worthy friend, Colonel SAMUEL CARMACK, are to receive on that occasion, a new and splended engine and other apparatus, by railroad from Baltimore.
2008. At a meeting of a convention of the different fire companies of the city of Frederick, held on the 14th last, at City Hall. The convention being organized by calling to the chair, Mr JACOB KELLER, and appointing Mr EZRA BENTZ, Secretary. Following resolutions were passed: (1) A public procession to be held on Saturday 24th inst. (2) That

Mayor, City Council, and Alderman, be enlisted to attend and join in the procession. (3) That different fire companies assemble in Market Street opposite the Market House, at 1 an 1/2 o'clock, with their engines, hose, &c. (4) That SAMUEL CARMACK, be appointed Chief Marshal, with power to appoint Deputy Marshals from each company. The following gentlemen were appointed Deputy Marshals. For the Friendship: WINCHESTER CLINGAN. Sunrise: JACOB FAUBLE. Independent: DAVID BRENGLE. Juniors: WM. B. McLANAHAN. Washington: WM. REICH. Frederick Hose: WILLIAM I. ALBAUGH.

September 12, 1839 (MHS)

2009. (M) On Thursday morning last, at Cookerly's Hotel, by the Rev. John L. Pitts, Mr JOHN T. PERRY, to Miss MARY MULLIN, both of this co.

2010. (M) On the same day, by the same, Mr SAMUEL THOMAS, to Miss HARRIET ANN BALL, both of this co.

2011. (D) On the 1st, GEORGE ADOLPHUS, infant son of Mr Jacob and Catharine Keller, aged 7 months.

2012. (D) On the 8th inst., Mr JACOB CRUMBINE, in the 56th year of his age.

September 19, 1839 (MHS)

2013. (M) On Thursday the 12th inst., near Woodsborough, by the Rev. R. Weiser, Mr EZRA CYPHERD, to Miss MARY MORNINGSTARR, all of this co.

2014. (M) On Sunday evening last, by the Rev. Jno. L. Pitts, Mr WILLIAM WHITEFORD, Esq., to Miss MARY ANN WILLINGHAN, both of Baltimore.

2015. (D) On the 1st inst., near Lewistown, GEORGE H. WILES, aged 18 years, and 11 months. He leaves a wife and 1 child

2016. (D) At the residence of her brother-in-law, William Cookerly, Esq., of Frederick, on the 12th inst., Miss ANN GIBSON, daughter of Capt. Thomas Gibson, late of this co., in the 28th year of her age.

2017. (D) Near Middletown, MD., on the 8th of September, CHARLOTTE LOUISA, infant daughter of Mr Jacob Rudy, in the 1st year of her age.

September 26, 1839 (MHS)

2018. (F) On Tuesday last between 9 and 10 o'clock, A.M., fire was discovered to be in one of the back buildings of Mr G.

CONRADT's Carpet Factory. It was discovered before having made much progress. Only the roof of the small building in which the fire commenced was burned, thanks to the assistance of the different fire companies being immediately on the ground. Mr Conradt and his family were much alarmed, and no wonder since about 18 months ago this same establishment was destroyed by fire.

2019. (M) On Thursday September 19th, by the Rev. K. Clary, Mr DANIEL MILLER, of Middletown, to Miss ELIZA ANN WINDSON, of Jefferson, Frederick Co.

2020. (M) On Tuesday last, by the Rev. D. Zacharias, Mr JOSEPH LAMBERT, to Miss MARY ANN HEIM, all of this co.

2021. (M) On the 12th of September inst., by the Rev. Jos. L. Smith, Mr HENRY RHOADES, to Miss ANN E. ENGLES, both of this city.

2022. (M) At Prospect Hall on Thursday the 19th inst., by the Rev. Upton Beall, Miss MARY E. McPHERSON, to JOHN W. KENNEDY, Esq., of Washington Co.

October 17, 1839 (MHS)

2023. (M) On Thursday last, by the Rev. S. R. Waters, Mr ADAM BOWSER, to Miss ANN C. SPRINGFIELD, both of Middletown Valley.

2024. (M) On Tuesday morning the 8th inst., by the Rev. John McElroy, at Rose Hill the residence of William Slater, Esq., Mr JOHN A. HERN, of Philadelphia, to Miss ANN C. SLATER.

2025. (M) Near Darnestown, in this co., on the 24th of Sept., last by the Rev. J. H. Jones, Mr JAMES BIGGS, to Miss MARTHA MEEKS, all of this place. The circumstances connected with the above marriage are of a noval character. Bigg's was engaged to Miss C. _____, and "the wedding clothes provided" and the invited guest assembled to witness the ceremonies on the appointed night. The evening had far advanced but the bridegroom did not make his appearance-conjectures ran that he had eloped with a maiden fair in the neighborhood. A party sailied forth to ascertain the facts connected with the affair and to report to the bride as to the whereabout of her intended lord. The party were not long in discovering that he had married another lady. They aroused him from his comfortable quarters and escorted him to a neighboroing town, where they made a friendly proposition-either to pay the expenses the first lady had incurred in preparing for the wedding or take a coat of tar and feathers. He, as it may reasonably be supposed, assented to the first proposition. The lady has survived the disappointment. (Rockville Journal)

2026. (D) Recently at New Orleans, of yellow fever, Dr. RAPHAEL SMITH, in the 23rd year of his age.

2027. (D) At her residence near Tiffin, on Thursday the 7th ult., after a short but severe illness, Mrs ELIZABETH LUGENBEEL, consort of Andrew Lugenbeel, and second daughter of the late Maj. Charles Baltzell, of Frederick Co., MD., in the 33rd year of her age.

2028. (D) At Union Mills, MD., on the morning of the 27th ult., after a long illness, Mrs ELIZABETH, wife of Andrew Shriver, Esq., in the 74th year of her age.

2029. (D) At Urbanna, on the 9th inst., after a short illness, Miss CASANDRA BEALL.

2030. (D) On Friday evening the 4th inst., at Uniontown, Mr JOHN GARBER, in the 78th year of his age. A faithful and respectable member of the German Baptist or Tunker Society, leaving a wife and 6 children.

2031. (D) On Tuesday the 1st inst., Mr SIMON KELLER, of Uniontown District.

2032. (D) In Baltimore on the 6th inst., after a short but severe illness of 3 weeks, Mr ALFRED LOW, in the 29th year of his age.

October 24, 1839 (MHS)

2033. (F) On Tuesday evening last about 10 o'clock, when it appeared that the United States Hotel in this city, which is kept by Mr ROBERT, was on fire. Flames were arrested by several of the engines and numerous citizens were almost immediately on the spot, so that before it had time to process. It was on the 2nd story floor between the plasting and floor.

2034. (M) On the 17th inst., by the Rev. D. Feete, Mr REUBEN SAILOR, to Miss HANNAH SMITH, both of this co.

2035. (D) At Harrisburg on the morning of the 13th inst., JAMES McBRIDE, a native of Emmitsburg.

October 31, 1839 (MHS)

2036. (M) On Monday evening last, (at Cookerly Hotel) by the Rev. John L. Pitts, Mr RUFUS KING, to Miss AMANDA ELIZABETH MOBBERLY, both of this co.

2037. (M) On Tuesday last, by the same, Mr SAMUEL SHIPLY, to Miss ANN MICHAEL, both of this co.

2038. (M) On Thursday last, by the same, Mr ROBERT SMITH, to Miss REBECCA EICHELBERGER, both of this co.
2039. (M) In Baltimore, on the 22nd inst., by the Rev. Mr Myers, at Eutaw House, AUGUSTUS E. DORSEY, of Frederick City, to MARTHA C., daughter of Daniel Thomas, Esq., of Loudon Co., VA.
2040. (M) On Tuesday evening the 29th of October, by the Rev. S. W. Harkey, Mr EDWARD EADER, to Mrs MARY HALLER, both of this city.
2041. (M) On the 8th inst., by the same, Mr DANIEL EIGENBRODE, to Miss ELIZABETH HARP, both of this co.
2042. (M) On the 27th inst., by the Rev. D. Zacharias, Mr GEO. W. GIBBS, to Miss LYDIA BUZZARD, both of this co.
2043. (M) On Tuesday morning last, near Jefferson, by the same, Mr MICHAEL KEEFER, to Miss CATHARINE A. WARFIELD, all of Frederick Co.
2044. (D) On the 14th inst., in the 27th year of his age, Lieut. CHARLES S. RIDGELY, of the U. S. Navy, son of General Charles S. Ridgely, of Anne Arundel Co.
2045. (D) On Monday last at the residence of his mother in this town, JOHN P. FOUT, in the 22nd year of his age. The disease which he died from attacked him suddenly, and very soon proved fatal. He leaves a widowed mother, in her declining years.
2046. (D) On the 7th of October inst, GEORGE HANCOCK GRIFFIN, of the 6th infantry at Ft. Brooke, Tampa, Florida, after a illness of 7 days.
2047. (D) On Friday the 25th inst., Mr HENRY N. TRICE, merchant of this city, after a short illness.

November 7, 1839 (MHS)

2048. (M) On Thursday evevning last, by the Rev. Jno. L. Pitts, Mr FREDERICK WACHTELL, to Miss MARTHA ANN CROCKEN, both of this city.
2049. (M) On the same evening, at (Dorsey's City Hotel,) Dr. E. LINCOLN BROWN, to ANNA MARIA FUNDENBURG, and at the same time, by the same, GEORGE H. JOHNSON, Esq., to JULIANA FUNDENBURG, all of Mechanics-Town.
2050. (M) On Tuesday evening last, by the Rev. Mr Beall, Rev. Mr HOFF, of Creagerstown, to Miss JULIANNA J. ROSS, daughter of Wm. Ross, Esq., of Frederick.
2051. (M) On Thursday morning the 24th inst., in St. John's Church, by the Rev. A. A. Lipscomb, Mr WM. B. PYFER,

formerly of Frederick, to HANNAH MELVILLE, daughter of the late Henry Pyfer, of George-Town, D.C.

2052. (M) On the 29th of October, by the Rev. A. P. Freeze, Mr JOHN W. BARRICK, to Miss CATHARINE SOPHIA, daughter of Capt. G. Develbiiss, all of this co.

2053. (M) At West Alexandria, on the 17th ult., by the Rev. Samuel Montgomery, E. BURKE FISHER, Esq., Editor of the Pittsburg Saturday Evening Visiter, to Miss NARCASSA McKEEHAN, of the former place.

2054. (M) Near Mechanicstown by the Rev. R. Weiser, on the 28th ult., Mr JOSEPH FREEZE, to Miss MARY ELIZABETH ROUZER, all of this co.

2055. (M) On Saturday morning the 2nd inst., by the Rev. Mr McCarthy, at the residence of J. Noonan, Esq., Mr D. GALWIN, of Hedgesville, Berkle Co., VA., to Miss BRIDGER E. BUCKLEY.

2056. (D) On Thursday last, the 31st of Oct., Mr CASPER MANTZ, aged 63 years, 4 months and 8 days. On last Friday afternoon, his remains were followed to the cemetery of the Reformed Church, where they now rest beside those of his father.

2057. (D) Copy from the Western Observer - Gloom was thrown over our little village, on Friday afternoon last, by the death of JOSEPH THORNTON, Esq., a native of Franklin Co., PA. Who migrated to this place about 47 years ago. He leaves a widow, and 2 sons, he left $5,000.00 to be appropriated to charitable purposes.

November 14, 1839 (MHS)

2058. (M) On Sunday last, by the Rev. John L. Pitts, Mr WARNER KAUFFMAN, to Miss HARRIET ANN LITTLE, all of Frederick City.

2059. (M) On Tuesday evening last, by the Rev. E. Keller, L. F. COPPERSMITH, Esq., of Columbia, IA., to Miss MARIA LOUISA, daughter of Isaac baugher, (merchant,) of Emmittsburg.

2060. (M) Miss JULIA WEBSTER, daughter of Daniel Webster, was married in London to SAMUEL APPLETON, Esq., of Boston. Mr Linn of Missouri, and Mr Young, of Illiniois, with a great number of distinguish Englishmen, and English leaders being present at the wedding.

November 21, 1839 (MHS)

2061. (M) On Thursday evening last, by the Rev. D. Zacharias, Mr

PETER C. CLEM, of Baltimore, to Miss RHODA BRUNNER, of Frederick Co.
2062. (M) On Tuesday evening last, by the same, Mr JOSEPH H. NEEL, to Miss ELIZA ANN STONER, all of this city.
2063. (D) On the 16th inst., in the 66th year of her age, Miss REBECCA COULTER, relict of Alexander Coulter, Esq., formerly of Frederick Co., for many years a residence of Baltimore City.
2064. (D) On Friday evening the 15th inst., at his residence in Prince George's Co., MD., Col. JOHN CONTEE, in the 45th year of his age.

November 28, 1839 (MHS)

2065. (D) Another Patriot Gone - At his residence near Westminster, in Carroll Co., MD., on Sunday the 17th at 10 an 1/2 o'clock, P.M., Col. JOSHUA GIST, at an advanced age of 93 years.
2066. (D) On Wednesday evening last week, a boy named EDWARD CHARLES TULY, and aged 9 years, 9 months and 19 days, came to death in our city, by being thrown from a horse. He was warned several times not to take the animal, unobserved, he loosen him from the yard where he was hitched, and rode him about the street. Several persons saw him whipping the horse and dashing through the town in a violent manner He was told to take the animal home, the horse took fright, throwing his rider off to one side, his left foot caught in the stirrup, and was dragged a considerable distances with his head dashing against the ground, and hitting stones amongest the feet of the horse, until he was nearly cut to pieces, and almost every bone was broken.
2067. (M) On Tuesday evening the 19th inst., by the Rev. S. W. Harkey, Mr DANIEL MICHAEL, to Miss HESTER ANN GEISBURT, all of the Manor
2068. (M) On Thursday the 21st inst., by the same, Mr WM. R. SUMAN, to Miss RACHAEL C. CROMWELL, all of Buckeystown.
2069. (M) At Clarksburgh, MD., on Tuesday the 5th ult., Mr HENRY W. MOORE, to Miss AMANDA MOBERLY, all of Montgomery Co., MD.
2070. (M) At Moul's Tavern, in Westminster, on Thursday the 14th inst., by the Rev. Isaac Webster, Mr ADAM BLOOM, of Carroll Co., to Miss MARY, daughter of Mr William Dudderar, of Frederick City.

2071. (M) At Nashville, TN., on the 9th inst., T. L. BUDD, Esq., to Miss ELIZA JANE, eldest daughter of the Rev. J. N. Maffit, both of that city.
2072. (M) At New York, on the 19th inst., Hon. LUTHER BRADISH, Lieutenant Governor of the State of New York, to Miss MARY E. HART, of the city of New York.
2073. (M) On Tuesday evening last, by the Rev. J. L. Pitts, Mr CHRISTIAN HECKATHORN, to Miss MARY WHEELER, of Frederick.
2074. (M) On the 19th ult., by the Rev. A. P. Freese, Mr EZRA E. BARRICK, to Miss HARRIET CRAMER, all of Frederick Co., MD.

December 5, 1839 (MHS)

2075. (M) On Thursday evening last, by the Rev. S. W. Harkey, WM. TOMPSON PALMER, Esq., to Miss MARY E. KEAFER, all of this co.
2076. (D) On Oct. 10th, near Buckeystown, CHARLOTTE REBECCA, daughter of Mr James Cary, in the 4th year of her age.

December 12, 1839 (MHS)

2077. (D) On the 5th inst., in Clearsprings, Washington Co., MD., Mrs CATHARINE ZACHARIAS, in the 53rd year of her age.

December 19, 1839 (MHS)

2078. (D) At his father's residence in Westminster, on Wednesday morning last, from the breaking of a blood vessel, Dr. GEO. SHRIVER, aged about 30 year.

December 26, 1839 (MHS)

2079. (M) In Baltimore, on the 15th inst., by the Rev. Mr Tippet, Mr DAVID F. SMITH, printer of Frederick, to Miss SUSAN E. FORD, of Baltimore.
2080. (M) On the 18th inst., by the Rev. Mr Bucher, Capt. AARON FITZGERALD, of the U. S. Army, to Mrs FRANCES ANN MILLER, of Middletown, MD.
2081. (M) By the Rev. Joseph Trapnell, on Thursday the 19th Mr CHRISTIAN HEMPSTON, to Miss M. A. DADE, at the house of Colonel Robert T. Dade, Montgomery Co.
2082. (M) In Frederick, on Tuesday the 17th inst., by the Rev. Joseph Trapnell, Mr JOSEPH R. FISHER, of Montgomery Co., to Miss MARY H. CARLLEY, of Frederick Co.

2083. (M) On Thursday evening last, by the Rev. Upton Beall, Dr. STOKES, of Mobile, AL., to Miss MARY TYLER, daughter of Dr. Wm. Bradley Tyler, of Frederick.

2084. (M) On Thursday evening the 10th inst., at Lansdowne, the residence of Dr. G. S. Townsend, by the Rev. Mr Burrows, HENRY BOSE, Esq., Editor of the Cecil Gazette, to Miss BELINDA P. HAMMER, all of Cecil Co., MD.

2085. (D) At the house of her son-in-law, (David Martin,) in this city, on the 15th inst., in the 72nd year of her age, MARGARET RECK, consort of Abraham Reck, Sen., formerly of Carroll Co., MD. She had the tedious and painful disease (dropsy at the heart,) she is survived by 2 sons who are engaged in the Lutheran Ministry.

2086. (D) Near Uniontown, on the 3rd inst., SAMUEL, eldest son of John and Mary Roop, in the 19th year of his age.

2087. (D) On Tuesday week near Uniontown, Mr PETER LITTLE, in the 38th year of his age.

2088. (D) On Thursday morning the 5th inst., in the 81st year of his age, SOLOMON HOLLAND, Esq., Register of Wills in Montgomery Co.

1840

THE VISITER

January 2, 1840 (MHS)

2089. (D) At Carlisle, PA., on the 25th ult., Mr DAVID S. FORNEY, a worthy and respectable citizen of that place.

January 9, 1840 (MHS)

2090. The Rev. J. CLARY, will preach on the subject of Temperance on Sunday night at 6 an 1/2 o'clock, the 12th inst., in the Ev. Lutheran Church in this city.

January 16, 1840 (MHS)

2091. (D) At his residence in Livingston Co., N. Y., on the 27th ult., Col. WM. FITZHUGH, in the 79th year of his age, formerly of Washington Co., MD. A patriot of the Washington School in the War of Independence, a Lieutenant of dragoones at the seize of Yorktown, and Aid-de-camp, of General Fish, of Maryland. Was an early settler in the valley of the Genessee, where he laid a foundation of affluence for a large family.

2092. The 19th anniversary of the Young Men's Bible Society of Frederick Co., was held in the Presbyterian Church on the evening of the 1st of January. Rev'd. UPTON BEALL, read a chapter from the Bible, and prayer was said by the pastor of the church, and address was given by the Rev. JOS. H. BROWN. The following members were elected for the ensuing year. Ev. Ref'd. Church: A. BARNEY, JNO. RAINSBURGH, GEO. SALMON, J. A. STEINER. Episcopal Church: DAVIS RICHARDSON, VAL. BIRELY, HORATIO WILCOXEN, EZEKIEL HUGHES. Lutheran Church: LEWIS BIRELY, JACOB KELLER, GEO. M. CONRADT, LEWIS MEDTART. Presbyterian Church: Doct. A. RITCHIE, ABRAHAM HUFF, S. R. HOGG, THOMAS GURLEY. Methodist Church: Rev. J. L. PITTS, ANDREW BOYD, A. H. HUNT, HENRY ROBINSON. Closing prayer was said by Rev. S. W. HARKEY.

January 23, 1840 (MHS)

2093. (M) In this city, on the Sabbath evening, by the Rev. J. H. Brown, Mr HOWARD HILLERY, to Miss ELIZABETH MARK, both of North Market.

2094. (M) On the 4th inst., by S. R. Waters, Mr JOHN SUMAN, to Miss SUSAN RIDENHOUR, all of Middletown Valley.

2095. (M) At Middletown, Frederick Co., MD., on the 16th of January 1840, by the Rev. J. C. Bucher, Mr ISAAC HOLLINGWORTH ALLEN, to Miss EVELINA, eldest daughter of Mr George Titlow, all of Middletown, MD.

2096. (D) In Middletown, Frederick Co., MD., on the 12th of Jan. 1840, Mrs. CHRISTIANA, consort of Mr Jacob Routzaun, in the 65th year of her age. She leaves a husband and a beloved daughter.

2097. Candidates for the Common Council - Mr HENRY C. LARE, representative of Ward #5. Mr GEORGE SALMON, of Ward #7. JOHN M. LOWE, of Ward #2.

January 30, 1840 (MHS)

2098. (D) Yesterday morning the 16th inst., the Rev. IRA A. EASTER, in the 46th year of his age. Pastor of Sherwood Chapel, Baltimore Co., and Home Agent of the Maryland State Colonization Society.

2099. (D) At New Orleans, on the night of the 21st ult., at Verandah Hotel, Gen. ROBERT T. LYTLE, of Cincinnati. A native of Ohio, and formerly represented Cincinnati in Congress, in the 38th year of his age.

2100. (M) In this city, on Thursday the 23rd inst., by the Rev. J. H. Brown, Mr MICHAEL UMBERGER, to Miss MARGARET MOBLEY, both of Frederick Co.

2101. (M) On Thursday the 23rd inst., by the Rev. S. W. Harkey, Mr HARRISON MILLER, to Miss ELIZABETH HALLER, all of this city.

2102. (M) On the 2nd inst., by the Rev. James Perro, Mr JOHN D. CLEMSON, of this co., to Miss RACHEL, daughter of Mr Nicholas Hoy, of Frederick Co.

2103. (M) On the 17th inst., by the same, Mr JOHN WOOD, to Miss MARTHA BRIGHTVILLE, both of Frederick Co.

2104. (M) On the 2nd ult., by the Rev. John L. Pitts, Mr BUNBURY BENNETT, to Miss MARY E. CREDMER, all of Harpers Ferry.

2105. (M) On Tuesday evening last, by the same, Mr JAMES HORTON, to Miss MARY A. C. HANE, all of this city.

2106. (M) On Thursday evening last, by the same, at the Pt. of Rocks, Mr WILLIAM LLOYD, to Miss ANN NICHOLS, all of this co.

2107. Candidates for the Common Council: Ward #1. A. P. BEATTY, GEO. METZGER. Ward #2. HENRY BOTELER, JOHN M. LOWE. Ward #3. P. L. STORM, G. McGAHEN. Ward #4. GEO. M. CONRADT. Ward #5. GEO. KOONTZ, JOHN ENGLEBRECHT. Ward #6. HENRY KELLEY, Sr., THOMAS CARLIN, WM. BRENNER. Ward #7. GEORGE SALMON.

February 6, 1840 (MHS)

2108. (M) On the 30th inst., by the Rev. Mr Reese, Mr ELIAS CRUTCHLY, of this co., to Miss LUCINDA BELL, of Montgomery Co., MD. Sweet Lucida is 17, her lord but 66.

2109. (D) On the 18th ult., Mrs CHRISTIANNA ANGLEBERGER, aged 91 years, and upwards of 10 months.

2110. (D) On the 1st of February, Mr FREDERICK FEAGA, after a painful an lingering illness, aged about 50 years.

2111. (D) On the 21st of February, Mrs MARY FOUT SMITH, aged 65 years, 7 months and 19 days.

2112. (D) On the 3rd of February, Mrs LEAB, at an advanced age.

February 13, 1840 (MHS)

2113. (M) On Thursday last, by the Rev. D. Zacharias, Mr

SOLOMON W. SHROYER, to Mrs LYDIA CHRIST, both of Frederick Co.

2114. (D) On Friday morning last, the 27th inst., Miss ELIZABETH RUTHERFORD, in the midst of blooming life.

2115. (D) On Monday evening last, CHRISTIAN KEMP, in the 74th year of his age.

2116. Junior Riflemen met on the 1st inst., the chairman called the meeting to order, the company then elected the following officers: Captain: W. M. B. McLANAHAN. 1st Lieutenant: J. B. HEIM. 2nd Lieutenant: DANIEL GRUMBINE. 3rd Lieutenant: JOHN ROBERTSON. Secretary: MILTON MANTZ. Treasurer: A. L. EADER. Chairman: S. C. SIMMONS.

2117. Following is list of members of the Junior Fire Company: President: EZRA HOUCK. Vice President: SAMUEL DUER. Secretary: EZRA DADYSMAN. Treasurer: EDMUND P. EBERTS. Standing Committee: ALEXANDER K. MANTZ, WILLIAM CARLTON, WILLIAM E. JOHNSON, GEORGE E. WEBSTER, JOHN BARTGIS. Engine Director: JAMES BRUNNER, HENRY BOTELER. Hose Director: GEORGE L. BRENGLE, PETER GOODMANSON. Superintend Director: SAMUEL CANBY, A. A. STAMBAUGH. Chief Engineer: JOHN BENDER. Assistant Engineers: JOHN W. BIRELY, JOHN D. HIMMELL. Axe men: GEORGE RICE, JOSHUA INGMAN, WM. MANTZ. Ladder men: JAMES BRUNNER, PETER GOODMANSON, HENRY BOTELER, SAMUEL CANBY, GEORGE L. BRENGLE, A. A. STAMBAUGH. Property Guards: WILLIAM ROSS, GEORGE BALTZELL, JOHN P. THOMSON, JACOB WIEST, JOHN BRUNNER, of J., RICHARD POTTS. Hose Carriage Guards: THOMAS HALLER, FREDERICK KELLY. Engine Keeper: WILLIAM DADYSMAN. Hose men: JOHN W. BIRELY, GEORGE K. BIRELY, ANDREW BOYD, WILLIAM CARLTON, JOHN DOLL, EDMUND P. EBERTS, NICHOLAS D. HAUER, THOMAS HALLER, JACOB KELLER, CHADWICK H. KUHN, JOHN B. KUNKEL, FREDERICK KELLY, WARNER KAUFMAN, W. M. B. McLANAHAN, EDWARD NICHOLS, THOMAS O'NEAL, GRAFTON J. RICE, ALBERT RICE, IGNATIUS D. RICHARDSON, WILLIAM YEAKLE. Engine men: GEORGE HARDT, JACOB B. HEIM, WILLIAM F. JOHNSON, WILLIAM EBERT, CH'N. GETZENDANNER, LEWIS LOGUE, EZRA DADYSMAN, JOHN MARTIN, Jr., WILLIAM GITTINGER, WILLIAM SNIDER, JAMES BARTGIS, JACOB SAHM, GEORGE F. WEBSTER, SAMUEL TYLER, A.

K. MANTZ, THOMAS BRASHEARS, WILLIAM S. BANTZ, FREDERICK SHROEDER, CYRUS WATERS, JOHN A. PORTER, DANIEL DOLL, JAMES PHEBUS, FREDERICK KREPP, SAMUEL M. ECKENRODE, WILLIAM RICHARDSON, WILLIAM HEIGHTON, JOHN A. SCHISSLER, J. H. CLAY MUDD, WILLIAM STONER, JOHN I. DAVIS, CHRISTIAN HECKATHORN, GEORGE W. POWELL, WILLIAM KAUFMAN, JOSEPH KEISER, HORATIO BENTZ, DANIEL HAUER, EPHRAIM EBERT, JOSEPH DAUGHADAY, WILLIAM DADYSMAN, LEWIS GEPHART, THOMAS M. MARKELL, EZEKIEL HUGHES, JAMES H. ROBERTSON, JOHN KREPP, LEWIS MARKELL, DANIEL ZACHARIAS, JOHN J. SMITH, HENRY DOYLE, WILLIAM T. DUVALL, FRANCIS BRENGLE, DANIEL SINN, GREEN H. DUKE, JOHN CONDRADT, WILLIAM WATERS, WILLIAM CONDRADT, JAMES M. COALE, LEWIS H. BENNETO, JOSEPH M. PALMER, WILLIAM H. RIGNEY, THOMAS GURLEY, CHARLES BRENGLE, LEWIS A. BRENGLE, VALENTINE S. BRUNNER, GEORGE W. MILLER, CHRISTIAN BRENGLE, Jr., LEWIS MEDTART, EZRA ROWE, JOHN L. PITTS, GEORGE R. WISONG, WILLIAM B. TYLER, WILLIAM S. BROWN, ALBERT RITCHIE, GEORGE HERSEY, JOHN BALTZELL, DAVID TITLOW, ROBERT JOHNSTON, JOSEPH M. EBERT, JACOB GONSO, DAVID H. MILLER, DAVID SCHLEY, HENRY TITLOW, JAMES A. GALLAGHER, GEORGE M. CONDRADT, Jr., JOHN HUDSON, ALFRED SCHLEY, WM. EBBERTS, of Jos., GEORGE W. TRISSLER, JOHN M. EBERT, THEO. F. ENGELBRECHT, JOSEPH G. MILLER, JOHN ROBINSON, WOODWARD A. HAMILTON, HENRY J. WALLING, FRANCIS A. BERGER, FREDERICK A. SCHLEY, Jr., McCLAIN CLINGAN, JOHN T. RIGNEY, JOHN TITLOW, HIRAM KEEFER. Honorary Members: DANIEL HAUER, WILLIAM ROSS, RICHARD POTTS, JOSEPH DAUGHADAY, GEORGE M. TYLER, LEWIS GEPHART, GEORGE BALTZELL, JACOB WIEST, EZEKIEL HUGHES, JOHN P. THOMPSON, JOHN KREPP, DANIEL ZACHARIAS, HENRY DOYLE, JOHN BENDER, FRANCIS BRENGLE, GEORGE HOSKINS, GREEN H. DUKE, WILLIAM WATERS, JAMES M. COALE, JOSEPH M. PALMER, THOMAS GURLEY, LEWIS A. BRENGLE, JOHN BRUNNER, of J., GEORGE W. MILLER, LEWIS MEDTART, JOHN L. PITTS, WILLIAM B. TYLER, ALBERT RITCHIE, JOHN BALTZELL, ROBERT JOHNSTON, JACOB GONSO, DAVID SCHLEY, JAMES A. GALLAGHER, NICHOLAS H. PITTS.

February 20, 1840 (MHS)

2118. (D) In Woodsboro, on the 10th inst., Mr HENRY W. DERR, in the 37th year of his age.

2119. (D) On the 14th inst., in the neighborhood, of Frederick, of dropsey in the chest, Mr DANIEL BOPST, in the 44th year of his age. He leaves a wife and dependent family.

2120. (M) On the 18th ult., by the Rev. R. Weiser, Mr FREDERICK CRUM, to Miss CASANDRA CAMPBELL, both of this co.

2121. (M) By the same, on the 26th ult., Mr ELIAS GROSHONG, to Miss MATILDA STAUB, both of Creagers-Town.

2122. (M) By the same, on Thursday the 18th inst., near Woodsboro, Mr ELI OTT, to Miss SOPHIA DUTTERO.

2123. (F) The midnight cry of "FIRE!" aroused our citizens from their slumber on Monday night last. When it was discovered that the slaughter house of Mr WM. KOLB, butcher, was wrapted in one sheet of flames. Being the dead hour of night, about 1 o'clock; the fire was not discovered by anyone, until the building was in one bright blaze, and beyond the possibility of being saved.

February 27, 1840 (MHS)

2124. (D) On the 7th inst., a train of cars in passing near Reils' Mill, ran over the leg of a man named HEZEKIAH BAILY, swirly managled it, amputation was performed above the knee, by Dr. J. H. T. COCKEY, of Urbana.

2125. (M) On the 13th inst., near Taney-Town, by the Rev. D. Feete, Mr NICHOLAS FRINGER, to Miss CATHARINE BUSHMAN, both of Carroll Co.

2126. (M) On Sunday evening the 16th inst., by the Rev. Mr Smith, JOSEPH W. WALKER, (printer,) formerly of Frederick, MD., to Miss SARAH FRANCES LEE, of Baltimore. (Washington Globe)

2127. (D) On the 20th inst., about 4 o'clock, A.M., MARY PROBUS TAYLOR, only daughter of A. P., and Mary Taylor, in South Street, aged 11 years and 26 days.

2128. (D) On the 18th inst., near Frederick City, Mrs REGINA LAMBRECHT, aged nearly 58 years.

2129. (D) On the 23rd of February, at the residence of her husband on the Manor Mrs JANE MICHAEL, consort of Mr Andrew Michael, aged 59 years, and 20 days.

2130. (D) On Wednesday afternoon, the 19th inst., on Linganore, JOHN DAVIS, only child of Maj. B. Washington and Margaret Bennett, aged 6 months and 18 days. Remains were interred in Clemson burial grounds, Sam's Creek, Frederick Co., MD.

2131. Rev. EZRA KELLER, of Taney-Town, MD., will deliver an address before the Temperance Society of Frederick City, on Wednesday evening next, the 4th of March, at 7 o'clock, at the Evangelical Reformed Church.

2132. Election held at the different Wards of this city, on Monday last, for members of the Common Council. The following gentlemen were elected. Ward #1. GEO. METZGER. Ward #2. HENRY BOTELER. Ward #3. L. P. STORM. Ward #4. GEO. M. CONRADT. Ward #6. WM. BRENNER. Ward #7. GEORGE SALMON. In the 5th Ward, there was a tie between Mr JOHN ENGELBRECHT, and Mr GEO. KOONTZ.

March 5, 1840 (MHS)

2133. (M) On Tuesday the 25th ult., by the Rev. Joseph Trapnell, near Barnesville, Mr JAMES A. CARLYLE, to Miss CHRISTY SPALDING.

2134. (M) On the same day, by the same, Mr THOMAS L. JONES, to Miss MARY T. POOL, both of Poolesville, Montgomery Co.

2135. (M) On Thursday evening last, by the Rev. S. W. Harkey, Mr FEDENAND BEDHEIMER, to Miss CHRISTIANNA NEWBRAND, both of this city.

2136. (M) On the 13th inst., by the Rev. Mr Hamilton, Mr RICHARD SIMPSON, to Miss JOANNA CLEMSON, all of Frederick Co.

2137. (D) On the 5th of February at Linganore, of protracted illness, LYDIA ELIZABETH, daughter of Mr Richard and Mrs Ann Howard, in the 11th year of her age.

March 12, 1840 (MHS)

2138. (F) A destructive fire occured near Buckeystown, on Saturday, it commenced in the woods, destroyed a consideral amount of timber, and 100 pannels of fencing belonging to Mr SNOUFFER, and consumed Mr HEBB's barn, and corn house, the latter containing about 200 barrels of corn, some clover seed &c. Destroyed Mr JOHN C. OSBORN's granary which contained 100 bushels of wheat &c., Mr Osborn's barn was also burnt about a week since. It originated from sparks thrown out by a locomotive engine in which wood was used. The day was windy and dry and fire burnt over about 20 acres before it was arrested.

2139. (M) On Thursday evening last, by the Rev. John L. Pitts, Mr JOHN HAMILTON to Miss MARY LEASE, all of this co.

2140. (M) In Baltimore on the 5th inst., by the Rev. J. G. Morris, Mr GREEN H. DUKE, to Miss ELIZABETH OGLE, all of this city.
2141. (M) On the 19th of February last, by the Rev. M. Swormsted, Mr JAMES WHITTAKER, of Cincinnati, to Miss OLIVA LYONS, of Fredericktown, MD.
2142. (D) On the 15th inst., JOHN W. KOLB, only child of Michael and Christianna Kolb, aged 2 years, 10 months and 1 day.
2143. (D) Near Liberty-Town, on the 22nd of Feb., ult., Mr JOHN WILLIAMS, in the 62nd year of his age, long a respectable inhabitant of that vicinity.

March 26, 1840 (MHS)

2144. (D) On Thursday last, Mr HENRY VOGLER, aged 85 years, 9 months and 26 days.

April 2, 1840 (MHS)

2145. (M) On Thursday evening last, by the Rev. S. W. Harkey, Mr JOHN DERR, to Miss CATHARINE ANN HALLER, all of this city.
2146. (M) On the 19th inst., by the Rev. A. P. Freese, Mr WILLIAM CASHOUR, to Miss MARTHA ALBAUGH, all of Frederick Co., MD.
2147. (M) On Thursday evening last, by the Rev. John L. Pitts, Mr GEORGE TRUSCOTT, to Miss HANNA MORMON, all of this city.
2148. (M) On Thursday morning last, by the Rev. D. Zacharias, Mr PETER GOODMANSON, to Miss MARY HALLER, both of this city.
2149. (M) By the same, Mr ISAAC BRUNNER, to Miss ANN SOPHIA SCHULTZ.
2150. (M) On Sunday evening last, by the same, Mr G. STUP, to Miss BARBARA HOUCK.
2151. (M) On Tuesday evening last, by the same, Mr DAVID E. HALLER, to Miss E. M. M. ROELKE.
2152. (D) On Friday afternoon the 13th inst., WILLIAM HENRY, infant son of Nimrod and Mary Ann M. Bantz, aged 6 months and 15 days.

April 9, 1840 (MHS)

2153. (D) In the 27th year of his age, Mr MICHAEL BARTGIS, son of Mathias E. Bartgis, Esq., of this place. The disease

2154. (M) On the 31st of March, by the Rev. John L. Pitts, Mr EDWARD D. HARD, to Miss MARGARET ANN HILTON, both of Frederick.

2155. (M) On Tuesday morning last, at 6 1/2 o'clock, by the same, Mr JOHN T. MITCHELL, to Miss ELIZABETH LEARNED, both of Jefferson.

April 16, 1840 (MHS)

2156. (D) Departed this life on the 7th of April, Mrs LILLY ANN, wife of the Rev. J. W. Hoffmier, aged 30 years, and 8 months. Lost of her mother and 3 small children over several years has made her last years of sorrow, 2 months previous to her death, she was taken with a sore throat, and violent cough, which at last terminated in consumption of the throat and lungs. She died in Boonesboro, where her husband was station. Her remains were taken to the house of her brother Mr G. Zimmerman, near Creagerstown. The discourse was delivered by the Rev. D. Zacharias, afterwards they were laid to rest beside her children.

2157. (D) In the neighborohood of Frederick City, MD., on the 7th of April, 1840. Mr MICHAEL STRAFFER, aged 70 years, 1 month and 28 days. A member of the Ev. Lutheran Church of Frederick, and served 8 years in the Vestry. He died from "dropsey of the heart," he raised a family of 11 children, 8 of whom are still living, several of his children reside in the West.

2158. (D) On Monday morning last, CATHARINE ELIZABETH, eldest daughter of Mr John Dear, aged 8 years, 7 months and 26 days.

2159. (D) On Friday last, Mr ALEXANDER TRUSCOTT, his funeral will take place this afternoon at 3 o'clock.

2160. (M) On Thursday morning last, by the Rev. S. W. Harkey, at Zimmerman's Hotel, in Frederick, Mr A. CLEM, to Miss ELIZA DEVILBISS, all of this co.

2161. (M) By the Rev. R. Weiser, near Mechanicstown, on Tuesday the 17th ult., Mr WILLIAM STAUFFER, to Miss SOPHIA SMITH, all of this co.

2162. (M) At Woodsboro, by the same, on Thursday evening the 26th ult., Mr GEORGE WASHINGTON SLANK, (merchant,) to Miss SEREPTA A., second daughter of Brooke Baker, Esq., of Woodsboro.

2163. (M) On the 9th inst., by the Rev. D. Zacharias, Mr CHRISTIAN SMITH, to Miss MARY BURKET, both of this co.
2164. (M) On Thursday morning last, by the same, the Rev. WM. H. ZIMMERMAN, to Miss MARY E., youngest daughter of Mr John Cronise, both of this co.

April 23, 1840 (MHS)

2165. (M) On Thursday morning last, by the Rev. S. W. Harkey, Mr DANIEL BAKER, to Miss MARY FOUT, both of this co.

April 30, 1840 (MHS)

2166. (M) On Tuesday the 21st inst., by the Rev. Henry G. Dill, Mr SAMUEL SHAFF to Miss MARY E. RHODES, all of this co.
2167. (M) On Tuesday last, by the Rev. S. W. Harkey, Mr GEORGE MILLER, to Miss MARY ANN CRAVER, all of this co.
2168. (M) On the same day last, by the Rev. Joseph Trapnell, Mr JAMES W. STRIDER, of Jefferson Co., VA., to Miss GEORGETTE WEBSTER, of this city.
2169. (M) On the same day, by the Rev. D. Zacharias, Mr DAVID DRAPER, to Miss MARGARET MISINGER, both of this co.
2170. (M) On Thursday morning last, by the same, THOMAS H. BINIX, of Shepherdstown, VA., to Miss MARGARET C. MOXLEY, of this city.
2171. (M) On Thursday morning, by the Rev. Daniel Zacharias, Mr GEORGE MARKELL, to Miss SOPHIA MARKELL, both of this city.
2172. (D) On Tuesday last, Mr NICHOLAS W. GOLDSBOROUGH, son of the late William Goldsborough, Esq.

May 7, 1840 (MHS)

2173. (M) On Sunday morning last, by the Rev. Jno. L. Pitts, Mr ISAAC TITLOW, to Miss ELIZABETH ELY, both of this city.
2174. (M) On Tuesday morning last, by the Rev. D. Zacharias, Mr CHRISTIAN GETZENDANNER, to Miss MARY ANN NICHOLS, both of this city.
2175. (M) On the 10th ult., by the Rev. R. Weiser, Mr HENRY HINIER, to Miss LYDIA KRISE, all of this co.
2176. (M) On the 6th ult., by the same, Mr FRANCIS HAHN, to Miss CATHARINE ELSHRODES, all of this co.
2177. (M) On the 19th ult., at Emmittsburg, by the Rev. John F. Hickey, Mr GEORGE M. GROVER, merchant, to Miss

ELMINA J. CRAPSTER, only daughter of Mr John Crapster, merchant of Simponsville, KY., formerly of this co.

2178. (D) Of consumption, on the 24th ult., at the residence of his mother, near New Market, WILLIAM FARQUHAR, aged 26 years.

2179. (D) On the 28th ult., of consumption, Mrs MARY MARKLE, widow of William Markle, the (first proprietor of the Visiter,) and only daughter of George and Catharine Salmon, of this city. She was 14 months a wife, 12 months a widow, and only 20 years of age.

May 14, 1840 (MHS)

2180. (D) Murder was committed near the Pt. of Rocks, on the night of the 6th inst., the atrocity of which is not often equaled. A woman named DAVIS, and her child, living in the family of her brother, at one of the locks of the canal, were both murdered in their bed-rooms in the dead of night; at least the woman was left in a sensible, and it was supposed would not recover, and the brains of the boy, who was about 11 years old, were completely battered out and scattered about the room. The club with which this horrible outrage was committed was left standing in the room. The woman and her child slept in the lower story and several persons who were asleep up stairs were not awakened. The fiend who is supposed to have committed this midnight murder has been arrested, and committed to the Frederick County jail.

2181. (D) Mr PETER HALLER, died in this city on the 30th ult., after a lingering illness, an affection of the heart, accompanied by the dropsy, in the 70th year of his age. He was sick and confinded to his house, and part of the time to his bed for about 1 year.

2182. (M) On Thursday morning last, by the Rev. R. S. Grier, Mr JOHN K. LONGWELL Editor of the Carrolltonian, SARAH H., youngest daughter of Major John McKaleb, of Taney-Town.

2183. (M) On Wednesday evening the 6th inst., by the Rev. Eli Hinkle, Mr JOHN WINEBRENNER, of Hanover, York Co., PA., to Miss HANNAH GROVE, daughter of Jacob Grove, Esq., Sheriff of Carroll Co.

2184. (M) On the 30th ult., by the Rev. S. W. Harkey, W. FRAZIER, to Miss MARGARET HALLER, both of this city.

2185. (M) On Thursday evening last, the 7th inst., by the Rev. D. Reese, Mr JACOB WALKER, to Miss ANN MARY RAMSBURGH, all of this vicinity.
2186. (M) On Thursday evening last, by the Rev. John L. Pitts, Mr CHARLES McLANE, to Miss JULIAN EICHELBERGER, both of this co.
2187. (M) On Tuesday the 12th inst., at the house of James A. Galligher, Esq., by the Rev'd. Father McElroy, Mr CHARLES McCOLGAN, of Baltimore City, to Miss ANN MARIA GALLIGHER, of Nashville, TN.
2188. Rev. JOHN McCROU, of Pittsburg is to preach in the Ev. Lutheran Church in this city, next Sabbath morning and evening.
2189. On last Sunday a week, May 3rd, the consecration of the newly finished Church, the property of the Ev. Lutheran and German Reformed congregation of Woodsboro.

May 21, 1840 (MHS)

2190. (M) On Thursday the 7th of May, by the Rev. Mr Schreiber, THOMAS SIMM LEE, of Needwood, Frederick Co., MD., to JOSEPHINE, daughter of Gen. Columbus O'Donnell, of Baltimore.
2191. (M) On Thursday evening last, by the Rev. S. W. Harkey, Mr FREDERICK SCHROEDER, to Miss CATHERINE HURNUNG, both of this city.
2192. (D) On Saturday the 16th inst., at the residence of Mr John Hoffman, of Francis, near Jefferson, FREDERICK WM. HOFFMAN, aged 48 years, and 7 months.
2193. (D) On the 7th inst., ANDREW D., son of Perry Young, aged 18 months.

May 28, 1840 (MHS)

2194. (M) On Sunday last, at the Lutheran Parsonage in this city, by the Rev. S. W. Harkey, Mr ISAAC COOPER WATSON, to Miss MARY ANN BITZENBERGER, both of this co.
2195. (M) On Tuesday evening last, by the same, Mr CHRISTIAN SCHIEWETZ, to Miss ELIZABETH RAELING, both of this city.
2196. The Temperance meeting of Frederick City was held on Tuesday evening last, in the Ev. Lutheran Church. Exercise commenced at 8 o'clock, when L. P. W. BALCH, Esq., President of the Society, took the chair, prayer was said by the Rev. R. WEISER, of Woodsboro. President introduced Rev. JOHN McCRON, of Pittsburg, PA., who addressed the

congregation for about 40 minutes. Then the Rev. Weiser, followed him with a few remarks. President appointed the following delegates to represent the society in the county convention to be held in this city on the 6th of June next. Rev. J. H. BROWN, Rev. S. W. HARKEY, L. P. W. BALCH, Esq., JACOB KELLER, GEORGE W. MILLER, A. P. BEATTY, ISRAEL C. O'NEAL, GEO. M. CONRADT, FREDERICK SCHROEDER, A. I. BARNEY, JOHN C. ENGLEBRECHT, THOMAS GURLEY, VALENTINE DOUB, ABRAHAM HAFF, PHILIP J. HAWAN, WILLIAM KAUFFMAN, JESSE WINECOFF.

June 4, 1840 (MHS)

2197. (D) On Sunday night last, Mrs CATHARINE FEAGA, aged 48 years, 4 months and 22 days. Mrs Feaga, her last illness was long, continue, and very severe, she leaves a devoted husband and a interesting family of children.

2198. (D) On Saturday last, Mr EZRA SCHELL, of this city, aged 49 years, 5 months and 25 days.

2199. (D) On the evening of the 25th of May, EUGEVN DEGRANGE, aged 7 months and 17 days.

2200. (M) On Sunday evening last, at the Lutheran Parsonage of this city, by the Rev. Simeon W. Harkey, Mr WILLIAM HARTBAUER, to Miss LOUISA SAHM, both of this city.

2201. (M) On Tuesday morning last, at the Parsonage of the Lutheran Church of this city, by the same, Mr ROBERT H. DUTROW, to Miss RACHAEL C. FELTY, all of this co.

June 11, 1840 (MHS)

2202. (M) On Thursday the 4th inst., by the Rev. Henry G. Dill, Mr JACOB KUSER, to Miss REBECCA MAGEE, both of Frederick Co.

2203. (M) In this county, on the 7th inst., by the Rev. John L. Pitts, Mr JOSEPH CRAMER, to Miss SUSAN RODEROCK.

2204. (D) On the 4th inst., near Emmittsburg, Mrs ELIZABETH WITMORE, wife of a Revolutionary soldier, aged 95 years. She was born in 1745, a member of the Lutheran Church for 75 years, mother of 11 children, 33 grandchildren, 35 great grandchildren, was confinded to bed for the last 10 years.

2205. (D) On Thursday last, on the 4th inst., Mrs CATHARINE MARIA MOYER, aged 44 years, 5 months and 25 days.

2206. The 1st annual meeting of the Frederick County Union Temperance Society, was held in the Evangelical Lutheran

Church of this city on Saturday last, on 6th of June. Meeting was organized at 1/2 past 10 o'clock, A.M., by calling Mr VALENTINE DOUB, to the chair (in the absence of the President,) and appointing Mr JESSE WINECOFF, Secretary. Prayer was said by the Rev. R. WEISER. The following delegates were present to represent their societies: Frederick City - Rev. S. W. HARKEY, Rev. J. H. BROWN, Mr GEO. W. MILLER, L. P. W. BALCH, Esq., VALENTINE DOUB, JESSE WINECOFF, ABRAHAM HAFF, ISRAEL C. O'NEAL, JAMES M. HARKEY. Woodsboro - Rev. R. WEISER, MALICHI BERNETT, Esq. Jefferson - Rev. R. W. H. BRENT, THOMAS THRASHER, ABRAHAM BLESSING. Middletown - Dr. JACOB BAER. St. John's - T. WINFIELD, DANIEL LEATHERMAN, CONRAD EASTERDAY, JOHN GLADHILL, JOHN DUPLE, JACOB JOHNSON.

June 25, 1840 (MHS)

2207. (M) Near Petersville, Frederick Co., MD., at the house of Mr David Catzendaffner, on the 4th of June, by the Rev'd. J. C. Bucher, Mr JOHN KEMP, to Miss MARTHA A. M. LAKINS, all of Middletown Valley.

2208. (M) Near Jefferson, on the 11th of June, by the same, Mr FRANCIS HOFFMAN, to Miss ANN REBECCA, daughter of Mr Henry Crum, all of Middletown Valley.

2209. (M) On Thursday morning last, by the Rev. Mr Zacharias, Mr JAMES W. OSBORN, to Miss SOPHIA SHEARER, all of this co.

2210. (M) On Thursday evening the 6th inst., by the Rev. S. W. Harkey, Mr ISAAC TURNER, to Miss PERMELIA KANEPP, all of this city.

2211. (M) On Thursday evening, by the Rev. John A. Gere, CHARLES A. KIRBY, to Miss ANN SOPHIA, daughter of Col. Wm. Ogden Niles, of Baltimore City.

2212. (D) In Middletown, Frederick Co., MD., on the 27th of May 1840, after a painful illness, AMANDA CATHARINE, daughter of Mr Henry and Mrs Mary Ann Brendel, in the 1st year of her age.

2213. (D) On the 3rd of June, near Middletown, MD., ANN N., daughter of Mr John and Mrs Catharine Miller, aged 2 years, 2 months and 3 days.

2214. (D) On the 9th of June, near Middletown, SARAH ELIZABETH, daughter of Mr Dan'l Keafauver, aged 3 years, 4 months and 19 days.

July 1, 1840 (MHS)

2215. (M) On Thursday evening last, by the Rev. James H. Brown, Mr WILLIAM TUCKER, to Miss CATHERINE KEPHART, both of this city.

2216. (M) On the Sabbath evening last, by the same, Mr JACOB NUSSBAUM, to Mrs MATILDA EVERHEART, all of this city.

2217. (M) On Thursday the 14th inst., by the Rev. John L. Pitts, Mr JOSEPH OGLE, to Miss MATILDA KESSLER, both of this city.

2218. (M) On Thursday the 25th inst., by the same, Mr WILLIAM CARLTON, (City Register,) to Miss MARY P. NEILL, of Philadelphia.

2219. (D) On Saturday last, JOSEPH V. S. BRENNER, son of William Brenner, Esq., of this city.

July 9, 1840 (MHS)

2220. (M) On the 30th of June, by the Rev. Daniel Zacharias, Mr HENRY FOGLER, to Miss MARTHA DUNCAN, both of Frederick.

2221. (D) HENRIETTA SWEADNER, an interesting child, aged 9 years. (Liberty-Town June 25th 1840)

July 16, 1840 (MHS)

2222. (D) Near Middletown, Frederick Co., MD., on the 28th of June 1840, after a protracted illness, Mrs MAGDALINE, consort of Mr John Kepler, aged 69 years, 7 months and 6 days. She leaves 6 children and a husband.

2223. (D) On the 5th of July, VIRGINIA BRENGLE HOUCK, daughter of Henry and Mary Houck, aged 7 months and 1 day.

2224. (D) On Saturday last, in this city, Mr JACOB STRICK-STRUCK, in the 46th year of his age.

2225. The Church Street School, will open in the room above the lecture room of the Ev. Reformed Church. Reference: F. A. ROUCH, D.D., President of Marshall College. Rev. D. ZACHARIAS, GIDEON BANTZ, DAVID SCHLEY, A. BARNEY, Esq., Mr WM. PHILLIP, will be the instuctor.

July 23, 1840 (MHS)

2226. (M) On Thursday last, at Dorsey's City Hotel, by the Rev. D. Zacharias, Mr B. T. POFFINBERGER, to Miss LOUISA S. GELWICKS, both of Washington Co., MD.

2227. (D) On Saturday last, JOSEPH GRAHAM STOUP, aged 1 year, 10 months and 22 days.

2228. (D) On Thursday the 11th ult., JAMES ROPER, formerly of Richmond, VA., lately of this place, aged about 45 years.
2229. (D) On Saturday the 18th inst., DAVID HENRY BAER, aged 15 years, 8 months and 28 days. He was severely afflicted for the last 7 years, 6 being perfectly helpless and blind, constantly confinded to his bed.
2230. (D) In Frederick, at the dwelling of Mr John Bailey, on the 10th ult., Mr WILLIAM LENHART, in the 53rd year of his age. A native of York, spent part-time in York, and partly in Frederick; from a injury received early in life has been generally confinded to the house. His principal occupation there has been the improvement of his mind and the extension of philosophical research.

July 30, 1840 (MHS)

2231. (M) At the Point of Rocks, on Thursday last, by the Rev. John L. Pitts, Mr JOHN LITCHFIELD, to Miss MARY HERST, all of VA.
2232. (M) On the 21st, by the Rev. S. W. Harkey, Mr JOSHUA SCHLUND, to Miss MARGARET SCHEITZ, all of this city.
2233. (D) In Frederick, on Tuesday morning last, Mr ROBERT McCLEARY, in about the 51st year of his age. He leaves a wife and several children, a member of the Presbyterian Church.
2234. (D) Murder - Inquest yesterday on the body of MARGARET O'BRIEN, woman of intemperate habits, lately married to Terrence O'Brien. From testimony, that the husband and wife were constantly quarrelling, and that the husband was in the habit of beating his wife. The verdict of the jury was, Margaret O'Brien, had died in a fit, but whether caused by violence or not, they were unable to determine; but are satisfied she had been beaten by her husband. O'Brien, who is but 19 years of age, his father James O'Brien, and his mother Margaret, were all arrested by order of the coroner and committed to a wait futher examination.

August 5, 1840 (MHS)

2235. (D) At his residence in Middletown Valey, on Sunday last, in the 86th year of his age, Sergeant LAWRENCE EVERHART. The immediate cause of death was apoplexy. Funeral took place on Tuesday last, and was attended by 3 military companies.

2236. (M) On Friday the 31st of July, by the Rev. Benjamin C. Flowers, Dr. WM. HARRISON BAKER, to Miss MARGARET FOX, both of Woodsboro.

August 13, 1840 (MHS)

2237. Funeral sermon for Sergeant LAWRENCE EVERHART, will be preached at the Methodist Episcopal Church, in Middletown, on Sunday the 23rd inst., A. M.
2238. (D) On the 5th of August in this city, HARRIET ANN, daughter of James and Emeline Alexander, aged 2 years, and 22 days.
2239. (D) On the 31st of July last, Mr GEORGE W. KAUFMAN, infant son of Mr William and Emily Kaufman, aged 10 months and 20 days.
2240. (D) On the 9th inst., very suddenly and unexpectedly after a short illness, Mrs SOPHIA MICHAEL, consort of Mr Michael, and daughter of Mr Geo. Thomas, of the Manor. She leaves a infant only a few months old, and affectionary husband.

August 20, 1840 (MHS)

2241. (D) A young man by the name of GRIM, residing within a few miles of this place, on the Liberty road, committed suicide on Sunday night last, by hanging himself in the woods. He was a man of exemplary deportment, and no cause is known for this rash act.

August 27, 1840 (MHS)

2242. (M) On Thursday afternoon last the 21st, by the Rev. S. W. Harkey, Mr HENRY M. FIRESTONE, to Miss MARY ANN MAHONEY, all of the Manor, Frederick Co., MD.
2243. (M) On the same day, by the same, Mr BARTLE MAYER, to Miss PHILIPPENA YOUNG, both of this city.
2244. The Rev. Mr PARKINSON, will preach in the Baptist Meeting House on next Sabbath morning at 10 o'clock, A. M.
2245. (F) The barn of Mr GEORGE THOMAS, of the Manor was entirely consumed with all its contends, by lightning on Sunday evening last, the 23rd inst. There was about 20 tons of hay, 100 bushles of rye, horse gears, &c, destroyed. It was with great difficulty that the corn house and other out buildings in the neighborhood were saved.

September 3, 1840 (MHS)
2246. REBECCA GORDON, LUCY COOMES, and WILLIAM WARREN, (alias) BILL BUTT, blacks, were brought before the Mayor, for being blue and obstreperous; by constable HALLER, and committed.

September 17, 1840 (MHS)
2247. (M) On Sunday evening last, by the Rev. James H. Brown, Mr ALONZO RAMSDELL, of New York, to Miss MARGARET ANN WALKER, of this city.

2248. (M) On Thursday morning last, by the Rev. S. W. Harkey, Mr THOMAS HALLER, (printer,) of Baltimore, to Miss LYDIANN SHEARER, of this vicinity.

September 24, 1840 (MHS)
2249. (M) On Tuesday evening last, by the Rev. Jno. L. Pitts, Mr JOHN W. HARGATE, to Miss MARY ELLEN THOMAS, all of this co.
2250. (M) On Thursday last, by the same, Mr JONATHAN SMITH, to Miss NANCY CUTSAIL, all of this co.
2251. The Rev. WM. ROLLINSON WHITTINGHAM, D.D., was consecrated as Bishop of the Protestant Episcopal Church, for the Diocese of Maryland, on the 17th inst., in St. Paul's Church, Baltimore.
2252. Candidates for Mayor: Captain GEORGE HOSKINS, JAMES M. HARDING, JOSHUA DILL.
2253. A camp meeting of the Temperance was held a few weeks ago near Liberty in this co. The address was delivered to the gathering by Mr McKEENER, of Baltimore, MD.

October 1, 1840 (MHS)
2254. (M) On Thursday evening last, by the Rev. Jno. L. Pitts, Mr MAHLON INGMAN, to Miss MARY NOLAND.
2255. (M) On Thursday the 17th inst., by the Rev. S. W. Harkey, Mr PETER CLINE, to Miss HENRIETTA, fourth daughter of Michael Straeffer, deceased, all of this vicinity.
2256. Candidate for Mayor: Captain WILLIAM SMALL.

October 8, 1840 (MHS)
2257. (D) Melancholy accident and loss - The Harpers Ferry Constitutionalist of of Thursday last, says that on Tuesday evening last, as a son of Mr JOHN O'HARA, of this place, was engaged in moving some cars, ladden with stone, upon

a temporary railroad, that had been laid down during the day, for the purpose of conveying the stone to the edge of the embankment making for the further extension of the Baltimore and Ohio Railroad, at this place, the grade of the road being very great, the car commenced rapidly descending, and before he could escape from before them, where he had been pulling, while they were on the level, he was caught, and falling across the rail, with one leg inside, the cars passed obliquely over the lower part of the body severing the left leg, at the hip joint, and cutting off a portion of the body, he survived but a few minutes. He was about 18 years old, and the only son of fond parents.

2258. Candidate for Mayor: P. L. STORM.

October 15, 1840 (MHS)

2259. Corporate election results: Whigs - NEILL - 2,884, RICHARDSON - 2,935, MOTTER - 2,895, WILLIAM LYNCH - 2,891, E. A. LYNCH - 2,890. Van Buren Party: QUYNN - 2,701, McKEEHAN - 2,709, DUNLOP - 2,704, SCHLEY - 2,695, GEYER - 2,688. For the Levy Court: 1st District - WILLIAM LARKIN - 819, GEORGE ZOLLINGER (V. B.) - 802, ISRAEL RAMSBURG - 811. 2nd District - WILLIAM DUDDERAR - 1,466, DANIEL DUVALL - 1,478, VALENTINE ADAMS - 1,480, JACOB TRAYER (W) - 1,488. Democrates not elected for the 1st District - KINZER - 1,167, TANZEY - 1,162. 3rd District - DANIEL HOOVER - 816, JACOB ROOT - 825, GEORGE KUHN - 818, REESE - 725, CURTIS - 726, ROWE - 703.

2260. (M) On Tuesday the 6th inst., by the Rev. John L. Pitts, Mr WILLIAM CURFMAN, to Miss ANN YARDLY, all of this co.

2261. (D) The life, on the 1st inst., at the residence of her husband, in this co., Mrs SARAH ANN DORSEY, consort of Henry W. Dorsey, in the 29th year of her age.

2262. (D) On Sunday last, after a painful illness of some days, in the 24th year of her age, Mrs ELIZABETH, wife of Edward Turbutt, Esq., of this city.

2263. If FREDERICK LEOHR, will consent to serve as a candidate for the next Mayoralty.

October 29, 1840 (MHS)

2264. The October term of the Frederick County Court commenced on Monday last, the following is a list of the juriors. Grand: JOHN R. CURTIS, Forman, PHILIP ROHR, ZEBULON KUHN, HENRY HARBAUGH, JAMES CASTLE, WM.

JOHNSON, BASIL D. DOWNEY, JOHN T. MITCHELL, JOSEPH W. BIGGS, BASIL BAKER, DANIEL GALLAGHER, JACOB YOUNG, of D., JACOB HYDER, RICHARD JOHNSON, of Wm., THOMAS NORWOOD, DANIEL BRENGLE, ABDIEL UNKEFER, DANIEL GITTINGER, THOMAS I. CLAGGETT, JACOB THOMAS, of Jno., THOMAS CASTLE, DAVID HINES, and SAMUEL PRESTON. Petite Jury: EDWARD SCHLEY, DAVID GAMBLE, JACOB TRAYER, DANIEL DUVALL, CHRISTOPHER MICHAEL, GEORGE SALMON, THOMAS J. WORTHINGTON, NICHOLAS HOLTZ, GIDEON D. CRUMBAUGH, THOMAS CRAMPTON, JOSHUA DILL, THOMAS CLABAUGH, SOLOMON FORREST, THOMAS HAMMOND, JOHN MILLER, JOHN COLEGATE, JOHN ZIMMERMAN, of N., ELI SMITH, PATRICK O'NEIL, PHILEMON S. McELFRESH, ROBERT FLEMING, WASHINGTON BURGESS, SEBASTIAN RAMSBURGH, Jr., THOMAS FLEMING, THOMAS SAPPINGTON.

2265. (M) At Oakland, Baltimore Co., on Thursday morning the 15th inst., by the Rev. Mr Lipscomb, HARRISON T. CLEMSON, Esq., of Frederick Co., to ANN ELIZABETH, eldest daughter of Col. Jesse Bennett.

2266. (M) On Thursday morning last, by the Rev. Jno. L. Pitts, Mr JOHN B. THOMAS to Miss CHARLOTTE THOMAS, both of this co.

2267. (M) On Wednesday evening (at Turbutts Hotel,) by the same, Mr HARRISON P. CLOWE, to Miss MARIA YOUNG, of VA.

2268. (D) At Cumberland, MD., on the 13th inst., of pulmonary affection, in the 21st year of her age, CATHARINE, daughter of Col. Wm. Durbin, formerly of this co.

2269. (D) At his residence on Monday last in Frederick Co., Mr NATHAN HAMMOND, about 56 years his of age.

November 5, 1840 (MHS)

2270. (M) On Tuesday evening last, by the Rev. D. Zacharias, Mr CONRAD BUCKBUMMER, to Miss ELIZABETH BRENGLE, both of this city.

2271. (M) At Utica Mills, on the 29th inst., by the Rev. W. F. Colliflower, Mr ADAM WILSON, to Miss MARY ANN SHRYOCK, both of Frederick Co.

2272. (M) On Sunday morning last, at Dorsey's Hotel, by the Rev. John L. Pitts, Mr JOHN G. BISER, to Miss ELEANOR ANN JARBOR, both of this co.

November 12, 1840 (MHS)
2273. (M) Near Lewistown, on the 3rd inst., by the Rev. William F. Colliflower, Dr. TIDEMAN HALL, formerly of Dutchess Co., N. Y., to Miss ELIZA, only daughter of John W. Derr, Esq., of Frederick Co.

November 19, 1840 (MHS)
2274. (M) At Rockhill Church, on the 12th inst., by the Rev. W. F. Colliflower, Mr DENNIS SHOEMAKER, to Miss LYDIA ANN FOGLE, both of this co.
2275. (D) At Hagerstown, on Monday evening last, after a protracted illness, at his residence, BENJAMIN PRICE, Esq., a member of the Hagerstown Bar, in the 42nd year of his age.

November 26, 1840 (MHS)
2276. The Chesapeake and Ohio Canal offices have been removed to Frederick, and is kept at the Episcopal Orphan Assylum House in Church Street. Mr TURNER, late of Georgetown, is the Chief Clerk, and Mr EDWARD SHRIVER, of Frederick, is the Assistant Clerk. Mr SAMUEL TYLER, of Frederick is the Treasurer, and Mr EZRA HOUCK, the Assistant Treasurer, and Mr ALBERT MAYBERRY, Messenger.
2277. (M) Near Woodsboro, on Tuesday evening the 17th inst., by the Rev. W. F. Colliflower, Mr HENRY SAYLOR, to Miss CATHARINE E. DONSEIF, both of this co.
2278. (M) At Willow Broake, Prince George's Co., MD., on the 12th inst., THOMAS DUCKETT, Esq., to Mrs CATHARINE CLARKE, daughter of the late William Bowie.
2279. (M) On the 12th inst., (at Gilbert's Hotel,) by the Rev. John L. Pitts, Mr JOEL MYERS, of Ohio, to Miss SARAH A. HOOVER, of this co.
2280. (M) On Tuesday morning last, (at Etna Glass Works,) by the same, Mr ROBERT GORSUCH, of Baltimore, to Miss SOPHRONIA ANGELL, of this vicinity.
2281. (M) Near Middletown, Frederick Co., MD., on the 12th of November 1840, by the Rev. J. C. Bucher, Mr HENRY J. JARBOE, to Miss EVELINE E. FLOOK, daughter of Mr Jacob Flook, of Jno., Esq., all of Middletown Valley.
2282. (D) Another hero of the '76 gone - FREDERICK SEMPLE, died on Monday last, at his residence in Middletown, Frederick Co., MD. The decease served in the Revolutionary War.

December 3, 1840 (MHS)

2283. (F) The barn on the farm belonging to Mr DANIEL GIT-TINGER, a few miles North of this place was destroyed by fire a few nights since. It was unquestionably the work of an incendary.

2284. Major General MACOMB, has recently suffered an attack of apoplexy, he has recovered.

2285. (M) On Tuesday the 1st inst., by the Rev. Jos. Smith, JAMES M. HARDING, Esq., to Mrs SARAH HULL, all of this city.

2286. (D) In this city, on Monday last, Mr DANIEL HIMBURY, in the 23rd year of his age.

2287. (D) On Thursday the 29th inst., at the residence of James C. Harry, near Emmittsburg, WILLIAM HIDE, in the 10th year of his age, late student of Mount Saint Mary's College.

2288. Sheriffalty candidates: EZRA DADYSMAN, GEORGE RICE, ADAM CUSTARD.

December 17, 1840 (MHS)

2289. (M) On Tuesday last, by the Rev. John L. Pitts, Mr ALFRED ANDREWS, to Miss ADELAIDE A. WOOD, both of VA.

2290. (M) Near Charlestown, VA., on the 10th inst., by the Rev. Mr Jones, Mr ROBERT G. McPHERSON, of Frederick, MD., to Miss MILICENT F., daughter of William T. Washington, Esq., of Jefferson Co., VA.

2291. (M) On Thursday evening last, by the Rev. D. Zacharias, Mr WILLIAM YOUNG, to Miss MARY DERTZBAUGH.

2292. (M) Near Middletown, Frederick Co., MD., on the 26th day of Nov., ult., by the Rev. J. C. Bucher, Mr MATHIAS LEAPOLD, to Miss MARY FINK, both of Middletown Valley.

2293. (M) On the 3rd of December inst., by the same, Mr JACOB POFFENBERGER, to Miss ELIZA ANN WALLECK, daughter of the late John Walleck.

2294. (D) On Saturday evening the 28th November, SABINAH CLAY, consort of Adam Clay, about 69 years of his age.

2295. (D) Near Burkettsville, Frederick Co., on the 3rd day of December, inst., after a protracted and painful illness, Mr JACOB WINPIGLER, aged about 66 years.

2296. (D) On Sunday the 29th, Mr JACOB SHELMAN, at the advance age of 91 years. The decease was a native of this place, and served as a volunteer in the Revolutionary War.

December 24, 1840 (MHS)

2297. (M) On Thursday morning, the 10th inst., by the Rev. S. W.

Harkey, Mr ADAM SNIDER, to Miss MARIA HARNUNG, both of this city.

2298. (M) On Tuesday morning, the 22nd inst., by the same, at Dorsey's City Hotel, Mr LEVI BUFFINGTON, to Miss MARY ANN WAGNER, both of this co.

2299. (D) On Monday evening the 21st inst., Mrs ELIZABETH LEWIS, of this city. She leaves a husband and a large family of children.

2300. (D) On Friday morning last, in the 93rd year of her age, Mrs MARY WHITTER, wife of Thomas Whitter, Esq., of this city. Subject was in good health, until within a few days of her death, nor was her friends and family aware of the near approach of her separation from them, so insidious was the stroke, till within a few hours time the spirit had left her.

December 31, 1840 (MHS)

2301. (M) On Thursday evening last, by the Rev. Jno. L. Pitts, Mr J. W. ANDERSON, to Miss SOPHIA HECKATHORN, both of this city.

2302. (M) On Sunday last, by the same, (at Trubutt's Hotel,) Mr CHARLES A. YOUNG, to Miss CATHARINE ALDRIDGE, both of VA.

2303. (D) On Saturday evening last, in the 64th year of her age, Mrs ANN MARGARET SHRIVER, wife of the Hon. Abraham Shriver, of this city. Her mortal remains were interred on Monday evening in the family burying grounds.

1835

POLITICAL EXAMINER & PUBLIC ADVERTISER

May 6, 1835 (MHS)

2304. (F) We regret to learn, that two dwellings belonging to Mr ISAAC APPLER, near Union Town were entirely consumed by fire, together with their contents, on Monday evening last. Whilst the family and several hands who were employed in putting up a new house for Mr A., were eating their suppers, in the old dwelling, they were alarmed by the noise produced by fire, and on going to the door, great as was their astonishment to find the new house engulfed in flames, and the old house burning rapidly over their heads, both buildings were soon reduced to the ground. It is suppose that fire was communicated to the combustible matter in or about the new house, by some children who had been left out side near a bake-oven, in which a fire had kindled. (Westminster Carrolltonian)

2305. The Hon. GEORGE C. WASHINGTON, will be supported at the ensuring Congressional elections by many of the voters of the 6th Congressional District.

2306. A large meeting of the Whig voters of the 6th Congressional District, met at the house of Mr LYNN N. WOODS, in Woodsborough, on the 2nd inst., to nominate a committee to attend the convention to be held at New Market on the 27th inst. On a motion of Mr PHILIP HINES, GEORGE BARRICK, of Jacob, was called to the chair, and JOSHUA DOUB, appointed Sectretary. Mr CHARLTON, moved that the chair nominate 6 persons to repesent the object of the meeting, whereupon ELIAS CRUTCHLEY, GEORGE M. POTTS, S. G. COOKEY, Dr. T. W. JOHNSON, C. SHRINER, and Colonel NOAH PHILLIPS, were appointed the said committee, returned with the following resolutions: That 9 delegates be appointed from this district to attend the convention. That they go untrammeled and free to vote for the candidate who will best promote the interest of the district. Captain FULTON, moved for a vote to be taken which passed, except the 2nd resolution was rejected. Dr. GOLDSBOROUGH, now moved that the house appoint the following 9 persons to said committee. Captain FULTON, JACOB ROOT, DAVID HINES, LEWIS BALTZELL, Doct. GOLDSBOROUGH, GEORGE BARRICK, of Peter, GIDEON D. CRUMBAUGH, Dr. SIMIN, and JOSEPH DELAPLANE, the resolution was carried.

2307. Creagers Town District of the Whig voters were held at BRECKENBAUGH, Tavern, on Saturday 2nd inst., Colonel JACOB CRAMER, was called to the chair, and WM. P. JONES, appointed Secretary, a committee to draft resolutions was appointed. It consisted of Dr. GOLDSBOROUGH, Z. KUHN, VALENTINE SHRYOCK, MARTIN EICHELBERGER, and WM. H. GRIMES. A resolution was accepted to appoint the following named gentlemen a committee to represent the district in said convention: Dr. ROB'T. C. CRUMMINGS, WM. P. JONES, ZEBULON KUHN, WARREN T. GRIMES, and VALENTINE SHRYOCK.

2308. (M) On Tuesday evening last, by the Rev. David F. Schaeffer. Mr DANIEL ORDNER, to Miss SUSAN B. HANSHEW, both of this city.

2309. (M) On the 28th ult., by the Rev. J. W. Hoffmier, Mr ANDREW D. WORMAN, to Miss SOPHIA M., second daughter of Mr John Cronise.

2310. (M) On the 23rd ult., by the Rev. M. Wachter, Mr EZRA SHANK, to Miss ANN E. BECK, both of this co.

2311. (M) On Thursday last, by the Rev. David F. Schaeffer, Mr WASHINGTON MATHIAS, to Miss ELIZA ANN HENRY, all of this co.

2312. (M) On Sunday evening the 19th ult., by the Rev. Mr McGee, Mr JACOB YAKLE, to Miss SARAH ANN GALEZIO, all of this city.

2313. (D) Departed this life on Tuesday the 21st April, in the 22nd year of his age, JOSEPH W. PANCOAST, a native of Frederick Co., MD. He left a disconsolent parent and sister who will long larment his loss. He obeyed the precept laid down in the 5th Chapter and 14th & 15th verses of the Gospel according to St. James, and with Christian fervor and devotion, died in full communion with the Roman Catholic Church. (Muakingum (Ohio) Messenger)

2314. (D) On Friday last, MARIA FRANCES, daughter of Lewis Birely, Esq., aged 2 years, and 5 months.

2315. (D) In Greenbush, N. Y., at the house of John Venderzee, GETTY VENDERZEE, aged 84 years, widow of Teunis Venderzee, and mother of S. F. Venderzee, Esq., of Troy. The deceased was the last of 4 sisters, who together with a number of other leaders, assisted by Ensign, gallantly defending the Middle Fort at Schoharie during the Revolutionary War. The place was surprise by a large number of British and Indians, at a time when the troops and male inhabitants were sent to the lower Fort, situtate about 4 miles distant, which was expected to be attacked by the enemy. The females with their children reparred to the fort for protection. It was under the care of a Major and Ensign BECKER, who was then only 16 years old. The Major ensisted on surrinding, but the young Ensign objected to such a course. The women joined the Ensign and decided to resist the enemy. They confinded the Major to the cellar, then they went to work and manned the guns with great bravery and skill. The enemy were kept at a distance, and prevented from taking the Fort until reinforcement arrived from the Fort below, when the enemy were routed and the Fort saved. The Major was broke for his cowardly conduct, and the gallant Ensign promoted to his place. The above incident will give some idea of the spirit that animated even our mothers during the critical period of the Revolution.

May 13, 1835 (MHS)

2316. It is announced that PETER H. BROWN, Esq., is now the proprietor of the "Citizen."

2317. The musical entertainment which Mr STULL, proposed to give this evening, at the rooms of the Mechanics' Lyceum, will afford to lovers of music a rich treat.

2318. The Whig meeting of the New Market District, assembled at ENOS SCHELL's Tavern, on the 9th inst. ABEL RUSSELL, was appointed chairman, JOHN LEASE, assistant chairman, and JACOB CRONISE, secretary. The following named gentlemen; to wit: NATHAN HAMMOND, of Ormond, JACOB CRONISE, WASHINGTON BURGESS, SINGLETON WOOTTON, GEO. P. BUCKEY, ABEL RUSSELL, WM. NORRIS, GEO. PHELPS, WILLIAM MORSELL, NATHAN NELSON, ABRAHAM JOHNS, ZACHARIAS McELFRESH, JOHN KLAY, ENOS SCHELL, JOHN HOUCK, and JNO. BARTHOLOW, are appointed a committee to represent this District in the convention to be held in New Market, on the 27th.

2319. Taney Town District meeting of the Whig voters of the 6th District met at S. SULTZER's Hotel, on the 19th inst. DAVID KEPHART, Esq., was called to the chair, and S. SULTZER, appointed Secretary. The following gentlemen were appointed to represent this District at the convention in New Market: JAMES SMITH, Dr. SAMUEL SWOPE, Col. THOMAS HOOK, STERLING GALT, JACOB ZUMBRUN, ELIAS GRIMES, DAVID FOUTZ, JOHN MATHIAS, and SAMUEL McKINSTRY.

2320. (M) On Thursday the 30th, by the Rev. M. Wachter, Mr JACOB HULL, to Miss MARGARET BARNHART, all of this co.

2321. (M) On Thursday last, by the Rev. David F. Schaeffer, Mr DANIEL HOUCK, to Miss CATHARINE STALEY, all of this co.

2322. (M) On Sunday evening last, by the same, Mr PETER STOFFEL, merchant, to Miss SUSAN COX, all of this city.

2323. (M) On Yesterday morning, by the same, Mr JOHN WACHTER, to Miss MARGARET ANN STONE, all of this co.

2324. (D) On Monday evening the 4th inst., Mrs BARBARA O'NEAL, in the 63rd year of her age.

2325. (D) On Saturday the 2nd inst., Mrs MARY QUINN, in the 70th year of her age.

May 27, 1835 (MHS)

2326. Military appointments by the Executive, for Frederick Co., May 1835. For the 29th Regiment, Frederick Co: LEWIS BALTZELL, Captain of a Uniform Rifle Company; BENJAMIN SMITH, 1st Lieutenant, CHARLES HESSER, 2nd Lieutenant.
2327. EVAN McKINSTRY, has been apppointed an additional Justice of the Levy Court, of Frederick Co., and JAMES CORNELL, and JOHN H. HOPPE, an additional Justices of the Peace of Frederick Co.
2328. The Whig meeting of the 2nd Election District of Frederick Co., convened on Wednesday evening the 20th inst., at the Court House, in Frederick. CYRUS MANTZ, Esq., was called to the chair, and WM. OGDEN NILES, appointed Secretary. The object of the meeting was explained by NEILSON POE, Esq., he submitted the following resolutions, which was 2nd by FRANCIS BRENGLE. (1) That the chair appoint 12 persons to represent the 2nd Election District at the convention. (2) That the chair appoint 10 persons to act as a General and Central Committee of Correspondence. The chair appointed the following gentlemen to the convention: MOSES WORMAN, LEWIS REMSBURG, ISRAEL MYERS, VALENTINE BIRELY, Dr. WM. S. McPHERSON, ABRAHAM KEMP, JONA. GETZENDANNER, PATRICK TORMEY, CHAS. H. BURKHART, JACOB FAUBEL, GIDEON BANTZ, LAWRENCE J. BRENGLE. Central Committee of Correspondence: Dr. W. B. TYLER, NICHOLAS H. PITTS, RICHARD POTTS, WM. J. ROSS, Col. G. M. EICHELBERGER, M. B. LUCKETT, Col. J. McPHERSON, CHAS. A. GAMBRILL, Dr. JOHN BALTZELL, GEO. J. FISCHER.
2329. Whig voters of the Buckeys Town District convened at the house of ALLEN SAIN, in Buckeys Town, on Saturday last. Col. DANIEL DUVALL, was appointed chairman, W. E. KING, assistant chairman, and JOSEPH L. SMITH, Esq., Secretary. The following persons appointed as delegates: Dr. JONATHAN MANROE, JOSPEH L. SMITH, PHILEMON McELFRESH, A. H. BROWN, B. A. CUNNINGHAM, HENRY KEMP, GEORGE KEPHART, E. HOWARD, ZADOCK WINDSOR, and PATRICK MURPHY, to attend the convention, to be held in New Market on Wednesday the 27th.

The following gentlemen composed a delegation to attend the convention to be held in Frederick, on the 1st Saturday of August, to nominate candidates for the next General Assembly: DANIEL DUVALL, J. G. COBBS, GEORGE HASSELBOCK, CONRADT DUDROW, ALLEN SAIN, OTHO THOMAS, Dr. J. LAMBERT, Maj. J. SIMMONS, C. DANNEHILL, Z. T. WINDSOR, R. B. MURDOCK, M. M. MAHONEY, SAMUEL JARBOE, JAMES L. DAVIS, and THOMAS KING. Gentlemen for the Committee of Correspondence: B. A. CUNNINGHAM, Dr. J. VAN BUSKIRK, Dr. JONATHAN MANROE, JAMES A. JOHNSON, THOMAS L. DAVIS, CHARLES JOHNSON, ELISHA HOWARD, and Dr. JAMES JOHNSON.

2330. Whig voters of the 13th Election District, met at the house of JACOB GLAZIER, in Uniontown, on Saturday the 23rd inst. The meeting was organized by calling JAMES L. BILLINGSLEA, to the chair, and appointed Dr. JOSHUA JONES, Secretary, the following gentlemen appointed as delegates to the general convention: EVAN McKINSTRY, JAMES C. ATLEE, JOHN ROBERTS, Dr. J. JONES, WILLIAM SHEPHERD, DANIEL ENGLE, and JOHN SMITH.

2331. (M) At the Union Mills, on Tuesday the 12th inst., by the Rev. Mr Geiger, Mr L. J. BRENGLE, to Miss ELIZA, daughter of Andrew Shriver, Esq., all of this co.

2332. (M) On Monday evening last, by the Rev. D. F. Schaeffer, Mr PHINEHAS BUCKMAN, to Miss ELEANOR A. PENN, all of this co.

June 3, 1835 (MHS)

2333. The connection existing between Col. JAMES M. SHELMAN, and EDWARD LYNCH, Esq., in the publication of the "Weekly Times," have expired by limitation, on the 22nd of May. The latter has withdrawn from the establishment and the paper will hereafter be conducted by Col. Shelman, the founder and original proprietor.

2334. J. W. MILLS, who was tried at the last term of our criminal court, on charges of robbing Mr E. L. MAGRUDER, of $800.00 has, we preceived by the Baltimore paper been arrested on a charge of forging the check of W. H. Fowble, & Company, for $200.00, and attempting to obtain the money for it at the Merchanics ank.

2335. Constables appointed by the Levy Court, at the May term 1835, for the respective Election Districts of Frederick County: District #1. Buckeys Town - JOHN CAREY, WM.

CRAWFORD, ARTHUR DELASHMUTT and JAMES W. SIMMONS. District #2. Fredericktown - JOHN BENDER, JOSHUA DILL, LEWIS CROSS, SAMUEL McDADE, JAMES CARLIN, JOHN M. LOWE, DANIEL HALLER, ROBERT G. RUSSELL, FREDERICK STONER, and HUGH MULLEN. District #3. Middletown - JOHN ALEXANDER, ABRAHAM MILLER, PETER YOUNG, JACOB YOUNG, of Dewalt, WM. HOUSE, of Daniel, and JOHN WISE. District #4. Creagerstown - CYRUS WALKER, JOSEPH LIDAY, GEORGE KUHN, ISAAC KOONTZ, EPHRAIM CARMACK, and ARNOLD R. FAHS. District #5. Emmittsburg - SAMUEL DUPHORN, ISAAC WILSON, and JESSE MARTIN. District #6. Taney Town - JOHN CLABAUGH, WM. KOONTZ, JOHN THOMPSON, ABRAHAM KOONTZ, and DANIEL McKENZIE. District #7. Westminster - JACOB FRINGER, ABRAHAM H. BUSBY, JOHN CROUSE, FREDERICK YIN GLING, DANIEL BANKERT, JOHN FEASER, and DANIEL ENGLE. District #8. Liberty - JOEL WOOD, DANIEL SWEADNER, DANIEL ROOT, AARON GOSNELL, and WILLIAM H. CONDON. District #9. New Market - WM. S. HOWARD, JONATHAN BROWNING, CHARLES STEVENS, and LEVI VANFOSSEN. District #10. Hauver's - HENRY NEED, and WM. H. BROWN. District #11. Woodsborough - JOHN BARRICK, and FREDERICK GRIMES, District #12. Petersville - JOHN G. DABELSTERN, THOMAS CLINGAN, and ADAM CUSTARD. District #13. Union Town - ISAIAH PEARCE, WM. COOPER, and TOBIAS COVER. District #14. Jefferson - WM. B. TABLER, and JACOB B. HALLER.

2336. Delegates appointed by several Election Districts composing the 6th Congressional District of Maryland. Assembled at New Market on Wednesday the 27th of May, for the general convention. EVAN McKINSTRY, Esq., was appointed President, JACOB MATHIAS, and JOHN SIMMONS, Esqrs., Vice Presidents, and JOSEPH L. SMITH, and HENRY KEMP, Secretaries. Gentlemen from Montgomery: Major WM. M. STEUART, read the proceeding of the Montgomery Convention, held in Rockville. Dr. R. DORSEY, offered the following resolution, not to nominate a candidate to represent this District in the next Congress and that the convention adjourn until August. The resolution was rejected. WASHINGTON BURGESS, Esq., put in the nomination the Hon. WM. COST JOHNSON. On counting the ballots received the unanimous vote of the District representatives. On motion of Dr. JOSHUA JONES, Jr., a committee of 5 be appointed to draft an address to the voters of the District. Chair appointed: Dr. J. JONES, Jr., Dr. J. MANRO, W. BURGESS, Esq., Dr. WM. WILLIS, and Mr S. McKINSTRY, and that a committee consisting of JACOB MATHIAS, JOSEPH L. SMITH, and HENRY KEMP, be appointed to inform WILLIAM COST JOHNSON, of his nomination.

2337. (M) On the 31st inst., by the Rev. David F. Schaeffer, Mr WILLIAM EADER, to Miss ANN STALLINGS, of this city.

2338. (M) Same evening by the same, Mr MICHAEL KEEFER, to Miss ANN MARIA FAREL, all of this city.

2339. (M) Same evening by the same, Mr JACOB GREENHOLTZ, to Mrs BARBARA ANN MULHORN, of this place.

2340. (D) On Wednesday last, in Union Town, MD., Mr DAVID STEM, at an advanced age, an old resident of this place.

June 10, 1835 (MHS)

2341. Baron KRUDENER, (Russian Minister,) and date arrived in Frederick, on yesterday morning, and took lodging at Talbott's City Hotel.

2342. The Rev. SAMUEL A. DAVIS, will preach in the Court House this (Wednesday) evening at 1/2 past 7 o'clock.

2343. The Rev. THOMAS WILKS, will preach in the Baptist Church this evening at at early candlelight.

2344. (M) On Tuesday the 2nd inst., by the Rev. David F. Schaeffer, Mr SEBASTIAN G. COCKEY, to Miss ELIZABETH SPRIGG, all of this place.

2345. (M) On Thursday evening last, by the same, Mr JOSHUA CRAVER, to Miss ELIZABETH LECHLEITER, all of this co.

December 2, 1835 (MHS)

2346. A hog only 20 months old was slaughtered in the city some days since, by Mr L. DOYLE, which weighted 488 pounds. It was raised by Mr HATTON DIXON, who resided on the farm of Caspar Mantz, Esq., near the city.

2347. (M) Near Woodsborough, on the 25th inst., by the Rev. J. W. Hoffmeier. Mr JOHN WOOD, to Miss SOPHIA WENRICK.

2348. (M) On the same day by the same, near Creagerstown, Mr DANIEL MAGN, of Jefferson Co., VA., to Miss ALICE, youngest daughter of Mr Michael Zimmerman.

2349. (M) On the 19th of Oct., at Camp Meeting, in Madison Co., MS., by the Rev. John McCruely, Dr. JOHN P. RICHMOND, formerly of Middletown, Frederick Co., MD., to Mrs AMERICAN TALLY, of Carthage Lake Co., MS.

2350. (M) On Tuesday evening in New York, by the Rev. Mr

Eastburn, the Hon. CHURCHILL C. CAMBRELENG, to PHEBE, daughter of the late John J. Glover.

2351. (M) On the 22nd ult., at Fort Jackson, on board of the canal boat Genesee E. B. Briggs, Captain. Mr THOMAS MAYNHOOD, of Saratoga, to Miss _____, a widow lady from Ohio. The lady came aboard at Buffalo, and the gentleman at Jordan - strangers to each other. After a long courtship of 143 miles, they proceeded to tie the nuptial knott. A magistrate at Fort Jackson officiated.

2352. (M) On Monday evening last, by the Rev. Henry V. D. Johns, WILLIAM PINKNEY MAULSBY, Esq., of Baltimore, to Miss EMILY CATHARINE TYLER second daughter of the late Roger Nelson.

December 9, 1835 (MHS)

2353. The members of the Reform Central Committee, are requested to assemble at Mr JOHN DILL's Tavern on Thursday (to-morrow,) evening at 7 o'clock.

2354. (M) On Thursday last, by the Rev. David F. Schaeffer, Mr DAVID YOWLER, to Miss HARRIET ANGLEBERGER, all of this co.

2355. (M) On yesterday evening, by the same, Mr CONSTANTINE LARGE, Professor of Music, to Miss SOPHIA RELKE, all of this co.

December 16, 1835 (MHS)

2356. List of jurors for the December term of Frederick, Co., Court. Grand jurors: JOSEPH TANEY, Sen'r., SAM'L. BAUMGARDNER, JOHN BRUNNER, of J., RICHARD CROMWELL, GEORGE DERTZBAUGH, WILLIAM DURBIN, GEO. W. FALCONER, SAMUEL GEYER, EZRA GOMBAR, ELIAS GRIMES, ALEXANDER HUDSON, GEORGE KUHN, LEWIS MOTTER, BENJAMIN NEIDIG, JOSHUA RUSSELL, PETER SCHLOSSER, HUGH SHAW, THOMAS SHEPHERD, JOSHUA SMITH, SAMUEL STEVENS, JACOB STITELY, Jr., LLOYD THOMAS, THOMAS THRASHER. Petite jurors: GEORGE BEER, HENRY BOTELER, THOMAS CASTLE, JOSEPH M. CROMWELL, CHARLES DEVILBISS, DAVID B. DEVITT, JACOB GLAZIER, WILLIAM GRAFF, SOLOMON HARBAUGH, FREDERICK HAWMAN, WILLIAM P. JONES, WILLIAM LOWE, JOHN MILLER, JOHN OTT, WM. H. POOLE, JACOB POWDER, JACOB ROWE, UPTON SCOTT, GEORGE B. SHRINER, GEORGE SMITH, DAVID SWITZER,

WILLIAM TODD, SAMUEL WILHIDE, CHARLES WORTHINGTON, DANIEL YOUNG.

December 23, 1835 (MHS)

2357. (D) A negro man was frozen to death on Friday night near this city. We are also informed that an individual was discovered in the river near Berlin in this co; a day or two since; how his death was occasioned is not certainly known. And yet another, a Mr MILLER, who was frozen to death, on the night of Thursday last, on the road between this city and Middletown.

2358. RODERICK DORSEY, Esq., who 2 years since was the competitor of WM. C. JOHNSON, Esq., as a candidate for Congress, was last week elected Sergeant-at-Arms to the House of Representatives. The salary attached to this office is 1500 dollars.

2359. In accordance with a resolution of the Central Reform Committee of Frederick Co. The following named persons have been appointed to accompany the memorial on this subject to be presented to the next Legislature to be held in Annapolis on the 25th of January next. GIDEON BANTZ, FRANCIS BRENGLE, L. P. W. BALCH, GEORGE BOWLUS, HENRY BRIEN, ISAAC BAUGHER JAMES M. COALE, WM. H. DANGERFIELD, WM. COST JOHNSON, JOHN STIFFORD, Col. JOHN THOMAS, Capt. DAVID KEMP, Col. A. KIMMEL, BENJAMIN PRICE, SAMUEL TYLER, ABDIEL UNKEFER, MADISON NELSON, JOHN ROBERTS, WM. P. JONES, Dr. WM. S. McPHERSON, LEWIS RAMSBURG, Doct. GWINN, GEO. WARFIELD, JOHN RIGNEY, JACOB MATTHIAS, JAMES A. SHORB.

2360. Disgraceful offense - A case of a very flagrant and enormous character, which has excited a great deal of conversation and anti-madversion in this city, and more especially in the 1st Ward; came before the court and jury this morning, CATHARINE HUGHES, a white woman, being in the neighborhood of Mr KRAFTS' Bakery, on Pennsylvania Ave., was indicted on 2 counts; (1st) charging her with keeping a house of ill-fame. (2nd) with enticing a young girl, apprentice to Mr Kraft, and only 15 years of age; and aiding in the seduction of the unfortunate girl. The circumstance, as disclosed by the testimony of the girl, Mr Kraft, and Mr Tyler, and the character given of the prisioner's house by L. Ashton, police officer in the 1st Ward. She was found guilty of both counts and indictment. She appeared at the bar very well dressed, having on her head a straw bonnet and veil.

2361. (M) On the 6th inst., by the Rev. Daniel Zacharias, Mr ABIJAH SHEPHERD, to Miss CHARLOTTE KELLER.

2362. (M) On Thursday last by the same, Mr JOHN A. HEDGES, to Miss MARY A. WHITMORE.

2363. (M) On the same day by the same, Mr HENRY S. STALEY, to Miss ANN REBECCA CONNERS, all of this city.

2364. (M) On Thursday last, at the residence of John Ellicott, Elkridge Landing by the Rev. Mr Cookman, GEORGE POE, to ELIZABETH R. ELLICOTT, all of Anne Arundel Co.

2365. (D) Suddenly on the 30th of November, in the 84th year of his age, SOLOMON SHEPHERD, a member of the Society of Friends, and one of the oldest and most respectable inhabitants of this co.

2366. (D) Departed this life, at his residence in Tiffin, on the 7th inst., Dr. THOMAS BOYER, aged about 60 years. Dr. Boyer was a native of Kent Co., MD. He removed to the Western Shore, and resided several years in Baltimore Co., and subsequently for a longer period of time in Frederick Co. From Frederick County he emigrated, about 3 years since, and settled among numberous friends from the same part of Maryland in this co. (Tiffin Gazette)

1836

POLITICAL EXAMINER

January 6, 1836 (MHS)

2367. R. B. TANEY, has been nominated by the President to the Senate as Chief Justice, and Mr BARBOUR, of VA., as Associate Justice, and AMOS KENDALL, the acting Postmaster is also before the Senate.

2368. The Rev. JOSEPH JONES, will preach in the Baptist Church, on Saturday evening next, at early candlelight.

2369. (M) On Tuesday the 15th ult., by the Rev. Mr Best, Col. JOHN A. WARFIELD, (merchant of Union Town) to Miss HENRIETTA, daughter of Suratt D. Warfield, Esq., all of this co.

2370. (D) On the 27th December 1835, at the residence of his mother in this city, of a pulmonary disease, Mr HENRY HICKSON, in the 49th year of his age.

2371. (D) On Monday morning the 28th ult., after a painful and lingering illness Mrs MARY ANN BROOKE, in the 44th year of her age.

2372. (D) At Planeville, Baltimore Co., on Friday night 25th of Dec., RINALDO, infant son of Vachel B. Todd, aged 6 months and 2 days.

January 13, 1836 (MHS)

2373. (M) On Thursday evening last, by the Rev. D. F. Schaeffer, THOMAS PURCELL, Esq., to Miss REBECCA YOUNG, all of this co.

2374. (M) On the 8th inst., by the Rev. John W. Hoffmier, Mr WILLIAM STAUP, of Creagerstown, to Miss MARY BECKER.

2375. (M) Yesterday evening by the Rev. Henry V. D. Johns, Dr. WM. M. KEMP, of this city, to Miss SUSAN W., daughter of Dr. Thomas W. Johnson, of this co.

2376. (D) In the city, on Sunday the 10th inst., ROSANNA, only surviving daughter of Mrs John McAleer, aged 7 years and 6 months.

2377. (D) On Monday night last, in the 39th year of his age, LAWRENCE BRENGLE, son of Mr Christian Brengle.

January 27, 1836 (MHS)

2378. (D) In Warrenington, Ms., on the 9th last, after a short illness, Mr HUGH HAGAN, aged 21 years, second son of Mr Peter Hagan.

February 3, 1836 (MHS)

2379. The Rev. WM. POOLE, a Reformed preacher, will deliver a discourse upon the merits of the Doctrine of Universal Salvation, on next Sunday afternoon in the Court House, at 1/2 past 2 o'clock.

2380. The Rev JOSEPH H. JONES, will preach in the Baptist Meeting House, on Friday evening at candlelight, and on Saturday evening also at candlelight.

2381. (M) In this city, on Tuesday evening last, by the Rev. P. F. Phelps, Mr CHARLES A. GAMBRILL, to Miss ANN ELIZABETH EICHELBERGER, daughter of Colonel George M. Eichelberger, all of this city.

2382. (M) On the same evening, by the same, Mr WILLIAM DEAN, to Miss CATHARINE BARRICK, daughter of George Barrick, all of Frederick Co.

February 10, 1836 (MHS)

2383. Candidate for the Common Council: Ward #2. PETER STOFFEL. Ward #7. WILLIAM KOLB.
2384. Funeral discourse for the Rev. F. D. SCHAEFFER, D.D., will be held on Sunday next, the 14th inst., at 10 o'clock, A.M. By the Rev. Dr. Schmuker, professor of Theology in the Seminary of the Lutheran Church, at Gettysburg.
2385. The Independent Hose Company held it annual meeting on the 30th of January, 1836, the following is list of officers for the ensuing year. G. M. CONRADT, President. JACOB DOLL, Vice President. GIDEON BANTZ, Sr., Treasurer. D. J. MARKEY, Secretary. Directors: JOHN FESSLER, and WILLIAM SMALL. Principal Engineer: D. B. DEVITT. Assistant Engineer: GEO. HOSKINS, DANIEL HALLER. The Standing Committee appointed the following stations to the members viz: Pipe Director: G. M. CONRADT. Hose Director: JACOB DOLL. Engineer: JOHN FESSLER. Lane Director: WILLIAM SMALL. Property Guards: WILLIAM SCHLEY, JOSEPH SCHELL. Superintendent of fire plugs: JOHN STRAFER, MARK BISHOP. Laddermen: FREDERICK A. SCHLEY, SAMUEL CARMACK, CASPAR QUYNN. Axmen: JOHN HENSHEW, HENRY RHODES. Hosemen: GEORGE SALMON, PHILIP RHODES, JOHN SHRIVER, HENRY YOUNG, V. J. BRUNNER, HENRY HENSHEW, EDWARD TRAIL, GEORGE J. FISCHER, GIDEON BANTZ, Sr., WM. C. RUSSELL, EDWARD MANTZ, WM. M. KEMP.
2386. (M) On Thursday last, by the Rev. M. Wachter, Mr PETER TRINGSTRUM, to Miss MARY ASENETH SIMMONS, all of this co.
2387. (M) On Thursday last, by the Rev. M. Wachter, Mr JACOB HINER, to Miss ANN MARTIN, all of this co.
2388. (M) On Tuesday morning, the 2nd ult., by the Rev. John L. Pitts, Mr NATHAN HAMMOND, of Vach'l. to Mrs MARGARET BURGESS, all of this co.
2389. (M) On Thursday evening the 4th., by the same, Mr TALBOTT B. ANDERSON, to Miss SARAH ANN RIGGS, all of this co.
2390. (M) On Sunday evening last, by the Rev. D. F. Schaeffer, Mr JOHN GEORGE SINN, to Miss CATHERINE E. STUTLER, all of this city.
2391. (D) On the evening of Monday the 1st inst., near Emmittsburg, JOHN GRABILL, Sr., in the 61st year of his age.
2392. (D) In the 6th year of her age, at the residence of her fa-

ther, HENRIETTA CATHERINE, eldest daughter of Joseph P. Fleming.

February 17, 1836 (MHS)

2393. JAMES M. COALE, Esq., of this city, has been appointed by the Governor of Pennsylvania, Commissioner within and for the State of Maryland, with power and authority to examine witnesses under commissions, and to take the acknowledgement, authentication, and probate of all instruments or proceeding relating to the State.

2394. The Rev. Mr DORSEY, agent for the Maryland State Temperance Society, will deliver an address on the subject of Intemperance this evening in the Methodist Church, on Thursday evening, in the German Reformed Church, and on Friday evening, in the Episcopal Church commencing at early candlelight.

2395. The annual meeting of the Washington Hose Company, was held at the house of Mr COOKERLY, on the 2nd of January. The following gentlemen were elected officers for the ensuing year: LEWIS MEDTART, President. JOHN ENGELBRECHT, Vice President. GODFREY KOONTZ, Secretary. GEORGE W. ENT, Treasurer. THOS. C. PRINCE, Principle Engineer. HORATIO WATERS, FRANCIS LUEBER, Assistant Engineers. Property Guards: WM. OGDEN NILES, L. A. BRENGLE. Superintendants of fire plugs: G. W. ENT, JAMES CARLIN. Laddermen: EZRA SCHELL, DAVID HANE. Axemen: J. LITTLE, C. GETZENDANNER. Hosemen: JACOB HALLER, P. R. SHAFFNER, PHILIP HAWMAN, JACOB DADDISMAN, CHAS. A. GAMBRILL, JAMES RAYMOND, WM. BRENNER.

2396. (M) On Tuesday morning the 7th inst., at Shrinerea, Frederick Co., MD., by the Rev. Mr McElroy, Dr. O. H. OWINGS, of Unionville, MD., to Miss MARGARET S., daughter of Capt. John S. Lawrence, of the former place.

2397. (M) On Sunday evening last, by the Rev. M. Wachter, Mr MATHIAS BEARD, to Miss ELIZA ANDES, all of this co.

February 24, 1836 (MHS)

2398. Civil Court of this co., commenced its February term on Monday last. The following is a list of the jurors in attendance: JOHN ANNAN, JOHN B. BOYLE, JOHN COST, GIDEON D. CRUMBAUGH, ISAAC DERN, DANIEL GETZENDANNER, JOHN HOUCK, JAMES McCOSKERY, WILLIAM OTTER, JOHN SMITH, MICHAEL SULIVAN, ABDIEL

UNKEFER, JOHN YOUNG, HENRY BOTELAR, of Edward, WM. BROWN, THOMAS CRAMPTON, JOSHUA DELAPLANE, JACOB FRINGER, THOMAS HAMMOND, LLOYD LUCKETT, EVAN McKINSTRY, GEORGE RICE, FREDERICK STONER, JOHN THOMAS, of Gab., SAMUEL YEAST.

2399. The Rev. Mr EVERETT, an universalist, from Baltimore, will deliver a discourse on Sunday next, in the Court House, at the ringing of the bell.
2400. (M) Near Middletown, Frederick Co., MD., on Thursday the 4th inst., by the Rev. J. C. Bucher, Mr ABRAHAM WILLIARD, to Miss HARRIET, eldest daughter of Mr Henry Hersperger, all of Middletown Valley.
2401. (M) On Wednesday morning last, by the Rev. Mr Zacharias, Mr WOODWARD A. E. HAMILTON, to Miss CATHERINE ELY, both of this city.
2402. (M) On yesterday evening at Creagerstown, by the Rev. M. Wachter, Mr HENRY ORNDORFF, to Miss HARRIET WICKHAM, all of this co.
2403. (M) On Thursday last, by the Rev. David F. Schaeffer, Mr JOSEPH ANGELBERGER, to Miss ELIZABETH MARTZ, youngest daughter of Major George Martz, all of this co.
2404. (D) On Wednesday the 17th inst., near Utica Mills, Mr JACOB D. SHRYOCK, aged 52 years.

March 2, 1836 (MHS)

2405. At the commencement of St. John's College, on the 22nd ult., the degree of Doctor of Devinity was conferred on the Rev. DAVID F. SCHAEFFER, of this city.
2406. Election results for the Common Council; on Monday last. Ward #1. JACOB FAUBLE. Ward #2. CHARLES GETZENDANNER. Ward #3. P. L. STORM. Ward #4. JACOB ENGLEBRECHT. Ward #5. JAMES WHITEHILL. Ward #6. GEORGE HOSKINS. Ward #7. WILLIAM KOLB.
2407. The Rev. Mr DORSEY, will deliver an address, this evening to members of the Temperance Society, in the Lutheran Church, at 6 an 1/2 o'clock.
2408. The Rev. JOSEPH H. JONES, will preach in the Baptist Meeting House, on next Lord's Day at 3 o'clock.
2409. (M) On Wednesday last, by the Rev. David F. Schaeffer, Mr GEORGE COLEGATE, to Miss ELIZABETH POOLE, all of this city.
2410. Candidate for Sheriff: HENRY HOUCK.

March 9, 1836 (MHS)

2411. (M) On the 28th ult., by the Rev. J. W. Hoffmier, Mr JOHN WELKER, of Yorke Co., PA., to Miss SARAH BAKER, near Woodsboro, Frederick Co., MD.
2412. (M) On Thursday last, by the Rev. David F. Schaeffer, Mr ENOS BUSSARD, to Miss BARBARA RAMSBURG, all of this co.
2413. (M) On Sunday evening last, by the same, Mr WILLIAM E. SULTER, to Miss MARIAN KILLAN, all of this co.
2414. (M) On Thursday evening the 3rd inst., by the Rev. Mr McGee, Mr WILLIAM D. LEWIS, to Miss COLUMBIA E. RIGDON, all of this city.
2415. (M) On yesterday evening, by the same, Mr STEPHEN S. MANN, to Miss ANN M. HARTSOCK, all of this city.
2416. (M) On Thursday last, by the Rev. M. Wachter, Mr JAMES NEILL, to Miss CATHERINE HOOVER, all of this co.
2417. (M) On Sunday last, by the same, Mr DAVID FOGLE, to Miss ELIZABETH HEFFNER, both of this co.

March 16, 1836 (MHS)

2418. Post office has been established at Ijamsville, and LEMUEL MUSSETTER, appointed Postmaster.
2419. (M) On Thursday the 8th inst., by the Rev. Mr Reese, Mr J. LANDIES, of Mount Pleasant, to Miss SOPHIA STONER, both of Frederick Co.
2420. (D) On the 1st inst., at his residence near McKinstry's Mill, CHRISTIAN SENSENY, aged about 65 years.
2421. (D) Departed this life on Wednesday last, Miss ELIZABETH RINGGOLD, daughter of the late, General Samuel Ringgold, of Washington, Co.

March 23, 1836 (MHS)

2422. (M) On Thursday the 17th of March, in Gettysburg, by the Rev. Frederick Ruthrauff, Mr CALEB SHELEY, to Mrs ANN GILLELEN, eldest daughter of Mr Thomas Jones, Esq., both of Frederick Co.

March 30, 1836 (MHS)

2423. On Monday last the following persons were on joint ballot elected officers of the corporation of Frederick, for the present year. Register: GEORGE ROHR. Collector: HENRY BAER. Corporation Printer: WM. OGDEN NILES. Town Commissioner: J. FESSLER. Hay Weighter: SOLOMON STICKLE. Market Master: CLEM. HILTON.

Lamp Lighters: J. FINCH, J. H. HOFF. Superintendent of the Streets and Pumps: JOHN BENDER, and JAMES CARLIN. City Constables: J. BENDER, J. CARLIN, J. H. HOFF. Clock Winder: JOHN FESSLER. Commissioners: ROBERT McCLEERY, ANDREW HEIM, FREDERICK NEZS. Messenger: C. MYERS.

2424. Whig meeting of the Liberty District, assembled at JOSEPH WAGNER's Tavern, on Saturday the 26th inst. ABRAHAM JONES, Esq., was called to the chair, and THOMAS CARR, appointed Secretary. The following persons will represent this Election District at the convention to be held in New Market, on the 5th of April, in order to designate an elector for President and Vice President of United States. Dr. RICHARD DORSEY, JOHN CLEMSON, WM. DUDDERAR, RICHARD SIMPSON, WM. A. ALBAUGH, CHRISTOPHER OWINGS, WM. H. POOLE, A. H. OWINGS, THOMAS CARR, ANTHONY KIMMELL, SURRAT D. WARFIELD.

2425. Bill to establish a Magistrate Court has been passed by the State Senate.

2426. At the Whig meeting held at the house of ENOS SCHELL, in New Market, on Saturday the 26th inst., to appoint delegates to the convention. ABEL RUSSELL, was called to the chair, and THOMAS C. BRASHEAR, appointed Secretary. The following persons were named as delegates SINGLETON WOOTON, PLUMMER IJAMS, Sen., WASHINGTON BURGESS, AB'M. JOHNS, JOHN CLAY, THOMAS C. BRASHEAR, JOHN HOUCK, HENRY NICHOLS, NATHAN HAMMOND, of V., WILLIAM NORRIS, JOHN LOWE, GEORGE P. BUCKEY, JOHN LEASE, NICHOLAS BRENGLE, PRADBY JAMES, HENRY NELSON, Doctor GEO. HUGHES, GEORGE PHELPS, WARFIELD TODD, JESSE RUSSELL, ZACHARIAH McELFRESH, ENOS SCHELL, HAMILTON STIER.

2427. The Whigs of Buckeystown District convened on the Tavern of ALLEN SAIN, on Saturday 26th of March, CHARLES JOHNSON, Esq., was called to the chair, and Dr. J. MANRO, appointed Secretary. The following gentlemen were appointed a committee to meet the convention at New Market, on 2nd Tuesday in April next. J. H. F. COCKERLY, CHARLES JOHNSON, JOHN LEATHER, B. A. CUNNINGHAM, Major JAMES SIMMONS, Doctor J. MANRO, THOMAS J. DAVIS.

2428. The Rev. OBADIAH B. BROWN, from Washington, and JOSEPH H. JONES, will preach in the Baptist Meeting

House, next Lord's Day at 3 o'clock, afternoon, also on Monday at 10 o'clock. A. M.
2429. (M) On Thursday last, by the Rev. D. Zacharias, Mr JOHN H. ROHRER, to Miss REBECCA SAMSEL.
2430. (M) On Tuesday the 22nd, by the Rev. P. F. Phelps, Mr ISAAC EMMERT, of Washington, Co., to Miss SUSAN D., daughter of David Hershey, Esq., of Montgomery.
2431. (M) Near Middletown, Frederick Co., MD., on the 17th inst., by the Rev. J. C. Bucher, Mr JOHN JONES, to Miss LEE ANN, daughter of Mr John Stottlemyer, deceased, all of Middletown Valley.
2432. (M) On Sunday evening last, by the Rev. Mr Pitts, Mr CHARLES J. FOX, to Miss CATHARINE E. GETZENDANNER, both of this city.
2433. (M) On Sunday last, by the Rev. D. F. Schaeffer, Mr HENRY ZIEGLER, to Miss MARGARET DERTZEBACH, all of this city.
2434. (M) On the same day, by the same, Mr CHARLES L. MISS, to Miss ELIZABETH LANTZ, all of this vicinity.
2435. (M) Near Middletown, on the 24th of March, by the Rev. J. C. Bucher, Mr JOHN M. LINTHICUM, to Miss MARY ANN, daughter of Mr John Welker, all of Middletown Valley, MD.
2436. (D) Near Jefferson, Frederick City, MD., on the 23rd of March, 1836, after a short illness, JOHN ADAM KREMER, in the 7th year of his age.
2437. (D) Near Middletown, MD., on the 27th of March, after a very short illness, CATHARINE, daughter of Mr Johnathan Keller, in the 5th year of her age.

April 6, 1836 (MHS)

2438. (M) On Tuesday the 29th ult., by the Rev. P. F. Phelps, ARCHIBALD ROBERTSON, of Frederick, to LYDIA ANN, daughter of Mr Joseph Stier, of Loudon Co., VA.
2439. (M) On Tuesday evening last, by the Rev. Daniel Zacharias, Mr GRAFTON J. RICE, to Miss ANN M. R. BIRELY.
2440. (M) In Baltimore, on Tuesday evening last, by the Rev. B. Kurtz, Mr GEORGE M. TYLER, to Miss ANN MARIA LATE, all of Frederick City, MD.
2441. (M) On Thursday evening last, by the Rev. Daniel Zacharias, Mr HENRY KAUFMAN, to Miss CHARLOTTE DOLL, all of this city.
2442. We are informed that commissions have been directed to GEORGE BALTZELL, GIDEON BANTZ, and JOHN H.

BEALL, as Justices of the Magistrate Court, for Frederick Co.

2443. Appointments by the Governor and Council for Frederick County, Levy Court: WILLIAM MILLER, MARTIN EICHELBERGER, FREDERICK TROXELL, SOLOMON FOREST, THOMAS SPRINGER, JEREMIAH G. MORRISON, WILLIAM LYNCH, WILLIAM DUDDERAR, MOSES WORMAN, JAMES SIMMONS, JACOB MATHIAS, JAMES SMITH, JAMES L. HIGGINS, EVAN McKINSTRY. Magistrates: PATRICK McGILL, Sr., THOMAS BAKER, JACOB CRAMER, JOSEPH TANEY, Jr., WILLIAM GRIMES, SURRATT D. WARFIELD, THOMAS HAYS, JACOB BAER, MALACHI BERNARD, GEORGE BLESSING, AL. BARNEY, GIDEON D. CRUMBAUGH, JOHN W. WALTMAN, JOHN W. CHARLTON, DANIEL DUVALL, JOSHUA DOUB, LLOYD DORSEY, JOHN McDONALD, HENRY W. DERR, WILSON HAYS, THOMAS J. HAMMOND, GEORGE HARNER, THOMAS W. JOHNSON, of Wm., JACOB JOHNSON, ZEBULON KUHN, EDWARD KNOTT, MICHAEL LEASE, JOHN S. LAWRENCE, PATRICK McGILL, Jr., PHILEMOR S. McELFRESH, JOHN MONTGOMERY, MARTIN MAHONEY, NICHOLAS NORRIS, NATHAN H. OWINGS, WILLIAM MOONEY, NOAH PHILLIPS, GEORGE PHELPS, WILLIAM B. PITTINGER, JOHN W. DERR, ELIHA H. ROCKWELL, GEORGE RINER, JOHN SMITH, SAMUEL BAUMGARDNER, JACOB THOMAS, HENRY YOUNG, HENRY BANTZ, GEORGE YANTIS, JAMES M. HARDING, GEORGE KUHN, WILLIAM DURBIN, GEORGE BECKENBAUGH, BURGESS NELSON, ABDIEL UNKEFER, TILGHMAN BISER, SOLOMON FORREST, HENRY HOUCK, JOSEPH TALBOTT, GEORGE BOWLUS, EMANUEL SLIFE, JONATHAN MANRO, PETER STEM, GEORGE RICE, JACOB CASSELL, WILLIAM LOWE, LEONARD PICKING, WILLIAM COOKERLY, JEREMIAH G. MORRISON, ABNER CAMPBELL, JAMES G. CABBS, REZIN E. TILLARD, EBENEZER B. HEBBARD, DAVID ROOP, of Jos., HENRY HERSHBERGER, CHARLES H. BURKHART, O. H. OWINGS, WILLIAM NORRIS, DANIEL KOLB, MICHAEL BALTZELL, RICHMOND JOHNSON, of Roger, GEORGE W. WINDSOR, HENRY BUTLER, CHARLES E. MARKLAND, JACOB FIROR, WILLIAM R. KING, THOMAS J. WORTHINGTON, GEORGE MANTZ, GEORGE BALTZELL, GIDEON BANTZ, THOMAS SAPPINGTON, ABRAHAM JONES, THOMAS HAMMOND, GRAFTON DUVALL, LEWIS MOTTER, WILLIAM VAN BIBBER, JOHN HINES, ANDREW

SHRIVER, CHRISTIAN BOWER, ABRAHAM LICHTENWALTER, JOSHUA JONES, LLOYD LUCKETT, PETER BANKHERD, WASHINGTON BURGESS, JACOB COBLENTZ, ISAAC DERR, CHARLES DEVILBISS, DANIEL ENGLE, STEPHEN GORSUCH, BENJAMIN HONER, THOMAS HOOK, THOMAS W. JOHNSON, JOSEPH KEEFER, GEORGE MATTHIAS, Jr., WM. V. MORGAN, JOHN McDOWELL, JACOB POWDER, PHILIP BIRELY, MICHAEL SULLIVAN, JAMES SMITH, JOSHUA SMITH, Jr., BENJAMIN SHUNK, SOMERSET R. WATERS, ZACHARIAH T. WINDSOR, JOHN M. A. ZOLICKOFFER, HENRY STEVENS, THOMAS SMITH, of Jos., ABRAHAM WAMPLER, JOHN SMITH, of Jos., DANIEL STONESIFER, JACOB REESE, JOHN McNEIL, JOHN ROBERTS, JOSHUA STEVENSON, GEORGE TITLOW, JOHN K. LONGWELL, EHTHA HOUSE, DANIEL H. BISER, WILLIAM H. GRIMES, JAMES CORNELL, JOHN H. HOPPE, GEO. ROHR, NIMROD FRIZZLE, JONATHAN NORRIS, WM. BEAM, WM. ZOLICKOFFER, GEO. GILDS, JOHN H. BEALL, MAHLON HARLEY, JOHN SWOPE, JOHN BAUMGARDNER, JACOB FOX, JOS. M. CROMWELL, WM. SHEPHERD, JOHN L. HARDING, and DAVID RICHARDSON. Coroners: DAVID KEPHART, DENNIS D. HOWARD, JACOB BAER, WILLIAM KOLLICKOFFER, HENRY BOTELER, and GEORGE HUGHES.

April 13, 1836 (MHS)

2444. A boy, 12 and 14 years old, attempting to enter between two of the train of burden cars near the deposite, fell on the rail and the wheels of the train passed over him. The body we are informed was literally cut asunder.

2445. JAMES M. COALE, Esq., has been nominated as a Presidential elector by the recent convention held in Hagerstown, of the Whigs of the 6th Congressional District.

2446. The Whig delegates from the several election Districts of the 6th Congressional District, of Maryland, assembled this day, in general convention to nominate a suitable candidate to be placed on the electoral ticket of the State. The meeting was organized by calling Dr. M. A. FINLEY, to the chair, and appointing Messrs: HENRY FIERY, and ELIAS DAVIS, Secretaries. Motion by WILLIAM SEBLY, Esq., of Frederick, that a committee of 9 were appointed to recommend to the consideration of the convention an electoral candidate, to report, for the action of the convention appropriate resolution. WILLIAM SCHLEY, R. M. TIDBALL, WILLIAM VAN-

TEAR, WILLIAM MURPHY, JOSEPH WEAST, ISAAC NESBITT, EDWARD A. LYNCH, G. W. STUBBLEFIELD, and JOSEPH GABBY. They returned with the following resolution: To approve the nomination of WILLIAM HENRY HARRISON, of Ohio, as candidate for President of U. States, and approve JOHN TYLER, of VA., as candidate for the office of Vice President of the U. States. That JAMES M. COALE, Esq., of Frederick, be nominated, on behalf of the 6th Congressional District of Maryland, as an electoral candidate for President and Vice President of the U. States. On motion, in the convention, Messrs: EDWARD A. LYNCH, WILLIAM SCHLEY, and ROBERT M. TIDBALL, Esqrs, were appointed a committee to prepare for publication an address to the people, expressive of the views of the convention.

2447. (M) On Sunday evening last, by the Rev. Michael Wachter, Mr JAMES TITLOW, to Miss CATHERINE MILLER, all of this city.

2448. (M) On Tuesday evening last, by the Rev. P. F. Phelps, Mr ASHBURY H. HUNT, to Miss ZERUAH M. McLANAHAM, all of this city.

2449. (M) On the 24th of March, by the Rev. John W. Hoffmier, Mr DAVID COBLENTZ, of Middletown, to Miss MARY M., youngest daughter of Col. Jacob Cramer, near Utica.

2450. (M) On Thursday evening last, by the Rev. Dr. Schaeffer, Mr JOHN J. STOCKMAN, to Miss MARY A. WEBSTER, all of this co.

2451. (M) On Sunday, by the same, Mr HEINRICK FISCHER, to Miss CHRISTINA SCHWARTZ, both from Germany.

2452. (M) On the 31st ult., by the Rev. Mr Ruthruff, Mr GEORGE GROVER, to Miss MARY ANN WHITE, all of this co.

2453. (D) In Baltimore, at the house of J. R. Kemp, on the morning of the 30th of March, Mr THOMAS WOODROW, a native of Frederick Co., MD., but of later years a resident of N. C. He was a scholar and a mathematician, a few years since he held the office of Surveyor of Frederick Co., in which he was the successor of his father. (Republican)

2454. (D) On Sunday evening, 3rd of April, SARAH C. LUCKETT, eldest daughter of Lloyd Luckett, aged 21.

2455. (D) On Sunday evening, 10th inst., at Oakland, Merryland Tract, after a painful illness, of 6 days, Mrs PRISCILLA ANN DUVALL, relict of the late Samuel Duvall, in the 80th year of her age. Mrs Duvall was remarkable for her charity, and tolerance, and died a member of the Protestant Episcopal Church, to which she had been attached upward of 50 years. She was a native of Prince George's Co., and settled in this co., in 1774 immediately after her marriage.

April 20, 1836 (MHS)

2456. Reform meeting was held in the court house in Frederick on Saturday evening the 16th inst., the following resolutions were adopted. Motion made by MADISON NELSON, Esq., to appoint a committee of 15 persons to represent this District in a County Convention, to be held in Frederick on Thursday the 19th of May next, for the purpose of choosing a delegation to represent this county in a State Reform convention, to be held in Baltimore on the 1st Monday of June next. In pursurance of the resolution; the following were appointed a committee: GIDEON BANTZ, JOHN RIGNEY, PETER H. BROWN, JAMES RAYMOND, MADISON NELSON, WM. OGDEN NILES, WM. H. DAINGERFIELD, JOHN H. WILLIAMS, GEO. W. ENT, FRANCIS BRENGLE, Col. JOHN McPHERSON, EDWARD A. LYNCH, HENRY NIXDORFF, DANIEL KOLB, and WILLIAM J. ROSS. Resolve that the County convention to be held on the 3rd Thursday, being the 19th day of May next, instead of Saturday the 21st of May. On a motion by EDWARD A. LYNCH, that friends of the Reform in several election districts of this county be requested to hold a meeting in their district and appoint committees to attend the county convention.

2457. At a large meeting of the voters of the 2nd Election District of Frederick Co., at the Court House, in Frederick City, on Monday the 18th of April. Meeting was organized by calling GEO. W. ENT, to the chair and to appoint CYRUS MANTZ, Secretary. A bill by the State Ways and Means Committee of the House of Delegates, to make large appropriation to various works of Internal Improvement. Giving the counties and opportunity to express their views. A resolution was called for to take in consideration the propriety of memorializing the legislation in relation to a cross cut canal, from the main stem of the C. & O. Canal through or near Frederick City and West to Baltimore, and that 20 delegates from this District be appointed to attend the convention. The following gentlemen were appointed: G. W. ENT, MOSES WORMAN, GEO. M. EICHELBERGER, WM. M. BEALL, HENRY R. WARFIELD, WM. BRADLEY TYLER, MADISON NELSON, WM. SCHLEY, Dr. JNO.

BALTZELL, EDWARD A. LYNCH, T. C. WORTHINGTON, JOHN H. WILLIAMS, GIDEON BANTZ, JOSEPH M. PALMER, MICHAEL BYRNE, CYRUS MANTZ, JOHN RIGNEY, PETER H. BROWN, JOHN McPHERSON, PATRICK O'NEILL

April 27, 1836 (MHS)

2458. (M) On Tuesday, the 19th inst., by the Rev. S. D. Finckle, Major JOHN REINDOLLAR, to Miss ELIZABETH JONES, second daughter of Thomas Jones, Esq., both of the vicinity of Taney-Town.

2459. (D) At his residence in Gettysburg, on Friday the 16th inst., in the 79th year of his age, ALEXANDER RUSSELL, Esq. The decease left the quiet pursuits of Princeton College at an early age, united himself with the destinies of his country in the battlefield. From this regiment, with the Pennsylvania Line, Commanded by Col. Irvine, into which he first entered. He was commissioned Ensign, and subsequently 1st Lieutenant, in Capt. Alexander's Company, and continue to serve until 1779, having borne his part in battles of Bandywine, White-Horse, Paoli, Germantown, and Monmouth.

May 3, 1836 (MHS)

2460. Col. DAVID CROCKETT, it is stated, is not dead, he was taken up from among the dead and wounded, covered himself with wounds, and taken to a place of safety, where he was slowly recovering.

2461. The Rev. Mr EVERETT, an universalist preacher from Baltimore, will preach at the schoolhouse recently fitted out for that purpose, near Mr MICHAEL GRINDER. One mile from Woodsborough on the road leading to Frederick, on Monday the 8th of May.

2462. (M) On Sunday evening last, by the Rev. John L. Pitts, Mr ELI PHILLER, to Miss MARIA DAYHOFF, both of Frederick.

2463. (M) On Thursday last, by the Rev. David F. Schaeffer, Mr JOSEPH STANDBURY, to Miss ELIZABETH TANEY, all of this co.

2464. (M) On the same day, by the Rev. M. Wachter, Mr JOHN BURRIER, to Miss BARBARA NUSBAUM, all of this co.

2465. (M) On Thursday evening last, by the Rev. Mr Young, Mr JOHN ROHRER, to Miss MARY, daughter of William Baile, Esq., all of this co.

2466. (D) At Richmond, VA., on Friday last, in the 53rd year of his age, Mr JOHN F. COOK, one of the editors of the Richmond Enquirer.
2467. (D) At Washington, on Saturday morning, in the 38th year of his age, FRANCIS G. BLACKFORD, Esq. A native of New York, and for the last 10 years a clerk in the General Post Office. He was standing at the foot of the steps leading to the city post office, when a hog, chased by a dog, ran violently against him, and threw him on his back; when his head came in contact with the curbstone, and received the injury which produced his death.

May 11, 1836 (MHS)

2468. Juriors for the May term of Frederick County Court now in session. Grand Jury: PHILIP ANGELBERGER, JOHN H. BEALL, MALACHI BERNARD, ROBERT BOON, BENJAMIN W. BENNETT, PHILIP BIRELY, WASHINGTON BURGESS, EZRA CRAMER, ADAM CUSTARD, EDWARD A. CROMWELL, JACOB LANDES, ROBERT FLEMING, DANIEL GALLAKER, WILSON HAYS, ABRAHAM KEMP, DANIEL KEMP, WILLIAM PATTERSON, DANIEL ROOT, GEORGE SCHLOSSER, JACOB THOMAS, NICHOLAS WHITMER, JOHN ZIMMERMAN, JACOB ZUMBRUN. Petit Jury: HENRY BAER, HENRY BOWERSOX, THOS. C. BRASHEAR, WILLIAM CRAPSTER, JACOB GROVE, JOHN HANE, THOMAS HOOK, JOHN HYDER, JOHN KEEFAUVER, ADAM KELLER, DAVID KEMP, ABRAHAM LICHTENWALTER, PHLN. S. M'ELFRESH, GEORGE MILLER, WILLIAM MOONEY, ISRAEL NORRIS, PHILIP REICH, JAMES SMITH, JOSEPH SMITH, GEORGE SPALDING, JOHN F. STRASBURGER, GEORGE H. WAESCHE, ABRAHAM WAMPLER, WM. WIRTENBAKER, JOHN M. A. ZOLLICKOFFER.
2469. Meeting of the people of Liberty Town District convened at the house of JOSEPH L. WAGNER, on the 7th of May. According to public notice, for the purpose of considing the subject of Internal Improvement. Mr ABRM. JONES, and Dr. JOHN W. DORSEY, were called to the chair, and Dr. WM. COALE, and JOSEPH SMITH, appointed Secretaries. A committee of 5 were appointed to draft resolutions. Dr. RICHARD DORSEY, A. UNKEFER, Dr. WM COALE, NICHOLAS HOY, and THOMAS HAMMOND. The following persons were appointed to attend the convention to be held in Frederick on Wednesday the 18th inst. Dr. RICHARD DORSEY, JOSEPH SMITH, A. UNKEFER, T. HAM-

MOND, NICHOLAS HOY, Capt. G. DEVILBISS, SURRATT D. WARFIELD, WILLIAM H. POOLE, WILLIAM DUDERAR, WM. A. ALBAUGH, JOHN CLEMSON, Jr., Dr. WM. COALE, R. SIMPSON, and JOHN WOLF.

2470. Meeting of the voters of Woodsboro, the 11th Election District of Frederick Co., was held on Saturday evening the 7th inst. JACOB POE, Esq., was called to the chair, and WILLIAM GRIMES, appointed Secretary. Eight delegates were appointed to attend the convention, the following gentlemen were appointed: NOAH PHILIPS, ELIAS CRUTCHLEY, WILLIAM MILLER, GEORGE M. POTTS, BROOK BAKER, DANIEL KEMP, GEORGE BARRICK, and BENJAMIN NEIDIG.

2471. (D) Near Jefferson, Frederick Co., on the 29th of April 1836, Mr MICHAEL DORSEY, in the 66th year of his age, the deceased left a widow, and 2 sons and 2 daughters.

2472. (D) Near Middletown, MD., on the 19th of April 1836, after a short but distressing illness, Mrs SOPHIA, consort of Mr George McBride, in the 28th year of her age. The deceased left 4 small children and her husband to deplore her loss.

2473. (M) By Charles B. Young, on the 31st ult., Mr WILLIAM SMITH, to Miss MARGARET EURY, both of this co.

2474. (M) By the same, on Thursday the 28th inst., Mr JOHN BAKER, to Miss MARY BAIL, all of Frederick Co.

2475. (M) On the evening of the 5th inst., by the Rev. John L. Pitts, Mr CHRISTIAN CARMACK, to Miss MARY SPRINGER, all of Frederick.

May 18, 1836 (MHS)

2476. The "Everhart Gray's" and "Frederick Volunteers" handsomely equipped military companies of the city, purpose paying a visit to Winchester, VA., on the 25th inst.

2477. Meeting of the Buckeystown voters, Maj. JAMES SIMMONS, was called to the chair, and JONATHAN MANRO, appointed Secretary. The following persons were authorized to draft resolutions on the subject of Reform. ALEXANDER H. BROWN, Maj. H. KEEFER, GEORGE W. BEALL, HENRY KEMP, and A. DELASHMUTT. To draft on Internal Improvement: Dr. JAMES JOHNSON, M. M. MAHONEY, Col. J. COLEGATE, GEO. THOMAS, and ELIAS D. DELASHMUTT. The delegates appointed to the convention are: DANIEL KEMP, Dr. JONATHAN MARROE, Col. JOHN H. SIMMONS, Maj. JAMES SIMMONS, Maj. HENRY KEEFER, JOHN COLEGATE, MARTIN M. MAHONEY, A. H. BROWN,

HENRY KEMP, GEORGE W. BEALL, CHARLES JOHNSON, GEORGE THOMAS, JOHN F. SIMMONS, and RICHARD B. MURDOCK.

2478. The Reform meeting of Middletown was held on the 14th of May, Capt. SAMUEL YOSTE, called to the chair, and Dr. WM. H. CREAGER, appointed Secretary. A committee of 10 was appointed to attend the convention. Capt. SAMUEL YOSTE, Dr. THOMAS SPRINGER, JOHN SIFFORD, CHRISTIAN RAMSBURG, PETER SCHLOSSER, Dr. JACOB BAER, ISRAEL RAMSBURG, DANIEL ROUTZENY, GEORGE BOWLUS, and DANIEL S. BISER.

2479. The Reform meeting of the New Market District, met on Saturday the 14th. DENNIS DORSEY, and JACOB CRONISE, were called to the chair, and Dr. J. W. GEYER, appointed Secretary. The following persons were appointed to attend the convention: WASHINGTON BURGESS, Esq., Dr. E. W. MOBBERLY, PLUMMER IJAMS, HENRY W. DORSEY, GRAFTON HAMMOND, Dr. J. W. GEYER, WILLIAM WERTENBAKER, THOMAS C. SHIPLEY, JACOB CRONISE, DENNIS DORSEY, THOMAS C. BRASHEAR, ARTHUR TANZEY, THOMAS ANDERSON, SINGLETON WOOTON, NATHAN HAMMOND, of O., ENOCH G. FALCONAR, JOHN HILLEARY, Dr. J. H. ANDERSON, ELIAS BOTELER, HENRY SMITH, HAMILTON STIER.

2480. Middletown meeting for the purpose of Internal Improvement was held on the 14th inst. Mr JOHN YOUNG, was called to the chair, and Dr. JACOB BAER, appointed Secretary. The following gentlemen were appointed as delegates to the convention: JOHN YOUNG, JACOB BAER, JOHN SIFFORD, GEORGE BOWLUS, Dr. W. H. CREAGER, JOHN HENRY, of C., DANIEL S. BISER, JOHN McNIEL, ISRAEL RAUSBAYLE, JONAS. SMITH, Dr. THOMAS SPRINGER, JAMES KENNA, GEORGE BLESSING, ADAM KELLER, JOHN SHENDLER, JACOB YOUNG, and JACOB HOOK, of John, DANIEL ROUTZENY, JACOB B. THOMAS, of John, PETER SCHLOSSER.

2481. Union Town District meeting was held on Saturday 7th of May, at the house of JACOB GLAZIER. JACOB GLEIM, Esq., was called to the chair, and WM. ROBERTS, and JOHN ROBERTS, appointed Secretaries. Following persons appointed delegates: JACOB GLIEM, JACOB LANDIS, EVAN McKINSTRY, JOHN M. A. ZOLLICKOFFER, Col. THOS. HOOK, BASIL ROOT, NIMROD FRIZZLE, JESSE SLINGLUFF, Dr. J. L. BILLINGSLEA, JOHN HYDER,

TOBIAS COVER, DAVID FOUTZ, WM. ROBERTS, Col. JAMES C. ATLEE, JOSEPH SWIGART, WM. SHEPHERD, and DAVID SWITZER.

2482. (M) On Thursday last, by the Rev. M. Wachter, Mr MICHAEL FRIEZE, to Miss SUSAN WETZEL, all of this co.

2483. (M) On Thursday last, by the Rev. Daniel Zacharias, Mr CHRISTIAN ZACHARIAS to Miss SARAH PICKING, all of this co.

2484. (M) On Thursday evening the 5th inst., by the Rev. Dr. Schaeffer, Mr FREDERICK MEYEALE, to Miss CATHARINE ROTH.

2485. (M) On the same evening, by the same, Mr PHILIP ATTIG, to Miss MARY KESSLER, all of this city.

2486. (M) On Monday evening last, by the Rev. Dr. David Schaeffer, Mr EDWARD O. GRIM, to Miss AMANDA M. NEILL, all of this city.

2487. (M) Another Patriot Gone - On Monday evening the 4th inst., Mr GEORGE HOLBROOKS, a soldier of the Revolution, in the 93rd year of his age, to Mrs BROILS, aged about 50 years. (Vincennes Sun)

May 25, 1836 (MHS)

2488. (M) On Tuesday the 10th inst., by the Rev. Wm. Butler, Mr DANIEL KELLER, to Miss MARY ANN SUTLER, both of Frederick Co. MD.

2489. (M) On Monday the 16th inst., by the same, Mr SAMUEL BURHMAN, of Frederick Co., MD., to Miss MARY ANN GORDON, of Adams Co., PA.

2490. (M) On Tuesday evening last, by the Rev. Daniel Zacharias, Mr GEORGE A. ROELKE, to Miss MARY ANN TURNER, all of this city.

2491. At a meeting of the delegates of the Reform Convention of Frederick Co., held at Town Hall, on Thursday the 19th of May, was organized by the appointment of GIDEON BANTZ, chairman, and GEORGE W. ENT, and GEORGE BOWLUS, as Assistant Chairman, and WM. H. DANGERFIELD, and WM. J. ROSS, Secretaries. Delegates to attend the Reform Convention to be held in Baltimore in June next, and that said delegation have the power to fill any vacancies which may occur. Buckey's Town: Col. JNO. H. SIMMONS, DANIEL KEMP, HENRY KEMP, JAMES CASTELL, MARTIN M. MAHONEY, Maj. JAMES SIMMONS, HENRY KEEFER, B. A. CUNNINGHAM, JONATHAN MANRO, CHARLES JOHNSON, THOMAS J. DAVIS. Petersville: Col. JOHN

THOMAS, BENEDICT BOONE, ADAM CUSTARD, J. G. MORRISON, SOLOMON BLESSING, Dr. GRAFTON DUVALL, O. HORSEY, RICH'D. JOHNSON, of W., Col. DUNLAP. Jefferson: PATRICK McGILL, Sr., MICHAEL THOMAS, HENRY KELLER, SEBASTIAN RAMSBURGH, EMANUEL THOMAS, WM. COST JOHNSON. Hauvers: GEORGE P. FOX, SOLOMON FORREST, WILLIAM HAYS, GEORGE LONG, J. C. SCHULTZ, GEORGE HARMAN. Frederick: M. E. BARTGIS, WM. H. DAINGERFIELD, HENRY R. WARFIELD, JACOB MARKELL, MADISON NELSON, WM. P. MAULSBY, JAMES RAYMOND, L. P. W. BALCH, GIDEON BANTZ, FRANCIS BRENGLE, SAMUEL TYLER, Col. JOHN McPHERSON, GEORGE W. ENT, E. B. McPHERSON, PETER H. BROWN, JOHN BRUNNER, of J., JOHN RIGNEY, JAMES DIXON, WM. J. ROSS. Westminster: JACOB MATHIAS, ABRAHAM WAMPLER, JOHN FISCHER, NIMROD FRIZLE, CHARLES DEVILBISS, WASHINGTON VAN BIBBER. Union Town: Col. THOMAS HOOK, ISRAEL NORRIS, JOHN ROBERTS, SAMUEL M'KINSTRY, DAVID FOUTZ, MOSES SHAW. Emmittsburg: ISAAC BAUGHER, JOSHUA MOTTER, SAMUEL BAUMGARDNER, Doct. SHIELDS, Major WM. MOONEY, JOSEPH DANNER, JOSEPH TANEY, JOHN HARRIT. Woodsborough: BROOK BAKER, GEORGE SMITH, MASON PARSON, DAVID KEMP, Doct. J. C. LIGGETT, ROB'T. Y. STOKES, JOSPEH WOOD, PAUL CARMACK. Creager's Town: WM. R. JONES, JOHN R. CURTIS, GEORGE BRECKENBAUGH, ZEBULON KUHN, DANIEL WELLER, L. W. GOLDSBOROUGH. Liberty: Col. ANTHONY KIMMEL, Dr. ABDIEL UNKEFER, JOSEPH SMITH, Dr. JOHN W. DORSEY, Dr. WILLIAM COALE, SURATT D. WARFIELD, GEORGE DEVILBISS. Taney Town: JOHN M'KALEB, AB'M. LICHTENWALTER, Dr. GWINN, UPTON SCOTT, Dr. J. SWOPE. Middletown: JOHN SIFFORD, GEORGE BOWLUS, DANIEL S. BISER, ADAM LORENTZ, JACOB HOFFMAN, ADAM KELLER, JOHN HERRING.

June 1, 1836 (MHS)

2492. Appointment by the Governor and Council for the 16th Regiment, in Frederick Co., under the command of Col. JAMES M. SHELMAN.
Maj. CHARLES H. BURKHART - Lieutenant Col.
Vice Lieutenant Col. PRICE, moved from this co.
Capt. WILLIAM SMALL - Major Vice.

Maj. BURKHART - Promoted.
Rv'd. JOHN L. PITTS - Chaplain.
GEORGE SCHLEY - Paymaster.
CHRISTIAN B. ARTZ - Quartermaster.
AFFRABEE P. BEATTY - 1st Lieutenant, in the Everhart Grays.
Vice Lieutenant JACOB FAUBLE, - Resigned.
HENRY RHODES - 2nd Lieutenant, in the Everhart Grays.
Vice Lieutenant BEATTY - Promoted.

2493. (M) On Tuesday last, by the Rev. Daniel Zacharias, Mr JOHN PHEBUS, to Miss ELIZABETH ELLIS, all of this co.

2494. (M) On Tuesday evening last, by the Rev. H. V. Johns, Mr JOSHUA H. MILLER, of Baltimore, to Miss SUSAN S. CRUM, of this city.

2495. (M) On Tuesday the 17th ult., by the Rev. Dr. Reese, Mr UPTON CLEARY, to Miss THEODOSIA WEAVER, all of this vicinity.

2496. (D) In George-Town, on Monday the 2nd inst., Mr WILLIAM JARBOE, for many years a respectable citizen of this co.

June 8, 1836 (MHS)

2497. (D) Departed this mortal life, on Friday last, at his residence in Williamsport, HORATIO McPHERSON, Esq., in the 35th year of his age. His remains were coveyed to the family vault, in the cemetery of the Protestant Episcopal Church, of which he had been a member.

2498. (D) On the 21st ult., in Cumberland Co., PA., Mrs MARGARET HARPER, in the 25th year of her age.

2499. (D) In Louisville, GA., on the 5th of May last, HENRY STEINER SHELMAN, son of the Rev. T. P. C. Shelman, aged 7 months.

2500. Appointment of constables by the Levy Court of Frederick Co., for the year 1836. District #1. JAMES S. SIMMONS, JOHN CAREY, SAMUEL H. HOUSER. District #2. JAMES M. DAYHOFF, DANIEL HALLER, JOHN BENDER, JOHN M. LOWE, JAMES WALLING, JOSHUA DILL, JAMES CARLIN, ROBERT G. RUSSELL, and JOS. S. McGAREY. District #3. JAMES WILLIAMSON, JOHN ALEXANDER, JACOB YOUNG, of D., JOHN H. YOUNG, of H., PETER YOUNG, and ADAM RENNER. District #4. GEORGE KUHN, CYRUS WALKER, ARNOLD R. FAHS, WARNER T. GRIMES, and JOSEPH LIDEY. District #5. SAMUEL DUPHOUR, JOHN MARTIN, and ISAAC WILSON. District #6. HENRY WANTZ, DAVID KEPHART, and JOHN CLABAUGH. District

#7. JACOB FRINGER, WM. CRUMBINE, FREDERICK YINGLING, and JACOB H. KEMP. District #8. DANIEL SWEADNER, DANIEL ROOT, OWEN BURGESS, JOHN WOOD, AARON GOSNELL, and JOEL WOOD. District #9. FREDERICK COVELL, THOMAS INGMAN, WM. HOWARD, LEVI VANFOSSEN, and JONATHAN BROWNING. District #10. HENRY NEED. District #11. JOHN BARRICK, and FREDERICK GRIMES. District #12. ADAM CUSTARD, JOHN G. DABLESTINE, and HENRY BOTELER, of Edw'd. District #13. TOBIAS COVER, and ISAIAH PEARCE. District #14. JACOB B. HALLER, WILLIAM B. TABLER, and JESSE M. LITTLE.

June 15, 1836 (MHS)

2501. (M) On the 31st ult., by the Rev. Charles B. Young, Mr WILLIAM LITZINGER, of Baltimore, to Miss MARY CURTIS, of Liberty Town.
2502. (M) On Thursday the 2nd inst., by the same, Mr JACOB GRINDER, to Miss ANN HAY, both of Frederick Co.
2503. (D) In this city, on the 20th ult., (where he was serving as a jurior,) JOHN MAURIUS AUGUSTUS ZOLLICKOFFER, Esq., at the age of 51 years, 3 months and 10 days. His remains were conveyed to Union-Town, the residence of the deceased, and deposited in the graveyard of the Methodist Protestant Church.
2504. (D) On Wednesday last, the 8th inst., Mrs HANNAH MARGARET ELIZABETH GETZENDANNER, in the 58th year of her age, an old and respectable citizen of this place.
2505. Medical and Chirurgical Faculty of Maryland, met in Baltimore on the 6th of June 1836. They appointed the following persons as censors for Frederick Co. Dr. WM. WILLIS, JEFFERSON SHIELDS, JAS. L. BILLINGSLEA.
2506. Mr BARZILLAI MARRIOTT, late of Anne Arundel Co., has become a partner in the editorial duties of the Times and Democratic Advocate.

June 22, 1836 (MHS)

2507. (M) On Thursday morning last, by the Rev. Daniel Zacharias, Mr JOHN M. KOLB, to Miss CHRISTINNA C. HANE, all of this city.
2508. (M) On the same day, by the Rev. P. Phelps, the Rev. DANIEL NEWEL, of Philadelphia, to Miss ANNALENAH RITCHIE, daughter of the late John Ritchie, Esq., of Frederick City, MD.

2509. (M) On the same, by the same, Mr BENJ. F. REED, to Miss CATHERINE E. PANCOST, all of this city.
2510. (D) At Monte Video, South America, on the 20th of March, Mr WM. FOLTZ, all of this city, in the 21st year of his age. He entered Nassau Hall, Princeton, N. J., he soon developed symptoms of a pulmonary affection thus he left the institution. It was though that a voyage at sea and southern climate would help. He set sail early autumn under the protection of his uncle Mr Valentine Birely, for Rio Janeiro, the capital of Brazil. Staying there for a month his health still declining, the physician there recommended he go to Monte Video. They set sail for Monte Video and landing their a few weeks before his death at Monte Video. The U. S. Consul at that post, Mr John Patrick, Esq., of Baltimore, offered his kindness on this occasion.
2511. A Post office called Bridgeport, has recently been established at Monocacy Bridge, between Emmittsburg and Taney Town.
2512. The Rev. T. W. DORSEY, agent of the Maryland State Temperance Society, will deliver an address on the subject of Temperance, at Linganore Church, on Thursday the 23rd inst., at 11 o'clock, and in Liberty Town, on Friday the 24th, at 11 o'clock.
2513. The Rev. JOSEPH H. JONES, will preach in the Baptist Meeting House next Lord's Day, at 3 o'clock, in the afternoon.
2514. Additional Justices of the Peace for Frederick Co: JOSHUA MOTTER, JACOB MATHIAS, ABRAHAM BAILE, JOHN BROOKE BOYLE, ROBERT BOONE, ADDISON WHITE, HENRY H. HARBAUGH, JOSEPH KEMP.

June 29, 1836 (MHS)

2515. Military Visit - We will be visited on the 4th of July by the Independent Blues of Baltimore, under the command of Captain SPURRIER, and the Highland Blues, of Winchester, VA., under the command of Captain THOMAS ROBERTS.
2516. (M) On the 26th ult., at the residence of Mr Hanson Marlow, by the Rev. Wm. Butler, Mr ENOCH SHIRGLEY, to Miss MARTHA E. MARLOW, all of Frederick Co.
2517. (D) Departed this life, on the Merryland Tract, on the 20th inst., WILLIAM WILCOXON, Jr., aged 19 years, 1 month and 3 days.

July 6, 1836 (MHS)

2518. (M) On Tuesday the 21st ult., by the Rev. Dr. John Reese, Dr. THOS. SIM, to Miss MARY C. WAGNER, both of Woodsborough, Frederick Co., MD.

2519. (M) On Wednesday the 15th of June, by the Rev. Dr. John S. Reese, ELIAS SCHOLL, to Miss MARY ANN DUDEROW, both of Frederick Co.

2520. Dr. REESE, will deliver an address at the Sabbath School, at Retreat School House, on the Sabbath next, at 3 o'clock.

2521. Accident - Whilst a very heavy cloud was passing over this place on Wednesday evening last, one of the flashes of lightning discharge from it, struck a house in the West end of Patrick Street. Knocking the chimney down, and severely, although not fatally injuring Mrs LEAB, an old lady residing in the house. We are informed that she and her daughter were on the garret at the time the lightning struck, and was not injured. (Citizen)

July 13, 1836 (MHS)

2522. The Whig voters of the 2nd Election District of Frederick Co., was held at the Court House, in this place, on Saturday evening last the 9th inst. On a motion, DANIEL KOLB Esq., (Mayor of this city,) was called to the chair, and Col. JOHN M. SHELMAN, was appointed Secretary. Several resolutions were submitted by Gen. THOMAS C. WORTHINGTON, and adopted. One called for the chair to appoint 25 delegates to meet at a general convention, in this city on the 6th of August next, and also a Committee of Correspondence, to consist of 15 persons, and a Committee of Vigilance, to act as a committee for the District. The Nominating Committee: THOMAS C. WORTHINGTON, MOSES WORMAN, WILLIAM SCHLEY, CHARLES H. BURKHART, GEORGE WACHTER, LEWIS BIRELY, JACOB FAUBEL, PHILIP ROHR, WILLIAM WHITE, FRANCIS BRENGLE, CHARLES A. GAMBRILL, WM. S. McPHERSON, Dr. WILLIAM WATERS, WILLIAM DURBIN, JOHN H. WILLIAMS, JAMES M. SHELMAN, GIDEON BANTZ, GEORGE GITTINGER, WILLIAM J. ROSS, JAMES RAYMOND, JACOB LITTLE, FREDERICK NUSZ, PATRICK O'NEIL, DANIEL GETZENDANNER, GEORGE ADAM EBERT. Correspondence Committee: RICHARD POTTS, GEO. M. EICHELBERGER, CYRUS MANTZ, MAHLON TALBOTT, HENRY R. WARFIELD, LAWRENCE J. BRENGLE, JOHN MILLER, AB'M. KEMP, Dr. WM. B. TYLER,

PATRICK TORMEY, EDWARD TRAIL, JAMES M. COALE, Dr. E. T. GOLDSBOROUGH, GEORGE M. CONRADT, GEORGE RICE. Committee of Vigilance: GEORGE BALTZELL, WM. R. SANDERSON, NICHOLAS H. PITTS, WILLIAM LEASE, WM. C. SMALLWOOD, L. P. W. BALCH, JOHN J. STEINER, JOHN H. BEALL, Dr. JOHN BALTZELL, MOUNTJOY B. LUCKETT, JOHN MARKELL, JAMES WHITEHILL, JAMES CARLIN, GEORGE WEBSTER, EDWARD A. LYNCH, CHARLES DEBUTS, WM. D. JENKS, JOHN McDONALD, GEORGE SCHLEY, JAMES BRUNNER, VAL. J. BRUNNER, ABRAHAM F. SHRIVER, JOHN M. LOWE, WILLIAM C. HOFFMAN, EZRA DOLL, CHARLES WILSON, SAMUEL FLEMING, GEORGE FISCHER, JOSEPH SMITH, EDWARD GAITHER, EZRA DOUB, JOHN HANSHEW, FREDERICK KLINE, BENJAMIN RUTHERFORD, HENRY SMITH, JOHN HANE, GREENBURY FOUT, PETER NICHOLS, VALENTINE ADAMS, JOHN ENGELBRECHT, FREDERICK HAWMAN, ELI MOBERLY, PHILIP HALLER, ROBERT BOON, JACOB DADISMAN, AQUILLA TULLY, GEORGE LARE, HENRY STEINER, JAMES W. PRYOR, Dr. THOS. A. FLEMING, JAMES M. DAYHOFF.

2523. The Rev. GEORGE C. M'CUNE, of the Universalist Church, will preach at the school house, adjacent to Mr M. Grinder's, near Woodsboro, Frederick Co., MD., on Sunday morning next, 17th inst., at 10 o'clock, A. M.

2524. (D) On Friday the 18th of July, at her residence in Frederick, Mrs REBECCA JOHNSON, widow of Thomas Johnson, of James, and daughter of Governor Thomas Johnson, deceased. But 10 days ago she was called to sympathize and mourn with her daughter the loss of a grandchild; ANN CAMPBELL GRAHAM.

July 20, 1836 (MHS)

2525. The Rev. JOSEPH H. JONES, will preach in the Baptist Meeting House, on next Saturday evening, at early candlelight.

2526. (D) On Friday the 18th inst., CATHERINE DAVIS, infant daughter of Dr. Albert Ritchie, aged 2 months.

2527. (D) At Bolivar, Tuscarawas Co., Ohio, on the 25th of June, in the 26th year of his age, RICHARD JOHNSON, son of Richard Johnson, formerly a resident of Frederick Co.

2528. (D) At his residence in Louisville, GA., on Friday the 10th inst., Dr. AUGUSTUS D. SHELMAN, in the 31st year of his age, leaving a wife and 4 nteresting children. Dr. Shelman, was surgeon of the GA., Battalion of Cavalry, commanded by Maj. Douglass, served his company during the last campaign in Fla., and it is supposed contracted the fatal disease, in consequence of the exposure and privations included in the sickly region of the Country. He is the 5th of a gallant company from Jefferson, who has died since the campaign commenced, and the 3rd since the company returned here.

July 27, 1836 (MHS)

2529. (D) On the 17th inst., at his residence near Middletown, WILLIAM MOTTER, in the 40th year of his age.

August 8, 1836 (MHS)

2530. The VAN BUREN, convention which assembled in this place on Saturday last, made the following nominations. For Elector of the Senate: WM. M. BEALL, and JOHN FISHER, Esqrs. For Delegates to the Assembly: JOHN SIFFORD, HENRY KEEFER, ISAAC SHRIVER, and J. W. GEYER, of these 6, 3 are bank officers.

2531. Appointments for the 29th Regiment, Frederick County. Captain: WILLIAM JONES. 1st Lieutenant: JOSEPH WILHIDE. 2nd Lieutenant: CHARLES GILPIN, of the Mechanicstown Guard. EDWARD CROMWELL, Justice of the Peace. ROBERT ANNAN, one of the Justices of the 5th District Court of Frederick Co. Vice: BAUMGARDNER, declined.

2532. (M) On the 19th of July, by the Rev. Dr. Schaeffer, Mr ABRAHAM SAUM, to Miss ELEANOR SONNENSTEIN.

2533. (M) On the 21st, by the same, HUGH W. IRWINE, Esq., to Miss MARY C. WISE, of VA.

2534. (D) On the 26th inst., near the Glade, Mrs SUSAN REINHART, relict of Geo. Reinhart, deceased, after the short illness of a few days, aged about 56 years.

August 10, 1836 (MHS)

2535. (M) On Tuesday the 2nd inst., by the Rev. Mr Reese, FRANCIS BRENGLE, Esq., to Miss MARIA DOWNEY, eldest daughter of the late William Downey, Esq., all of Frederick Co.

2536. (D) On Wednesday afternoon last, Mr FREDERICK STEINER, by a discharge of electricity.

2537. (D) On Wednesday evening last, of a pulmonary disease,

Miss MARY LYON, daughter of Dr. Isaac Lyon, in the 20th year of her age.

2538. (D) On Wednesday evening last, in this city, after a short illness, Mrs SARAH BEATTY, in the 59th year of her age.

2539. (D) In this city, on Monday last, EDWARD WEAVER, in the 32nd year of his age.

2540. (D) On the 8th inst., at his residence near Woodsborough, Frederick Co., MD., ROBERT FULTON, Esq., aged 67 years.

2541. The members of the Central Reform Committee for Frederick County: GEORGE BALTZELL, LEWIS BIRELY, GIDEON BANTZ, VALENTINE J. BRUNNER, JOHN H. BEALL, LEWIS A. BRENGLE, FRANCIS BRENGLE, JONATHAN BRUNNER, WM. COOKERLY, JAMES M. COALE, DAVID B. DEVITT, WM. DURBIN, G. M. EICHELBERGER, GREENBURY FOUT, JACOB FAUBEL, JONA. GETZENDANNER, DANIEL GETZENDANNER, GEORGE GITTINGER, JOHN HANSHEW, EZEKIEL HUGHES WM. D. JENKS, ABRAHAM KEMP, DAVID KEMP, GEORGE KOONTZ, DANIEL KOLB, EDWARD A. LYNCH, MOUNTJOY B. LUCKETT, JACOB LITTLE, ELI MOBBERLY, JOHN MILLER, CYRUS MANTZ, ISRAEL MYERS, WM. S. McPHERSON, PATRICK O'NEILL, RICHARD POTTS, JAMES M. PRYOR, NICHOLAS H. PITTS, GEORGE RICE, BENJ. RUTHERFORD, JAMES RAYMOND, WM. J. ROSS, PHILIP ROHR, WM. R. SANDERSON, WM. C. SMALLWOOD, JAMES M. SHELMAN, WM. SCHLEY, HENRY SMITH, WM. BRADLEY TYLER, THOS. C. WORTHINGTON, WM. WATERS, JOHN H. WILLIAMS, MOSES WORMAN.

August 17, 1836 (MHS)

2542. The Van Buren, convention assembled in this place on Saturday, they nominated: CASPAR QUYNN, Esq., of this city, one of the candidates for Electors of the Senate, instead of WM. M. BEALL, who declines serving.

2543. The Rev. JOSEPH H. JONES, will preach in the Baptist Meeting House, on next Lord's Day, at 3 o'clock, P. M.

2544. (M) On the 4th inst., by the Rev. Dr. Schaeffer, Mr JACOB GROSSNICKLE, to Miss ELIZABETH HOUSE, all of this co.

2545. (D) On the 12th inst., at the residence of his father, near Popular Springs, Dr THEODORE K. MILLER, in the 37th year of his age.

August 24, 1836 (MHS)

2546. Election to take place on the 1st Monday in September, for

Frederick Co., for Elector of the Senate of Maryland. EVAN McKINSTRY, GIDEON BANTZ. For Montgomery Co: HENRY HARDING, EPHRAIM GAITHER.

2547. (F) The barn of Mrs ELIZABETH HILLERY, about 6 miles West of Frederick, was consumed by fire on Monday evening last between 9 and 10 o'clock. There was a quantity of grain and hay in the barn. It is suspected to be the deed of an incendiary from the fact and the fire being observed simultaneously in 3 distinct parts of the barn.

2548. (M) On Sunday morning last, by the Rev. Dr. Schaeffer, JOHN P. JEFFERY, Esq., to Miss LOUISA GARDINIER. all of this city.

2549. At a meeting held in the court house, in Frederick, on the 22nd day of August, on the subject of the monument to be erected to the memory of Washington. RICHARD POTTS, Esq., was called to the chair, Col. GEO. M. EICHELBERGER, appointed assistant chairman, and JAMES M. SHELMAN, Secretary, on motion of WM. P. MAULSBY, Esq., Resolve; that this meeting approve the design of erecting to the memory of Washington, a monument as a memorial of nation's gratitude, and recommended Mr STEVENSON, the agent of the National Monument Society.

August 31, 1836 (MHS)

2550. (M) On the 17th inst., by the Rev. Mr Burges, of Hartford, FREEMAN CONVERSE, Esq., principal of Frederick College, MD., to Miss EMILY MILLER, daughter of Giles Miller, Esq., of Middletown, Conn.

2551. (D) In this city, on Thursday last, after a lingering illness, Mr FREDERICK STONER, son of Mr Frederick Stoner, whose death by lightning was recorded but a few weeks since. He was in the 28th year of his age.

September 7, 1836 (MHS)

2552. (F) The barn of DAVID DUDDERAR, Esq., about 3 miles below Liberty was burnt to the ground on Thursday evening. The barn was valuable and contained at thrashing mill, chopping mill, all the grain and the chief part of the hay of Mr D. Two negros have been committed on suspicion of having set the barn fire.

2553. (D) At his residence on Owing Creek, near Graceham, in this co., on Friday last, Mr CHRISTIAN HOOVER, in the 58th year of his age. Mr Hoover's decease was congestion of

the brain. He was taken suddenly and violently ill on Monday night the 22nd ult.
2254. (D) On the 24th ult., Mrs ELIZABETH KEMP, wife of Mr Peter Kemp, aged 31 years.

September 14, 1836 (MHS)

2555. Election results: Van Buren - FISHER - 3,144, QUYNN - 3,168. Whig - BANTZ - 2,658, McKINSTRY - 2,647.

September 21, 1836 (MHS)

2556. (F) Another fire - The barn of Mr JOHN FIESTER, was burnt to the ground on Friday evening last, a large quantity of grain &c, was consumed with the barn.
2557. (M) On Thursday evening last, in New Market, by the Rev. John L. Pitts, THOMAS J. JOHNSON, Esq., to Miss JULIA ANN OGLE, all of this co.
2558. (M) On Thursday last, by the Rev. Mr Geiger, Mr G. W. SLINGLUFF, of Dover, Ohio, to Miss MARY SHRIVER, eldest daughter of Col. Jacob Shriver, of Fred'k, MD.
2559. (M) On same day, by the Rev. Dr. Reese, Dr. JOSEPH SLINGLUFF, of Dover, Ohio, to Miss ELIZABETH JONES, daughter of Abraham Jones, Esq., of Liberty Fred'k. Co., MD.
2560. (D) At his residence, near Burketsville, on the 9th inst., Mr JOHN SLIFER, Sen., after an illness of 9 days, aged 68 years, 8 months and 28 days, was worthy farmer of this co.
2561. (D) On Thursday last at Staten Island, AARON BURR, in the 81st year of his age.
2562. (D) On Saturday night the 17th inst., of congestive fever, HENRY MONTAGUE, infant son of Henry Montell, Esq., of this co.

October 5, 1836 (MHS)

2563. (M) On the 30th last month, by the Rev. Dr. Schaeffer, Mr LAWRENCE GOSZ, of Baltimore, to Miss ANNA MAGDALENA LEILICH, of this city.
2564. (M) On Thursday evening last, by the same, Mr JOSEPH LEONARD, to Miss CATHARINE MARTIN, all of this co.
2565. (D) On Friday the 30th of September at Baltimore, Mrs CATHARINE E. W. DUCKETT, wife of Thomas Duckett, Esq., of Annapolis and only daughter of the late Wm. Goldsborough, of Frederick Town. She was returning from a visit to her friend in Frederick Co., where she contracted the disease.

October 12, 1836 (MHS)

2566. General HARRISON, arrived in this city on yesterday evening.
2567. Election returns. Whigs for the Assembly: DOUB - 3,092, BOWLUS - 3,093, BRENGLE - 3,103, MATTHIAS - 2,821. Van Burens for the Assembly: SIFFORD - 197, SHRIVER - 171, KEEFER - 197, GEYER - 197. For Sheriff: GURLEY - 2,643, HOUCK - 2,344, CAMPBELL - 1,285, PARSONS - 262, BAUMGARTNER - 1,207, HARRITT - 376, HOWARD - 196, WATERS - 1,373.
2568. The Rev. JOSEPH H. JONES, will preach in the Baptist Meeting House, next Lord's Day, at 3 o'clock, in the afternoon.
2569. The Rev. G. C. McCUNE, a universalist from Baltimore, will preach in Jefferson, on the 4th Sunday, and 23rd day of October inst., at 3 o'clock, P.M.

October 19, 1836 (MHS)

2570. NEILSON POE, Esq., is now the sole editor of and proprietor of the Baltimore Chronicle.
2571. The house of Dr. JOHN BALTZELL, of this city was entered on Monday evening last by some rogues for the purpose of robbing. They entered the cellar and found their way thenced into the 1st story of the building. Here they broke the lock of a sideboard one rifled it of its contends, and deposit this, with other valuables plunder in a basket, near the street door, which they opened. Not yet satisfied they proceeded up stairs, where the light they carried shinning through the keyhole of a chamber door attracted the attention of the inmates, who, supposing that the sickness of some member of the family had occasioned this unreasonable stir, came to the door. The thieves, in fulfilment of the old proverb, precipitately fled although no one pursued them, leaving all their plunder, and probably more frighten than the family whose repose they distrubed.
2572. (M) On Tuesday the 27th day of September last, by the Rev. Mr Hickey, Mr ALEXANDER SHORB, of Adams Co., PA., to Miss MARY ANN WISE, daughter of Mr John Wise, of Emmittsburg.
2573. (M) On Sunday evening the 9th inst., near Burkettsville, by the Rev. Michael Wachter, Mr GEORGE POTTER, to Miss ARABELLA OHR, both of this co.
2574. (M) On Tuesday evening the 11th inst., by the Rev. John

McElroy, Mr HENRY CONNER, to Miss MARGARET McGLENNEN.

2575. (M) On last Monday evening, by the Rev. Joseph H. Jones, Mr NOAH WHITMORE, to Miss MARY BRIETENBAUGH, of Harpers Ferry.

October 26, 1836 (MHS)

2576. The Whig voters of Liberty District will meet at the Tavern of JOSEPH L. WAGNER, in Liberty, on Saturday week at 2 o'clock, P.M., an addresses are expected.

November 2, 1836 (MHS)

2577. (D) On the 17th ult., MARK BISHOP, Sen., in the 60th year of his age.

2578. The Whig voters of Middletown District will meet at the Middletown Academy on Saturday next at 2 o'clock, P.M.

November 16, 1836 (MHS)

2579. (D) On the 29th of October, in the 46th year of his age, LLOYD LUCKETT, leaving a widow and 7 children.

November 23, 1836 (MHS)

2580. The following gentlemen are appointed Justices of the Levy Court of Frederick County: WILLIAM DUDDERER, MARTIN EICHELBERGER, SOLOMON FORREST, JAMES L. HIGGINS, WILLIAM LYNCH, WILLIAM MILLER, JEREMIAH MORRISON, EVAN McKINSTRY, THOMAS SPRINGER, JAMES SIMMONS, JAMES SMITH, FREDERICK TROXELL, ABRAHAM WAMPLER, MOSES WORMAN.

2581. (M) On Tuesday the 15th inst., by the Rev. George Flautt, Mr ANDREW WELTY, to Miss REBECCA BLACK, both of Emmittsburg.

2582. (M) On Tuesday evening last, near Middletown, by the Rev. M. Wachter, Mr SAMUEL D. RIDDLEMOSER, to Miss ELIZABETH C. MAGRUDER, both of this co.

2583. (M) On Tuesday evening by the Rev. Dr. Schaeffer, Mr WILLIAM WAGNER, to Miss ADELINE WENSICK, all of this co.

2584. (M) On Thursday evening by the same, JONATHAN KERSHNER, Esq., of Washington Co., to Miss CATHERINE McGAHIN, of this co.

2585. (M) On Tuesday morning last, by the Rev. Daniel Zacharias, Mr JOSEPH BEVAN, of Baltimore, to Miss SARAH C. FISCHER, of this city.

2586. (D) Mr JAMES H. McCULLOCH, the Collector of the Port of Baltimore, he died at his residence on the borders of this city. On Thursday evening after an illness of a few days. He was a disciple of Washington, a true friend of this country, and one of the bravest defenders in the Revolution, as well as the Battle of N. Point, where he was a volunteer, and had his leg shattered and broken by a shot from the enemy.

2587. (D) Departed this life, at his residence in Fort Bull, Ohio, on the night of the 9th inst., Doct. ROBERT C. J. CARY, aged 35 years, 11 months and 20 days, formerly of this city.

2588. (D) Departed this transitory existence in New Market, on Tuesday the 15th inst., CHARLES B. Y. DAY, son of E. G. Day, in the 3rd year of his age.

November 30, 1836 (MHS)

2589. The following officers have arrived and taken rooms at Talbott's City Hotel. Major General MACOMB, and SCOTT, Brigadier General ATKINSON, General SANFORD, Colonel BANKHEAD, and KENAN, and LINDSAY, Major HUSON, Captain COOPER, and McCALL, and HITCHCOCK, and GREEN, and DAMMOCK, and LEE. NEWCOMB, resigned, formerly U. S. A.

2590. (M) At Hillsborough, Ohio, Thursday the 17th inst., by the Rev. Henry Defenbaugh, Mr JACOB M. STRAEFFER, of Cincinnati, formerly of Frederick Town, MD., to Miss REBECCA CALEY, daughter of George Caley, Esq., of the first mentioned place.

December 7, 1836 (MHS)

2591. The following officers have arrived since Saturday, at Talbott's City Hotel: Brigadier General EUSTIS, Major KIRBY, and GRAHAM, Captain THORNSTON, Lieutenant ALEXANDER, Aid to General ATKINSON.

2592. (D) At his residence on Big Pipe Creek, Frederick Co., MD., on Thursday the 24th ult., Mr DAVID KEPHART, in the 74th year of his age.

2593. (D) In Frederick, on Thursday last, Mrs NUSZ, mother of Frederick Nusz, of this place.

2594. Free School meeting - At a meeting of the citizens of New Market District, held at JOHN STEVENS, Tavern. MICHAEL LEASE, was called to the chair, and GEORGE HUGHES, appointed Secretary. Following gentlemen were appointed delegates to attend the Free School convention, to be held in Frederick, on the 10th: WILLIAM WERTENBAKER, PLUMMER IJAMS, JACOB CRONISE, WM. MORSELL, JOHN WOOD, MICHAEL LEASE, Dr. E. W. MOBBERLY, Capt. GEO. RINER, LEBRUS GRIFFITH, THOMAS BRASHEAR, WASHINGTON BURGESS, Dr. J. W. GEYER, JONATHAN BROWNING, ABEL RUSSELL, JOHN ROADRUCK, SAMUEL CANBY, HENRY SMITH.

2595. Meeting of the Creagers Town District was held at Mr Breckenbaugh's Hotel, on Saturday 3rd of December. Mr JOSHUA DELAPLANE, called to the chair, and WM. R. PITTENGER, Esq., appointed Secretary. A resolution was passed, calling for a committee of 7 persons to attend the "Free School Convention for Frederick Co.," to be held in Frederick on the 10th of December inst. JOSHUA DELAPLANE, Captain WM. P. JONES, WILLIAM TODD, WILLIAM BIGGS, JOHN CURTIS, GEORGE BRECKENBAUGH, and Dr. L. W. GOLDSBOROUGH.

December 14, 1836 (MHS)

2596. (M) ISAAC MOTTER, of Williamsport, formerly of Emmittsburg, and son of Lewis Motter, to MARY A., daughter of Joseph Snively, of Franklin Co., PA.

2597. (D) On the 26th ult., LOUISA, daughter of Mr Edward McPherson, in the 6th year of her age.

2598. Members of the jurors for the December term of Frederick County Court now in session. Grand: JACOB POE, BASIL HEYDEN, FRANCIS MATTHIAS, ISAAC SHRIVER, JOHN H. WORTHINGTON, SAMUEL WILHIDE, GEO. THOMAS, FELIX B. TANEY, JOHN GROSHON, JOHN A. BAKER, JOSEPH C. SCHULTZ, TOBIAS COVER, MASON PARSONS, CHRISTIAN KEMP, GEORGE WACHTER, NIMROD FRIZZLE, GEO. SMITH, WILLIAM FISHER, NICHOLAS NORRIS, GEORGE HOSKINS, JOHN JONES, ABDIEL UNKEFER, CHRISTOPHER MICHAEL. Petite: JOHN ADELSPERGER, DANIEL S. BISER, BENEDICT BOONE, JAMES CASTLE, CHARLES DEVILBISS, DAVID FOUTZ, JOHN FINK, ELIAS GROSHON, ELIAS GRIMES, THOMAS HAMMOND, WILSON HAYS, MICHAEL MORELOCK, EDWARD McBRIDE, JOHN POUDER, JOSEPH PAYNE, JOHN SIFFORD, SAMUEL SWOPE, WM. R. SANDERSON, JOHN SMITH, GEO. TITLOW, WM. J. THOMPSON, JACOB TRAGER, JOSEPH WELTY, CH'S. WORTHINGTON, WM. WERTENBAKER.

December 21, 1836 (MHS)
2599. Appointment by the Governor: GEO. KUHN, Captain of the Graceham Sentinels, WM. M. BRECKENBAUGH, 1st Lieutenant, JOHN WELLER, 2nd Lieutenant.
2600. (M) On Sunday evening, at Talbott's City Hotel, by the Rev. John L. Pitts, WILLIAM HICKS, Esq., to Miss MARY AVIS, both of Charlestown, VA.
2601. (M) Near Union Town, by the Rev. Daniel Zollickoffer, on Thursday 15th, JOHN Y. SHAER, Esq., to Miss RACHEL A. N. DEVILBISS, both of this co.
2602. (D) At his residence, in Burkettsville, on Wednesday the 7th inst., in the 70th year of his age, Mr HENRY BURKETT, after a long and severe illness, he was the founder of the village bearing his name, and had resided there for the last 40 years.
2603. (D) At his residence, in Jefferson, Frederick Co., on Tuesday the 14th inst., in the 65th year of his age, GEORGE HOFFMAN, for the last 45 years of his life an active and efficient member of the Methodist Episcopal Church.
2604. (D) In this city, on Monday the 12th inst., Miss ROSANNA HUGHES.

1837

January 4, 1837 (MHS)
2605. A protracted meeting under the direction of the Rev. JOHN WINEBRENNER, commencing on Saturday evening next, will be held in the Baptist Meeting House, of this city.

January 11, 1837 (MHS)
2606. The Rev. D. F. SCHAEFFER, will preach on Sunday next in the Baptist Church, and administered the sacraments in German and English, he will also preach on the Saturday previous, commencing on both days at 10 A.M.
2607. Divine service by the Rev. S. W. HARKEY, may be expected in the Lutheran Church on Friday evening next at candle-light.
2608. At a meeting of the citizens of District #5., in Frederick Co., was held at the house of Mr ISAAC HAHN, in the town of Emmittsburgh, ROBERT ANNAN, Esq., was called to the chair, and appointing SAMUEL BAUMGARDNER, Esq.,

Secretary. The following list of delegates to meet the Free School Convention, in Frederick Town, on the 9th of January 1837. ISAAC BAUGHER, JEFFERSON SHIELDS, THOMAS HAYS, JOSEPH WELTY, WILLIAM KOONTZ, JOHN STEWART, ROBERT ANNAN, SAMUEL BAUMGARDNER, and MICHAEL C. ADLESPERGER.

2609. At a meeting of the citizens of the Hauver's District, at HENRY NEED's Tavern, on Saturday, 31st of December, 1836. Mr JACOB POORMAN, was called to the chair, and JOSEPH WISE, appointed Secretary. The following list of gentlemen to attend the Free School Convention for Frederick Co., to be held in Frederick, on the 9th of January inst. MICHAEL SWOPE, WILSON HAYS, SOLOMON FOREST, HENRY HARBAUGH, PETER STEIN, Esqrs., and Captain GEORGE ZOLLINGER.

2610. (M) On Tuesday evening, the 27th ult., by the Rev. David F. Schaeffer, Mr SAMUEL ZIMMERMAN, to Miss SUSAN GREENWALD, both of this co.

2611. (M) On the 29th ult., by the same, Mr JAMES NICKUM, to Miss EMELINE JONES, all of this co.

2612. (M) On Thursday last, near New Market, by the Rev. John L. Pitts, Mr. JOSHUA SHIPLEY, to Miss MARGARET SPONSELLER, all of this co.

2613. (M) Matrimonial Tydings - On Tuesday evening last, by the Rev. Mr Poisal, Mr JOSEPH TYDINGS, of Anne Arundel Co., to Miss SARAH TYDINGS, of Annapolis.

2614. (M) Strange doing in Ill. - The following announcement is from Galena (Ill) Gazette, of Dec., 3rd. "Married by the Rev. Mr Weigley, on the 24th of November, Mr ASAHEL BULL, to Miss LYDIA ISLER, all of Small Pox."

2615. (D) Departed this life on the morning of the 27th ult., at his residence near Frederick, JACOB BRENGLE, in the 63rd year of his age.

2616. (D) At his residence, in the neighborohood of Buckey's Town, on Wednesday last, after a short illness, Mr GEORGE KESSLER, an aged and highly esteemed citizen of this co.

2617. (D) Departed this life, on the 28th ult., in the 5th year of her age, MARTHA JANE BEAM, third daughter of Robert M. Beam, of Clarksburg, Montgomery Co., MD.

2618. (D) In this city, on Friday December 3rd ult., Mrs MARIA SMALL, consort of Captain Wm. Small, of this town, in the 30th year of her age.

2619. (D) In this city, on Tuesday after last, CHARLTON HUNT, Esq., aged about 35, death was due to scarlett fever. He was attacked by the malady on Sunday evening the 18th inst. Mr Hunt was born in Lexington, in the year 1801, completed his academical studies at Transylvania University, and graduated in 1821. He studied law in Frederick, MD., with the Hon. R. B. Taney, present Chief Justice of U. S. He set up practice in Paris KY., where he resided until 1825, when he moved to Lexington, and became a member of the Fayette Bar. As a speaker, he was bold, ardent and impassioned and in debate, frequently sarcastic and severe, but all ways respectful to his opponent. In 1835' 36, he was solicited to become a candidate for the Legislature, which he declined.

January 18, 1837 (MHS)

2620. (M) On Thursday the 24th of November last, at Talbott's Hotel, by the Rev. Daniel Zollickoffer, JOHN SWITZER, Esq., to Miss ELIZABETH WOLF, daughter of Abraham Wolf, Esq., of Sam's Creek.
2621. (M) On Thursday morning last, by the Rev. John L. Pitts, Mr REUBEN OSLOR, to Miss CATHARINE GILBERT, both of Mechanics-Town.
2622. (D) On Friday morning the 16th inst., JAMES HENRY, son of James and Harriet Ogle, in the 3rd year of his age.
2623. (D) At Saint Mary's College, Baltimore, on the 12th of January, in the 29th year of his age, the Rev. JOHN H. HOSKYNS, A. M., Vice President of that institution.
2624. The Rev. S. W. HARKEY, may be expected to preach in the Lutheran Church, on Sunday next at 3 o'clock, P.M.
2625. SANTA ANNA, arrived in this place, yesterday, and took lodging at the hotel of Mr Roberts.

January 25, 1837 (MHS)

2626. (M) On Wednesday last, by the Rev. Jacob Reinhart, Mr JACOB BAER, of Frederick Co., to Miss SARAH FUNK, of Washington Co., MD.
2627. (M) On Thursday evening last, by the Rev. D. Zacharias, Mr HENRY HOUCK, to Miss MARY C. BRENGLE.
2628. (M) On Thursday last, by the Rev. Dr. Schaff, Mr ADAM RITCHIE, to Mrs ANN ULERICK, all of this city.
2629. (M) On the same day, by the same, ISAAC LONG, Esq., to Miss REBECCA LINGANFELTER, all of this co.

2630. (D) On Friday last, Mrs ELIZABETH SCHAEFFER, daughter of G. Krebs, Esq., late of Philadelphia, and consort of the Rev. Dr. Schaeffer, of this city, after a long and tedious illness, she leaves an affectionate husband and 6 children.

2631. Mr JACOB FAUBLE, as candidate for the Common Council, for Ward #1. GEORGE SOLOMON, for Ward #7.

February 1, 1837 (MHS)

2632. Aurora Borealis - This phenominon appeared with great splender on Wednesday evening last, an arch of brilliant, red light gradually formed across the Northern heavens, quickly changing its appearances and position. The light was so vivid as to give a reddish hase to the snow with which the ground was covered.

2633. A court martial will speedily assemble at Frederick, for the purpose of trying Major GATES, who was lately dismissed from the Army, and reinstated by the President.

2634. The Washington Hose Company, of Ward #2., met on Saturday evening the 28th ult., the following officers were elected for the present month. President - GEO. W. ENT, Secretary - P. L. STORM, Treasurer - CYRUS MANTZ. Directors - WM. SMALL, VALENTINE BIRELY, HENRY HANSHEW. Engineer: DAVID B. DEVITT. Principal Engineer: EZRA BANTZ. Assistant Engineer: GEO. McCAHAN. Hosemen: WM. H. RIGNEY, EZRA HOFFMAN, PHILIP J. HAWMAN, WM. REICH, NICHOLAS KEEFER, HENRY N. TRICE, ZEPHENIAH HARRISON, ABRAHAM HOOPER. Lanemen: GEORGE C. GELWICKS, EZRA DILL, CHAS. A. GAMBRILL, PETER STOFFEL, RICHARD HARPER, WM. M. KEMP, CYRUS MANTZ. Property Guard: JOHN RIGNEY, JACOB KELLER, GEORGE W. ENT, JOHN SHOLL, JOHN C. FRITCHIE. Bagmen: JOHN HOOPER, ALEXANDER TRUSCOTT, JOHN BALDERSON, DAVID HANE, CHRISTIAN STEDDING. Laddermen: JACOB LEIDIG, GEORGE MOORE, RICHARD BLOWERS, JACOB HALLER, HENRY STEINER, WM. COOKERLY. Hookmen: JOHN KUNKEL, PHILIP HALLER, WM. C. COLE, JAMES CARLIN, NIMROD BANTZ, LEWIS STEIN. Axmen: JACOB LITTLE, CHARLES GETZENDANNER.

2635. Candidates for the Common Council: Ward #1. Mr CASPER KLEIN, and Mr WILCOXON. Ward #2. GEORGE MOORE. Ward #3. GEORGE HAUER. Ward #5. HIRAM KEEFER, and MICHAEL HALLER. Ward #6. GEORGE

HOSKINS, and DAVID J. MARKEY. Ward #7. GEORGE SALMON, WILLIAM KOLB, and WILLIAM ELY.

2636. The Rev. Dr. SCHAFF, will preach and administer the Lord's Supper, in the Baptist Church, on Sunday next at 10 o'clock, A.M., in both languages.

2637. The Rev. JOSEPH H. JONES, will preach in the Baptist Meeting House, on next Lord's Day at 3 o'clock, P.M.

February 8, 1837 (MHS)

2638. The Independent Hose Company officers for the ensuing year: President: CASPAR QUYNN. Vice President: EZRA BANTZ. Secretary: D. J. MARKEY. Treasurer: GIDEON BANTZ. Principal Engineer: HENRY RHODES. DANIEL HALLER, Assistant Engineer. JOHN HENSHAW, Engine Director. EZRA BENTZ, Pipe Director. G. J. FISCHER, Hose Director. CASPAR QUYNN, Lane Director. EZRA M. GAMBER, JOHN RHODES, Ax-men. DAVID J. MARKEY, HENRY YOUNG, Laddermen. SAM'L. CARMACK, GIDEON BANTZ, HENRY HENSHAW, ISAIAH MEALEY, Lane men. VALENTINE BIRELY, E. A. LYNCH, JOHN SCHRINER, JACOB DOLL, Property Guards. JOSEPH SCHELL, EDWARD TRAIL, JACOB ENGLEBRECHT, PATRICK TORMEY, GEO. M. CONRADT, JAMES WALLING, Dr. WM. M. KEMP, A. D. O'LEARY, NIMROD BANTZ, JOHN H. WILLIAMS, JOHN SHAEFFER, DAVID STEINER, Hosemen.

2639. (D) On the 3rd inst., FRANCES VIRGINIA, daughter of Mr John Richardson, in the 4th year of her age.

2640. (D) Departed this life, on the 16th ult., DAVID DUDERAR, aged 63 years, and 7 months, he leaves a widow and several children.

2641. Candidates for the Common Council: Ward #2. CHARLES GETZENDANNER, JOHN RIGNEY, NIMROD BANTZ. Ward #4. JOHN A. SIMMONS.

February 22, 1837 (MHS)

2642. Coroner's jury - An inquisition taken at the house of JOHN WEHNER, on the 17th day of February 1837, before me HENRY BAER, one of the Coroners of Frederick Co., upon the view of the body of John Wehner. Upon the oaths of JOHN KUNKLE, DANIEL KOLB, LEWIS BIRELY, JOHN HANE, JACOB KELLER, JACOB BERGER, W. H. ALBAUGH, ISAAC WYSONG, RICHARD HARPER, GEORGE RICE, CHARLES A. GAMBRILL, JACOB FAUBEL, JOHN FAUBEL, DANIEL BRENGLE, the above citizens were duly sworn to inquire when, where, how, and after what matter the said John Wehner, came to his death from taking of ise of Lobelia.

2643. (M) On Carroll's Manor, on Thursday evening last, by the Rev. John L. Pitts, Mr JOHN ELLIOT, to Miss ELLEN NICHOLAS.

2644. (D) On Sunday night last, MARY JANE KOONTZ, daughter of Mr George Koontz, aged 2 years, and 1 month.

2645. (D) On Tuesday last, infant son of WILLIAM P. MAULSBY, Esq., of this place.

2646. (D) On Monday last, in Middletown Valley, Mrs MARGARET CAUFMAN, wife of William Caufman, and daughter of Michael Straffer, Sr., of this place, in the 38th year of her age. She leaves 6 children, one of whom is a infant.

March 1, 1837 (MHS)

2647. The February term of the Frederick County Court commenced on Monday last, the following gentlemen composed the jury: GEORGE W. BEALL, CHARLES W. BIGHAM, THOMAS CRAMPTON, LUKE DAVIS, JOSEPH DANNER, JACOB KELLER, JOHN KINZER, ALPHEUS W. MARRIOT, FRANCIS RICHMOND, FREDERICK SHRINER, JOHN STEWART, JOSEPH WILHIDE, GEORGE ZOLLINGER, HENRY BOTELER, CHESTER COLEMAN, DAVID B. DEVITT, JOSHUA DELAPLANE, JOSHUA HERRING, DAVID KEMP, JOHN LEATHER, MICHAEL McCARTNEY, JOHN T. SCHLEY, JOHN SMITH, MICHAEL THOMAS, JOHN WOLF.

2648. The Friendship Fire Company, of Ward #5, elected the following officers: President: JOHN McDONALD. Vice President: HENRY SHULTZ. Secretary: GEORGE KOONTZ. Treasurer: HENRY KAUFMAN, Jr. Directors: MATHIAS E. BARTGIS, GEORGE DOFFLER. Engineer: CHRISTIAN STEIN, WINCHESTER CLINGAN, ORMAND F. BUTLER. Lanemen: GEORGE RICE, JOSEPH PAYNE. Axmen: JOHN SPONSELLER, MICHAEL LAMBRECHT, JACOB SCHABACHER, JACOB STRICKSTRUCK. Bucketmen: MICHAEL EBBERT, FREDERICK LAMBRECHT, THEOPHILUS KELLER, JOHN OTT. Laddermen: JACOB NUSZ, GEORGE KANTNER, JOSEPH EBBERTS, ADAM RITCHIE, FREDERICK KOLB, CECILIUS HEAD. Hookmen: JACOB KNOUF, JOHN D. HEMMELL, WILLIAM ELY, LEWIS GEPHART, PERRY RICE, HENRY FOGLER, Jr. Bagmen: ADAM SCHABACHER, PETER NICHOLS, JOHN

TITLOW, JACOB NUSSBAUM. Property guard: FREDERICK NUSZ, GEORGE HOUCK, THOMAS CARLIN, HENRY KELLEY. Keys men: GODFREV KOONTZ, EDWARD KOONTZ, PERRY RICE, CHRISTIAN STEINER. To serve until the last Saturday in December next.

2649. (M) On Thursday evening last, by the Rev. Daniel Zacharias, Mr WILLIAM WALKER, to Miss SARAH SHEARER, all of this co.

2650. (M) On this morning March 1st, at the Episcopal Methodist Parsonage, by the Rev. S. Byson, Mr MORGEON LEATHER, to Miss LUCINDA BARKER, all of Stephensburg, VA.

2651. (D) On the 22nd inst., GEORGE W. TRICE, infant son of Nicholas Trice, of this city, aged 1 year, 6 months and 24 days.

March 8, 1837 (MHS)

2652. (F) A large portion of the building on West Patrick Street, occupied by Mr G. M. CONRADT, as a Carpet Factory was destroyed by fire on Thursday morning last. The adjoining building, belonging to Mr GELWICKS, suffered but little injury; the roof and uppermost floor of the building, adjoining that of Mr Conradt on the East, was destroyed. Mr Conradt loss will be between $4,000 and $5,000. dollars.

2653. At a meeting held in the court house, Monday evening last, to take into consideration the losses of the suffers by the last fire. DANIEL KOLB, was called to the chair, and MAHLON TALBOTT, appointed Secretary. A committee of 7 were appointed to investigate the amount loss by the recent fire and the best method of relieving the suffers; the committee to report on Wednesday evening: GIDEON BANTZ, LEWIS MEDTART, A. B. HANSON, WM. ROSS, Sr., JACOB FAUBLE, BASIL NORRIS, LEWIS BIRELY, made up the committee.

2654. (M) On Thursday last, by the same, Mr JAMES BOOTH, to Miss MARY FRY.

2655. (M) On Tuesday the 28th ult., near Johnsville, by the Rev. John Garber, GEORGE PFOUTZ, Esq., to Miss CATHARINE, second daughter of the Rev. Jacob Saylor.

2656. (D) Near New Market, on Tuesday last, Mr JAMES L. HIGGINS, for a long time a member of the Methodist Episcopal Church, and a local preacher.

2657. (D) On Thursday last, at his residence in Emmittsburgh, LEWIS MOTTER, Esq.

March 22, 1837 (MHS)

2658. Colonel WM. COST JOHNSON, is announced in the Rockville Journal as a candidate for Congress in the 5th Congressional District. Dr. T. O. WHARTON, is announced in the Hagerstown paper, as a candidate for Congress in the 6th District.

2659. Dr. WASHINGTON DUVALL, one of the glorious 19, is nominated as a candidate for Congress in the adjoining District.

2660. Captain COOPER, the indefatigable Judge Advocate of the late Military Court in this place has been appointed Chief Clerk of the War Department.

2661. (M) On yesterday evening, by the Rev. S. W. Harkey, Mr OTHO G. ENT, to Miss LYDIA LAMBRECHT, all of this city.

2662. Appointment for Frederick County Justices of the Levy Court: JAMES SIMMONS, ABRAHAM KEMP, WILLIAM MILLER, MARTIN EICHELBERGER, F. TROXEL, SOLOMON FORREST, THOMAS SPRINGER, JEREMIAH G. MORRISON, WM. LYNCH, WM. DUDDERAR, JACOB CRONICE. Coroners: JACOB THOMAS, DENNIS D. HOWARD, GEORGE HUGHES, HENRY BAER, HENRY BOTELER, JACOB BAER. Orphan's Court: JOHN L. HARDING, DAVID RICHARDSON, NICHOLAS TURBUTT. Justices of the Peace: PATRICK McGILL, Sr., THOMAS BAKER, JACOB CRAMER, JAMES TANEY, Sr., WILLIAM GRIMES, SURAT D. WARFIELD, THOMAS HAYS, JOSHUA JONES, JACOB BAER, MALACHI BERNARD, WASHINGTON BURGESS, GEORGE BLESSING, A. L. BARNEY, GIDEON D. CRUMBAUGH, JOSEPH W. WALTMAN, JOHN W. CHARLTON, DANIEL DUVALL, JOSHUA DOUB, LLOYD DORSEY, JOHN McDONALD, HENRY W. DERR, WILSON HAYS, THOMAS J. HAMMOND, GEORGE HAUER, THOMAS W. JOHNSON, JACOB JOHNSON, ZEBULON KUHN, EDWARD KNOTT, MICHAEL LEASE, JOHN S. LAWRENCE, PATRICK McGILL, Jr., PHILEMON S. McELFRESH, JOHN MONTGOMERY, JOHN McDONALD, MARTIN MAHONEY, NICHOLAS NORRIS, NATHAN H. OWINGS, WM. MOONEY, NOAH PHILIPS, GEO. YANTIS, JAMES M. HARDING, GEORGE KUHN, WM. DURBIN, GEORGE BECKENBAUGH, BURGESS NELSON, ABDIEL UNKEFER, TILGHMAN BISER, SOLOMON FORREST, HENRY HOUCK, JOSEPH TALBOTT, GEO. BOWLUS, EMANUEL SLIFER, JONATHAN MANROE, PETER STEM, GEORGE RICE, JACOB CASSEL, W. LOWE, LEONARD PICKING, WM. COOKERLY, Jr., G. MORRISON,

HENRY BANTZ, ABNER CAMPBELL, J. G. COBB, RESIR E. TILLARD, E. B. HEBBARD, DAVID ROOP, of Jno., HENRY HERSHBERGER, CHARLES H. BURKHART, O. H. OWINGS, WILLIAM NORRIS, DANIEL KOLB, MICHAEL BALTZELL, RICHARD JOHNSON, of R., GEO. W. WINDSOR, HENRY BEATTEE, C. E. MACKLAND, JONATHAN NORRIS, WILLIAM BEAM, JACOB FERIOR, WM. R. KING, THOMAS WORTHINGTON, GEORGE GELDS, GEORGE MANTZ, JOHN H. BEALL, MAHLON HARLEY, GEO. BALTZELL, GIDEON BANTZ, THOMAS SAPPINGTON, ABRAHAM JONES, THOMAS HAMMOND, JACOB POE, GRAFTON DUVALL, JOSEPH M. CROMWELL, J. L. HARDING, DAVIS RICHARDSON, JOSHUA MOTTER, ROBERT BOONE, JACOB HOFFMAN, EDWARD A. CROMWELL, JOSEPH KEMP, ROBERT ANNAN, HENRY BAKER, JOSEPH C. SHOLTZ, GEO. ZOLLINGER, BEN. NEIDIG, PETER COBLENTZ, of P., VALENTINE ADAMS, GEO. FRANCIS, JOHN COST, ADAM KELLER, GEO. BURHMAN, GODFREY KOONTZ, JACOB FAUBLE, ADAM WHITE, GEO. PHELPS. WM. B. PITTENGER, JOHN W. DERR, ELIHA H. ROCKWELL, GEORGE RINER, JOHN J. SMITH, SAMUEL BAUMGARTNER, JACOB THOMAS, ZACHARIAH T. WINDSOR, HENRY YOUNG.

March 29, 1837 (MHS)
2663. Robbery - General EDWARDS, the cashier of the Branch of the Valley Bank, at Leesburg, VA., was robbed in this place on Wednesday last, of $26,000. He had been accustomed to conveying money to and from Leesburg, as the agreement of the bank. He arrived at the City Hotel, in this place about dinner time. The landlord placed his saddlebags on shelf. After dinner, he ordered his horse and Mr JOSEPH TALBOTT, the keeper of the house, upon looking for the saddlebags, could not find them. The possibility exist that the bags might have been placed on one of the stagecoaches heading West, by mistake. The General took pursuit, and soon overtook the stages, but could not obtain a thorough examination until he arrived at Funkstown. The bags were not there. A special messenger, sent from Frederick, informed him they had been located in Frederick, and with the contends locked up at Mr Talbotts. The next day he met a friend in Middletown, was informed the saddlebags had been rifled of their contends. They were found in the cellar of the Hotel cut open. A reward of $5,000. is

offered. Since then the money had been found. One parcel contained about $11,000. was found on Saturday morning last, between the head boards of the bed, and the wall in one of the chambers of the Hotel. The other was found on Sunday last, by some negro children among the rubbish in the stable yard belonging to the Hotel.

2664. (M) On Monday evening last, at Chamber Hotel, by the Rev. John L. Pitts, Mr OTHO COOK, to Miss MARY ANN MONTGOMERY, all of this co.

2665. (D) Departed this life, on Thursday morning the 23rd inst., ELIZABETH, wife of George Hardt, in the 31st year of her age.

2666. (D) On the 24th inst., in the 2nd year of her age, LOUISA JANE BAKER, daughter of James and Harriet Baker, of this city.

2667. (D) On Thursday the 16th inst., HENRY BAKER, infant son of Isaac and Elizabeth Wysong, aged 9 months and a few days.

April 5, 1837 (MHS)

2668. The investigation, which was made last week of the late robbery at the City Hotel, resulted in the holding EDWARD McPHERSON. To set bail in the sum of $500. to appear at the next session of the criminal court of this co., which will take place in May.

2669. (M) On Thursday, the 30th ult., by the Rev. John L. Pitts, Mr JACOB YON, to Miss NANCY MYERS, both of Carroll Co.

2670. (M) On Tuesday morning last, by the Rev. Daniel Zacharias, Mr CHARLES SHRIVER, second son of the Hon. Abraham Shriver, of this place, to Miss ANN ELIZA, only daughter of Samuel Thomas, late of Frederick Co.

2671. (D) Near Middletown, on the 28th ult., Mr JOHN BAKER, in the 35th year of his age.

2672. (D) At Linganore, on Saturday, the 1st inst., after a short illness, MARIAN LOUISA, only daughter of Colonel Anthony and Sidney Ann Kimmel, aged 3 years, 7 months and 3 days.

April 12, 1837 (MHS)

2673. Messrs, WASON and McGILL, the two recusant electors from Washington, Co., are added to the list of persons proposed as candidates for Congress from the 3rd District.

2674. (M) On Tuesday week, Mr EDWARD TURBUTT, of Frederick, to Miss ELIZABETH S. SPANGLER, daughter of the late Colonel Michael Spangler, of York, PA.

2675. (M) On the 30th ult., at the Eutaw House in Baltimore, by the Rev. Mr Duncan, Mr FRANCIS S. JONES, of Liberty to Miss HARRIET DOWNEY, daughter of the late William Downey, of New Market District.

2676. (D) On Monday 3rd inst., near Lewistown, WILLIAM AUGUSTUS, son of Wm., and Naomi Stait, in the 7th month of his age.

2677. (D) On the 10th inst., Mrs TERESA JAMISON, widow of the late Oswald Jamison, Esq., in the 55th year of her age.

2678. The Rev. Prof. BERG, of Marshall College, is expected to preach in the German Reformed Church this evening. April 12.

April 19, 1837 (MHS)

2679. Dr. WM. D. JENKS, has planted this Spring in the vicinity of this town, 20,000 white mulberry trees. On the growth of 1 year, for the purpose of feeding silk worms, and purpose of planting the same number next year.

2680. Mr GEORGE KOONTZ, was appointed a constable at the local meeting of the Levy Court.

2681. (M) On the evening of the 6th inst., by the Rev. Mr Slaughter, of Georgestown, D.C., WILLIAM GREEN, attorney-at-law, and DANIEL S. GREEN, M. D., of the U. S. Navy, the former to COLUMBIA, and the latter to VIRGINIA, daughter of Samuel Slaughter, Esq., of Western View, Culpepper Co., VA.

2682. (M) On Thursday last, by the Rev. D. Zacharias, Mr ELIAS BAST, to Miss MARY LAMBERT, all of this co.

2683. (M) On the same day, by the same, Mr DANIEL CULLER, to Miss ANNA MARIA HARGET, both of Frederick Co.

2684. (M) On the evening of the same day, by the same, Mr JOHN A. STEINER, of this city to Miss ANN SOPHIA MYERS, of this vicinity.

2685. The Aurora Borealis made its second appearance over the city last week.

April 26, 1837 (MHS)

2686. Divine service at Saint John's Church, will commence this day, at 10 o'clock, precisely - no admittance before that hour, and no person whatever admitted without a ticket. Sermon by the Right Rev. Dr. ENGLAND.

June 14, 1837 (MHS)
2687. Medical and Chirugical Faculty, at their annual meeting appointed the following Censors for Frederick Co. Dr. RICHARD DORSEY, JEFFERSON SHIELDS, JACOB BAER.

July 12, 1837 (MHS)
2688. The Maryland State Bible Society has chosen RICHARD POTTS, of Frederick, as Vice President to represent Frederick Co.

July 19, 1837 (MHS)
2689. (M) On Tuesday morning, by the Rev. S. Brison, Mr JOHN KANODLE, of Washington Co., to Miss VIOLETA B. MEIXELL, of this city.
2690. (D) On the 17th inst., Mr JAMES BOWDEN, respectful citizen of Emmittsburgh.
2691. (D) At Jefferson, Frederick Co., on the 2nd of July, 1837, Mrs BARBARA, consort of Mr Henry Crum, in the 59th year of her age. The mother of 10 children, 8 of whom, with her disconsol husband still survive.
2692. (D) On Saturday last, ANNA MARY MARTZ, aged 86 years, and 3 months and 26 days.
2693. (D) In Graceham's section Meeds, Co., Ohio, on the 22nd June 1837, Mrs POLLY HOLDER, in the 39th year of her age.
2694. (D) Departed this life, July 6th, after a lingering illness, Mrs WILLIAMINA GOODMANSON, consort of Peter Goodmanson, aged 22 years, 4 months and 25 days.

August 2, 1837 (MHS)
2695. (M) On Tuesday last, by the Rev. Mr Harkey, JOHN HENRY WILLIAM VAN BUREN, Esq., late of Amsterdam, to Miss MARY PHILLIPS, of this city.
2696. (D) In Cincinnati, on the 9th of July, in the 17th year of her age, Mrs REBECCA STRAEFFER, consort of Jacob M. Straeffer, and daughter of George Caley, Esq., of Hillsborough, Ohio, she died of bilious fever.

August 9, 1837 (MHS)
2697. Election results for the 5th Congressional District. KIMMEL - 648, JOHNSON 807. part of Carroll - 324, - 327. Part of Montgomery - 461, - 392. Johnson, wins by a majority of 93 votes.

2698. (M) On Tuesday evening last, by the Rev. Mr Harkey, Mr THOMAS C. PRINCE, to Miss MARY CATHERINE GRUMBINE, both of this city.

2699. The Rev. Mr BLOOD, will preach on next Sunday evening at 1/2 past 6 o'clock, in an orchard at the end of Patrick Street and Bentz Town, the situation is most beautiful.

August 23, 1837 (MHS)

2700. (M) In New Orleans, Mr ALEXANDER PHILIP SOCRATES EMILIAS CAESAR HANNIBAL MARCELLUS GEORE WASHINGTON TREADWELL, to Miss CAROLINA SOPHIA MARIA JULIANNE WORTLEY MONTAGUE JOAN of ARC POPE, all of that city.

August 30, 1837 (MHS)

2701. The National Gazette says - The sudden death of WM. KUHN, son of Mr Charles Huke, of this city, in the 20th year of his age. He was gunning on Monday, when by the accidental discharge of his piece and its contends entered his body. A graduate of Mt. Saint Mary's College, and had just returned home from their, after having taken the highest honors, and before he entered upon active life.

September 27, 1837 (MHS)

2702. (D) On the 21st inst., after a long and painful illness, JOHN ALEXANDER HALLER, son of Christopher Haller, deceased, in the 36th year of his age.

November 15, 1837 (MHS)

2703. The Rev. Mr BLOOD, will preach in the Presbyterian Church, on Sunday evening next, at 10 o'clock, A.M.

November 26, 1837 (MHS)

2704. It is with great pleasure we announce that Mr L. P. W. BALCH, Jr., son of L. P. W. BALCH, Esq., of this city has been unanimously chosen Rector of St. Andrew's Church, in Philadelphia. We learned that it is one of the largest congregation in that city.

2705. (D) On the 2nd inst., WILLIAM, eldest son of Mr Jacob Fogle, in the 45th year of his age, occasion by a wagon loaded with green oak wood, passing over his breast.

December 13, 1837 (MHS)

2706. Our attention has been directed by Mr P. O'NEILL, to a cure of scropula effected by his prescription. The patient is Mrs KAUFFMAN, an aged woman of this city. The disease has been of 10 years stealing, and has disfigured her face in the most shocking manner. The excruciating pain and other ailing symptoms have entirely subsided, the ulcerated portion of the face is healing.

2707. (M) On Thursday evening last, by the Rev. Henry R. Wilson, GEORGE M. PHILLIPS, Senior editor of the Carlislie Herald, to Miss JANE, youngest daughter of the late John Colwell, of South Hampton Township.

1838

January 17, 1838 (MHS)

2708. (M) On Tuesday, January 2nd, by the Rev. James Pearre, Mr GEORGE ALDRIDGE, to Miss ARA GILBERT, both of this co.

February 7, 1838 (MHS)

2709. (M) On Tuesday morning, January 30th, at the residence of George Price, Esq., near Point of Rocks, by the Rev. L. H. Johns, JAMES SMITH, Esq., attorney-at-law, Cumberland, MD., to Miss ANN E. PRICE.

2710. (D) On Sunday, at his residence, near Bladensburg, Prince George's Co., MD., GEORGE CALVERT, Esq.

February 14, 1838 (MHS)

2711. Temperance meeting of the citizens of Mechanicstown, and its vicinity met in the United Brethren's Church, on Saturday the 20th of January 1838, to form a Temperance Society. After prayer by the Rev. R. WEISER, SAMUEL STEM, was called to the chair, and appointed Mr R. WEISER, Secretary. A constitution was adopted and 75 gentlemen and ladies immediately subscripted their names and pledging their honor. Motion by R. WEISER, that the following gentlemen were elected officers for the ensuing year. President - SAMUEL STEM. Vice President - DANIEL ROGER. Secretary - HENRY McHENRY. Directors - WILLIAM SIFTON, GEO. STOKES, _____ RIDER.

February 21, 1838 (MHS)

2712. Appointment by the Governor and Council: Levy Court -

WILLIAM MILLER, MARTIN EICHELBERGER, FREDERICK TROXELL, SOLOMON FORREST, THOMAS SPRITGER, JEREMIAH S. MORRISON, WILLIAM LYNCH, WILLIAM DUDDERAR, PATRICK O'NEILL, ABEL RUSSELL, DANIEL DUVALL. District Court: Middletown - GEO. BOWLUS, GEORGE SMITH, HENRY HERSHBERGER. Creagerstown - ZEBULON KUHN, GEO. BECKENBAUGH, WILLIAM P. JONES. Emmittsburgh - JOSHUA MOTTER, THOMAS HAYS, FELIX B. TANEY. Liberty - THOMAS SAPPINGTON, AB'M. JONES, THOMAS HAMMOND. New Market - GEORGE PHELPS, WASHINGTON BURGESS, GEORGE RINER. Hauver - SOLOMON FORREST, WILSON HAYS, GEORGE BURHMAN. Woodsborough - JACOB POE, NOAH PHILLIPS, WILLIAM GRIMES. Petersville - GRAFTON DUVALL, JEREMIAH G. MORRISON, EMANUEL SLIFER. Frederick - GIDEON BANTZ, GEO. RICE, J. M. HARDING. Jefferson - JACOB THOMAS, PATRICK McGILL, WILLIAM LYNCH. Buckeystown - JONATHAN MANRO, Z. T. WINDSOR, P. S. McELFRESH. Magistrates: PATRICK McGILL, Sr., THOMAS BAKER, JACOB CRAMER, JOSEPH TANEY, Jr., WILLIAM GRIMES, SURRATT D. WARFIELD, THOMAS HAYS, JACOB BAER, MALACHI BERNARD, GEORGE BLESSING, AL BARNEY, G. D. CRUMBAUGH, JAMES W. WALTMAN, JOHN W. CHARLTON, DANIEL DUVALL, JOSHUA DOUB, LLOYD DORSEY, JOHN McDONALD, HENRY W. DERR, WILSON HAYS, THOS. J. HAMMOND, GEORGE HAUER, THOMAS W. JOHNSON, JACOB JOHNSON, ZEBULON KUHN, EDWARD KNOTT, MICHAEL LEASE, JOHN S. LAWRENCE, P. McGILL, Jr., PHILIMORE S. McELFRESH, JOHN MONTGOMERY, JN. McDONALD, M. MAHONEY, NICHOLAS NORRIS, NATHAN H. OWINGS, WILLIAM MOONEY, NOAH PHILLIPS, GEO. PHELPS, WILLIAM B. PITTINGER, JOHN A. DERR, ELIHU H. ROCKWELL, GEORGE RINER, JOHN SMITH, SAMUEL BAUMGARTNER, JACOB THOMAS, Z. T. WINDSOR, HENRY YOUNG, GEO. YANTIS, J. M. HARDING, GEORGE KUHN, WILLIAM DURBIN, GEORGE BRECKENBAUGH, BURGESS NELSON, ABDIEL UNKEFER, TILGHMAN BISER, SOLOMON FORREST, HENRY HOUCK, JAMES TALBOT, GEORGE BOWLUS, EMANUEL SLIFER, JONATHAN MANRO, PETER STEM, GEORGE RICE, JACOB CASSELL, WM. LOWE, LEONARD PICKING, WILLIAM COOKERLY, J. G. MORRISON, HENRY BANTZ, ABNER CAMPBELL, JAMES G. COBB, REZIN E. TILLARD, O. H.

OWINGS, WILLIAM NORRIS, DANIEL KOLB, MICHAEL BALTZELL, RICHARD JOHNSON, of R., EBENEGER HEBBARD, DAVID ROOP, of Jos., HENRY HERSHBERGER, CHARLES H. BURKHART, GEORGE W. WINDSOR, HENRY BOTELER, CHARLES E. MARKLAND, WILLIAM BEAM, JACOB FIROR, WM. R. KING, THOMAS J. WORTHINGTON, GEORGE GELTZS, GEO. MANTZ, MAHLON HARLEY, GEORGE BALTZELL, GIDEON BANTZ, THOMAS SAPPINGTON, ABRAHAM JONES, THOMAS HAMMOND, JACOB POE, GRAFTON DUVALL, DAVIS RICHARDSON, JOSHUA MOTTER, ADDISON WHITE, ROBERT BOONE, JACOB HOFFMAN, JOS. KEMP, ROBERT ANNAN, JOSEPH C. SHULTZ, GEO. ZOLLINGER, BENJ. NEIDIG, PETER COBLENTZ, of P., VALENTINE ADAMS, GEORGE FRANCIS, ADAM KELLER, GEORGE BURHMAN, GODFREY KOONTZ, JACOB FAUBLE, PHILIP McGAUGHREN, PHILIP BIRELY, MASON PARSON, JOHN BAILY, JACOB FLOOK, of Jno., SAMUEL CARMACK. Coroners - HENRY BAER, JOHN BAILY, HENRY BOTELER, GEORGE HUGHES, JACOB BISER, DENNIS D. HOWARD, JACOB THOMAS.

March 7, 1838 (MHS)

2713. Colonel JOHN McPHERSON, has been compelled, by ill health to resign his situation as cashier of the Branch Bank of this city. CYRUS MANTZ, Esq., a gentleman in all respectes qualified for the office, has been elected to fill the vacancy.

March 21, 1838 (MHS)

2714. (M) At Boston, by the Chaplain of the House of Representatives, Rev. EDWARD N. HARRIS, member of the House, from Malden, to Miss SARAH GEORGE, of Noston. Mr H., being a widower with 3 children saw Miss G., through the window of a Milliner's shop, and being impressed by her appearance popped his head into the door, and popped the question of marriage to her. She, blushed, and hesitated, he gave her a brief account of himself, said he would give her a week to consider and determine, and left the shop. At the expiration of the term, he again appeared. Consent was given, the ceremonies were at once performed. Mr H., re signed his seat in the House, and has taken his young bride (only 17,) off to Methuen, where he has received a call for settlement, over a Universalist Society, at $800. per annum.

May 9, 1838 (MHS)

2715. (M) On Thursday evening last, by the Rev. Daniel Zacharias, Mr CHRISTIAN THOMAS, to Miss MARY ELIZABETH, daughter of Walter King, both of Frederick Co.

2716. (D) On the night of the 1st inst., at the residence of her son-in-law, Col. Wm. Ogden Niles, in the 76th year of her age, Mrs MARY VINCENT relict of Samuel Vincent, Esq., of Baltimore. The decease was born in the vicinity of Annapolis, MD., and descendant from one of the oldest and respectable familes in the state, for more than 50 years a resident of Baltimore.

May 16, 1838 (MHS)

2717. Jurors. Grand: T. ANDERSON, Foreman, LEWIS LINK, JAS. WILHIDE, JACOB FOX, WILLIAM OTTER, HENRY W. DERR, JOHN WISE, JOS. SMITH, THOMAS WINTERS, JOS. WOOD, LAURENCE MAUGHT, JAMES HALL, CHRIST. HARBAUGH, THOS. I. HAMMOND, WARFIELD SIMPSON, CHAS. W. BIRHAM, FRANCIS KNOTT, WILLIAM MOONEY, JOS. ALEXANDER, JOS. STORM, JON. APPLEMAN, WM. WERTENBAKER, JAMES CHAMBERS. Petite jury: WM. H. ALBAUGH, WM. BRENNER, GEORGE BOWERSOX, AL. BARNEY, JAS. CASTLE, ELIAS L. DELASHMUTT, JOHN E. ELDER, GEO. W. ENT, JOHN W. GEYER, DAN'L. GROVE, ENOS HEDGES, ADAM HOLBRUNER, RICH'D. JOHNSON, of W., JAS. LEGGITT, JNO. LAMAR, WM. C. MARTIN, JACOB RIDDLEMOSER, JONAS SMITH, JNO. STOCKMAN, EZRA SMITH, HY. K. SMELSER, PETER STEM, GEO. THOMAS, UPTON WORTHINGTON, JOHN ZIMMERMAN.

2718. (M) On the 10th of May, by the Rev. S. W. Harkey, Mr TOBIAS WILLIAM HALLER to Miss JULIAN CATHERINE SUMAN, all of this city.

2719. (M) On same day, by the same, Mr JACOB WACHTER, to Miss ELIZABETH BARBARA REESE, all of this co.

2720. (M) On Thursday evening last, at Dorsey's City Hotel, by the Rev. D. Zacharias, Mr ROBERT J. W. POLK, of Woodstock, VA., to Miss SARAH J. SOMERVILLE, of Winchester, VA.

2721. (D) On the 27th of March last, at Rising Sun, Indiana, the place to which he emigrated, and settled in 1806, JOHN JAMES, a native of the Linganore, Frederick Co., MD., in the 72nd year of his age.

2722. (D) In Middletown Valley, Frederick Co., MD., on the 29th of April, 1838. ELIJAH WASKEY, son of the late Christian Waskey, near Jefferson, Frederick Co., MD. The decease was aged 13 years, 4 months and 4 days. His mortal remains were borne from his uncle's Mr Ramsburgh's above Middletown, (where he died,) in the neighborohood of Jefferson, and interred in the cemetery on the farm of the late Mr Hoffman, on Tuesday the 1st of May.

2723. (D) Near Middletown, Frederick Co., MD., on the 9th of May, 1838, of a protracted illness, Mrs ANNA EVERHART, wife of Jacob Everhart, Senior, aged 65 years, 4 months and 25 days. She leaves a husband and 5 children.

2724. (D) In Lancaster, PA., on the 4th inst., JOHN ROSS, Esq., long a respectable inhabitant of that city.

May 23, 1838 (MHS)

2725. Another military court of inquire to be held in Frederick, on the conduct of Gen. JESSUP.

June 27, 1838 (MHS)

2726. Medical and Chircugical Faculty, at their annual meeting appointed the following Censor for Frederick Co. Dr. RICHARD DORSEY, Dr. JACOB BAER, JEFFERSON SHIELDS.

July 11, 1838 (MHS)

2727. The Rev. Dr. SCHMUCKER, of the institution of Gettysburg, will preach in the Lutheran Church of this city, on next Sabbath.

August 8, 1838 (MHS)

2728. (M) In Aberdeen, on Monday evening the 23rd inst., by Esquire Shelton, J. B. CLEMENT, Esq., to Miss ELIZABETH, daughter of Colonel A. C. Repass, all of this city.

August 15, 1838 (MHS)

2729. A thunderstorm on Thursday evening last did some damage in this neighborohood, the barn of Mr JACOB DOUB, is said to have been consumed.

August 22, 1838 (MHS)

2730. (D) Mr HENRY BRAWNER, Esq., of Charles Co. He served his country in several ways, as a Legislator, and was one of 21 Senatorial Electors, who probably stood for the cause of the Constitution and law, when they were threaten with violence.

2731. (M) On Tuesday the 14th inst., by the Rev. T. Riley, of Frederick City, Mr TILGHAM B. BENNETT, to Miss CATHARINE SHIPLEY, all of Frederick Co.

2732. (D) On Friday night the 24th inst., MARY JANE, infant daughter of Dr. Andrew and Elizabeth Annan, of Emmittsburgh, aged 3 years, 5 months.

September 5, 1838 (MHS)

2733. (M) On Tuesday evening last, (at Stevens Hotel,) by the Rev. John L. Pitts, Mr VACHAEL L. CLEARY, to Miss MARY ANN NORRIS, both of this co.

September 12, 1838 (MHS)

2734. (M) In Philadelphia, on the 28th of August, by the Rev. Mr Riegart, Mr MICHAEL ENGLEBRECHT, of Frederick, to Miss REBECCA R. McMULLIN, both of this co.

September 19, 1838 (MHS)

2735. (M) Near Woodsboro, on Sunday evening the 9th inst., by the Rev. R. Weiser, Mr JOSHUA W. PITTINGER, to Miss SABINA MARTIN.

2736. (M) On the 30th ult., near Creagerstown, by the Rev. R. Weiser, Mr LEVI BOWERS, to Miss ALICE SNOOK.

2737. (M) On the 9th ult., by the same, Mr MICHAEL ILER, to Miss REBECCA FOGLE, all of this co.

2738. (M) On the 16th inst., near Woodsboro, by the Rev. R. Weiser, Mr ELI SMITH, to Miss TERESA SMITH, all of Frederick City.

2739. (M) On Wednesday morning at Dorsey's City Hotel, by the Rev. John L. Pitts, Captain WILLIAM SMALL, to Mrs ELIZABETH HEWETT, both of Frederick.

2740. (D) On the 28th ult., SAMUEL CLAY, infant son of Mr Samuel Wilhide, of Woodsboro.

2741. (D) On Saturday the 18th inst., at the residence of Mr Joseph Roman, in Cecil Co., JAMES DIXON, Esq., a member of the Frederick Bar, and for many years the State Attorney, for the 5th Judicial District.

2742. (D) On Friday the 24th ult., at the residence of her father Joseph M. Cromwell, in this co., after a lingering illness of consumption, Dr. EDWARD A. CROMWELL, aged about 30 years.

October 3, 1838 (MHS)
2743. (D) On Sunday the 16th inst., at the residence of her brother, James Hopwood, Miss CATHARINE HOPWOOD.

October 10, 1838 (MHS)
2744. EDWARD A. LYNCH, Esq., has been appointed Deputy Attorney General, for the counties of Washington and Allegany Co., in the place of JAMES DIXON, Esq., deceased.

October 24, 1838 (MHS)
2745. (D) In Hagerstown, on the 18th inst., after a lingering illness, Mrs SUSANNA BELL, mother of the editor of the Torch Light, aged 68 years, wanting 8 days.
2746. (D) On Monday the 15th inst., at his residence in Hagerstown, Mr HENRY YEAKLE, Sen'r., at an advanced age.

November 14, 1838 (MHS)
2747. (M) On the 17th ult., near Chambersburg, PA., the Rev. FREDERICK RAHAUSER, of Tiffin, OH., formerly of Chambersburg, PA., to Mrs HANNAH KIEFFER, of Franklin Co., PA.
2748. (M) On Tuesday evening last, by the Rev. M. Harris, Mr JAMES WILLOUGHBY, merchant (formerly of calvert Co.,) to Miss ELLEN JANE, youngest daughter of the late Captain David Lynn, of the Maryland Line, all of Cumberland Co.
2749. (M) On the 25th ult., by the Rev. B. R. Hall, Mr JACOB LEWIS SLENTZ, editor of the "Bedford Inquirier" (formerly of this borough,) to Miss JANE HOLLIDAY, of Bedford. (Gettysburg Star)

November 28, 1838 (MHS)
2750. (D) On Saturday last, Mr MICHAEL JEFFERSON GETZENDANNER, near Frederick, in the 37th year of his age, leaving a wife and 8 children.

December 5, 1838 (MHS)
2751. (M) On Thursday the 15th of November, by the Rev. Josiah Varden, Mr JOHN OMERGOAST, to Miss BARBARA LEISTER, all of this co.

December 26, 1838 (MHS)
2752. (M) At Fort Hill, S. C., November 12th, by the Rev. Mr

Porter, THOS. C. CLEMSON, of Philadelphia, to ANNA, daughter of the Hon. John C. Calhoun.

2753. (M) In Middletown, Frederick Co., MD., on the 16th inst., by the Rev. J. C. Bucher, Mr ISAAC ROWLAND, of Washington Co., to Mrs SUSAN UPDEGRAFF, of Hagerstown MD.

2754. (M) On the 11th ult., J. W. NEED, Esq., to LETITIA MARY, only daughter of the late Major General Hall.

2755. (M) In Philadelphia, on Tuesday the 11th inst., by the Rev. J. H. Jones, ALEXANDER HAMILTON DODGE, of George Town, D. C., to ANNA, daughter of the late Dr. Samuel L. Howell, of Princeton, N. J.

2756. (D) On Tuesday the 18th inst., LAURIA ADELIA, and ALICE, daughter of Mr Jacob Yeakle, of this city, the one in the 3rd, and the other in the 1st year of her age.

1839

January 9, 1839 (MHS)

2757. Candidates for the Common Council: Ward #1. SAMUEL HERGESHEIMER, GEORGE METZER. Ward #2. JACOB MARKELL, JOHN M. LOWE, HORATIO WATERS. Ward #3. GEORGE McCAHEN, DAVID B. DEVITT. Ward #4. WILLIAM SMALL, LEWIS MEDTART. Ward #5. HENRY C. LARE, DAVID BOYD. Ward #6. THOMAS CARLIN, Sen'r. Ward #7. WINCHESTER CLINGAN.

January 16, 1839 (MHS)

2758. (D) On the 10th inst., in Baltimore, ALEXANDER FRIDGE, in the 74th year of his age.

January 23, 1839 (MHS)

2759. (F) The dwelling of DANIEL S. BISER, Esq., one of the delegates of this co., in the House of Delegates, was destroyed by fire on Saturday night last.

2760. Candidate for the Common Council: Ward #6. HENRY KELLEY, Senr.

January 30, 1839 (MHS)

2761. (D) On Saturday night last, suddenly, JAMES ANDERSON, attorney-at-law, of Yorke, PA.

2762. Candidates for the Common Council: Ward #7. JOHN MILLER. Ward #2. HENRY BUTLER. Ward #4. WILLIAM C. HOFFMAN, GEORGE J. FISCHER, GEORGE M. CONRADT.

February 20, 1839 (MHS)
2763. (M) Near Middletown, Frederick Co., on Thursday last, by the Rev. M. Wachter, Mr ELIAS DELAUTER, to Miss LYDIA DERR, all of Middletown Valley.
2764. (M) On same day, by the same, Mr JOHN EMMISS, to Miss DELANA WEAVER, all of Middletown Valley.

February 27, 1839 (MHS)
2765. Election results for the Common Council: Ward #1. GEORGE METZGAR - 49, SAM'L. HAY - 24. Ward #2. HENRY BOTELER - 35, J. M. LOWE - 29. Ward #3. P. L. STORM - 50, GEORGE McGAHEN - 29. Ward #4. GEORGE M. CONRADT - 94. Ward #5. GEORGE KOONTZ - 51, JOHN ENGELBERGER - 48. Ward #6. D. J. MARKEY - 54, HENRY KELLY - 43. Ward #7. J. W. MILLER - 55, PATRICK DEGRANGE - 42.
2766. Civil Court of this co., commenced its February term on Monday last. The following is a list of jurors in attendance. Grand Jurors: NICHOLAS HOLTZ, JOHN MAUGHT, JACOB ROOT, GEORGE OTT, HENRY SMITH, JOHN HAGAN, SAMUEL DUTROW, JOHN JAMES, of T., EDWARD SCHLEY, NATHAN NELSON, DAVID BOYD, HENRY BOTELER, PETER RHOADES, GEORGE SMITH, FREDERICK WELLER, PETER CRAMER, WILLIAM BROWN, JOHN YOUNG, of C., SAMUEL WOLFE, DAVID KEMP, PETER STEM, DAVID DUDDERAR, DEWALT WILLIARD. Petite Jurors: MICHAEL BALTZELL, JERAMIAH BLACK, THOMAS CASTLE, RICHARD ENGLISH, PETER GOODMANSON, THOMAS JOHNSON, JACOB T. C. MILLER, JOHN OTT, PETER H. ROUSE, VALENTINE SHRYCOCK, JOHN STRASBURY, JOHN WOLFE, SAMUEL YASTE, AB'M. BLESSING, FREDERICK CRABBES, JOHN CRAPSTER, EZRA GOMBER, WILLIAM HYATT, HENRY KEMP, PHILLIP McGAHEN, JOSEPH PAYNE, HENRY SIMMS, JOHN B. STIMMELL, CHARLES WORTHINGTON, JOSEPH B. WEBB.
2767. Appointments for Frederick County, by the Governor and Council: Justices for the Orphans Court - C. QUYNN, rejected, JNO. HARRITT, confirmed E. HOUCK, confirmed. Coroners - A. LORENTZ, DAVID YANTIS, GEORGE

GROVER, CHAD STEVENS. Levy Court - (laid on the table) JOSEPH WOOD, GEO. ZOLLINGER, GEORGE SMITH, ISRAEL RAMSBURG, JOSEPH SMITH, of M., BENEDICT BOONE, JOHN JONES, of Thomas, MICHAEL THOMAS, JOHN H. SIMMONS, WILLIAM WERTENBAKER, JACOB CRISE. Notaries Public - (confirmed) WM. SMALL, GEORGE HOSKINS, OTHO G. ENT, ABNER CAMPBELL. Surveyor - THOMAS H. O'NEAL, confirmed. District Justices - Ward #1. ELIAS DELASHMUTT, JACOB KEIFER, CHRISTIAN THOMAS. Ward #2. MICHAEL BALTZELL, SAMUEL CARMACK, CORNELIUS STALEY. Ward #3. JOHN SIFFORD, MICHAEL McCARTNEY, SAMUEL YASTE. Ward #4. Confirmed; JACOB FIROR, JOHN R. CURTIS. Rejected: WM. CREAGER. Ward #5. WILLIAM MOONEY, JAMES M'KEEHAN. MICHAEL C. ADELSPERGER, confirmed. Ward #6. ABDIEL UNKEFER, confirmed. JOHN GLISSAN, rejected. JOHN KINZER, Sen., confirmed. Ward #9. Confirmed; JOHN H. M. SMITH, SAMUEL WRIGHT, LEBLEUS GRIFFITH. Ward #10. Confirmed; GEORGE P. FOX, PETER STEM, OVERTON HARNE. Ward #11. BROOKE BAKER, EZRA CRAMER, PETER H. RUSS, confirmed. Ward #12. JOHN FINK, THOMAS CRAMPTON, confirmed. Ward #14. THOMAS JOHNSON, of Wm., MICHAEL THOMAS, WM. LAKINS, confirmed. Justices of the Peace: WM. MOONEY, JOHN R. CURTIS, JAMES McKEEHAN, WILLIAM CREAGER, MICH'L. C. ADELSPERGER, CHARLES WORTHINGTON, WILLIAM LOWE, JOSEPH W. BIGGS, GEORGE HAUER, JAMES LEGGET, Sen., BROOKE BAKER, WILLIAM VALENTINE, EZRA CRAMER, WILLIAM TODD, PETER H. ROUSS, WM. HEWIRR, JACOB REESE, PETER EICHELBERGER, JOHN NORRIS, FRANCIS J. HOOVER, JACOB BEARD, Sen., JOHN AGNEW, JOHN JACKSON, GEORGE FRANCIS, JACOB KELLER, JOHN HOUCK, MICHAEL BYRNE, HENRY KEEFER, EZRA BENTZ, JAMES A. GALAGHER, WM. C. MARTIN, HENRY KELLY, Sr., ABNER CAMPBELL, EZRA DADISMAN, CHARLES SHRIVER, GEORGE SALMON, JOHN KUNKLE, ISAAC WYSONG, JOHN S. MILLER, JOHN BRUNNER, of J., MICHAEL BALTZELL, WILLIAM KOLB, Jr., JOHN McDONALD, HENRY KAUFFMAN, Sr., DAVID BOYD, HENRY NIXDORFF, ANDREW HEIM, SAMUEL CARMACK, PHILIP KEYSER, JOHN DERR, RICHARD HARPER, JOSEPH C. SCHULTZ, SAMUEL YASTE, MICHAEL McCARTNEY, GEORGE W. MARIS, FREDERICK

WHEREAFELT, GEORGE P. FOX, JOHN SIFFORD, JACOB T. C. MILLER, SAMUEL GROVE, GEORGE KOONTZ, JONAS. SMITH, JONATHAN LINEBAUGH, DAVID KELLER, ISAAC PROFFENBERGER, HENRY BOWERS, SOMERSET R. WATERS, WM. G. HOWARD, ARTHUR TANZY, ALFRED BAKER, JOHN BLOOM, Jr., HENRY SCHOLL, THOMAS NORWOOD, THOMAS C. SHIPLEY, WM. CAIN, of Eph'm., MASON MARSH, JOHN THOMAS, Jr., JACOB FEASTER, Senr., JOHN WISE, LEWIS RAMSBURG, of M., JOHN H. M. SMITH, SAMUEL WRIGHT, LEBLEUS GRIFFITH, MARTIN S. GROVE, JOHN B. STIMMEL, FRANCIS SHAW, DANIEL MARTZ, BASIL BAKER, ELIAS L. DELASHMUTT, JACOB KEEFER, CHRISTIAN THOMAS, GEO. W. BEALL, JAMES A. JOHNSON, WM. R. KING, JAMES CASTLE, PETER HOFFMAN, PHILLIP M'GAHAN, Z. T. SIMMONS, ISAAC RENN, N. W. CLAYBAUGH, NELSON HOFFMAN, JOHN SMITH, of Jacob, NICHOLAS HOLTZ, PHILIP LOWE, JOHN MEASEL, GEORGE W. ENT, GEORGE MARTZ, GEORGE SMITH, LEWIS BRUNNER, G. ZIMMERMAN, of M., JOHN MAYN, SAMUEL WACHTER, GEORGE STRAILMAN, GEORGE FEAGA, ABDIEL UNKEFER, JOHN KINSER, Sen., JOHN W. DORSEY, WILLIAM McCOLLUM, MASON MARSH, BASIL HAGDER, ARCHIBALD ESTLER, JOSEPH JAMES, Jr., JOHN WOLFE, PETER STEM, CHARLES W. BIGHAM, GEORGE LONG, JOHN MORGAN, Jr., OVERTON HARNE, DAVID KAILOR, PETER PALMER, JACOB FLOOK, of Jno., JACOB SUMMERS, of Wm., MICHAEL THOMAS, WM. LAKINS, JOHN LAMAR, HENRY DUNLOP, JOHN FINK, THOMPSON CRAMPTON, JOHN WILLIARD, BARTON GARROT, DAVID GROVE, THOMAS HOWARD, ADEN ANDERSON, WM. H. RIGNEY, JACOB FIROR, confirmed. Armourer - EZRA HOFFMAN. Leather Inspector - GEO. MALAMBRE, rejected, HENRY KAUFFMAN, nomi'd. Flour Inspector - HENRY ROBINSON, confirmed.

March 6, 1839 (MHS)

2768. (D) At Liberty Town, on the 20th ult., the infant son of FRANCIS S., and HARRIET JONES, aged 12 days.

March 13, 1839 (MHS

2769. (M) At New York, on Tuesday morning at the residence of James H. Ray, by the Rev. Fitch Reed, the Rev. H. B. BASCOM, D.D., professor of Moral Science, and Belle Letters, Augusta College, KY., to Miss ELIZA VAN ANTWERP, daughter of the late Thomas Van Antwerp, of that city.

March 20, 1839 (MHS)

2770. Returns of the special election for Frederick Co. JOHN GEYER - 947, WILLIAM GRIMES - 69, KINZEY HARRIS - 32, DENNIS D. WAGNER - 32.

April 3, 1839 (MHS)

2771. (M) Yesterday morning by the Rev. E. Heiner, CHAD D. SCHELL, to Miss CORNELIA ANN BEATTY, both of New Market, Frederick Co.
2772. (M) On the 19th ult., at St. Joseph's, Fla., JAMES CANTWELL, of Baltimore, to SOPHIA, daughter of the late Baker Johnson, Esq., of Frederick Co., MD.

April 10, 1839 (MHS)

2773. Negro BROWN, will be executed at Rockville, on the 12th inst., the day appointed by the Executive.
2774. (D) At the residence of his uncle Dr. R. W. Davis, Hagerstown, on the morning of the 4th inst., JOHN H., eldest son of Thomas J. Davis, Esq., of Frederick Co., in the 8th year of his age.
2775. (D) In Hagerstown, on the morning of Tuesday 2nd inst., MARGARET H., second daughter of Dr. R. W. Davis, of the above place, in the 12th year of her age.

April 17, 1839 (MHS)

2776. (M) On Thursday evening last, by the Rev. Daniel Zacharias, Mr PHILIP H. SINN, to MARY E. BIRELY, both of this city.
2777. (M) On the 14th inst., by the Rev. James Pearre, Mr ENOCK BEALL, to Miss MARIA CANOUGH, both of this co.
2778. (M) On Wednesday evening the 10th inst., by the Right Rev. Bishop Onderdonk, the Rev. LEWIS P. W. BALCH, Rector of St. Bartholomew's Church, N. Y., and son of L. P. W. Balch, Esq., of Frederick MD., to ANNA, eldest daughter of the late Hon. William Jay, of Bedford.
2779. (D) On the 20th ult., near Chilicothe, OH., Dr. JEREMIAH F. KUHN, in the 34th year of his age, formerly of this city.
2780. (D) On the morning of Tuesday the 11th inst., at her boarding house of a protracted illness, Mrs FRANCES ROSS, late Miss Frances Ross, formerly of Savanah, GA., and wife of Wm. B. Ross, Esq., formerly of New York.

April 24, 1839 (MHS)

2781. (M) On Tuesday evening the 16th inst., by the Rev. John L. Pitts, Mr WILLIAM P. STOCKMAN, to Miss MATILDA A. UTCHERSON, both of Jefferson, in this co.
2782. (M) On the same evening, by the same, Mr HENRY SHIELDS, to Miss ANN HANEY, both of this co.
2783. (D) On the night of the 15th inst., CHARLES REIGHLY, infant son of David Steiner, aged 4 months and 23 days.
2784. (D) Suddenly on Monday the 22nd inst., whilst upon a visit to his connexions, in this co., Dr. H. B. TUCKER, of Philadelphia.

May 1, 1839 (MHS)

2785. Postmasters appointed for the following communities: HENRY CURTIS, of Liberty Town, and JOHN WICKHAM, of Creagers Town, Frederick Co., MD.

May 8, 1839 (MHS)

2786. (F) The barn of Mr PETER CULP, near Gettysburg was struck by lightning, and burnt to the ground.
2787. (D) On Thursday evening last, at his residence in Harbaugh's Valley, Frederick Co., in the 84th year of his age, Captain DANIEL SMITH, a soldier of the Revolution. He lived on the farm where he was born, was a regular member from early life of the Lutheran Church, and was buried on Saturday last, by Captain Jone's Uniform Company with honors due a soldier.

May 15, 1839 (MHS)

2788. (M) On Thursday last, by the Rev. John L. Pitts, Mr WILLIAM SNYDER, of New Market, to miss SARAH ANN PLAIN, of that vicinity.
2789. (M) On the 1st inst., by the Rev. S. R. Fischer, Mr ELIJAH CLOSE, of Frederick Co., to Miss SUSAN, daughter of Frederick Biggs, Esq., of Carroll Co.
2790. (M) On Thursday the 2nd, by the Rev. Joseph G. Hays, Mr ZACHARIAH H. DAVIS, of Carroll Co., to Miss CORDELIA ANN, eldest daughter of Jesse Clay, of Frederick Co.

May 29, 1839 (MHS)

2791. Appointments by the Levy Court for Frederick Co. Trustees of the Alms House - PHILLIP ROHR, GEO. HAUER, VALENTINE DOUB. Constables: District #1. (Buckeystown) JOHN H. RENN, JAMES L. SIMMONS, GEO. LATE. District

#2. (Frederick) GEO. KOONTZ, JOHN H. HOFF, JOSHUA DILL, FRED'K. REINHART, JAMES M. CARNN, JOHN M. LOWE, HENRY LOWE, FRED'K. HAWMAN. District #3. (Middletown) JACOB YOUNG, of D., MAHLON RODRICK, JAMES WILLIAMSON, JOHN H. YOUNG. District #4. (Creager's Town) DANIEL MATHEWS, SAMUEL HEARD, WARNER T. GRIMES, JOHN ZIMMERMAN. District #5. (Emmittsburgh) SAMUEL DUPHORN, JNO. MARTIN. District #8. (Liberty) DANIEL ROOT, of D., JOHN A. WARFIELD, RICHARD GALLAGHER, JOEL WOOD, ADAM GOSNELL. District #9. (New Market) THO'S. MOUNT, HENRY LYDAY. District #10. (Hauver) HENRY NEED. District #11. (Woodsborough) JOHN BARRICK, CH'S. HESSER, BENJAMIN STULL, ADAM CREAGER. District #13. (Petersville) WILLIAM HAYS, JOHN SLIFER. District #14. (Jefferson) JACOB B. HALLER, LLOYD H. KESSLER. GIDEON BANTZ, EDWARD TRAIL, and SAMUEL CARMACK, were appointed Judges of Election of the District. JOSHUA RUSSELL, was appointed Inspector of Primary School, in place of WASHINGTON BURGESS, who resigned.

June 5, 1839 (MHS)
2792. (M) On the 26th of May, Mr ROBERT BOUREE, to Miss MARY A. HOFFMAN, both of Boonesboro.

June 19, 1839 (MHS)
2793. (D) A boy about 4 years old, while playing in a field a few miles from Emmittsburgh, approached too near a burning stump by which fire was communicated to his clothes. His father, who was ploughing in the same field, did not discover him until he was shockingly burnt and in the last agonies of death.

June 26, 1839 (MHS)
2794. A black man was arrested in this place on Monday last, charged with having fired the property of Mr HORATIO WATERS, in the month of March. The information came from the mother-in-law of the accused, who we are informed is a white woman. The negro has been released for want of satisfactory testimony.
2795. (M) In Annapolis on Tuesday evening last, by the Rev. L. Humphreys, the Rev. JOS. TRAPNELL, of Upper Marlbow, to Miss EMILY WATKINS, of Annapolis.

2796. (M) On the 19th inst., in Gettysburg, by the Rev. J. C. Watson, Mr GEORGE TOOT, of Cumberland Township, to Miss MARTHA M'NAIR, of Emmittsburgh.
2797. (D) On Sunday last, in Baltimore, CHAR. J. WHITE, aged 36 years, a native of Baltimore and agent of the Union Lines of Steamboats and of the Stage Lines of Messrs, Reeside and Company.
2798. (D) In this city, on Sunday last, Mr PETER PHEBUS, a brickmaker, at advanced age, leaving a large family.
2799. Medical and Chircugical Faculty, at their annual meeting appointed the following Censors for Frederick Co. Dr. C. L. GOLDSBOROUGH, and Dr. WM. WATERS.

July 3, 1839 (MHS)

2800. (M) On Wednesday morning the 26th inst., by the Rev. Mr Wyley, GEO. SCHLEY Esq., to Miss MARY HALL, third daughter of the late Thomas B. Hall, Esq., of Hagerstown.

July 10, 1839 (MHS)

2801. (M) On the 1st inst., Mr PELEY THRASHER, to Miss ZEBRINA PEASE.
2802. (M) In Gettysburg, on Saturday last, by Professor Jacobs, Mr HENRY DEMUTH, to Miss MARY ANN SHORB, both of Frederick Co., MD.
2803. (D) Departed this life on Tuesday the 2nd of July, in the 40th year of her age, Sister GENEVIEVE, Superior of St. John's Female Academy and Orphan Asylum in Frederick. Her family name was ROSETTA TYLER, born in New Hampshire, of a respected family, educated in the Church of England. She was lead by the example of her cousin, the Rev. Virgil H. Barber, who, from a distinguished minister of the Episcopal Church, who became a Catholic Priest, she entered the Sisters of Charity.
2804. (D) On Friday the 5th, near Dam #6, of the Chesapeake and Ohio Canal, ARTHUR WELLESLEY STAIT, son of William Stait, Esq., of the County of Closter, England.
2805. (D) On the 7th inst., MINERVA, youngest daughter of Patrick and Louisa O'Neill, aged 3 years.

July 24, 1839 (MHS)

2806. (D) On Saturday morning the 20th inst., at the home of her son near Woodsborough, in the 65th year of her age, Mrs BARBARA FULTON, relict of Robert Fulton, Esq., late of this co.

2807. (D) Departed this life, in the 58th year of his age, on the 14th inst., RICHARD JOHNSON, eldest son of the late Major Roger Johnson.

2808. (D) On Friday 19th inst., ROSE ELLEN, daughter of Patrick and Louisa O'Neill, in the 5th year of her age, the disease was scarlett fever the same of which her sister died about 10 days before.

July 31, 1839 (MHS)

2809. (M) On Thursday the 18th inst., by the Rev. J. Cline, Mr JOHN BOWMAN, to Miss JULIA FORREST, daughter of Mr Solomon Forrest, all of Hauver's District, Fred'k. Co.

2810. (D) On the 26th of June, last at Viciennes, IN., in the 61st year of his age, the Right Rev. G. S. BRUTE, formerly, and for many years a resident of MD.

2811. (D) At Pennsylvania College, of Frederick last, EDWARD S. KEY, son of Henry St. G. Key, of St. Mary's Co., MD., in the 18th year of his age. His remains were removed to the residence of his father for interment.

August 7, 1839 (MHS)

2812. (M) In Frederick Co., MD., on the 1st of August, by the Rev. Upton Beall, JOHN PICKLE, Esq., late of the Army, to SARAH ELIZABETH, eldest daughter of Capt. David Geisinger, U. S. Navy.

2813. (M) In Frederick on Saturday the 20th ult., by the Rev. Upton Beall, Mr CHARLES W. BURNES, of this co., to Miss MARY MASON, late of England.

August 14, 1839 (MHS)

2814. (M) On Wednesday morning last, by the Rev. D. Zacharias, Mr WILLIAM GITTINGER, to Miss ANN R. BRENGLE, all of this city.

2815. (M) On Sunday morning last, by the Rev. J. L. Pitts, Mr RICHARD LAMAR, to Miss MALINDA WELSH, both of this co.

2816. (D) On the 30th of July, Mr JOHN FREDERICK WISE, in the 48th year of his age.

2817. (D) On the 4th of August, Mrs SUSAN REYNOLDS, consort of James Reynolds.

2818. (D) On the 30th ult., WILLIAM COST, infant son of Colonel Thomas Johnson, near Jefferson, aged 4 years, 6 months and 15 days.

August 21, 1839 (MHS)
2819. Mr ELIAHU S. RILEY, has announced the publication of a paper at Emmittsburgh, called the "Gazette."

August 28, 1839 (MHS)
2820. (M) On Tuesday the 27th inst., by the Rev. J. A. Henning, the Rev. R. W. H. BRENT, to Miss CATHARINE E., eldest daughter of G. W. Miller, of Frederick City.

September 4, 1839 (MHS)
2821. (M) On Thursday morning last, by the Rev. John L. Pitts, Mr JNO. F. RAMSBURG, to Miss ANN M. E. BARRICK, both of this co.

September 11, 1839 (MHS)
2822. (D) On Friday night September 5th, of a short but severe attack of billious fever, SAMUEL MERRITT, Sen., of Baltimore.

September 18, 1839 (MHS)
2823. (M) On Tuesday last, (at Walling's Hotel) by the Rev. John L. Pitts, Mr STEWART BENNETT, to Miss MARGARET LEVISHER.

September 25, 1839 (MHS)
2824. (D) On the 21st of September, after a few days illness, DAVID HENRY, son of John and Catharine Holtz, aged 20 years, 1 month and 26 days. On the day following his mortal remains were conveyed to the graveyard attached to the Glade Church.
2825. (D) At Kakaskia, ILL., in the present month JOHN OWINGS, Esq., aged upwards of 60 years. Recently left this state to visit and resided with his son. He had just reached there when the disease hit him, and in 9 days it terminated his life. He was born in Pennsylvania, early in life he moved to Baltimore.

October 30, 1839 (MHS)
2826. The October term of the Frederick County Court commenced on Monday last, the following is a list of the jurors. Grand: DANIEL DUVALL, HENRY BOTELER, of E., SAMUEL CARMACK, THOMAS HAMMOND, DANIEL ROUTZONG, LEWIS HAYS, SEBASTIAN RAMSBURG, UPTON WORTHINGTON, DANIEL WELTY, JOS. EICHEL-

BERGER, DAVID SCHLEY, DAVID B. DEVITT, EMANUEL SMITH, JOSEPH WILHIDE, WM. MILLER, JOHN RIGNEY, JOHN WOOD, JOHN FINK, NOAH PHILLIPS, OTHO THOMAS, THOMAS HOWARD, JOSEPH WEST, JOSHUA DILL. Petit Jurors: ABDIEL UNKEFER, ANTHONY KIMMEL, GEO. W. ENT, DAVIS RICHARDSON, MOSES WORTHINGTON, AB'M. WILLIARD, THOMAS C. BRASHEAR, GEORGE HARMAN, WM. TODD, JACOB REESE, BASIL HAYDEN, JOS. DANNER, FELEX B. TANEY, SAMUEL WRIGHT, JOS. HARBAUGH, JOHN SIFFORD, GEO. W. HOFFMAN, PETER SOWDER, JAMES CASTLE, THOMAS LAMAR, THOS. A. FLEMMING, JOHN T. JOHNSON, JOHN CRAMPTON, MICHAEL SLUSS, CHARLES BIGHAM.

November 16, 1839 (MHS)

2827. (M) On Thursday evening the 17th inst., by the Rev. Mr Harrison, HAMMOND DORSEY, Esq., to Miss LUCRETIA BROAN, both of Elkridge, Anna Arundel Co.

2828. (D) On the 6th of September last, in New Lancaster, Ohio, Mrs MARY A. H. BLAIR, wife of Henry Blair, and daughter of Michael J., and Anne Stacy Jacobs, of this co.

2829. (D) In Springfield, Jefferson Co., Ohio, on the 20th inst., of apoplexy, Mr DAVID J. LEVY, of Carrollton, Ohio.

November 20, 1839 (MHS)

2830. A man named JOHNSON, charged with stealing a horse was tried in our county court, yesterday, and convicted, and sentence to the penitentiary for 7 years.

November 27, 1839 (MHS)

2831. (M) On Tuesday evening last, by the Rev. D. Zacharias, Mr HENRY NEELD, to Miss ELIZA ANN STONER, all of this city.

1840

January 8, 1840 (MHS)

2832. (D) At sea on board the schooner "Henry Captain Clark" on his passage from Galveston to New Orleans, Dr. ANTY. HERMANGE, a native of Baltimore, formerly professor of

Chemistry, of Mount St. Mary's College, Emmittsburgh, MD.

January 15, 1840 (MHS)

2833. (M) On the 6th inst., by the Rev. Joseph Trapnell, Mr ASAEL ROBERTS, to Miss ELIZABETH LEASHER, all of Frederick Co.

January 29, 1840 (MHS)

2834. (M) On the 22nd inst., by the Rev. Joseph L. Smith, Mr HENRY BAKER, to Miss SARAH CATHARINE BUTLER.

February 5, 1840 (MHS)

2835. (M) On Thursay evening last, (at Cookerly's Hotel) by the Rev. John L. Pitts, Mr BASIL RUNKLES, to Miss REBECCA HENRY, both of Frederick Co.

March 4, 1840 (MHS)

2836. (M) On Thursday evening last, by the Rev. John L. Pitts, Mr JOHN HAMILTON to Miss MARY LEASE, all of this co.

May 20, 1840 (MHS)

2837. The Levy Court appointed Mr JOHN SIFFORD, Collector of Taxes.

May 23, 1840 (MHS)

2838. (M) On Sunday evening by the Rev. John L. Pitts, Mr JACOB BAILY, to Miss MARY ANN LIGER, both of this co.

May 27, 1840 (MHS)

2839. (M) On Thursday evening last, by the Rev. Jno. L. Pitts, Mr PETER SMITH, to Miss ELIZABETH CRAMER, both of this co.

2840. (M) In Burkittsville, on Thursday evening last, by the Rev. Michael Wachter, Mr JOHN T. EDWARDS, of Cumberland, MD., to Miss ELIZABETH A. GREY, of Pleasant Valley, MD.

2841. (D) On the 10th inst., in the 33rd year of her age, at Eller's residence in Elkridge, MD., Mrs ELIZABETH DORSEY, relict of the late Caleb Dorsey, of Thomas.

August 5, 1840 (MHS)

2842. (M) On Thursday last, by the Rev. John L. Pitts, Mr HAMILTON SELVEY, to Miss REBECCA YINGLING, both of this co.

September 9, 1840 (MHS)

2843. (M) At Jefferson, Frederick Co., MD., on the 1st of September, 1840, by the Rev. J. C. Bucher, Mr ALEXANDER H. YOUNG, to Miss SERENA S. COST, daughter of the late Mr Christian Cost, all of Frederick Co., MD.

2844. (M) On Tuesday morning last, by the Rev. D. Zacharias, W. M. B. McLANAHAN, Esq., one of the editors of the "Citizen," to Miss ANN R. SMITH, all of this city.

2845. (M) On Thursday last, by the Rev. Jno. L. Pitts, Mr ALBERT GRIMES, to Miss ELLEN EDMONSON, both of this co.

2846. (M) On the same day, by the same, Mr EMANUEL R. GRIFFITH, to Mrs MARY A. HOOKER, all of this co.

2847. (D) In Cumberland, on Wednesday last, WILLIAM McMAHON, Esq.

December 9, 1840 (MHS)

2848. (M) At Philadelphia, on the 26th ult., by the Rev. W. H. Odenheimer, the Honorable HENRY A. WISE, of VA., to SARAH, daughter of the Hon. John Sergeant.

2849. (D) At Clearsprings, MD., on the 30th ult., Mr ELIE K. FRIEND, formerly of this place.

1831

MARYLAND JOURNAL AND TRUE AMERICAN

January 26, 1831 (LC)

2850. Elder JAMES McVERY, is expected to preach in the Court House on next Friday evening at candlelight.

February 9, 1831 (LC)

2851. (M) On Tuesday evening, by the Rev. J. H. Jones, Mr WILLIAM WEST, to Miss SARAH GATTON, daughter of the late Aquila Gatton.

2852. (M) On the same evening, Mr NICHOLAS LYDDANE, to Miss MARY ANN BARRET, all of this co.

2853. (M) On Saturday the 29th ult., by the Rev. J. H. Jones, Mr BENJAMIN HANEY, to Miss ELIZA SIMMS, both of this co.

2854. (D) At the residence of her father, Mr Nathan Dickerson, on the 25th ult., Miss ELIZABETH DICKERSON, in the 25th year of her age. She was the victim of a protracted pulmonary complaint; a disease which is like the canker.

2855. (D) On Friday the 21st ult., Mrs GEMIMA J. GRIFFITH, consort of Howard Griffith, Esq., in the 72nd year of her age. A member of the Baptist Church for over 42 years.

2856. Appointment by the Governor and Council of Maryland, for Montgomery Co. Orphan's Court - HENRY HARDING, JESSE LEACH, WILLY JAMES. Justices of the Levy Court - LLOYD MAGRUDER, ROGER BROOK, HORACE WILLSON, HENRY GRIFFITH, of L., and NATHAN WHITE, of N. Justices of the Peace - JESSE LEACH, LYDE GRIFFITH, JAMES DAY, JOHN M. WILLIAMS, JOHN L. TRUNDLE, LEVI VEIRS, JOHN CANDLER, WILLIAM SCOTT, HENRY HOWARD, of J., JAMES LYDDANE, ABRAHAM S. HAYS, THOMAS L. OFFUTT, ARNOLD T. WINDSOR, THOMAS SCOTT, CHARLES BUNTING, ABSALOM THRIFT, ROBERT W. WILLETT, THOMAS L. PERRY, BENJAMIN PERRY, EVAN THOMSON, ERASMUS PERRY, GEORGE I. JUDY, ASA HYATT, WILLIAM CHISWELL, THOMAS DAWSON, of R., JAMES M. DAWSON, SAMUEL DARBY, ADEN DARBY, of B., WASHINGTON DUVALL, HENRY A. COLLIER, OSBORN S. WILLSON, JESSE ALLNUTT, HENRY W. TALBOTT, HENRY HARDING, WILLIAM O. CHAPPEL, JOHN POOL, JOSEPH ANDERSON, WILLIAM TALBOTT, LEMUEL CLEMENTS, WILLIAM DARNE, THOS. F. W. VINSON, LEWELLYN LODGE, BURGESS WILLETT, JAMES HAWKINS, Jr., LOTT LINTHICUM, WILLIAM T. GLAZE, WILLIAM B. BENNETT, MERCER BROWN, RICHARD CROMWELL, R. Y. GOLDSBOROUGH, Z. L. MAGRUDER, SAMUEL P. GILPIN, ELIJAH P. ETCHISON, BENJAMIN LYON, NATHAN DICKERSON, WILLIAM GAITHER, JOHN LOWE, WILLIAM PRATHER, Jr., ROGER B. THOMAS, NATHAN HOLLAND, Senr., JOHN BONNIFANT, WILLIAM BROWN, SAMUEL D. WATERS, BENJAMIN ROBEY, WILLIAM TRAIL, EDWARD PORTER, NATHAN T. HEMPSTON, THOMAS L. F. HIGGINS, SAMUEL PERRY, HANSON CLARK, JOHN GASSAWAY, JAMES N. ALLNUTT, JAMES L. PLATER, JOHN GOTT, GEORGE W. HEMPSTON, GEORGE W. DAWSON, JOHN YOUNG, of L., ELISHA W. WILLIAMS, JACOB NICHOLLS, ROBERT LYLES, WILLIAM PEARRE, ANDREW CLEMENTS.

February 16, 1831 (LC)

2857. (M) Last evening, by the Rev. J. Mives, Dr. JOHN W. ANDERSON, to Miss MIRA MAGRUDER.

2858. (M) Also on the same, Mr JOHN S. BALL, to Miss TABITHA RIGGS.

2859. (M) By the same, on Thursday evening last, Mr THOS. B. OFFUTT, to Miss MARY ANN HARRIS.

2860. (M) By the Rev. J. H. Jones, JAMES N. AUSTIN, of KY., to Miss MARGARET WEST.

April 20, 1831 (LC)

2861. Elder JAMES McVERY, is expected to preach in the Court House on tomorrow evening at candlelight.

May 4, 1831 (LC)

2862. Rev'd. JOHN HEALY, from Baltimore, is expected to preach in the Baptist Meeting House, on Tuesday evening next at 1/2 past 7 o'clock.

June 8, 1831 (LC)

2863. Appointments by the Levy Court for Montgomery Co. EVAN THOMPSON, appointed Commissioner of the School Fund, for Clarksburg District, WILLIAM WILLSON, of Jno., declined to serve. Judges of the Election District #1. Cracklin - LYDE GRIFFITH, THOS. RIGGS, of Sam'l., NICHOLAS D. WARFIELD. District #2. Clarksburg - ZADOK SUMMERS, JAMES NEEL, JAMES MAGRUDER. District #3. Medley's - CHAS. WILLSON, RECHIL L. GOTT, JOHN YOUNG, of Ludowick. District #4. Rockville - ZACHARIAH GATTON, THOS. FISHER, JOHN JONES, of Nath. District #5. Berry's - WASHINGTON OWENS, RICHARD HOLMES, ROBERT Y. BRENT. Constables. District #1. JOSHUA HILTON, WARREN ADAMS. District #2. JAMES ANDERSON, JOSHUA PURDOM, Jr., JOHN McDONALD, ROBERT SOPER. District #3. GEO. W. FLETHALL, ARCH'D. M. LYLES, NICH'S. L. DAWSON, ELIAS SPAULDING. District #4. OTHO BOSWELL, WILLIAM HARRIS, RICH'D. B. GITTINGS, CASPER YOST, MICH'L. R. BERRY. District #5. REUBEN BAKER, NICH'S. G. THOMAS, BENJAMIN BURGESS. Clarksburg - DANIEL COLLINS. Hyatts-Town - WILLSON L. PHILIPS. Rockville - MOSES LUGENBED, Constable and town bailiff.

June 22, 1831 (LC)

2864. BENJAMIN S. FORREST, Esq., has declined serving as an Elector for this District.

July 6, 1831 (LC)

2865. (M) In Bath, Stuben Co., New York, on the 11th ult., Mr MOSES ALEXANDER, age 98, to Mrs FRANCIS TOMKINS, age 105! (They were taken out of bed the following day)

2866. (D) In Logan Co., Ohio, on the 2nd of June, Mrs MARY MAGRUDER, wife of the the Rev. J. B. Magruder. She was taken with a violent chill on the 31st of May, which was followed by high fever, and continued until abated by the cold chill of death, on the 2nd of June. The bereaved husband vents his sorrow in the word of the Rev. John Newton.

July 13, 1831 (LC)

2867. Right Reverend Bishop STONE, will preach at St. Bartholomews Church, on Saturday the 23rd., and Sunday the 24th., in the Protestant Episcopal Church, in Rockville.

August 3, 1831 (LC)

2868. (D) On the Lord's Day last, GREENBURG GRIFFITH, aged 70 years, and 3 days.

August 10, 1831 (LC)

2869. (D) At the residence of her mother, in Rockville, MD., on Monday night last, Miss ELIZABETH HAGAN, in the 16th year of her age. The disease which terminated the death of this lady, was of a complicated nature.

August 24, 1831 (LC)

2870. (D) On Wednesday last, near this place, Mr CHARLES S. LANSDALE, age about 40 years, he leaves a wife and 1 child.

September 7, 1831 (LC)

2871. National Republican Convention of the 3rd Congressional District, is to be held on Saturday next, at New Market, Frederick Co., MD. Delegates from Montgomery Co. District #1. OTHO MAGRUDER, JOHN W. DARLY, and HENRY GRIFFITH, of Lyde. District #2. JOSHUA PURDOM, WILLIAM T. GLAZE, and ROBERT M. BEAM. District #3. Gen. T. T. WHEELER, ARCHIBALD LEE, and JOHN CASSAWAY. District #4. RICHARD BOWIE, WILLIAM DARNE, and ZACHARIAS McCUBLIN. District #5. ROGER B. THOMAS, THOS. I. BOWIE, and THOS. WORTHINGTON.

September 14, 1831 (LC)

2872. (D) On Monday evening last, near this place, at the residence of her father, Miss ERNSLEY OFFUTT, in the 14th year of her age.

October 19, 1831 (LC)

2873. (D) At the residence of Mrs Martha Wooton, at about 10 o'clock, last Monday evening (10th inst.,) ELIZA MARY, aged 5 years, and daughter of Dr. William M. B. Wilson, of Frederick City.
2874. (D) On Tuesday following, Mr OSGOOD OFFUTT, about 70 years, a long and highly respected citizen of this co.
2875. (D) On Monday the 10th inst., Miss MILLY SMITH, age about 50 years.
2876. (M) By the Rev. J. Mines, on the 7th inst., Mr GREENBURY M. WATKINS, to Miss KITTY ANN GATTON.
2877. (M) By the same, on Monday evening last, the Rev. JOHN BURGER MAGRUDER, to Miss HELEN GATTON.

November 16, 1831 (LC)

2878. List of Grand Jurors for the November term, 1831. LYDE GRIFFITH, THOMAS BEALL, of Tyson, SAMUEL MAGRUDER, WILLIAM PRATHER, Jr., JOHN RIGGS, ASA HYATT, WILLIAM CHISWELL, LLOYD DORSEY, THOMAS RAWLINGS, NATHAN COOK, THOMAS POOLE, DAVID TRUNDLE, JOSEPH NEEL, HARVEY GRIFFITH, JAMES HILLARD, HENRY YOUNG, WASHINGTON DUVALL, WILLIAM S. HAYS, BENJAMIN I. PERRY, HANSON CLARKE, ADAMSON WATERS, BERNARD GILPIN, BASIL BROOK.

December 7, 1831 (LC)

2879. (D) At 1/2 past 6 o'clock, this morning, at his residence in this village, ZADOK MAGRUDER, Esq., attorney-at-law, in the 37th year of his age. The decease will be buried on Friday next at 1/2 past 10 o'clock, A.M., at the residence of his mother, Mrs Martha Magruder.

December 14, 1831 (LC)

2880. (D) On Monday last, in this village, Mr JOHN LANSDALE, age about 40 years. He was in the vigor of health, about an hour before he fell a corpse.
2881. (D) On same day, in this co., very suddenly, Mr JAMES ATWOOD, age about 50 years.

1832

January 3, 1832 (LC)

2882. (D) In Philadelphia, on Monday last, STEPHEN GIRRARD, Esq., age 85 years. In his will, he named 10 gentlemen as trustees to settle his affairs of his banking house. He had lived there for 50 years, his net capital is estimated at 10 million dollars,, and probably the richest person in the world. He distributed $2,000,000.00 dollars for the establishment of a great public school for the county, and city of Philadelphia, which is to be endowed with his real estate in that district. To the State of Pennsylvania, $300,000.00 dollars, to be invested in Danville, and Pottsville Railroad, a 1/2 a million dollars, for improving the docks and the Eastern front of the city. He began his career as a cabin-boy, and died the richest banker in America.

2883. (D) At his residence near Rockville, on Monday last, Mr JOHN ADAMSON, age 85 years.

January 17, 1832 (LC)

2884. (D) In Clarksburg, on Wednesday mornng, Mr WILLIAM WILLSON, an old and respectable citizen, and formerly a residence of this place.

March 6, 1832 (LC)

2885. List of Grand Jurors for Montgomery County, for the March term. ROBERT WALLACE, ASA CLAGETT, ARNOLD T. WINSOR, SAMUEL SOPER, LEMUEL HOLLAND, ARCHIBALD NICHOLLS, HENRY GRIFFITH, of L., THOS. B. BENSON, CALEB GARTRELL, SAMUEL M. BEALL, ROBERT BROWN, BENJAMIN DUVALL, REUBEN B. CARLEY, HENRY A. COLLIER, REMUS DORSEY, ELIAS PERRY, STANISHUS KNOTT, JAMES MAGRUDER, Jr., JOHN D. KING, JAMES M. HAWKINS, RICHARD SNOWDEN,, JAMES B. BEALL, WILLIAM O. LODGE, THOS. C. NICHOLLS, Bailiff.

2886. List of appointments made by the Governor and Council, for Montgomery County. No changes have been made in the Orphans' or the Levy Courts. Justices of the Peace - THOMAS L. OFFUTT, JESSE LEACH, JOHN M. WILLIAMS, JOHN CANDLER, JAMES LYDDANE, THOMAS SCOTT, ABSALOM THRIFT, BENJAMIN PERRY, ERASMUS PERRY,

ASA HYATT, SAM DARBY, of Basil, WASHINGTON DUVALL, OSBORN S. WILLSON, HENRY W. TALBOTT, JAMES HAWKINS, Jr., WM. T. GLAZE, RICHARD CROMWELL, BENJAMIN LYON, NATHAN HOLLAND, Senr., BARRY ROBY, Senr., NATHAN T. HEMPSTONE, JAS. N. ALLNUTT, GEORGE W. DAWSON, ALEXANDER WINSOR, GEORGE W. DARBY, JOSEPH C. WHITE, RICHARD K. WATTS, JOSEPH ANDERSON, JAMES DAY, LEVI VEIRS, WILLIAM SCOTT, ABRAHAM S. HAYS, ARNOLD T. WINSOR, CHARLES BUNTING, ROBERT W. WILLETT, EVAN THOMPSON, GEORGE I. JUDY, JAMES M. DAWSON, ADEN DARBY, HENRY A. COLLIER, JESSE ALLNUTT, HENRY HARDING, LOTT LINTHICUM, MERCER BROWN, ZACHARIAH L. MAGRUDER, JOHN LOWE, JOHN BONIFANT, WILLIAM TRAIL, T. L. F. HIGGINS, GEO. W. HEMPSTONE, ELISHA R. GAITHER, ROBERT M. BEAM, THOMAS W. GREEN, WILLIAM B. HOWARD, BENJAMIN HIGGINS, THOMAS OWEN. Coroners - ABRAHAM DAWSON, WILLIAM O. CHAPPELL.

2887. (M) On last Tuesday evening, by the Rev. Mr Hemphill, Mr HORATIO CLAGGETT, to Miss MARGARET ELIZABETH, daughter of Thomas Scott, Esq., both of this co.

2888 (D) In Rockville, on Wednesday morning last, at about 2 o'clock, after a long and lingering illness, Mr JOHN PORTER, editor of the Maryland Free Press, in the 31st year of his age. He leaves a wife, and 1 child.

2889. (D) On the 10th of February last, in this co., Mrs ELEANOR AGLON.

March 20, 1832 (LC)

2890. (M) On Sunday evening the 4th of March, by the Rev. J. H. Jones, Mr JOHN H. THOMPSON, to Miss MARY BURNS, both of Montgomery Co.

2891. (M) On Tuesday evening the 6th, by the Rev. J. H. Jones, Mr DENNIS HARRISON, to Miss SERENY SPARROW, both of this co.

April 3, 1832 (LC)

2892. (M) On Thursday evening last, by the Revd. J. H. Jones, Mr LEONARD D. SHAW, to Mrs ANN H. BENNETT, both of this co.

April 16, 1832 (LC)

2893. Appointment of Supervisor of Public Roads, in Montgomery

County, made by the Levy Court, in April 1832. District #1. JAMES BROWN, WILLIAM PRINCE, NATHANIEL POPE. District #2. ARCHIBALD BROWNING, ADEN DARBY, MERCER BROWN. District #3. SAMUEL S. HAYS, HENRY W. TALBOTT, JOHN B. DYSON. District #4. SAMUEL CLEMENTS, THOMAS WATKINS, THOMAS SCOTT. District #5. AMOS FARQUHAR, JAMES HOLLAND, ERASMUS PERRY.

2894. (M) On Thursday the 5th inst., by the Rev. Mr Gilliss, Mr ELBERT HEETER, to Miss LYDIA C. OFFUTT, all of this co.

April 24, 1832 (LC)

2895. (D) Departed this life, on Thursday morning the 17th inst., in this place Mrs HANNAH A. POLLARD, widow of the late Rev. Charles Pollard, in the 31st year of her age, she leaves a son and daughter.

May 1, 1832 (LC)

2896. (M) On Thursday evening the 19th of April, by the Rev. J. H. Jones, Mr KEMP G. CARTER, of Washington City, D.C., to Miss JANE TRAMELL, all of this co.

2897. (M) On Tuesday evening last, by the same, Mr WILLIAM THOMPSON, to Miss JANE BURNS, both of this co.

May 29, 1832 (LC)

2898. (M) At Baltimore, on Tuesday evening last, the 29th ult., by the Rev. E. J. Reis, Dr. JESSE WILLET LEACH, of this place, to Miss ELIZABETH ANN, eldest daughter of Edward Morgan, esq., of Baltimore.

2899. Appointment of the Levy Court, for Montgomery Co. Judges of Election District. District #1. LYDE GRIFFITH, THOS. RIGGS, of Sam., NICHOLAS D. WARFIELD. District #2. ZADOK SUMMERS, JAMES NEEL, JAMES MAGRUDER. District #3. CHARLES WILLSON, RICHARD GOTT, Sen., JOHN YOUNG, of Ludowick. District #4. ZACHARIAH GRATTON, THOMAS FISHER, JOHN JONES, of Nath. District #5. WASHINGTON OWENS, RICHARD HOLMES, ROBERT Y. BRENT. Constables: District #1. JOSHUA HILTON, WARREN ADAMS, NIMROD DAVIS. District #2. ROBERT SOPER, JOSHUA PURDOM, Jr., EDEN GLOYD. District #3. ELIAS SPAULDING, DAWSON ALLNUTT, HEIRMAN F. BENNETT. District #4. JOHN McDONALD, CASPER YOST, OTHO BOSWELL, WILLIAM HARRIS, RICHARD B. GITTINGS, MICH'L. R. BERRY. District #5.

BENJAMIN BURGESS, HENRY B. DULANY, REUBEN BAKER. Hyattstown - CHAS. H. MURPHY. Berry - THOMAS WATKINS. Rockville - MOSES LUGENBED, Constable and town bailiff.

July 3, 1832 (LC)

2900. (D) At Mr Walter Magruder, in this co., on Sunday the 24th of June, Miss ELIZABETH CHILDS, age about 43 years, and daughter of William Childs, a member of the Methodist Episcopal Church, for about 20 years.

August 14, 1832 (LC)

2901. (D) At his residence in this co., on last Lord's Day morning, after 3 weeks sickness of bilious fever, Mr JESSE WILCOXEN, aged 60 years, leaves a widow and several children.

September 18, 1832 (LC)

2902. (M) On Wednesday the 5th inst., by the Rev. J. H. Jones, Mr SAMUEL CROWN, to Miss MARY CAMBELL, all of this co.

2903. (M) On Thursday last, by the Rev. L. J. Gillis, Mr JOHN S. BAILEY, of this co., to Miss ELIZA HICKS, of Fairfax Co., VA.

2904. (D) On Monday the 27th of August ult., at his residence in Montgomery Co., MD., Captain NICHOLAS L. DAWSON, in the 80th year of his age. For more than 24 years past he has open the polls of every election held in this district.

2905. (D) On the 14th inst., in this co., JOHN BASEY, Esq., age about 50 years leaves a widow and children.

November 13, 1832 (LC)

2906. (M) On Thursday evening last, by the Rev. J. H. Jones, Mr CHARLES W. WOODS, to Mrs TRACY CARY, both of this co.

2907. (D) On Monday evening last, Mrs MARY HERRON, consort of the late John Herron, in the 74th year of her age.

1833

February 12, 1833 (LC)

2908. (M) On Thursday evening last, by the Rev. J. H. Jones, Mr

CHARLES RIGGS, to Miss ANN AMERICA NORTHCRAFT, all of this co.

2909. (D) Departed this life on Friday last, THOMAS DAVIS, Esq., of this co., age about 65 years. Was a officer in the Army that went to quell the insurrection in Pennsylvania. Served as Delegate to the General Assembly, and as Council to the Governor.

2910. (D) On last Lord's Day, near Brookeville, Mrs HOLLAND, wife of the late James Holland.

2911. (D) On the same day, in the vicinity of Rockville, the late TYSON BURGESS, age about 12 years.

February 27, 1833 (LC)

2912. (M) On Tuesday evening last, by the Rev. J. H. Jones, Mr THOMAS F. CHRISWELL, to Miss MARY E. JONES, both of this co.

2913. (M) On same evening, by the Rev. F. Waters, Mr JOSHUA DORSEY, to Miss CATHARINE WATERS, all of this co.

2914. (D) On Last Lord's Day evening near this place, JOSEPH ALBY, in the 34th year of his age, leaving a wife and 5 small children.

March 20, 1833 (LC)

2915. (D) On Friday evening last, after a severe illness, MARY HILTON BRADDOCK, only daughter of Mr John Braddock, of this place, age, nearly 8 years.

April 3, 1833 (LC)

2916. (D) JOHN W. HILLERY, was drowned in a well, in this village on Monday last. He had gone to the well to examine the pump stock, about half way he slipped and fell to the bottom, where he remained underwater for about 30 minutes. He resided in Baltimore, where he kept a oyster house.

April 17, 1833 (LC)

2917. (D) Departed this life, on Wednesday the 3rd inst., after a protracted illness of nearly 2 years duration, JEREMIAH G. ORME, eldest son of Doct. Richard Orme, of this co., age about 26 years.

May 15, 1833 (LC)

2918. (M) On Tuesday evening the 7th inst., by the Rev. Mr Drane, RICHARD I. BOWIE, Esq., of this place to Miss

CATHARINE L., second daughter of General O. H. Williams, of Hagerstown.

May 22, 1833 (LC)

2919. (M) Last evening by the Rev. J. H. Jones, Mr NOAH E. DORSEY, of Baltimore Co., to Miss SARAH DORSEY, of Montgomery Co.

June 5, 1833 (LC)

2920. (M) Last evening by the Rev. J. H. Jones, Mr WILLIAM W. MAGRUDER, to Miss LEANNA BENTON, both of this co.

July 17, 1833 (LC)

2921. (D) On the Sabbath afternoon last, Mrs ISABELLA NEEL, wife of Mr Joseph Neel, near Clarksburg. She leaves a husband and 3 children. She was killed suddenly by lightning while sitting at the end of the bed of her afflicted son.

July 31, 1833 (LC)

2922. (D) A patriarch - At Hickory Hill, in Baltimore Co., MD., on the 22nd inst., Mr WILLIAM THOMPSON, aged 111 on the 1st day of February.
2923. (D) General JOHN COFFEE, on the 7th inst., in the 62nd year of his age, at his residence near Florence, AL.
2924. (D) In Philadelphia, Commodore WILLIAM BRAINBRIDGE, of the Navy, of the United States.

August 7, 1833 (LC)

2925. (D) Another Revolutionary character gone - Captain THOMAS ROGERSON, in the 77th year of his age. A member of the Maryland Legislature, acted as chairman of the Committee of Military Pensions, of Charles Co.
2926. (D) At Alexandria, Dr. THOMAS SEMMES, age 65 years.

August 14, 1833 (LC)

2927. (M) In Washington, THOMAS L. SPEAKE, Esq., to Miss MARY ANN ROWE.
2928. (M) At George Mills, Smithfield, on the 14th ult., Col. THOMAS WESTGATE, a patriot of the Revolution, aged 83 years, to Miss SUSAN CARD, of South Kingston, age 14.
2929. (D) In Baltimore, PHILLIP A. JONCHEREZ, aged 21, of Washington City.
2930. (D) In Newburn, N. C., the Hon. JOHN STANLEY.

2931. (D) Of chorlea, at Bardstown, KY., after a few hours illness, WM. ROWAN, and his wife, A. H. ROWAN, and MARY JANE STEELE, son and daughter in-law, and granddaughter of Judge John Rowan.
2932. (D) Near Knoxville, TN., JAS. MARTID, in the 106 year of his age, a soldier of the Revolution.

August 21, 1833 (LC)

2933. (D) WILLIAM TRAIL, an old and respected citizen of this co., and lately of Barnestown, in the 64th year of his age, after a long and protracted illness, he leaves a widow and 9 children.
2934. (D) In London, ANNA, second daughter of Sir Walter Scott, cause of death was brain fever.

August 28, 1833 (LC)

2935. (M) At Leesburg, VA., by the Rev. Mr Adie, on the 8th inst., Gen. THS. T. WHEELER, of this co., to Miss HESTER ANN McLEOD, of New York.
2936. (M) In Alexandria, on the 16th ult., by the Rev. T. W. Newman, Mr ANDREW SALES, to Miss LUCY FORTUNE, of Prince Williams Co., VA.
2937. (D) In Washington City, on Sunday morning last, ELIZABETH ANN, consort of Dr. Jesse W. Leach, of VA., and eldest daughter of Edward Morgan, Esq., of Baltimore.

September 18, 1833 (LC)

2938. (M) On Thursday evening last, by the Rev. Thomas Birkly, Mr LORENZO D. NIXON, of this place, to Miss ELIZA A. SHAW, of Leesburg.

October 2, 1833 (LC)

2939. (M) On Tuesday the 10th of September, by the Rev. John Mines, RICHARD CROMWELL, Esq., to Miss ELIZABETH ANN, eldest daughter of Mr Zachariah Williams, of this co.
2940. (M) On Thursday evening last, by the Elder J. H. Jones, Mr ELISHA RIGGS, of Montgomery Co., to Miss AVOLINA WARFIELD, of Anne Arundel Co.

October 16, 1833 (LC)

2941. Right Rev. Bishop STONE, will visit this co., service will be held at St. Bartholomews on Saturday next, and at St. John's Church, in Rockville, on the Sabbath, and at Monocacy Chapel, on the 22nd.

October 30, 1833 (LC)

2942. (M) At Graden, on Wednesday last, by the Rev. W. A. Smallwood, JOHN BOWIE, Esq., to ANNA M. L. GRANT, daughter of the late Levi Grant, all of Prince George's Co., MD.

2943. (D) Departed this life, on the 24th of May, last, at West Liberty, Ohio, Mrs HELLEN MAGRUDER, formerly Hellen Gatton wife of Rev. John Magruder, in the 50th year of her age.

November 13, 1833 (LC)

2944. (D) Departed this life, on Wednesday the 6th inst., at Rockville, THOMAS EDWARD, only son of Dr. J. W. Leach, of Va., aged 7 months and 7 days.

2945. (D) On same, at his residence, near Rockville, Mr LLOYD A. BURRIS, age about 30 years.

2946. (D) On Thursday the 7th inst., Mr LLOYD A. LANNUM, age about 40.

1834

January 15, 1834 (LC)

2947. (M) On Thursday evening last, by the Rev. John Mines, Mr BENJAMIN BAKER, to Miss SOPHIA CROWN, both of this co.

2948. (M) From the Liverpool (PA) Mercury - Married in this borough on Tuesdayy last, PELEG STURTEVANT, Esquire, editor of the "Liverpool Mercury" to Miss _____, she doesn't like to see her name in print, but she's a pretty girl any how.

February 26, 1833 (LC)

2949. (D) WILLIAM WIRT, died in Washington, on Tuesday evening the 18th inst.

2950. (D) At the residence of his father, on Tuesday evening the 18th inst., after a protracted illness, Mr NICHOLAS LYDDANE, printer, in the 22nd year of his age.

2951. (D) On Thursday morning last, in this place, Mrs MAHALAH DOWDEN, consort of James Dowden.

1835

July 8, 1835 (EP)

2952. Levy Court met on Monday last, and appointed THOMAS H. OFFUTT, Constable.

1829

December 2, 1829 (MHS)

2953. (M) On Tuesday the 17th of November, by the Rev. J. H. Jones, Doct. JAMES H. CLAGETT, of this co., to Miss ELIZABETH A. GERROTT, of Washington Co.
2954. (M) On the same day, by the same, JOHN P. GERROTT, of Frederick Co., to Miss MATILDA GERROTT, of Washington Co.
2955. (M) In Frederick Co., on Tuesday the 24th, by the same, Mr AARON RIGGAL, to Miss ELIZABETH MAYNARD, both of Frederick Co.
2956. (M) On last evening, by the same, Mr WILLIAM COUNSELMAN, to Miss EDITH SHOEMAKER, both of this co.

1831

April 13, 1831 (MHS)

2957. On Monday the 4th inst., the Levy Court appointed the following School Commissioners. 1st District - Cracklin - SAMUEL P. GILPIN, WILLIAM I. DORSEY, BASIL MAGILL. 2nd District - Medley's - BENONI DAWSON, COLMORE WILLIAMS, SAMUEL S. HAYS. 3rd District - Clarksburg - WILLIAM WILLSON, of John, JAMES M. THRIFT, ADEN DARBY. 4th District - Rockville - WILLIAM HUDDLESTON, THOMAS I. PERRY, WILLIAM DARNE. 5th District - Berry's - THOMAS GITTINGS, ABRAHAM BROOKE, THOMAS P. STABLER. Additional appointments: MOSES LUGENBEEL, Constables and bailif for Rockville.
2958. On Monday last, the Levy Court appointed the following gentlemen Supervisors of Roads for the county. 1st District - Cracklin - JAMES BROWN, WILLIAM PRICE. 2nd District - Medley's - ADAM DARBY, BASIL SOPER, MERCER

BROWN. 3rd District - SAMUEL S. HAYS, JOHN M. WILLIAMS, HENRY YOUNG. 4th District - Rockville - JOHN LANSDALE, WILLIAM TALBOT, BENJAMIN PERRY. 5th District - Berry's - ISAAC HOLLAND, ERASMUS PERRY, JOHN RABBITT. Inspector of weights and measures - OBED HURLEY. Appointment by the Commissioners of Tax Assessors - 1st District - Cracklin - JOSHUA HILTON. 2nd District ROBERT SOPER. 3rd District - JAMES N. ALLNUTT. 4th District - Rockville - WILLIAM O. CHAPPELL. 5th District - ROGER B. THOMAS.

1839

EMMITSBURG GAZETTE

August 17, 1839 (LC)

2959. (D) Melancholy death - On 6th inst., MARY VIRGINIA, infant daughter of Rev. Geo. St. C. Hussey, of Fayetteville. Whilst at play fell from the porch of her dwelling into a vessel, used for the purpose of collecting water, and was drowned. The child had escaped parental vigilance but a short time before its situation was discovered.

2960. (D) On 4th inst., Mrs ELIZABETH WEAVER, of this place, aged 62 years.

2961. Mr JAMES WISE, of Emmitsburg raised a tomato measuring 16 1/2 inches around the grit, and weighting 16 ounces. A potato from the same garden weighting 2 1/4 pounds.

2962. A onion raised at St. Joseph's by Mr WASHINGTON MARTIN, measured 14 inches around grit, and weighting 16 ounces.

2963. A cabbage stalk raised by JACOB L. GELWICKS, measured 5 feet 2 1/2 inches, they can be seen at the Union Hotel.

1831

FREDERICKTOWN HERALD

January 22, 1831 (MHS)

2964. Protestant Female Free School - The second anniversary of this institution was held in the Lutheran Church of Frederick, on the evening of the 17th inst. Meeting was organized by calling Major GEO. M. EICHELBERGER, to the chair, and appointed LEWIS MEDTART, Secretary. Meeting was open by religious exercise by the Rev. Mr GEHR, Rev. Mr SCHAEFFER, & Rev. Mr SMALTZ. Managers elected for 1831, are: Mrs SMALTZ, Mrs ELIZA, Mrs MANTZ, Mrs HUGHES, Miss MARY JACKSON, Miss CATH. REYNOLDS, Mrs ELIZA STEINER, Mrs CATH. RITCHIE, Miss ANNA RITCHIE, Mrs OTT, Miss ROBINSON, Miss GETZENDANNER, Mrs EBERT, on motion by the Rev, Mr SCHAEFFER.

INDEX

This index references the **paragraph** numbers, not the page numbers. All titles such as Doctor, Reverend, General, etc. have been removed. Titles are used when no other names are given in the newspapers.

ABBOTT John 371; 1098; John H. 167; 468; Margaret 167; Savinia 135; Thomas 167.
ABEARM Thos. 1288.
ACCIDENT 1227; 2257; 2521.
ACHROMATIC MICROSCOPE 1563.
ADAMS John 1282; Samuel 1282; Valentine 376; 1718; 2259; 2522; 2663; 2712; Warren 2863; 2899.
ADAMSON John 2883.
ADELSPERGER John 2598; Joshua 1405; Michael C. 2767.
ADER Matilda Shivers 53; Susan 53.
ADIE Mr 2935.
ADKINS Margaret 754; Rebecca 1181.
ADLESPERGER Michael C. 2608.
ADLUM Joseph 1098.
ADMINISTRATION CANDIDATES 1773.
AFRICAN COLONIZATION SOCIETY 780; 1396.
AGLON Eleanor 2889.
AGNEW John 1178; 1509; 1515; 2767.
AHALT M. 1832; Samuel 1513.

AHOLT Mathias 1952.
ALBAUGH Albert 1951; Catherine 908; Daniel 1040; Elizabeth 272; Lewis 601; Martha 2146; Samuel 1364; Sarah 1951; Solomon 1306; 1338; Valentine 1505; Valentine A. 1505; W. A. 985; W. H. 2642; William 970; William A. 360; 842; 1040; 1313; 1642; 1718; 1951; 2424; 2469; Wm. H. 2717; William Henry 1642: Wm. I. 2008.
ALBERT C. H. A. 1757; Mr 482; 1348.
ALBY Joseph 2914.
ALDRIDGE Catharine 2302; George 2708.
ALEXANDER 1309; Captain 2459; Emeline 2238; Harriet Ann 2238; Henry 869; James 2238; John 985; 1372; 1513; 2335; 2500; Joseph 2717; Lieutenant 2591; Mary 869; Moses 2865; Robert 1513.
ALLEN Isaac Hollingworth 2095; Mr 796.
ALLISON John 1614.
ALLNUTT Dawson 2899; James N. 2856; 2886; 2958; Jesse

ALLNUTT (continued) 2856; 2886.
ALLSTON John 1044.
AMERICAN BIBLE SOCIETY 1130.
AMERICAN HOTEL 236.
ANDERS Eliza 1018; Paul 624; Sarah Ann 802.
ANDERSON Abel 650; Aden 2768; J. H. 2479; J. W. 2301; James 2761; 2863; John Hamilton 1670; John W. 2857; Joseph 2856; 2886; Mary J. 350; T. 2717; Talbott B. 2389; Thomas 1670; 1735; 2479.
ANDES Eliza 2397.
ANDRE Major 144.
ANDREWS Alfred 2289.
ANGELBERGER Christianna 2109; David F. 775; Harriet 2354; Joseph 2403; Philip 2468.
ANGELL Sophronia 2280.
ANNA Santa 2625.
ANNAN Andrew 1047; 2732; Elizabeth 2732; John 970; 1047; 2398; Mary Jane 2732; Robert 724; 1047; 1093; 1127; 1377; 1509; 2531; 2608; 2662; 2712.
ANTIETAM FURNACE 1879.
ANTIETAM IRON WORKS 962; 1171.
APPLEBEE Sarah Ann 57.
APPLEMAN John 1952; Jona. 2717; Jonathan S. 1832.
APPLER Isaac 2304; Jacob Sr. 623.
APPLETON Samuel 2060.
APPOINTMENTS BY THE CITY 996.
APPOINTMENT OF DEPUTIES 1323.
APPOINTMENTS BY THE EXECUTIVE 43; 375; 507; 1056; 1217; 1395; 1436; 2322.
APPOINTMENTS FOR FREDERICK COUNTY 275.
APPOINTMENTS BY THE GOVERNOR 1239; 1312; 2599.
APPOINTMENTS BY THE GOVERNOR & COUNCIL 24; 325; 500; 993; 1074; 1297; 1303; 1318; 1339; 1341; 1379; 1382; 1412; 1699; 2443; 2492; 2712; 2767; 2856; 2886.
APPOINTMENTS OF JUSTICES OF THE LEVY COURT 2327; 2580; 2662.
APPOINTMENTS BY THE LEVY COURT 94; 277; 360; 985; 1372; 1718; 2335; 2500; 2680; 2791; 2837; 2863; 2893; 2899; 2952; 2957; 2958.
APPOINTMENTS BY THE PRESIDENT OF U. S. 1321.
ARCHER Thomas 650.
ARMOR J. U. 1205.
ARMOUR Chas. 708; Jane M. 583; Julia 135.
ARMSTRONG James 1253; Jane 1253; William 267.
ARNOLD Ann Sophia 696; Catharine 286; James M. 690; July Ann 966.
ARTHUR Charles 902; John 1832.
ARTS Capt. 760.
ARTZ C. B. 1098; Christian B. 2492.
ARVARD Thomas L. 156.
ASHBURY Prudence 981.
ASHTON L. 2360.

ASKEW Margaret 355; Peter 355.
ATKINSON General 2589; 2591.
ATLEE James C. 24; 1049; 1178; 2330; 2481.
ATTICK Philip 1811.
ATTIG Philip 1414; 2485.
ATWOOD James 2881; John L. 251.
AURORA BOREALIS 2632; 2685.
AUSTIN James N. 2860.
AVIS Mary 2600.
BABYLON William 1911.
BACKUS Mr 1985.
BACON Amelia A. 1337.
BAER Anne E. 1814; Anne R. 756; David Henry 2229; George 360; 915; Henry 24; 94; 360; 377; 879; 892; 985; 1025; 1098; 1297; 1313; 1339; 1428; 1718; 2423; 2468; 2642; 2662; 2712; Jacob 24; 275; 780; 1048; 1297; 1339; 1368; 1396; 1832; 1968; 2206; 2443; 2478; 2480; 2662; 2687; 2712; 2726; Julian 1850; Philip 150; Sarah Ann 262; Vice 1393.
BAIDERSTON Eli 757; Mary 757.
BAIL Mary 2474.
BAILE Abraham 2514; Mary 2465; William 2465.
BAILEY John 377; 2230; John S. 2903.
BAILY Hezekiah 2124; Jacob 2838; John 1394; 1397; 1485; 2712.
BAKER Alfred 2767; Basil 1394; 2264; 2767; Belinda 1963; Benjamin 2947; Brook 667; 2470; 2491; Brooke

BAKER (continued) 808; 1155; 1332; 1509; 1963; 2162; 2767; Daniel 2165; Harriet 2667; Henry 24; 275; 1040; 1297; 1339; 1396; 1509; 1662; 1965; 2662; 2834; J. A. 1968; James 2667; John 2474; 2671; John A. 1645; 2598; John H. 372; 544; Joseph Milton 603; Louisa Jane 2667; Lucinde 2650; Mary Ann 667; Mary Ann Rebecca 1788; Reuben 2863; 2899; Samuel 735; Sarah 2411; Serepta A. 2162; Thomas 2443; 2662; 2712; William 1827; Wm. Harrison 2236.
BALCH 765; L. P. W. 233; 377; 707; 745; 976; 1098; 1161; 1260; 1832; 1953; 1968; 1995; 2196; 2206; 2359; 2497; 2522; 2704; 2778; L. P. W. Jr. 2704; Lewis P. W. 2778.
BALDERSON John 2634.
BALDWIN James H. 405.
BALEY Eliza 1777.
BALL Harriet Ann 2010; John S. 2858.
BALLINGER Ann 595.
BALLON ASCENSION 1075; 1084.
BALTIMORE & OHIO RAILROAD 110; 207; 1279; 2257.
BALTZELL 1238; 1422; Aaron H. 360; Barbara 415; Belinda 363; Charles 415; 432; 1280; 1361; 2027; Charles Jr. 1280; Elizabeth 432; George 94; 206; 358; 359; 377; 1055; 1155; 1368; 1770; 2117; 2442; 2443; 2522; 2541; 2662; 2712; J.

BALTZELL (continued)
1155; Jacob 1774; John
119; 206; 255; 366; 377;
553; 654; 2117; 2328; 2457;
2522; 2571; Lewis 2306;
2326; M. 113; 120; Michael
43; 233; 256; 275; 276;
1015; 1026; 1073; 1156;
1191; 1204; 1218; 1297;
1339; 1394; 1397; 1485;
1830; 2443; 2663; 2712;
2766; 2767.
BANKER Daniel 985; Peter 24.
BANKERT Daniel 2335; Peter 275; 1339.
BANKHEAD Colonel 2589.
BANKHERD Peter 2443.
BANKHERT Peter 1297.
BANTZ 1238; 2555; Ezra 2634; 2638; Gideon 44; 206; 242; 255; 256; 276; 278; 359; 976; 1196; 1198; 1202; 1218; 1306; 1338; 1368; 1397; 1485; 1632; 2225; 2328; 2359; 2442; 2443; 2456; 2457; 2491; 2522; 2541; 2546; 2638; 2653; 2663; 2712; 2791; Gideon Jr. 199; 459; 951; 1098; 1327; 1414; Gideon Senr. 1098; 1414; 2385; Gordon 30; Henry 24; 275; 1297; 1339; 1515; 2443; 2662; 2712; John 730; Mary Ann M. 2152; Nimrod 326; 1338; 1414; 2152; 2634; 2638; 2641; Uriah 858; 878; Uriah S. 976; 1098; 1218; 1338; William Henry 2152; William S. 2117.
BARBER Mr 194; 372; Virgil H. 2803.
BARBOUR Mr 2367.

BARKER Elizabeth 901.
BARNARD Malachi 24.
BARNES Cordella 1708; Hannah Jane 516; John 94; 1509; Moses 1708; Mr 220; Samuel 602.
BARNET Raymond 115.
BARNEY A. 2092; 2225; A. L. 1297; 1339; 2196; 2443; 2662; 2712; 2717.
BARNHART Jacob 360; Margaret 2320; Margaretta 1956; William 784.
BARON Dr 489; Isabel Ann 489.
BARRET Mary Ann 2852.
BARRETT Thomas 407.
BARRICK Ann M. E. 2821; Catharine 2382; Ezra E. 2074; Frederick 959; George 1043; 1149; 1718; 2306; 2382; 2470; Henry 968; Jacob 235; 1258; 2002; 2306; John 1372; 1405; 1711; 1718; 2002; 2335; 2500; 2791; John W. 2052; Levi 1372; Peter 2306; Rosannah 1258; Samuel 433; Sarah Ann Elizabeth 673; Susan 959; William 1149.
BARRITT Wm. 1288.
BARROW T. 1131.
BARTGIS 765; 1238; 1671; Benjamin F. 43; Central Hotel 1585; Hotel 891; 1075; 1306; James 2117; John 2117; M. E. 30; 183; 206; 891; 996; 1025; 1161; 1202; 1218; 2491; Mathias E. 1196; 1320; 1397; 2648; 2153; Matthias E. 597; 598; 1306; 1460; 1485; Michael 2153.

BARTHOLOW E. M. 1737; John 1396; 1405; 2318; Michael 1895; Pressly J. 1394.
BARTLETT Josiah 1282.
BARTLEY James 461.
BARTLY James 1098.
BASCOM H. B. 2769.
BASEY John 2905.
BAST Elias 2682; Israel 1996; Susan 441.
BATES Aquilla 626.
BAUGH Edward F. 1441.
BAUGHER H. L. 1090; Isaac 1047; 1155; 1396; 2059; 2360; 2491; 2608; Joshua 724; Joseph 1047; Maria Louisa 2059; Wm. 31.
BAUGHMAN C. 715; Charlotte 135; 715; John W. 708.
BAUMBAUGH Mary Ann 180.
BAUMGARDNER J. Sr. 360; Jacob 1313; John 970; 2443; S. 808; 1332; Samuel 724; 1297; 1368; 2356; 2443; 2491; 2608; 2662; Vice 2351.
BAUMGARTNER 2567; Jacob 1042; John 24; 1368; S. 24; Samuel 1047; 1339; 2662; 2712.
BAXTER D. 550.
BAYARD J. H. 758; John H. 771.
BAYER Anna Maria 143; Jacob 143.
BAYLEY Catharine 612; John 612; 1098.
BAYNE John A. 1297; 1339; John G. 375; 1339.
BAYNER John G. 94.
BEAGLEY Catherine 83; John H. 83.
BEAHEY Eliza J. 1159; John 859; Joseph 1159.

BEAL Julian 1795.
BEALL 1395; Ann Lee 1821; Casandra 2029; Celena Caroline 1430; Enock 2777; Frances Z. S. 691; George W. 267; 2477; 2647; 2767; James B. 936; 2885; John H. 740; 1368; 2442; 2443; 2468; 2522; 2541; 2662; Lucilia 1275 Mary Jane 429; Mr 2050; Rev. 1832; Samuel M. 2885; Sarah Eleanor P. 1854; Theophilus 360; Thomas 1275; 2878; Tyson 2878; Upton 1712; 1873; 2022; 2083; 2092; 2812; 2813; William M. 206; 255; 429; 691; 1155; 1278; 1312; 2457; 2530; 2542.
BEAM Martha Jane 2617; Robert M. 2617; 2871; 2886; William 2443; 2662; 2712.
BEAN Mr 1182.
BEAR Anne R. 756; Charlotte 254; George 723; 985; Jacob 119; 1952; 2626; John 756.
BEARD Jacob Jr. 1333; Jacob Sen. 2767; Mary 1294; Mathias 2397; Matthias 1730; Solomon 1964; Susan M. 1448.
BEATTEE Henry 2662.
BEATTY 1671; A. P. 199; 1338; 1364; 1371; 1407; 1485; 1515; 1609; 2107; 2196; Affrabee P. 2492; Alfred B. 1369; Cornelia Ann 2771; Eli 1938; Elizabeth 1938; Otho 1255; Sarah 2538.
BEAUMONT Ann 497.
BECHTOL Sarah 596.
BECK Ann E. 2310; Edward 1778; Mary Ann 124; Nimrod 846.

BECKENBAUGH 1779; C. 24; George 722; 798; 1339; 1396; 1769; 2443; 2662; 2712; Jane Elizabeth 798; Susanna 836.
BECKER Ensign 2315; Mary 2374.
BEDHEIMER Fedenand 2135.
BEEMER Mary 532.
BEER George 94; 2356.
BEFORGODLEFEVER John 1934.
BEIGHLY John Henry 47.
BELL Elisha 1408; Joseph 110; Lucinda 2108; Susanna 2745.
BELT Margaret 1507.
BENDER J. 2423; John 94; 892; 985; 1428; 2117; 2335; 2423; 2500; Mr 1022.
BENET Washington A. 909.
BENNETO Lewis H. 2117.
BENNETT Ann Elizabeth 2265; Ann H. 2892; Benjamin W. 2468; Bunbury 2104; B. Washington 2130; Heirman F. 2899; Jesse 2265; John Davis 2130; Lucy 319; Margaret 2130; Perry 1349; Sarah Ann 920; Sarah J. 1873; Stewart 2823; Tilgham B. 2731; William B. 2856.
BENSON Thos. B. 2885.
BENTLINGER Frederick 1789.
BENTON Leanna 2920.
BENTZ 1238; Charles 264; Christiana 1947; Daniel 795; E. 981; Elizabeth 331; Ezra 878; 1218; 1414; 1460; 1515; 2008; 2638; 2767; Gideon 1414; George 692; Horatio 2117; Louisa 769; Margaret 692; Susan 396.
BERG Prof. 2678.

BERGER Catharine 1717; Elizabeth 949; Francis A. 2117; Jacob 256; 276; 2642; Thomas 160.
BERGSTRASSER Dieder 201.
BERLIN Louisa 1573.
BERNARD Malachi 275; 1297; 1339; 2443; 2468; 2662; 2712.
BERNNARD Malachi 1645.
BERNETT Malachi 2206.
BERRIER Ely 1523; Philip 1523.
BERRY John 650; Mich'l. R. 2863; 2899.
BEST John F. 797; Mr 2369.
BETES Fanny 297.
BEVAN Joseph 2585.
BEVERLY Eglantine 1347.
BICKLE Christian 847; Henry 1133.
BIDWELL Sylvester 673.
BIGGS Elizabeth 1176; Frederick 2789; J. 722; James 2025; Joseph W. 2264; 2767; Susan 451; 2789; William 722; 1718; 2595; William Sr. 851.
BIGHAM Charles 2826; Charles W. 1514; 2647; 2767.
BILLINGSLEA J. L. 2481; James L. 1331; 2330; 2505.
BINIX Thomas H. 2170.
BIRELY 1238; 1671; Ann M. R. 2439; Charlotte C. 458; Elizabeth 666; George K. 2117; Jacob 1718; John 1557; John W. 2117; Joseph 985; Lewis 256; 276; 377; 1026; 1098; 1218; 1322; 1397; 1485; 1623; 1632; 1832; 1953; 1968; 1995; 2092; 2314; 2522; 2541; 2642; 2653; Maria Frances

BIRELY (continued)
2314; Mary 135; Mary E.
2776; P. 1339; Philip 275;
970; 1297; 2443; 2468;
2712; Samuel 1043; Valentine 199; 255; 256; 276;
1098; 1161; 1250; 1338;
1953; 2092; 2328; 2510;
2634; 2638.
BIRHAM Chas. W. 2717.
BIRKLY Mr 564; Thomas 2938.
BIRTSCH Mary 1.
BISER 1571; 1779; D. S. 1339;
Daniel 895; 899; 1035;
Daniel H. 2443; Daniel S.
275; 1297; 1513; 1530;
1773; 2478; 2480; 2491;
2598; 2759; Daniel Sr. 899;
Eli 1390; Elizabeth 895;
Gideon 1401; George 1313;
1718; 1952 George C. 1041;
1405; Jacob 2712; John
924; John G. 2272; Mariah
899; Mary Catharine 1391;
Peter 893; 1390 Sarah 924;
Tilghman 24; 275; 1297;
1339; 1391; 1396; 1509;
2443; 2662; 2712.
BISHOP Mark 2385; Mark Jr.
1098; Mark Sen. 2577; Mary
1066.
BITZENBERGER Mary Ann
2194.
BLACK Frederick 94; Jeramiah
2766; Josiah 600; Rebecca
2581.
BLACKBURN Richard S. 796.
BLACKFORD Francis G. 2467.
BLACKWOOD Thomas O. 56.
BLAIR Henry 2828; John 1261;
Justice 5; Mary A. H. 2828.
BLASKEY Susan 1100.
BLESSING Abraham 2206;
2766; George 275; 723;

BLESSING (continued)
1048; 1297; 1338; 1968;
2443; 2480; 2662; 2712;
Michael 1421; Rebecca
1555; Solomon 2491.
BLIZZARD Isaac 1088.
BLOCHER John 1697.
BLOOD Parker 498; Mr 1378;
1406; 1623; 2699; 2703.
BLOOM Adam 2070; Catharine
502; John Jr. 2767.
BLOOMSBURG 40; 442; 1092.
BLOWER Richard 2634.
BLUME Peter 373.
BLUMINOUR Catharine 935.
BLUE LING 389.
BOARD OF HEALTH 1260;
1265; 1268; 1270; 1272.
BOCK Elizabeth 1103.
BODMAN P. 367.
BOGART Dr. 680.
BOGNER John 1513.
BOILEAN David 1513.
BOLABAUGHER Margaret 958.
BOLLENBAUCHER Julian
1771.
BOMGARDNER Elizabeth 625;
Jacob Jr. 94; Samuel 275.
BOND Peter 1523.
BONIFANT John 2886.
BONNIFANT John 2856.
BOOCHER Elizabeth A. 1796.
BOON Benedict 359; Jefferson
1718; Robert 2468; 2522.
BOONE Alexius 1124; Ben. 94;
Benedict 985; 1313; 2491;
2598; 2767; R. 708; Robert
24; 708; 1297; 1395; 2514;
2663; 2762; Thomas J.
1796.
BOOTH James 2654.
BOPST Daniel 2119.
BORIN Levi 1387.
BORING Sarh 1924.

BOSE Henry 2084.
BOSLER M. 536.
BOSTION William 755.
BOSTON Catharine 714; Jacob 714; 1334.
BOSWELL Otho 2863; 2899; Priscilla 263.
BOTELAR Edward 2398; Henry 2398.
BOTELER Bartholomew 1223; Dr. 1519; E. 2826; Edw'd. 2500; Elias 2479; Henry 24; 36; 275; 1297; 1338; 1405; 1718; 2107; 2117; 2132; 2356; 2443; 2500; 2647; 2662; 2712; 2765; 2766; 2826; Thomas 1041.
BOTES Asher B. 1275.
BOTLER Ed. 1372; Henry 1372; 1413.
BOUDET M. 726.
BOUGHER Henry 1040.
BOULDEN William 1853.
BOUREE Robert 2792.
BOURK Michael 1288.
BOURNE 572.
BOWDEN James 2690
BOWER Christian 275; 1339; 2443.
BOWERS Ann Elizabeth 1578; Christian 43; 1297; Daniel 1711; Henry 2767; John 1578; Levi 2736.
BOWERSOX George 2717; Henry 2468; Jacob 889.
BOWIE John 2942; Richard 2871; Richard I 740; 2918; Robert G. 740; Thos. I. 2871; William 2278.
BOWLUS 2566; Andrew 85; Catharine 398; David 1931; George 1048; 1155; 1339; 1368; 1396; 2359; 2443; 2478; 2480; 2491; 2662;

BOWLUS (continued) 2712; John 1396; John William 1788; Jona. 85.
BOWMAN John 2809;
BOWSER Adam 2023.
BOYD 1238; 1671; Andrew 1953; 2092; 2117; David 24; 70; 233; 256; 276; 278; 1161; 1191; 1196; 1202; 1218; 1249; 1397; 1485; 1632; 2757; 2766; 2767; E. 1169; Elijah 1169; Elisha 763; Mary 763; Mary Ann 1825.
BOYER Frances Hannah 1630; Henry 1787; Jacob 1172; Peter 1698; Thomas 2367.
BOYLE Daniel S. 1573; James 985; John B. 2398; John Brooke 2514.
BRACKENRIDGE Martha 306.
BRADDOCK John 2915; Mary Hilton 2915.
BRADISH Luther 2072.
BRADLEY Wm. 1169.
BRADY Geo. 1371.
BRAGONIER D. C. 1908; Eliz. S. 1908; John Melville 1908.
BRAINBRIDGE William 2924.
BRANCH John 76; Rebecca B. 76.
BRANDENBURG Daniel 420.
BRANE Geo. 1971; Henry 1948.
BRASHEAR Ann 1888; Belt 24; 275; 1045; 1297; 1888; 1923; Capt. 1117; Dr. 1045; Elias 1045; Thomas 1509; 2594; Thomas C. 1045; 1332; 2426; 2468; 2479; 2826.
BRASHEARS Thomas 2117.
BRASHIER Belt 1150; 1339.
BRAWNER Henry 2730; Louisa Ann 1088.

BRAXTON Carter 1282.
BREAHAN Catherine 1336.
BREATHITT George 659.
BRECKENBAUGH 1571; George 1368; 1536; 2491; 2595; 2712; Hotel 2595; Mr 2595; Tavern 2307; Wm. M. 2599.
BRECKENBRIDGE Mr 1063; Robert J. 1337.
BRECKENRIDGE George 1309.
BREEDY George 644.
BREAHAN Catherine 1336.
BRIETENBAUGH Mary 2575.
BRENDEL Amanda Catharine 2212; Henry 2212; Henry G. 1860; Mary Ann 2212.
BRENEMAN Frederick 863.
BRENGLE 2567; Alfred F. 345; Amelia Ann 1780; Ann R. 2814; Caroline 2; Catharine 481; Charles 262; 1098; 1936; 2117; Christian 377; 2377; Christian Jr. 1098; 2117; Daniel 1379; 1421; 1679; 2264; 2642; David 1414; 2008; Elizabeth 2270; Francis 324; 377; 707; 976; 996; 1093; 1127; 2117; 2328; 2359; 2456; 2491; 2522; 2535; 2541; George L. 2117; Jacob 377; 2616; John 1025; 1329; L. A. 1098; 2395; L. J. 1405; 2331; Lawrence 377; 481; 2377; Lawrence J. 976; 2328; 2522; Lewis A. 972; 2117; 2541; Louisa 345; Luther 1936; M L. J. 1354; Mary C. 2627; Nicholas 1045; 1405; 2426; Peter 592; 598; Sarah 1936; Sheriff 60; 105.
BRENNER Joseph V. S. 2219; William 906; 1411; 1485;

BRENNER (continued) 1515; 2107; 2132; 2219; 2395; 2717.
BRENT R. W. H. 2206; 2820; Robert Y. 2863; 2899.
BREVITT Elizabeth Beraston 603; Joseph 603.
BREWER Nicholas Jr. 1395; Senr. 1930.
BREXTON Thos. C. 1177.
BRIAN David Benjamin 1424; Elizabeth 1424; Henry A. 1396; Peter 1424.
BRIEN Anna E. 944; Coleman 944; Edward 134; Henry 1462; 2359; Henry A. 722; 1039; John 134; 1055; 1166; 1171; John McPherson 489; John Sen. 1033; Robert Coleman 658; William 1166; Wm. Coleman 1171.
BRIEN'S Iron Works 1462.
BRIGGS E. B. 2351.
BRIGHTVILLE Martha 2103.
BRINCKLEY Mr 1091.
BRINGERIE Louis 1943.
BRISH John M. 704.
BRISON Mr 1403; 1573; Rev. 1480; S. 2689; Saml 1617.
BROADRUP George 1840; Margaret 1840.
BROADRUPT George 126; Sarah 126.
BROAN Lucretia 2827.
BROILS Mrs 2487.
BROMETT Michael 1019.
BROMWELL John Edward 1188.
BROOK Basil 2878; Roger 2856.
BROOKE Abraham 2957; Mary Ann 2371; R. 708; Roger 708.

BROOKOVER Lucy Ann 570.
BROWER Isaac 1523.
BROWN Alexander H. 1311;
2477; A. H. 2329; 2477;
Catharine 472; Christian 24;
E. Lincoln 2049; Elizabeth
298; F. H. 985; Henry 893;
920; Isaac 1394; J. H. 361;
1968; 2093; 2100; 2196;
2206; James 2893; 2958;
James H. 1975; 2215; 2216;
2248; Jas. M. 763; Jos. H.
2092; Magdalen 473; Mahala
893; Matthew 239; Mercer
2856; 2886; 2893; 2958; Mr
576; 1387; Negro 2773; O.
B. 378; Obadiah B. 2428; P.
H. 360; 1515; Peter 94; Peter
H. 1313; 1460; 1515; 2316;
2456; 2457; 2491; Rev. 1953;
Robert 2885; Samuel Jr.
1803; Susan 1305; Susanna
1027; William 1306; 1338;
1405; 2398; 2766; 2856;
Wm. H. 94; 985; 2335; William S. 2117.
BROWNER Michael 1051.
BROWNING Archibald 2893;
Jonathan 985; 1372; 1718;
2335; 2500; 2594.
BRUCE A. 1169; Andrew 1829.
BRUCHA Jacob 1098.
BRUNNER 1238; 1671; Barbara
135; Elizabeth 135; Isaac
2148; J. 233; 970; 1003;
2117; 2356; 2491; 2767;
Jacob 342; 377; 970; 1098;
1202; 1218; 1421; James
1098; 1360; 1407; 1485;
1609; 2117; 2522; John
233; 970; 1003; 1509; 2117;
2356; 2491; 2767; Jonathan
347; 2541; Lewis 2767;
Margaret 342; Mary 135;

BRUNNER (continued)
Peter 175; Rhoda 2061;
Sophia 817; V. J. 30; 377;
2385; Valentine J. 70; 375;
1098; 1191; 1306; 1338;
1597; 2522; 2541; Valentine
S. 2117.
BRUTE C. S. 2810.
BRYSON S. 1656.
BUCHANAN Elizabeth 649;
James 649; John 490; 722;
1039; Justice 93; Mr 1899;
T. 1940; Thomas 1250;
Thos. Elie 490.
BUCHER J. C. 32; 46; 66; 67;
68; 82; 83; 286; 289; 294;
295; 352; 398; 400; 401;
409; 420; 516; 620; 631;
642; 703; 790; 813; 831;
855; 888; 893; 898; 899;
937; 966; 967; 988; 989;
1050; 1086; 1251; 1350;
1516; 1517; 1567; 1568;
1615; 1672; 1673; 1690;
1691; 1692; 1835; 1855;
1857; 1867; 1868; 1869;
1900; 1921; 1952; 2095;
2207; 2208; 2281; 2292;
2293; 2400; 2431; 2435;
2753; 2843; Mr 64; 559;
1024; 2080.
BUCKBUMMER Conrad 2277.
BUCKENHAM Greenburry 219.
BUCKEY Catharine Louisa
1981; Daniel 377; David 24;
Edward 24; Elisa 564; Elizabeth 312; Elizabeth M. 1808;
G. P. 1045; George 866;
George P. 24; 2318; 2426;
Jacob 672; 1098; 1414;
Mary E. 621; Michael 250;
906; 1260; Mrs 250; Peter
564; Susan 1714.
BUCKINGHAM William 1041.

BUCKLES M. 1583.
BUCKLEY Bridger E. 2055.
BUCKMAN Phinehas 2332.
BUCKY Daniel 1969; Evelina Virginia 1969.
BUDD T. L. 2071.
BUFFINGTON Levi 2298.
BULL Asahel 2614.
BUNTING Charles 2856; 2886; James 1745.
BURCH Sarah A. 1851.
BURCHART George 1840.
BURCKHART Charles 976; Chas. H. 377.
BURGEE Grafton 94.
BURGES Mr 2550.
BURGESS Benjamin 2863; 2899; Margaret 2388; Mary Ann 1531; Owen 1372; 1718 2500; Richard 81; Tyson 2911; W. 2336; Washington 24; 275; 1045; 1297; 1339; 1368; 1531; 1718; 2264; 2318; 2336; 2426; 2444; 2468; 2479; 2594; 2662; 2712; 2791.
BURHMAN George 2662; 2712; Henry 275; 1718; Samuel 2489.
BURKET Mary 2163.
BURKETT Henry 2602; John 1041.
BURKHARD Charlotte 886.
BURKHARDT Chas. H. 1339.
BURKHARL Charles 359.
BURKHART C. H. 24; Charles 1421; Charles H. 275; 375; 707; 1056; 1297; 1382; 2328; 2443; 2492; 2522; 2662; 2712.
BURKLEY Mr 1375
BURNAP Mr 216.
BURNES Charles W. 2813.
BURNETT J. R. 2003.

BURNS Jane 2897; Mary 2890; Michael 1515.
BURR Aaron 680; 2561.
BURRIER John 2464.
BURRIS Lloyd A. 2945.
BURROWS Mr 2084.
BURSKIRK Van 1041.
BURTON Mary Parks 1996.
BUSBY Abraham H. 2335.
BUSH John 979; Margareth 1283.
BUSHMAN Catharine 2125; Henry 1396.
BUSKIRK J. Van 2329.
BUSSARD Enos 2412.
BUTCHER John 662.
BUTLER Ann Elizabeth 644; Elias 1509; Henry 2443; 2762; Jeremiah 811; Mr 1159; Ormand F. 2468; Patrick 1288; Pierce 990; Sarah Catharine 2834; William 2488; 2489; 2516.
BUTT Bill 2246; Hazel 1400.
BUXTON John W. 1718.
BUZZARD John 1394; 1514; Lydia 2042.
BYER Geo. W. 1890.
BYERS Jacob 593; 1251.
BYRNE Martha Rebecca 1950; Michael 1155; 1460; 1950; 2457; 2767; Rebecca 1950.
BYSON S. 2650.
CABBS James G. 2443.
CADDEN Mr 930; 987; 1349; R. 816; 1088; 1089; Robt 814.
CAHOON Daniel K. 1316.
CAIN Eph'm. 2767; Letitia 640; 651; Wm. 2767.
CALEY George 2590; 2696; Rebecca 2590.
CALHOUN A. P. 1292; Alexander 1591; J. C. 1292; Mary 1591.

CALHOURN Anna 2752; John C. 2752.
CALN Mary A. 1658.
CALVERT George 2710.
CAMBRELENG Churchill C. 2350.
CAMPBELL 765; 2567; Abner 24; 275; 1098; 1320; 2443; 2662; 2712; 2767; Casandra 2120; Edward 975; James Mason 980; Mary 2902.
CANBY Samuel 2117; 2594.
CANDIDATES FOR ELECTIONS 25; 181; 192; 229; 242; 256; 261; 274; 276; 569; 586; 607; 616; 741; 742; 743; 751; 840; 844; 850; 858; 872; 1007; 1015; 1021; 1057; 1060; 1073; 1093; 1145; 1147; 1156; 1192; 1196; 1202; 1204; 1209; 1212; 1215; 1218; 1219; 1220; 1237; 1308; 1314; 1320; 1364; 1377; 1397; 1407; 1409; 1411; 1413; 1485; 1496; 1501; 1530; 1532; 1536; 1609; 1632; 1666; 1735; 1740; 1746; 1769; 1773; 2097; 2107; 2252; 2256; 2258; 2263; 2288; 2305; 2358; 2383; 2410; 2530; 2542; 2631; 2635; 2641; 2658; 2659; 2673; 2757; 2760; 2762.
CANDLER Daniel H. 1814; John 2856; 2886.
CANE Solomon 901.
CANON Hannah 766.
CANNON Ann Lavina 1365.
CANOUGH Maria 2777.
CANTWELL James 2772.
CAPES Thomas 613.
CARD Susan 2928.
CAREN J. 894.

CARES Mr 951.
CAREY John 94; 360; 985; 2335; 2500.
CARLEN Thomas 25.
CARLEY Reuben B. 2885.
CARLIN David 1688; J. 2423; J. Q. A. 708; James 94; 360; 377; 794; 892; 906; 985; 1098; 1372; 1718; 2335; 2395; 2423; 2500; 2552; 2634; Joseph 708; Matilda 715; Thomas 996; 2107; 2648; Thomas Ser'r. 2757.
CARLISLE David 1041.
CARLLEY Mary H. 2082.
CARLTON 387; Ann Rebecca 972; Edward A. 375; 1183; Eliza 1510; Thomas 192; 206; 233; 256; 276; 278; 553; 827; 972; 1155; 1183; 1191; 1198; 1278; 1332; 1339; 1510; William 2117; 2218.
CARYLE James A. 2133.
CARMACK Catharine 1189; Christian 2475; Christian S. 1415; Ephraim 2335; Evan 30; 1189; 1306; Hanson 1912; Jacob 808; 1332; Jno. 1875; Paul 1043; 2491; Samuel 30; 70; 255; 256; 276; 278; 375; 970; 994; 996; 1007; 1025; 1073; 1156; 1306; 1338; 1382; 1414; 1460; 1465; 2007; 2008; 2385; 2638; 2712; 2767; 2791; 2826; Sarah 1875.
CARNELL Thomas 286.
CARNES Ann 1955.
CARNN James M. 2791.
CARPENTER Stephen 32.
CARPET FACTORY 1322; 2010; 2018; 2652.

CARR Sarah 1719; Thomas 2424.
CARROLL Charles 362; 1279; 1282; Harriet 362; James 1288; Mary Ann 1223.
CARTER J. A. 740; John A. 740; Kemp G. 2896.
CARY Charlotte Rebecca 2076; James 2076; Robert C. J. 2587; Tracy 2906.
CASHOUR Jacob 776; William 2146.
CASSAWAY John 2871.
CASSEL Jacob 2662.
CASSELL Ann 1158; Eliza Ann 1554; G. 24; 1339; George 275; 1049; 1158; 1297; J. 24; Jacob 24; 275; 1040; 2442; 2712; James E. 1102; John 275; 1049; 1297; 1339; John A. 1520.
CASTELL James 2491.
CASTLE James 94; 827; 1122; 1332; 1371; 2264; 2598; 2717; 2767; 2826; James T. 1041; Mary Ann 68; Margaret Ann Rebecca 1122; Thomas 68; 723; 1048; 1394; 2264; 2356; 2766.
CATHOLIC CHURCH 1307.
CATOCTIN IRON WORKS 1033.
CATON Richard 1279.
CATZEBERGER Daniel 664.
CATZENDAFFER Joseph 1041.
CATZENDAFFNER David 2207.
CAUFMAN Margaret 2646; William 2646.
CECIL Hammedatha 1592.
CHAMBERS Hotel 1402; 1461; 1880; 2664; James 2717; Levi 1499; S. A. 1731.
CHANDLER Joseph R. 681.
CHAPMAN S. 660.

CHAPPEL William O. 2856.
CHAPPELL Eugenia 1292; J. J. 1292; William O. 2856; 2886; 2958.
CHARLESTOWN NUNNERY 1427.
CHARLESWORTH Solomon 449.
CHARLTON John N. 1339; John W. 1297; 1339; 2443; 2662; 2712; Louisa B. 310; Mr 2306.
CHASE Samuel 1282.
CHESAPEAKE & OHIO CANAL 787; 1169; 2276; 2457; 2804.
CHILCOTE Richard 1041.
CHILDS Elizabeth 2900; William 2900.
CHILTON Joshua 1542.
CHOAT Edward 709; 781; Mr. 862.
CHRIST Lydia 2113.
CHRISWELL Thomas F. 2912; William 2856; 2878.
CHURCH S. C. 1525; S. S. 1041.
CHURCH'S INN 1041.
CHURCH STREET SCHOOL 2225.
CISSELL Philip 1719.
CITY ELECTION 278.
CITY HOTEL 1228; 2663; 2668.
CLABAUGH Harriet 1912; John 94; 360; 985; 1912; 2335; 2500; Mary R. 984; Susan 301; Thomas 2264.
CLAGETT Asa 2885; James H. 2953.
CLAGETT Horatio 2887; Thomas I. 2264.
CLAPP Mr 1943.
CLAPSADDLE Louisa 526.

CLAREY Nathaniel 223.
CLARK Abraham 1282; Hanson 2856.
CLARKE Catharine 2278; David 1380; Hanson 2878; Wm. 985; Wm. B. 1675.
CLARY Burgess N., 864; J. 2090; Jesse 24; K. 2019; Nathaniel 94; Upton 1372.
CLAY Adam 2294; Codelia Ann 2790; Henry 446; 1148; Henry Jr. 4912; Jesse 2790; John 2426; Mr 208; 224; Sabinah 2294.
CLAYBAUGH N. W. 2767.
CLEARY Cornelius 1593; J. 1952; 1958; 1965; 1968; Lucinda 1816; Upton 2495; Vachael L. 2733.
CLERY Nathaniel 360.
CLEM A. 2160; Peter C. 2061.
CLEMENT Aaron 1091; Elizabeth Levis 1091; J. B. 2728.
CLEMENTS Andrew 2856; Lemuel 740; 2856; Samuel 2893.
CLEMM Catharine 321; Georgiana M. 98; Josephine E. 209; Wm. 98; 209; 321.
CLEMSON 2130; Harrison T. 2265; James 1442; Joanna 2136; John 2424; John D. 2102; John Jr. 2469; Mary Ann 609; Mordeca 609; Thos. G. 2752.
CLEVELAND Jane 894.
CLIFTON Miss 182.
CLINE Caspar 1407; 1411; J. 2809; Peter 2255.
CLINGAN John F. 288; McClain 2117; Thomas 2335; W. 1515; Winchester 1218; 2008; 2648; 2757.

CLOSE Elijah 2789; Elizabeth 695.
CLOUSE Philip 110.
CLOWE Harrison B. 2267.
CLYMER George 1282.
COA George 94.
COALE Jas. 1318; James M. 324; 359; 377; 707; 976; 996; 1098; 1215; 1382; 2117; 2359; 2393; 2445; 2446; 2522; 2541; John 1405; Mary 1302; Richard 1862; Richard Sen. 1030; William 879; 1302; 2469; 2491.
COBB J. G. 2662; James G. 2712.
COBBS J. G. 1046; 2329.
COBENTZ Henry 620; Jno. 620.
COBLENTS Eve 1086; John P. 1086; Peter 1048.
COBLENTZ Daniel 988; 1048; David 2449; Elizabeth 813; H. 1968; Henry 1952; J. P. 1855; Jacob 24; 275; 1297; 1339; 2443; John P. 813; John Philip 289; Leonora 1855; P. 1832; 2662; 2712; Peter 24; 1952; 2662; 2712; Peter Sen. 46; Philip Jr. 1513; Rebecca 46; Sarah 289; Solomon 988.
COBOURN James R. 116.
COCHRAN Henry 896; John William 896.
COCHRANE Martha E. 1659.
COCKEY Caroline C. 267; J. H. T. 1648; 2124; John H. T. 1394; 1495; Sebastian G. 2344; T. H. T. 1006; William 1045; 1405.
COCKERLY J. H. F. 2427.
COE Thomas 1297; 1339.

COFFEE John 2923.
COKE George 1614.
COLE Edward J. 517; Emily 1366; John 24; 94; 360; 604; 779; 1044; 1718; Mary Catherine 779; Wm. C. 2634; William G. 1460.
COLEGATE George 2409 J. 2477; John 808; 1332; 2264; 2477.
COLEHORSE Frederick 1975.
COLEMAN Chester 780; 1396; 1953; 2647; George 1098.
COLLGER Dr. 1563.
COLLIER Henry A. 2856; 2885; 2886.
COLLIFLOWER W. F. 2271; 2274; 2277; William F. 1245; 2273.
COLLINS Daniel 2863.
COLONIZATION SOCIETY 1396.
COLTON Mr 366.
COLWELL Jane 2707; John 2707.
CONDON John H. 94; 985; William H. 2335.
CONDRADT George M. Jr. 2117; John 2117; William 2117.
CONLEY Harrison 1655.
CONN Thos. 1514.
CONNELLY John 1288.
CONNER Eviline 1240; Henry 2574; Michael 385.
CONNERS Ann Rebecca 2363.
CONOWAY Solomon Freeborn 1725.
CONRAD George M. 586; John 1910.
CONRADT 1238; Frederica S. 1600; G. 2018; G. M. 30; 1098; 1260; 1832; 2385; 2652; George M. 25; 591; 844;

CONRADT (continued) 878; 1191; 1218; 1306; 1338; 1830; 2092; 2107; 2132; 2196; 2522; 2638; 2762; 2765.
CONROD Wm. 1987.
CONSECRATION 2189.
CONSTABLE Albert 650.
CONTEE John 2064.
CONTER John 1065.
CONVERSE F. 1249; Freeman 1206; 2550; Mr 1817; Sarah M. 1206.
COOK Eliza Ann 815; Elizabeth 1837; James 398; John 687; John F. 2466; Nathan 740; 2878; Otho 2664; W. G. 1075.
COOKERLY George 1430; Hotel 2009; 2036; 2835; Mr 2395; William 24; 722; 1039; 2016; 2443; 2541; 2634; 2712; Wm. Jr 2662.
COOKEYS G. 2306.
COOKMAN Mr 2364.
COOKS Joseph M. 1587.
COOKSON Esther 884.
COOLY Ruth Ann 1375.
COOMES Finnetta 574; Jesse 574; 986; Lucy 2246.
COOPER Adam 531; Captain 2589; 2660; James Sen. 1798; William 985; 2335.
COPPER MINES 701; 1458.
COPPERSMITH Hannah 900; L. F. 2059.
CORNELL James 2327; 2443.
CORONER'S JURY 2642.
COST Ann Rebecca 1690; Christian 1690; 2843; Henry 94; 1041; 1396; 1690; John 24; 74; 277; 970; 1155; 1297; 1396; 1612; 2398; 2662; Serena S. 2843.

COULTER Alexander 2063; Rebecca 2063.
COUNSELMAN William 2956.
COURT MARTIAL 2633.
COVELL Frederick 1481; 2500.
COVER Ephraim 1523; Jacob 1041; John 1041; Josiah S. 718; Tobias 808; 985; 1178; 1332; 2335; 2481; 2500; 2598.
COX G. 360; George 985; 1313; 1718; Geo. W. 213; Susan 2322.
COXE R. S. 1169.
CRABBES Frederick 2766.
CRABBS Frederick Jr. 1509.
CRAFT George 1970.
CRAILEY Mary Ann 1233.
CRAMER 1571; Absalom 94 360; Catharine 797; Elizabeth 1957; 2839; Ezra 24; 1465; 1530; 2468; 2767; Harriet 2074; Henry 797; J. 1039; Jacob 24; 275; 722; 970; 1297; 1339; 1718; 2307; 2443; 2449; 2662; 2712; Joseph 2203; Mary M. 2449; Peter 319; 2766.
CRAMERS Jacob 162.
CRAMPTON John 2826; John W. 1402; Thomas 1339; 2264; 2398; 2647; 2767; Thompson 2767.
CRANE Elizabeth 155.
CRAPSTER Elmina J. 2177; John 724; 1047; 1405; 2177; 2766; William 2468; William L. 1042.
CRAVER Joshua 2345; Mary Ann 2167.
CRAWFORD William 985; 2335.
CREAGER Adam 1718; 2791; Daniel 1043; 1149; Leah Mary 1149; Manassus 1078;

CREAGER (continued) Margaret 352; Solomon 959; W. H. 2480; William 1421; 2767; Wm. H. 1048; 2478.
CREDMER Mary E. 2104.
CREED 995.
CREEP Jacob 1288.
CREIGH Mr. 1833.
CRIMINAL COURT 808; 827; 879; 970; 1332; 1394; 1405; 1421; 1509; 2264; 2356; 2398; 2468; 2598; 2647; 2717; 2766; 2826; 2878; 2885.
CRISE Elizabeth 1859; Jacob 2767.
CROBY Ann R. 1299.
CROCKEN James S. 1098; Martha Ann 2048.
CROCKET Jas.94.
CROCKETT David 829; 843; 2460; James 360; 985; 1313; 1718; Mary 829.
CROMB Stephen B. 1716.
CROMWELL 260; Edward 2531; Edward A. 2468; 2662; 2742; George 1098; 1781; George W. 700; Harriet Ann Rebecca 1781; John 778; Joseph M. 1297; 2356; 2443; 2662; 2742; Mary Ann 1781; Nicholas 321; 377; 1421; Philemon Jr. 819; R. 1178; Rachael C. 2068; Richard 145; 778; 1046; 2356; 2856; 2886; 2939; Stephen Curtiss Crubb 145; Thomas T. 1800.
CRONE Henry 1952.
CRONICE J. 1045; Jacob 520; 1045; 2662; Samuel 377; 1953.
CRONISE Jacob 905; 1314; 2318; 2479; 2594; Jane

CRONISE (continued)
Rebecca 905; John 818; 2164; 2309; Mary E. 2164; Rachael 818; S. 1832; Samuel 976; 1968; Sophia M. 2309.
CROOKS Robert 1396.
CROPSEY Francis J. 646.
CROSS Lewis 985; 2335; Robert 1946.
CROUSE John 360; 652; 985; 2335.
CROWN Samuel 2902; Sophia 2947.
CRUM Ann Rebecca 2208; Barbara 2691; Catharine 926; Frederick 2120; G. W. 1041; Henry 925; 926; 1041; 2208; 2691; Hetty 433; John 1301; Louisa 925; Susan S. 2494; William 78.
CRUMBAUGH G. D. 1339; 2712; Gideon D. 275; 1297; 2264; 2306; 2398; 2443; 2662; John D. 985; 1313; 1718.
CRUMBINE Jacob 1098; 2012; Wm. 2500.
CRUMMINGS Robt. C. 2307.
CRUNDALL Miss 744.
CRUSE C. F. 1226.
CRUSHON George S. 1624.
CRUTCHLEY Elia 985; Elias 94; 360; 1313; 1436; 1710; 2306; 2470; Rosanna 1710.
CRUTCHLY Elias 2108.
CUDDY 670.
CUGHLAN Wm. 24.
CULBRETH Robert Emmet 1560; Th. 325; Thos 1560.
CULLER Daniel 1718; 2683; David 1041; Henry 1309; 1339; 1832; John Jr. 1041; Philip 1041.

CULLERYS John 594.
CULP Peter 2786.
CUMMING Robert C. 722.
CUNNINGHAM B. A. 1311; 2329; 2427; 2491; Edward C. 1489; Mrs 105; 1198; Tavern 1764; William 708.
CURFMAN William 2260.
CURLEY THomas Jr. 793.
CURR Amos 1041.
CURRAN Elijah 927.
CURTIS 2259; Henry 2785; John 2595; John R. 24; 2264; 2491; 2767; Mary 2501.
CUSHMAN Elizabeth 348.
CUSTARD Adam 94; 970; 2288; 2335; 2468; 2491; 2500.
CUTIS John R. 1465.
CUTRO Henry 287.
CUTSAIL Nancy 2250.
CYPHERD Ezra 2013.
DABBLESTEAD John G. 1372.
DABEESTEIN John G. 1718.
DABELSTERN John G. 2335.
DABLESTINE John G. 2500.
DADE M. A. 2081; Robert T. 2081.
DADDISMAN Jacob 2395.
DADISMAN Ezra 1180; 1428; 1515; 2767; Jacob 377; 1098; 2522.
DADYSMAN Ezra 2117; 2288; William 2117.
DAINGERFIELD William H. 1003; 2456; 2491.
DAMMOCK Captain 2589.
DAMPHOUX Dr. 859.
DANAHEW Patrick 1288.
DANDRIDGE A. S. 490; Ann S. 490; Mrs 490; Sarah 490.
DANGERFIELD Wm. H. 2359; 2491.
DANNEHILL C. 2329.

DANNER Joseph 2491; 2647; 2826.
DARBY Adam 2958; Aden 2856; 2886; 2893; 2957; B. 2856; Basil 2886; George W. 2886; John 360; John W. 740; Samuel 2856; 2886.
DARE John 1509.
DARLY John W. 2871.
DARNE William 740; 2856; 2871; 2957.
DARNER John 966; Joseph 1396.
DARTZEBAUGH Geo. 377.
DAUB George 723; Valentine 985; 1313.
DAUGHADAY Joseph 2117.
DAUGHERTY Jos. 1098.
DAVIDSON Alexander B. 1052; George 16.
DAVIS 2180; Ann Maria 89; Asabel 8; Delila 1822; Elizabeth Ann 323; Elias 2446; G. L. L. 1968; George L. 1831; 1832; George L. L. 199; 1396; 1953; James 1112; 1509; 1807; James L. 557; 1046; 1396; 1482; 2329; John 89; 1066; John H. 724; 2774; John I. 2117; Levi 923; 1918; Luke 2647; Margaret H. 2775; Mary 1624; Meredith 199; 459; 1098; 1131; 1327; Mrs 8; Nimrod 2899; R. W. 2774; 2775; Richard T. 756; Richard W. 1923; Robert 24; Samuel A. 2342; Sarah 1123; Sarah C. 1923; Sevilla 1417; Thomas 2909; Thomas J. 1396; 1610; 2427; 2491; 2774; Thomas L. 2329; Zachariah H. 2790.

DAWSON Abraham 2886; Benoni 2957; George W. 740; 2856; 2886; James M. 2856; 2886; Nicholas L. 2863; 2904; Philip 193; R. 2856; Thomas 2856.
DAY 861; Charles B. Y. 2588; E. G. 2588; Enoch G. 82; James 200; 2856; 2886.
DAYHOFF Andrew 1098; James M. 1372; 1718; 2500; 2522; Josiah 360; 985; 1098; Maria 2462; Nancy G. 567.
DEAFOBOUGH Catharine 1683.
DEAN Margaret Ann 1833; William 2382.
DEAR Catharine Elizabeth 2158; John 2158
DEATZEBACH Christenia 1878.
DEAVER Abraham 1394; Susan 1402.
DEBATING SOCIETY 1096.
DEBORAH L. 526.
DEBUTS Charles 2522.
DEBUTTS Charles 1098; Elisha 71.
DEFENBAUGH Henry 2590.
DEGRANGE Eugevn 2199; Margaret 333; 1247; P. 1422; Patrick 2765; Peter 1407; 1411; 1485; 1830.
DEGROFA Abraham 650.
DEKRAFT Frederick W. 805.
DELANEY Dr. 1138.
DELAPLANE E. 1858; Joseph 2306; Joshua 2398; 2595; 2647.
DELASHMUTT A. 2477; Arthur 94; 985; 2335; Elias 2767; Elias D. 2477; Elias L. 1509; 2717; 2767.
DELAUTER Elias 2763.

DELAWTER Mary Ann 559.
DELL Wm. 94.
DELPHY Margaret 824; Philander 824.
DEMUTH Henry 2802.
DENN Jacob 1952.
DENNY Mr 1591.
DERN Isaac 24; 275; 802; 970; 1297; 1339; 1960; 2398; Susan 1960.
DERR Daniel 813; 1104; 1952; Eliza 1245; 2273; Elizabeth 1764; H. W. 1832; Henry W. 1043; 1297; 1339; 1645; 2118; 2443; 2662; 2712; 2717; Isaac 2443; Israel 1859; Jacob 19; 813; John 1509; 1701; 1952; 2145; 2767; John A. 2712; John W. 24; 275; 722; 970; 1039; 1245; 1297; 1339; 1405; 2273; 2443; 2662; Lydia 2763.
DERTZEBACH Margaret 2433.
DERTZBAUGH Catharine 1104; George 808; 1332; 2356; Mary 2291.
DESHON John C. 650.
DEVELBISS Catharine Sophia 2052; G. 2052; John T. 1992.
DEVILBISS Adam W. 2006; Charles 24; 275; 1049; 1297; 1339; 2356; 2443; 2491; 2598; Eliza 2160; G. 2469; George 842; 2491; John Henry 2006; Joseph 184; Rachel A. N. 2601; Rosanna 2006.
DEVINE Charles 1288; Mary 401.
DEVITT 1238; D. B. 44; 255; 1191; 2385; David B. 25; 30; 256; 276; 1098; 1131; 1218;

DEVITT (continued)
1306; 1338; 1364; 1414; 2356; 2541; 2634; 2647; 2757; 2826.
DICKERSON Elizabeth 2854; Nathan 2854; 2856.
DIETERICH John C. 1005.
DIGGS Juliet 1633.
DILL 1238; Ezra 2634; George 708; Henry G. 2166; 2202; John 377; 1098; 1154; 2353; John Little 1028; Joshua 94; 192; 840; 878; 985; 1015; 1073; 1156; 1192; 1196; 1202; 1218; 1372; 1414; 1718; 2252; 2264; 2335; 2500; 2790; 2826; Leonard Augustus 1365; Tavern 1098; 1154; 2453.
DILLEHUNT Elizabeth 1962.
DIXON 765; 1178; Ann Rebecca 1725; Eliza 922; Haines 1725; Hatton 2346; James 255; 553; 650; 745; 1464; 2491; 2741; 2744; William 903; 1098.
DOBBS Dr. 1992.
DODDRIDGE Philip 518.
DODDS Robert 275; 713; 1297.
DODGE Alexander Hamilton 2755.
DOFFLER George 1362; 2648.
DOFLER Ann Mary 1877; George 1877.
DOLL Ann Elizabeth 1089 Caroline 266; Catharine 1696; Charles Edward 1549; Charlotte 2441; Daniel 2117; Ezra 377; 569; 586; 780; 840; 1098; 1191; 1260; 1549; 2522; George 1098; J. 30; Jacob 377; 1306; 1338; 2385; 2638; John 2117;

DOLL (continued)
Margaret 135; Michael 676; Thomas 266; 1098.
DONALDSON William 1199.
DONNELLY Rose 135.
DONSEIF Catharine E. 2277.
DORCAS John 1240; 1241.
DORF Julianna 371.
DORSEY 765; Augustus E. 2039; Caleb 1500; 2841; City Hotel 1471; 1851; 1961; 2049; 2226; 2272; 2298; 2720; 2739; Dennis 2479; Eli 1092; Elizabeth 2841; Ely 712; Evan 712; Hammond 2827; Henry W. 2261; 2479; John L. 712; John W. 1185; 1394; 1523; 2469; 2491; 2768; Joshua 2913; Lloyd 275; 1297; 1339; 1396; 1832; 1968; 2443; 2662; 2712; 2878; Michael 1283; 2471; Mr 904; 2394; 2407; Noah E. 2919; R. 2336; R. E. 1098; 1161; Remus 2885; Richard 1040; 1396; 2424; 2469; 2687; 2726; Richard G. 541; Roderick 745; 751; 1155; 1228; 1315; 2358; Sarah 2919; Sarah Ann 2261; Sarah Johnson 1092; Susan H. 1982; T. W. 2512; Thomas 1500; 2841; Upton 1982; Wm. H. 678; 1256; William I. 2957; William J. 678.
DOUB 2567; Ezra 377; 2522; Jacob 2729; Joshua 275; 1235; 1297; 1339; 1396; 2306; 2443; 2662; 2712; V. 1832; 1968; Valentine 360; 1718; 1953; 2196; 2206; 2791.
DOUGHERTY Bridget 715.

DOUGLASS A. J. 1041; Maj. 2528.
DOUR Margaret E. 1101.
DOUTY James 1040; Moses 1659.
DOW Lorenzo 852.
DOWDEN James 2951; Mahalah 2951.
DOWNEY Basil D. 2264; Harriet 2675; Maria 2535; William 2535; 2675.
DOWNS Paris 1633.
DOYLE Ephraim 77; George 280; Henry 654; 2117; John 377; L. 2346.
DRAINE Mr 185.
DRANE Mr 75; 2918; R. 1106.
DRAPER David 2169.
DRESSEL Elizabeth 99.
DRONE William G. 650.
DRONENBURG Andrew 1804.
DRONESBURG Sarah 736.
DUBLE Jacob 1041.
DUCATEL Julius F. 1309.
DUCKET T. Buchanan 1899.
DUCKETT Catharine E. W. 2565; Sally 1126; Thomas 1126; 2278; 2565.
DUDDERAR Col. 1832; Conrad 101; 1046; David 1040; 2552; 2766; Elizabeth 1469; George W. 1832; John 1040; Mary 2070; Sarah 1468; William 24; 101; 275; 1297; 1339; 1396; 1468; 1469; 2070; 2259; 2424; 2443; 2662; 2712.
DUDDERER Daniel 94; Hezekiah 845; John 66; Mahela 66; William 2580.
DUDDERO Jacob 1139.
DUDDEROW Henry 1350.
DUDERAR David 2640; William 1436; 2469.

DUDEROW Ezra 1776; Mary Ann 2519.
DUDRER Jacob 1523.
DUDROE Rebecca 1528.
DUDROW Conradt 2329.
DUER Samuel 2117.
DUKE Green H. 2117; 2140.
DULANY E. 715; Elizabeth 715; Henry B. 2899.
DUNCAN Charles 766; John M. 1253; Martha 2220; Mr 756; 1266; 2675.
DUNDDAR Elizabeth 784.
DUNHAM Isaac 24; 1098; Lewis 1098.
DUNLAP Col. 2491; Henry 1405.
DUNLOP 2259; Harriet Margaret 525; Henry 1465; 2767; James 525.
DUNNE John 1288.
DUPHORN Samuel 985; 1372; 1718; 2335; 2791.
DUPHOUR Samuel 2500.
DUPLE John 2206.
DURBIN Catharine 2268; Elizabeth 1697; James 24; 211; 275; 1297; 1339; Jno. 275; T. 24; Thos. 1297; 1339; William 275; 500; 827; 1332; 1339; 1697; 2268; 2356; 2443; 2522; 2541; 2662; 2712; Wm. Jr. 1098; Wm. Sr. 1098.
DUTROW Elias 831; Eliza 1654; John 117; Robert H. 2201; Samuel 2766.
DUTTERO Sophia 2122.
DUVALL 765; A. T. H. 1297; Benjamin 2885; Daniel 24; 275; 1046; 1127; 1297; 1339; 1405; 1436; 2259; 2264; 2329; 2443; 2662; 2712; 2826; David 745;

DUVALL (continued) 1093; Delila 1827; Eliza 1991; Elizabeth W. 79; Grafton 24; 79; 275; 2443; 2491; 2662; 2712; John 1414; 1674; John Henry 1967; Priscilla Ann 2455; Rebecca 1967; 1965; Thomas 24; 94; 360; 1045; 1313; Washington 2659; 2856; 2878; 2886; William 1967; William T. 2117.
DYSON John B. 2893.
EADER A. L. 2116; Edward 2040; Johnathan 850; Jonathan 976; 1594; T. 30; Thos 1306; 1338; Wm 2337.
EADOR Jonathan 24.
EAGLE Hotel 1480; 1573; 1722; 1852; 1972; Wm. 1375.
EARNST Solomon 1523.
EASTBURN Mr 2350.
EASTER Ira A. 2098; Mr 1130.
EASTERDAY Anna Rebecca 582; Conrad 2206; Harriet Ann 338; Sarah Ann C. 1812.
EASTIN Mary A. 320.
EASTON Johnsey 244.
EATON Henry 1801; 1851.
EBBERT Augustus 1098; George A. 1098; Mathias 1371; Michael 2648; Valerius 1371.
EBBERTS Joseph 2117; 2648; Wm. 2117.
EBERLY J. 1356.
EBERT A. F. 1327; Ann Rebecca 1137; Augustus 976; Augustus F. 199; 459; 1131; 1161; 1327; Ephraim 2117; G. Adam 377; George Adam 707; 2522; John 24; 94; 275; 360; 377; 985; 1137;

EBERT (continued)
1297; 1313; 1718; John M.
2117; Joseph M. 2117; Mrs
2964; Valerius 199; 459;
1098; 1131; 1327; William
2117.
EBERTS Edmund P. 2117;
Frederick 608; Wilhelmimina
1328.
EBRECHT Jonathan 122.
ECCLESTON Mr 733.
ECKENRODE Samuel M. 2117.
ECKER Jacob 1468; Mary Ann
617.
EDDY Mr 1275.
EDES Benjamin 425.
EDMONSON Elen 2845.
EDMONSTON Enoch 380.
EDWARDS General 2663;
Harriet 531; John T. 2840;
Mr 1444; Mrs 1410; Richard
H. 12.
EGE Andrew Galbraith 1000.
EICHELBERGER Ann Elizabeth
2381; Ann Maria 1988;
Colonel 1264; Frederick
1456; G. M. 206; 377; 996;
2328; 2541; George M. 255;
654; 1098; 1155; 2381;
2457; 2522; 2549; 2964;
Joseph 722; 1039; 1509;
2826; Julian 2186; M. 1339;
Martin 24; 74; 275; 277; 722;
1156; 1297; 1396; 1436;
2307; 2443; 2580; 2662;
2712; Niles 1414; Peter
1988; 2767; Rebecca 2038.
EIDENMILLER Elizabeth 664.
EIGENBRODE Daniel 2041;
Sarah 1722.
ELBERT Catharine 135.
ELDER C. 715; Catharine 715;
Elizabeth H. 1439; John E.
2717; Mr 610; 1439.

ELDRED Daniel 1194.
ELECTIONS 25; 30; 44; 70;
199; 278; 569; 586; 591;
654; 765; 840; 844; 878;
892; 906; 1055; 1238; 1271;
1306; 1338; 1414; 1422;
1428; 1571; 1671; 1779;
1843; 2092; 2117; 2116;
2132; 2259; 2385; 2395;
2406; 2423; 2546; 2555;
2567; 2634; 2638; 2648;
2697; 2765; 2770.
ELKINS Margaret 1826; Mary
Ann 1474; William 1474.
ELLER 2841.
ELLERY William 1282.
ELLICOTT Elizabeth R. 2364;
John 2364.
ELLIOT John 2643.
ELLIOTT Jonathan 187; Sarah
187; 571.
ELLIS Elizabeth 2493; Margaret
636; Mr 1163.
ELMWOOD 98; 209.
ELSHRODES Catharine 2176.
ELWOOD Anna 1525; J. 1525.
ELY 1238; Agnes 231; Catherine 2401; Christian 231;
Elizabeth 2173; Ezra 1098;
Givenia 1887; Hugh 650;
William 25; 278; 586; 591;
1218; 1323; 1887; 2635;
2648.
EMMERT Isaac 2430.
EMMETT Jane 1587.
EMMISS John 2764.
EMMITT Abigail 1660.
ENGEL Peter 615.
ENGELBERGER John 2765.
ENGELBRECHT George 255;
1953; Jacob 30; 1364; 1509;
1968; John 25; 44; 377;
906; 1414; 2132; 2395;
2522; Theo. F. 2117.

ENGLAND Dr. 2686; John G. 740; Julia Ann 82; Mary 715; Nathan 24.
ENGLAR Ephraim 231; David 231; Rev. 1895.
ENGLE Daniel 24; 275; 1049; 1297; 1339; 2330; 2335; 2443; Mary Ann 882; Susanna 718.
ENGLEBRECHT 1238; 1671; Ann 1997; Ann M. 1997; George 1098; 1953; 1997; Jacob 25; 840; 1098; 1306; 1411; 1953; 2406; 2638; John 906; 1407; 1485; 2107; John C. 2196; Michael 1371; 2734.
ENGLER D. 548; David 491.
ENGLES Ann E. 2021; Christianna 1334.
ENGLISH George 199; 459; 1131; 1327; Richard 586; 2766.
ENT 1238; 1571; G. W. 256; 276; 1057; 1073; 1156; 2395; 2457; George W. 24; 206; 255; 278; 586; 906; 996; 1025; 1155; 1161; 1218; 1228; 1278; 1460; 1515; 1530; 1843; 2456; 2491; 2634; 2717; 2767; 2826; O. G. 1371; Otho G. 1830; 2661; 2767.
EPISCOPAL ORPHAN ASSYLUM HOUSE 2276.
ERAST Susan 1139.
ERB John 24; P. 24; Peter 1042.
ERNST Catharine 1251.
ERVIN Thomas 1713.
ERVINE Elizabeth Ann 1727.
ERVING William 1041.
ESCAPE PRISONER 599.

ESTLER Archibald 2767; Dennis 1089.
ETCHISON Elijah P. 2856.
ETNA GLAS HOUSE 611; 2280.
ETTING S. 1169.
ETZLER Arthur 911; David 1509.
EULER Margaret 1964.
EURY Lydia 965; Margaret 2473.
EUSEBME Bishop 1226.
EUSTIS Brigadier General 2591.
EUTAW HOUSE 2039; 2675.
EVANS Harriet 54.
EVERETT Mr 2399; 2461
EVERHART Anna 2723; Jacob 43; Jacob Sen. 2723; Lawrence 1025; 2235; 2237; Mary Ann 703; Sarah 530; William 703.
EVERHEART Matilda 2216.
EVERIST John W. 1767.
EVERT Mr 871
EVITT Geo 1141; Joseph 1246.
EWING David 964.
EYCLER John 1552; Mary 1552.
EYLER Adam 1405; 1676; Elizabeth 1343; John 1254; Peter 882; Robert 1396.
EYSTER Daniel 269.
FABOR John 589.
FAGAN G. 1428.
FAHNESTOCK Derrick 130; Matilda 130.
FAHS Arnold R. 1372; 2335; 2500; Tobias 1832.
FAIR Elizabeth 227.
FAIRBANKS Franklin 389.
FALCONAR Enoch G. 249.
FALCONER Ann 361; G. W. 361; Geo. W. 2356; John 361.

FAREL Ann Maria 2338.
FARMERS'S BANK 1055; 1770.
FARQUHAR Amos 740; 2893; George A. 984; 1042; 1297; William 2178; William P. 24; 248.
FAUBEL 1238; David 333; 1218; 1247; Jacob 70; 256; 276; 360; 377; 591; 985; 1015; 1073; 1098; 1156; 1161; 1204; 1218; 1364; 2328; 2522; 2541; 2642; John 1097 2642.
FAUBLE 1671; David 1407; 1411; 1485; Jacob 94; 278; 375; 586; 878; 970; 976; 1260; 1313; 1396; 1397; 1485; 1718; 2008; 2406; 2492; 2631; 2653; 2662; 2712; John 840; Joseph 1861; Lydia A. 141; Solomon 1414.
FAULKNER Charles James 763.
FAVORITE Samuel 94.
FEAGA Catharine 2197; Frederick 2110; George 2767.
FEAGEA Geo. 1371.
FEARHAKE Adolphus 1098.
FEASER John 985; 2335.
FEASTER Jacob Senr. 2767; Jonathan 1041.
FEET Harrison 1689.
FEETE D. 1859; 1860; 2034; 2125; Daniel 1392; 1912; John Henry 1081; Mary A. 1860.
FELTY Rachael C. 2201.
FERIOR Jacob 2662.
FERREE Daniel 922.
FERRON V. 940.
FERTICH Johannes 694.
FESLER John 1953.
FESSLER Henry 1414; J. 2423; John 30; 256; 276; 892;

FESSLER (continued) 1163; 1202; 1218; 1306; 1338; 1428; 1843; 1968; 2385; 2423; Rosanna C. 1163.
FICHTER Barbara 847.
FICKLE Daniel 1107.
FIDDLER Mr 172.
FIERY Henry 2446.
FIESTER John 2556.
FIEZER Ann E. 1051.
FILLER Samuel 1952.
FINCH J. 2423; Margaret 135.
FINCKLE Rev. 1011; S. D. 2458.
FINK John 2598; 2767; 2826; Margaretta A. 1274; Mary 2292.
FINKLE Mr 927; 935; 936; 984.
FINLEN Robert 63.
FINLEY M. A. 2446; Thomas 650; 1236.
FINNEY James 254.
FIRE 7; 17; 260; 336; 520; 891; 987; 1151; 1304; 1355; 1400; 1420; 1455; 1462; 1909; 2018; 2033; 2123; 2138; 2245; 2283; 2304; 2547; 2552; 2556; 2652; 2653; 2759; 2786; 2793.
FIRE CONVENTION 2008.
FIRESTONE Henry M. 2242.
FIROR Daniel 1405; Jacob 24; 2443; 2712; 2767.
FISCHER G. J. 2638; Catherine 488; George 2522; George J. 1230; 2328; 2385; 2762; Heinrick 2451; James 1339; John 2491; Margaret 382; Philip 1839; S. R. 2789; Sarah C. 2585; William 25; 30; 70; 206; 229; 242; 255; 256; 276; 278; 377; 586; 707; 1306.

FISH General 2091; Henrietta 956; Marian 422.
FISHER 2555; Adam 1098; E. Burke 2053; Elizabeth 635; George 332; Geo. I. 1161; Geo. M. J. 1414; James 24; 275; 1297; John 2530; Joseph R. 2082; Samuel R. 1486; Susan 351; Thomas 2863; 2899; William 2598.
FISTAR Captain 1839.
FITZGERALD Aaron 2080.
FITZHUGH Mr 834; Wm. 2091.
FLAHERTY J. 1832.
FLANAGAN Dorcas 688; Wm. 24; 275; 1297.
FLAUT George 24; Mr 4.
FLAUTT George 275; 970; 1297; 1339; 2581.
FLEMING Henrietta Catherine 2392; John 923; Joseph 970; Joseph P. 2392; Robert 724; 879; 1047; 1394; 2264; 2468; Samuel 2522; Thomas 2264; Thomas A. 1098; 1421; 2522.
FLEMMING J. P. 377; Thomas 1628; Thomas A. 377; 2826.
FLETHALL Geo. W. 2863.
FLEWETT William 1741.
FLOOK Elizabeth 1867; Eveline E. 2281; Henry 989; J. 1832; Jacob 24; 1048; 1509; 1867; 1952; 1999; 2281; 2712; 2767; Jacob Jr. 68; John 1867; 2281; 2712; 2767; Mary Ann 989; Mary Jane 1999.
FLOUR INSPECTION 273; 357; 842; 1483; 2767.
FLOWERS B. 1832; Benjamin C. 1657; 2236.
FLOYD William 1282.
FLYNN T. 715; Teresa 135; 715.

FOGLE David 2417; Jacob 2705; Lydia Ann 2274; Rebecca 2737; William 2705.
FOGLER Henry 2220; Henry Jr. 2648.
FOLTZ Wm. 2510.
FORD Susan E. 2079.
FOREST Solomon 879; 1297; 2443; 2609.
FORNEY David S. 2089.
FORRANCE James 1041.
FORREST B. S. 1309; Benjamin S. 376; 2864; Jonathan 427; Julia 2809; Solomon 24; 74; 275; 277; 1339; 1396; 1436; 2264; 2443; 2491; 2580; 2662; 2712; 2809.
FORTNEY Mary 699.
FORTUNE Lucy 2936.
FOUT Baltzer 377; 1915; Catharine 1695; Grafton 1958; Greenberry 1879; Greenbury 2522; 2541; John H. 1460; John P. 2045; Mary 2165; Mary M. 1929; Otho 1232; Philip P. 1414.
FOUTZ David 24; 74; 275; 277; 897; 1297; 2319; 2481; 2491; 2598; Esther 491; John 491; Susanna P. 549.
FOWBLE W. H. 2334.
FOWLER Margaret 1017.
FOX Baltzer 717; Charles J. 2432; George 377; 663; 1509; George P. 24; 1514; 2491; 2767; Jacob 24; 2443; 2717; John 1795; Jonathan 1101; Margaret 2236; Susan 601; Susannah 752.
FRAAD George 1956.
FRANCES Mary 424.
FRANCIS George 2662; 2712; 2767.
FRANCISCO Peter 14.

FRANKLIN Bank 945; Benjamin 1282.
FRAZER J. 1968.
FRAZIER Caroline 715; Mahala 430; Mary 135; Sam'l. H. 418; W. 2184.
FREDERICK College 2550; Elizabeth 1920.
FREDERICK COUNTY BANK 654; 915.
FREDERICK COUNTY SAVINGS INSTITUTE 70.
FREDERICK WATER COMPANY 1310.
FREE SCHOOL 2594; 2595; 2608; 2609.
FREEMAN Wm. H. 650.
FREESE A. P. 1772; 1875; 1898; 1974; 2074; 2146.
FREEZ Andrew P. 1621.
FREEZE A. P. 2052; Joseph 2054.
FRENCH COURT 148.
FRENCHBAUGH Frederick 1100.
FRESHOUR Adam 141; Geo. W. 1850; Sophia 791.
FRESHOWER Wm Henry 1820.
FREYTAG George 485.
FREZE J. 1832.
FRIDBY James Edward 1410; Richard 1410.
FRIDGE Alexander 2758.
FRIEND Elie K. 2849.
FRIENDSHIP FIRE COMPANY 2648.
FRIEZE Michael 2482.
FRINGER Jacob 94; 360; 652; 985; 2335; 2398; 2500; Jacob Jr. 94; 360; Jacob Sen. 1012; Nicholas 2125.
FRISBY Eleanor M. 1444; James Edward 1444.
FRITCH Master 487.
FRITCHIE John 1830; John C. 654; 2634.
FRITZPATRICK James 1495.
FRIZLE Nimrod 2491.
FRIZZLE Nimrod 24; 2443; 2481; 2598.
FROG TOWN 1276.
FRY Mary 2654.
FRYDINGER Christian 113; 120.
FULLERTON M. L. 210; Matthew L. 750.
FULTON Alexander 1478; Barbara 2806; Captain 2306; John 1344; 1562; 1875; Robert 2540; 2806; Sabina 1562.
FUNDENBURG Anna Maria 2049; David 877; Henry 275; 1039; 1297; 1339; Julian 2049.
FUNDENBURGH H. 24; Henry 722.
FUNK Jacob 1385; Sarah 2626.
FUNSTON John 102.
FURRAY Abraham 930.
FURRON Robert 1043.
GABBY Eliza 1899; Joseph 1899; 2446.
GADULITIG Ezra 94.
GAINS Edmund P. 1943.
GAITHER Edward 2522; Elizabeth Ann 1446; Elisha R. 2886; Ephraim 740; 2546; Evan 216; George 1287; Henry C. 740; John 1523; Perry 768; S. 30; Steuart 70; Stuart 233; 377; 459; 1125; 1249; 1306; 1322; 1338; William 654; 827; 917; 1332; 1446; 2856.
GALAGHER James A. 2767.
GALEZIO Margaret 551; Sarah Ann 2312.

GALLAGHER Daniel 2264; James A. 2117; Richard 2791.
GALLAHER Betsy 445; James A. 2118.
GALLAKER Daniel 2468.
GALLIGHER Ann Maria 2187; James A. 2187.
GALLION Sarah Ann 919.
GALT Samuel 985; Sterling 629; 808; 1042; 1332; 2319; William 970.
GALWIN D. 2055.
GAMBER Ezra M. 2638.
GAMBLE David 2264; William 635.
GAMBRILL Ann S. 329; Charles A. 329; 392; 2328; 2380; 2395; 2522; 2634; 2642; Launcelot 1756; Maria 392.
GAPES Eliza Jane 1115; Elizabeth 1115; Thomas 1115.
GARBER John 2030; 2655; Martin B. 1458.
GARDENER Peter 1371.
GARDINER Oliver P. 1808.
GARDINIER Louisa 2548.
GARDNER John P. 949; Peter W. 1041.
GARFORD Martha 1471.
GARLIN Mary R. A. 1810.
GARRETT Geo. 1586.
GARROT Barton 2767.
GARROTT Barton 350.
GARTRELL Caleb 2885.
GASSAWAY John 2856.
GATES Major 2633.
GATTON Aquila 2851; Helen 2877; Hellen 2943; Kitty Ann 2876; Sarah 2851; Zachariah 2863.
GAVER George 1513.
GEAR John A. 55.
GEARY Michael 1041.

GEESEY Elizabeth 909; John 1010.
GEHR Margaret Ann 662; Mrs 2964.
GEIGER Mr 2331; 2558.
GEISBERT Samuel 1707.
GEISBURT Hester Ann 2067.
GEISINGER David 2812; Sarah Elizabeth 2812.
GEITZ Mary 2004.
GELDS George 2662.
GELMITH Peter 94.
GELTZS George 2712.
GELWICKS George C. 1098; 2634; Jacob L. 2963; Louisa S. 2226; Mr 2652.
GENEVIEVE Sister 2803.
GEORGE Sarah 2714.
GEPHART Charlotte 1786; Eleanor 1786; George 708; John 39; 504; 1786; Lewis 1098; 2117; 2648; O. C. 708; Oliver C. 708; Simon 708.
GERE John A. 2211.
GERNAND Emanuel 1049.
GERROTT Elizabeth A. 2953; John P. 2954; Matilda 2954.
GERRY Elbridge 1282.
GESEY Charlotte 1629.
GETZ Mary Ann 1301.
GETZENDANNER Abraham W. 621; Adam 1098; Alexander 37; C. 1093; 1421; 2395; Catharine 69; Catharine E. 2432; Charles 886; 1364; 1413; 1422; 2406; 2634; 2641; Ch'n. 2117; Christian 1060; 1278; 1515; 1752; 2174; Daniel 377; 976; 2398; 2522; 2541; Hannah Margaret Elizabeth 2504; J. 24; 1405; Jacob 359; 1494; Jonathan 377; 2328; 2541;

GETZENDANNER (continued) Josiah 177; Mary 437; Michael Jefferson 2750; Miss 2964; Nathan 24; Solomon 980; 1414; Tavern 23.
GEYER 1571; 1779; 2259; 2567; J. W. 2479; 2530; 2594; John 2770; John W. 1530; 1773; 2717; Samuel 1509; 2356.
GIBBS Geo. W. 2042.
GIBBSON Mr 646.
GIBSON Ann 2016; J. 603; Thomas 2016; William 328.
GIDDINGS James 674.
GIGAN Joseph 610.
GILBERT Ara 2708; Catharine 2621; Daniel 955; Eli 1325; Hotel 2279; Julietta 1488.
GILDEA Jno. B. 1803.
GILDS Geo. 2443.
GILLELAN Wm. R. 275.
GILLELEN Ann 2422.
GILLES Mr 773.
GILLIN Wm. R. 985.
GILLIS L. J. 2903.
GILLISS Mr 2894.
GILMOR R. 489.
GILMORE William 961; 1608.
GILPIN Bernard 740; 2878; Charles 2531; Samuel P. 2856; 2957; William H. 623.
GILSAN John 94.
GILSON Elizabeth 590; Richard 1396.
GIRRARD Stephen 237; 2882.
GIST Joshua 2065; Newton H. 1337; Thos Hammond 1252.
GITTING John 1297; 1339.
GITTINGER Daniel 2264; 2283; Elizabeth 287; George 2522; 2541; J. 708; John 889; 1455; John H. 708; Susan 889; William 2117; 2814.

GITTINGS Catharine 1864; Lloyd 926; 1864; Mary Elizabeth 1864; Richard B. 2863; 2899; Thomas 2957.
GIVEN James 1737; Mary Jane 1737.
GLADHILL John 2206.
GLAZE William T. 2856; 2871; 2886.
GLAZIER Jacob 1782; 2330; 2356; 2481.
GLEIM Jacob 2481.
GLENN 375.
GLESSAN John Sen. 985.
GLESSING Mr 1551; 1552.
GLESSNER William 822.
GLISAN John Sr. 360.
GLISON John 1151; 1313; John Sr. 1523.
GLISSAN John 2767.
GLOVER John J. 2350; Phebe 2350.
GLOYD Eden 2899.
GOES Maria 485.
GOLDSBOROUGH C. L. 2799; Chas. 1309; Dr. 2306; 2307; E. T. 2522; Edward 1906; Edward Y. 1906; L. 1396; L. W. 722; 1039; 2491; 2595; Nicholas W. 2172; R. Y. 2856; William 2172; 2565.
GOMBAR Ezra 2356; John 186.
GOMBER Ezra 2766; Ezra M. 382; 1414.
GONSO Jacob 2117; John 1881.
GOOD Wm. A. 932.
GOODMANSON Peter 1328; 1460; 2117; 2148; 2694; 2766; Rebecca Ann 1541; Williamina 2694.
GORDON Daniel 1763; James W. W. 1426; John H. 360; Mary Ann 2489; Rebecca

GORDON (continued)
1541; 2246; Thomas 777;
William 368.
GORE Ann 1165.
GORSUCH A. P. 696; Robert
2280; Stephen 24; 275;
1297; 1339; 2443.
GOSLIN Henry S. 290.
GOSNELL Aaron 1372; 1718;
2335; 2500; Adam 2791.
GOSZ Lawrence 2563.
GOTT John 2856; Rechil 2863;
Richard Sen. 2897.
GOWER Mary Ann 1178.
GRABILE Catharine Ann 1090;
John 1090.
GRABILL John Sen. 2391.
GRADEN 2942.
GRAFF Sebastian 1168; Sophia
Jane 1644; William 2356.
GRAHAM Ann Campbell 2524;
Ann J. 1504; James 1288;
Jno. 1504; Major 2591.
GRAHAME Caroline W. G. 232;
John 61; 377; Thos J. 232.
GRANT Anna M. L. 2942; Levi
2942.
GRANTHAM S. 715; Sarah 715;
Wm. 708.
GRAPHENSTEINER Ollen-
backenoffen 1384.
GRASON Rebecca 34.
GRATTON Zachariah 2899.
GRAVER Mary 1516.
GRAVES Dietrich 605.
GRAYSON Agnes 629; Wm 629.
GREASON William 1396; Wil-
liam Sen. 257.
GREEN Ann Laura 378; Cap-
tain 2589; Daniel S. 2681;
Duff 378; Jane 1897; Jonas
650; Thomas W. 2886;
Timothy 1611; William 2681.
GREENALL Catherine 600.

GREENE Thomas 657.
GREENHOLTZ Jacob 2339.
GREENTREE Benjamin 1045.
GREENWALD Emanuel 1193;
Susan 2610.
GREENWOOD Wm. 409.
GREER Mr 34.
GREY Eliza Ann 1497; Eliza-
beth A. 2840.
GRIER Mr 1463; R. S. 1000;
1540; 1667; 1813; 1893;
2182; Robert S. 1587.
GRIFFIN George Hancock 2046;
T. 708; Thomas 708.
GRIFFFITH Alfred 219; Eman-
uel R. 2846; Gemima J.
2855; Greenburg 2868;
Harvey 2878; Henry 740;
2856; 2871; 2885; Howard
2855; L. 2856; 2885; Lebbe-
us 1891; Lebleus 2767;
Lebrus 2594; Lyde 740;
2856; 2863; 2871; 2878;
2899; Lyde Jun. 740; Phili-
mon 1709.
GRIM 2241; Edward O. 2486.
GRIMES Albert 2845; Elias
1042; 2319; 2356; 2598;
Frederick 985; 2335; 2500
Gasaway 1982; Mary Ann
Elizabeth 846; S. Sen. 808;
1332; Samuel 722; Warner
T. 1718; 2791; Warren F.
1372; Warren T. 2307; 2500;
William 24; 275; 846; 1039;
1297; 1339; 1368; 1405;
2443; 2470; 2662; 2712;
William H. 722; 2307; 2443.
GRINDER Jacob 2502; M.
2523; Michael 1527; 2461.
GROFF John C. 410; 1263.
GROFT Abraham De. 650.
GROSHON Elias 2598; Elias A.
808; 1332; John 2598.

GROSHONG Elias 2121.
GROSNICKLE J. 1968.
GROSS Charles 132; Henry 1041; John J. 650.
GROSSNICHOL Peter 519.
GROSSNICKLE Jacob 2544.
GROVE Ann Elizabeth Post 1879; Daniel 888; 2717; David 2767; Elizabeth 1581; George 24; Hannah 2183; Jacob 808; 1332; 1405; 1581; 1958; 2183; 2468; John 1879; John D. 947; Lauretta 1958; Leonard S. 1513; Lewis J. 1495; 1708; Martin S. 1513; 2767; Mary 947; Samuel 2767.
GROVER Dr. 1085; George 970; 2452; 2767; George M. 2177; Mary A. 1984; Susanna 295.
GRUMBINE Daniel 2116; Margaret 655; Mary Catherine 2698.
GRUSHON Abraham E. 1988.
GUITEAU Mr 1700.
GURLEY 765; 2567; Martha 1463; Thomas 1320; 1323; 1414; 1460; 1463; 2092; 2117; 2196.
GUTELIUS Mr 1017.
GWINN Doct. 2491; 2359.
GWINNET Button 1282.
GWYNN W. 1155.
HABLISTONE Henry 623; 701; 702.
HACKNEY Barton 24; 275.
HADERMAN C. J. 939.
HAFF Abraham 2196; 2206.
HAFF & DAVIDSON 16
HAGAN Elizabeth 2869; Hugh 2378; John 912; 1513; 2766; Peter 2378.
HAGDER Basil 2767.

HAHN Francis 2176; Isaac 2608; Jacob 24; Jacob Jr. 1042; Susan 1742.
HAINES Andrew 314; Daniel 1331; I. P. 1682; 1683; Israel P. 1894; Rebecca 1894; Ruth 173; Stephen 884; Susan 1331; Thomas 1227.
HAKERSMITH E. 1856.
HALE Edward 331.
HALL Ann Eliza 213; B. R. 2749; Jacob 1509; James 2717; Joel 1816; John Henry 1641; Letitia Mary 2754; Lyman 1282; Major General 2754; Mary 2800; Mary Ann 1834; Richard M. 213; Thos B. 2800; Tideman 2273.
HALLER Catharine Ann 2145; Catherine 136; Charles 1805; Charlotte Lucretia 1296; Christopher 522; 2708; Constable 2246; Daniel 985; 1278; 1414; 2335; 2385; 2500; 2638; David 1414; David E. 2151; Elisha 297; Eliza 522; Elizabeth 2101; Ezra 312; 1414; Henry 471; Henry H. 1296; Henry Heichler 509; Jacob 2395; 2634; Jacob B. 985; 1041; 2335; 2500; 2791; John 30; 454; 928; John Alexander 2702; L. 715; Margaret 2184; Mary 2040; 2148; Michael 2635; Michael H. 458; 1411; 1414; N. 1371; Nicholas 1098; Peter 30; 157; 1260; 2181; Philip 1098; 2522; 2634; Samuel 665; 1411; Sarah Matilda 471; Thos 1371; 1866; 2117; 2248; Tobias William 2718.

HALLEY Mary Ann 1261.
HAMBLETON H. A. 1297; John 546.
HAMILTON Benjamin 1833; Catharine 77; F. G. 985; Francis B. 360; H. A. 24; Henry A. 1339; John 247; 2139; 2836; Mary Bartin 185; Mr 2136; Woodward A 2117; Woodward A. E. 2401.
HAMMETT David 1772.
HAMMOND 765; 1271; 1779; Adelia 761; Ann Maloine 1451; Armond 52; Barbara Ann 302; Charles 761; Denton 1045; Eden 94; 992; Eliza Ann 1451; Grafton 654; 780; 1045; 1396; 1769; 2479; Harriet D. 914; Henry Clay 535; Jno. L. 1252; Julia Ann Macubbin 1252; Mary Ann 1356; N. C. 1523; N. E. 24; Nathan 214; 914; 1045; 1799; 2269; 2318; 2388; 2426; 2479; Nathaniel 302; Nicholas W. 1451; O. 1045; 2479; Ormond 2318; Singleton Wooton 1799; T. 2469; Thomas 535; 745; 761; 970; 1040; 1228; 1252; 1281; 1368; 1396; 2264; 2398; 2443; 2469; 2598; 2662; 2712; 2826; Thomas J. 1297; 1339; 2443; 2662; 2712; Thos. I. 2717; V. 2426; Vach'l. 2388; Walter C. 1273; Wm. 1718.
HAMMER Belinda P. 2084; Elizabeth G. 557.
HAMNER J. G. 557; 1187; James G. 429; 612; 1175; Mary 1175; Mr 382.
HANCOCK John 1282.
HANDS John 1297.
HANE 1238; Catharine M. 1584; Christinna C. 2507; David 872; 1098; 2395; 2634; Jacob 1842; John 1098; 1218; 1409; 1485; 1584; 2468; 2522; 2642; Mary A. C. 2105.
HANER George 1297; Margaret A. 1669.
HANES Simeon 1747.
HANEY Ann 2782; Benjamin 2853; John 1241.
HANK Mr 334.
HANKS Mr 1737.
HANKEY Eliz 1010; Peter 1638.
HANN Matthias 38.
HANNA Isaac 217.
HANSER Sam'l. H. 1372.
HANSHEW Henry 1306; 1338; 1414; 2634; J. 1327; 1414; J. L. 1131; John 30; 199; 459; 1161; 1306; 1327; 1338; 1414; 2522; 2541; Susan B. 2308.
HANSON A. B. 1414; 1515; 2653; Alexander B. 720; 1025; James M. 302; Margaret Wilson 720; Mr 981; 1112.
HAPE Inn 81; Wm. 81.
HARBAUGH C. 1514; Chris'. 2717; Eliza 1343; Henry 1405; 1514; 2264; 2609; Henry H. 2514; J. 1421; 1514; Jacob 808; 1332; 1509; 1514; John 1514; Jos. 2826; S. G. 1952; Sevilla 1362; Solomon 1514; 1550; 2356.
HARD Edward D. 2154.
HARDEN Mrs 533; Sarah Ann 533.

HARDING Hannah 1575; Henry 2546; 2856; 2886; J. L. 261; 2662; J. M. 2712; James G. 1309; James M. 375; 1098; 1297; 1339; 1395; 2252; 2285; 2443; 2662; John 1575; John L. 24; 256; 275; 500; 1098; 1260; 1339; 1590; 2443; 2662; Julia Ann 1575; Louisa 715; Norman 1098; 1720; Sarah Ann 1182; Vice 1395; William 1098.
HARDMAN Sarah Ann 1346.
HARDT Ann Rebecca 1998; Elizabeth 2665; Frederick Peter 1070; George 1070; 1183; 1202; 1218; 1414; 1777; 2117; 2665; Jacob 1830.
HARGATE David 1528; John W. 2249; Marian 332.
HARGET Anna Maria 2683; Jon. 1371; P. 1371.
HARKEY James M. 2206; Mr 1555; 1556; 2695; 2698; Rev. 1832; S. W. 1447; 1448; 1449; 1487; 1488; 1489; 1490; 1498; 1510; 1555; 1695; 1696; 1814; 1826; 1831; 1836; 1837; 1852; 1880; 1910; 1919; 1920; 1929; 1954; 1955; 1956; 1968; 1988; 1989; 1995; 2004; 2040; 2041; 2067; 2068; 2075; 2092; 2101; 2135; 2145; 2160; 2165; 2167; 2184; 2191; 2194; 2195; 2196; 2206; 2210; 2232; 2242; 2243; 2248; 2255; 2297; 2298; 2607; 2624; 2661; 2718; 2719; Simeon W. 2200; 2201.
HARKLEY Thomas 650.

HARLEY Elizabeth 299; Mahlon 275; 722; 2443; 2662; 2712.
HARLEM HEIGHTS 680.
HARM Overton 1509.
HARMAN Frederick 94; George 94; 360; 827; 985; 1313; 1332; 1405; 1465; 1718; 2491; 2826; Jacob 1926; Susan 1345.
HARNE Horatio N. 360; Overton 2767.
HARNER George 1297; 2443.
HARNUNG Maria 2297.
HARP Elizaebth 2041; Joseph L. 1118.
HARPER Charles Carroll 991; John 1907; Margaret 2498; R. 1832; Richard 950; 1098; 1953; 1968; 2634; 2642; 2767; Robert Goodloe 991; William 627.
HARRIS Drusilah 1004; Edward N. 2714; Elizabeth 1726; Kinzey 2770; M. 2748; Mary Ann 2859; Vice 1395; William 2863; 2899.
HARRISON Ann E. 669; Ann Elizabeth 675; Benjamin 1282; Dennis 2891; General 2566; Mr 2827; William G. 344; 669; 675; William Henry 2446; Zepheniah 2634.
HARRIT John 2491.
HARRITT 1779; 2567; Catharine 1257; John 970; 1060; 1093; 1257; 1465; 1773; 2767.
HARRY James C. 2287; Parmenio R. 1039; William Hide 2287.
HART Elvira 87; George 1196; Jacob 906; 1405; 1979; John 1282; John Caspar

HART (continued)
1979; Mary 1979; Mary E.
2072; Mary Elizabeth 1979;
Susanna 446; Thomas 446.
HARTBAUER William 2200.
HARTMAN John 951; Julia 951.
HARTSOCK Ann M. 2415; Mary
1574.
HARTZ Joseph 867.
HASSELBOCK George 2329.
HASWELL John C. 1579.
HAUER D. J. 530; 531; 532;
730; 731; Daniel 139; 985;
1098; 2117; Daniel J. 515;
634; Elizabeth 296; George
94; 296; 360; 1098; 1313;
1339; 1397; 1428; 1718;
1843; 2635; 2662; 2712;
2767; 2791; Nicholas D.
2117; Wm. 1098.
HAUMAN Frederick 1098;
Philip 1098.
HAUPT Ann Rebecca 1835;
Philip 1411.
HAUPTMAN Philip 256; 276;
Phillip 1666.
HAUSER Wm. P. 985.
HAVE 1671; John 1666.
HAWAN Philip J. 2196.
HAWKINGS James 687.
HAWKINS Alexander Thomas
153; James 687; James Jr.
2856; 2886; James L. 153;
1462; James m. 2885; Tho.
79.
HAWLEY Dr. 346; Mr 320;
1684.
HAWMAN Frederick 360; 377;
985; 2356; 2522; 2791;
Philip 2395; Philip J. 2634.
HAY Ann 2502; Jacob 281;
Sam'l. 2765; Susanna 281.
HAYBERGER Mr 638.

HAYDEN Basil 970; 1421;
1523; 2826; Margaret
Josephine 161; Mr 161;
Thomas 161.
HAYES Wilson 94; 275; 360;
1297.
HAYS Abraham S. 2856; 2886;
Benjamin 1128; Ellen B.
1849; John 1849; Joseph G.
2790; Lewis 2826; Samuel S.
2893; 2957; 2958; Sophia B.
75; Thomas 1047; 1339;
2443; 2608; 2662; 2712;
William 1332; 2791; William
S. 2878; Wilson 24; 808;
985; 1313; 1339; 1368;
1396; 1718; 2443; 2468;
2491; 2598; 2609; 2662;
2712.
HAYWARD Thomas 1282.
HEAD Benidict I. 1395; Cecilius
2648; John 827; 1332; W. B.
837; Wm. B. 722; 1297; Wm.
R. 275.
HEALY John 1062; 2862.
HEARD Benedict J. 1631;
Samuel 2791.
HEARN Thos. A. Sr. 1288; John
A. 2024.
HEATH Jas. P. 650; William
284.
HEBB Edward T. 1178; Mr
2138;
HEBBARD E. B. 2662; Ebene-
ger 2712; Ebenezer B. 2443;
W. A. 1525; 1732; William B.
997; 1042.
HECKATHORN Christian 2073;
2117; Sophia 2301.
HEDGES Dorcas 373; Eliza
1404; Enos 2717; Isaac 377;
Isaac Jr. 812; John A. 2362;
Josiah 1404; Susan 204.

HEETER Elbert 2894.
HEFFERMAN John 155.
HEFFNER Benjamin 24; 275; 377; 1297; 1339; Elizabeth 2417; Sophia 1325.
HEICHLER Anna Margaret 142; Henry 2000.
HEIGHTON William 2117.
HEIKE Mr 87.
HEIM 1238; 1671; Andrew 256; 276; 278; 586; 892; 1191; 1218; 1397; 1421; 1428; 1485; 1632; 1953; 2423; 2767; David 1371; J. B. 2116; Jacob B. 2117; Lewis 397; Mary Ann 2020; William D. 459; 769; 1131; 1327.
HEINBLETON H. A. 275.
HEINER E. 1113; 1546; 1969; 2771; Mr 946; 1342; 1343.
HEIST Anna 268.
HEITER Elias 1042.
HELDEBRAND Catharine 1890.
HELMAN Michael 351; 1342.
HEMMELL John D. 2648.
HEMPHILL Andrew 1559; Mr 2887.
HEMPSTON Christian 2081; George W. 2856; Nathan T. 2856.
HEMPSTONE Geo. W. 2886; Nathan T. 2886.
HEMSWORTH Eliza A. 794.
HENDERSON George G. 243; Joseph 595; Mary Ann 1242.
HENESTOFEL Owen 323.
HENNING J. A. 2820.
HENRY C. 2480; Eliza Ann 2311; John 2480; Levi 528; Mr 1292; Rebecca 2835; Robert 649; Sabina 65.
HENSHALL James 933.

HENSHAW Dr. 854; 1023; Henry 2638; John 2638.
HENSHEW Henry 2385; J. P. K. 396; John 1098; 2385; Mr 130.
HERBERT Ann 874; Dr. 874; Mrs 823.
HERD Ruth 140; Samuel 1718.
HERGESHEIMER James 1460; Samuel 2757.
HERMAN Peter 670.
HERMANGE Ant'y. 2832.
HERRING Daniel 1509; 1523; Daniel C. 1513; Geo. 1698 John 1405; 2491; Jonathan 723; 1048; Joshua 1345; 2647; Margaret 626; Mary 1698.
HERRINGTON Timothy A. 1471.
HERRON John 2907; Mary 2907.
HERSBERGER Henry 1395.
HERSEY George 2117.
HERHBERGER H. 24; Henry 723; 1297; 2443; 2658; 2662; 2712.
HERSHEY David 2430; Susan D. 2430.
HERSPERGER Harriet 2400; Henry 2400.
HERST Mary 2231.
HESS Phaebe 792.
HESSER Charles 1372; 1718; 2326; 2791.
HESSON Catherine 215; Levi 1968.
HETHINGTON Julian 349.
HEWES Ann 346; Joseph 1282; Samuel 346.
HEWET Jacob 1764.
HEWETT Elizabeth 2739; William 1741.
HEWIRR Wm. 2767.

HEYDEN Basil 2598.
HICKEY Dr. 1934; John F. 2177; Mr 2572.
HICKMAN Emily 1298.
HICKORY CLUB 1278.
HICKS Eliza 2903; Thos. F. 1631; William 2600.
HICKSON Henry 2370.
HICKY John 1984.
HIDE Jonathan 1682; William 2287.
HIGGINS Basil D. 91; Benjamin 2886; Eleanor 1349; J. L. 1339; James L. 907; 2443; 2580; 2656; Mr 919; T. L. F. 2886; Thomas L. F. 2856.
HILDEBRAND Catherine 228.
HILL Fanny B. 1028; Henry 1620; Maria 37.
HILLARD James 2878.
HILLARY Susan 581.
HILLEARY John 2479; John H. 970; Perry 24; 1509; Thomas 1790; William 848.
HILLERY Elizabeth 2547; Howard 2093; John W. 2916.
HILLS Mary 131.
HILTEBRIDLE Jacob 1893; Mary Ann 1893.
HILTON Ann Maria Christinan 685; C. 892; 1428; Clem 2423; Henry K. 1098; 1869; Joshua 2863; 2899; 2958; Margaret Ann 2154; Rossanna 1787; William 1098.
HIMBURG Daniel 1414; John 1414.
HIMBURY Daniel 2286; Elizabeth 1548; Mary 801.
HIMBUY John B. 1668.
HIMMELL John D. 2117.
HIMMILL John 194.
HINDS John 43; 275;

HINER Jacob 2387.
HINES David 2264; 2306; John 24; 1339; 2443; Philip 2306; Philip Jr. 325.
HINIER Henry 2175.
HINKLE Eli 2183; John 1269.
HITCHOCK Captain 2589.
HITESHEW Sally 1556.
HOBBS Lewis I. 275; Lewis L. 722; 1297; 1339; Reasin 551; Wm. 1523.
HOCKENSMITH Jno. 1823.
HOCKERSMITH Eveline 1387.
HOES Barent 1445.
HOFF Abraham 1953; Elizabeth 697; J. H. 2423; John H. 2791; Mr 2050; Peter 1886.
HOFFER Caroline 1679.
HOFFMAN 1671; Charlotte 511; David 1894; David M. 1122; Elizabeth 1892; Ezra 2634; 2767; Francis 2192; 2208; Frederick Wm. 2192; George 436; 511; 1098; 2603; George W. 1396; 2826; Hannah 146; J. W. 1398; Jacob 24; 275; 443; 814; 1178; 1297; 1339; 1368; 1523; 2491; 2662; 2712; John 24; 49; 2792; John N. 29; 227; 351; Mary A. 2792; Mary Ann 1102; Mr 300; 1474; 2722; Mrs 436; Nelson 275; 1041; 2767; Peter 2767; Sarah 634; Sarah A. 1971; Susan 12; Washington 283; Wm 146; Wm C. 275; 377; 1407; 1485; 2522; 2762.
HOFFMEIER J. W. 797; 959; 2347; 2348; John W. 1149; John Wm. 1139; 1140.
HOFFMIER Ann Elizabeth Cockey 1537; Lilly Ann

HOFFMIER (continued)
2156; J. W. 983; 1527;
1537; 2156; 2309; 2411;
John W. 1356; 1879; 2374;
2449; Mr 889; 1385.
HOFFMIRE Gertrude 1376;
John 1376.
HOGG Rachel B. 1853; S. R.
1832; 1968; 1995; 2092;
Samuel R. 1098; 1131;
1327; 1414; 1853; William
1834.
HOLBROOKS George 2487.
HOLBRUNER Adam 2717.
HOLBRUNNER Casper 952.
HOLDER Polly 2693.
HOLLAND Isaac 2958; James
2893; 2910; Joseph 1862;
Lemuel 2885; Mrs 2910;
Nathan Senr. 2856; 2886;
Solomon 2088.
HOLLENBERGER Charity 623.
HOLLER Eleanor 1533; Jacob
1533; Mary 1533.
HOLLIDAY Jane 2749.
HOLLIS Richard F. 650.
HOLMAN Wilson 1288.
HOLMES David 1262; Marian
957; Mary Amanda 1539;
Richard 2863; 2899.
HOLODAY Margaret 1934.
HOLTZ Catharine 2824; David
Henry 2824; Jacob 508; 879;
John 11; 2824; N. 1278;
Nicholas 24; 94; 360; 985;
1313; 1460; 1515; 1718;
2264; 2766; 2767; Sophia
135.
HOLTZMAN Samuel 754.
HOOD Charles W. 1459;
Hannah H. 1459.
HOOK Jacob 723; 1339; 2480;
John 723; 2480; T. 997;
Thos 43; 275; 970; 997;

HOOK (continued)
1042; 1297; 1339; 1368;
2319; 2443; 2468; 2481;
2491.
HOOKER Mary A. 2846.
HOOPER Abraham 1098; 2634;
John 1098; 1598; 2634;
Joseph T. F. 1598; Julian
1668; William 1282.
HOOVER Catherine 2416;
Christian 2553; Col. 1396;
Daniel 24; 985; 1047; 1313;
1718; 2259; Elizabeth 1774;
Francis J. 2767; Juliann
806; Mary 1429; Sarah
1440; Sarah A. 2279.
HOPKINS Dr. 1470; Lambert N.
1754; Harriet L. Finch 1470;
Stephen 1282.
HOPKINSON Francis 1282.
HOPPE John H. 24; 1297;
2327; 2443; John W. 275.
HOPWOOD Catharine 2743;
James 954; 1414; 2743.
HORINE Tobias 24.
HORNER Andrew 1178; 1450;
Benjamin 2444.
HORSEY O. 2491; Outerbridge
916; 1155; 1228; Thomas
Sim Lee 916.
HORTON James 2105.
HOSHOUR Mr 202.
HOSKINS 1238; 1671; G. 1414;
Geo 1218 1306; 1338; 1364;
1397; 1422; 1465; 1515;
1830; 2117; 2252; 2385;
2406; 2598; 2635; 2767; J.
N. 360; John N. 1313.
HOSKINSON John N. 985;
1044.
HOSKYNS John H. 2623.
HOSSELBOCK George 1182;
John 94.
HOUBLESTINE Mr 617.

HOUCK 2567; Barbara 2150; Catharine 1744; Catherine 483; Daniel 2321; E. 2767; Elizabeth 315; 409; Ezra 970; 1460; 1515; 1830; 2117; 2276; George 1744; 2648; Henry 94; 1323; 1339; 1414; 2223; 2410; 2443; 2627; 2662; 2712; Jacob 409; John 94; 483; 645; 970; 1045; 1460; 2318; 2398; 2426; 2767; Margaret 645; Mary 2223; Michael 502; Virginia Brengle 2223.
HOUSE Ann Rebecca 160; Catherine Ann 64; Daniel 2335; Ehtha 2443; Elisha 94; Elizabeth 2544; Sarah Ann R. 1791; Stephen 64; Wm. 2335.
HOUSER Michael 1080; Samuel H. 1718; 2500.
HOVES John 203.
HOWARD 2567; Ann 2137; Arnold 52; Dennis D. 24; 275; 1297; 1339; 2443; 2662; 2712; E. 2329; Edward 1509; Elisha 1046; 1178; 2329; Elizabeth 938; George 121; Henry 740; 2856; Isaac H. 462; J. 2856; James 253; John 1925; John C. 112; Lydia Elizabeth 2137; Richard 2137; Robert 650; Thomas 2767; 2826; Wm. 2500; William B. 2886; Wm. G. 2767; Wm. S. 2335.
HOWELL Anna 2755; J. 963; Samuel L. 2755.
HOY Nicholas 907; 2102; 2469; Noah 1639; Rachel 2102; Ruth 907.
HOYBERGER Catharine 630.

HUDDLESTON William 2957.
HUDSON Alexander 2356; Dr. 1876; John 2117; Menelius 1876.
HUFF Abraham 2092; John H. 1718.
HUFFER George 372.
HUFFNER Margaret 881.
HUGHES Ann F. 1224; Barbara 123; Catharine 2360; Christopher 479; D. 1322; Daniel 274; 275; 377; 1055; 1098; 1770; Dr. 1045; Ezekiel 1396; 1953; 2092; 2117; 2541; Floridia 135; George 24; 275; 1297; 1339; 1396; 2426; 2443; 2594; 2662; 2712; John 190; 1601; Laura Sophia 479; Mr 362; 681; Mrs 1753; 2964; Rosanna 2604; Senova 1601; Victoria 135; Zenobia 135.
HUKE Charles 2701; Wm. Kuhn 2701.
HULL David 808; 1332; Harriet 177; Jacob 2320; Sarah 2285; Tideman 1245.
HUMPHREYS L. 2795.
HUNT A. H. 2092; Asbury 1098; 1131; 1327; 1414; 1623; 1750; Ashbury H. 2448; Charlton 2619; Fletcher 1734; Mary Elizabeth 1750; Wm. 1708.
HUNTER A. 1169; Samuel M. 391.
HUNTINGTON Samuel 1282.
HURLBUT Elizabeth Ann 1648; L. 1648.
HURLEY Obed 2958.
HURNUNG Catherine 2191.
HURST Joseph 599.

HUSON Major 2589.
HUSSEY Geo. St. C. 2959; Mary Virginia 2959.
HUTZELL John 1857.
HYATT Asa 2856; 2878; 2886; Maria 1248; William 1513; 2766.
HYDER Jacob 94; 360; 970; 985; 1313; 2264; John 1049; 2468; 2481.
IJAMS Plummer 24; 1155; 2479; 2594; Plummer Sr. 1045; 2426.
ILER Michael 2737.
INDEPENDENT HOSE COMPANY 30; 1306; 1338; 1414; 2385; 2638.
INGLE J. P. 1169.
INGLES Rebecca 822.
INGMAN Ambrose 195; 1414; 1460; 1981; Joshua 1098; 2117; Mahlon 2254; Thomas 1372; 2500.
INSTITUTION FOR THE DEAF AND DUMB 2003.
INTERNAL IMPROVEMENTS 1169.
INZOR Lydia 1585.
IRVINE Col. 2459.
IRWINE Hugh W. 2533.
ISLER Lydia 2614.
ITHIRE William 1567.
JACKSON Andrew Jr. 220; Charles 811; Charlotte 811; J. E. 62; 116; John 2767; Mary 2964; Mary C. 62; Mr 209; 238; 291; 310; Thos 62.
JACOBS 1128; Ann Stacy 2828; Charles W. 395; 413; Joel 327; Julia 1611; Michael J. 2828; Professor 2802; Roswell P. 515.
JAMES Catharine 1883; Daniel 1768; Isaac Jr. 24; John

JAMES (continued) 2721; 2766; John Wesley 1883; Joseph 24; 842; Joseph Jr. 2767; Joshua 136; Pradby 842; 2426; T. 2766; Washington 1883; Willy 2856
JAMESON Leonard 1058; Mary 1058.
JAMISON Baker 1545; Exile 465; H. M. 30; 1507; Henry 465; Henry M. 1260; 1539; Lawrence 161; Oswald 2677; Samuel 118; Teresa 2677.
JARBOE Henry J. 2281; J. 24; Samuel 2329; W. 24; William 275; 1041; 2496.
JARBOR Eleanor Ann 2272.
JARRET Abraham 650.
JAY Anna 2778; William 2778.
JEFFERSON College 939; Thomas 1282.
JEFFERY John P. 2548.
JEFFREYS Jacob 963.
JENKINS C. 708; Charles 708; Elizabeth J. 1803; Helena 823; Henry 1803; Mr 1129; Tannery 1129; William 650.
JENKS W. D. 826; William D. 2522; 2541; 2679.
JENNINGS Maria 29.
JESSUP Gen. 2725.
JOHNS Abram 1045; Abraham 2318; 2426; Dr. 1426; H. V. 2494; H. V. D. 1130; 1191; 1198; 1374; Henry V. D. 439; 2352; 2375; J. 1152; 1492; 1755; John 253; 344; 1685; L. H. 89; 1223; 2709; Mr 213; 489; 568; 674; 832; 1252.
JOHNSON 765; 1271; 2697; 2830; Anne Rebecca W. 1225; Arthur 772; Baker

JOHNSON (continued)
232; 1457; 2772; Benjamin
611; 1932; C. C. 370;
Charles 1046; 2329; 2427;
2477; 2491; Cyrene 150;
Dorothea 854; ELisha S.
259; Eliza 1256; Elizabeth
1266; 1558; George H. 2049;
Henry W. 1225; Henry V. D.
439; Jacob 1041; 1297;
1339; 1968; 2206; 2443;
2662; 2712; James 1754;
2329; 2477; 2524; James A.
2329; 2767; James J. 1396;
Jane 447; 453; John 293;
1603; John T. 2826; Joshua
D. 1874; Juliet C. 423;
Louisa C. 674; Maria A.
1256; Mary 1932; Mary F.
1211; Mary R. 1754; Mathias 1266; Milton 293; R.
1169; 2662; 2712; Rebecca
2524; Richard 1041; 1155;
2264; 2491; 2527; 2662;
2712; 2717; 2807; Richmond 2443; Roger 40; 1092;
1558; 2443; 2807; Sophia
2772; Susan W. 2375; T. 24;
T. W. 2306; Th. 360; 1339;
Th. W. 1339; Thomas 275;
611; 879; 985; 1041; 1297;
1313; 1394; 1396; 1457;
1465; 1504; 1718; 2524;
2766; 2767; 2818; Thomas
J. 2557; Thomas W. 275;
447; 453; 1043; 1297; 2375;
2443; 2662; 2712; W. 24;
1169; 2491; 2717; W. F.
1407; 1411; 1485; William
275; 360; 879; 985; 1155;
1256; 1297; 1339; 1396;
1718; 2264; 2443; 2767;
William C. 607; 745; 751;
1281; 1308; 2358; William

JOHNSON (continued)
Cost 324; 1098; 1319; 1377;
2336; 2359; 2491; 2658;
2818; William E. 2117;
William F. 1631; 2117; William S. 1041; 1225; 1603;
William T. 10; Worthington
377; 1211.
JOHNSTON Ann M. 904; Arthur
1230; Isabella 1230; Robert
2117.
JONCHEREZ Philip A. 2929.
JONES 1238; Abraham 24; 74;
275; 277; 654; 808; 1040;
1332; 1368; 1718; 2424;
2443; 2469; 2559; 2662;
2712; Andrew 1041; Ann
Maria 887; Aubury G. 1825;
Benjamin 681; Captain
2787; Edward 1889; Elizabeth
2458; 2559; Emeline 2611;
Francis S. 267; 2675; 2768;
H. V. 408; J. 1043; 1152;
2330; J. Jr. 2336; J. H.
2025; 2755; 2851; 2853;
2860; 2890; 2891; 2892;
2896; 2897; 2902; 2906;
2908; 2912; 2919; 2920;
2940; 2953; 2954; 2955;
2956; John 30; 827; 841;
1218; 1332; 1339; 2431;
2598; 2767; 2662; 2863;
2899; Joseph 411; 1277;
2368; Joseph A. 953; Joseph
H. 857; 953; 1061; 1094;
1120; 1145; 1351; 1891;
2380; 2408; 2428; 2513;
2525; 2543; 2568; 2575;
2637; Joshua 24; 275; 1297;
1339; 1657; 2330; 2443;
2662; Joshua Jr. 2336;
Maria H. 681; Mary Ann
1657; Mary E. 2912; Mr 41;
97; 129; 159; 189; 205; 230;

JONES (continued)
249; 313; 394; 408; 486;
514; 1195; 2290; Sarah 841;
Thomas 94; 2422; 2458;
2767; Thomas L. 2134; W. P.
355; William 24; 1039; 1040;
2531; William P. 1395; 2307;
2356; 2359; 2595; 2712;
Wm. R. 2491.
JORDON Catharine 1896.
JOURDON J. L. 1583.
JOY Mary Ann 1983.
JUDY George I. 2856; 2886;
Jane 1416.
JULIUS Daniel 552.
JUMEL Eliza 680.
JUNIOR FIRE COMPANY 1824;
2007; 2117.
JUNIOR RIFLEMEN 2116.
KAHLER Henry 1397.
KAILOR David 1513; 2767.
KANEPP Permelia 2210.
KANODLE John 2689.
KANTNER George 2648.
KARNE William 1299.
KAUFAUVER John 1024.
KAUFFMAN 1671; Henry 1407;
1485; 1515; 2767; Henry Jr.
1371; Henry Sr. 2767; John
H. 1266; 1364; Mrs 2706;
Warner 2058; William 1098;
2196.
KAUFMAN Emily 2239; George
W. 2239; Henry 1843; Henry
Jr. 2648; Warner 2117;
William 2117; 2239.
KAUNTNER George Jun. 1606.
KEAFAUVER 1571; Daniel 596;
1952; 2214; Geo. 1952;
Harry 899; Jacob 1855;
John 723; 808; 1332; 1952;
Sarah Elizabeth 2214.
KEAFER Mary E. 2075.
KEAN Edmund 684.

KEANS Joseph 1004.
KEEFAUVER G. 24; J. 24; John
2468.
KEEFER 1238; 2567; Barbara
1167; Christian 254; 808;
1332; Frederick 1414; 1548;
George 753; H. 2477; Henry
1460; 2477; 2491; 2530;
2767; Hiram 1098; 1218;
1364; 1411; 1414; 1422;
2117; 2635; Jacob 1111;
1371; 1405; 2767; Joseph
275; 1297; 1339; 2443;
Michael 2043; 2338; Mrs
1814; Nicholas 791; 2634;
Susanna 614.
KEENE Arthur 931; Arthur F.
1091.
KEFAUVER Ann Rebecca 1568;
George 1568; John 994;
1536.
KEHLER Henry Sen. 256; 276;
1218.
KEIFER Hiram 906; Jacob
2767.
KEIL Catharine 170; Tobias
1336.
KEISER Joseph 2117.
KELLER 1238; 1671; Adam
723; 970; 2468; 2480; 2491;
2662; 2712; B. 1973; Catharine 2011; 2437; Chas.
1371; Charlotte 2361;
Conrad 1020; D. 1968;
Daniel 399; 1952; 2488;
David 2767; E. 2059; Elizabeth 1020; Ezra 1856; 1858;
2131; Frederick 24; George
Adolphus 2011; Henry 1665;
2491; J. 1832; Jacob 586;
591; 844; 1198; 1218; 1397;
1452; 1485; 1515; 1632;
1830; 1968; 1995; 2008;
2011; 2092; 2117; 2196;

KELLER (continued)
2634; 2642; 2647; 2767;
John 48; Johnathan 2437;
Michael 352; Mr 1578; 1640;
1957; Mrs 1665; Rebecca
1326; Simon 2031; Sophia
950; Theophilus 2648.
KELLEY Henry 2648; 2760;
William 166.
KELLY 1238; 1671; Catharine
1180; Edward 1288; Frederick 1826; 2117; George
1782; Henry 1407; 1485;
2765; Henry Sr. 2107; 2767;
Margaret A. 859; Patrick
599; 1367; Thomas 859.
KEMBLE Charles 990; Fanny
990.
KEMP Abraham 233; 242; 256;
276; 278; 359; 377; 707;
1098; 1191; 1196; 1202;
1203; 1209; 1407; 1409;
1414; 1953; 2328; 2469;
2522; 2541; 2662; Catharine
H. 1393; Christian 1046;
2115; 2598; Christian
Franklin 1783; Col. 993;
Daniel 130; 1371; 1382; 1394;
1718; 1735; 1783; 1838;
2468; 2470; 2477; 2491;
David 377; 2359; 2468;
2491; 2541; 2647; 2766;
Elizabeth 2554; Frederick
69; H. 821; Henry 24; 130;
275; 377; 825; 942; 1046;
2329; 2336; 2477; 2491;
2766; Hy. 1382; J. R. 2453;
Jacob H. 2500; John 2207;
Joseph 2514; 2662; 2712;
Lewis 24; 360; 780; 1313;
Peter 1654; 2554; Walter
1393; William M. 1832;
1995; 2375; 2385; 2634;
2638.

KENAN Colonel 2589.
KENDALL Amos 2367.
KENEGA Mary 1688.
KENNA James 2480.
KENNEDY Alexander 963; Ann
Eliza 963; Anthony 490; J.
P. 1169; John 971; 1566;
John F. 1522; John W.
2022; Louisa 1566; Sarah
Ann 971; Thomas 487; 495.
KENT Elizabeth 578.
KEPHART Catharine 135;
Catherine 2215; David 724;
1042; 1297; 1339; 2319;
2443; 2500; 2591; George
879; 2329; P. J. 94; Peter
1098.
KEPLAR John Jr. 1952.
KEPLER John 2222; Magdaline
2222; Mr 1369.
KEPPLER Mr 1712; Rev. 1623.
KERLY Morris 1288.
KERSHNER Jonathan 2584.
KESSLER Andrew Jr. 1519;
Catharine 923; Catherine
715; George 2616; Henry
263; 1098; Lloyd 1718; Lloyd
H. 2791; Mary 2485; Matilda
2217; Rachel 790; Susannah
1087.
KETRO Geo. 60; 1371.
KETROW Mr 1913.
KEY Edward D. 2811; F. S.
1511; Francis S. 1324;
Henry St. G. 2811; John R.
1106; 1511; Philip 677;
Susan 1652.
KEYON COLLEGE 147.
KEYSER Catharine Ann 1954;
Jacob 1898; Philip 2767;
Sam'l. 1870.
KIEFFER Hannah 2747.
KILGOUR Charles J. 1542; Vice
1395.

KILL Thomas 1028.
KILLAN Marian 2413.
KIMMEL 2697; A. 2359; Anthony 842; 970; 1155; 1405; 1493; 2424; 2491; 2672; 2826; Edmund Clemson 1493; Marian Louise 1493; 2672; Sidney Ann 1493; 2672.
KIMMELL Anthony 1040; 1718.
KING Catharine 1449; Eliza Jane 1820; George 820; John 94; John D. 2885; Mary Elizabeth 2715; Mr 6; Rufus 2036; Thomas 2329; W. E. 2329; Walter 2715; William R. 24; 275; 1297; 1339; 1434; 1509; 2443; 2662; 2712; 2767.
KINLEY Dorcas 200.
KINNA Nathan 559.
KINZER 2259; John 24; 1155; 1523; 2647; John Jr. 879; 1165; John Sen. 2767; P. 775.
KINZEY Barbara 1079.
KIPE Maria Catharine 1973.
KIRBY Charles A. 2211; Major 2591.
KITZMILLER Jacob 1479.
KIZER Philip 1515.
KLAY Cornelius 1045; John 1045; 2318.
KLEIM Jacob 1782.
KLEIN Ann Sophia 322; Casper 2635; George 222; Maria 579; William 360; 985.
KLEISZ Rebecca 812.
KLINE Caspar 1414; 1485; Casper 1716; Daniel 636; 985; E. 715; Elizabeth 715; Frederick 2522; George 1514; Harriet 1716; Jonathan 1186; Mary 1285; Mary

KLINE (continued)
Ann 1038; Stephen Jr. 1135; William 1038.
KLISE Frederick E. 908; John 360.
KNIGHT John 691.
KNODE Archibald B. 1565.
KNOTT Constantia 135; 715; Edward 24; 275; 1297; 1339; 2443; 2662; 2712; Francis 2717; Francis A. 937; Stanishus 2885.
KNOUF Jacob 2648.
KNOUFF Jacob 1260; John 1039; Margaret 1869.
KNOX Saml 414; 2001; Wm 24; 275; 1297; Zeruiah 2001.
KNOXE Christianna 1674.
KOESTER Henry 671.
KOHLENBURG Thomas 985.
KOHLHASS Henry 1847; Judith 1846.
KOLB 1238; 1422; 1671; Christianna 2142; Daniel 2; 25; 44; 94; 206; 242; 256; 276; 278; 360; 375; 377; 707; 985; 1015; 1073; 1098; 1156; 1191; 1204; 1218; 1238; 1313; 1397; 1485; 1718; 2443; 2456; 2522; 2541; 2642; 2653; 2662; 2712; Frederick 2648; John M. 2507; John W. 2142; Margaret E. 1143; Michael 2142; William 278; 1278; 1370; 1397; 1422; 1460; 1485; 1515; 1632; 1695; 2123; 2383; 2406; 2635; William Jr. 2767; William Sr. 256; 276; 1213; Wilson W. 993; 1143; 1371.
KOLLICKOFFER William 2443.
KOONTZ Catharine 1067; Isaac 1067.

KOONTZ Abraham 2335;
Edward 1515; 2648; G.
1995; George 1414; 1428;
1513; 1718; 2107; 2132;
2541; 2644; 2648; 2680;
2765; 2767; 2791; Godfrev
2648; Godfrey 906; 1428;
1832; 1843; 2395; 2662;
2712; Henry 196; 1405;
Isaac 2335; Jane E. 1884;
John 1098; Mary Jane 2644;
Minerva 715; William 2335;
2608.
KRAFTS BAKERY 2360.
KRAMER Mary 790.
KRAMMER D. J. 24; F. J. 94.
KRAUTH J. P. 1132; 1133.
KREBS G. 2630.
KREBY Ann Maria 753.
KREMER John Adam 2436.
KREPP Frederick 2117; John 2117.
KRIDLER James 1645; 1882.
KRISE Lydia 2175; Mary Ann 1638.
KROMMER Frederick W. 566.
KROUSE John 94.
KRUDENER Baron 2341.
KUHN Chadwick H. 2117;
George 24; 275; 722; 985;
1339; 1372; 1421; 2259;
2335; 2356; 2443; 2500;
2599; 2662; 2712; Harriet
67; Henry 875; Jeremiah F.
2779; John 23; William 985;
1722; Z. 2307; Zebulon 24;
275; 722; 1039; 1297; 1339;
1368; 2264; 2307; 2443;
2491; 2662; 2712.
KULLER Henry 1371.
KUNKEL Jacob 708; John 256; 276; 2634; John B. 2117.
KUNKLE Catherine 776; J. 1832; John 278; 906; 1191;

KUNKLE (continued)
1198; 1968; 1995; 2642;
2767; Philip 1414.
KUNTZ Abraham 94.
KURTZ B. 2440; Benjamin 1453; 1591.
KUSER Jacob 2202; Michael 640; 651.
LABAREE Mr 829.
LACKLAND Dennis 1023; Margaret Ann 1023.
LADIES OF ALL SAINTS CHURCH 238.
LADY MACBETH 182.
LAFAYETTE 1025.
LAGGET Isabella Keith 1565; James 1565.
LAIN Allen 1046.
LAKIN Daniel 688; Washington 582.
LAKINS Martha A. M. 2207; Wm. 2767.
LAMAR Ann Drusil 1557;
Archibald 1557; Eliz 63;
John 2717; 2767; Laurettz
1519; Richard 2815; Susan
1557; Thos 63; 985; 1313;
1509; 1519; 1718; 2826;
Wm 1041; 1643; Wm B. 299.
LAMB Mary Elizabeth 1194; Sarah 1647.
LAMBER Frederick 1219.
LAMBERT Daniel 228; Elizabeth 58; Frederick 1290;
1371; 1515; J. 2329; Jacob
Sen. 24; 275; 1297; 1339;
John 1515; Joseph 2020;
Mary 2682.
LAMBRECHT Catherine E.
1290; Frederick 1179; 1515;
2648; George 1729; Lydia
2761; Marian 783; Michael
2648; Rachael 135; Regina
2128; Susan 1487.

LAMBRIGHT Jacob 567.
LANDERS William C. 1667.
LANDES Jacob 2468.
LANDIES J. 2419.
LANDIS Jacob 2481.
LANE John 377.
LANNUM Lloyd A. 2946.
LANSDALE Charles C. 2870; John 2880; 2958.
LANTZ Elizabeth 2434.
LARE Charlotte 1634; Edward 1326; 1327; 1414; George 1098; 1414; 1634; 1653; 2522; Henry 1098; Henry C. 1617; 2097; 2757.
LARGE Constantine 2355.
LARKIN Julia Ann 450; William 2259.
LATE Ann Maria 2440; Geo. 2791; John D. 180; Mary A. C. 291; Michael 291.
LAURENCE J. M. 367.
LAURENSON Philip 650.
LAUVER S. A. 1523.
LAWLER Martin 1288.
LAWMAN Margaret 1948.
LAWRENCE Elizabeth 466; John S. 842; 1297; 1339; 2396; 2443; 2662; 2712; Margaret 135; Margaret S. 2396.
LAYMAN John 1555; Margaret 203.
LEAB Charlotte 665; Mrs 2112; 2521.
LEACH Elizabeth Ann 2937; J. W. 2944; Jesse 2856; 2886; Jesse W. 2937; Jesse Willett 2898; Thomas Edward 2944.
LEADER Lenary 29.
LEAKIN William 1405.
LEAMAN Mary Ann 880.
LEAPOLD Mathias 2292.

LEARNED Elizabeth 2155.
LEASE Catherine 194; Elizabeth 1794; Jacob 275; John 827; 1045; 1332; 2318; 2426; Mary 2139; 2836; Michael 24; 275; 1045; 1297; 1339; 2443; 2594; 2662; 2712; William 2522.
LEASER Daniel 1516.
LEASHER Elizabeth 2833.
LEATHER John 158; 2427; 2647; Mary 464.
LEATHERMAN Daniel 2206; Jacob 1048.
LEATHERS Morgeon 2650.
LECHLEITER Elizabeth 2345.
LEE 765; Archibald 2871; Captain 2589; David 415; Eliza Horsey 1728; Francis Lightfoot 1282; John 362; 607; 616; 745; 1044; 1308; Richard Henry 1282; Sarah Frances 2126; Thomas Simm 2190; William 1728.
LEEDS Eliz 210; Lodowick 210.
LEEKINGS William 919.
LEGGET James Sen. 2767.
LEGGITT Jas. 2717.
LEIDIG Jacob 2634.
LEIGHTER Catharine Ann 1567; Joseph 1567.
LEILICH Ann Magdalena 2563; Jacob 935.
LEIS Jacob 65.
LEISTER Barbara 2751.
LENHART William 2230.
LEOHR Frederick 2263.
LEONARD Joseph 1414; 2564.
LEOPOLD George A. 583.
LEVISHER Margaret 2823.
LEVY Ann Rebecca 36; David J. 2829; Elizabeth 1588; Jonathan 1588.

LEWIS Asa 516; Elizabeth 2299; Francis 1282; Isaac 421; 1662; Samuel B. 256; 276; 278; 586; 591; 842; 878; 906; 1098; 1414; William D. 2414.
LIBERTY COPPER MINES 1458.
LIDAC Jacob 1370.
LIDAY Jacob 360; Joseph 2335.
LIDEY Joseph 2500.
LIDY Jacob 94; John 1672.
LIFE Sarah Ann 814.
LIGER Mary Ann 2838.
LIGGETT J. C. 2491.
LIGGINS Deborah 1099.
LIGHTENWALTER A. 24; 808; 1332; A. P. 24; Abraham 1297; 1339; 2443; 2468; 2491.
LIGHTER George M. 702; Henry 1692; Mary Ann 1692.
LILLY Thomas 1539.
LIND Chars. T. 1873.
LINDSAY Colonel 2589.
LINDSEY John 1288.
LINEBAUGH Jonathan 2767.
LINGANFELTER Rebecca 2629.
LINGENFELTER 828.
LINK Adam 1880; Adam Sen. 1852; Anna Mary 417; Lewis 2717; Sarah 1706.
LINN Mr 2060.
LINTHICUM Ann Maria 1650; John M. 2435; Lott 740; 2856; 2886.
LIPSCOMB A. A. 2051; Mr 2265.
LIPSICOMB Mr 1676.
LISPCOND Mr 1808.
LITCHFIELD John 2231.
LITTLE 1238; 1671; Harriet Ann 2058; J. 2395; Jacob 25; 256; 276; 278; 377; 906; 1098; 1218; 1364; 1397;

LITTLE (continued) 1485; 2522; 2541; 2634; Jesse M. 94; 1372; 1718; 2500; John 94; 360; Peter 2087.
LITTLEJOHN Elizabeth T. 622; Harriet 135; Teresa 135.
LITZINGER William 2501.
LIVERS Cecilia 33.
LIVINGSTON Philip 1282.
LLOYD Elizabeth 1014; James 72; William 1014; 2106.
LOCK Catharine 755; George W. 1541.
LOCKE Ellen Ridgely 602; Nathaniel 602.
LODGE Lewellyn 2856; William O. 2885.
LOEHR Frederick 256; 276; 377; 1098.
LOFFUS Anthony 401.
LOFTUS J. 708; John 708.
LOGUE Lewis 2117.
LOKEY Jos. 1414.
LONG Charlotte 1874; Ephraim 1513; George 2491; 2767; H. K. 1874; Isaac 2629; James 94; 360; Joseph 1556; Nancy A. 1836.
LONGWELL J. K. 997; John K. 2182; 2443.
LORENTZ A. 2767; Adam 2491; Elizabeth 402; Jacob Sr. 402.
LOTS Philip 100.
LOTZ Barbara 762.
LOVEDER Ann 948; Catharine 1721; Elizabeth 873.
LOVIER Richard M. 1098.
LOW Alfred 2032.
LOWE 765; Alexander 842; Barbara 1749; E. L. 708; Enoch L. 708; George 842; Henry 2791; J. M. 2765;

LOWE (continued)
John 24; 1045; 2426; 2856;
2886; John M. 94; 360; 985;
1098; 1718; 1749; 1980;
2097; 2107; 2335; 2500;
2522; 2757; 2791; Philip
2767; W. 2662; William 842;
937; 1040; 1320; 2356;
2443; 2712; 2767.
LOWNDLES Elizabeth Lloyd
1802; Richard T. 1802.
LUCKET Lloyd 1332.
LUCKETT Eleanor 1259; Lloyd
224; 275; 808; 1041; 1297;
1339; 1383; 2398; 2443;
2454; 2579; Lloyd W. L.
1383; M. B. 2368; Mountjoy
B. 1098; 2522; 2541; N.
1041; Nelson 24; 1259;
Sarah C. 2454.
LUDWICK Jacob 94; 360.
LUDY E. 1350.
LUEBER Francis 906; 2395.
LUGENBED John 233; Moses
2863; 2899.
LUGENBEEL Andrew 432;
2027; Basil 245; Elizabeth
2027; John 1278; Moses
2957; Peter 308.
LYDAY Henry 2791.
LYDDANE James 2856; 2886;
Nicholas 2852; 2950.
LYLES Arch'd. M. 2863; Robert
741; 2856.
LYNCH 1178; E. A. 2259; 2638;
Edward 2333; Edward A.
993; 1228; 1312; 1414;
2446; 2456; 2457; 2522;
2541; 2744; Eliza 258; Eliza
H. 1059; Sarah 1059;
Thomas 1282; 1983; William
1394; 1436; 2259; 2443;
2580; 2662; 2712.

LYNTAN John 1181.
LYNN David 2748; Ellen Jane
2748; Isaac 1043; Joseph
360; Tavern 1043.
LYON Benjamin 2856; 2886;
Isaac 2537; James 1647;
James L. 578; Mary 2537.
LYONS Adriam 641; Geo. W.
1704; Isaac 1288; Oliva 2141.
LYTLE Robert T. 2099.
M'CABE Eliza G. 1547; John
1547.
M'CLEERY Robert 892.
M'CUNE George C. 2523.
M'ELFRESH Phln. S. 2468.
M'ENALLY John 570.
M'GAHAN Phillip 2767.
M'GOWAN Michael 1288.
M'IIHENNY A. 1049.
M'KALEB J. A. 997; 1042;
James A. 1042; John 1000;
2491; Margaret Ann 1000.
M'KEAN Thomas 1282.
M'KEEHAN James 2767.
M'KINSTRY Daniel 1042;
Samuel 2491.
M'LEAN C. G. 1732.
M'MULLEN M. 715.
M'NAIR Martha 2796.
M'NEILL J. 360.
MACKLEY 113; John 4; 5; 6;
18; 59; 86; 93; 96; 105; 111;
113; 114; 120.
MACKLAND C. E. 2662.
MACKLIN Rives 1293; Sarah
1293.
MACOMB General 2284; 2589.
MACRANDER Jacob 1449.
MAEGILL W. D. 367.
MAFFIT Eliza Jane 2071; J. N.
2071.
MAGN Daniel 2348.
MAGEE Rebecca 2202; Mr 986.

MAGENNIS J. 708; James 708.
MAGILL Basil 2957; Patrick 275; Patrick Jr. 1297; Patrick Sen'r. 1297.
MAGISTRATES COURT 2425.
MAGISTRATES COURT APPOINTMENTS 1368; 2442.
MAGLAUGHLIN Catherine 135.
MAGRATH John 1097.
MAGRUDER Dennis F. 1117; E. L. 2334; Elizabeth C. 2582; Hellen 2943; J. B. 2866; James 2863; 2899; James Jr. 2885; John 2943; John A. 1513; John Burger 2876; Lloyd 2856; Martha 2879; Mary 2866; Mira 2856; Otho 2871; Samuel 2878; W. 367; Walter 2900; William W. 2920; Z. L. 2856; Zachariah L. 2886; Zadok 2879.
MAGUIRE B. 708; Bernard 708; James 1360.
MAHARNA Martin M. 1490.
MAHN Cornelius 1976; David 1976.
MAHONEY David 736; M. 2712; M. M. 2329; 2477; Martin 1297; 2443; 2662; Martin M. 1046; 2477; 2491; Mary Ann 2242; Wm. 1727.
MAHONY M. M. 1339.
MAINE Jesse 1941.
MALAMBRE George 1414; 1460; 1515; 2767.
MALONY Sarah Jafe 1540.
MALOTT Daniel 834.
MANAHAN Dennis 298.
MANDAVILLE Ellen 1961.
MANE John G. 1305.
MANN Charles 62; Stephen S. 2415.
MANRO J. 1339; 2336; 2427; Jonathan 1046; 1396; 2443;

MANRO (continued) 2477; 2491; 2712; Jonathan Jr. 544.
MANROE Jonathan 2329; 2662.
MANTZ A. K. 1414; 2117; Alexander K. 2117; C. 1832; Caspar 1025; 1155; 2346; Casper 978; 1439; 1770; 2056; Charles 947; 1879; Cyrus 206; 377; 707; 1098; 1161; 1995; 2328; 2457; 2522; 2541; 2634; 2713; Daniel 835; Edward 377; 1414; 2385; George 2443; 2662; 2712; John 1949; John A. 962; Josias V. 835; Matilda 1916; Milton 2116; Mrs 2964; Peter 24; 275; 326; 563; 840; 1218; 1364; Wm. 2117.
MARIS George W. 1513; 1517; 2767.
MARK Elizabeth 2093.
MARKEL Mrs 456.
MARKELL George 1131; 1414; 2171; J. 1278; Jacob 1460; 1515; 2491; 2757; John 377; 2522; Lewis 2117; Samuel 1249; Sophia 2171; Thomas M. 2117; Wm. 1414; William W. 1656; 1866; 1928.
MARKER Philip 1103.
MARKEY D. J. 1422; 2385; 2638; 2765; David 396; David J. 1409; 1411; 1414; 1485; 2635; 2638.
MARKLAND Charles E. 2443; 2712.
MARKLE Mary 2179; Wm 2179.
MARLOW Harman 1718; Hanson 1396; 2516; Martha E. 2516.

MARMAN Thomas 1098.
MARONEY Michael 1288.
MARQUART Michael 197.
MARQUERT George 1843.
MARRIOT Alpheus W. 2647.
MARRIOTT Alpheus Waters 761; Barzillai 1515; 2506; Wm. H. 650.
MARROE Jonathan 2477.
MARSH Mason 2767; Mr 1648.
MARSHALL College 1939; 2225; 2678; Joseph 1903; Richard H. 1414; William 210.
MARTID Jas. 2932.
MARTIN Andrew 1159; Ann 2387; Barbara 1911; Catharine 2564; Charles 1510; Daniel 121; 185; David 2; 164; 386; 427; 2085; Elizabeth 1162; Jane 928; 1975; Jesse 94; 360; 985; 2335; John 892; 1372; 1718; 2500; 2791; John A. 1372; John Jr. 2117; John S. 1098; Joseph 1288; Mary 715; Mrs 164; Sabina 2735; Stephen 1370; Susan 56; Washington 2962; William C. 1414; 1460; 1515; 2717; 2767.
MARTS Geo. 1371.
MARTZ Anna Mary 2692; Daniel 1518; 2767; Elizabeth 2403; George 1460; 1515; 2403; 2767; George Sen. 1506; Maj. 234; 431; Margaret 431; Mary Ann 234; Rosanna 1506.
MARYLAND STATE BIBLE SOCIETY 2688.
MARYLAND STATE COLONIZATION SOCIETY 2098.
MARYLAND PENITENTIARY 1116; 2830.

MASBURY Eliza 303.
MASON Hezekiah 558; Mary 2813.
MATHEWS Daniel 2791.
MATHIAS Benjamin 1348; George Jr. 275; 1297; 1339; Jacob 879; 1049; 1157; 1297; 1339; 1368; 2336; 2443; 2491; 2514; John 2319; Marian 929; Mary 1157; Washington 2311.
MATTERN John 303; Sarah 830.
MATTHEWS Mr 490.
MATTHIAS 2567; Francis 2598; George Jr. 24; 2443; Henry 1524; Jacob 997; 2359; John 1042; Virginia 1524.
MATTOX Nicholas 1298.
MAUGENS David 1513.
MAUGHT John 2766; Laurence 2717.
MAULSBY Elizabeth 1751; J. D. 650; William 1751; William P. 2491; 2549; 2645; William Pinkney 2352.
MAUS Rachel 226.
MAY Daniel M. 1486; Ellen E. 1486; Mr 1524.
MAYBERRY Albert 2276; Justinian 1069; Thomas 24; 870.
MAYER Bartle 2243; Dr. 1486.
MAYN John 2767.
MAYNARD Elizabeth 2955; Thomas 1105.
MAYHOOD Thomas 2351.
MAYO Enoch M. 1162.
MAYU Susanna H. 1589.
McADAMISED ROAD 1316.
McALEER John 271; 2376; Rosanna 2376.
McBRIDE Edward 827; 1332; 1677; 2598; George 2472;

McBRIDE (continued)
James 2035; John A. 1677;
Sophia 2472.
McCAHAN Geo. 2634.
McCAHEN George 2757.
McCALL Captain 2589.
McCALLUM Mr 980.
McCARTHY John 1460; Mr 2055.
McCARTNEY Michael 1513; 2647; 2767.
McCHRYSTAL R. 715; Rosanna 135; 715.
McCLANE Joseph 1552.
McCLAIN John 1514.
McCLAY Mr 297.
McCLEARY Joseph 1198; Robert 780; 1428; 2233.
McCLEERY Robert 1953; 2423.
McCLELLAN Sam'l. 650.
McCLURE Georgiana Virginia 212; John 212
McCOLGAN Charles 2187.
McCOLLUM William 2767.
McCOLLUN Ephraim 1405.
McCOMB Alexander 1684; Czarina 1684; John Navarre 1684.
McCOSKERY James 2398.
McCOUBERY Margaret Jane 339.
McCOY Thomas W. 107.
McCRON John 2196.
McCROSKY John 813.
McCROU John 2188.
McCRUELY John 2349.
McCUBLIN Zacharias 2871.
McCULLOCH J. 1169; James H. 2586.
McCULLOH J. H. 854; J. W. 1309.
McCUNE G. C. 2569.
McDADE Catharine 1673; Samuel 985; 2335.

McDANIEL Francis 478.
McDEVITT John 1285.
McDONALD 1238; Alexander 1206; 1288; John 24; 233; 256; 275; 276; 377; 1098; 1196; 1202; 1218; 1297; 1339; 1371; 1394; 1397; 1485; 2443; 2522; 2647; 2662; 2712; 2767; 2863; 2899.
McDOWELL John 1297; 1339; 2443.
McELFRESH 1779; Charles 1762; Charles T. 460; Elizabeth 1762; Henry 94; J. A. 553; J. H. 206; 1515; Jane 1686; John 970; 1045; John H. 1155; 1465; 1773; P. S. 970; 1297; 1339; 2712; Phil. S. 24; 275; Philemon 2329; Philemon S. 1046; 1368; 2264; 2662; Philemor S. 2443; Philimore S. 2712; W. L. 24; Wilson L. 1421; Zachariah 2426; Zacharias 2318.
McELROY Father 2187; J. 1416; John 135; 708; 806; 1367; 1526; 2024; 2574; Mr 193; 442; 2396.
McENELLY J. 697.
McGACHIN George 783.
McGAHAN George 1411.
McGAHEN G. 2107; George 2765; Philip 2766.
McGAHIN Catherine 2584.
McGAREY Jos. S. 2500.
McGAUGHREN Philip 2712.
McGEE Mr 541; 761; 986; 1105; 1164; 1198; 2312; 2414; 2415; Thomas 632; 768; 839; 1191.
McGILL 2673; P. Jr. 2712; Patrick 2712; Patrick Jr. 24;

McGILL (continued) 1041; 1339; 2443; 2662; Patrick Sen. 24; 1041; 1259; 1339; 2443; 2491; 2662; 2712.
McGINNIS Elizabeth 715; Michael 715.
McGLANGHLIN John 487.
McGLENNEN Margaret 2574.
McHENRY Henry 2711.
McIIHENNY Alexander 24; 275; 970; 1212; 1297; 1339; John 487.
McKALEB J. A. 1042; John 1042; 2182; Sarah H. 2182.
McKALH John 1155.
McKECHAN Samuel L. 781.
McKEEHAN 2259; James 2767; Narcassa 2053; S. L. 459; 1327; Sam'l. 24; Sam'l. L 996.
McKEENER Mr 2253.
McKENNEY John 1631; Mr 780.
McKENZIE Daniel 985; 2335.
McKERNAN Peter 377; 1098.
McKIM Alexander 252.
McKIMMEL Wayne 734.
McKINSIE Dan'l. 360.
McKINSTRY 2555; Charles W. 948; Evan 609; 985; 1313; 2327; 2330; 2336; 2398; 2443; 2481; 2546; 2580; Mill 1518; 2420; S. 2336; Samuel 609; 1042; 2319.
McKNIGHT J. 1169.
McLANAHAN Martha A. 735; W. M. B. 2116; 2217; 2844; Wm. B. 2008; Zeruah 2448.
McLANE Charles 2186.
McLEAN Cornelius 650; Henry 1016; Samuel 1921.
McLEOD Hester Ann 2935.
McMAHON William 2847.

McMANUS John 1288; Owen 1288; Thos. 1288.
McMEAL John P. 1984.
McMECHON Judge 506.
McMIEL John 2480.
McMULLEN A. L. 708; Augustine L. 708; Mary 135; 715; T. 715; Teresa 135; 715.
McMULLIN Charles P. 296; Rebecca R. 2734
McNAIR Ann 1974.
McNEALE John 879.
McNEEL John 275.
McNEIL John 24; 1339; 2443.
McNEILL John 372; 723; 1297; Sarah Ann 372; William 829.
McNIEL John 1313; 2480.
McNULTY James 1405.
McPHEARSON William S. 1055.
McPHERSON 1779; E. B. 2491; Edward 2597; 2668; Edward B. 377; 1373; Henry 547; Horatio 199; 238; 459; 628; 2497; Howard 547; Howard H. 534; J. 2328; John 70; 206; 255; 336; 377; 628; 707; 976; 996; 1003; 1098; 1155; 1414; 1465; 1515; 1773; 1792; 24556; 2457; 2491; 2713; Louisa 2597; Mary E. 2022; Mary Eliza 1792; Robert G. 2290; Sarah 897; Sarah Ann 540; W. S. 206; 1203; William 897; William S. 256; 261; 377; 534; 540; 547; 707; 976; 1055; 1228; 1770; 2328; 2359; 2522; 2541.
McSHERRY Wm. 794.
McVERY James 2850; 2861.
McVICKER Elizabeth 135; 613; Mary 449.
MEALEY Isaiah 1414; 2638; Michael Jr. 1297.

MEALY Harriet 902; Michael 275; Michael Sen. 1339.
MEASEL John 2767.
MEASELL John 1515.
MEASLER Solomon 1718.
MEAZLE George 431.
MECHANICS INSTITUTE LYCEUM SOCIETY 255; 1154; 1161; 2317.
MEDCALF Thomas 970.
MEDICAL CHIRCUCICAL FACULTY 119; 367; 1006; 2505; 2687; 2726; 2799.
MEDTARDT Lewis 906.
MEDTART Lewis 181; 192; 233; 256; 276; 278; 377; 780; 1055; 1098; 1191; 1198; 1260; 1270; 1310; 1396; 1421; 1770; 1830; 1953; 2092; 2117; 2395; 2653; 2757; 2964; Mr 463.
MEEKS Martha 2025.
MEHRING John Jr. 300.
MEIXELL Violeta B. 2689.
MENDENHALL Hannah 1572.
MENTZER Catherine 128; Samuel 128.
MERCHANT Joseph 1098.
MERRICK Joseph I. 75.
MERRIKEN Mr 1649; 1650.
MERRITT Samuel Sen. 2822.
MERRYLAND TRACT 55; 2455.
MERRYMAN Nicholas R. 650.
MERTZ David S. 1358; George 1358; John P. 513.
MESSLER William 999.
METCALF Thomas 1394.
METZ John W. 94; Wm. 1515.
METZER George 2757.
METZGAR George 1411; 2765.
METZGER George 1422; 1830; 2107; 2132.
MEYEALE Frederick 2484.
MEYER Charles 215.

MEYERLY George 301.
MICHAEL Adelia Emeline 529; Andrew 1526; 2129; Ann 2037; Christopher 630; 631; 1900; 2264; 2598; Daniel 2067; Eliz 1526; Israel 1844; James 294; Jane 2129; John 1570; Malinda 988; Margaret 176; Mr 2240; Rebecca 391; 631; Susan 1900; Sophia 2240; Wm. 521; 1098.
MIDDLEKAUF Sarah 347.
MIDDLETON Arthur 1282.
MIDDLETOWN ACADEMY 2578.
MILES Robert 1748.
MILHAU Rosella De. 148.
MILITARY APPOINTMENTS 1382; 2326; 2492; 2531; Court 2591; 2725.
MILITARY VISIT 335; 749; 760; 994; 1071; 1075; 2476; 2515.
MILLER 387; 1238; Abraham 94; 360; 985; 2335; Anna Maria 1179; Ann N. 2213; Casper 170; Catharine 2213; 2447; Catharine E. 2820; Chas 1502; Danl 484; 2019; David H. 2117; Eliz A. 1689; Emily 2450; Frances Ann 661; 2080; Francis S. 527; 1354; Frederick D. 886; G. W. 2820; Geo 1626; 1858; 2167; 2468; Geo W. 2117; 2196; 2206; Giles 2550; Harrison 2101; J. W. 1191; 2765; Jacob 1513; Jacob T. C. 43; 1421; 1735; 2766; 2767; John 487; 1045; 1429; 1514; 1551; 2213; 2264; 2356; 2522; 2541; 2762; John S. 256; 276; 527; 2767; John Sen. 1711;

MILLER (continued)
John W. 586; 722; 840; 878;
1218; 1364; 1413; Joseph G.
2117; Joshua H. 2494;
Leonard 967; Magdalena
269; Martin 1041; Mary Ann
845; Matilda 967; Mr 2357;
Mrs 1664; Philip 1957;
Rebecca 643; Samuel 1364;
1812; Susanna H. 1551;
Theodore K. 2545; William
24; 74; 275; 277; 845; 1067;
1297; 1339; 2443; 2470;
2580; 2662; 2711; 2826.
MILLS J. W. 2334.
MILNOR Dr. 2003.
MINEAR Adam 1221.
MINES J. 2876; 2877; John
2939; 2947; Mr 525.
MISINGER David 1759; Margaret 2169.
MISS Charles L. 2434.
MITCHELL Charles 106; John
T. 1405; 2155; 2264; Samuel
L. 154.
MITE SOCIETY 238.
MIVES J. 2857; 2858; 2859.
MIX Robert 1872.
MOBBERLEY E. W. 974; Eliza 974.
MOBBERLY Amanda Elizabeth
2036; E. W. 1396; 1465;
2479; 2594; Eli 2541; Levi
1098; 1414.
MOBERLY Amanda 2069; Eli 2522.
MOBLEY Margaret 2100.
MOELLER John F. 788.
MOFFETT William 487.
MOLESWORTH Thos I. 1658.
MONROE Jonathan 1368; Mr
1165; 1889; Thomas H. W.
28; William 1983.

MONTELL Henry 2562; Henry Montague 2562.
MONTGOMERY John 24; 275;
1297; 1339; 2443; 2662;
2712; John Sen. 3; 34;
Joshan 3; Mary Ann 2664;
Samuel 2053.
MOONEY William 24; 275;
1297; 2443; 2468; 2491;
2662; 2712; 2717; 2767.
MOONY Wm. 1339.
MOORE Bishop 657; George
2634; 2635; Henry W. 2069;
Margaret 715; Philip 945;
Sam'l. 650; William 697.
MORE George 1364.
MORELAND John 60.
MORELOCK Jacob 1027;
Michael 2598.
MORGAN Charles W. 689;
Daniel 1297; E. 715; Edward
2898; 2937; Eleanor 135;
Elizabeth Ann 2898; Ellen
715; John Jr. 2767; Margaret 715; Mary Ann 116; Mr
108; Sarah J. 715; Sarah
Jane 715; Sophia R. 715; T.
W. 1196; 1202; Th. W. 256;
276; Thomas 1595; 1599;
Thomas W. 278; 1025; 1098;
1209; Thos W. 278; 377;
W.V. 30; William 1595;
1599; William V. 275; 377;
1098; 1297; 1339; 2443.
MORMAN Sarah 1980.
MORMON Hanna 2147.
MORNINGSTARR Mary 2013;
Susan 545.
MORRARTY Dennis 1288.
MORRIS Anna Maria 1170; J.
E. 1523; J. G. 1470; 2140;
Lewis 1282; Richard A.
1726; Robert 1282.

MORRISON G. 2662; J. G.
1297; 1339; 2491; 2712;
Jeremiah 2580; Jeremiah G.
24; 275; 970; 1436; 1509;
2443; 2662; 2712; Jeremiah
S. 2712; John 95; Michael
131; Wm. 1523.
MORROW James B. 1193.
MORSELL William 1045; 2318;
2594.
MORTON John 1282.
MOSER James 643.
MOTTER 2259; Ann Cecelia
Sophia Catherine 1036;
Elizabeth 285; Elizabeth Ann
1517; George 1517; Isaac
724; 1047; 2596; John 727;
Joshua 724; 1047; 2491;
2514; 2663; 2712; Lewis 24;
275; 1297; 1339; 1368;
2356; 2443; 2596; 2657;
Mary A. 2596; Susan 1517;
William 1036; 1945; 2529.
MOUL Ann 1582; Conrad 1582;
Tavern 2070.
MOUNT Thomas 1045; 1372;
1718; 2791.
MOUNT PROSPECT 321.
MOUNT SAINT MARY'S 115;
College 916; 1304; 2287;
2701; 2832; Seminary 33;
733.
MOUNT VERNON 1598.
MOXLEY Margaret C. 2170.
MOYER Catharine Maria 2205.
MUDD J. H. Clay 2117.
MULHORN Barbara Ann 2339.
MULKEY Mr 1249.
MULLEN David 1288; Hiram H.
1774; Hugh 985; 2335; John
J. 987; Teresa 135.
MULLIN Mary 2009.
MUMMEY Margaret Ann 1466;
Samuel J. 1466

MUNDSHOWER Joseph 623.
MUNROE James 1224; Mr
1937; Thomas W. H. 632.
MURDER 995; 1022; 1178;
2180.
MURDOCK Benjamin 982; R. B.
2329; Richard 1046; Richard
B. 2477; William 808; 1332.
MURPHEY Wm. Sr. 275.
MURPHY C. 715; Caroline 715;
Chas. H. 2899; James H.
1123; John 556; 1288;
Joshua 1009; Patrick 1718;
2329; William 1046; 2446;
Wm. Sen. 24; 1297; 1339.
MURRAY Mr 422; T. 599.
MURRY Joshua 970.
MUSGRAVE Mr 1162.
MUSSETER Christ 24.
MUSSETTER Lemuel 2418.
MYERHEIFFER Catherine
1160.
MYERLY Mr 513; Mrs 513.
MYERS Ann Sophia 2684; C.
1428; 2423; Catharine 1942;
Christopher 892; 985; E.
311; George 699; Israel 359;
377; 707; 976; 1941; 2328;
2541; Jacob 94; 985; 1585;
Joel 2279; Lewis 99; Margaret E. 1776; Mary 311; Mr.
2039; Nancy 2669; Thomas
1645; 1719; Thomas Jefferson 732.
NAGLE Charles 562; 1098;
Mary Ellen 562.
NAIL D. W. 1311.
NAILL David W. 1040; Samuel
1178.
NATIONAL Hotel 1161;
Monument Society 2549.
NAUMANN John C. V. 2004.
NAYLOR James 67.
NEAL Minerva 1543.

NEED J. W. 2754; Henry 94;
    985; 1718; 2335; 2500;
    2609; 2791.
NEED'S Tavern 2609.
NEEDWOOD 2190.
NEEL Isabella 2921; James
    2863; 2899; Joseph 686;
    2878; 2921; Joseph H. 2061;
    Mrs 686.
NEELD Henry 2831.
NEGRO Child 810.
NEIDIG Ben. 2662; Benjamin
    2356; 2470; 2712.
NEIGH John 1488.
NEIGHBORS John 1041.
NEIGHBOURS Wm. 1041.
NEIHOFF Christian 614.
NEILL 2259; Alexander Jr.
    1492; Amanda M. 2486; Dr.
    964; James 2416; Mary P.
    2218.
NELSON B. 1210; Burger 1968;
    Burgess 275; 1339; 2443;
    2662; 2712; Burgess Jr.
    1832; Elisha 1045; 1214;
    1297; Emily Catharine Tyler
    2352; Frances Columbia
    305; Henry 24; 2426; James
    650; John 305; 553; 1492;
    1685; Madison 206; 742;
    1314; 1515; 1828; 2359;
    2456; 2457; 2491; Mary S.
    1492; Nathan 1045; 2318;
    2766; Roger 1828; 2352;
    Thomas Jr. 1282.
NESBITT Isaac 2446.
NEWBRAND Christianna 2135.
NEWCOMB Captain 2589.
NEWEL Daniel 2508.
NEWEY 59; 113; John 86;
    Lydia 86; Mr 4; 6.
NEWHALL Lydia 1222; Winthrop 1222.

NEWKIRK John 1900.
NEWMAN Francis 442; T. W.
    2936; Susan Bird 442.
NEWTON John 2866.
NEWTOWN Trap 258.
NEZS Frederick 2423.
NICHOLAS Ellen 2643.
NICHOLLS Archibald 2885; Col.
    1944; Jacob 2856; Mary
    1944; Thos. C. 2885.
NICHOLS Ann 2106; Ann Cecilia
    1246; Catharine 341; 476;
    Edward 2117; Henry 2426;
    John Randolph 1942; Mary
    Ann 2174; Peter 341; 377;
    827; 1098; 1332; 2522;
    2648; Seth. 199; 459; 476;
    1327; Sophia 1729; Thomas
    1472; William 54.
NICKEL Adam 803; Elizabeth
    803.
NICKLE Daniel 1414; Louisa
    1723.
NICKLES Jacob 356.
NICKUM James 2611; John 94;
    360.
NICODEMUS Isaac 1049.
NIGH John Sr. 1098.
NILES Ann Sophia 2211; Hezekiah 152; 1169; 1927;
    Nathaniel 148; Robert Duer
    152; Robert Eichelberger
    383; Wm. 229; William
    Ogden 199; 206; 255; 324;
    377; 383; 459; 553; 780;
    906; 976; 996; 1003; 1098;
    1239; 2211; 2328; 2395;
    2423; 2456; 2716.
NIXDORF Henry 1191.
NIXDORFF Henry 233; 256;
    276; 278; 996; 1025; 1260;
    1278; 1371; 1460; 1515;
    2456; 2767.

NIXON Lorenzo D. 2938.
NOLAND Lawrence 538; Mary 2254.
NOLL Levi 894.
NOOMAN Bridget Eliza 1959; Catherine 1959; John 1959.
NOONAN J. 2055.
NORRED Samuel 898; 1041; Wm. 1041.
NORRIS Aaron T. 1382; Amos 28; 45; 108; 162; 879; 1421; Basil 80; 2653; Catharine 45; Israel 360; 985; 1313; 2468; 2491; James L. 459; 1131; 1327; John 1357; 2767; John E. 1775; Jonathan 24; 2443; 2662; Lot 1446; Mary Ann 28; 2733; Nicholas 24; 275; 827; 1040; 1297; 1332; 1339; 2443; 2598; 2662; 2712; Nimrod 666; Samuel 1056; 1515; Susanna 108; William 24; 970; 1045; 2318; 2426; 2443; 2662; 2712.
NORTHCAFT Ann America 2908.
NORWOOD Thomas 1509; 2264; 2767.
NOWLAND Patrick 33.
NULL Abraham 1042.
NUSBAUM Barbara 2464; Daniel 1924; E. 715; Ellen 715; Rachael 715.
NUSSBAUM Jacob 2216; 2648; Samuel 1432.
NUSZ Catharine 240; Catherine 1065; Ezra F. 343; Frederick 240; 377; 892; 1098; 1202; 1218; 2522; 2593; 2648; Henry 1065; Jacob 2648; Mrs 2593.
O'BEALL Alexander 733.
O'BOYLE J. 1098.

O'BRIAN Levi 24; Mr 1347.
O'BRIEN James 2234; Levi 275; 1339; Lewis 1297; Margaret 2234; Patrick 1288; Terrence 2234; Thomas 384.
O'CONNER Joseph 1178.
O'DONNELL Columbus 2190; Josephine 2190.
O'FARRELL John 1288.
O'HARA John 2257.
O'LEARY A. D. 1414; 2638.
O'NEAL Barbara 2324; Horatio G. 1303; 1341; Israel C. 2196; 2206; Maria 1617; P. 233; Thomas 2117; Thomas H. 2767.
O'NEALL Thomas H. 1460.
O'NEIL Israel C. 1696; Mary 135; Patrick 2264; 2522.
O'NEILL Eliza 715; J. 708; Louisa 2805; 2808; Minerva 2805; P. 2706; Patrick 377; 1379; 1436; 2457; 2541; 2711; 2805; 2808; Rose Ellen 2808.
O'ROUKE William 1650.
OAKLAND 2265; 2455.
OBERMEYER Rebecca 115.
ODEN William 1229.
ODENHEIMER W. H. 2848.
OFFUTT Ernsley 2872; Henry A. 740; Lydia C. 2894; Osgood 2874; Thos. B. 2859; Thomas H. 2952; Thomas L. 2856; 2886.
OGDEN 725.
OGLE Ann Maria 1720; Benjamin 985; Elizabeth 715; 2140; Harriet 2622; James 2622; James Henry 2622; Joseph 2217; Julia Ann 2557; Margaret 421; Samuel 377.
OGSTON John 1142.

OHR Arabella 2573; H. 94;
  Henry 360; 985; 1313; Jacob
  J. 985.
OLCOTT George M. 667.
OMERGOAST John 2751.
ONDERDONK Bishop 2778.
ORDNER Daniel 2308.
ORENDORFF Samuel 1157.
ORME Jeremiah G. 2917;
  Richard 2917.
ORNDORFF Henry 2402; John
  80.
ORPHAN ASYLUM 2803.
ORPUT Richard 58.
ORTNER Elizabeth 1291; Peter
  1835.
OSBORN Anne E. 1880; Granary 2138; J. C. 1046; James
  W. 2209; John C. 2138;
  Richard 981.
OSBORNE Phebe 2003.
OSBURN Ann 1852.
OSGOOD 555.
OSLOR Reuben 2621.
OTIS William 291.
OTT Elizabeth 1082; Frederick
  94; 360; 722; 985; 1313;
  George 2766; John 2356;
  2648; 2766; Mrs 2964; Peter
  1098.
OTTER William 2398; 2717.
OTTO Eli 1382; Mary Ellen 624.
OURAND Daniel 786.
OWEN Thomas 2886.
OWENS Washington 2863;
  2899.
OWING 1271; 1571; A. H. 2424;
  Belford 1922; Christopher
  2424; Deborah 1374; John
  2825; N. H. 275; 1339;
  Nathan H 24; 1040; 1297;
  1536; 2443; 2662; 2712;
  Nimrod 1460; 1509; 1515;

OWING (continued)
  O. H. 367; 2396; 2443;
  2662; 2712; Patrick 94; 360;
  561; Rachael Ruth 576;
  Susan 730; Thomas B. 576;
  Washington 1140; 1922.
OYSTER David Wm. 1672.
PACA William 1282.
PAGE Calvin 1414.
PAINE Robert T. 1282.
PAINTER Ignatius 1837.
PALMER 765; 1271; Joseph H.
  1496; Joseph M. 206; 743;
  1317; 1515; 2117; 2457;
  Jno. M. 729; Mr 679; Peter
  1513; 2767; Wm. T. 1414;
  Wm. Tompson 2075.
PANCOAST Joseph W. 2313.
PANCOST Catherine E. 2509.
PARE Elizabeth 543.
PARKINSON Mr 2244.
PARKS George 1495.
PARSON 2567; Mason 1043;
  1323; 2491; 2598; 2712.
PATINGAL W. 1396.
PATRICK John 2510; Mary Ann
  987.
PATTENGALE Robert 1619.
PATTERSON Ann Catharine
  785; Bailey 1128; John 785;
  M. E. 1732; Ruth 785; William 2468.
PAUBLE Jacob 70.
PAVILIAN CIRCUS 679.
PAXTON D. 284; Mr 1550.
PAYNE Joseph 256; 276; 1515;
  2598; 2648; 2766.
PEACOCK Belle Jane 438; Eliz
  1649; 1718; Thomas 236.
PEARCE Isaiah 2335; 2500.
PEARRE George A. 1414;
  James 1658; 1659; 1968;
  2708; 2777; William 2856.

PEARSON Hannah A. 1985; I. E. 1047; Isaac E. 724; 1047; Jas. 1985.
PEASE Zebrina 2801.
PEDDICORAD Joseph 1499.
PEDICORD Reason M. 965.
PEDICORN Greenbery 1973.
PENN John 1282; Eleanor A. 2332.
PERKINS Ebenezer 918; Joseph C. 815.
PERRO James 2102; 2103.
PERRY Ann L. 1615; Benjamin 2856; 2886; 2958; Benjamin I. 2878; Elias 2885; Erasmus 2856; 2886; 2893; 2958; John T. 2009; Mr 1446; Samuel 2856; Tavern 723; Thomas I. 2957; Thomas L. 2856; Wm. 723; 1048.
PERSELL John B. 33.
PERSEY Benjamin 1098.
PETERS Charles 94; 360; 1114; 1338; John Francis 27; Michael 1966.
PETTIT Henry M. 429.
PEYTON Yelverton T. 15.
PFOUTZ George 2655.
PHEBUS Elizabeth 690; James 2117; John 2493; Peter 2798.
PHELPES Harriet 1713.
PHELPS F. P. 1190; George 24; 275; 1297; 1339; 1368; 2318; 2426; 2443; 2662; 2712; P. 2508; 2509; P. F. 2381; 2382; 2430; 2438; 2448; R. W. 94.
PHEOBUS Ann 193.
PHILIPS Almeda 816; Catharine 1885; John 907; Levi 1041; Minerva 112; Noah 112; 168; 907; 1043; 1055; 1297;

PHILIPS (continued) 1339; 1770; 2470; 2662; R. H. 1357; Thomas H. 94; Willson L. 2863; Wilson L. 1041.
PHILLER Eli 2462.
PHILLIP Wm. 2225.
PHILLIPS Ann 78; Augustus Ann 839; Elizabeth S. 1775; George M. 2707; Greenbury 1649; John 28; 682; 1775; Levi 360; Mary 2695; Mary Ann 682; Noah 24; 275; 839; 1368; 2306; 2443; 2712; 2826; Thomas 360.
PICKING Leonard 722; 879; 2443; 2662; 2712; Sarah 2483.
PICKINS Elizabeth 1229.
PICKLE John 2812.
PIERCE Ann America 1756; Dr. 1756; Mr 212.
PIEREE Isaiah 985.
PIETER Catherine E. 201.
PIGMAN Hanson B. 1715.
PINKNEY Wm. 1802.
PIPHER Mrs 1780.
PITTENGER Catharine Rosanna 1367; W. B. 1339; Wm. B. 2662; Wm. R. 2595.
PITTINGER Joshua W. 2735; Louis Dunkin 573; W. B. 24; 1178; Wm. 573; William B. 722; 970; 1039; 1297; 1368; 2443; 2712; Vice 1395.
PITTS 1832; J. L. 905; 1396; 1402; 1572; 1592; 1593; 1624; 1722; 1723; 1911; 1933; 1968; 1980; 1981; 2073; 2092; 2815; John L. 1188; 1386; 1430; 1431; 1471; 1472; 1481; 1491; 1561; 1585; 1637; 1652; 1655; 1669; 1697; 1713;

PITTS (continued)
1714; 1716; 1777; 1787;
1788; 1789; 1794; 1795;
1796; 1800; 1801; 1816;
1821; 1827; 1830; 1850;
1851; 1854; 1871; 1872;
1924; 1925; 1961; 1971;
1972; 1982; 1987; 1996;
2009; 2010; 2014; 2036;
2037; 2038; 2048; 2058;
2104; 2105; 2106; 2117;
2139; 2147; 2154; 2155;
2173; 2186; 2203; 2217;
2218; 2231; 2248; 2250;
2254; 2260; 2266; 2267;
2272; 2279; 2280; 2289;
2301; 2302; 2388; 2389;
2462; 2475; 2492; 2557;
2600; 2612; 2621; 2643;
2664; 2669; 2733; 2739;
2781; 2782; 2788; 2821;
2823; 2835; 2836; 2838;
2839; 2842; 2845; 2846; Mr
2432; Nicholas H. 1096;
1098; 2117; 2328; 2522;
2541.
PLANE Elizabeth 1895; Wm. 1895.
PLAIN Jonathan 1098; Sarah Ann 2788.
PLAINE Stephenson 1801.
PLASTER Susan R. 515.
PLATER James L. 2856.
PLEASANT DALE PAPER MILL 126; Retreat 1899.
PLOUGHMAN Nathan 641.
PLUMMER Abner M. 173; John 1288; Thomas M. 1045; William 404; William W. 1470; Yate 1512.
POE Anna M. 107; George 2364; George Jr. 107; Jacob 98; 209; 1555; 1368; 2470; 2598; 2662; 2712; Neilson

POE (continued)
199; 206; 209; 324; 377;
459; 553; 707; 780; 976;
996; 1098; 1131; 1260;
1327; 2328; 2570.
POFF Fanny 973.
POFFENBEAGER John 631.
POFFENBERGER George 1625; Jacob 2293; Rachel 1625.
POFFINBERGER B. T. 2226.
POINDEXTER George 346.
POISAL J. 1946; Mr 2613.
POISIONED 168
POLK Lucius J. 320; Robert J. W. 2720.
POLLARD Charles 2895; Hannah A. 2895.
POMEROY Ebenezer 1217.
POOL Ann C. 1870; Eli 1098; John 2856; Mary T. 2134; Walter 377.
POOLE Achasah 1529; Brice 1529; Catharine 1481; Dennis 768; Eli 451; 849; 1176; Elizabeth 565; 2409; Geo. W. 1529; Henrietta Hanson 768; John 1690; Mary 50; 558; Mary Ann 1135; Susan 849; Thomas 2878; Thornton 576; 842; William H. 24; 275; 1040; 1845; 2356; 2424; 2469; WM. 2379.
POORMAN Jacob 360; 2609.
POPE Carolina Sophia Maria Julianne Wortley Montague Joan of Arch 2700; Nathaniel 2893.
PORTER Edward 2856; Elizabeth 715; J. W. 1776; John 279; 2888; John A. 2117; John W. 1725; Mr 214; 215; 2752.
POSEY Sarah Ann 1357.

POST OFFICE 575; 820; 1207; 1276; 2418; 2511; Master 308; 575; 820; 865; 1128; 1276; 1311; 1434; 1477; 1495; 1518; 2418; 2785.
POTEET Thomas 709.
POTTER George 1041; 2573.
POTTS 1779; George 827; 1333; George M. 510; 1394; 1396; 2306; 2470; George Murdoch 510; John 731; John Lee 265; Mary Ann B. 1076; R. 233; 377; 1130; Richard 206; 255; 359; 780; 1055; 1098; 1161; 1396; 1769; 1770; 1953; 2117; 2328; 2522; 2541; 2549; 2688.
POUDER Jacob Jr. 24; John 2598.
POULTNEY Evan 1476; Philip 1129.
POWDER Jacob 827; 1332; 2356; 2443; Jacob Jr. 275; 1297; 1339.
POWELL Alfred H. 133; George W. 2117; Peter 349; Thomas 24; 275.
PRAFT John W. 24.
PRATHER William Jr. 2856; 2878.
PRATT John W. 275; 324; 808; 1332; Thos. G. 1631.
PREBLE Edward 1185.
PRENTISS William 960.
PRESTON Samuel 2264; Sarah B. 1805.
PRETTYMAN Mr 1832; Wm. 1657.
PRICE Ann E. 2709; Benjamin 255; 324; 359; 377; 553; 650; 707; 971; 976; 993; 1003; 1098; 2275; 2359; Colonel 1739; 2492; G. 708; George 24; 275; 708; 1339;

PRICE (continued) 2709; Margaret A. 633; Rebecca 1739; Sarah 1596; Sophia 1675; V. 1056; William 1596; 1675; 2958.
PRINCE 1238; 1671; T. C. 1414; Th. C. 233; Thomas C. 906; 970; 1007; 1073; 1147; 1218; 1397; 1405; 1485; 1532; 1632; 2395; 2698; William 2893.
PROBY James 390.
PROFFENBERGER Isaac 2767.
PROSPECT HALL 2022.
PROTESTANT FEMALE FREE SCHOOL 2964.
PROTHER Maria Julia 492; Thomay 492.
PROVOST M. 715; Paul 705; Thaddeus 708.
PRYOR J. W. 1327; James M. 2541; James W. 587; 976; 1098; 2522.
PURCELL Dr. 773; Thomas 2373.
PURDOM Joshua 740; 2871; Joshua Jr. 2863; 2899.
PURSLE Lucy 1177.
PURVEST Linvel 1288.
PUSEY B. 1339.
PYFER Hannah Melville 2051; Henry 2451; Wm. B. 2051.
QUINN Mary 2325.
QUYNN 2259; 2555; C. 2767; Caspar 278; 1414; 1509; 1515; 2385; 2542; 2638; Casper 256; 276; 1260; 1338; Louisa Isabella 1977; Margaret 715; Mary 715.
RABBITT John 2958.
RADCLIFF Joseph 1523.
RAELING Elizabeth 2195.
RAGAN Catherine 1823; Elizabeth 356; Richard 1823.

RAHAUSER Frederick 2747.
RAILROAD 1153.
RAINSBURGH Jno. 2092.
RAISING OF LAZARUS 726.
RAMBLER RETREAT 674.
RAMESBURG John 339.
RAMICH Michael 1993.
RAMSBERG Christian 1952; David 1952; Jane Rebecca 1241.
RAMSBURG 1271; Barbara 2412; C. 1968; Catharine 775; Christian 723; 1048; 2478; Daniel 1248; Elias 483; Elizabeth 1841; George 1355; Henry 1629; Israel 1513; 2259; 2478; 2767; Jacob 199; 459; 1137; John 1327; 1414; Jno F. 2821; Lewis 30; 377; 1338; 1396; 1414; 2359; 2767; M. 2767; Mary Ann 1693; Sebastian 1421; 2826; Sebastian Jr. 1718; Sophia 496; Stephen 198; 1460; 1841.
RAMSBURGH Ann Mary 2185; Israel 1509; 1513; John 339; 1098; Lewis 1098; Mr 2722; Sebastian 2491; Sebastian Jr. 2264.
RAMSDELL Alonzo 2247.
RAMSEY Mr 1200; William 178.
RANDALL Vachel W. 499.
RANDOLPH Edwin 746; Mr 585; P. 746; Robert B. 1347.
RANEBERGER Philip 1399; 1605; Rebecca 1399; 1605.
RANNEBAGER Philip 1854.
RATHRAUFF F. 1051.
RAUSBAYLE Israel 2481.
RAWLINGS thomas 2878.
RAY James H. 2769.
RAYCLIFF Elizabeth 1173.

RAYMOND 725; James 377; 1098; 2456; 2491; 2522; 2541; Mr 1178.
REA Andrew J. 1540.
READ George 1282.
REAL Otho 1584.
REAL ESTATE BANK 1228; 1235.
REARDON Ellen 715.
REASER Jacob 377.
REAVER John 1578.
REBAUGH J. 947.
RECH Eliza 1011.
RECHTOL Lewis 1952.
RECK Abraham Sen. 2085; John 227; Margaret 2085; Mr 136; 924; 926.
REDDICH Eve 100.
REDDICK John 1099; Leonard 1405; 1523; 1972.
REED Benj. F. 2509; E. B. 1327; Enos B. 459; 1131; 1327; Fitch 2769; Henry 360; 1372; Isaac Shelby 378; John Wesley 1240; Rebecca Theresa 1427.
REEK Mr 63.
REEL Thomas 1288.
REES Susan 998.
REESE 2259; Catharine 1432; D. 1698; 2185; Dr. 1654; 2495; 2520; 2559; Elizabeth Barbara 2719; J. T. 914; Jacob 1049; 1318; 1339; 2443; 2767; 2826; John 2518; John S. 2519; Mr 2108; 2419; 2535.
REESIDE AND COMPANY 2797.
REGG John 1920.
REICH Isaac 1577; John 1098; P. 30; Philip 377; 1098; 1306; 1338; 2468; William 1371; 2008; 2634.

REID William 956.
REIGART Elizabeth Lydia 1546; P. 1546.
REIGHLEY Charles 815; 934; 969; 1002; 1113; 1335; G. 913; Mr 965.
REIGHLY C. 1130; Charles 738; 769; 782; 795.
REIHL Jacob 1414; John 1414.
REILEY James 1210.
REILY Rev. 1832.
REINDOLLAR John 2458.
REINER George 1140; Hannah 1140.
REINHART David 905; Elizabeth 482; Fred'k. 2791; Geo. 2534; Jacob 2626; Susan 2534.
REIS E. J. 2898.
REITZEL Elizabeth 1733; John 1733.
RELIEF OF THE POOR 233; 1191; 1198; 1203; 1216; 1830.
RELKE Sophia 2355.
REMSBERG Christian 1692; Josiah 1692.
REMSBURG Elizabeth Louisa 1388; J. 1131; Lewis 2328; Samuel 1388; 1569; Sarah Ann Maria 1569; Sebastian Jr. 1041.
REMSBURGH Christian 1048; Wm. 1041.
RENN Isaac 1718; 1986; 2767; John H. 1791; 2791; Lucretia Permelia 1986; Martha 1986.
RENNER Adam 1372; 2500; Elizabeth 294; Solomon 294.
REPASS A. C. 2728; Elizabeth 2728.
REPP Henry 1040; Jacob 1703; Susannah 1703.

RESSLER Lloyd A. 1372.
RETREAT SCHOOL HOUSE 2520.
RETTGERING Joanah A. 1989.
REYNOLDS Cath. 2964; James 1414; 2817; Louisa 952; Margaret 1861; 1904; Samuel 1904; Susan 2817
RHEA John 365.
RHEIL Harriet 179.
RHINEHART W. R. 287; Sarah 1663.
RHOADES Henry 2021; Peter 2766.
RHOADS George 1897.
RHODES Amos 1222; Catharine 1520; H. 1414; Henry 1131; 1473; 2385; 2492; 2638; John 1414; 2638; Mary E. 2166; Philip 2385; Susan 1473; Wm. 1288.
RHODNICK Joseph 703.
RHOR Philip 94.
RICE Albert 2117; George 176; 275; 377; 1297; 1339; 1397; 1414; 2117; 2288; 2398; 2443; 2522; 2541; 2642; 2648; 2662; 2712; Geo. B. 64; Grafton J. 2117; 2439; Hannah 1937; Jared 698; Levi N. 1134; Mary Ann D. 452; Mr 581; Nathaniel 985; Perry 1202; 1209; 2648; Perry Sen. 452; 1041; William 270.
RICHARDS Cornelia 1804; John 1098; Luther 1733; Wm. 1403; Wm. M. 1109.
RICHARDSON 2259; David 2443; Davis 1198; 1260; 1297; 1339; 1830; 2092; 2662; 2712; 2826; Frances Virginia 2639; Ignatius D. 2117; John 1535; 2639;

RICHARDSON (continued)
John Henry 1535; Mary
1535; William 2117.
RICHMOND Floyd N. 1347;
Francis 1311; 1513; 2647;
Jacob 46 John P. 2349.
RIDDLEMOSER Ephraim 1077;
Jacob 2717; Saml D. 2582.
RIDENHOUR Susan 2094.
RIDENOUR Margaret 1078;
Sarah 202.
RIDER 2011; F. 1832.
RIDGELY Charles S. 2044;
Jane Olivia 719; Nicholas H.
719.
RIEGART Mr 2734.
RIEHL Catharine 484; Jacob
1411.
RIGDON CoLumbia E. 2414;
John V. 42.
RIGGAL Aaron 2955.
RIGGS Charles 2908; Elisha
2940; Henry Jr. 459; 1327;
John 2878; Sam'l. 2863;
2899; Sarah Ann 2389;
Tabitha 2858; Thos 2863;
2899.
RIGNER John 206.
RIGNEY Frederick A. 1414;
1460; George Morlimer
1136; John 25; 192; 233;
553; 586; 808; 856; 1136;
1260; 1278; 1332; 1405;
1460; 1477; 1515; 2359;
2456; 2457; 2491; 2634;
2641; 2826; John T. 2117;
Sophia Elizabeth 856; William H. 2117; 2634; 2767;
William Heisely 1242.
RIGNY John 25.
RILEY Eliahu S. 2819; James
45; T. 1831; 2731; Tobias
1726; 1727; 1747; 1804;
1805; 1825.

RILY Ann W. D. 88.
RILING Henry 1053.
RIMEL George 1774.
RINE Jesse W. 570.
RINEDOLLAR Amelia J. 927.
RINEHART Geo. 1929; John
599.
RINER George 24; 275; 1045;
1297; 1339; 2443; 2594;
2662; 2712.
RINGGOLD Chester 1419;
Elizabeth 2421; Samuel
1106; 2421; Virginia 1106.
RINGLAND Eliza 930.
RINOR George 1140; Hannah
1140.
RITCHIE 1238; A. 1034; 1098;
1327; 1995; 2092; Adam
2628; 2648; Albert 199; 459;
1131; 1196; 1202; 1218;
1396; 1485; 1623; 1832;
1968; 2117; 2526; Anna
2964; Annalenah 2508;
Cath. 2964; Catherine Davis
1034; 2526; John 103;
2508; Mary Roane 657;
Rosanna 805; Thomas 199;
459; 657; Wm. N. 103.
RITENMYER Conrad 1098.
RITER Elizabeth 1933.
RITNER Geo. 1368.
RIVES Mr 148.
ROACH Mary A. 135.
ROADRUCK John 2594.
ROBBERY 979; 2334; 2571;
2663; 2668.
ROBECKER Rosanna 1502.
ROBERT Mr 2033.
ROBERTS Asael 2833; Dr. 1547;
1748; George 602; Hotel
2621; John 1049; 1368;
2330; 2359; 2443; 2481;
2491; Mr. 2625; Samuel
1738; Thomas 2515; William

ROBERTS (continued)
856; 1049; 1093; 1127; 1297; 2481.
ROBERTSON Archibald 2438; James H. 2117; John 2116; Susan Catherine 290.
ROBINSON Ann E. 715; Capt. 760; H. 1483; 1764; Henry 418; 452; 1134; 2092; 2767; John 1623; 2117; Miss 2964.
ROBEY Benjamin 2856.
ROBY Barry Senr. 2886.
ROCHESTER Wm. 260.
ROCKDALE FACTORY 257.
ROCKWELL Eliha H. 24; 2443; 2662; H. 1339; Elihu 275; 2662; 2712; Elihu H. 1297.
RODERICK Mahlon 1718.
RODEROCK Susan 2203.
RODES William 1200.
RODGERS James 94.
RODNEY Ceasar 1284.
RODRIC Benjamine 1480.
RODRICK Lewis 1041; 1054; Mahlon 903; 989; 2791; Margaret Ann Elizabeth 1054.
RODUCK Mahlon 1372.
ROELKE Christiana 671; E. M. M. 2151; George A. 2490.
ROGER Daniel 2711.
ROGERS James 1297; 1339.
ROGERSON Thomas 2925.
ROHR Catharine 1363; George 24; 275; 1297; 1339; 2423; 2443; Jacob 865; 1477; Mrs 865; P. 1428; Peter 1098; Philip 278; 360; 377; 586; 591; 707; 985; 1025; 1098; 1313; 1363; 1718; 1830; 2264; 2522; 2541; Phillip 2791.

ROHRER John 2465; John H. 2429.
ROLLINGTON Ellen 1019; Wm. M. 764.
ROMAN J. Dixon 1566; James D. 1327; Joseph 2742.
ROOP David 1892; 2443; 2662; 2712; John 2086; 2662; Joseph 1892; 2443; 2712; Mary 2086; Samuel 2086.
ROOT Basil 1276; 1311; 2481; D. 2791; Daniel 94; 985; 1372; 1418; 1523; 1718; 2335; 2468; 2500; 2791; David 1013; Emanuel 1013; Jacob 307; 879; 1043; 1509; 2259; 2306; 2766; Mary 308; 1418; Rachel Elizabeth 1418.
ROOTE Daniel 360.
ROPER James 2228.
RORHER John 2465.
ROSE Jn. 1371; Martha Ann 156.
ROSEBERRY Miss 1480.
ROSEHILL 2024.
ROSENSTEEL George T. 526.
ROSS Ann E. 344; Anna M. 1743; Catherine M. 253; Frances 2780; George 1282; John 2723; Julianna J. 2050; W. J. 976; 1396; William 206; 232; 253; 344; 669; 675; 721; 1025; 1055; 1770; 2050; 2117; Wm. B. 2780; William J. 89; 199; 377; 459; 707; 721; 1098; 1131; 1327; 1414; 1743; 2328; 2456; 2491; 2522; 2541; Wm. Sr. 2653.
ROTH Catharine 2484; Nicholas 792.
ROTHAUVER Catharine 694.

ROUCH F. A. 2225.
ROUSE Peter H. 364; 2766.
ROUSS Peter H. 2767.
ROUTGANER George L. 1086.
ROUTHZAHN Benjamin 723; Daniel 723; John 289; Joseph 723.
ROUTZAUN Ann Magdalene 620; Benjamin 620; Christiana 2096; Jacob 2096.
ROUTZENY Daniel 2478; 2480.
ROUTZONG C. 1968; Daniel 1396; 2826; John 1694; Joseph 1952; 1968; Solomon 1513.
ROUZER Mary Elizabeth 2054.
ROW Charles G. 695.
ROWAN A. H. 2931; John 2931; Wm. 2931.
ROWE 2259; Elizabeth 838; Ezra 2117; Jacob 25; 2356; John K. 650; Mary Ann 2927.
ROWHAN Catherine 219.
ROWLAND Isaac 2753.
ROWLES Catharine Elenora 1426; Rezin 1426.
ROYER Jhu. 1503.
RUCK Jacob 762.
RUDDACH Joseph 318.
RUDDERAR Conrad 1046.
RUDISCEL William 1042.
RUDISEL Thomas 1640.
RUDY Charlotte Louisa 2017; Hanson 1050; Jacob 1952; 2017.
RUNKEL William 503.
RUNKLES Basil 2835; Brice 1607; Samuel 1045.
RUNNELS Wm. 1630.
RUNZER Daniel 1667; Sarah A. 1667.
RUPEL Joshua 1313.
RUSH Benjamin 1282.

RUSS Peter H. 2767.
RUSSELL Abel 1045; 1436; 2318; 2426; 2594; 2712; Alexander 2459; Jesse 1045; 2426; Joshua 360; 985; 1718; 2356; 2791; Robert G. 1098; 2335; 2500; W. C. 30; William C. 1306; 1338; 1414; 1806; 2385.
RUSSIAN MINISTER 2341.
RUSSLE John 1392.
RUTHERFORD Benjamin 377; 1072; 1784; 2522; 2541; Elizabeth 2114; Sophia 1072; Virginia 715.
RUTHRAUFF Frederick 2422; Mr 1018.
RUTHRUFF Mr 2452.
RUTLEDGE Edward 1282.
RYPMA Karl J. 1386.
SAHM Jacob 2117; Louisa 2200.
SAILER F. 549.
SAILOR Reuben 2034.
SAIN Allen 360; 2329; 2427; Tavern 2427.
ST. ANDREW'S CHURCH 1152; 1712; 2704.
ST. BARTHOLOMEW CHURCH 2778; 2867; 2941.
ST. JOHN'S CHURCH 2051; 2686; 2941; College 2405; Female Academy 1810; 2803; Female Institute 135; Female School 715; Literary Institute 708; 1312; 1360.
ST. MARY'S CHAPEL 610; College 2287; 2623.
ST. THOMAS MANOR 1539;
SALES Andrew 2936.
SALMON Catharine 2179; George 199; 1260; 1295; 1338; 1405; 1411; 1414; 1485; 1830; 1953; 1968;

SALMON (continued)
2092; 2097; 2107; 2132;
2179; 2264; 2385; 2635;
2767; M. A. 715; Mary A.
715; Mary A. E. 1656; Richard D. 200; Susan Amelia 1295.
SALTER Wm. E. 1414.
SAMFORD Mr 1756.
SAMSDEN Mr 460.
SAMSEL Rebecca 2429.
SANDERS John L. 1221.
SANDERSON Elizabeth 1819; Raymond 1414; 1687; Thos. 1985; W. R. 906; William R. 1098; 1819; 1953; 2522; 2541; 2598; Wm R. Jr. 377.
SANDS George W. 1509.
SANFORD General 2589.
SAPPINGTON Catharine 1482; Francis 7; 708; Thomas 708; 1368; 1396; 1482; 2264; 2443; 2658; 2712.
SARGENT Thomas 833.
SAUM Abraham 2532; Isaac 1785.
SAUNDERS John 832; John L. 199; 459; 636.
SAYLOR Catharine 2655; Henrietta 593; Henry 2277; Jacob 2655.
SCHABACHER Adam 2648; Jacob 2648.
SCHAFFER Ann Maria 1389; John 1389; Peter 1389.
SCHAEFFER Catharine Ann 1050; D. F. 37; 65; 69; 100; 122; 123; 124; 149; 150; 151; 160; 179; 201; 203; 204; 228; 254; 268; 269; 296; 303; 311; 312; 314; 316; 322; 323; 331; 332; 337; 348; 349; 350; 356; 371; 374; 390; 391; 417;

SCHAEFFER (continued)
421; 422; 430; 431; 446;
451; 458; 459; 461; 484;
485; 488; 529; 545; 558;
565; 566; 567; 579; 580;
593; 594; 595; 608; 626;
627; 637; 643; 644; 645;
655; 663; 664; 665; 670;
671; 672; 699; 700; 718;
752; 753; 754; 762; 766;
767; 791; 792; 801; 811;
817; 822; 830; 838; 847;
853; 856; 863; 880; 912;
929; 954; 955; 956; 957;
958; 972; 1005; 1027; 1053;
1076; 1077; 1087; 1099;
1100; 1101; 1102; 1103;
1122; 1123; 1176; 1179;
1180; 1181; 1194; 1198;
1242; 1244; 1248; 1273;
1274; 1290; 1291; 1305;
1326; 1327; 1328; 1329;
1334; 1365; 2332; 2373;
2390; 2433; 2434; 2606;
David 2486; David F. 1; 70;
88; 114; 140; 141; 175; 176;
177; 199; 217; 218; 244;
245; 262; 263; 285; 397;
732; 733; 734; 783; 812;
886; 887; 903; 948; 949;
950; 998; 999; 1019; 1065;
1066; 1135; 1137; 1186;
1229; 1283; 1285; 1298;
1299; 1300; 1301; 1336;
1358; 1359; 1371; 2308;
2311; 2321; 2322; 2323;
2337; 2338; 2339; 2344;
2345; 2354; 2355; 2403;
2405; 2409; 2412; 2413;
2463; 2610; 2611; Dr. 1602;
2450; 2451; 2484; 2485;
2532; 2533; 2544; 2548;
2563; 2564; 2583; 2584;
2630; Elizabeth 2630; F.D.

SCHAEFFER (continued)
1244; 1358; 1359; 2384;
Frederick 1291; Frederick C.
51; George 1050; George
Krebs 1602; Jno. A. 1515;
Mr 11; 12; 50; 11; 169; 170;
423; 694; 695; 696; 2964;
Rev. 96; Rosana 1244.
SCHAFF Dr. 2628; 2629; 2636.
SCHEITZ Margaret 2232.
SCHELL Chad D. 2771; Enos 377; 1045; 1705; 2318; 2426; Ezra 906; 1098; 2198; 2395; J. 30; Joseph 358; 1090; 1306; 1338; 1414; 2385; 2638; Rosanna E. 1655; Tavern 2318.
SCHENCK Abraham H. 104.
SCHIEWETZ Christian 2195.
SCHISLER Charles 149.
SCHISSLER J. 708; John 9; John A. 708; 2117.
SCHLEIGH D. H. 1778; John 487; Mary 832.
SCHLEY 765; 1271; 1571; 1779; 2359; Alfred 2117; David 24; 98; 275; 1237; 1281; 1317; 1414; 1501; 1746; 2117; 2225; Edward 1394; 1515; 2264; 2826; F. A. 206; 255; 553; 654; 1178; 1396; Frederick A. 1025; 1155; 1306; 1322; 1338; 1414; 1464; 2385; Frederick A. Jr. 2117; George 1536; 1769; 2492; 2522; 2800; H. 435; Henry 206; 553; 654; 996; 1025; 1414; James M. 1651; John E. 1414; John T. 1216; 2647; John Thos 212; Wm 30; 206; 377; 553; 584; 1098; 1155; 1178; 1288; 1306; 1338; 1395; 2385; 2446; 2457; 2522; 2541.

SCHLOSSER Ann 1871; Elias 1691; George 2468; Peter 24; 1405; 1718; 1952; 2356; 2478; 2480.
SCHLUND Joshua 2232.
SCHMAL Henry 579.
SCHMUCKER Dr. 2727.
SCHMUKER Dr. 2384.
SCHNEIDER John M. 268.
SCHOLL Daniel 377; Dennis 1098; 1414; Elias 13; 1001; 2519; Elizabeth 795; Henry 256; 276; 2767; John 374; 1460; Margaret 566; Mr 710; Susan 1001.
SCHREIBER Mr 2190.
SCHREINER J. 1338; John 1098; 1306.
SCHRINER Henry J. 127; John 2638; Virginia Mary 127.
SCHRIVER A. F. 1049; Andrew 275; Isaac 1155; Jacob 275; Judge 934; Mary 934.
SCHROB James A. 1006.
SCHRODER Henry H. 1989.
SCHROEDER A. 715; Arabella 715; Frederick 2191; T. H. 1865.
SCHUGUR Elizabeth 1133.
SCHULTZ Ann Sophia 2149; Henry 1509; J. C. 2491; Joseph C. 2598; 2767.
SCHWARTZ Christian 2451.
SCOTT A. M. 683; Ann 2934; E. H. 804; Eli 739; 789; Gen 2589; Margaret Elizabeth 2887; Robert 58; Thomas 2856; 2886; 2887; 2893; Upton 2356; 2491; Walter 2934; William 2856; 2886.
SEAMAN Christian 1098; Jacamiah 637.
SEARS Cassandra Ann 637; Jonathan 1076.

SEBLY William 2446.
SEGAN Ann 1806.
SEINBACH Daniel 83.
SEIVER Elizabeth 860.
SELLMAN Beall 1158.
SELVEY Hamilton 2842.
SEMMES Thomas 2926.
SEMPLE Frederick 2282.
SENSENY Christian 2420.
SERGEANT John 2848; Sarah 2848.
SHAAFF Margaret Jane 1755.
SHAEFFER Daniel 221; John 2638; Mr 50.
SHAER John 2601.
SHAFER Ann SOPHIA 175; J. A. 1371; Jacob 879; 1371; John 710; 1041; Noah A. 275; 377; 1098; 1297; 1339; Susan 337.
SHAFF Samuel 2166.
SHAFFER George 1952; 1968; John 24; Noah A. 840.
SHAFFNER John 806; P. R. 2395.
SHAIFER A. K. 290; 619; Sarah An 619.
SHANEBERGER Samuel 1554.
SHANK Benjamin 879; Ezra 2310; Jacob 32; Joseph 1706; Maria 32.
SHARER Catharine 853; Lewis 970; Maria 288; Susanna 13.
SHARP G. W. 30; 255; George W. 206; 807; 1260; 1278; 1306; 1338.
SHARPE Edith 1330.
SHARRER Valentine 1771.
SHAW Eliza A. 2938; Francis 1421; 2767; Grizelda Jamison 353; Hugh 2356; Leonard D. 2892; Moses 94; 353; 360; 985; 1049; 1313; 2491;

SHAW (continued) Mrs 1170; Susan 1385; Thomas 434; William 1228; Zachariah 1933.
SHAWAN Eliza 647; Richard 647.
SHAWBAKER J. 1515.
SHAWWN Ann 627; Dan'l. Sen. 1515; David Sen. 1834; Grafton 1947; Joseph 285; Rebecca R. 397.
SHEARER Lydiann 2248; Sarah 2649; Sophia 2209.
SHEETS Ephraim 57; Greenbury 94; Henry 900.
SHEFFER Mary Ann 1694; Philip 1952.
SHEHAUN Nelly 556.
SHEID J. G. 1278; James G. 560.
SHELEY Caleb 2422.
SHELL Joseph 1718.
SHELLMAN Jacob 1098; James M. 1218.
SHELMAN Augustus D. 2528; Henry Steiner 2499; Col. 1382; 2334; J. M. 1327; Jacob 2296; James 1204; James M. 199; 233; 459; 553; 780; 892; 993; 996; 1130; 1131; 1161; 1191; 1322; 1327; 1352; 2333; 2492; 2522; 2541; 2549; John M. 2522; Mr 1064; T. P. C. 1187; 2499; Thomas P. C. 1095.
SHELLI Catharine 670.
SHELLY Frederick 1098;
SHELTON Esquire 2728.
SHENDLER John 2480.
SHEPHERD 1271; Abijah 1098; 2361; Mr 635; Solomon 1031; 2365; Susan 334; Susanna 1031; Thomas 469;

SHEPHERD (continued) 2356; W. 360; William 94; 1368; 2330; 2443; 2481.
SHERMAN Roger 1282.
SHERWOOD Chapel 2098; Samalva 1579.
SHETENHELM Reuben 1794.
SHIED James G. 550.
SHIELDS Amelia 149; Doct. 2491; Henry 2782; J. 1047; Jefferson 724; 985; 1006; 1313; 1396; 1718; 2505; 2608; 2687; 2726; Susan 580.
SHINDLER D. 1968; David 1513; John 1048.
SHINDTER David 1952.
SHIPLEY Catharine 2731; Elizabeth Hall 1188; Greenbury 2005; Joshua 2612; Mary 1273; Sarah Ann Selman 216; Thomas C. 24; 1188; 1394; 1421; 2479; 2767; Wm. 26; 216.
SHIPLY Samuel 2037.
SHIPMAN Frederick 348.
SHIRGLEY Enoch 2516.
SHIVERS Thomas 986.
SHOEMAKER Amy 300; Dennis 701; 2274; Edith 2956; Elizabeth 1868; Francis 853; Sarah 1403.
SHOLL Catharine 732; Jacob 533; John 1098; 2634; Mrs 533.
SHOLTZ Joseph C. 2662.
SHOOK Daniel 542; Peter 377.
SHOPE G. B. 1219; George B. 256; 276; 278.
SHOPER George B. 586.
SHORB Alexander 2572; James A. 2359; Mary 921; Mary Ann 2802.

SHOTTS Henry 1098; Margaret 1490.
SHOUB Frances 1757.
SHOUMAN Isavena N. 898.
SHOUP Elizabeth 416; Susan 1707.
SHOWERS Adam 737.
SHOWMAN David 962; Eliza Ann 962.
SHRINER C. 2306; Cornelius 1809; Frederick 2647; George B. 2356; Michael 1604; Mr 556; Rebecca 1809.
SHRINEREA 2396.
SHRIVER 1671; 2567; A. F. 1048; Abraham 206; 1848; 2303; 2670; Abraham F. 1297; 2522; Abr'm. P. 970; Andrew 24; 172; 275; 481; 1297; 1339; 2028; 2331; 2443; Ann M. S. 172; Ann Margaret 2303; Charles 1414; 1460; 1848; 2670; 2767; D. 1169; Edward 1025; 1414; 1422; 1515; 1546; 1666; 1815; 2276; Eliza 2331; Elizabeth 2028; Geo. 2078; Isaac 997; 1918; 2530; 2598; Jacob 24; 1460; 1515; 2558; John 2385; John S. 1715; Joseph 1169; Judge 18; 329; Julianne 1918; Mary 2558; Mary E. 1715; Philip Abraham 1815; Sarah 1586.
SHROEDER Frederick 2117.
SHROYER John 1616; John Henry 1616; Solomon W. 2113.
SHRYCOCK Valentine 2766.
SHRYOCK Ann 1741; Jacob D. 722; 2404; Mary Ann 2271;

SHRYCOCK (continued)
  Valentine 722; 985; 1313; 1718; 2307.
SHUE Mr 1892; 1894.
SHUEMAKER Daniel 831; Sally 831.
SHUK Christaina 983.
SHULTZ George 256; 276; 278; 976; Henry 2648; Joseph C. 2712; Margaret 135; Sophia 135.
SHUNK Benjamin 34; 1297; 2442; Mich 970.
SHUP Sarah Ann 222.
SHUTZ George 242.
SHYLER Elizabeth 1627.
SIDES Ann Sabina 2005.
SIEVER Elizabeth 859.
SIFFORD 765; 2567; John 1060; 1093; 1155; 1317; 1421; 1465; 1513; 2478; 2480; 2491; 2530; 2598; 2767; 2826; 2837; Maria 912.
SIFTON Andrew 1832; William 2711.
SIGNERS OF THE DECLARATION 1282.
SIM Thomas 448; 2518.
SIMIN Dr. 2306; Thomas 1382.
SIMMONS 1671; Eliza Amelia 539; J. 2329; James 24; 74; 275; 277; 1046; 1155; 1297; 1339; 1396; 2427; 2443; 2477; 2491; 2580; 2662; James L. 1372; 2791; James S. 1718; 2500; James W. 2335; John 808; 985; 1313; 1332; 1396; 2336; John A. 1163; 1397; 1414; 1422; 1460; 1485; 1515; 1632; 2641; John F. 2477; John H. 970; 2477; 2491; 2767; John T. 539; Mary Ann

SIMMONS (continued)
  Rebecca 539; Mary Aseneth 2386; S. C. 2116; Z. T. 2767.
SIMMS Eliza 2853; Henry 2766.
SIMPSON Mr 1084; R. 2469; Rachel 1765; Rachel Raitt 1765; Richard 1040; 1178; 2136; 2424; Warfield 1523; 1765; 2717.
SIMS Eliza Jane 1068; Mary 214; Thomas 1068; 1396.
SINCLAIR Elizabeth Ann 1747.
SINGLETON Richard 1817; Sarah Angelica 1817.
SINN Charles Henry 1902; Daniel 1487; 2117; George 1902; Jacob 1366; John George 2390; Philip H. 2776; Thomas 1721.
SKINNER Henry S. 88; Otis A. 1146.
SLAGER Frederick 1144; Henry A. 1144.
SLAGLE Elizabeth 1489; Ruth 937.
SLANK George Washington 2162.
SLANSLEUTE Mary 1384.
SLATER Ann C. 2024; William 2024.
SLAUGHTER Columbia 2681; Mr 1755; 2681; Samuel 2681; Virginia 2681.
SLAYBAUGH E. 1856.
SLEIGH Daniel 124.
SLENTZ Jacob Lewis 2749.
SLICER Mr 1497.
SLICK Louisa 1009; Thomae 226.
SLIFER Asneth 1032; Emanuel 924; 1044; 1339; 1718; 2443; 2662; 2712; John 55; 2791; John Sen. 2560; Mary 151; Samuel 151; Wm 642.

SLINGLUFF G. W. 2558; Jesse 2481; Joseph 2559.
SLOAN J. 1968; Walter J. 1758; 1832.
SLUSS Jno. 724; M. 94; 1047; Michael 360; 970; 985; 1313; 1718; 2826.
SMALL 1238; Eli 957; Maria 2618; William 30; 44; 256; 276; 278; 375; 908; 994; 1025; 1196; 1202; 1218; 1278; 1306; 1465; 2256; 2385; 2492; 2618; 2634; 2739; 2757; 2767; Wm. J. 996.
SMALLWOOD Benjamin 1289; Robert 1281; W. A. 2942; W. C. 1286; 1289; Wm. 1098; William C. 70; 377; 1414; 2522; 2541; Wm. Cooper 708.
SMALTZ J. H. 77; 315; 449; 450; John 272; 483; John H. 13; 31; 36; 56; 57; 90; 180; 183; 184; 211; 222; 223; 234; 235; 284; 288; 319; 333; 339; 345; 347; 496; 502; 508; 521; 542; 543; 552; 583; 596; 597; 613; 614; 621; 622; 641; 656; 661; 662; 693; 736; 1247; 1284; 2964; M. 716; Mr 98; 155; 156; 171; 706; 728; 748; 2964; Mrs 2964.
SMELSER D. 1832; Hy. K. 2717.
SMELTZER Daniel 1952; Henry R. 1048.
SMIDMER Mr 1760.
SMITH Ann 689; Ann Maria 90; Ann R. 2844; Augustus C. 904; Barbara 668; 1053; Benjamin 1382; 2326; Carey Anna 457; Catharine 1333;

SMITH (continued)
Catharine R. 1392; Catherine 235; Charlotte 1637; Christian 1371; 2163; Daniel 1676; 2787; Daniel G. 564; David F. 2079; David Sylvester 1037; Edward 412; 419; 440; Eli 2264; 2728; Elizabeth 11; 183; Emanuel 645; 1515; 2826; Ezra 311; 1294; 2717; Frederick 1287; Frederick Sr. 1045; George 24; 505; 827; 1332; 1460; 1515; 2356; 2491; 2598; 2712; 2766; 2767; H. 245; Hannah 2034; Henry 94; 360; 985; 1313; 1396; 1717; 2479; 2522; 2541; 2594; 2766; J. 360; 1831; J. H. M. 1396; J. J. 1037; Jacob 420; 1297; 1683; 2767; James 24; 275; 1042; 1282; 1297; 1313; 1339; 1368; 2319; 2443; 2468; 2580; 2709; Job. Jr. 650; John 827; 910; 970; 1018; 1332; 2330; 2398; 2443; 2598; 2647; 2712; 2767; John D. 22; John H. M. 1405; 2767; John J. 24; 723; 985; 1048; 1297; 1313; 1339; 1718; 2117; 2662; John L. 275; 1857; John Speak 457; John Sr. 393; Jonathan 808; 1332; 2250; 2480; 2717; 2767; Joseph 94; 360; 691; 723; 735; 807; 985; 1297; 1313; 1435; 1465; 1509; 1523; 1718; 1961; 2285; 2443; 2468; 2469; 2491; 2522; 2717; 2767; Joseph L. 2021; 2329; 2336; 2834; Joshua 1339; 2356; Joshua Jr. 24; 275; 827; 997; 1049;

SMITH (continued) 1297; 1332; 1339; 1368; 2443; Lydia 1941; Lydia A. 1342; M. 2767; Margaret M. 22; Maria 594; Mary Ann 1730; Mary Besore 1676; Mary Fout 2111; Mid. 360; Milly 2875; Mr 112; 497; 1026; 2126; Peter 2839; Professor 1939; Raphael 2026; Rev. 1832; Roger 606; Robert 2038; S. P. 367; 1739; Samuel 479; 1131; Sarah 1761; Sarah Ann 1857; Sophia 1112; 2161; Susanna 420; 999; Sybilla 245; Teresa 2738; Th. 1339; Thomas 1297; 2443; Thomas Perrin 354; Washington 723; William 316; 2473; William M. 1760.
SNEATH Richard 1293.
SNELSER Henry Sr. 723.
SNIDER Adam 2297; Ann Mary 1640; Miss 487; Nicholas 1025; 1236; 1640; William 2117.
SNIVELY Joseph 2596; Mary A. 2596.
SNOOK A. 722; Adam 722; Agnes 508; Alice 2736; Daniel 1284.
SNOUFFER George 1335; Mr 2138.
SNOWDEN Richard 2885.
SNYDER Caroline R. 807; Denton J. 338; Ezra J. 1398; Henry M. 816; Jacob 946; John 1164; Joseph R. 1023; Joshua 1968; Mr 1711; Nicholas 807; 1278; William 2788.
SOCIETY OF FRIENDS 20; 340; 2365.

SOLLERS Adrianna 1105; Sabrett 1029; 1105; Sabritt 302; Thomas E. 302.
SOLOMON George 2631.
SOMERVILLE Sarah J. 2720; Vice 1935.
SONNENSTEIN Eleanor 2532.
SOPER Basil 2958; Robert 2863; 2899; 2958; Samuel 2885.
SOUDER Jacob 24.
SOWDER Peter 2826.
SOWER Eli 1714.
SPALDING Christy 2133; Francis 1042; 1405; George 2468.
SPARROW Sereny 2891; Wilson 1041; 1919.
SPAULDING Elias 2863; 2899.
SPAYTH Lydia E. 1221.
SPEAKE Thomas L. 2927.
SPEALMAN Mr 1.
SPEELMAN Elizabeth 1925.
SPENCE Jervis 1823; Robert 1396.
SPONSELLER Agnes 461; Amanda Ann 1789; Ann 1789; Christianna 1491; F. 708; John 1098; 2648; Margaret 2612; Michael 475.
SPANGLER Elizabeth S. 2674; Michael 2674.
SPRENGLE D. 30; David 25; 455.
SPRIG Sarah Ann Dorsey 462.
SPRIGG Columbia 1945; Elizabeth 2344.
SPRING Geo. 1896.
SPRINGER Daniel 512; 1098; 1411; Dr. 1048; John 512; Mary 2475; Rebecca 1164; Thomas 74; 277; 723; 1048; 1297; 1339; 1436; 2443; 2478; 2480; 2580; 2662.

SPRINGFIELD Ann C. 2023.
SPRITGER Thomas 2712.
SPURRIER Ann 1635; Barbara 1472; Captain 2515.
STABLER Edward 20; Thomas P. 2957.
STAGES 1484; 2797.
STAIT Arthur Wellesley 2804; Naomi 2676; William 2676; 2804; William Augustus 2676.
STALEY Catharine 2321; Christiana E. 656; Conrad 1515; Cornelius 1394; 1460; 1515; 2767; Elizabeth 885; Eve Elizabeth 597; Ezra 817; Frederick 7; Henry S. 2363; J. 885; John 94; Moses 1515; P. S. 377; Solomon 171; Susanna 544; 1284; Susanna Barbara 171; William 1693.
STALLINGS Ann 2337; Rebecca 903.
STAMBAUGH A. A. 1414; 2117.
STANDBURY Joseph 2463.
STANLEY John 2930.
STANSBURY John F. 94.
STAR Edmund 497; Jesse W. 162; John N. 1042; John Norris 92; Maurice T. 839; Rebecca 92.
STAUB Matilda 2121; Samuel 1742.
STAUBS Sarah Ann 1398.
STAUFFER Elizabeth 1431; William 2161.
STAUP William 2374;
STAYMAN George F. 1414.
STEDDING Christian 1371; 2634.
STEDING Christian L. 488.
STEEL Ann 1940; James 650; John N. 1940.

STEELE Mary Ann 701; Mary Jane 2931; Miranda 911.
STEGER Mr 84.
STEHLEY Malinda 1691; Stephen 809.
STEIGERS Wm. T. 172.
STEIN Christian 2648; Elizabeth 1111; Lewis 2634; Peter 2609.
STEINER 1671; Charles Reighly 2783; Christian 1098; 1407; 1485; 2648; Daniel 450; David 24; 30; 70; 377; 892; 1098; 1306; 1338; 1414; 2638; 2783; David C. 1414; 1681; Eliza 2964; Elizabeth 618; 1184; Frederick 360; 381; 2536; Henriett A. 1187; Henry 618; 1243; 2523; 2634; Henry Jr. 24; 25; J. A. 1968; 2092; Jacob 24; 275; 1184; 1264; James 1098; John A. 1414; 1830; 1953; 2684; John J. 1630; 2522; Margaret 1987; Rachel Rebecca 1243; William 30; 1098; 1234; 1306; 1338.
STEM David 2340; Margaret 1553; Peter 1074; 1553; 2443; 2662; 2712; 2717; 2766; 2767; Samuel 1832; 2711.
STEPHENS Jas. 94; Rezin 1087.
STEPHENSON Henry 1297; Mr 633.
STEUART Wm. M. 2336.
STEVENS Chad 2767; Charles 94; 2335; Henry 2443; Hotel 1629; 2733; James 360; 1414; John 2594; Mr 1626; Rezin 1045; Samuel 2356; Tavern 2594; William J. 1526.

STEVENSON Henry 1374; Joshua 1040; 2443; Mr 2549; R. B. 24; Saml 1045.
STEWART Alexander 416; Benson 1618; Henry 830; John 1155; 2608; 2647; John B. 417; John S. 1813; Wm. 1863; Wm. M. 1169.
STICKELL S. 1428.
STICKLE 1238; Mary 135; Solomon 879; 1218; 1843; 2423; William 202.
STIER Hamilton 914; 2426; 2479; Joseph 2438; Lydia Ann 2438; Mr 54.
STIFFORD John 2359.
STIMBLE Harriet 81.
STIMMEL John B. 970; 2767; Joseph 545; Sarah 244.
STIMMELL John B. 1509; 2766.
STINCHCOMB Beal C. 247; Mary 247.
STINGER Charles 1098; George 1098.
STITCHER John 1914; Peter 94; 1443.
STITELY Jacob Jr. 2356; John 876.
STITLEY Jacob 360; Lyia 719.
STOCKER Elizabeth 1138.
STOCKMAN David 1447; Elizabeth 1919; Jno. 2717; John J. 2450; Joseph 1041; Lawson D. 1538; William P. 2781.
STOCKTON Richard 1282; Richard C. 1613.
STOCKWELL John 661.
STOFFEL Peter 1830; 2322; 2383; 2634.
STOKES Dr. 2083; G. 1832; Geo. 2711; James 1968; Robert Y. 568; 1509; 2491.

STOLEY Isaac 337.
STOLL Adam 1515.
STONE 260; Bishop 2867; 2941; Charles 708; Ellen 715; Geo. F. 1161; Helen 715; Joseph 708; Lewis 1183; Margaret Ann 2323; Nancy 765; Rebecca 1682; Thomas 1282; Wm. Murray 1423.
STONEBRAKER Arnold S. 496.
STONER Adeline 125; Ann Elizabeth 211; Ann Rebecca 639; Christian 90; David E. 491; Dennis 1637; Eliza Ann 2062; 2831; Frederick 94; 892; 985; 2335; 2398; 2551; Frederick Sen'r. 1098; George 94; John 211; 639; 1405; John L. 35; Sophia 2419; William 2117.
STONESIFER Cassa Ann 1348; Daniel 1339; 1348; 2443.
STONESTREET Samuel T. 740.
STOOP Jas. 1371; Joseph 1515.
STOOPS John 1381.
STORM Jos, 2717; L. P. 2132; Mary A. 670; P. L. 1371; 1422; 1830; 2107; 2258; 2406; 2634; 2765; Peter L. 179; 1411.
STOTTLEMYER Jacob 94; John 2431; Lee Ann 2431.
STOUFFER Caroline 184; Catherine 1800; Jacob 892; Miranda E. 646.
STOUP Joseph Graham 2227.
STOUT John L. 1300.
STRAEFFER Esther Charlotte 537; Henrietta 2225; Jacob M. 2590; 2696; John 30; 1306; 1338; Michael 99; 537; 2255; Rebecca 2696.

STRAFER John 2385.
STRAFFER John 1098; 2385; Michael 2157; Michael Sr. 2646.
STRAILMAN George 2767.
STRASBURGER John F. 2468.
STRASBURY John 2766.
STRAWBRIDGE Mr 1210.
STRICKLAN Samuel 1553.
STRICKSTRUCK Jacob 2224; 2648.
STRIDER James W. 2168.
STRINE Catharine 1254; John 617.
STROUP Elizabeth 374.
STUB David 441; Joseph 315.
STUBBINS John A. 322.
STUBBLEFIELD G. W. 2446.
STUCHBURY Dorethea M. A. 241.
STULL Amanda 793; Benjamin 1330; 2791; Elie Williams 1267; Ellen N. 1651; George 204; Jacob 597; 767; John Henry 426; Joseph 881; Mr 1639; 2317; O. H. W. 1267; 1651; Otho H. W. 426; Susan 1639.
STUP G. 2150.
STURTEVANT Peleg 2948.
STUTLER Catherine E. 2390.
SUDDARELS Mr 1646.
SUE John 148; Rosella DeMilhau 148.
SUICIDE 366; 861.
SULIVAN Michael 2398.
SULLIVAN Michael 24; 275; 827; 1297; 1332; 1339; 2443; William 24.
SULTER William E. 2413.
SULTZER Hotel 1042; 2319; S. 2319; Sebastian 24; 275; 1297; 1339.

SUMAN John 282; 2094; Julian Catherine 2718; Wm. R. 2068.
SUMMERS Jacob 1425; 2767; James 43; 275; 1297; Mr 1820; Samuel 1513; Wm. 2767; Zadok 2863; 2899.
SUMPTER Samuel 364.
SUNDERLAND James 1224.
SUTER Henry 1041.
SUTLER Mary Ann 2488.
SWEADNER Daniel 275; 360; 985; 1040; 1372; 1718; 2335; 2500; David 94; Henrietta 2221; Upton 109.
SWEARINGEN Charles V. 758; 771.
SWEENY Israel 169.
SWIGART Jos 2481; Sarah 314.
SWIGERT David 880.
SWITZER David 2356; 2481; John 2620.
SWOPE J. 2491; John 1368; 2443; Michael 2609; Samuel 1042; 2319; 2598.
SWORMSTED M. 2141.
SYKES William 1098.
TABLER Christian 94; 360; 1041; 1323; Julia Ann 1077; Mr 925; W. B. 985; William 1041; William B. 923; 1372; 1718; 2335; 2500.
TAILER Moses 1652.
TALBOT James 2712; Joseph 1332; Mahlon 375; 1320; William 2958.
TALBOTT 765; 1671; Adjutant 993; City Hotel 2341; 2589; 2591; 2600; 2620; Henry W. 2856; 2886; 2893; Jacob 1007; John Jr. 1302; Joseph 827; 1156; 1218; 1339; 2443; 2662; 2663; Mahlon

TALBOTT (continued)
310; 996; 1098; 1297; 1323; 1397; 1422; 1740; 1830; 2522; 2653; William 2856.
TALEY Hiram 140.
TALLEY American 2349.
TANEY Adriann Elizabeth 2800; Anna Arnold 980; Eliabeth 2463; Ethelbert 800; Felix B. 1047; 1421; 2598; 2712; 2826; James Sr. 2662; Joseph 24; 1515; 2491; Joseph Jr. 24; 1297; 1339; 2443; 2712; Joseph Sr. 275; 1339; 2356; Mrs 388; Octavius 292; R. B. 980; 1321; 2367; 2619; Roger B. 388.
TANZEG Arthur 43.
TANZEY 2259; Arthur 1339; 2479.
TANZY Arthur 2767.
TAYLOR A. P. 2127; George 1282; Isaac P. 404; Mary 2127; Mary Probus 2127; William 920; William W. 406.
TEASE Bernard 1098.
TEHAN Ann Maria Stanislaus 1990; Catharine 317; Elizabeth A. 1990; James 708; John 1990; Wm. 708.
TEIRNAN Luke 944.
TEMPERANCE SOCIETY 1002; 1645; 1832; 1952; 1953; 1968; 1995; 2090; 2131; 2196; 2206; 2253; 2394; 2407; 2512; 2711.
TENANT Matilda 1685; Thomas 1685.
THISTLE Bayard 758; 771; Geo. 758; 771.
THOMAS 765; 1779; Ann Eliza 2670; Anna Maria 1231; Ann R. 1134; C.K. 1969; Caroline E. 1329; Cassandra 223;

THOMAS (continued)
Catharine 165; Catharine A. 1386; Catharine Contee 174; Charles Bedford 1678; Charlotte 2266; Christian 1008; 2715; 2767; Daniel 2039; Daniel W. 1083; David O. 1431; E. 1056; Eli 983; 1405; Emanuel 507; 1509; 2491; Francis 206; 616; 745; 1155; 1237; 1501; 1530; Francis Ephraim 1543; Gab. 2398; George 790; 879; 1231; 1421; 1465; 2240; 2245; 2477; 2598; 2717; H. 1231; Henry 890; 1098; Hotel 552; 587; Isaiah 73; Jacob 24; 275; 723; 1041; 1048; 1134; 1297; 1405; 1769 1952; 2264; 2443; 2468; 2662; 2712; Jacob B. 2480; James 1346; John 165; 174; 330; 723; 759; 796; 1056; 1155; 1396; 1769; 1952; 2264; 2359; 2398; 2480; 2491; John B. 2266; John Junr. 507; 1311; 2767; John M. 174; 477; 525; 1201; John W. 650; Lloyd 1396; 1421; 2356; Martha C. 2039; Mary Ellen 2249; Michael 508; 1056; 1421; 1978; 2491; 2647; 2767; Nich's. G. 2863; Otho 94; 360; 985; 1046; 1313; 1718; 2329; 2826; Perry G. 452; 1678; Peter 1543; Richard 1253; Roger B. 740; 2856; 2871; 2958; Samuel 423; 723; 985; 2010; 2670; Sarah A. E. 796; Sophia 1844; Thomas Turener 477; William 377; 1098; 1161; 1371; 1386.

THOMPSON 387; Charles 188; Eliza Ann 1672; Evan 2863; 2886; J. P. 206; John 188; 2335; John H. 2890; John P. 1025; 1098; 1953; 2117; Mary 188; Mary Ann 1592; Richard 1592; Sarah 1790; William 1011; 2897; 2922; Wm. J. 2598.
THOMSON Evan 2856; F. 1832; Fielder 1041; James 1893; John P. 304; 377; 654; 1175; 2117; Mary 304; William J. 191.
THORNTON Joseph 2057; Matt. 1282; Mr 1775.
THRASHER Pley 2801; Thomas 2206; 2356.
THRIFT Absalom 2856; 2886; James M. 2957.
THRONSTON Captain 2591.
THSEN John 808.
THSON 1332.
THUNDERSTORM 977; 1711; 2729.
TIDBALL R. M. 2446; Robert M. 2446.
TIDY Harriet 1946.
TILGHMAN William 23.
TILLARD Resir E. 2662; Rezin E. 1217; 2443; 2712.
TIPPET Mr 2079.
TIPPIS Jacob 868.
TITLOW David 2117; Evelina 2095; George 24; 275; 1513; 1869; 2095; 2443; 2598; Henry 2117; Isaac 2173; James 2447; John 508; 569; 586; 591; 1025; 1197; 1260; 1509; 1515; 1793; 2117; 2648; Juliana 672; Margaret 1910; Tavern 1869.
TODD Benjamin 24; 1045; Rinaldo 2372; Vachel B.

TODD (continued) 2372; Warfield 2426; William 1155; 1396; 1509; 2356; 2356; 2595; 2767; 2826.
TOFF Wm. 855.
TOMKINS Francis 2865.
TOMPKINS Jane 955.
TOMS Jacob S. 1868; Samuel 1952.
TOOT George 2796.
TORMEY P. 30; Mary Jane 715; Patrick 233; 377; 586; 707; 976; 1098; 1191; 1198; 1218; 1301; 1338; 1414; 2328; 2522; 2638.
TORNADO 653.
TORRANCE James 654.
TOWNSEND G. 650; G. S. 2084.
TRAGER Jacob 2598;
TRAIL Edward 30; 233; 377; 976; 1025; 1098; 1260; 1306; 1322; 1338; 1414; 1830; 1953; 2385; 2522; 2638; 2791; William 2856; 2886; 2933.
TRAIN ACCIDENT 2444.
TRAMELL Jane 2896.
TRAPNELL Joseph 1369; 1896; 1897; 1945; 2080; 2082; 2133; 2134; 2168; 2795; 2833; Joseph Sen. 1941; Sarah 1369.
TRAYER Jacob 2259; 2264.
TREADWELL Alexander Philip Socrates Emilias Caesar Hannibal Marcellus George Washington 2700.
TREFZER Ann Mary 1005.
TRICE George W. 2651; Henry N. 2047; 2634; Nicholas 2651.
TRIG Samuel 543.
TRINGSTRUM Peter 2386.

TRISCOTT George 1414.
TRISLER George 377; 774; 1098; 1438.
TRISSLER George W. 2117.
TRITTEPO Thomas 634.
TROUT Airy 1872; Matilda 863.
TROUTMAN Ann Catharine 1186. TROXALL Frederick 24; 275; 277.
TROXEL Frederick 74; F. 2662.
TROXELL Daniel 1962; Frederick 879; 1297; 1339; 1436; 2443; 2580; 2712; Jacob 808; 1332; Joseph 1047; Margaret 1503; Mary Ann 536; Sabilla 946.
TRUBUTT Hotel 70; 2267; 2302; N. 70.
TRUMBO Mary 1580.
TRUNBULL Wm. 1832.
TRUNDELL David Sen. 740.
TRUNDLE David 2878; Hezekiah L. 1944; John L. 2856; William 1433.
TRUSCOTT Alexander 30; 1306; 2159; 2634; George 2147.
TUCKER H. B. 2784; William 2215.
TULBOTT Joseph 1073; 1204.
TULEY Hiram 140.
TULLY Aquilla 1098; 2522; Ruth 731.
TULY Edward Charles 2066.
TUNKER SOCIETY 2030.
TURBUTT Capt. 826; Edward 1098; 1131; 1191; 1318; 1680; 2262; 2674; Elizabeth 2262; Hotel 2267; Lawrence Brengle 1680; N. 377; Nicholas 233; 256; 276; 821; 906; 1260; 1339; 2662; Nicholas H. 1021.
TURNER Catharine 1935; Isaac 2210; James 650; John 123;

TURNER (continued) John C. 622; Mary Ann 2490; Mr 2276; Thomas 174; 480.
TYDINGS Joseph 2613; Sarah 2613.
TYLER Anna L. P. 1767; Catherine Contee 163; Eleanor M. 1818; George M. 1414; 2117; 2440; Harriet D. 568; John 163; 1025; 1055; 1098; 1770; 2446; Mary 1818; 2083; Mr 2360; Rosetta 2803; Samuel 612; 1412; 2117; 2276; 2359; 2491; W. B. 119; 206; 238; 367; 654; 1396; 2328; William 206; 238; 679; 725; 1155; 1278; 1414; 1465; William B. 553; 707; 1155; 1953; 2117; 2522; William Bradley 568; 712; 780; 1098; 1130; 1310; 1767; 2083; 2457; 2541; Wm. C. 1818; Wm. Jr. 1414; 1515.
UHLER David 360; 985; 1313.
ULERICK Ann 2628.
UMBERGER Michael 2100.
UNGLEBERGER George 1371; Philip 1509.
UNION ACADEMY 724; 1047; Lines and Steamboats 2797.
UNITED STATES HOTEL 2033.
UNIVERSALIST SOCIETY 2714.
UNIVERSITY OF MARYLAND 71.
UNKEFER 765; 1271; 1779 A. 1523; 2469; Abdiel 24; 1060; 1093; 1281; 1317; 1405; 1736; 1773; 2264; 2359; 2398; 2443; 2491; 2598; 2662; 2712; 2767; 2826.
UPDEGRAFF Susan 2753.
UPTON Levi T. 529.

URNER Samuel 108.
UTCHERSON Matilda A. 2781.
VAGNER Christian 246.
VALENTINE William 2767.
VALLEY BANK 2663.
VAN ANTWERP Eliza 2769; Thomas 2769.
VAN BIBBER Isaac 1766; W. 24; 1297; Washington 275; 1049; 1155; 1339; 1368; 2491; William 2443.
VAN BUREN Abraham 1817; Jane 1445; John Henry William 2695.
VAN BUSKIRK J. 2329.
VAN FOSSEN Levi 360; 985; 2335; 2500.
VAN TEAR William 2446.
VARDEN Josiah 1110; 2751; Mr 1208.
VEASEY Thomas W. 1631.
VEIRS Levi 2856; 2886.
VENDERZEE Getty 2315; John 2315; S. F. 2315; Teunis 2315.
VERANDAH HOTEL 2099.
VERNON N. 1249.
VINCENT Joseph 523; Mary 2716; Samuel 719; 2716.
VINSON Thos. F. W. 2856.
VOGLER Henry 2144.
VORE Harriet 1921; Mordecal 1636; W. N. 1731; William 1513.
WACHTELL Frederick 2048.
WACHTER Daniel 1954; George 2522; 2598; Harriet 1358; Jacob 2719; John 2323; Jno. C. 1757; M. 666; 667; 784; 793; 802; 864; 881; 882; 883; 908; 909; 910; 911; 921; 922; 952; 1111; 1325; 1330; 1333; 1344; 1345; 1346; 1731; 1812;

WACHTER (continued) 2310; 2320; 2386; 2387; 2397; 2402; 2416; 2417; 2464; 2482; 2582; 2763; 2764; Michael 363; 600; 601; 1254; 1294; 1371; 1688; 1689; 1694; 2447; 2573; 2840; Mr 21; 81; 243; 415; 416; 432; 433; 624; 625; 673; 689; 717; 755; 776; 784; 845; 846; 1009; 1010; 1078; 1079; 1104; 1554; Philip Jr. 998; S. 1358; Samuel 2767.
WAESCHE George H. 1332; 2468.
WAGGONER Fanny S. 460.
WAGNER Denis D. 2770; Joseph 2424; Joseph L. 94; 360; 1040; 1745; 2469; 2576; Mary Ann 2298; Mary C. 2518; Nicholas 1491; Sophia 1745; Tavern 1040; 2424; 2576; William 2583.
WAGONER Barbara 1016; Michael 1016; 1901.
WAINWRIGHT Dr. 1865.
WAITMAN Joseph 1044.
WALDECK John 855; Lydia Ann 642; Theresa 855.
WALDMAN Michael 580.
WALKER Cyrus 94; 360; 722; 985; 1372; 1718; 2335; 2500; Isaac 1405; Jacob 2185; Joseph W. 2126; Margaret Ann 2247; Mary Ann 954; W. 5; Wm 2649.
WALL Caroline 733.
WALLACE Robert 2885.
WALLECK Eliza Ann 2293; John 2293.
WALLING Emma 715; Henry 467; Henry J. 2117; Hotel 2823; James 256; 276;

WALLING (continued)
1364; 1414; 2500; 2638;
Jane 715; John 137; Juliana
137; Louisa 1797; Martha
715; Mary Ann 467; Mrs
1917; Susan 913; Tavern
1796.
WALLS Anna Louisa 1052; Dr.
1052.
WALPOLE Emily 550; Miss 560.
WALSH Robert 1138.
WALTMAN James W. 2712;
John W. 2443; Joseph W.
2662; Peter 1836.
WALTON George 1282.
WALTZ Elias 1079; Jamimah
1972; Tobias 1497.
WAMPLER Abraham 24; 74;
277; 970; 1049; 1297; 1339;
2443; 2468; 2491; 2580;
John 94.
WANTZ Henry 2500.
WAR John 752.
WARD Albert B. 422; W. H.
708; Wm. H. 708.
WARE Thos. 1288.
WARFIELD 1779; Alexander
1210; Alexander A. 147;
Avolina 2940; Catharine A.
2043; George 2359; Henrietta 2369; Henry R. 1515;
1905; 2457; 2491; 2522; J.
L. 1049; John A. 2369;
2791; Mr 1464; Matilda 147;
Nicholas D. 2863; 2899; S.
D. 24; 1339; Sarah Ann 632;
Sarat D. 275; Surat D. 1297;
1396; 1769; 2662; Suratt D.
147; 1040; 2369; 2491;
Surrat D. 2424; Surratt D.
2443; 2469; 2712.
WARNER Christopher 1723;
John 652; 1382.

WARREN William 494; 2246.
WASHINGTON General 1457;
George C. 616; 745; 1169;
2305; Hose Company 906;
2395; 2634; John A. 369;
Medical College 1185;
Memorial 2549; Milicent F.
2290; William T. 2290.
WASKEY Christian 2722; Elijah
2722; Elizabeth 1447.
WASON 2673.
WATERS 1671; 2567; Adamson
2878; Catharine 2913;
Cyrus 2117; Dorothea 55;
Eliza 21; F. 2913; Hazel 418;
Henry C. 21; 1509; Horatio
906; 1397; 1485; 1632;
1699; 1909; 2395; 2757;
2794; Ignatius 1534; James
H. 1871; Mary Ann 418;
Rachel M. S. 544 Richard
544; S. R. 24; 1429; 1952;
1968; 2023; 2094; Samuel
D. 2856; Somerset R. 275;
1155; 1297; 1339; 1380;
1396; 1502; 1513; 1534;
2443; 2767; William 976;
1098; 1396; 1995; 2117;
2522; 2541; 2799; Zadock
M. 740.
WATKINS Cassaway 740;
Decimus Eugene M. 577;
Emily 2795; Greenbury M.
2876; John 1669; Thomas
2893; 2899; Tobias 577;
Wm. W. 1495.
WATSON Elizabeth 663; Isaac
Cooper 2194; J. C. 2796;
James C. 1503; Phineas
377;
WATTS H. M. 1169; Rachael
390; Richard K. 2886.
WAUGH Bishop 1994.

WAYS Samuel D. 913; 1882; Susan 1882; Susan Ann Cecelia 1882.
WEANER Michael 1564.
WEASCHE Geo H. 827; 1322.
WEAST Joseph 2446.
WEAVER Andrew 708; Christian 1041; David 1017; Delana 2764; Edward 2539; Elizabeth 2960; George 536; Henerietta 1438; James S. 1438; Mary Ann 243; P. 94; Samuel 482; Theodosia 2495; Valentine 1098.
WEBB J. B. 1098; Joseph B. 273; 357; 2766; Richard J. 1220.
WEBER George R. 334; 469; John B. Jr. 463; Susan 469; William 199; 459; 1337.
WEBSTER Daniel 2060; George 233; 780; 1161; 1191; 1260; 1830; 2522; George F. 2117; Georgette 2168; Isaac 428; 470; 501; 524; 1468; 1469; 2070; John Bradley 430; Joseph 1547; Julia 2060; Mary A. 2450; Rev. 901; 902.
WEHNER John 2642.
WEIGLEY Mr 2614.
WEISER D. F. 1645; R. 1638; 1639; 1706; 1707; 1730; 1741; 1742; 1758; 1759; 1963; 1964; 1968; 2013; 2054; 2120; 2121; 2122; 2161; 2162; 2175; 2176; 2196; 2206; 2711; 2735; 2736; 2737; 2738; Rev. 1832; 1953.
WEIST Jacob 377; 648; 1098.
WEISTLER Lydia 400.
WELCH Elizabeth 403; Vachael 403.

WELKER John 1521; 2411; 2435; Mary Ann 2435.
WELLER Daniel 1467; 2491; Frederick 2766; John 2599; Jonathan 625; Mary 1758.
WELLING Amos L. 1416.
WELLS Joshua 1052; Martha Ann 964; Zenas 964.
WELSH Malinda 2815.
WELTY Andrew 2581; Daniel 2826; Joseph 724; 827; 1047; 1332; 2598; 2608; Joshua 724.
WELTZHEIMER Lewis 1174.
WENNER John 530.
WENRICK Sophia 2347.
WERNFELS Peter 295.
WERNSICK Adeline 2583.
WERTENBAKER William 1518; 2479; 2594; 2598; 2717; 2767.
WEST B. W. 1396; Dr. 480; Joseph 24; 94; 1396; 2826; Levin 24; Margaret 2860; William 2851.
WESTGATE Thomas 2928.
WETHERALD Thomas 340.
WETNIGHT Jacob 1421; 1513.
WETZEL Susan 2482.
WEYL Mr 301.
WEYLE Charles 226.
WHARTHON Francis 1702.
WHARTON John O. 1237; T. O. 2658.
WHEAT J. C. 1130; 1131; 1327.
WHEELER Elias 838; Mary 2073; T. T. 2871; Thomas T. 740; Ths. T. 2935.
WHELAN Catharine Ann 610; Thomas 610.
WHEREAFELT Frederick 2767.
WHIPP George 256; 276.
WHIPPLE Wm. 1282.

WHITE Adam 2662; Addison 94; Addisson 500; 2514; 2712; Benjamin 740; Bishop 990; Char. J. 2797; Hiram 565; John 770; Joseph C. 2886; Mary Ann 2482; N. 2856; Nathan 740; 2856; Stephen N. C. 740; William 377; 2522.
WHITEFORD William 2014.
WHITEFIELD James 1121.
WHITEHILL James 1098; 1218; 1228; 1364; 1414; 2406; 2522; John C. 1561.
WHITFIELD George 588.
WHITMER Nicholas 1515; 2468.
WHITMORE Lydia 1550; Mary A. 2362; Nicholas 1460; Noah 2575.
WHITNEY Daniel Clark 1943; Mary Clark 1943.
WHITTAKER James 2141.
WHITTER Mary 2300; Thomas 2300.
WHITTINGHAM Wm. Rollinson 2251.
WHITTLESEY Elisha 1169.
WICKHAM Harriet 2402; John 2785.
WICKUM Eleanor 910.
WIEST Elizabeth 135; 1681; Henrietta 135; Jacob 2117.
WILCOXEN Horatio 1830; 2092; William 1098; 1178.
WILCOXON Jesse 2901; Louisa 936; Mr 2635; William 1407; 1411; 1485; William Jr. 2517.
WILES George H. 2015.
WILEY Mr 1651; 1675; 1823.
WILHIDE Ann Maria 169; Elizabeth 1759; Jas. 2717; Joseph 879; 1039; 2531;

WILHIDE (continued) 2647; 2826; Margaret Ann 1527; Sabina 1344; Samuel 94; 1421; 1527; 1562; 2356; 2598; 2740; Samuel Clay 2740.
WILKS Thomas 2343.
WILLARD Charles 275.
WILLETT Burgess 2856; Robert W. 2856; 2886.
WILLHIDE Frederick 1467; Joseph 360; Samuel 360.
WILLIAMS Catharine L. 2918; Colmore 2957; David 144; Elisha W. 2856; Elizabeth Ann 2939; Ferry 405; Henry S. 1955; James W. 650; John 2143; John H. 1414; 1428; 2456; 2457; 2522; 2541; 2638; John M. 2856; 2886; 2958; Livinia 1193; Nat. F. 650; O. H. 2918; Peter 1193; R. W. 76; Stephen 1437; Robert 1041; T. P. 1523; William 1282; Wm. H. 1098; Zachariah 2939.
WILLIAMSON Isaac 360; 1515; James 493; 985; 2500; 2791; Jos. 94; Warren R. 1372; 1718.
WILLIAR Charles 24; 970.
WILLIARD Abraham 2400; 2826; Charles 1297; 1339; Dewalt 1394; 1867; 2766; George 1041; John 1509; 2767; John Sr. 888; Juliann 888.
WILLINGHAN Mary Ann 2014.
WILLIS 660; Henry 309; Margaret 1300; W. 199; 267; William 997; 1006; 1297; 2336; 2505.
WILLOUGHBY James 2748.
WILLOW Broake 2278.

WILLS George 1098; Rebecca 122; William 377.
WILLSON Charles 2863; 2899; Edward F. 1524; Horace 740; 2856; Jno. 2863; 2957; O. 367; Osborn S. 2856; 2886; William 2863; 2884; 2957.
WILLYARD John 26.
WILLYS Epgraim 1340.
WILSON Adam 2271; Charles 934; 1098; 1414; 2522; Daniel 1611; Eliza Mary 2873; Elizabeth 1722; Henry R. 2707; Isaac 94; 360; 985; 1372; 1394; 1718; 2335; 2500; James 1282; John C. 581; John I. 1770; John J. 1767; Jonathan T. 377; 1055; William 1463; William M. B. 1155; 2873.
WINCHESTER George 650.
WINCOUGH Jesse 1968.
WINDER Wm. S. 650.
WINDSON Eliza Ann 2019.
WINDSOR Arnold T. 2856; Emma 1593; George W. 94; 985; 2443; 2662; 2712; Lorenzo B. 575; Robert B. 1405; Z. T. 1368; 2329; 2712; Zachariah T. 24; 275; 970; 1297; 1339; 2443; 2662; Zadock 1593; 2329.
WINEBRENNER Elizabeth E. 1760; Jacob 39; 724; 1047; 1760; John 2183; 2605; Sophia 39.
WINECOFF Jesse 2196; 2206.
WINECOOP Mr 971.
WINFIELD T. 2206.
WINKS Joshua 66; 723.
WINN Isabella 1610.
WINPIGLER Catherine 608; Jacob 2295.

WINSOR Alexander 2886; Arnold T. 2885; 2886.
WINTER Frederick 1717.
WINTERS Thomas 2717.
WINULL William 459.
WIRT William 2949.
WIRTENBAKER Wm. 2468.
WIRTS Mary 1335.
WISE Elizabeth 1380; Henry A. 2848; J. B. 1513; James 2961; John 2335; 2572; 2717; 2767; John Frederick 2816; Joseph 2609; Mary Ann 2572; Mary C. 2533; Valentine 400.
WISEMAN Mr 115.
WISER Mr 1565.
WISONG George R. 2117; Issac 1306.
WISSENGER George 25.
WISSINGER 1238; George 44; 138; 206; 233; 256; 276; 278; 554; 1218; Jacob 138.
WITHEROW John 1405; 1813; Margaret B. 1813.
WITHERSPOON John 1282.
WITMORE Elizabeth 2204.
WITTER Elizabeth 715; Rebecca 715.
WITTINGER Nancy 747.
WOLCOTT Oliver 1282.
WOLF Abraham 2620; Anna Mary C. 882; Elizabeth 2620; John 1523; 2469; 2647; Josiah 1821; Samuel 1394.
WOLFE 1113; Jacob 921; John 2766; 2767; Mary E. 1113; Samuel 2766.
WOLFENSBERGER Sarah 552.
WOLTZ John B. 463; Sarah 463.
WOOD Adelaide A. 2289; D. 1372; Hannah 1621; Jacob

WOOD (continued)
1372; James 548; Joel 985; 1718; 2335; 2500; 2791; John 985; 1045; 1396; 1718; 1790; 1891; 2103; 2347; 2500; 2594; 2826; John D. 985; Joseph 94; 1235; 2491; 2717; 2767; Sarah Ann 1891.
WOODBRIDGE Frederick 1340; Geo. 238; Jonathan E. 199.
WOODMAN Jona. 225.
WOODROW Thomas 2453.
WOODS Charles W. 2906; James 842; John D. 94; 360; Lynn N. 2306; Tavern 842.
WOODWARD Baldwin 218; Lydia A. 218.
WOODYEAR Edward G. 379.
WOOTEN Singleton 1045.
WOOTON Martha 2873; Singleton 2426; 2479.
WOOTTEN Singleton 74; 277.
WOOTTON Singleton 24; 275; 2318; 2479
WORLEY Joseph 444; Louis D. 1572.
WORMAN Andrew D. 2309; Barbara D. 1561; Josiah 1469; Moses 24; 275; 277; 359; 377 654; 707; 1025; 1155; 1297; 1339; 1379; 1396; 1405; 1420; 2328; 2443; 2457; 2522; 2541; 2580; William 1040; 1297; 1339; 1561.
WORRALL Edward H. 435; Elizabeth 435; Elizabeth Rachael 435.
WORTHINGTON Ann Matilda 1889; Charles 87; 1523; 2356; 2598; 2766; 2767; J. 1523; J. F. 1822; J. H. 1405; John H. 2598; Martha 259;

WORTHINGTON (continued)
Moses 74; 2826; Samuel 259; T. 1832; T. C. 206; 2457; Thomas 740; 1645; 2662; 2871; Thomas C. 377; 1098; 1312; 1412; 2522; 2541; Thomas I. 1396; Thomas J. 1889; 2264; 2443; 2712; Upton 2717; 2826; Walter 1459. Wm. 740; 1515.
WRIGHT Charles A. 1042; Eliza Ann 734; James 967; Jesse 1394; John 1098; Judgematical 1177; Samuel 879; 2767; 2826; Wm. C. 94.
WYATT Dr. 1610; 1715; 1754.
WYGERT Maria M. 35.
WYLEY Mr 2800.
WYNKOOP Mr 1230; Richard 1566.
WYSONG Elizabeth 474; 2667; Henry Baker 2667; I. 30; Isaac 24; 474; 1830; 2642; 2667; 2767; Sarah Ellen 474.
WYTHE George 1282.
YAKLE Jacob 2312.
YANTIS Daniel 84; David 2767; David F. 1963; George 24; 275; 1297; 1339; 2443; 2662; 2712; Mary 84; Mrs 1235; Tavern 1235.
YARDEY John 50.
YARDLY Ann 2260.
YASTE Samuel 1952; 2766; 2767.
YEAGLE Jacob 1515.
YEAKEY John 532.
YEAKLE Alice 2756; Henry Sen. 2746; Jacob 2756; Lauria Adelia 2756; William 2117.
YEAST Elizabeth 1626; Samuel 1394; 1513; 2398.

YEISER Daniel 827; 1332.
YINGLING Frederick 94; 360; 985; 2335; 2500; Rebecca 2842.
YON Jacopb 2669.
YONITZ Christian 941; Susan 715.
YORKE Peter 220; Sarah 220.
YOST Casper 2863; 2899; Elizabeth 702.
YOSTE Samuel 2478.
YOUNG Alexander H. 2843; Andrew D. 2193; C. 2766; C. B. 78; 338; 551; Catharine 1024; Charles A. 2302; Charles B. 2473; 2474; 2501; 2502; D. 1372; 1718; 2264; 2500; 2791; Daniel 24; 1048; 1568; 2356; Dewalt 360; 985; 2335; H. 30; 1372; 2500; Henry 24; 275; 1297; 1306; 1338; 1339; 1405; 1414; 2385; 2443; 2638; 2662; 2712; 2878; 2958; J. 1718; Jacob 360; 985; 1372; 1615; 1718; 2264; 2335; 2480; 2500; 2791; John 655; 827; 985; 1332; 1414; 1509; 1513; 1718; 1953; 1968; 2398; 2480; 2766; 2856; 2863; 2899; John H. 1372; 1718; 2500; 2791; L. 2856; Ludowick 2863; 2899; Maria 2267; Mary Jane 1661; 2193; McClintock 442; Men's Bible Society 199; 459; 1130; 1131; 1327; 1623; 1831; 2092; Men's National Republican 377; Mr 298; 299; 462; 2060; 2465; Nicholas 958; Perry 1414; 1661; 2193; Peter 94; 360; 970; 985; 2335; 2500; Philippena

YOUNG (continued) 2243; Rebecca 2373; Samuel 929; Sarah 217; William 2291.
YOURTE Aaron 1673.
YOWLER David 2354.
ZACHARIAS Catharine 2077; Christian 2483; D. 1528; 1541; 1548; 1583; 1584; 1586; 1629; 1674; 1681; 1717; 1791; 1822; 1844; 1861; 1870; 1884; 1890; 1947; 1948; 2020; 2042; 2043; 2061; 2062; 2113; 2148; 2149; 2150; 2151; 2156; 2163; 2164; 2169; 2170; 2174; 2225; 2226; 2270; 2291; 2429; 2627; 2682; 2683; 2684; 2720; 2814; 2831; 2844; Daniel 1366; 1432; 1520; 1668; 1693; 1720; 1721; 1771; 1941; 1942; 2117; 2171; 2220; 2361; 2362; 2363; 2439; 2441; 2483; 2490; 2493; 2507; 2585; 2649; 2670; 2715; 2775; Mr 1626; 1679; 2209; 2401; Rev. 1832.
ZEALER An 521.
ZECHER Caspar 1274.
ZEGAFOOSE Eleanor 548.
ZEIGLER Henry 1414.
ZEPP D. 1832; Thomas 1884.
ZIEGLER Henry 2433.
ZIMMERMAN Alice 2348; Ann Elizabeth 1576; Anna Maria 316; Calvin 943; Catharine 1898; Elizabeth 31; G. 2156; 2767; George 234; 799; 1405; George F. 1974; H. 1203; Henry 970; Hotel 2160; J. P. 722; Jacob 24; Jacob Alexander 799; John

ZIMMERMAN (continued)
1509; 1576; 2264; 2468;
2717; 2791; John Nicholas
272; John P. 785; 1509;
Joshua J. 1448; M. 2767;
Michael 656; 1108; 1621;
2348; N. N. 2264; Wm. H.
2164; Samuel 2612; Sarah
864.
ZOCCHI N. 1157.
ZOLICKOFFER John M. A.
2423; Wm. 2443.
ZOLLINGER Mr 653.

ZOLLICKOFFER Daniel 884;
90; 2601; 2620; J. M. A. 24;
1339; Jno. M. 275; John M.
A. 1297; 2468; 2481; John
Maurius Augustus 2503.
ZOLLICOFFER Daniel 609.
ZOLLIKOFFER Daniel 1331.
ZOLLINGER George 1514;
2259; 2609; 2647; 2663;
2712; 2767.
ZUMBRAN Jacob 985.
ZUMBRUN George 549; Jacob
2319; 2468.